Dear Student,

What did you think of your Dearborn PassTrak study materials? We'd like to know!

We invite you to fill out the PassTrak Survey below. Your responses will help us as we develop even better exam preparation materials. Please tear this page out of your book, fold it, seal it and mail it to us. Your comments are greatly appreciated.

Dearborn Financial Institute, Inc.®
155 North Wacker Drive
Chicago, Illinois 60606-1719

Sincerely,

Linton Farrelly, Executive Editor

Book title and edition: _____

Please rate the PassTrak materials using the following scale:

1 = Poor   2 = Satisfactory   3 = Very Good

License Exam Manual				*Questions & Answers*			
Easy to read	1	2	3	Challenging	1	2	3
Easy to understand	1	2	3	Number of questions	1	2	3
Organized	1	2	3	Accurate	1	2	3
Up-to-date	1	2	3	Up-to-date	1	2	3
Complete	1	2	3	Matches the text	1	2	3
Accurate	1	2	3				

How well do you feel the PassTrak materials have prepared you for the exam?   1   2   3

Which chapter did you find most difficult?   Chapter number____

What other Dearborn study materials did you use?

____Classroom   ____Answer Phone   ____Videotapes   ____Audiotapes

____Practice Finals   ____Diagnostic Exams   ____Computer-based Q&A

Did you take your licensing exam?   No____ Yes____ Date_____ Score_____

Name: (optional) _____   **Firm:** _____

NOTE: This page, when folded over and taped, becomes an envelope, which has been approved by the United States Postal Service. It is provided for your convenience.

IMPORTANT—PLEASE FOLD OVER AND TAPE BEFORE MAILING

Return Address:

_____

_____

_____

NO POSTAGE
NECESSARY
IF MAILED
IN THE
UNITED STATES

BUSINESS REPLY MAIL

FIRST CLASS MAIL   PERMIT NO. 88175   CHICAGO, IL

POSTAGE WILL BE PAID BY ADDRESSEE:

**Dearborn
Financial Institute, Inc.**

Attn: Linton Farrelly
155 North Wacker Drive
Chicago, IL 60606-1719

IMPORTANT—PLEASE FOLD OVER AND TAPE BEFORE MAILING

NOTE: This page, when folded over and taped, becomes an envelope, which has been approved by the United States Postal Service. It is provided for your convenience.

PASSTRAK®

SERIES 7

GENERAL SECURITIES REPRESENTATIVE

LICENSE EXAM MANUAL

10TH EDITION

Dearborn
Financial Institute, Inc.®

The Series 7 qualification exam is copyrighted by the New York Stock Exchange. The exam contains the following notice:

> "The contents of this examination are confidential. Neither the whole nor any part of this examination may be reproduced in any form or quoted or used in any way without the written consent of the New York Stock Exchange, Inc."

Dearborn Financial Publishing, Inc. and its employees and agents honor the copyrights of the New York Stock Exchange. We specifically urge each of our students to refrain from any attempts to remove a copy of the exam; or to copy or record any of the questions on the exam.

At press time, this 10th edition of PASSTRAK® Series 7 contains the most complete and accurate information currently available for the NASD Series 7 license examination. Owing to the nature of securities license examinations, however, information may have been added recently to the actual test that does not appear in this edition.

This publication is designed to provide accurate and authoritative information in regard to the subject matter covered. It is sold with the understanding that the publisher is not engaged in rendering legal, accounting or other professional service. If legal advice or other expert assistance is required, the services of a competent professional person should be sought.

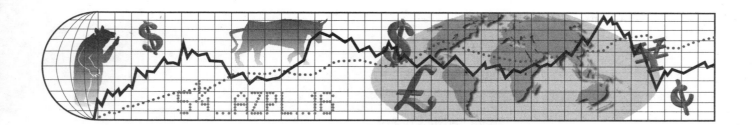

Contents

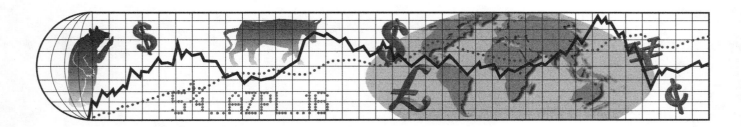

Acknowledgments

The 10th edition of *PASSTRAK® Series 7 License Exam Manual* and *Questions & Answers* reflects the combined efforts and contributions of hundreds of students, instructors and customers. In particular, I'd like to thank Dearborn instructors Gib Larson and Marcia Burak, whose contributions to the text and Q&A constitute a quantum leap in securities training standards. Instructors Marc Katz, Phil Keener, Jim Altier, Amy Murphy, Deirdre Patten, Tom Drinkard, Don Drews, Gigs Stephenson, Paul Leo, Rock Sytsma and Mark Skarstedt all helped raise the bar.

Many of our customers made invaluable recommendations for this edition as well. I'd like to thank Barry Cash, Judy Hallstrom, Calvin Plummer and Mitchell Siegel for their help, as well as many others who preferred to remain nameless.

Harvey Knopman, President of Knopman Financial Training Services Inc., made valuable contributions to the *Licence Exam Manual*, as did Dr. Colin Meredith to the *Questions & Answers* database from which we compile our practice exams.

I'd also like to extend my gratitude to production editors Nicky Bell, Brian Fauth, Rebecca Hicks and Nancy Whiteley whose talent, patience and perseverance made this book.

Wm. Linton Farrelly,
Managing Editor

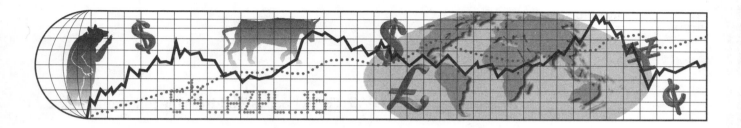

Introduction to PASSTRAK® Series 7

Welcome to PASSTRAK®. Because you probably have a lot of questions about the course and the exam, we have tried to anticipate some of them and provide you with answers to help you prepare.

The PASSTRAK® Series 7 Course

The *PASSTRAK® Series 7* course consists of a *License Exam Manual*, a *Questions & Answers* book and a set of practice exams, titled *Success Set*.

The *License Exam Manual* consists of seventeen lessons, each devoted to a particular area of general securities sales and regulation that you will need to know in order to pass the General Securities Registered Representative Exam (the Series 7). Each lesson is divided into study sections devoted to more specific areas with which you need to become familiar.

The *Questions & Answers* book contains review exams that test the topics covered in the *License Exam Manual*. The *Success Set* contains comprehensive and targeted practice exams.

What Topics Are Covered in the Course?

The Series 7 exam and PASSTRAK® Series 7 address the following topics:

Lesson	Topic	Estimated No. of Exam Questions
1	Equity Securities	10–15
2	Debt Securities	15–25
3	Municipal Securities	50–55
4	Options	40–45
5	Customer Accounts	10–20
6	Margin Accounts	5–10
7	Issuing Securities	10–15
8	Trading Securities	15–20
9	Brokerage Office Procedures	10–15
10	Investment Company Products	10–15
11	Retirement Plans	5–10
12	Variable Annuities	5–10
13	Direct Participation Programs	10–12
14	Economics and Analysis	10–15
15	Ethics, Recommendations and Taxation	10–20
16	U.S. Government and State Rules and Regulations	10–15
17	Other SEC and SRO Rules and Regulations	10–15

How Much Time Should I Spend Studying?

You should plan to spend approximately 90 to 120 hours reading the material and working through the questions. Your actual time may vary depending on your study habits and professional background.

Spread your study time over six to eight weeks before the date on which you are scheduled to take the Series 7 exam. Select a time and place for studying that will allow you to concentrate. There is a lot of information to learn, so be sure to give yourself enough time to understand the material.

What Is the Best Way to Approach the Q&A Review Exams?

Take each review exam in *Questions & Answers* after you have read the corresponding study section in the *License Exam Manual*. Read each question carefully in its entirety and write down your answer. Then check your answer against the key and read the accompanying rationale. This will increase your comprehension and retention of the information covered.

If, after reading the rationale, you still are uncertain about the answer, refer to the cross-referenced page in the *License Exam Manual,* where normally you will find a more complete explanation. (Note, however, that sometimes a question may not be answered on a specific page because it requires the application of multiple concepts.)

What Is the Best Way to Approach the Success Set Exams?

The *Exam Success Set* consists of 16 exams. These include:

- Practice Final exams
- a Special Exam Set consisting of
  - Questions From the Front exam
  - exams on options
  - exam on municipals
  - exam on margin accounts
- Alpha exams

Take the first two Practice Final exams as you did the review exams in *Questions & Answers;* as you answer each question, check your answer immediately against the rationale.

Take the next two Practice Final exams and the Questions From the Front exam each in its entirety before checking your answers against the rationale. Set aside a day to take the last two Practice Final exams as you would the actual Series 7, allowing three hours to take each one, with a break in between. Do not check your answers against the rationale until you have finished. This will simulate closely the actual Series 7 testing environment.

The Practice Final exams and Questions From the Front exam in the *Exam Success Set* test the same knowledge you will need in order to pass the Series 7.

The Special Exam Set and the Alpha exams offer a mechanism to take your exam preparation to the limit. The exams in the Special Exam Set provide an intensive review of the most difficult topics tested on the Series 7. The Alpha Exams are advanced review exams, and are more difficult than the actual Series 7. Do not be discouraged if your Alpha exam scores are much lower than your scores on the other exams.

The Series 7 Exam

Why Do I Need to Pass the Series 7 Exam?

Your employer is a member of the New York Stock Exchange (NYSE) or another self-regulatory organization that requires its members and employees of its members to pass a qualification exam in order to become registered. To be registered as a representative qualified to sell all types of securities, you must pass the Series 7 exam.

Are There Any Prerequisites I Must Meet Before Taking the Exam?

There are no prerequisite exams you must pass before taking the Series 7.

What Is the Series 7 Exam Like?

The Series 7 is a two-part, six-hour, 250-question exam administered by the National Association of Securities Dealers (NASD). The exam is given in two three-hour sessions, each covering different areas of general securities sales and regulation. It is offered as a computer-based test at various testing sites around the country. A pencil-and-paper exam is available to those candidates who apply to and obtain permission from the NASD to take a written exam.

What Score Must I Achieve in Order to Pass?

You must score at least 70 percent on the Series 7 exam in order to pass and become eligible for NYSE registration as a general securities representative.

What Topics Will I See Covered on the Exam?

The questions you will see on the Series 7 exam do not appear in any particular order. The computer is programmed to select a new, random set of questions for each test taker, selecting questions according to the preset topic weighting of the exam. Each Series 7 candidate will see the same number of questions on each topic, but a different mix of questions.

The Series 7 exam is divided into seven critical function areas:

	No. of Questions	*% of Exam*
Prospecting for and qualifying customers	9	3.6%
Evaluating customer needs and objectives	4	1.6%
Providing customers with investment information and making suitable recommendations	123	49.2%
Handling customer accounts and account records	27	10.8%
Understanding and explaining the securities markets, their organization and their participants to customers	53	21.2%
Processing customer orders and transactions	13	5.2%
Monitoring economic and financial events, performing customer portfolio analysis and making suitable recommendations	21	8.4%

Additional Trial Questions

During your exam, you will see up to ten extra trial questions. These are potential exam-bank questions that the NASD is testing by having examinees answer them during the course of an exam. These questions are not included in your final score, and you will be given extra time in which to answer them.

What Is PROCTOR®?

The Series 7 exam, like many professional licensing examinations, is administered on the PROCTOR® computerized testing system. PROCTOR® is a nationwide, interactive computer system designed for the administration and delivery of qualifications examinations. Included with your PROCTOR® enrollment, you will receive a brochure describing how the exam is formatted and how to use the computer terminal to answer the questions.

When you have completed the exam, the PROCTOR® System promptly scores your answers and within minutes displays your grade for the exam on the terminal screen.

How Do I Enroll for the Exam?

To obtain an admission ticket to the Series 7 exam, your firm must file the proper application form with the NASD, along with the appropriate processing fees. The NASD will then send you a directory of Sylvan Learning Centers and a PROCTOR® enrollment valid for a stated number of days. To take the exam during this period, you should make an appointment with a Sylvan Learning Center as far in advance as possible of the date on which you would like to take the test.

What Should I Take to the Exam?

Take one form of personal identification with your signature and photograph as issued by a government agency. You are not allowed to take reference materials or anything else into the testing area. Calculators are available upon request; you will not be allowed to use your own calculator.

Scratch paper and pencils will be provided by the testing center, although you will not be permitted to take them with you when you leave.

How Well Can I Expect to Do on the Exam?

If you study and complete all of the sections of this course, and consistently score at least 80 percent on the review and practice final exams, you will be well prepared to pass the Series 7.

Examination Results and Reports

At the end of the exam, your score will be displayed on your computer screen, indicating whether you passed. The next business day after your exam, your results will be mailed to your firm and to the self-regulatory organization and state securities commission specified on your application.

Successful Test Taking

Passing the Series 7 exam depends not only on how well you learn the subject matter but also on how well you take tests. You can develop your test-taking skills, and thus improve your score, by learning a few simple test-taking techniques:

- Read the full question.
- Avoid jumping to conclusions—watch for hedge clauses.
- Interpret the unfamiliar question.
- Look for key words and phrases.
- Identify the intent of the question.
- Recognize synonymous terms.
- Memorize key points.
- Eliminate/short-list Roman numeral choices.

- Use a calculator.
- Beware of changing answers.
- Pace yourself.

Each of these pointers is explained below, including examples that show how to use them to improve your performance on the exam.

Read the Full Question

You cannot expect to answer a question correctly if you do not know what it is asking. If you see a question that seems familiar and easy, you might anticipate the answer, mark it and move on before you finish reading it. This is a serious mistake and can result in errors. Be sure to read the full question before answering it—the questions are often written to trap people who assume too much. Here is an example of a question in which an assumption could produce a wrong answer.

> What is the term for a divided underwriting of municipal securities that is priced through a bidding process involving more than one investment banking firm?
>
> A. Eastern
> B. Western
> C. Negotiated
> D. Competitive

The answer is D—the question describes a situation in which competitive bidding sets the price, and therefore the spread, of the offering. This is an easy question to answer only for someone who has read the full question, because the point is made in the second half. If you read the question too quickly, you might get to the word "divided" and assume that you are being asked to remember whether a *divided* underwriting is also called an *Eastern* underwriting or a *Western* underwriting.

Avoid Jumping to Conclusions—Watch for Hedge Clauses

The questions on the Series 7 are often embellished with deceptive *distractors* as choices. To avoid being taken in by seemingly obvious answers, make it a practice to read each question *and each answer* twice before selecting your choice. Doing so will provide you with a much better chance of doing well on the test.

Watch out for hedge clauses embedded in the question. Examples of hedge clauses include the terms *if, not, all, none* and *except*. In the case of *if* statements, the question can be answered correctly only by taking into account the qualifier. If you ignore the qualifier, you will not answer correctly.

Qualifiers are sometimes combined in a question. Some that you will frequently see together are *all* with *except* and *none* with *except*. In general, when a question starts with *all* or *none* and ends with *except,* you are looking for an answer that is opposite to what the question appears to be asking. For example:

> All of the following are characteristics of Treasury bills EXCEPT that they
>
> I. mature in more than one year
> II. are sold at a discount
> III. pay interest semiannually
> IV. are very safe investments
>
> A. I and II
> B. I and III
> C. II and III
> D. II and IV

If you neglect to read the *except,* you will look for the choices that are characteristics of T bills. In fact, the question asks which choices are *not* characteristics of T bills (that is, the exceptions). T bills mature in one year or less and do not pay periodic interest; therefore, choices I and III are incorrect and the answer is B.

Interpret the Unfamiliar Question

Do not be surprised if some questions on the test seem unfamiliar at first. If you have studied your material, you will have the information to answer all the questions correctly. The challenge may be a matter of understanding *what* the question is asking.

Very often, questions present information indirectly. You may have to interpret the meaning of certain elements before you can answer the question. The following two examples concerning bond yields and prices highlight this point.

> What is the effect of a decline in purchasing power on the current yields of outstanding bonds?
>
> A. The yields decrease.
> B. The yields increase.
> C. The yields stay the same.
> D. This cannot be determined with the information given.

This question is asking you to apply your knowledge of economics, investment recommendations and the relationship between bond prices and yields. Consumer purchasing power declines during periods of inflation. Inflation causes interest rates to rise, and this in turn causes prices of outstanding bonds to decrease. You will learn that when a bond declines in price or sells at a discount, the current yield increases (answer B).

This same content could have been tested in a different way, as illustrated by the next example.

What is the effect of tight money on bond prices?

A. Bond prices decrease.
B. Bond prices increase.
C. Bond prices stay the same.
D. This cannot be determined with the information given.

When you study the sections on economics, you will see that tight money is closely related to high interest rates. When money is scarce (tight), interest rates rise. When interest rates rise, prices of outstanding bonds decrease (answer A).

At first glance, the two questions appear very different, but in fact they test the same relationship—the relationship between a bond's price and its yield. Be aware that the exam will approach a concept from different angles.

Look for Key Words and Phrases

Look for words that are tip-offs to the situation presented. For example, if you see the word "prospectus" in the question stem, you know the question is about a new issue.

Sometimes a question will even supply you with the answer if you can recognize the key words it contains. The following is an example of how a key word can help you answer correctly.

Whose Social Security number must appear on an account under the Uniform Gifts to Minors Act?

A. Minor
B. Donor
C. Legal guardian
D. Parent

Looking at the answers, answer A is a likely candidate. You will learn that under UGMA, the minor is the owner of the securities. As the owner, the minor's Social Security number must be listed on the account. Few questions provide clues as blatant as this one, but many do offer key words that can guide you to selecting the correct answer if you pay attention.

Be sure to read all instructional phrases carefully, as illustrated in the next example.

Rank the following persons in descending order of their claims against a corporation's assets when the corporation is forced into liquidation.

  I. General creditors
 II. Preferred stockholders
III. Bondholders
IV. Common stockholders

A. I, II, III, IV
B. I, III, II, IV
C. III, I, II, IV
D. III, II, IV, I

The most important aspect of this question is identifying the key word—*descending*. A descending order ranks a list from highest to lowest—in this question, the highest claim on assets to the lowest claim on assets. (The answer is C: bondholders, general creditors, preferred stockholders, common stockholders.) The question could have asked for the *ascending* order—lowest to highest. Or it could have asked you to rank the choices from junior claim to senior claim or vice versa. Take time to identify the key words to answer this type of question correctly.

Identify the Intent of the Question

Many questions on the Series 7 exam supply so much information that you lose track of what is being asked. This is often the case in story problems. Learn to separate the "story" from the question. For example:

You have decided to buy 100 shares of ArGood Mutual Fund, which prices its shares at 5:00 p.m. every business day. You turn in your order at 3:00 p.m. when the shares are priced at $10 NAV, $10.86 POP. The sales load is 7.9 percent. What will your 100 shares cost?

A. $1,000
B. $1,079
C. $1,086
D. 100 times the offering price that will be calculated at 5:00 p.m.

A clue to the answer is presented in the first sentence—the fund price at 5:00 p.m. Orders for mutual funds are executed based on the next price calculated (forward pricing); therefore, the answer to this question is D. You do not need to calculate anything.

Take the time to identify what the question is asking. Of course, your ability to do so assumes you have studied sufficiently. There is no magic method for answering questions if you don't know the material.

Recognize Synonymous Terms

The securities industry has a tendency to abbreviate terms and use acronyms. Several terms may be used interchangeably throughout the test, and you should be able to recognize them. Examples include:

- NAV = net asset value = bid price
- POP = public offering price = ask price
- periodic payment plan = contractual plan
- buy = long = own
- sell = short = owe
- registered representative (RR) = account executive (AE)
- tax-sheltered annuity (TSA) = tax-deferred annuity (TDA)
- Uniform Gifts to Minors Act (UGMA) = Uniform Transfers to Minors Act (UTMA)
- VLI = variable life insurance

Memorize Key Points

Reasoning and logic will help you answer many questions, but you will have to memorize a good deal of information. In particular, you should try to memorize these key points: sales charges for investment companies; sales charge refunds for contractual plan withdrawals; the difference between refunds from spread load plans and those from front-end load plans; and the difference between sales literature and advertising.

Eliminate/Short-List Roman Numeral Choices

Roman numeral (or *multiple-multiple*) questions are common on the Series 7 exam; they require you to distinguish between several likely answers. When you are confronted with Roman numeral choices, try to eliminate one or two of them. Doing so helps to narrow your choices. For example, if you can eliminate choice II in a Roman numeral question, and three of the four answers contain choice II, you have successfully narrowed down your options to the correct answer by the process of elimination. For example:

An owner of common stock has which of the following rights?

I. Right to determine when dividends will be issued
II. Right to vote at stockholders' meetings or by proxy
III. Right to determine the amount of any dividends issued
IV. Right to buy redeemed shares before they are offered to the public

A. I, III and IV
B. II
C. II, III and IV
D. II and IV

The answer to this question is B. Stockholders have the right to vote on certain corporate matters and the right to dividends if and when declared.

Stockholders do not vote on when a dividend is to be paid, nor on the amount of dividend to be paid. Knowing this, you can eliminate answers A and C. You are now left with only two answers from which to choose.

Use a Calculator

For the most part, the Series 7 exam will not require the use of a calculator. Most of the questions are written so that any math required is simple. However, if you have become accustomed to using a calculator for math, you will be provided with one by the testing center staff.

Beware of Changing Answers

If you are unsure of an answer, your first hunch is the one most likely to be correct. Do not change answers on the exam without good reason. In general, change an answer only if you:

- discover that you did not read the question correctly
- find new or additional helpful information in another question

Pace Yourself

Some people will finish the exam early; some will use the entire time allowed; and some do not have time to finish all the questions. Watch the time carefully (your time remaining will be displayed on your PROCTOR® screen) and pace yourself through the exam.

Do not waste time by dwelling on a question if you simply do not know the answer. Make the best guess you can, mark the question for "Record for Review," and return to the question if time allows. Make sure that you have time to read all the questions so that you can record the answers you do know.

To give yourself an indication of how much time you need to answer a 250-question exam, time yourself on the "Go/No Go Exam" in the *Success Set*. Remember that your ability to take an exam within an allotted time will improve with practice.

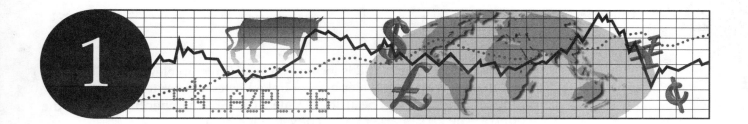

Equity Securities

OVERVIEW

The investment world is divided between owners (stock or equity) and lenders (bonds or debt). Owning equity in a company is perhaps the most visible and widely accessible means by which wealth is created. Individual investors become owners of a publicly traded company by purchasing stock in that company. In so doing, they can participate in the company's growth over time.

In this section, we will cover:

- common stock
- preferred stock
- related equity securities

What Is a Security?

In the simplest terms, a **security** is an investment that represents either an ownership stake or a debt stake in a company. An investor becomes part owner in a company by buying shares of the company's stock. A debt security is usually acquired by buying a company's bonds. A debt investment is a loan to a company in exchange for interest income and the promise to repay the loan at a future **maturity** date.

Stocks and bonds are normally purchased and sold on a stock exchange or in the over-the-counter (OTC) market. A stock exchange, such as the New York Stock Exchange (NYSE), is an auction market where buyers and sellers are matched by a specialist that maintains a fair and orderly market for a particular stock. The NYSE is located on Wall Street in New York City. The OTC market is an interdealer market linked by computer terminals to National Association of Securities Dealers (NASD) member firms across the country. The OTC market has no physical location.

Equity and Debt   Stock represents equity or ownership in a company, and bonds are a loan to a company. A company discloses the composition of its **total capitalization**—debt and equity—by publishing a **balance sheet**. The balance sheet summarizes the company's:

- **assets**—what the company owns: cash in the bank, accounts receivable (money it is owed), investments, property, inventory, etc.;
- **liabilities**—what the company owes: accounts payable, short- and long-term debt and other obligations; and
- **equity**—the excess of the value of assets over the value of liabilities—that is, the company's **net worth**.

 Take Note: A company's equity or net worth equals the value of assets left for stockholders after all liabilities have been paid. This can be summarized by the following balance sheet equation:

Assets – Liabilities = Stockholder's equity (net worth)

Common Stock

A company issues stock as its primary means of raising business capital. Investors who buy the stock buy a share of ownership in the company's net worth. Whatever a business owns (its assets) less its creditors' claims (its liabilities) belongs to the business owners (its stockholders).

Each share of stock entitles its owner to a portion of the company's profits and dividends and an equal vote in management. Most corporations are organized in such a way that their stockholders regularly vote for and elect a few people to a board of directors to oversee the company's business. By electing a board of directors, stockholders have a say in the company's management, but are not involved with the day-to-day details of its operations.

✓ *For Example:*   If a company issues 100 shares of stock, each share represents an identical 1/100—or 1 percent—ownership position in the company. A person who owns 10 shares of stock would own 10 percent of the company; a person who owns 50 shares of stock would own 50 percent of the company.

Types of Stock

Corporations may issue two types of stock: **common stock** and **preferred stock**. When speaking of stocks, people generally refer to common stock, as our discussion does. Preferred stock represents equity ownership in a corporation as well, but it usually does not have the same voting rights or appreciation potential as common stock. Preferred stock normally pays a fixed quarterly dividend and has **priority claims** over common stock; that is, the preferred is paid first if a company goes bankrupt.

Common stock can be classified in four ways.

Authorized Stock. As part of its original charter, a corporation receives authorization from the state to issue, or sell, a specific number of shares of stock. Often, a company sells only a portion of the authorized shares, raising enough capital for its foreseeable needs. The company may sell the remaining authorized shares in the future or use them for other purposes. Should the company decide to sell more shares than are authorized, it must amend its charter through a stockholder vote that approves more shares.

Issued Stock. Issued stock has been authorized and distributed to investors. When a corporation issues or sells fewer shares than the total number authorized, it normally reserves the **unissued** shares for future needs, such as:

- raising new capital for expansion;
- paying stock dividends;
- providing stock purchase plans for employees or stock options for corporate officers;
- exchanging common stock for outstanding convertible bonds or preferred stock; or
- satisfying the exercise of outstanding stock purchase warrants.

✎ *Take Note:* Authorized but unissued stock does not carry the rights and privileges of issued shares and is not considered in determining a company's total capitalization.

Outstanding Stock. Outstanding stock includes any shares that a company has issued, but has not repurchased—that is, stock the investors own.

Treasury Stock. Treasury stock is stock a corporation has issued and subsequently repurchased from the public. The corporation can hold this stock indefinitely or can reissue or retire it. A corporation could reissue its treasury stock to fund employee bonus plans, distribute it to stockholders as a stock dividend or, under certain circumstances, redistribute it to the public in an additional offering.

Treasury stock does *not* carry the rights of other common shares, such as voting rights and the right to receive dividends.

By buying its own shares in the open market, the corporation reduces the number of shares outstanding. If fewer shares are outstanding and operating income remains the same, earnings per share increase.

A corporation buys back its stock for a number of reasons, such as to:

- increase earnings per share;
- have an inventory of stock available to distribute as stock options, fund an employee pension plan and so on; or
- use for future acquisitions.

 Take Note: Issued stock – Outstanding stock = Treasury stock

Common Stock Values

The laws of **supply and demand**, which are based largely on the perception of a company's profitability and business prospects, determine the company's stock price in the market. Although a stock's market price is the most meaningful measure of its value, other measures include **par value** and **book value**.

Par Value

For investors, a common stock's par value is meaningless. It is an arbitrary value the company gives the stock in its articles of incorporation, and it has no bearing on the stock's market price. If a stock has been assigned a par value for accounting purposes, such as $1 or $.01, it is usually printed on the face of the stock certificate.

When the corporation sells stock, the money received exceeding par value is recorded on the corporate balance sheet as capital in excess of par, also known as *paid-in surplus, capital surplus* or *paid-in capital*.

Book Value

A stock's book value per share is a measure of how much a common stockholder could expect to receive for each share if the corporation were liquidated. Most commonly used by analysts, the book value per share is the difference between the value of a corporation's tangible assets and its liabilities, divided by the number of shares outstanding. The book value per share can—and usually does—differ substantially from a stock's market value.

Market Value

The most familiar measure of a stock's value is its market price, the price investors must pay to buy the stock. Market value is influenced by a company's business prospects and the consequent effect on supply (the number of shares available to investors) and demand (the number of shares investors want to buy).

Before You Go On: The market value of RST Corp.'s stock is $17 per share. The company has total tangible assets of $30 million and total liabilities of $18 million. With 4 million shares outstanding, what is the book value per share?

Answer: $30m (assets) − $18m (liabilities) = $12m equity ÷ 4m shares = $3 per share.

The Rights of Stock Ownership

Because stockholders are owners of a company, they have certain rights that protect their ownership interests.

Voting Rights   Common stockholders exercise control of a corporation by electing a board of directors and by voting on corporate policy matters at annual meetings, such as:

- issuance of convertible bonds (dilutes stockholder equity when converted) or additional common stock; and
- substantial changes in the corporation's business, such as mergers or acquisitions.

Stockholders have the right to vote on the issuance of convertible bonds because, when converted, current stockholders' equity is diluted.

Calculating the Number of Votes

A stockholder can cast one vote for each share of stock owned. Depending on the company's bylaws and applicable state laws, a stockholder may have a **statutory** or **cumulative** vote.

Statutory Voting. Statutory voting allows a stockholder to cast one vote per share owned for each item on a ballot, such as candidates for the board of directors. A board candidate needs a simple majority to be elected.

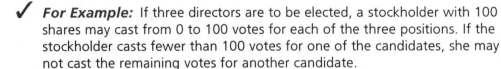 ***For Example:*** If three directors are to be elected, a stockholder with 100 shares may cast from 0 to 100 votes for each of the three positions. If the stockholder casts fewer than 100 votes for one of the candidates, she may not cast the remaining votes for another candidate.

Cumulative Voting. Cumulative voting allows stockholders to allocate their votes in any manner they choose.

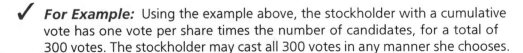 ***For Example:*** Using the example above, the stockholder with a cumulative vote has one vote per share times the number of candidates, for a total of 300 votes. The stockholder may cast all 300 votes in any manner she chooses.

The stockholder could cast all 300 votes for a single candidate or split them between two or more candidates, as illustrated below.

3 Candidates, 100 Shares	Statutory	Cumulative
Washington	100	0
Jefferson	100	0
Lincoln	100	300

Proxies Stockholders often find it difficult to attend the annual stockholders' meeting, so most vote on company matters by means of a proxy, a form of absentee ballot. Once it has been returned to the company, a proxy can be canceled automatically if the stockholder attends the meeting, authorizes a subsequent proxy or dies.

When a company sends proxies to shareholders, usually for a specific meeting, it is known as a *proxy solicitation*. Figure 1.1 illustrates a sample proxy ballot.

Companies that solicit proxies must supply detailed and accurate information to the shareholders about the proposals to be voted on. Before making a proxy solicitation, companies must submit the information to the Securities and Exchange Commission (SEC) for review.

If a proxy vote could change control of a company (a **proxy contest**), all persons involved in the contest must register with the SEC as participants or face criminal penalties. This registration requirement includes anyone providing unsolicited advice to stockholders about how to vote. However, brokers who advise customers who *request advice* are not considered participants.

A stockholder may revoke a proxy at any time before the company tabulates the final vote at its annual meeting.

Nonvoting Common Stock

Companies may issue both voting and nonvoting (or limited voting) common stock, normally differentiating the issues as Class A and Class B, respectively. Issuing nonvoting stock allows a company to raise additional capital while maintaining management control and continuity without diluting present ownership.

FIGURE 1.1 Sample Proxy Ballot

> ### DATAWAQ, INCORPORATED
> #### Proxy for Annual Meeting of Stockholders, August 24, 1996
>
> The undersigned, having received the Notice of Meeting and Proxy statement dated July 24, 1996, hereby appoints Maurice Saltzman and Gerald Kurland, and each of them, proxies of the undersigned, with full power of substitution and revocation, to attend the annual meeting of the stockholders of the Company, to be held at the Company's executive offices at 6000 Data Place, Chula Vista, California, on Thursday, August 24, 1996, at 10:00 am (Pacific Time), and any adjournment thereof, and thereat to vote all the shares of stock of the undersigned in the Company which the undersigned would be entitled to vote if personally present, upon the following:
>
> (1) The election of seven (7) Directors; _____ For _____ Abstain
>
> (2) The adoption of the Employees' Savings Plan of Datawaq, Inc.; _____ For _____ Against
>
> (3) The ratification of the appointment of Max Leveridge & Co. as independent auditors; _____ For _____ Against
>
> (4) In their discretion, on any matters coming before the meeting, or any adjournment thereof;
>
> hereby ratifying and confirming all that said proxies may lawfully do or cause to be done by virtue hereof, and hereby revoking any proxies heretofore given by the undersigned to vote at said meeting or any adjournment thereof.
>
> **This proxy will be voted as directed or, if no direction is indicated, will be voted in favor of the proposals listed as items (1), (2) and (3).**
>
> **THIS PROXY IS SOLICITED BY THE MANAGEMENT.**
>
> (To be signed on the reverse side.)

Preemptive Rights

When a corporation raises capital through the sale of additional common stock, it may be required by law or its corporate charter to offer the securities to its common stockholders before the general public; this is known as an **antidilution agreement**. Stockholders then have a **preemptive right** to purchase enough newly issued shares to maintain their proportionate ownerships in the corporation.

✓ *For Example:* A person who owns 1 percent of the stock of Microscam Corporation (MCS) has a preemptive right to purchase 1 percent of any new stock issue. Therefore, if the company issues an additional 1 million shares, the stockholder has a preemptive right to purchase up to 10,000 shares.

Limited Liability   Stockholders cannot lose more than the amount they have paid for a corporation's stock. Limited liability protects stockholders from having to pay a corporation's debts in bankruptcy.

Inspection of Corporate Books   Stockholders have the right to receive annual financial statements and obtain lists of stockholders. Inspection rights do not include the right to examine detailed financial records or the minutes of directors' meetings.

Residual Claims to Assets   If a corporation is liquidated, the common stockholder, as owner, has a residual right to claim corporate assets after all debts and other security holders have been satisfied. The common stockholder is at the bottom of the liquidation priority list.

Stock Splits

Although investors and executives are generally delighted to see a company's stock price rise, a high market price may inhibit trading of the stock. To make the stock price attractive to a wider base of investors—that is, retail versus institutional investors—the company can declare a **stock split**. A stock split increases the number of shares and reduces the price without affecting the total market value of shares outstanding.

 For Example: In a four-for-one split, a company would distribute three additional shares of new stock for each share outstanding. An investor holding 100 shares before the split would receive an additional 300 shares and own 400 shares afterward. Each new share is worth one-fourth of the presplit price. The stockholder's 100 shares worth $100 each become 400 shares worth $25 each. The total market value remains $10,000 immediately before and after the split.

A **reverse split** has the opposite effect on the number and price of shares. After a reverse split, investors own fewer shares worth more per share. After a 1-for-2 reverse split, for example, a stockholder who owned 100 shares with a market value of $5 per share will own 50 shares worth $10 per share. If operating income remains the same, earnings per share increase because fewer shares are outstanding. The following chart illustrates the effect of stock splits on holdings.

Split Type	Old Shares	Old Price	Old Value	New Shares	New Price	New Value
4 for 1	100	$80	$8,000	400	$20	$8,000
1 for 4	100	$5	$500	25	$20	$500

Benefits and Risks of Owning Common Stock

Generally, and throughout this course, we assume an investor buys or owns shares of stock with the intent of selling them at a higher price at some point in the future—buy low, sell high later. An investor who buys shares is considered **long** the stock.

An investor may also sell shares before he owns them, with the intent of buying them back at a lower price in the future—sell high, buy low later. Such a transaction, known as a *short sale*, involves borrowing shares to sell that the investor must eventually replace. An investor who sells borrowed shares is considered **short** the stock until he buys and returns the shares to the lender.

Benefits of Owning Stock

People generally expect to receive financial growth, income or both from common stock investments.

Growth. An increase in the market price of shares is known as *capital appreciation*. Historically, owning common stock has provided investors with high real returns.

✔ *For Example:* An investor buys shares of RST for the market price of $60 per share on January 1, 1998. On December 31, 1998, the shares are worth $90, an increase of 50 percent in the market price.

Income. Many corporations pay regular quarterly cash dividends to stockholders. A company's dividends may increase over time as profitability increases. Dividends, which can be a significant source of income for investors, are a major reason many people invest in stocks.

✔ *For Example:* RST also paid a dividend of $2 per share during 1998, providing the investor with a dividend yield of 3.3 percent ($2 ÷ $60 = 3.33%) in addition to the market price appreciation.

✎ *Take Note:* The increase in the price of RST stock in the example above is referred to as an **unrealized gain** until the stock is sold; when it is sold, it becomes a **realized gain**. Capital gains are not taxed until they are realized. Dividend income is taxed in the year in which it is received.

Risks of Owning Stock

Regardless of their expectations, investors have no assurances that they will receive the returns they expect from their investments.

Market Risk. The chance that a stock will decline in price at a time the investor needs her money is one risk of owning common stock. A stock's price fluctuates daily as perceptions of the company's business prospects change and affect the actions of buyers and sellers. An investor has no assurance whatsoever that she will be able to recoup her investment in a stock at any point in time.

A long investor's losses are limited to his total investment in a stock. A short seller's losses are theoretically unlimited because there is no limit to how high a stock's price may climb.

Decreased or No Income. Another risk of stock ownership is the possibility of dividend income decreasing or ceasing entirely if the company loses money.

Low Priority at Dissolution. If a company enters bankruptcy, the holders of its bonds and preferred stock have priority over common stockholders. Therefore, a company's debt and preferred shares are considered senior securities. Common stockholders have only residual rights to corporate assets upon dissolution.

Preferred Stock

Preferred stock has features of both equity and debt securities. Preferred stock is an equity security because it represents ownership in the corporation. However, it does not normally offer the appreciation potential associated with common stock. Like a bond, preferred stock is usually issued as a fixed-income security with a fixed dividend. Its price tends to fluctuate with changes in interest rates rather than with the issuing company's business prospects unless, of course, dramatic changes occur in the company's credit quality. Unlike common stock, most preferred stock is nonvoting.

Although preferred stock does not typically have the same growth potential as common stock, preferred stockholders generally have two advantages over common stockholders:

1. When the board of directors declares dividends, owners of preferred stock receive their dividends before common stockholders.
2. If a corporation goes bankrupt, preferred stockholders have a priority claim over common stockholders on the assets remaining after creditors have been paid.

Fixed Rate of Return

A preferred stock's fixed dividend is a key feature for income-oriented investors. Normally, a preferred stock is identified by its annual dividend payment stated as a percentage of its par value, which is usually $100. (A preferred stock's par value is relevant, unlike that of a common stock.) A preferred stock with a par value of $100 that pays $6 in annual dividends is known as a *6 percent preferred*. The dividend of preferred stock with no par value is stated in a dollar amount, such as a *$6 no-par preferred*.

Adjustable-Rate Preferred

Some preferred stocks are issued with adjustable, or variable, dividend rates. Such dividends are usually tied to the rates of other interest rate benchmark, such as Treasury bill and money-market rates, and can be adjusted as often as quarterly.

Limited Ownership Privileges

Except for rare instances, preferred stock does not have voting or preemptive rights.

No Maturity Date or Set Maturity Value

Although a fixed-income investment, preferred stock, unlike bonds, has no preset date at which it matures and no scheduled redemption date.

Categories of Preferred Stock   Separate categories of preferred may differ in the dividend rate, in profit participation privileges or in any number of other ways. All, however, maintain a degree of preference over common stock. Preferred stock may have one or more of the following characteristics.

Straight (Noncumulative)

Straight preferred has no special features beyond the stated dividend payment. Missed dividends are not paid to the holder.

Cumulative Preferred

Buyers of preferred stock expect fixed quarterly dividend payments. The directors of a company in financial difficulties can reduce or suspend dividend payments to both common and preferred stockholders. Most likely, the corporation will never make up any dividends common stockholders miss. Any and all dividends due cumulative preferred stock accumulate on the company's books until the corporation can pay them. When the company can resume full payment of dividends, cumulative preferred stockholders receive their current dividends plus the total accumulated dividends—dividends in arrears—before any dividends may be distributed to common stockholders. Therefore, cumulative preferred is safer than straight preferred.

 For Example: In 1994, RST Corporation had both common stock and cumulative preferred stock outstanding. The common paid a dividend of $1, and the preferred paid a $2 dividend. Due to financial difficulties, the company stopped paying dividends during 1994. Having resolved its problems in 1998, the company resumed dividend payments and paid the cumulative preferred holders an $8 dividend for the arrears in years 1994, 1995, 1996 and 1997 before paying any dividend to the common stockholders.

Convertible Preferred

A preferred stock is convertible if the owner can exchange the shares for shares of common stock.

✓ *For Example:* A $100 preferred stock is convertible at $25. This means one preferred share may be exchanged for four shares of common stock ($100 par divided by the $25 conversion price). As long as the common stock price remains below $25 per share, the preferred stockholder has no incentive to convert. If the common stock price rises above $25 per share, however, the preferred stockholder could profit by converting shares into common stock at the preset below-market conversion price. Because the value of convertible preferred is linked to the value of common stock, its price fluctuates in line with the common.

✎ *Take Note:* Because the value of a convertible preferred stock is linked to the value of a common stock, the convertible preferred's price fluctuates in line with the common.

Convertible preferred may be issued with a lower stated dividend rate than nonconvertible preferred because the investor may have the opportunity to convert to common shares and enjoy capital gains. In addition, the conversion of preferred stock into shares of common increases the total number of common shares outstanding, which decreases earnings per common share and may decrease the common stock's market value.

Participating Preferred

In addition to fixed dividends, participating preferred stock offers its owners a share of corporate profits that remain after all dividends and interest due other securities are paid. The percentage to which participating preferred stock participates is noted on the stock certificate. If a preferred stock is described as "XYZ 6% preferred participating to 9%," the company pays its holders up to 3 percent in additional dividends in profitable years if the board declares so.

Callable Preferred

Corporations often issue callable, or redeemable, preferred, which a company can buy back from investors at a stated price after a specified date. The right to call the stock allows the company to replace a relatively high fixed dividend obligation with a lower one.

When a corporation calls a preferred stock, dividend payments and conversion rights generally cease on the call date. In return for the call privilege, the corporation usually pays a premium exceeding the stock's par value at the call, such as $103 for a $100 par value stock.

Return on Investment

An investment's *total* return is a combination of the dividend income and price appreciation or decline over a given period of time. You will need to know how to calculate current return, or yield, for the exam.

Dividends   Dividends are distributions of a company's profits to its stockholders. Investors who buy stock are entitled to dividends only when the company's board of directors votes to make such distributions. Stockholders are automatically sent any dividends to which their shares entitle them.

Cash Dividends

Cash dividends are normally distributed by check if an investor holds the stock certificate or are automatically deposited to a brokerage account if the shares are held in **street name**—that is, held in a brokerage account in the firm's name to facilitate payments and delivery. Dividends are usually paid quarterly and taxed as ordinary income in the year they are received.

 Take Note: The calculation to determine a stock's yield is:

Cash dividend ÷ Current price = Yield

Stock Dividends

If a company uses its cash for business purposes rather than to pay cash dividends, its board of directors may declare a stock dividend. Under these circumstances, the company issues shares of its common stock as a dividend to its current stockholders. A stock's market price and par value decline after a stock dividend, as with a stock split, but the company's total market value remains the same.

Calculating Return   To evaluate the return on a stock investment, combine the dividend yield
on Investment   with any change in the stock's price. The dividend yield is the annual dividend (normally four times the quarterly dividend) divided by the price paid for the stock.

 For Example: If the annual dividend for General Widget's (GW's) common stock is $1 (a quarterly dividend of $.25 × 4 = $1), at $20, the yield for GW is 5 percent ($1 ÷ $20 = 5%). If the stock price rises to $25 and the dividend remains the same, the yield declines to 4 percent ($1 ÷ $25 = 4%).

Transferability of Ownership

The ease with which stocks and other securities can be bought and sold contributes to the smooth operation of the securities markets. When an investor buys or sells a security, the exchange of money and ownership requires little or no additional action on his part.

The Stock Certificate   A stock certificate is a receipt for the shares of a corporation a person owns. The vast majority of stock transactions are for **round lot** numbers of shares—that is, share amounts evenly divisible by 100. **Odd lot** transactions are share amounts of fewer than 100 shares, such as 4 or 99. Individual stock certificates may be issued for any number of shares. For example, an investor who buys 100 shares of General Gizmonics receives one certificate for 100 shares.

Stock certificates identify the company's name, number of shares and investor's name, among other things. In addition, each certificate is printed with the security's CUSIP number.

CUSIP Numbers   A Committee on Uniform Securities Identification Procedures (CUSIP) number is a universal security identification number. Each issue of common stock, preferred stock, corporate bonds and municipal bonds has its own CUSIP number, which helps identify and track the certificate in the event it is lost or stolen. The CUSIP number is also used in trade confirmations and correspondence regarding specific securities.

Negotiability   Shares of stock are negotiable; that is, a stockholder can give, transfer, assign or sell shares he owns with few or no restrictions.

To transfer ownership of a stock, the registered owner must sign the stock certificate or a **stock power**, a form that duplicates the back of a stock certificate for transfer purposes. When securities are held in a brokerage account but registered in the owner's name, the stock power facilitates the transfer of securities when they are sold. Once the certificate or stock power has been signed, an exchange member, an authorized person of a broker-dealer or an officer of a national bank must guarantee the signature.

Transfer Procedures   The transfer and registration of stock certificates are two distinct functions that, by law, cannot be performed by a single person or department operating within the same institution. Issuers typically use commercial banks and trust companies to handle these functions.

Transfer Agent. The transfer agent for a corporation has the following responsibilities:

- ensures that its securities are issued in the correct owner's name
- cancels old and issues new certificates
- maintains records of ownership
- handles problems relating to lost, stolen or destroyed certificates

The transfer agent distributes additional shares in the event of a stock split or new certificates in the event of a reverse split. If a stock dividend or stock split results in fractional shares, under most circumstances the transfer agent sends the beneficial owner a check for a fractional share's value.

Registrar. Any stock or bond transaction requiring the registration and issuance of new certificates is routed through a registrar as well as the transfer agent. The registrar does not, however, keep a list of the names of the owners of the company's securities.

The registrar ensures that a corporation does not have more shares outstanding than have been authorized. The registrar is also responsible for certifying that a bond represents a legal debt of the issuer. Unlike the transfer agent, the registrar must be independent of the issuing corporation and is usually a bank or trust company.

Tracking Equity Securities

Common and preferred stock prices are listed in the financial sections of daily newspapers and in other financial publications.

A stock's market price is quoted in whole dollars, also known as *points*, plus fractions of a dollar.

✓ *For Example:* A half-point equals a half-dollar, or $.50. If a stock is quoted at 25, the stock's market price is $25 per share; a stock quoted at 25½ sells for $25.50 per share.

Exchange-Listed Stocks

Figure 1.2 is an example of an NYSE composite transactions listing as it might be printed in *The Wall Street Journal*. These consolidated stock tables, which present the most complete information available, report activity for the previous day.

The range of prices is shown for the previous 52 weeks, but does not include the latest trading day. ALFA, for instance, has had a 52-week high of 42⅝ ($42.625) and a low of 26⅞ ($26.875) per share.

The stock name and annual dividend follow the 52-week price range. The dividend is quoted as an annual dollar amount based on the most recent quarter. ALFA is paying an annual dividend of $2.40 per share. The "Yld" column reports the security's current yield. For ALFA, the yield is 5.6 percent ($2.40 ÷ 42⅝ = 5.6%).

FIGURE 1.2   NYSE Composite Transactions

New York Stock Exchange Composite Transactions

Tuesday, September 13, 1999
Quotations include trades on the Chicago, Pacific, Philadelphia, Boston and Cincinnati Stock Exchanges and reported by the National Association of Securities Dealers and INSTINET.

52 Weeks High	Low	Stock	Div	Yld %	PE Ratio	Sales 100s	High	Low	Close	Net Chg.
80	40	ABCorp	.75	.1	12	3329	78	71	73	- 1 1/2
n 8 3/8	6 1/2	ACM IncFd	1.01	12.4	...	178	8 1/4	8 1/8	8 1/8	- 1/8
42 5/8	26 7/8	ALFA	2.40	5.6	12	x 1265	42 5/8	41 1/4	42 5/8	+1 1/4
35	24 5/8	Anchor	1.48	4.9	36	1960	30	29 3/4	30	+ 1/4
27 1/4	25	ANR pf	2.67	10.3	...	6	26	26	26	...
6	1 7/8	ATT Cap wt	...	...	...	20	5 7/8	5 3/4	5 3/4	- 1/4
s 22 3/4	14	AVEMCO	.40	1.9	17	6	21 1/2	21 3/8	21 1/2	...
84 1/4	40	BrlNth	2.20	3.7	13	2701	59 3/8	58 1/4	58 3/4	+ 1/2
4 3/4	1/2	Brooke rt	...	...	...	26	4 5/8	4 5/8	4 5/8	...
7	2 1/2	CV REIT	.25	4.0	...	10	6 3/8	6 1/4	6 1/4	...
3 1/8	2 1/4	CalifREIT	.40	13.9	...	3	2 7/8	2 7/8	2 7/8	...
39 3/8	17 7/8	Circus wi	...	...	...	14	39 1/4	38 7/8	39 1/4	+ 5/8
82 1/2	39 5/8	Dsny	.32	.6	17	6211	53 3/4	52	53 1/4	+1 1/4
38 3/8	19 1/2	Fubar	.24	.9	13	z 1454	28	26 7/8	27 3/8	+ 1/4
8 3/4	3 5/8	Navistr	...	...	...	6484	4 1/2	4 1/8	4 1/4	...

EXPLANATORY NOTES

The following explanations apply to New York and American Exchange listed issues and the National Association of Securities Dealers Automated Quotations system's over-the-counter securities. The 52-week high and low columns show the highest and lowest price of the issue during the preceding 52 weeks. Dividend rates, unless noted, are annual disbursements. Yield is the dividends paid by a company on its securities, expressed as a percentage of price. The PE ratio is determined by dividing the price of a share of stock by its company's earnings. Sales figures are quoted in 100s (00 omitted). a-Extra dividend. b-Annual rate of the cash dividend and a stock dividend was paid. n-Newly issued in the past 52 weeks. pf-Preferred. rt-Rights. s-Stock split or dividend greater than 25% in the past 52 weeks. vi-In bankruptcy or receivership. wd-When distributed. wi-When issued. wt-Warrants. ww-With warrants. x-Ex-dividend or ex-rights. xw-Without warrants. z-Sales in full, not in hundreds.

The "PE Ratio" (price-earnings ratio) column follows the "Yld" column. It gives the ratio of the stock's current price to its earnings during the past 12 months. ALFA's PE ratio is 12.

The "Sales" column reports the number of shares traded during the day. Trading is reported in round lots of 100 shares. The entry for ALFA is 1265, which means that 126,500 shares of stock were traded. The "x" before the sales volume indicates that the stock is selling ex-dividend, or ex-rights, meaning that a buyer will not receive the next dividend check.

The two columns after "Sales" list the daily range of prices—the security's high and low prices for the day. ALFA sold for a high of 42⅝ and a low of 41¼. The column labeled "Close" shows the final price for the day. ALFA closed at 42⅝, at the top of its 52-week range.

The final column reports the net change in price. The net change is the difference between the closing price on the trading day reported and the previous day's closing price. ALFA closed up 1¼ points from the previous day's close.

Over-the-Counter Stocks

Thousands of securities trade in the OTC market. Daily transactions for these securities and the names of market makers who trade each of them are found in the *Pink Sheets*. These are interdealer quotations subject to change.

Nasdaq Small Cap Issues

OTC stocks that have national interest are listed on the National Association of Securities Dealers Automated Quotation system (Nasdaq). Quotes for these securities can be found on a quote machine, a computer that facilitates OTC trading.

Listings for more frequently traded Nasdaq securities may appear in *The Wall Street Journal*. Figure 1.3 provides an example of Nasdaq small cap transactions. The listing shows the stock name, its dividend, its sales volume in round lots, the execution price of the day's last transaction and the net change from the previous day's last transaction.

Nasdaq National Market Stocks

OTC stocks with very high national interest may be listed on the Nasdaq National Market (NNM). Although these securities may be eligible for listing on an exchange, the companies have chosen to sell OTC instead. Intel is an example of a well-known company that does not list its stock on an exchange. NNM listings contain similar information as is supplied for exchange-listed securities, as illustrated in Figure 1.4.

FIGURE 1.3   Nasdaq Small Cap Transactions

Nasdaq Small Cap Issues

Quotations as of 4 pm Eastern Time
Tuesday, September 13, 1998

Stock & Div	Sales 100s	Last	Net Chg.	Stock & Div	Sales 100s	Last	Net Chg.
A&A Fd g	29	4 5/8	- 1/16	FtnPh un	5	15	...
ACS En	12	1 3/8	...	Frnchtx .03e	118	5 1/2	+ 1/8
ACTV	14	1 7/8	...	FrntAd .04e	20	2 1/2	...
ACTV wt	86	3/4	...	FutCm	472	6 3/4	- 1/16
AFN s	390	1 7/8	...	BG Fds	209	4 1/2	+ 1/16
AGBag	162	4 5/8	...	GTEC 56pf .90	6	10 1/2	...
APA	40	4 1/2	...	GTEC 5pf 1.00	z65	11 1/2	...

FIGURE 1.4   NNM Transactions

Nasdaq National Market Issues

Quotations as of 4 pm Eastern Time
Tuesday, September 13, 1998

52 Weeks High	Low	Stock	Symbol	Div	Yld %	PE Ratio	Sales 100s	High	Low	Close	Net Chg.
37 3/4	20	A&W Brands	SODA	.40	1.1	26	237	36 3/4	35 3/4	36	- 1/2
8 1/2	5 1/8	Acme Steel	ACME	.32	5.1	20	3	6 1/4	6	6 1/4	+ 1/4
s 13 1/2	4 1/8	Adobe Sys	ADBE	.16	1.6	20	59	10 1/4	9 3/4	10 1/4	+ 1/2
43 1/2	15 1/4	AdvMktg	ADMS	...	...	21	226	41 1/4	40 1/4	40 1/4	- 1/4
30	7 5/8	AffBkshCo	AFBK	t	...	3	x 3764	11 1/2	9 1/8	10 7/8	+1 7/8
7 1/4	4	Aldus	ALDS	...	...	18	3211	6 1/2	6 1/8	6 1/2	...
41 1/2	26 5/8	AmGreetgs	AGREA	.70	2.1	13	1511	34 1/2	33 3/8	33 3/8	- 1

Nasdaq Symbol Explanation

Securities in the Nasdaq system are identified by a four or five letter symbol. The fifth letter, as described below, indicates issues that aren't common stock, or which are subject to restrictions or special conditions. A-Class A. B-Class B. C-Exempt from Nasdaq listing qualifications for a limited period. D-New issue. E-Delinquent J-Voting. K-Nonvoting. L-Miscellaneous. M-Fourth preferred. N-Third preferred. O-Second preferred. P-First preferred. Q-In bankruptcy. R-Rights. S-Shares of beneficial interest. T-With warrants or rights. U-Units. V-When issued or when in required SEC filings. F-Foreign. G-First convertible bond. H-Second convertible bond. I-Third convertible bond. distributed. W-Warrants. Y-American Depositary Receipt. Z-Miscellaneous situations.

Rights and Warrants

Preemptive rights entitle existing stockholders to maintain their proportionate ownership shares in a company by buying newly issued shares before the company offers them to the general public. A **rights offering** allows stockholders to purchase common stock below the current market price. The rights are valued separately from the stock and trade in the secondary market during the **subscription period**. A stockholder who receives rights may:

- **exercise the rights** to buy stock by sending the rights certificates and a check for the required amount to the rights agent;
- **sell the rights** and profit from their market value (rights certificates are negotiable securities); or
- **let the rights expire** and lose their value.

Approval of Additional Stock

The board of directors must approve decisions to issue additional stock through a rights offering. If the additional shares will increase the stock outstanding beyond the amount authorized in the company charter, the stockholders must vote to amend the charter.

Characteristics of Rights

Once a rights offering has been issued, investors may buy or sell the rights in the secondary market just as they do stocks. If the holder of a right does not sell it, he may either exercise it to buy the stock specified in the right or let it expire.

Subscription Right Certificate

A subscription right is a certificate representing a short-term (typically 30 to 45 days) privilege to buy additional shares of a corporation. One right is issued for each common stock share.

Terms of the Offering

The terms of a rights offering are stipulated on the subscription right certificates mailed to stockholders on the payable date. The terms describe how many new shares a stockholder may buy, the price, the date the new stock will be issued and the final date for exercising the rights.

Significant Trading Dates and Prices of Rights Offerings

Associated Industries, Inc. (AII), plans to raise capital by issuing additional stock and, on April 1, declares a rights offering. Common stockholders as of May 1 can subscribe to one new share, at a price of $70, for each five shares of stock they own. AII stock trades for $100 per share. The rights will expire on June 18.

The number of rights required to buy one new share is based on the number of shares outstanding and the number of new shares offered. Associated Industries has 5 million shares outstanding and will issue 1 million additional shares. Because each existing share is entitled to one right, the company will issue 5 million rights. Because 5 million rights entitle stockholders to buy 1 million shares, it will require five rights to buy one new share. Between April 1 and June 18, the stock tables in newspapers and other publications will show two entries for Associated Industries:

- the price of the stock with rights (**cum rights**) or, after the rights distribution ex-date, without rights (**ex-rights**); and
- the price of the rights, either on a **when issued** basis—before they are issued—or after they have been issued.

The corporation will issue rights May 8 to stockholders of record May 1. Stock is traded cum rights until the ex-date. An investor who buys the stock cum rights receives the right. An investor who buys the stock ex-rights does not.

The Rights Agent

The **rights agent** keeps a record of who owns each right, just as a transfer agent records each stockholder's name. When a right is sold, the rights agent records the new owner's name. The rights agent may or may not be the same individual or trust that acts as transfer agent.

Standby Underwriting

If the current stockholders do not subscribe to all the additional stock, the issuer may offer unsold rights to a broker-dealer in a standby underwriting. A standby underwriting is done on a firm commitment basis, meaning the broker-dealer buys all unsold shares from the issuer and resells them to the general public.

Characteristics of Warrants

A **warrant** is a certificate granting its owner the right to purchase securities from the issuer at a specified price, normally higher than the current market price. Unlike a right, a warrant is usually a long-term instrument, giving the investor the option of buying shares at a later date at the exercise price.

Origination of Warrants

Warrants are usually offered to the public as sweeteners in connection with other securities, such as debentures or preferred stock, to make those securities more attractive. Such offerings are often bundled as **units**.

✓ *For Example:* Datawaq may make an offering of 1 million shares of new preferred stock, bundling it into units of two shares of preferred and one warrant for one share of common stock exercisable at a specific price. An investor who purchases 100 units receives 200 shares of preferred stock plus warrants redeemable for 100 shares of common (100 units times one warrant for 1 share of common per unit).

Warrants may be detachable or nondetachable from other securities. If detachable, they trade in the secondary market in line with the common stock's price. When first issued, a warrant's exercise price is set well above the stock's market price. As the stock's price increases, the owner can exercise the warrant and buy the stock below the market price or sell the warrant in the market.

Table 1.1 compares rights and warrants.

TABLE 1.1 Comparison of Rights and Warrants

Rights	Warrants
Short-term	Long-term
Exercisable below market value	Exercisable above market value
May trade with or separate from the common stock	May trade with or separate from the units
Offered to existing shareholders with preemptive rights	Offered as a sweetener for another security(ies)

American Depositary Receipts

American depositary receipts (ADRs), also known as *American depositary shares (ADSs)*, facilitate the trading of foreign stocks in U.S. markets. An ADR is a negotiable security that represents a receipt for shares of stock in a non–U.S. corporation, usually from 1 to 10 shares. ADRs are bought and sold in the U.S. securities markets like stock.

Rights of ADR Owners

Most of the rights common stockholders normally hold ADR owners also hold. These include voting rights and the right to receive dividends when declared. ADR holders do not normally have preemptive rights.

Delivery of Foreign Security.   ADR owners have the right to exchange their ADR certificates for the foreign shares they represent. They can do this by returning the ADRs to the depository banks, which cancel the ADRs and deliver the underlying stock.

Currency Risk.   In addition to the normal risks associated with stock ownership, ADR investors are also subject to currency risk. Currency risk is the possibility that an investment denominated in one currency, such as the Mexican peso, could decline if the value of that currency declines in its exchange rate with the U.S. dollar. Because ADRs represent shares of stock in companies located in foreign countries, currency exchange rates are an important consideration.

Registration Requirements Foreign corporations often use ADRs as a means of generating U.S. investment in their securities. By issuing ADRs, foreign corporations do not have to go through the SEC registration process typical for new U.S. issues.

Custodian Bank Foreign branches of large commercial U.S. banks issue ADRs. A custodian, typically a bank in the issuer's country, holds the shares of foreign stock that the ADRs represent. The stock must remain on deposit as long as the ADRs are outstanding because the ADRs are the depository bank's guarantee that it holds the stock.

Registered Owner. ADRs are registered on the books of the U.S. banks responsible for them. The individual investors in the ADRs are not considered the stock's registered owners. Because ADRs are registered on the books of U.S. banks, dividends are sent to the custodian banks as registered owners. The banks collect the payments, convert them into U.S. funds for U.S. owners and withhold any required foreign tax payments.

Real Estate Investment Trusts

A real estate investment trust (REIT) is a company that manages a portfolio of real estate investments in order to earn profits for shareholders. REITs are normally traded publicly, and serve as a source of long-term financing for real estate projects.

A REIT pools capital in a manner similar to an investment company. Shareholders receive dividends from investment income or capital gains distributions.

REITs are organized as trusts or corporations where investors buy shares or certificates of beneficial interest either on stock exchanges or in the OTC market. Under the guidelines of Subchapter M of the Internal Revenue Code, a REIT can avoid being taxed as a corporation by receiving 75 percent or more of its income from real estate and distributing 95 percent or more of its taxable income to its shareholders.

Summary

Buying stock in companies is the most common means by which investors become owners of companies. As owners of a company, stockholders enjoy certain rights and privileges that are not available to the company's other constituents. A company's owners enjoy the fruits of a company's success more than any other group. Conversely, the owners generally have the lowest priority claims on a company's assets in the event of failure. By far the most widely known type of stock is common stock. Common stockholders have voting rights and also may receive periodic dividends when declared by the board of directors.

Preferred stock is almost always a fixed-income security. Preferred shares take priority over common shares in the liquidation of the company and in payment of dividends.

Rights and warrants are securities that allow the holder to buy common stock under specified conditions. Rights allow the holder to buy common stock within a short timeframe at a price lower than the market price. Warrants allow the holder to buy the stock at a price higher than the current market price over a long timeframe.

ADRs represent common or preferred stock in foreign companies. Traded on a U.S. exchange or in the OTC market, the ownership privileges of ADRs may be different from those for domestic stocks.

Key Concepts

To prepare for your license exam, you should learn the following concepts.

In addition to studying these key concepts, use the Equity Securities Hot Sheet on page 633 for further review.

American depositary receipt (ADR)	participating preferred stock
authorized stock	par value
book value	preemptive right
callable preferred stock	preferred stock
cash dividend	real estate investment trust (REIT)
convertible preferred stock	registrar
cumulative preferred stock	residual claim
cumulative voting	reverse split
CUSIP number	rights offering
dividend	statutory voting
equity security	stock dividend
issued stock	stock split
market value	transfer agent
negotiability	treasury stock
outstanding stock	warrant

Review Questions

1. Which of the following represent(s) owner-ship (equity) in a company?

    I. Corporate bonds
    II. Common stock
    III. Preferred stock
    IV. Mortgage bonds

    A. I and IV only
    B. II only
    C. II and III only
    D. I, II, III and IV

2. Which of the following statements describe treasury stock?

    I. It has voting rights and is entitled to a dividend when declared.
    II. It has no voting rights and no dividend entitlement.
    III. It has been issued and repurchased by the company.
    IV. It is authorized but unissued stock.

    A. I and III
    B. I and IV
    C. II and III
    D. II and IV

3. In which of the following ways may a company declare dividends?

    I. Cash
    II. Stock
    III. Stock of another company

    A. I only
    B. I and II only
    C. II and III only
    D. I, II and III

4. ALFA Enterprises currently has earnings of $4 and pays a $.50 quarterly dividend. The market price of ALF is $40. What is the current yield?

    A. 1.25 percent
    B. 5 percent
    C. 10 percent
    D. 15 percent

5. A corporation must have stockholder approval to

    A. issue bonds for capital improvements
    B. repurchase 100,000 shares of stock for the treasury
    C. declare a 15 percent stock dividend
    D. declare a cash dividend

6. Limited liability regarding ownership in a large, publicly held U.S. corporation means all of the following EXCEPT

    A. investors might lose the amount of their investment
    B. investors might lose their investment plus the difference between their investment and par value
    C. investors' shares are nonassessable
    D. investors are not liable to the full extent of their personal property

7. Stockholders' preemptive rights include which of the following rights?

    A. Right to serve as an officer on the board of directors
    B. Right to maintain proportionate ownership interest in the corporation
    C. Right to purchase treasury stock
    D. Right to a subscription price on stock

8. Common stockholders' rights include a

   I. residual claim to assets at dissolution
   II. vote for the amount of stock dividend to be paid
   III. vote in matters of recapitalization
   IV. claim against dividends that are in default

   A. I
   B. I and III
   C. II and III
   D. III and IV

9. When a corporation holds treasury stock, it has the option of

   A. reissuing it as debt securities
   B. not disclosing it to the registrar
   C. retiring it
   D. registering it under any name it chooses

10. A corporation issuing stock has informed its stockholders that they can buy the newly issued stock for $21.50 per share with 20 rights. The outstanding stock is currently trading at $40. To purchase a share of the stock at the subscription price takes

    A. $21.50 with one right
    B. $21.50 with 20 rights
    C. $21.50 with 21 rights
    D. $40 with one right

11. Datawaq Corporation has declared a rights offering. An investor who owns 100 shares on the record date is entitled to 100 subscription rights to be sold on a when issued basis. The change of ownership is recorded by the

    A. registrar
    B. rights agent
    C. transfer agent
    D. issuer

12. Which of the following instruments does NOT receive dividends?

    A. Warrants
    B. Common stock
    C. Preferred stock
    D. Convertible preferred stock

Answers & Rationale

1. **C.** Owning either common or preferred stocks represents ownership (or equity) in a corporation. The other two choices represent debt instruments. Clients purchasing corporate or mortgage bonds would be considered lenders, not owners.

2. **C.** Treasury stock is stock a corporation has issued but subsequently repurchased from investors in the secondary market. The corporation can either reissue the stock at a later date or retire it. Stock that has been repurchased by the corporation has no voting rights and is not entitled to any declared dividends.

3. **D.** Cash dividends are normally declared by corporations, but corporations can also declare stock dividends (where stockholders receive additional shares) or declare dividends that are securities in another company the corporation owns. This type of dividend is known as a *property dividend*.

4. **B.** The current yield on a stock is calculated by dividing the yearly dividend by the current market price of the stock.

5. **A.** Stockholders are entitled to vote on whether to issue bonds because bonds have a priority claim to corporate resources over common stock. The other choices are decisions that are made by the board of directors and don't require a stockholder vote.

6. **B.** An advantage of owning stock is that an investor's liability is limited to the amount of money he invested when the stock was purchased.

7. **B.** Preemptive rights deal with stockholders maintaining their proportionate ownership when the corporation wants to issue more stock. If a stockholder owns 5 percent of the outstanding stock and the corporation wants to issue more stock, the stockholder has the right to purchase enough of the new shares to maintain a 5 percent ownership position in the company.

8. **B.** Choices I and III are common stockholder rights. Dividend declarations are decided by the board of directors, not by the stockholders. Claims against dividends in default can be made only by preferred stockholders.

9. **C.** The corporation always has the option of retiring treasury stock. Stock cannot be reissued as debt. The registrar has to know how many shares are outstanding at any given time in order to keep accurate records.

10. **B.** With 20 rights, a stockholder would pay $21.50 per share of the new stock.

11. **B.** The rights agent does for rights what the transfer agent does for stocks. The rights agent keeps a record of who owns each right.

12. **A.** A warrant is not evidence of ownership in a corporation qualifying for dividends. It is a certificate giving the holder the right to purchase securities from the issuer at a stipulated price. Eventually the warrant expires.

2

Debt Securities

OVERVIEW

Whether issued by corporations, municipalities, the U.S. government or its agencies, bonds are **debt securities**; that is, they represent an investor's loan to an issuer. As a borrower, the issuer promises to repay the debt on a specified date and to pay interest on the loan amount. Because the interest rate the investor receives is set when the bonds are issued, they are known as *fixed-income securities*. Individual bonds usually have a face (par) value of $1,000.

Although government, corporate and municipal bonds each have characteristics that distinguish them from the others, all bonds share certain features.

Characteristics of Bonds

Unlike stockholders, bondholders have no ownership interest in the issuing corporation or voice in management. As creditors, bondholders receive preferential treatment over common and preferred stockholders if a corporation files for bankruptcy. Because creditor claims are settled before the claims of stockholders, bonds are considered **senior securities**. Therefore, stockholders' interests are subordinate to those of bondholders.

Issuers

Corporations issue bonds to raise working capital or funds for capital expenditures such as plant construction or equipment and other major purchases. Corporate bonds are commonly referred to as *funded debt*. Funded debt is any long-term debt payable in five years or more.

The federal government is the nation's largest borrower and the most secure credit risk. Treasury bills (maturities of one year or less), notes (1- to 10-year maturities) and bonds (10- to 30-year maturities) are backed by the full faith and credit of the government and its unlimited taxing powers.

Municipal securities are the debt obligations of state and local governments and their agencies. Most are issued to raise capital to finance public works or construction projects that benefit the general public.

Interest   Both the interest rate an issuer pays its bondholders and the timing of payments are set when a bond is issued. The interest rate, or coupon, is calculated from the bond's par value. Par value, also known as *face value*, is normally $1,000 per bond, meaning each bond will be redeemed for $1,000 when it matures. Interest on a bond accrues daily and is paid in semiannual installments over the life of the bond.

> **For Example:** An investor who owns a bond that pays 7 percent interest will receive $70 ($1,000 × 7% = $70) in income each year in two $35 semiannual installments.

The final interest payment is made when the bond matures, and it is normally combined with repayment of the principal amount. If a bondholder has been receiving semiannual payments of $350 from 10 bonds, he will receive a check for $10,350 when the bonds mature.

Maturities   On the maturity date, the loan principal is repaid to the investor. Each bond has its own maturity date. The most common maturities fall in the 5- to 30-year range.

Three basic types of bond maturity structures are term, serial and balloon.

Term Maturity. A term bond is structured so that the principal of the whole issue matures at once. Because all of the principal is repaid at one time, most issuers establish a **sinking fund** account in which to accumulate money that will be due at maturity.

Serial Maturity. A serial bond issue schedules portions of the principal to mature at intervals over a period of years, until the entire balance has been repaid

Figure 2.1 illustrates bonds issued with serial maturities.

Balloon Maturity. An issuer sometimes schedules its bond's maturity using elements of both serial and term maturities. The issuer repays part of the bond's principal before the final maturity date, as with a serial maturity, but pays off the major portion of the bond at maturity. This bond has a balloon, or **serial and balloon**, maturity.

FIGURE 2.1   Example of Bonds with Serial Maturities

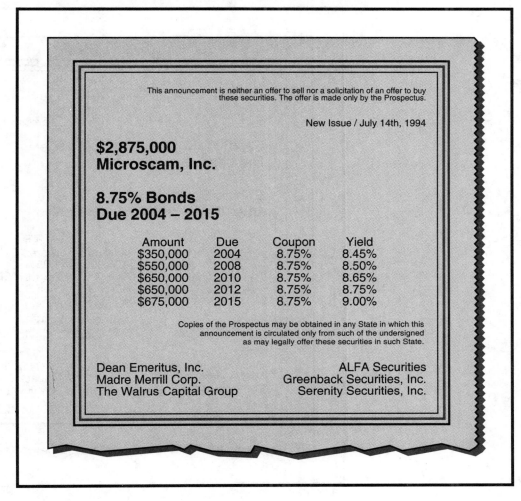

This announcement is neither an offer to sell nor a solicitation of an offer to buy these securities. The offer is made only by the Prospectus.

New Issue / July 14th, 1994

$2,875,000
Microscam, Inc.

8.75% Bonds
Due 2004 – 2015

Amount	Due	Coupon	Yield
$350,000	2004	8.75%	8.45%
$550,000	2008	8.75%	8.50%
$650,000	2010	8.75%	8.65%
$650,000	2012	8.75%	8.75%
$675,000	2015	8.75%	9.00%

Copies of the Prospectus may be obtained in any State in which this announcement is circulated only from such of the undersigned as may legally offer these securities in such State.

Dean Emeritus, Inc.	ALFA Securities
Madre Merrill Corp.	Greenback Securities, Inc.
The Walrus Capital Group	Serenity Securities, Inc.

Series Issues. Instead of placing all of its bonds in the hands of investors at one time, any bond issuer may spread out its borrowing over several years as its needs dictate by issuing the bonds in separate series. Figure 2.2 lists such bonds.

Bond Certificate   Bonds have traditionally been issued as certificates, physical evidence that designates the bond's ownership and characteristics—in essence, an IOU.

Each bond certificate contains the following information:

- name of issuing company
- type of bond
- principal amount

FIGURE 2.2   Example of Bonds Issued in Series

This announcement is neither an offer to sell nor a solicitation of an offer to buy these securities. The offer is made only by the Prospectus.

New Issue / July 14th, 1994

$1,250,000
Datawaq, Inc.

Series Bonds
Due 2014 – 2030

Series	Issue Date	$ Amount of Issue	Interest Rate	Maturity Date
L	Jul 1994	$400,000	7.25%	Jul 2014
M	Nov 1996	$250,000	7.35%	Dec 2016
N	Jun 1998	$400,000	7.65%	Jun 2025
O	Jul 2000	$200,000	7.50%	Jul 2030

Copies of the Prospectus may be obtained in any State in which this announcement is circulated only from such of the undersigned as may legally offer these securities in such State.

Dean Emeritus, Inc.   ALFA Securities
Madre Merrill Corp.   Greenback Securities, Inc.
The Walrus Capital Group   Serenity Securities, Inc.

- date of issue
- maturity date
- call feature(s)
- interest rate and payment date
- where interest is payable (coupon bond only)
- reference to the trust indenture

Registration of Bonds

Bonds are registered, in varying degrees, to record ownership should a certificate be lost or stolen. Tracking a bond's ownership through its registration has been common in the United States only since the early 1970s.

Coupon (Bearer) Bonds

Though rare today, in past years most bonds were issued in coupon, or bearer, form. Issuers kept no records of purchasers, and securities were issued without an investor's name printed on the certificate. Because coupon bonds are not registered, whoever possesses them can collect interest on, sell or redeem the bonds.

Interest coupons are attached to bearer bonds, and holders collect interest by clipping the coupons and delivering them to an issuer's paying agent. Individual coupons are payable to the bearer. When a bond matures, the bearer delivers it to the paying agent and receives his principal.

No proof of ownership is needed to sell a bearer bond.

Registered Bonds

The most common form of bond currently issued is the registered bond. When a registered bond is issued, the issuer's transfer agent records the bondholder's name. The buyer's name appears on the bond certificate's face.

Fully Registered. When bonds are registered as to both principal and interest, the transfer agent maintains a list of bondholders and updates this list as bond ownership changes. Interest payments are automatically sent to bondholders of record. The transfer agent transfers a registered bond whenever a bond is sold by canceling the seller's certificate and issuing a new one in the buyer's name. Most corporate bonds are issued in fully registered form.

Registered as to Principal Only. Principal-only registered bonds have the owner's name printed on the certificate, but the coupons are in bearer form.

When bonds registered as to principal only are sold, the names of the new owners are recorded (in order) on the bond certificates and on the issuer's registration record. Like bearer bonds, bonds registered as to principal only are no longer issued.

Book-Entry Bonds

Book-entry bond owners do not receive certificates. Rather, the transfer agent maintains the security's ownership records. While the names of buyers of both registered and book-entry bonds are recorded (registered), the book-entry bond owner does not receive a certificate—the registered bond owner does. The trade confirmation serves as evidence of book-entry bond ownership. Most U.S. government bonds are available only in book-entry form.

Pricing   Once issued, bonds are bought and sold in the secondary market at prices determined by conditions unique to the issuer or common to all debt securities.

Par, Premium and Discount

Bonds are issued with a face, or par, value of $1,000. **Par** represents the dollar amount of the investor's loan to the issuer, and it is the amount repaid when the bond matures.

In the secondary market, bonds can sell for any price—at par, below par (at a **discount**) or above par (at a **premium**). The two primary factors affecting a bond's market price are the issuer's financial stability and overall trends in interest rates. If an issuer's credit rating remains constant, interest rates are the only factor that affect the market price.

Bond quotes are commonly stated as percentages of par. A bid of 100 means 100 percent of par, or $1,000. A bond quote of 98⅛ means 98 and ⅛ percent (98.125 percent) of $1,000, or $981.25. Bond price changes are quoted in newspapers in points. One point is 1 percent of $1,000, or $10; ¼ point equals $2.50; a basis point in yield is equal to 10¢ in price. The minimum variation for most corporate and municipal bond quotes is ⅛ (.125 percent, or $1.25).

Table 2.1 shows the dollar values of prices for bonds with $1,000 par values.

TABLE 2.1   Example of Corporate Bond Pricing

A Price of . . .	Means . . .	Or . . .
92	92% of $1,000	$920.00
93⅛	93⅛% of $1,000	$931.25
94¼	94¼% of $1,000	$942.50
95⅜	95⅜% of $1,000	$953.75
96½	96½% of $1,000	$965.00
97⅝	97⅝% of $1,000	$976.25
98¾	98¾% of $1,000	$987.50
99⅞	99⅞% of $1,000	$998.75
100	100% of $1,000	$1,000.00
105	105% of $1,000	$1,050.00

FIGURE 2.3 Bond Ratings

Standard & Poor's	Moody's	Interpretation
Bank grade (investment grade) bonds		
AAA	Aaa	Highest rating. Capacity to repay principal and interest judged high.
AA	Aa	Very strong. Only slightly less secure than the highest rating.
A	A	Judged to be slightly more susceptible to adverse economic conditions.
BBB	Baa	Adequate capacity to repay principal and interest. Slightly speculative.
Speculative (non-investment grade) bonds		
BB	Ba	Speculative. Significant chance that issuer could miss an interest payment.
B	B	Issuer has missed one or more interest or principal payments.
C	Caa	No interest is being paid on bond at this time.
D	D	Issuer is in default. Payment of interest or principal is in arrears.

Rating and Analyzing Bonds

Rating services, such as Standard & Poor's and Moody's, evaluate the credit quality of bond issues and publish their ratings. Standard & Poor's and Moody's rate both corporate and municipal bonds. Both base their bond ratings primarily on an issuer's creditworthiness—that is, the issuer's ability to pay interest and principal as they come due. Figure 2.3 summarizes the rating services' bond ratings.

A plus or minus sign in a Standard & Poor's rating indicates that the bond falls within the top (+) or bottom (−) of that particular category. Moody's uses A1 and Baa1 to indicate the highest quality bonds within those two categories. Moody's also provides ratings for short-term municipal notes, designating MIG-1 as the highest quality and MIG-4 as the lowest.

The rating organizations rate those issues that either pay to be rated or have enough bonds outstanding to generate constant investor interest. The fact that a bond is not rated does *not* indicate its quality; many issues are too small to justify the expense of a bond rating.

Basis for Bond Ratings   Bond ratings are based on an issuer's financial stability. The rating services apply a series of financial tests to assess a corporation's financial strength.

Specific criteria used to rate corporate and municipal bonds include:

- the amount and composition of existing debt;
- the stability of the issuer's cash flow;
- the issuer's ability to meet scheduled payments of interest and principal on its debt obligations;
- asset protection; and
- management capability.

A bond's rating may change over time as the issuer's ability to make interest and principal payments changes.

Investment Grade. The Comptroller of the Currency, the Federal Deposit Insurance Corporation (FDIC), the Federal Reserve and state banking authorities have established policies determining which securities banks can purchase. A municipal bond must be investment grade (a rating of BBB/Baa or higher) to be suitable for purchase by banks. Investment-grade bonds are also known as *bank-grade bonds*.

Relationship of Rating to Yield   Generally, the higher a bond's rating, the lower its yield. Investors will accept lower returns on their investments if their principal and interest payments are safe. Bonds with low ratings due to the issuer's instability pay higher rates because of the risks to principal and interest associated with such uncertainties.

Qualitative Analysis. In addition to financial statistics, qualitative factors such as an industry's stability, the issuer's quality of management and the regulatory climate may be considered when bonds are rated.

Comparative Safety of Debt Securities   Although there are exceptions to the rule, a hierarchy exists in the degree of safety associated with different categories of debt securities. Normally, the higher the degree of safety, the lower the yield relative to other investments at the same point in time.

U.S. Government Securities. The highest degree of safety is in securities backed by the full faith and credit of the U.S. government. These securities include:

- U.S. Treasury bills, notes and bonds, as well as Series EE and HH bonds;
- Government National Mortgage Association bonds (GNMAs or Ginnie Maes); and
- New Housing Authority bonds (NHAs).

Government Agency Issues. The second highest degree of safety is in securities issued by government agencies and government-sponsored corporations, although the U.S. government does not back the securities. These organizations include:

- Federal Farm Credit Banks
- Federal Home Loan Bank (FHLB)
- Federal National Mortgage Association (FNMA or Fannie Mae)

Municipal Issues. Generally, the next level of safety is in securities issued by municipalities. General obligation bonds (GOs), backed by the taxing power of the issuer, are usually safer than revenue bonds. Revenue bonds are backed by revenues from the facility financed by the bond issue.

Corporate Securities. Corporate debt securities cover the safety spectrum, from very safe (AAA corporates) to very risky (junk bonds). Corporate bonds are backed, in varying degrees, by the issuing corporation. Usually, these securities are ranked from safe to risky, as follows:

1. equipment trust certificates
2. first mortgage bonds
3. debentures
4. subordinated debentures
5. income bonds

However, these rankings serve only as a rough guideline.

Liquidity   Liquidity is the ease with which a bond or any other security can be sold. Many factors determine a bond's liquidity, including:

- quality
- rating
- maturity
- call features
- coupon rate and current market value
- issuer
- existence of a sinking fund

Debt Retirement

The schedule of interest and principal payments due on a bond issue is known as the **debt service**.

Redemption   When a bond's principal is repaid, the bond is **redeemed**. Redemption usually occurs on the maturity date.

Sinking Fund. To facilitate the retirement of its bonds, a corporate or municipal issuer establishes a sinking fund operated by the bonds' trustee. The trust indenture often requires a sinking fund, which can be used to call bonds, redeem bonds at maturity or buy back bonds in the open market.

To establish a sinking fund, the issuer deposits cash in an account with the trustee. Because a sinking fund makes money available for redeeming bonds, it can aid the bonds' price stability.

Calling Bonds

Bonds are often issued with a call feature, or call option. A call feature allows the issuer to redeem a bond issue before its maturity date, either in whole or in part (**in-whole** or **partial calls**). The issuer does this by notifying bondholders that it will redeem the bonds at a particular price on a certain date.

Call Premium. The right to call bonds for early redemption gives issuers flexibility in their financial management. In return, an issuer usually pays bondholders a premium, a price higher than par, known as a *call premium*. Various municipal bonds, corporate bonds and preferred stocks are callable at some point over their terms, although many are not.

Advantages of a Call to the Issuer. Callable bonds can benefit the issuer in numerous ways:

- If general interest rates decline, the issuer can redeem bonds with a high interest rate and replace them with bonds with a lower rate.
- The issuer can call bonds to reduce its debt any time after the initial call date.
- The issuer can replace short-term debt issues with long-term issues, and vice versa.
- The issuer can call bonds as a means of forcing the conversion of convertible corporate securities.

Term bonds are generally called by random drawing. Serial bonds, on the other hand, are usually called in inverse order of their maturities because longer maturities tend to have higher interest rates. Calling the long maturities lowers the issuer's interest expense by the largest amount.

If a bond issue's trust indenture does not require a call, the issuer normally can buy bonds in the open market, known as **tendering**, to retire a portion of its debt.

Call Protection. Bonds are called when general interest rates are lower than they were when the bonds were issued. Investors, therefore, are faced with having to replace a relatively high fixed-income investment with one that pays less; this is known as **call risk**. A newly issued bond normally has a noncallable period of 5 or 10 years to provide some protection to investors. During this period, the issuer cannot call any of its bonds. When the call protection period expires, the issuer may call any or all of the bonds, usually at a premium. A call protection feature can be an advantage to bondholders in periods of declining interest rates.

Effects of a Call on Trading. After a call notice is issued, but before the call date, called bonds continue to trade in the open market. When bonds are called, a bondholder can turn in the bonds to the issuer immediately or sell them in the open market. The bonds will trade at a slight discount to the call price during this period. By selling at the small discount, the investor doesn't have to wait until the call date to get her money.

Notice of Redemption

Call dates and prices are specified in the bond contract when a bond is issued. A company notifies investors of its intent to call a bond issue by press release or advertisements in financial publications 30 to 90 days before the call. *The Bond Buyer*, a trade paper for the municipal securities industry, publishes a called bond list for municipal issues.

Refunding Bonds

Refunding is the practice of raising money to call a bond. Specifically, the issuer sells a new bond issue to buy back the old bond issue. Refunding, like a call, can occur in full or in part. Generally, an entire issue is refunded at once.

Refunding is common for bonds approaching maturity. An issuer may not have enough cash to pay off the entire issue, or it may choose to use its cash for other needs.

Prerefunding

When a bond issue is **prerefunded**, also known as *advance refunding*, a new issue is sold at a lower coupon before the original bond issue can be called. An issuer prerefunds a bond issue only to lock in a favorable interest rate. The proceeds from the new issue are placed in an escrow account and invested in U.S. government securities. Interest received from the investment is used to pay interest on the original or prerefunded bonds, which are called at the first call date using the escrowed funds.

Prerefunded bonds are generally rated AAA or Aaa, the highest rating available. Advance refunding is a form of **defeasance**, or termination, of the issuer's obligation; prerefunded bonds are considered defeased and no longer count as part of the issuer's debt.

Tender Offers

When general interest rates are down, companies may wish to redeem callable and noncallable bonds and replace them with bonds paying less interest. A bond issuer may make a tender offer for its outstanding bonds, most likely at a premium price as an inducement to bondholders to tender their securities.

Put Bonds Some bonds issued with put options are known as **put**, or **puttable**, **bonds**. In return for accepting a slightly lower interest rate, an investor receives the right to put (sell) the bond to the issuer at full face value at some point before maturity.

Bond Yields

A bond's yield expresses the cash interest payments in relation to the bond's value. Yield is determined by the issuer's credit quality, prevailing interest rates, time to maturity and call features. Bonds can be quoted and traded in terms of their yield as well as a percentage of par dollar amount.

Comparing Yields Because bonds most frequently trade for prices other than par, the price discount or premium from par is taken into consideration when calculating a bond's overall yield. You can look at a bond's yield in several ways.

Nominal Yield

A bond's coupon yield, or nominal yield, is set at issuance and printed on the face of the bond. The nominal yield is a fixed percentage of the bond's par value. A coupon of 6 percent, for instance, indicates the bondholder is paid $60 in interest annually until the bond matures.

Current Yield

Current yield (CY) measures a bond's coupon payment relative to its market price, as shown in the following equation:

$$\text{Coupon payment} \div \text{Market price} = \text{Current yield}$$

Bond prices and yields move in opposite directions: as a bond's price rises, its yield declines, and vice versa. When a bond trades at a discount, its current yield increases; when it trades at a premium, its current yield decreases.

✓ *For Example:* A 6 percent coupon bond trading for $750 has a current yield of 8 percent ($60 ÷ $750 = 8%). Conversely, the current yield of a bond bought at a premium is lower than its nominal yield. An investor who buys a 6 percent bond for $1,200 receives a current yield of 5 percent ($60 ÷ $1,200 = 5%).

Figure 2.4 illustrates the relationships between nominal yield and current yield on premium, par and discount bonds.

FIGURE 2.4   Relationship Between Bond Prices and Current Yields

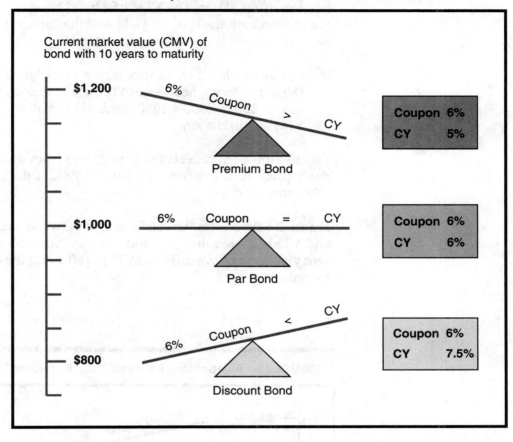

Yield to Maturity

A bond's yield to maturity (YTM) reflects the annualized return of the bond if held to maturity. In calculating yield to maturity, the bondholder takes into account the difference between the price paid for a bond and par value. If the bond's price is less than par, the discount amount is **accreted**. If the bond's price is greater than par, the premium is **amortized**.

✓ **For Example:** An investor who buys a 10% coupon bond at 105 ($1,050 per bond) with 10 years remaining to maturity can expect $100 in interest per year. If he holds the bond to maturity, the bondholder loses $50 ($1,050 – $1,000 = $50; $50 ÷ 10 years = $5 per year). This loss is included in the YTM approximation.

The YTM of a bond bought at a discount is always higher than both the coupon yield and the current yield because the investor has a gain when the bond matures at par. The YTM of a bond bought at a premium is always lower than both the coupon yield and the current yield because the investor has a loss when the bond matures at par.

✓ **For Example:** If an investor buys a bond with a 10 percent coupon for 95 ($950 per bond), he receives $100 a year in coupon interest payments and a gain of $50 ($1,000 – $950) per bond at maturity. This gain is included in the YTM approximation.

Because the YTM reflects the gain or loss from a discount or premium purchase price, it differs from the current yield if the bondholder pays a price other than par.

Figure 2.5 illustrates the relationships between coupon yield, current yield and YTM on premium, par and discount bonds. Two bonds with equal current yields may have different YTMs, reflecting the different amounts of time to maturity.

FIGURE 2.5   Relationship Between Bond Prices and Yields to Maturity

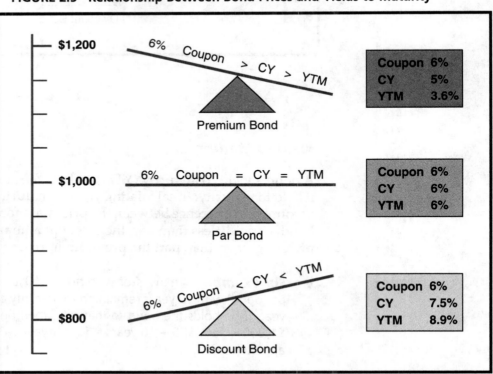

Yield to Call

A bond with a call feature may be redeemed before maturity at the issuer's option. Unless the bond was bought at par and is callable at par, yield to call (YTC) calculations reflect the early redemption date and consequent acceleration of the discount gain or premium loss from the purchase price.

The yield to call of a bond bought at par and called at par equals nominal yield.

 For Example: An investor who buys a callable 6% bond for $1,000 receives a 6 percent yield to call on the bond if it is called at par, no matter how long the investor holds it.

An investor who buys a callable bond at a premium, however, loses the premium faster when the bond is called at par than if held to maturity. Because a bond sells for a premium when its coupon rate is higher than current market rates, premium bonds are likely to be called so the issuer can save on interest expenses. The sooner the bonds are called, the sooner the premium the investor paid is lost. The YTC for a premium bond called at par, therefore, is *always* lower than the nominal yield, current yield and YTM. If a premium bond is called at a premium, the yield relationship is determined by the difference between the premium paid for the bond and the call premium.

For a bond bought at a discount, YTC is *always* greater than YTM because the accrual of the discount is accelerated.

For a bond bought at a premium, YTC *may be* greater than or less than YTM, depending on the relationship between the purchase price and call price. If a bond's purchase price is lower than the call price, YTM is lower than YTC; if the purchase price is higher than the call price, YTC is lower than YTM.

 For Example: The Mt. Vernon Port Authority issues a 20-year bond with a coupon rate of 6 percent. A customer buys the bond at the end of the 10th year for 105. The customer receives a current yield of 5.71 percent and a YTM of approximately 5.36 percent. However, if the issuer can call the bond after 15 years at 102, the investor's YTC is 5.22 percent. Both YTM and YTC calculations are based on the bond's average price for the duration (purchase price plus call or maturity value divided by 2). The following equations show how the investor's yield is calculated (note that the equations are approximations; the concept is critical, not the formula):

Current yield is:	$60 ÷ $1,050	= 5.71%
With 10 years to maturity, YTM is:	($60 − $5) = $55	
	$55 ÷ $1,025	= 5.36%
With 5 years to the call date, YTC is:	($60 − $6) = $54	
	$54 ÷ $1,035	= 5.22%

FIGURE 2.6   Relationship Between Bond Prices, Yields to Maturity and Yields to Call

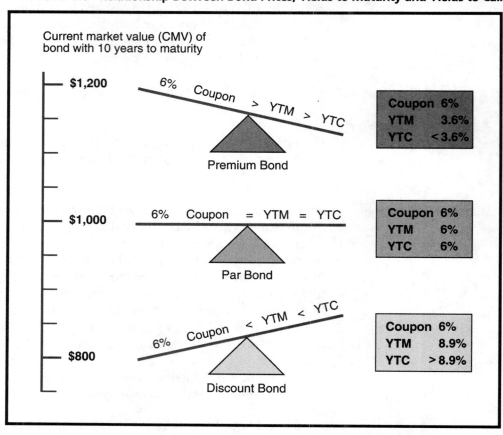

Figure 2.6 illustrates the relationships between coupon yield, yield to maturity and yield to call on premium, par and discount bonds. YTC can be calculated the same way as YTM, with the discount or premium adjusted to reflect the first call date and price.

Yield Curve

Bond prices and yields have an inverse relationship: as yields decline, bond prices rise.

In addition, under normal circumstances the longer a bond's maturity, the greater its yield will be. The increased yield reflects the potential for credit quality or inflation risks over time.

The difference in interest rates between short-term and long-term bonds of the same quality is known as the yield curve, as illustrated below. In a normal yield curve, the difference between short-term and long-term rates is about 3 percentage points (300 basis points), but may be much larger or smaller at any given time.

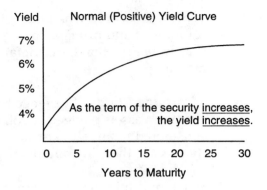

As interest rates change, long-term bond prices are more volatile than short-term bonds. As interest rates rise, long-term bond prices decline more than the price of short-term bonds.

When interest rates are high and expected to begin declining, long-term bond yields can be lower than short-term yields as their market price anticipates the declining rates. When long-term interest rates are lower than short-term rates the yield curve is considered inverted.

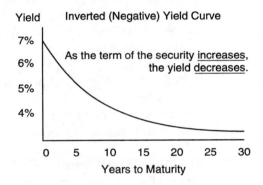

When short-term and long-term rates are the same, the yield curve is flat.

Corporate Bonds

Corporate bonds are issued to raise working capital or capital for expenditures such as plant construction and equipment purchases.

Types of Corporate Bonds

The two primary types of corporate bonds are secured and unsecured. Others are discussed in this section, as well.

Secured Bonds   A bond is secured when the issuer has identified specific assets as collateral for interest and principal payments. The trustee holds the title to the assets that secure the bond. In a default, the bondholder can lay claim to the collateral.

Mortgage Bonds. Mortgage bonds have the highest priority among all claims on assets pledged as collateral. While mortgage bonds, in general, are considered relatively safe, individual bonds are only as secure as the assets that secure them and are rated accordingly.

When multiple classes of a mortgage bond exist, the first claim on the pledged property goes to first-mortgage bonds, second claim to second-mortgage bonds and so on.

Open-End Indentures. An open-end trust indenture permits the corporation to issue more bonds of the same class later. Subsequent issues are secured by the same collateral backing the initial issue and have equal liens on the property.

Closed-End Indentures. A closed-end indenture does not permit the corporation to issue more bonds of the same class in the future. Often, a company issues all the bonds at once. Any subsequent issue has a subordinated claim on the collateral.

Prior Lien Bonds. Companies in financial trouble sometimes attract capital by issuing mortgage bonds that take precedence over first-mortgage bonds. Before issuing prior lien bonds, however, a corporation must have the consent of first-mortgage bondholders.

Collateral Trust Bonds. Collateral trust bonds are usually issued by corporations that own securities of other companies as investments. A corporation issues bonds secured by a pledge of those securities as collateral. The trust indenture usually contains a covenant requiring that a trustee hold the pledged securities.

Collateral trust bonds may be backed by one or more of the following securities:

- stocks and bonds of partially or wholly owned subsidiaries;
- pledging company's prior lien long-term bonds that have been held in trust to secure short-term bonds;
- another company's stocks and bonds; or
- installment payments or other obligations of the corporation's clients.

Equipment Trust Certificates. Railroads, airlines, trucking companies and oil companies use equipment trust certificates (or equipment notes and bonds) to finance the purchase of capital equipment.

Title to the newly acquired equipment is held in trust, usually by a bank, until all certificates have been paid in full. Because the certificates normally mature before the equipment wears out, the amount borrowed is generally less than the full value of the property securing the certificates.

Unsecured Bonds Unsecured bonds have no specific collateral backing and are classified as either debentures or subordinated debentures.

Debentures. Debentures are backed by the general credit of the issuing corporation, and a debenture owner is considered a general creditor of the company. Debentures are below secured bonds and above subordinated debentures and preferred and common stock in the priority of claims on corporate assets.

Subordinated Debentures. The claims of subordinated debenture owners are subordinated to the claims of other general creditors. Subordinated debentures generally offer higher income than either straight debentures or secured bonds due to their subordinate, therefore riskier, status, and they often have conversion features.

Guaranteed Bonds Guaranteed bonds are backed by a company other than the issuer, such as a subsidiary's parent company. This effectively increases the issue's safety.

Income Bonds Income bonds, also known as **adjustment bonds,** are used when a company is reorganizing and coming out of bankruptcy. Income bonds pay interest only if the corporation has enough income to meet the interest payment and the board of directors declares a payment.

Because missed interest payments do not accumulate for future payment, these bonds are not suitable investments for customers seeking income.

Zero-Coupon Bonds Bonds are normally issued as fixed-income securities. Zero-coupon bonds are an issuer's debt obligations that do not make regular interest payments.

Instead, zeros are issued at a deep discount from their face value and mature at par. The difference between the discounted purchase price and the full face value at maturity is the return (accreted interest) the investor receives.

The price of a zero-coupon bond reflects the general interest rate climate for similar maturities.

Zero-coupon bonds are issued by corporations, municipalities and the U.S. Treasury and may be created by broker-dealers from other types of securities.

Advantages and Disadvantages of Zero-Coupon Bonds

A zero-coupon bond requires a relatively small investment—perhaps $100 to $200 per bond—and matures at $1,000.

Zero-coupon bonds offer investors a way to speculate on interest rate moves. Because they sell at deep discounts and offer no cash payments, zeros are substantially more volatile than traditional bonds; their prices fluctuate wildly with changes in market rates. Moreover, the longer the time to maturity, the greater the volatility. When interest rates change, a zero's price changes much more as a percentage of its market value than an ordinary bond's price.

Taxation of Zero-Coupon Bonds

Although zeros pay no regular interest income, an investor who owns taxable (government or corporate) zeros owes income tax each year on the amount by which the bonds have accreted, just as if the investor had received it in cash. The income tax is due regardless of the direction of the market price. Because the annual interest is not prorated in equal amounts, the bond issuer must send each investor an Internal Revenue Service (IRS) Form 1099 annually showing the amount of interest subject to taxation.

Liquidation In the event a company goes bankrupt, the hierarchy of claims on the company's assets are as follows:

1. unpaid wages
2. IRS (taxes)
3. secured debt (bonds and mortgages)
4. unsecured liabilities (debentures) and general creditors
5. subordinated debt
6. preferred stockholders
7. common stockholders

The Trust Indenture

The Trust Indenture Act of 1939 requires corporate bonds to be issued under a **trust indenture**, a legal contract between the bond issuer and a trustee representing bondholders. Although the face of a bond certificate mentions the trust indenture, it is not automatically supplied to bondholders.

The trust indenture specifies the issuer's obligation and bondholders' rights, and it identifies the trustee.

The Trustee The Trust Indenture Act of 1939 requires a corporation to appoint a trustee— usually a commercial bank or trust company—for its bonds. The trustee ensures compliance with the covenants of the indenture and acts on behalf of the bondholders if the issuer defaults.

Exemptions Federal and municipal governments are exempt from the Trust Indenture Act provisions, although municipal revenue bonds are typically issued with a trust indenture to make them more marketable.

Protective Covenants In the trust indenture, the debtor corporation agrees to:

- pay the interest and principal of its bonds
- specify where bonds or coupons can be presented for payment
- defend the legal title to the property
- maintain the property to ensure that business can be conducted
- do nothing that diminishes the claims of the bonds
- insure the mortgaged property against fire and other losses
- pay all taxes and assessments (property, income, franchise)
- maintain its corporate structure and the right to do business
- record the mortgage and pay any recording fees

Other covenants might include provisions for a sinking fund, a replacement fund, minimum working capital or other requirements.

Mortgage bonds may be issued with either open- or closed-end covenants. Bonds issued with closed-end covenants have senior claim on the underlying assets, even if the corporation issues other bonds secured by the same assets. An open-end covenant permits subsequent issues to be secured by the same property and have equal liens on it.

Trading Corporate Bonds

NYSE–Listed Bonds The New York Stock Exchange provides a central marketplace for trading bonds. Unlike stocks traded on the Exchange, listed corporate bonds trade sporadically. Trading in listed bonds is thin for the following reasons:

- Most bonds are traded in the OTC market.
- As long-term investments, bonds are not traded as frequently as stocks.
- Many institutional investors, such as banks and insurance companies, are legally restricted in their investments and tend to be long-term holders.

Most corporations with stocks listed on the Exchange may list their bonds as well.

Trading Most brokerage firms do not maintain regular floor brokers to execute bond orders; they enlist bond brokers to execute the orders on their behalf. A bond broker charges a small fee, called a **give-up commission**, for each order executed.

Pricing The NYSE bond market operates under the same principles and auction procedures used on the stock trading floor.

Bids and Offers

Unlike bids and offers for stocks, bids to buy and offers to sell bonds are stated as a percentage of the bond's par value. A bid of 100 means 100 percent, not $100. For a $1,000 bond, it means the bidder will pay $1,000.

Convertible Bonds

Convertible bonds are corporate bonds that may be exchanged for a fixed number of shares of the issuing company's common stock. Because they are convertible into common stock, convertible bonds pay lower interest rates than nonconvertible bonds and generally trade in line with the common. Because they are bonds with fixed interest payments and maturity dates, convertible bonds are less volatile than common stock.

Advantages of Convertible Securities to the Issuer

A corporation adds a conversion feature to its bonds or preferred stock to make it more marketable. Other reasons corporations issue convertible securities include the following:

- Convertibles can be sold with a lower coupon rate than nonconvertibles because of the conversion feature.
- A company can eliminate a fixed interest charge as conversion takes place, thus reducing debt.
- Because conversion normally occurs over a period of time, it does not have an adverse effect on the stock price, as may occur after a secondary underwriting.
- By issuing convertibles rather than common stock, a corporation avoids immediate dilution of primary earnings per share.

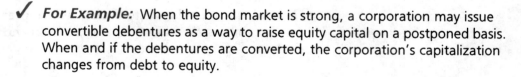 **For Example:** When the bond market is strong, a corporation may issue convertible debentures as a way to raise equity capital on a postponed basis. When and if the debentures are converted, the corporation's capitalization changes from debt to equity.

Disadvantages of Convertible Securities to the Issuer

On the other hand, convertibles have potential disadvantages for a corporation and its stockholders:

- When bonds are converted, shareholders' equity is diluted; that is, more shares are outstanding, so each share now represents a smaller fraction of ownership in the company.
- Because common stockholders have a voice in the company's management, a substantial conversion could cause a shift in the control of the company.
- Reducing corporate debt through conversion means a loss of leverage.
- The resulting decrease in deductible interest costs raises the corporation's taxable income; therefore, the corporation pays increased taxes as conversion takes place.

The Market for Convertible Securities

Convertible bonds offer the safety of the fixed-income market and the potential appreciation of the equity market. This provides investors with several advantages:

- As a debt security, a convertible debenture pays interest at a fixed rate and is redeemable for its face value at maturity, provided the debenture is not converted. As a rule, interest income is higher and surer than dividend income on the underlying common stock. Similarly, convertible preferred stock usually pays a higher dividend than does common stock.
- If a corporation experiences financial difficulties, convertible bondholders have priority over common stockholders in the event of a corporate liquidation.
- In theory, a convertible debenture's market price tends to be more stable during market declines than the underlying common stock's price. Current yields of other competitive debt securities support the debenture's value in the marketplace.
- Because convertibles can be exchanged for common stock, their market price tends to move upward if the stock price moves up. For this reason, convertible securities are more volatile in price during times of steady interest rates than are other fixed-income securities.
- Conversion of a senior security into common stock is not considered a purchase and a sale for tax purposes. Thus, the investor incurs no tax liability on the conversion transaction.

Conversion Price and Conversion Ratio

The conversion price is the stock price at which a convertible bond can be exchanged for shares of common stock.

The **conversion ratio**, also called *conversion rate*, expresses the number of shares of stock a bond may be converted into. A bond with a conversion price of $40, for instance, has a conversion ratio of 25-to-1 ($1,000 ÷ $40 = 25). Conversion terms are stated in the indenture agreement, either as a conversion ratio or as a conversion price.

✓ *For Example:* Silicon Microchip's convertible debenture has a conversion price of $40. This means each bond, with a par value of $1,000, can be converted into 25 shares of stock ($1,000 ÷ $40 = 25). If the stock price exceeds $40, the convertible can still be exchanged for 25 shares.

Stock Splits and Dividends. Conversion prices are adjusted if stock splits and stock dividends are declared on the underlying common stock during the life of the bond.

Additional Shares. The bond indenture fixes both the maximum number of additional shares the corporation can issue while convertible bonds are outstanding and the minimum price at which the corporation can issue them.

Mergers, Consolidations and Dissolutions. If the corporation ceases to exist because of any of these situations, convertible bondholders lose their conversion privileges.

Calculating Conversion Parity

Parity means that two securities, in this case a convertible bond and the common stock into which it can be converted, are of equal dollar value. If a corporation issues a bond that is convertible at $50, the conversion ratio is 20-to-1.

If a bond selling for 104 ($1,040) is convertible into 20 shares of common, the common stock price would have to be $52 to be at parity with, or equal to, the convertible bond price ($1,040 ÷ 20 = 52). If the common stock is selling below 52, the convertible bond is worth more than the stock. If the stock is selling above 52, the investor can make more money by acquiring the bond, converting to common and selling the shares.

The following formulas calculate the parity prices of convertible securities and their underlying common shares:

$$\frac{\text{Market price of convertible}}{\text{Conversion ratio}} = \text{Parity price of common}$$

$$\text{Market price of common} \times \text{Conversion ratio}$$
$$= \text{Parity price of convertible}$$

✓ *For Example:* The market price of RST common stock is $30. The RST bond is convertible at $25—that is, exchangeable for 40 shares of common stock. The bond's parity is $30 times 40, or $1200.

In a rising market, the convertible's value rises with the common stock's value. In a declining market, the convertible's market price tends to level off when its yield becomes competitive with the yield on nonconvertible bonds, and it may not decline in price as far as the common stock.

Convertible bonds normally sell at a premium above parity, which is why they are not constantly exchanged for common stock when the stock price is rising. Converting a bond or preferred stock into common stock is not a taxable event.

U.S. Government and Agency Securities

The U.S. Treasury Department determines the quantity and types of government securities it must issue to meet federal budget needs. The marketplace determines the interest rates those securities will pay. In general, the interest government securities pay is exempt from state and municipal taxation, but subject to federal taxation.

The federal government is the nation's largest borrower as well as the best credit risk. Securities issued by the U.S. government are backed by its full faith and credit, which is based on its power to tax.

Most government securities are issued in book-entry form, meaning no physical certificates exist.

Marketable Government Securities

Treasury securities are classified as bills, notes and bonds to distinguish an issue's term to maturity.

Treasury Bills T bills are short-term obligations issued at a discount from par in **competitive bid** auctions. Large U.S. government securities dealers submit bids, or **tenders**, for large blocks of T bills at weekly auctions held on Mondays. Each competitive tender is submitted for a price that reflects the interest rate the bidder wishes to receive. The Treasury awards the bills to the highest bidders (those that bid the lowest interest rates) beginning at the top of the list and working down. Not all bids are filled. Those bids that are filled settle in federal funds, as do all U.S. government securities.

T bills may be purchased by submitting a **noncompetitive bid** as well. The investor who submits a noncompetitive bid agrees to pay the average of the competitive bids accepted at that auction and is guaranteed to have his order filled. Noncompetitive bids are limited to a maximum of $500,000.

Rather than making regular cash interest payments, bills trade at a discount from par value; the return on a T bill is the difference between the price the investor pays and the par value at which the bill matures.

Maturities and Denominations. Treasury bills issued in denominations of $10,000 to $1 million mature in 13, 26 or 52 weeks. T bills with 13-week and 26-week maturities are auctioned weekly, while 52-week maturities are auctioned every four weeks.

Pricing. Treasury bills are quoted and sold at a discount from par. A quote of 5.5 percent, for instance, means a 52-week T bill is selling at 5½ percent less than its $1,000 face value. For a $10,000 52-week Treasury bill, that would be a price of $9,450.

✎ *Take Note:* The bid for a T bill is a higher number than the ask because the higher bid (interest rate) reflects the lower dollar price.

✔ *For Example:* A T bill may be quoted as "bid 5 percent, asked 4.875 percent." The bid reflects a higher yield than the ask, thus a deeper discount from par value, because the bidder wants to pay less for the bill.

Treasury Notes   Unlike Treasury bills, T notes pay interest every six months.

Maturities and Denominations. Issued in denominations of $1,000 to $1 million, T notes are intermediate-term bonds maturing in 1 to 10 years. T notes mature at par, or they can be refunded. If a T note is refunded, the government offers the investor a new security with a new interest rate and maturity date as an alternative to a cash payment for the maturing note. Bondholders may always request their principal in cash.

Pricing. T notes are issued, quoted and traded in $1/32$ of a percentage of par. A quote of 98.24, which can also be expressed as 98-24 or 98:24, on a $1,000 note means that the note is selling for $98\frac{24}{32}$ percent of its $1,000 par value. In this instance, .24 designates $\frac{24}{32}$ of 1 percent, not a decimal. A quote of 98.24 equals 98.75 percent of $1,000, or $987.50.

Other examples follow.

A bid of . . .	Means . . .	Or . . .
98.01	$98\frac{1}{32}$% of $1,000	$980.3125
98.02	$98\frac{2}{32}$% of $1,000	$980.6250
98.03	$98\frac{3}{32}$% of $1,000	$980.9375
98.10	$98\frac{10}{32}$% of $1,000	$983.1250
98.11	$98\frac{11}{32}$% of $1,000	$983.4375
98.12	$98\frac{12}{32}$% of $1,000	$983.7500

Treasury Bonds   Treasury bonds are long-term securities that pay interest every six months.

Maturities and Denominations. Treasury bonds are issued in denominations of $1,000 to $1 million and mature in 10 to 30 years.

Pricing. T bonds are quoted exactly like T notes.

Callable. Some Treasury bonds have optional call dates, ranging from three to five years before maturity.

✓ *For Example:* A quote of "5s^{11}⁄$_{16}$" indicates the 5% bond could be called at any time from 2011 until it matures in 2016. The Treasury department must give bondholders four months' notice before calling the bonds. U.S. government securities are always called at par.

Treasury Receipts   Brokerage firms can create **Treasury receipts** from U.S. Treasury notes and bonds. Broker-dealers buy Treasury securities, place them in trust at a bank and sell separate receipts against the principal and coupon payments. The Treasury securities held in trust collateralize the Treasury receipts. Unlike Treasury securities, Treasury receipts are not backed by the full faith and credit of the U.S. government.

To illustrate how Treasury receipts are created, think of a $1,000 10-year Treasury note with a 6 percent coupon as 21 separate payment obligations. The first 20 are the semiannual $30 interest payment obligations until maturity. The 21st is the obligation to repay the $1,000 principal at maturity. An investor may purchase a Treasury receipt for any of the 20 interest payments or the principal repayment. Each Treasury receipt is priced at a discount from the payment amount, like a zero-coupon bond.

STRIPS. In 1984, the Treasury department entered the zero-coupon bond market by designating certain Treasury issues as suitable for stripping into interest and principal components. These securities became known as *STRIPS*, which stands for Separate Trading of Registered Interest and Principal of Securities.

While the securities underlying Treasury STRIPS are the U.S. government's direct obligation, major banks and dealers perform the actual separation and trading.

Agency Issues

Congress authorizes the following agencies of the federal government to issue debt securities:

- Federal Farm Credit System (FFCS)
- Government National Mortgage Association (GNMA or Ginnie Mae)

Other agency-like organizations operated by private corporations include:

- Federal Home Loan Mortgage Corporation (FHLMC or Freddie Mac)
- Federal National Mortgage Association (FNMA or Fannie Mae)
- Student Loan Marketing Association (SLMA or Sallie Mae)

The term "agency" is sometimes used to refer to entities that are not technically government agencies, but that do have ties to the government. Fannie Mae is a privately owned but government-controlled entity. Whatever its technical status, therefore, it functions as a government agency.

Yields and Maturities. Agency issues have higher yields than direct obligations of the federal government, but lower yields than corporate debt securities. Their maturities range from short to long term. Agency issues are quoted as percentages of par and trade actively in the secondary market.

Backing. Agency issues are backed by revenues from taxes, fees or interest income from lending activities. They may also be backed by collateral, such as cash or U.S. Treasury securities, by a U.S. Treasury guarantee or by the full faith and credit of the government.

Taxation. Interest on government agency issues is sometimes exempt from state and local income taxes, but is always subject to federal income tax. Interest from Fannie Mae, Freddie Mac and Ginnie Mae securities, for instance, is taxed at the federal, state and local levels.

Government National Mortgage Association (Ginnie Mae)

The Government National Mortgage Association is a government-owned corporation that supports the Department of Housing and Urban Development. Ginnie Maes are backed by the full faith and credit of the government.

Types of Issues. GNMA buys Federal Housing Administration (FHA) and Department of Veteran Affairs (VA) mortgages and auctions them to private lenders, which **pool** the mortgages to create pass-through certificates for sale to investors. Thus, monthly principal and interest payments from the pool of mortgages pass through to investors. Like the principal on a single mortgage, the principal represented by a GNMA certificate constantly decreases as the mortgages are paid down.

GNMA pass-throughs pay higher interest rates than comparable Treasury securities, yet are guaranteed by the federal government. GNMA also guarantees timely payment of interest and principal. Because GNMAs are backed directly by the government, risk of default is nearly zero. Prices, yields and maturities fluctuate in line with general interest rate trends. If interest rates fall, homeowners tend to pay off their mortgages early, which accelerates the certificates' maturities. If interest rates rise, certificates may mature more slowly.

GNMAs are issued in minimum denominations of $25,000. Because few mortgages last the full term, yield quotes are based on a 12-year prepayment assumption; that is, a mortgage balance should be prepaid in full after 12 years of normally scheduled payments.

Taxation. Interest earned on GNMA certificates is taxable at the federal, state and local levels.

Federal Farm Credit Banks

The Farm Credit System (FCS) is organized into 12 geographic districts and is composed of 37 privately owned banks. The Farm Credit Administration (FCA), a government agency, oversees the system. The 37 member banks are made up of Federal Land Banks (FLBs), Federal Intermediate Credit Banks (FICBs), and Banks for Cooperatives (COOPs). The Federal Farm Credit Bank Consolidated Systemwide securities are the joint and separate obligations of all 37 Farm Credit Banks. The securities are *not* backed by the faith and credit of the U.S. government.

FCS banks issue securities to finance farmers' mortgages and operations. Figure 2.7 shows a tombstone announcing an issue of these securities. Consolidated Systemwide bonds are issued in book-entry form.

Taxation. Interest on Farm Credit System issues is paid every six months and is sometimes exempt from state and local income taxes, but it is always subject to federal income tax.

Federal Intermediate Credit Banks

Twelve Federal Intermediate Credit Banks provide short-term agricultural financing. The FICBs lend money to credit companies, agricultural institutions and commercial banks, which in turn lend the money to farmers. They issue short- and long-term debentures to raise funds for lending.

Taxation. Interest income from FICB securities is federally taxable and can be exempt from state and local income taxes.

Federal Home Loan Mortgage Corporation (Freddie Mac)

The Federal Home Loan Mortgage Corporation is a public corporation whose stock trades on the NYSE. It was created to promote the development of a nationwide secondary market in mortgages by purchasing residential mortgages from financial institutions and packaging them into mortgage-backed securities for sale to investors.

Pass-Through Certificates. A pass-through security is created by pooling a group of mortgages and selling certificates representing interests in the pool. The term "pass-through" refers to the mechanism of passing homebuyers'

FIGURE 2.7   Federal Farm Credit Bank Bonds Tombstone

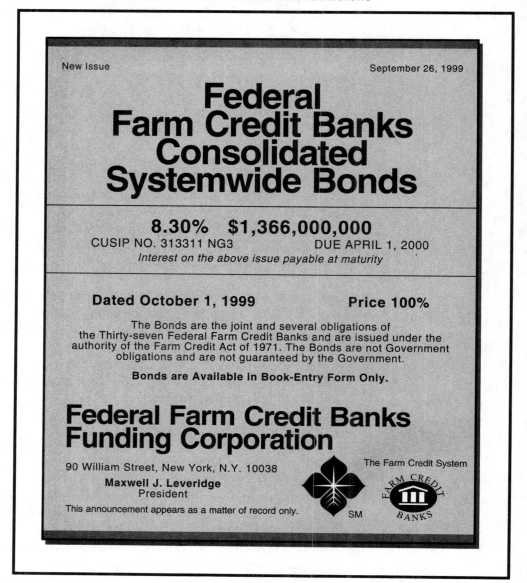

interest and principal payments from the mortgage holder to the investors. Both FHLMC and GNMA function this way.

FHLMC sells two types of pass-through securities: mortgage participation certificates (PCs) and guaranteed mortgage certificates (GMCs). PCs make principal and interest payments once a month; GMCs make interest payments twice a year and principal payments once a year.

Taxation. Income from FHLMC securities is subject to federal and state income taxes.

Federal National Mortgage Association (Fannie Mae)

The Federal National Mortgage Association is a publicly held corporation that provides mortgage capital. FNMA purchases conventional and insured mortgages from agencies such as the FHA and the VA. The securities it creates are pass-through certificates like Ginnie Maes, and are backed by FNMA's general credit, not by the U.S. government. FNMA stock also trades on the NYSE.

Types of Issues. FNMA issues debentures, short-term discount notes and mortgage-backed securities. The notes are issued in denominations of $5,000, $25,000, $100,000, $500,000 and $1 million. Debentures with maturities from 3 to 25 years are issued in minimum denominations of $10,000 in increments of $5,000. Interest is paid semiannually. They are issued in book-entry form only.

Taxation. Interest from FNMA securities is taxed at the federal, state and local levels.

Collateralized Mortgage Obligations

Collateralized mortgage obligations (CMOs) are mortgage-backed securities like the pass-through obligations Ginnie Mae and Fannie Mae issue. CMOs pool a large number of mortgages, usually on single-family residences. A pool of mortgages is structured into maturity classes called **tranches**. CMOs are issued by private sector financing corporations and by government-sponsored corporations such as FNMA and FHLMC.

A CMO pays principal and interest from the mortgage pool monthly; however, it repays principal to only one tranche at a time. In addition to interest payments, investors in a short-term tranche must receive all of their principal before the next tranche begins to receive principal repayments. Principal payments are made in $1,000 increments to randomly selected bonds within a tranche. Changes in interest rates affect the rate of mortgage prepayments, and this, in turn, affects the flow of interest payment and principal repayment to the CMO investor.

A CMO's yield and maturity are estimates based on historical data or projections of mortgage prepayments from the **Public Securities Association (PSA)**. The particular tranche an investor owns determines the priority of his principal repayment. The time to maturity, amount of interest received and amount of principal returned are not guaranteed. The following chart shows a sample CMO tranche structure.

		Estimated Life
Tranche	*Interest Rate*	*in Years*
1	5.125%	1.5
2	5.25%	3.5
3	5.5%	6
4	5.875%	8.5
5	6.125%	11

Classes of CMOs   In addition to the standard CMOs discussed above, some CMOs have been structured to suit specific needs of investors. Common CMO types include:

- principal-only
- interest-only
- planned amortization class
- targeted amortization class

Principal-Only CMOs (POs). The flow of income from underlying mortgages is divided into principal and interest streams and directed to the owners of principal-only CMOs (POs) and interest-only CMOs (IOs), respectively. For a PO, the income stream comes from principal payments on the underlying mortgages—both scheduled mortgage principal payments and prepayments. Thus, the security ultimately repays its entire face value to the investor.

A PO sells at a discount from par; the difference between the discounted price and the principal value is the investor's return. Its market value, like that of all deeply discounted securities, tends to be volatile. POs, in particular, are affected by fluctuations in prepayment rates. The value of a PO rises as interest rates drop and prepayments accelerate, and its value falls when interest rates rise and prepayments decline.

Interest-Only CMOs (IOs). IOs are by-products of POs. Whereas POs receive the principal stream from underlying mortgages, IOs receive the interest.

An IO also sells at a discount, and its cash flow declines over time, just as the proportion of interest in a mortgage payment declines over time. Unlike POs, IOs increase in value when interest rates rise and decline in value when interest rates fall because the number of interest payments changes as prepayment rates change. Thus, they can be used to hedge a portfolio against interest rate risk.

When prepayment rates are high, the owner of an IO may receive fewer interest payments than anticipated. Because the entire CMO series receives more principal sooner and, therefore, less overall interest, the IO owner does not know how long the stream of interest payments will last.

Planned Amortization Class CMOs (PACs). PACs have targeted maturity dates; they are retired first and offer protection from prepayment risk and extension risk (the chance that principal payments will be slower than anticipated) because changes in prepayments are transferred to **companion tranches**, also called *support tranches*.

Targeted Amortization Class CMOs (TACs). A TAC structure transfers prepayment risk only to companion tranches and does not offer protection from extension risk. TAC investors accept the extension risk and the resulting greater price risk in exchange for a slightly higher interest rate.

CMO Characteristics

Because mortgages back CMOs, they are considered relatively safe. However, their susceptibility to interest rate movements and the resulting changes in the mortgage repayment rate mean CMOs carry several risks:

- The rate of principal repayment varies.
- If interest rates fall and homeowner refinancing increases, principal is received sooner than anticipated.
- If interest rates rise and refinancing declines, the CMO investor may have to hold his investment longer than anticipated.

Yields. CMOs yield more than Treasury securities and normally pay investors interest and principal monthly. Principal repayments are made in $1,000 increments to investors in one tranche before any principal is repaid to the next tranche.

 Take Note: Due to changing interest rates, a CMO's actual maturity differs, often substantially, from its estimated life. As a result, a CMO's actual yield to maturity cannot be determined unless the CMO is purchased at par.

Taxation. Interest from CMOs is subject to federal, state and local taxes.

Liquidity. An active secondary market exists for CMOs. However, the market for CMOs with more complex characteristics may be limited or non-existent.

Certain tranches of a given CMO may be riskier than others. Some CMOs or certain tranches carry the risk that repayment of principal may take longer than anticipated.

Denominations. CMOs are issued in $1,000 denominations.

Suitability. Some varieties of CMOs, such as PAC companion tranches, may be particularly unsuitable for small or unsophisticated investors because of their complexity and risks. The customer may be required to sign a suitability statement before buying high-risk classes.

Money-Market Securities and Interest Rates

In the financial marketplace, a distinction is made between the *capital market* and the *money market*. The capital market serves as a source of intermediate-term to long-term financing usually in the form of equity or debt securities with maturities of more than one year.

The money market, on the other hand, provides very short-term funds to corporations, municipalities and the U.S. government. Money-market securities are debt issues with maturities of one year or less.

The Money Market

Money-market instruments provide businesses, financial institutions and governments a means to finance their short-term cash requirements.

Liquidity and Safety. Money-market instruments are fixed-income securities with short-term maturities—typically one year or less. Because they are short-term instruments, money-market securities are highly liquid. Money-market securities also provide a relatively high degree of safety because most issuers have high credit ratings.

Money-market securities issued by the U.S. government and its agencies include:

- Treasury bills that trade in the secondary market;
- Treasury and agency securities with remaining maturities of less than one year;
- Federal Farm Credit Bank notes and bonds maturing in one year;
- Federal Home Loan Bank (FHLB) short-term discount notes and interest-bearing notes;
- Federal National Mortgage Association short-term discount notes; and
- short-term discount notes issued by various smaller agencies.

Municipalities issue tax-exempt money-market instruments that include:

- bond anticipation notes (BANs)
- tax anticipation notes (TANs)
- revenue anticipation notes (RANs)
- construction loan notes (CLNs)

Corporations and banks have a number of ways to raise short-term funds in the money market, such as:

- repurchase agreements (repos)
- reverse repurchase agreements

- bankers' acceptances (time drafts)
- commercial paper (prime paper)
- negotiable certificates of deposit
- federal funds
- brokers' and dealers' loans

Money-Market Instruments

Repurchase Agreements   In a repurchase agreement (repo), a financial institution, such as a bank or broker-dealer, raises cash by temporarily selling some of the securities it holds with an agreement to buy back the securities at a later date. Thus, a repo is simply an agreement between a buyer and a seller to conduct a transaction (the purchase), then to reverse that transaction (the repurchase) in the future.

A repo contract includes both a repurchase price and a maturity date. If the agreement sets a specific date, the repo is considered a fixed agreement. If the maturity date is left to the initial buyer's discretion, the repo is known as an *open repo* and becomes a demand obligation callable at any time.

Though technically a sale of securities, a repo is similar to a fully collateralized loan. Instead of borrowing money and putting up securities as collateral for the loan, the dealer sells the securities and agrees to buy them back later at a higher price. The interest on the loan is the difference between the sale price and the repurchase price. The loan's interest rate is negotiated between the two parties and is generally lower than bank loan rates. If the dealer defaults on the agreement to buy back the securities, the lender can sell the securities in the secondary market.

In addition to serving as a way to raise short-term capital, repos are used as instruments to implement Federal Reserve monetary policy. Primary users of repos are:

- U.S. government and municipal securities dealers financing their inventories;
- commercial banks raising short-term funds; and
- the Federal Reserve adjusting member bank reserves.

Reverse Repurchase Agreements   In a repo, a dealer agrees to sell its securities to a lender and buy them back at a higher price in the future. In a reverse repurchase agreement (reverse repo), a dealer agrees to buy securities from an investor and sell them back later at a higher price. The difference between repos and reverse repos is that the dealer initiates the sale in a repo and an investor initiates the sale in a reverse repo.

Bankers' Acceptances   A banker's acceptance (BA) is a short-term time draft with a specified payment date drawn on a bank—essentially a postdated check or line of credit.

The payment date of a banker's acceptance is normally between 1 and 270 days.

American corporations use bankers' acceptances extensively to finance international trade—that is, a banker's acceptance typically pays for goods and services in a foreign country.

✓ *For Example:* A U.S. company enters into an agreement with a firm in another country to buy bolts of cloth. The U.S. company asks its bank to send a time draft to the foreign company as payment for the goods. The company wants the draft postdated six months in the future so it will have enough time to sell the cloth in the United States to raise the cash to cover the purchase. The foreign company accepting the time draft as payment for the cloth presents the draft to its local bank, which gives the company less than the face value in cash. The foreign firm now has immediate cash, and the U.S. company has the goods it needs.

The foreign bank sends the draft for payment to the U.S. bank on which the draft is drawn. The U.S. bank agrees to accept (guarantee) the draft and puts its own credit behind this guarantee of payment. When a bank accepts a time draft in this manner, the draft becomes a banker's acceptance, a security tradeable in the money market.

Once the U.S. bank accepts the returned time draft, the bank sells the new banker's acceptance in the money market at a discount from face value, thereby raising the cash to cover the payment to the foreign bank. When the acceptance eventually matures, the U.S. firm makes good on the amount it borrowed and the current holder redeems the banker's acceptance for its face value at the accepting bank.

A banker's acceptance is a secured money-market instrument because the holder has a lien against the trade goods in the event the accepting bank fails. Banks frequently use bankers' acceptances as collateral against Federal Reserve Bank (FRB) loans.

Commercial Paper Corporations issue short-term, unsecured commercial paper, or promissory notes, to raise cash to finance accounts receivable and seasonal inventory gluts. Commercial paper interest rates are lower than bank loan rates.

Commercial paper maturities range from 1 to 270 days, although most mature within 90 days. Commercial paper normally is issued in bearer form at a discount from face value.

Typically, companies with excellent credit ratings issue commercial paper. The primary buyers of commercial paper are money-market funds, commercial banks, pension funds, insurance companies, corporations and nongovernmental agencies.

Direct Paper. Direct paper is commercial paper sold by finance companies directly to the public without the use of dealers. General Motors Acceptance Corporation (GMAC) is a well-known issuer. High-quality commercial paper is sometimes called *prime paper*.

Dealer Paper. Dealer paper is commercial paper sold by issuers through dealers rather than directly to the public.

Tax-Exempt Commercial Paper. Municipal commercial paper is similar to corporate paper, but the municipality usually has acquired a credit line or letter of credit for the issue.

Certificates of Deposit

Banks issue and guarantee certificates of deposit (CDs) with fixed interest rates and minimum face values of $100,000, although face values of $1 million and up are more common. Some can be traded in the secondary market.

Nonnegotiable CDs. Most investors are familiar with the CD time deposits having set maturities and fixed interest rates and offered by banks and savings and loans. Banks offer nonnegotiable CDs with maturities ranging from 30 days to 10 years or more. Banks may issue nonnegotiable CDs for small or large amounts which are insured by the Federal Deposit Insurance Corporation (FDIC) for up to $100,000. Nonnegotiable CDs are not traded in the secondary market and are not money-market securities.

Negotiable CDs. Negotiable CDs are time deposits banks offer. They have minimum face values of $100,000, but most are issued for $1 million or more.

A negotiable CD is an unsecured promissory note guaranteed by the issuing bank. Most negotiable CDs mature in one year or less, with the maturity date often set to suit a buyer's needs. Because the CDs are negotiable, they can be traded in the secondary market before their maturity.

Interest Rates

The cost of doing business is closely linked to the cost of money; the cost of money is called *interest rates*. The money supply and inflation levels within the economy determine the level of *general* interest rates. The level of a *specific* interest rate can be tied to one or more benchmark rates, such as those described below.

Federal Funds Rate

The federal funds rate is the rate federal banks charge each other for overnight loans of $1 million or more. It is considered a barometer of the direction of short-term interest rates, which fluctuate constantly. The federal funds rate is listed in daily newspapers.

Prime Rate

The prime rate is the interest rate that large U.S. money center commercial banks charge their most creditworthy corporate borrowers for unsecured loans. Each bank sets its own prime rate, with larger banks generally setting a rate other banks use.

Banks lower their prime rates when the Fed eases the money supply, and they raise rates when the Fed contracts the money supply.

Discount Rate

The discount rate is the rate the New York Federal Reserve Bank charges for short-term loans to member banks. The discount rate also indicates the direction of FRB monetary policy: a decreasing rate indicates an easing of FRB policy; an increasing rate indicates a tightening of FRB policy.

Broker Loan Rate

The broker loan rate is the interest rate banks charge broker-dealers on money they borrow to lend to margin account customers. The broker loan rate is also known as the *call loan rate* or *call money rate*. The broker loan rate usually is a percentage point or so above other short-term rates. Broker call loans are callable on 24 hours' notice.

Interest Rate Summary

Interest rates reflect the cost of money and, therefore, the cost of doing business. The key interest rates people monitor include the following:

- **Federal funds rate**. The interest rate charged on reserves traded among member banks for overnight use in amounts of $1 million or more. The federal funds rate changes daily in response to the borrowing banks' needs.
- **CD rate**. Bank rate offered on non-negotiable CD's. Considered the least volatile of the rates listed.
- **Prime rate**. The base rate on corporate loans at large U.S. money center commercial banks. The prime rate changes when banks react to changes in FRB policy.
- **Discount rate**. The charge on loans to depository institutions by the New York Federal Reserve Bank (FRB).
- **Call money rate**. The charge on loans to brokers of stock exchange collateral.
- **Commercial paper**. The rate on commercial paper placed directly by finance companies or the rate on high-grade unsecured notes that major corporations sell through dealers.

Eurodollars and the Foreign Currency Markets

The cost of raising money and doing business is not restricted by national boundaries. International monetary factors, such as changes in foreign currency exchange rates, Eurodollars, Eurosecurities and the international interbank system, can also affect U.S. money markets and businesses.

Eurocurrency

Eurodollars are U.S. dollars deposited in banks outside the United States; that is, the deposits remain denominated in U.S. dollars rather than the local currency. Euroyen are Japanese yen deposited in banks outside Japan. In other words, when a currency is preceded by the prefix "euro," it refers to a bank deposit outside of the currency's home country.

Eurodollar time deposits tend to be short term, ranging from overnight to 180 days. European banks lend Eurodollars to other banks in much the same way that U.S. banks lend federal funds. The interest rate is usually based on the London Interbank Offered Rate (LIBOR).

Eurosecurities

A Eurobond is any long-term debt instrument issued and sold outside the country of the currency in which it is denominated. A U.S. dollar–denominated Eurobond (Eurodollar bond) is a bond issued and sold outside the United States, but for which the principal and interest are stated and paid in U.S. dollars. Foreign corporations, foreign governments, domestic corporations and domestic governments, including municipalities, can issue Eurodollar bonds.

The Eurobond market is largely unregulated, and investors usually demand a higher return because they enjoy few safeguards. Eurobonds are sometimes used by investors to diversify domestic portfolios.

Interbank Market

The **Interbank Market** developed as a means of handling, transacting business in, trading, lending and consolidating foreign currency deposits.

Regulation. The interbank market is an unregulated, decentralized international market that deals in the various major world currencies.

The U.S. Treasury department buys and sells U.S. dollars in an attempt to influence the dollar's exchange rate in the interbank market. The money for these transactions comes from the Treasury's **exchange stabilization fund**.

If Treasury officials decide that the U.S. dollar is priced too high in the interbank market, it can sell U.S. dollars in the market. As the supply of dollars in the market increases, the price should decrease and the exchange rate should drop. Conversely, if the Treasury decides that exchange rates for the U.S. dollar are too low, it can buy dollars in the market. Stabilizing a currency through its purchase and sale by the country's central bank is sometimes known as **pegging**.

FIGURE 2.8 Foreign Exchange Rate Quotations

Exchange Rates

Wednesday, September 23, 1998

The New York foreign exchange selling rates below apply to trading among banks in amounts of $1,000,000 and more, as quoted at 3 pm Eastern Time by Bankers Trust Co. and other sources. Retail transactions provide fewer units of foreign currency per dollar.

Country	US $ equivalent		Currency per US $	
	Fri.	Thu.	Fri.	Thu.
Australia (Dollar)	.7630	.7760	1.3106	1.2887
Britain (Pound)	1.7285	1.7370	.5785	.5757
Canada (Dollar)	.8696	.8703	1.1500	1.1490
France (Franc)	.17116	.17205	5.8425	5.8122
Germany (Mark)	.5807	.5839	1.7220	1.7125
Hong Kong (Dollar)	.12840	.12839	7.7880	7.7890
Japan (Yen)	.007257	.007283	137.80	137.30
Mexico (Peso)	.000328	.000328	3005.01	3005.01
Switzerland (Franc)	.6854	.6908	1.4590	1.4475
ECU	1.2000	1.2018	. . . . . .	. . . . . .

Trading. The interbank market for foreign currencies functions efficiently as a telephone/telex market conducting international monetary business and exchange from individual bank trading rooms around the world. Two types of trades are:

- **spot trades**, which settle and are delivered in one or two business days (sometimes referred to as the **cash market** or **spot market**); and
- **forward trades**, which settle in more than two business days, with settlement dates normally set from 1 to 18 months (also known as the **forward market**).

Exchange Rates   An exchange rate is the rate at which one currency can be converted into another. Affected by numerous factors, exchange rates fluctuate daily. Figure 2.8 depicts foreign currency exchange rates with the U.S. dollar. Exchange rates are usually quoted in terms of the currency of the country in which the quote is published. Figure 2.9 illustrates the exchange rates among key currencies.

FIGURE 2.9 *Currency Cross Rates*

Key Currency Cross Rates New York trading, September 23, 1998

	Dollar	Pound	SFranc	Guilder	Yen	Lira	DMark	FFranc	CDollar
Canada	1.1498	1.9869	.78743	.59274	.00834	.00090	.66744	.19670	. . . . .
France	5.8455	10.101	4.0032	3.1035	.04242	.00457	3.3932	. . . . .	5.0839
Germany	1.7227	2.0768	1.1798	.88808	.01250	.00135	. . . . .	.29471	1.4983
Italy	1278.4	2209.1	875.50	659.04	9.2770	. . . . .	742.09	218.70	1111.8
Japan	137.80	238.12	94.371	71.038	. . . . .	.10779	79.991	23.574	119.85
Netherlands	1.9398	3.3520	1.3284	. . . . .	.01408	.00152	1.1260	.33185	1.6871
Switzerland	1.4602	2.5232	. . . . .	.75276	.01060	.00114	.84762	.24980	1.2700
UK	.57870	. . . . .	.39632	.29833	.00420	.00045	.33593	.09900	.50331
US	. . . . .	1.7280	.68484	.51552	.00726	.00078	.58048	.17107	.86972

Appreciation. A currency is said to be *appreciating* if it is rising in value compared to other currencies on the foreign exchange market.

Depreciation. A currency is said to be *depreciating* when it falls in value on the foreign exchange market. In this case, it will buy fewer units of another country's currency. A declining U.S. dollar means that U.S. dollars are becoming cheaper for citizens of other countries, and American goods and services are becoming less expensive abroad.

 For Example: If U.S. dollars are depreciating, goods produced by other countries become more expensive in the United States as those countries' currencies appreciate relative to the dollar. A dollar that can buy 200 Japanese yen (or yen-denominated goods) can buy twice as much Japanese goods and services as a dollar that can buy 100 yen.

Valuation

The exchange rate between currencies changes, or floats, constantly. The **devaluation** or **revaluation** in relationship to the currencies of other countries can result from market factors or governmental decisions.

Speculating in Foreign Currencies

Foreign currencies provide speculative opportunities for sophisticated investors. Risks of foreign currency speculation include the following:

- The interbank market is unregulated.
- The interbank market is decentralized.

- Changes in a country's economic, governmental or social policies could have immediate and dramatic impact on its currency's value.

Tracking Debt Securities

Corporate Bonds

Bonds are listed in daily newspapers and other financial publications. Figure 2.10 is an example of a New York Stock Exchange bond table as it might appear in a financial publication. Take, for example, Alabama Power (AlaP). The description of its 9s 2000 bond indicates that the bond pays 9 percent interest and matures in the year 2000. The current yield is given as 8.9 percent, which indicates that the bond is selling at a premium. The "Vol" (volume, or sales) column states how many bonds traded the previous day (the day being reported). In this case, 18 bonds, or $18,000 par value, were traded in Alabama Power 9s of 2000.

The next three columns explain the high, low and closing prices for the day. For AlaP, the high was 100¾, the low was 100⅝ and the bonds closed at (last trade) 100¾. Net change (the last column) refers to how much the bond's closing price was up or down from the previous day's close. Alabama Power 9s of 2000 closed up ¼ of a point, or $2.50. AlaP closed yesterday at 100½ (100¾ - ¼).

FIGURE 2.10 Corporate Bond Quotations

New York Exchange Bonds
Quotations as of 4 pm Eastern Time
Friday, July 16, 1999
Corporation Bonds
Volume $45,198,000

Bonds	Cur Yld	Vol	High	Low	Close	Net Chg
AForP 5s 30r	9.6	50	52 1/4	51 7/8	52	+3/4
AbbtL 7 5/8s 96	7.6	21	99 3/4	99 3/4	99 3/4	...
Advst 9s 08	cv	72	103 1/2	103	103	...
AetnLf 8 1/8s 07	8.5	15	95 3/4	95 3/4	95 3/4	−1
AirbF 7 1/2s 11	cv	32	114	112	114	+1
AlaP 9s 2000	8.9	18	100 3/4	100 5/8	100 3/4	+1/4
AlaP 8 1/2s 01	8.6	13	98 3/8	98 3/8	98 3/8	−3/8
AlaP 8 7/8s 03	8.5	65	102 7/8	102 1/2	102 1/2	−3/8
AlldC zr 12	...	10	91 1/2	91 1/8	91 1/2	−1/8
viAmes 7 1/2s 14f	cv	79	15 1/2	14 3/4	15	+1
Ancp 13 7/8s 02f	cv	10	91	89 3/8	91	+2

EXPLANATORY NOTES

Yield is current yield. cld–Called. cv–Convertible bond. dc–Deep discount. f–Dealt in flat. m–Matured bonds, negotiability impaired by maturity. na–No accrual. r–Registered. zr–Zero coupon. vi–In bankruptcy or receivership or being reorganized.

Note that the Allied Chemical (AlldC) zr bonds have " ... " in the current yield column. This indicates that these are zero-coupon bonds that do not pay interest.

Tracking U.S. Government Securities

Quotes for Treasury bonds, notes and bills are listed in Figure 2.11. Reading from left to right under "Govt. Bonds & Notes," you can determine the coupon rate, maturity date, bid and asked prices, bid change from the previous trading day and the yield to maturity.

Treasury Bonds and Notes
Treasury bonds and notes are quoted at percentages of par. The first note shown in Figure 2.11 pays a rate of 7½ percent and matures in August 1999. (An "n" after the year indicates that the security is a Treasury note, and no letter after the year indicates it is a bond.) The bid and asked prices reflect the most recently reported over-the-counter market prices, and the bid change indicates how much the price has changed from the last report. At the current asked, this particular note would yield 7.37 percent. Other government

FIGURE 2.11   Treasury Securities Quotations

Treasury Bonds, Notes & Bills
Quotations as of mid-afternoon
Monday, August 1, 1999

Govt. Bonds & Notes

Rate	Maturity Mo/Yr	Bid	Asked	Chg	Ask Yld
7 1/2	Aug 99n	100:02	100:04	....	7.37
7 1/4	Aug 00	100:26	100:30	....	6.30
9 1/2	Oct 02	105:31	106:01	....	7.35
8 1/2	Apr 03	102:18	102:20	+1	7.92
9	May 04	104:24	104:26	....	8.07
3 1/2	Nov 04	94:05	95:05	- 1	4.28
13 3/8	Aug 07	134:26	135:02	....	8.19
10 3/4	Feb 09	117:27	118:03	- 1	8.28

U.S. Treasury STRIPS

Maturity	Type	Bid	Asked	Chg	Bid Yld
Nov 00	np	78:19	78:22	+1	7.46
Aug 01	ci	73:15	73:18	+1	7.78
Feb 07	ci	45:06	45:10	- 2	8.50
Nov 10	bp	32:19	32:23	....	8.62
Feb 11	ci	31:22	31:26	- 1	8.67
Nov 15	bp	20:19	20:22	....	8.83
May 21	ci	13:09	13:12	....	8.67
Aug 26	ci	9:11	9:14	....	8.33

EXPLANATORY NOTES
Colons in bid and asked quotes represent 1/32nds. 99:01 means 99 1/32. Net changes are in 1/32nds. n-Treasury note. Treasury bill quotes in hundredths, quoted on terms of a rate of discount. Yields are to maturity or to earliest call date.
U.S. Treasury STRIPS quotes are based on transactions of $1,000,000 or more. Colons represent 1/32nds. Abbreviations: ci-stripped coupon interest. bp-Treasury bond, stripped principal. np-Treasury note, stripped principal.

Treasury Bills

Maturity	Days to Maturity	Bid	Asked	Chg	Ask Yld
Aug 08 99	7	5.54	5.44	- 0.05	5.52
Oct 24 99	84	5.55	5.53	- 0.02	5.68
Dec 26 99	147	5.60	5.58	....	5.81
Apr 23 00	266	5.82	5.80	....	6.10
May 07 00	280	5.81	5.79	- 0.01	6.10

and agency issues are quoted in a similar fashion. In the second listing under "Govt. Bonds & Notes," the bonds have a 7¼ percent coupon rate and mature in August 2000. The bid was 100:26 (100 and ²⁶⁄₃₂); the asked price was 100:30 (100 and ³⁰⁄₃₂). The bonds have a YTM of 6.30 percent.

Treasury Bills Treasury bills are quoted at their annualized discount rates (or yields). The maturity date is given in the first column of the Treasury bills quotation in Figure 2.11. The second column shows the number of days remaining until the bills' maturity. The third column shows the discount rate that results from the bid prices dealers will pay to buy the bills. The fourth column is the ask price. The number reflects the discount from par, and the discount on the asked side is smaller than that on the bid side. Under the column headings "Bid" and "Asked" are listed the discounts from par that investors and broker-dealers will give and take for the bills. In Figure 2.11, the dollar bid on a May 7, 2000, $1 million T bill would be $941,900 ($1 million – $58,100). The dollar ask price would be $942,100 ($1 million – $57,900).

The first bill in the table matures August 8, 1999. It is being offered for sale at par less a discount computed at a rate of 5.44 percent, to yield 5.52 percent. On August 8, 1999, the bill is payable at par.

Summary

Corporations, the federal government and municipal governments issue bonds as a means to raise funds for expenses of operations, improvement and expansion.

Bonds are debt instruments. As such, a bond issuer is a borrower and the bond investor is a lender. A bond, as any other loan, requires the issuer to pay interest for a period of time—from very short- to very long-term—and repay the principal amount at maturity.

Because bonds are issued with a fixed interest rate payment (the coupon), they are known as fixed-income securities. However, the actual yield of a bond will change as its market price changes.

The market price of a bond will fluctuate in general with changes in interest rates, or in particular with changes in the financial stability of the issuer. As interest rates rise, bond prices decline; as interest rates decline, bond prices rise. If an issuer's financial stability improves, the price of its bonds will likely increase; if the issuer's financial stability deteriorates, the price of its bonds will likely decline.

Key Concepts

To prepare for your license exam, you should learn the following concepts.

In addition to studying these key concepts, use the Debt Securities Hot Sheet on page 634 for further review.

agency issue
balloon maturity
banker's acceptance (BA)
bearer bond
book-entry bond
book entry
broker loan (call) rate
call protection
cash market
certificate of deposit (CD)
closed-end indenture
collateralized mortgage obligation (CMO)
collateral trust bond
commercial paper
competitive bid
convertible security
coupon bond
current yield
dealer paper
debenture
debt service
devaluation
direct paper
Eurobond
Eurodollar
Eurosecurity
exchange stabilization
Federal Farm Credit Bank
federal funds rate
Federal Home Loan Mortgage Corporation (FHLMC)
Federal Intermediate Credit Bank (FICB)
Federal National Mortgage Association (FNMA)
foreign exchange rate
forward trade

funded debt
Government National Mortgage Association (GNMA)
interbank
investment grade bond
junk bond
London Interbank Offered Rate (LIBOR)
money market
nominal yield
noncompetitive bid
par
pass-through security
pegging
point
premium
prerefunding
prime rate
redemption
refunding
registered bond
repurchase agreement (repo)
revaluation
reverse repurchase agreement
Separate Trading of Registered Interest and Principal of Securities (STRIPS)
serial maturity
sinking fund
Treasury bill
Treasury bond
Treasury note
Treasury receipt
trust indenture
yield
yield to call (YTC)
yield to maturity (YTM)
zero-coupon bond

Review Questions

1. Bonds that mature with a smaller amount in the earlier years and a greater amount in the later years are called

   A. series bonds
   B. term bonds
   C. balloon bonds
   D. callable bonds

2. Which of the following are characteristics of bonds?

   I. They represent a loan to the issuer.
   II. They give the bondholder ownership in the entity.
   III. They are issued to finance capital expenditures or to raise working capital.
   IV. They are junior securities.

   A. I, II and IV only
   B. I and III only
   C. II and III only
   D. I, II, III and IV

3. Which type of bonds mature in stages over a succession of years?

   A. Series
   B. Callable
   C. Term
   D. Serial

4. As the maturity date approaches, the amount of interest paid out by the issuer would be most reduced on a(n)

   A. series bond
   B. adjustment bond
   C. serial bond
   D. income bond

5. Interest payments on bonds are based upon the security's

   A. par value
   B. discount value
   C. market value
   D. book value

6. A 5% bond is issued at par. It is now selling at 90 and is redeemable at par. What is the owner's annual income from this investment?

   A. $20
   B. $50
   C. $500
   D. $5,000

7. A trust indenture is a contract between the

   A. issuer and the investor
   B. issuer and the trustee
   C. trustee and the underwriter
   D. issuer and the underwriter

8. Bonds that are secured by other securities placed with a trustee are called

   A. mortgage bonds
   B. collateral trust bonds
   C. debenture bonds
   D. guaranteed bonds

9. Which of the following statement(s) concerning convertible bonds is(are) true?

   I. Coupon rates for convertible bonds are usually lower than for nonconvertible bonds of the same issuer.
   II. Convertible bondholders are creditors of the corporation.
   III. If the underlying common stock should decline to the point where there is no advantage to converting the bonds into common stock, the bonds will sell at a price based on their inherent value as bonds, disregarding the convertible feature.

   A. I only
   B. I and III only
   C. III only
   D. I, II and III

10. Greater Health, Inc. bonds are convertible at $50. If the bonds are selling in the market for 60 ($600) and the common stock is selling for $30, which two of the following statements are true?

    I. The bonds are trading below parity to the common.
    II. The stock is selling at conversion parity.
    III. There would be a profitable arbitrage situation.
    IV. The bonds can be converted into 20 shares of common.

    A. I and II
    B. I and III
    C. II and IV
    D. III and IV

11. Government bonds and notes are quoted

    A. in 1/8ths
    B. as a percentage of par
    C. on a yield to maturity
    D. as a percentage of par on a discounted annualized basis

12. The maximum maturity on a T note is

    A. One year
    B. Three years
    C. Five years
    D. Ten years

13. Which of the following statements are true regarding T bills?

    I. T bills trade at a discount to par.
    II. T bills have maturities of one year or less.
    III. Most T bill issues are callable.
    IV. A T bill is a direct obligation of the U.S. government.

    A. I and II
    B. I and III
    C. I, II and IV
    D. II and IV

14. Which of the following is an original issue discount obligation?

    A. GNMA certificate
    B. T bill
    C. corporate bond
    D. FNMA bond

15. If you invest $10,000 in T bills over a period of years, which of the following statements are true?

    I. The principal is stable.
    II. The interest is volatile.
    III. The interest is stable.
    IV. The principal is volatile.

    A. I and II
    B. I and III
    C. II and IV
    D. III and IV

16. Both 13-week and 26-week T bill auctions are held

    A. daily
    B. weekly
    C. monthly
    D. quarterly

17. A GNMA pass-through certificate pays interest

    A. monthly
    B. quarterly
    C. semiannually
    D. annually

18. All of the following are money-market instruments EXCEPT

    A. Treasury bills
    B. municipal notes
    C. commercial paper
    D. newly issued Treasury bonds

19. Which of the following describes money-market instruments?

    A. Short-term debt
    B. Long-term debt
    C. Short-term equity
    D. Long-term equity

20. The maximum maturity of commercial paper is how many days?

    A. 90
    B. 180
    C. 270
    D. 360

21. Which of the following statements are true of negotiable certificates of deposit?

    I. The issuing bank guarantees the instrument.
    II. Certificates of deposit are callable.
    III. Minimum denominations are $1,000.
    IV. Certificates of deposit can be traded in the secondary market.

    A. I, II and III only
    B. I and IV only
    C. II and III only
    D. I, II, III and IV

22. Which of the following characteristics describes commercial paper?

    A. Secured note issued by a corporation
    B. Guaranteed note issued by a corporation
    C. Promissory note issued by a corporation
    D. Promissory note issued by a broker

23. Which of the following money-market instruments finances imports and exports?

    A. Eurodollars
    B. Bankers' acceptances
    C. ADRs
    D. Commercial paper

24. A banker's acceptance is a

    A. promissory note
    B. capital-market instrument
    C. time draft
    D. means of facilitating the trading of foreign securities

25. A U.S. government bond dealer sells bonds to another dealer with an agreement to buy back the securities in a specified period of time. This is a(n)

    A. repurchase agreement
    B. reverse repurchase agreement
    C. open market certificate
    D. open market note

Answers & Rationale

1. **C.** Occasionally, an issuer will repay part of a bond's principal before the final maturity date but will pay off the major portion of it at maturity. This is known as a *balloon maturity.*

2. **B.** Bonds give the bondholder the status of lender, not of owner. Because they represent a debt the corporation owes, they are senior securities.

3. **D.** Some bond issuers schedule repayment of the bond over a period of time and structure their bond issues with serial maturities. In this case, portions of the bond will mature at intervals until the entire balance has been repaid.

4. **C.** With a serial bond issue, more of the earlier payments represent interest rather than principal. As maturity approaches, the opposite is true. A lesser amount of each payment represents interest and a greater amount represents principal.

5. **A.** $1,000 is considered a bond's par value or principal amount. If a bond is issued with a 6 percent coupon, this means the corporation will pay 6 percent of $1,000, or $60, each year in interest.

6. **B.** A 5% bond will continue to pay $50 a year, regardless of its market price in the secondary market.

7. **B.** As established by the Trust Indenture Act of 1939, a trust indenture is a legal contract between the bond issuer and a trustee on behalf of the bondholders.

8. **B.** Debt issued by a corporation that is backed by stocks or bonds of another issuer and held by a trustee for safekeeping is called a *collateral trust bond.*

9. **D.** Coupons on convertible bonds are lower because, in exchange for the conversion option, investors are willing to settle for lower interest income. Bondholders are creditors of the corporation. If the price of the underlying declines sharply, then the conversion feature is unimportant and the bond will sell in the secondary market as if it was a nonconvertible bond.

10. **C.** With a conversion price of $50 the investor would receive 20 shares ($1,000 par value ÷ $50 = 20). To calculate the parity of the common stock, divide the current market price by the number of shares at conversion: $600 ÷ 20 = $30. The stock is selling at parity.

11. **B.** U.S. government notes and bonds are issued, quoted and traded at a percentage of par.

12. **D.** Treasury notes are intermediate-term bonds maturing in one to a maximum of ten years.

13. **C.** Treasury bills are issued at a discount from par in a competitive bidding auction. They are short-term issues with maturities of one year or less and they are a direct obligation of the U.S. government. Because of their short maturity, they are not callable.

14. **B.** Treasury bills are issued at a discount from par. The other three choices are issued at or near par.

15. **A.** Because Treasury bills are short-term instruments, they are vulnerable to upward and downward changes in short-term interest rates. As they are direct obligations of the U.S. government, however, the principal is not at risk.

16. **B.** The competitive bid auctions for the 13- and 26-week Treasury bills are held weekly.

17. **A.** GNMAs pay principal and interest monthly.

18. **D.** Money-market instruments provide ways for businesses, financial institutions and governments to meet short-term financial requirements. By their nature they need to have short-

term maturities. Because Treasury bonds don't mature for at least ten years, they are not considered money-market instruments.

19.   **A.**   By definition, a money-market instrument is a debt security with a fixed interest rate and a short-term maturity, usually one year or less.

20.   **C.**   Commercial paper issues have fixed maturities that range from 1 to 270 days, although most are issued to mature in less than 90 days.

21.   **B.**   Negotiable certificates of deposit are issued and guaranteed by banks and can be traded in the secondary market. Negotiable CDs are not callable because they mature in one year or less. They are usually issued in minimum denom-

inations of $100,000, although sales of $1,000,000 are more common.

22.   **C.**   Commercial paper is an unsecured, short-term promissory note issued by corporations for short-term financial needs.

23.   **B.**   Bankers' acceptances are used extensively by U.S. corporations as a means of financing international trade (exports and imports).

24.   **C.**   A banker's acceptance is a short-term time draft with a specified payment date, drawn on a bank.

25.   **A.**   When a dealer lends securities to another dealer with an agreement to buy back the securities at a later date, this is a repurchase agreement.

3

Municipal Securities

OVERVIEW

Municipal securities are loans by investors to a state, local government or U.S. territory. They are issued to raise capital for public works and construction projects that benefit the general public, such as road maintenance or new sewer systems.

Municipal securities need not be registered with the SEC, but *no offering is exempt from the antifraud provisions* of the Securities Act of 1934.

Municipal Bond Characteristics

In the ranking of investment categories by safety of principal, municipal securities are considered second only to U.S. government and U.S. government agency securities. The degree of safety, of course, varies from issue to issue and municipality to municipality. Generally, a municipal issue's safety is based on the municipality's financial stability.

Each new municipal issue is accompanied by documentation that:

- sets forth the loan terms and the repayment schedule;
- attests to the issuing municipality's authority to issue the debt obligation;
- lists the issue's specific features;
- describes the intended use of the borrowed funds; and
- provides financial information about the municipality's and the community's economic health.

Tax Benefits   The federal government does not tax the interest from municipalities' debt obligations; municipalities reciprocate by not taxing the interest from federal debt securities. This **doctrine of reciprocal immunity**, also known as the **doctrine of mutual reciprocity**, was established by a Supreme Court decision in 1895. However, in 1986 a Supreme Court decision reversed the doctrine of mutual reciprocity, allowing Congress to tax the interest earned from municipal issues at any time, although this is unlikely.

To qualify for federal tax exemption, a municipal security must be issued to fund public, rather than private, activities. In most states, interest from municipal bonds is exempt from state taxes if a bond is:

- issued by a municipality in that state;
- sold to an investor who resides in the state; or
- issued by a U.S. territory.

The tax-advantaged status of municipal bonds allows municipalities to raise money at a lower cost than corporations. Municipalities pay lower interest rates on their tax-exempt bonds than those paid on taxable bonds. An investor's **after-tax rate of return** may be higher, lower or about the same as that on a taxable bond. Municipal securities are more appropriate for investors in high tax brackets than those in low brackets because the amount of tax savings for high tax bracket investors is larger. Investors should be aware of a bond's **tax-equivalent yield** when assessing its merits as an investment. Calculating the tax-equivalent yield is discussed later in this lesson.

Municipal bonds pay interest semiannually. The interest payment schedules are set when the bonds are issued.

Issuers   The three primary entities legally entitled to issue municipal debt securities are territorial possessions of the United States (such as Puerto Rico), state governments and legally constituted taxing authorities. Taxing authorities include county and city governments and the agencies they create. Public authorities that supervise ports and mass transit systems—such as the River Des Peres Port Authority—also can issue municipal bonds.

Maturity Structures   Municipal notes and bonds may be issued with maturities of 1 (or less) to 30 (or more) years. Municipal issuers use the three types of maturity schedules common to corporate debt issuers: **term**, **serial** and **balloon**.

Term Maturity. A term bond issue is structured so that all of the principal matures at once. Because all of the principal is repaid at one time, most issuers establish a sinking fund account in which to accumulate money that the issuers will use to pay principal on bonds at or before maturity.

Serial Maturity. In a serial maturity issue, the issuer designs principal repayment so that each bond matures on a specific date over a period of years until the entire balance has been repaid.

Balloon Maturity. Occasionally, an issuer repays part of a bond issue's principal before the final maturity date (as with serial maturities), but pays off the major portion of it at maturity. This type of maturity schedule is called a *balloon*, or *serial with a balloon, maturity*.

Types of Municipal Issues

Two categories of municipal securities exist. **General obligation bonds (GOs)** are backed by the full faith, credit and taxing powers of the municipality. **Revenue bonds** are backed by the revenues generated by the municipal facility the bond issue finances.

General Obligation Bonds   GOs are also known as *full faith and credit bonds* because the interest and principal payments are backed by the issuer's full faith and credit. GOs are used to raise funds for municipal capital improvements that benefit the entire community—road repairs, for instance. These improvements typically do not produce revenues.

Sources of Funds

GOs are backed by the municipality's taxing power. Bonds issued by states are backed by income taxes, license fees and sales taxes. Bonds issued by towns, cities and counties are backed by property (ad valorem) taxes, license fees, fines and all other sources of revenue to the municipality. School, road and park districts may also issue municipal bonds backed by property taxes.

Legal Limitations

The amount of debt a municipal government may incur can be limited by state or local statutes to protect taxpayers from excessive taxes. Debt limits can also make a bond safer for investors. The lower the debt limit, the less risk of excessive borrowing and default by the municipality.

Voter Approval. Because taxes back GOs, most municipalities require a vote of the taxpayers to approve new GO issues.

Tax Limits. Some states limit property taxes to a certain percentage of the assessed property value or to a certain percentage increase in any single year. Normally, the tax rate is expressed in **mills**; one mill equals $\frac{1}{10}$ of one cent ($.001).

Overlapping Debt. Several taxing authorities that draw from the same taxpayers can issue debt. Bonds issued by different municipal authorities that tap the same taxpayer wallets are known as **coterminous** debt.

For Example: A school district's debt is backed by property taxes in the district. Debt issued by the city or county in which the school resides may also be backed by these property taxes. The school district, therefore, issues debt that overlaps the city's or county's debt. Debt issued by states is not included when calculating overlapping debt.

Double-Barreled Bonds. Double-barreled bonds are GOs that have characteristics of revenue bonds. Interest and principal are paid from a specified facility's earnings. However, the bonds are also backed by the taxing power of the state or municipality and, therefore, have the backing of two sources of revenue. Although they are backed by revenues from the facility, double-barreled bonds are rated and traded as GOs.

Revenue Bonds

Revenue bonds can be used to finance any municipal facility that generates sufficient income.

Unlike GOs, revenue bonds are not subject to statutory debt limits and do not require voter approval. A particular revenue bond issue, however, may be subject to an **additional bonds test** before subsequent bond issues with equal liens on the project's revenue may be issued.

Sources of Revenue

Revenue bonds' interest and principal payments are payable to bondholders only from the specific earnings and net lease payments of revenue-producing facilities, such as:

- utility (water, sewer, electric)
- housing
- transportation (airports, toll roads)
- education (college dorms, student loans)
- health (hospitals, retirement centers)
- industrial (industrial development, pollution control)
- sports facilities

Debt service payments do not come from general or real estate taxes and are not backed by the municipality's full faith and credit.

Protective Covenants

The face of a revenue bond certificate usually refers to an indenture. This is a statement of the terms of agreement between the issuing municipality and the trustee appointed to act on behalf of the bondholders.

In the trust indenture, the municipality agrees to abide by certain protective covenants, or promises meant to protect bondholders. A trustee appointed in the indenture supervises the issuer's compliance with the bond covenants.

The trust indenture's provisions can vary, but a number of standard provisions are common to most bond issues:

- **rate covenant**—a promise to maintain rates sufficient to pay expenses and debt service;
- **maintenance covenant**—a promise to maintain the equipment and facility(ies);
- **insurance covenant**—a promise to insure any facility built;
- **additional bonds test**—whether the indenture is open ended (allowing further issuance of bonds with the same status and equal claims on revenues) or closed ended (allowing no further issuance of bonds using the same collateral unless the original bondholders agree);
- **sinking fund**—money to pay off interest and principal obligations;
- **consulting engineer;**
- **catastrophe clause**—a promise to use the insurance proceeds to repay investors if a facility is destroyed;
- **flow of funds**—details of the application;
- **outside audit of records and financial reports**; and
- **call features.**

Types of Revenue Bonds

There are a number of categories of revenue bonds, depending on the type of facility the bond issue finances.

Industrial Development Revenue Bonds. A municipality issues industrial development revenue bonds (IDRs or IDBs) to construct facilities or purchase equipment, which is then leased to a corporation. The municipality uses the money from lease payments to pay the principal and interest on the bonds. The ultimate responsibility for the payment of principal and interest rests with the corporation; therefore, the bonds carry the corporation's debt rating.

Technically, industrial revenue bonds are issued for a corporation's benefit. Under the Tax Reform Act of 1986, the interest on these bonds is usually taxable because the act reserves tax exemption for public purposes. Some IDRs remain exempt from taxation because of the use of the proceeds or their size.

Lease Rental Bonds. Under a typical lease-rental (or lease-back) bond arrangement, a municipality could create an authority or agency to construct a new building that benefits the municipality itself or its state or community.

✓ *For Example:* A municipality might issue bonds to raise money to construct a school and lease the finished building to the school district. The lease payments provide backing for the bonds. Lease payments come from funds raised through special taxes or appropriations, from the lessor's revenues, such as the school's tuition or fees, or from the municipality's general fund.

Special Tax Bonds. Special tax bonds are issued for specific projects. Interest and principal payments are made only from the proceeds of a special tax. Examples include excise taxes on tobacco, alcohol or hotel room rentals.

Special Assessment Bonds. Special assessment bonds are issued to finance the construction of public improvements such as streets, sidewalks or sewers. The issuer assesses a tax only on the property that benefits from the improvement and uses the funds to pay principal and interest.

New Housing Authority Bonds. Local housing authorities issue New Housing Authority bonds (NHAs) to develop and improve low-income housing. NHAs are backed by the full faith and credit of the U.S. government. NHAs are sometimes called **PHAs (Public Housing Authority Bonds)**. Because of their federal backing, they are considered the most secure of all municipal bonds.

Moral Obligation Bonds. A moral obligation bond is a state-issued or state agency-issued revenue bond. If revenues backing the bond are not sufficient to pay the debt service, the state legislature has the authority to appropriate funds to make the payments. The potential backing by state revenues tends to make the bond more marketable, but the state's obligation is not established by law; it is a moral obligation only.

Municipal Notes   Municipal notes are short-term securities that generate funds for a municipality that expects other revenues soon. They are repaid when the municipality receives the anticipated funds. Municipal notes fall into several categories:

- Municipalities issue tax anticipation notes (TANs) to finance current operations in anticipation of future tax receipts.
- Revenue anticipation notes (RANs) are offered periodically to finance current operations in anticipation of future revenues.
- Bond anticipation notes (BANs) are sold as interim financing that will eventually be converted to long-term funding through the sale of bonds.
- Construction loan notes (CLNs) are issued to provide interim financing for new projects.
- Variable rate demand notes have a fluctuating interest rate and are issued in anticipation of long-term funding.

Tax-Exempt Commercial Paper

Municipalities meet very short-term funding needs by issuing tax-exempt commercial paper. These promissory notes typically mature in 270 days or less. Tax-exempt commercial paper is similar to corporate commercial paper, is issued in registered form and is usually issued with the backing of a line of credit from a bank.

Municipal Security Registration Documents

Bond Contract A municipal issuer enters into a **bond contract** with the underwriters of, and investors in, its securities. The bond contract is a collection of legal documents that includes the bond resolution, the trust indenture, applicable state and national law, and any other legal documents pertaining to that particular issue and issuer. By issuing its securities, the issuer has agreed to abide by the terms and covenants contained in the various documents that compose the bond contract.

Bond Resolution The municipality authorizes the issue and sale of its securities through the **bond resolution**. The bond resolution contains a description of the issuer's obligations and duties toward its bondholders. Normally, this includes a flow of funds statement establishing the priority of payments made from a facility's revenues.

In some cases, the bond resolution consists of two separate documents: the **authorizing resolution**, which authorizes the bonds' issuance, and the **award resolution**, which authorizes the bonds' sale.

Indenture On the face of most municipal *revenue* bond certificates is a reference to the bonds' underlying **indenture**, also known as **bond indentures**. Although it is not required by law, most municipal issuers use indentures as part of revenue bond contracts. The indenture serves as a contract between the bond's issuer and a trustee appointed on behalf of the bond's investors.

The indenture is too long to supply to all bondholders, although the issuer must make a complete copy available upon request. The official statement outlines the indenture's covenants (protective promises).

Official Statement The **official statement (OS)** is the municipal securities industry's equivalent of the corporate prospectus. The official statement serves as a disclosure document and contains any material information an investor might need about an issue. Prepared by the issuer, the official statement identifies the issue's purpose, the source from which the interest and principal will be repaid and the issuer's and community's financial and economic backgrounds. The official statement also has information relating to the issue's creditworthiness.

Preliminary Official Statement. Municipal issuers may also prepare preliminary official statements that, like their corporate counterparts, are known as **red herrings**. The preliminary official statement discloses most of the same material information as the official statement, with the exception of the issue's interest rate(s) and offering price(s). An issuer uses a preliminary official statement to determine investors' and dealers' interest in the issue. As with any red herring, the preliminary official statement does not constitute an offer to sell the securities; only the final official statement can make that offer.

Legal Opinion   Attached to every bond certificate (unless the bond is specifically stamped "**ex-legal**") is a **legal opinion** written and signed by the **bond counsel**, an attorney specializing in tax-exempt bond offerings. The legal opinion states that the issue conforms with applicable laws, the state constitution and established procedures. If interest from the bond is tax exempt, that too is stated in the legal opinion. The legal opinion is issued either as a **qualified opinion** (that is, the bond counsel that issued the opinion has reservations about the issue or wants it known that certain conditions exist) or as an **unqualified opinion** (issued by the bond counsel unconditionally).

Issuing Municipal Securities

A uniform sequence of events leads to a new municipal issue. The issuer must first obtain a preliminary legal opinion, which determines whether and how the bonds may be offered. Then, the terms of the municipal bond offering may be set by either **negotiation** or **competitive bidding**.

Negotiated Underwriting   In a negotiated underwriting, the municipality appoints an investment banker to underwrite the offering. The underwriter works with the issuer to establish the interest rate and the offering price in light of the issuer's financial needs and market conditions. Most revenue bonds are issued through negotiated underwritings. The issue can be distributed as either a public offering or a private placement.

Competitive Bidding   With few exceptions, municipal GOs are awarded to an underwriter through competitive bidding. When a municipality publishes an invitation to bid, investment bankers respond in writing to the issuer's attorney or another designated official requesting information on the offering.

Official Notice of Sale

The notice of bond sale is usually published in *The Bond Buyer* and includes the following information:

- date, time and place of sale;
- name and description of issuer;
- type of bond;
- bidding restrictions (usually requiring a sealed bid);
- interest payment dates;
- dated date (interest accrual date) and first coupon payment date;
- maturity structure;
- call provisions (if any);
- denominations and registration provisions;
- expenses to be borne by purchaser or issuer;

- amount of good faith deposit that must accompany bid;
- paying agent or trustee;
- name of the firm, sometimes called the *bond counsel*, providing the legal opinion;
- details of delivery;
- right of rejection; and
- criteria for awarding the issue.

The bond's rating and the underwriter's name are not included in a notice of sale because they have yet to be determined.

Investment bankers prepare bids for the securities based on information in the notice of sale, comparable new issue supply and demand, and general market conditions.

Sources of Municipal Securities Information

A number of publications and services offer information on proposed new issues and secondary market activity for municipal issues. These include *The Bond Buyer, Munifacts* and *The Blue List*.

- *The Bond Buyer* is published every business day and serves as an authoritative source of information on both new and secondary market municipal bonds. The Thursday edition publishes the 30-day visible supply (the total dollar volume of municipal offerings expected to reach the market in the next 30 days) and the placement ratio indexes (the percentages of the previous week's new issues that have been purchased from the underwriters), among other information.
- *Munifacts* is a subscription wire service of *The Bond Buyer* that supplies prices, information about proposed new issues and general news relevant to the municipal bond market.
- *The Blue List* is a daily industry publication that provides a comprehensive source of municipal security information for the interdealer market. It lists the par values, issuers, interest rates, maturity dates, prices or yields and offering dealers for current municipal bond secondary offerings of banks and brokers across the nation. *The Blue List* also contains a limited amount of information about new issues—primarily new housing authority bonds and new-issue delivery dates. Underwriters and issuers often consult *The Blue List* to determine current yields and prices. Figure 3.1 illustrates a page as it might appear in *The Blue List*.

FIGURE 3.1   Sample Page from *The Blue List*

The Blue List

of Current Municipal and Corporate Offerings

A Division of Standard & Poor's Corporation

Published every weekday except Saturdays and Holidays
by The Blue List Publishing Company,
15 Broadway, New York, NY 10004
Telephone 212-555-8200   FAX 212-555-3000

The bonds set forth in this list were offered at the close of business
on the day before the date of this issue by the houses mentioned,
subject to prior sale and change in price. Every effort is made by
The Blue List Publishing Company and the houses whose offerings
are shown in The Blue List to avoid mistakes and inaccuracies, but
due to the fact that many offerings come in by wire and that the list
is published after the offering houses have closed for the day,
occasional errors are unavoidable. Neither The Blue List Publishing
Company nor the offering houses take responsibility for the accuracy
of the offerings listed herein.

INDEX

New Housing Authority Bonds	22	Corporate Bonds	36
Taxable Municipals	23	Bank Qualified	37
Industrial Development and		AMT Bonds	41
Pollution Control Bonds	24	Zero Coupon Bonds	45
Notes	26	Offerings Wanted	49
Unit Investment Trusts	29	AMBAC Insured Bonds	50
New Issue Delivery Dates	30	List of Advertisers	55
Pre-refunded Bonds	33	Late Breaking CUSIPs	
Federally Sponsored Bonds	35		

+ Items so marked did not appear in the previous issue of The Blue List.
\# Prices so marked are changed from the previous issue.
c Items so marked are reported to have call or option features. Consult
offering house for full details.

AMT. M	SECURITY	PURPOSE	RATE	MATURITY	YIELD OR PRICE	OFFERED BY
+ 2000	ALABAMA ST	CA @ 99.691	0.000	09/01/00 C99	7.10	GOLDMANY
+ 110	ALABAMA HSG FIN AUTH SINGLE	P/R @ 103	8.750	12/01/01	104 1/2	PORTER
350	ALABAMA ST UNIV REV	BK.QD	8.000	01/01/14	7.60	MOOSEACO
10	BALDWIN CNTY ALA EASTN SHORE	AMBAC	7.750	04/01/11 C02	# 7.40	WILEYBRO
+ 500	BIRMINGHAM ALA WTRWRKS & SWR	*REG*	7.200	01/01/17	98 3/4	ROBINHUM

Glass-Steagall Act of 1933

The Glass-Steagall Act of 1933 erected a wall between commercial banking
and investment banking activities, one that is being slowly dismantled in the
1990s. The act was intended to protect bank customers by preventing banks
from engaging in the investment banking, brokerage or underwriting
business.

The Glass-Steagall Act prohibits commercial banks from underwriting corporate securities and most municipal revenue bonds. The act, however, does
allow commercial banks to underwrite general obligation bonds and New
Housing Authority bonds without restriction. Banks also can underwrite
housing and education revenue bonds and moral obligation bonds. The revenue bonds that commercial banks are permitted to underwrite are known
as *bank eligible* bonds.

Formation of the Underwriting Syndicate

Once an issuer's notice of sale has circulated, those investment bankers interested in placing competitive bids for an issue form **syndicates**. A syndicate is an account that helps spread the risk of underwriting an issue among a number of underwriters. Although the bidding process is competitive, successive offerings of a particular municipality are often handled by the same syndicate, composed of the same members.

A firm makes the decision to participate as a syndicate member after it considers the:

- potential demand for the security
- existence of presale orders
- determination and extent of liability
- scale and spread
- ability to sell the issue

Participants formalize their relationship by signing a **syndicate letter** or **syndicate agreement** in a competitive bid or a **syndicate contract** or **agreement among underwriters** in a negotiated underwriting. About two weeks before the issue is awarded, the syndicate manager sends the syndicate letter or contract to each participating firm for an authorized signature. The member's signature indicates its agreement with the offering terms. Syndicate letters include the following:

- each member firm's level of participation, or **commitment**;
- priority of order allocation;
- duration of the syndicate account;
- appointment of the manager(s) as agent(s) for the account;
- fee for the managing underwriter and breakdown of the spread; and
- other obligations, such as member expenses, good faith deposits, observance of offering terms and liability for unsold bonds.

Types of Syndicate Accounts
The financial liability each underwriter is exposed to depends on the type of syndicate account. Underwriting syndicates use two arrangements: **Western account** and **Eastern account**.

Western account. The Western account is a **divided account**. Each underwriter is responsible only for its own underwriting allocation.

✓ *For Example:* If the underwriter is allocated 10 percent of the issue to sell, its financial liability ends once it has distributed its 10 percent participation.

Eastern Account. An Eastern account is an **undivided account**. Each underwriter is allocated a portion of the issue. After the issue has been substantially distributed, each underwriter is allocated additional bonds representing its proportionate share of any remaining bonds. Thus, an underwriter's financial liability might not end when it has distributed its initial allocation.

✓ **For Example:** If a 10 percent underwriter of a $10 million bond issue has sold its 10 percent share, but bonds worth $5 million remain unsold by other syndicate members, the underwriter is responsible for 10 percent of the unsold bonds—in this case, $500,000. The responsibility for any unsold bonds continues until the entire issue has been sold.

Due Diligence   Municipal underwriters must investigate an issuer's financing proposals thoroughly. With revenue bonds, this **due diligence** investigation is conducted through a **feasibility study**, which focuses on the projected revenues and costs associated with the project and an analysis of competing facilities.

Establishing the Syndicate Bid

A syndicate arrives at its competitive bid over a series of meetings during which member dealers discuss the proposed reoffering scale and spread for the underwriters. Their goal is to arrive at the best price to the issuer while still making a profit. At a preliminary meeting, the manager seeks tentative agreement from members on the prices or yields of all maturities in the issue, as well as the gross profit or underwriting spread. A final bid price for the bond is set at a meeting conducted just before the bid is due. If the member dealers cannot all agree on a final bid, the syndicate can go ahead with its bid as long as the syndicate members agree to abide by the majority's decision.

In bidding for the issue, the underwriter establishes the **reoffering yield** (or **price**) for each maturity, which is the price at which the bonds will be offered to the public. This is called **writing a scale**. A scale is the list of the bond issue's different maturities. If the coupon rate has already been determined, each maturity listed is assigned a yield. If the rate has not been set, each maturity is assigned a coupon. A normal scale has higher yields for long-term bonds. Table 3.1 shows an example of a GO bond scale.

Once the underwriters have written a scale that allows them to resell the bonds, they prepare the final bid. Before they submit the bid, the underwriters ensure that they have met any unique specifications the issuer has set.

Firm Commitment. Competitive bids are submitted as firm commitments: the underwriters buy the bonds from the issuer and assume all financial responsibility for unsold bonds. The underwriters have no profit guarantee.

Disclosure of Fees. Fees to be paid to a clearing agency and the syndicate manager must be disclosed to syndicate members in advance. Normally, this disclosure is part of the syndicate letter or the agreement among underwriters. Management fees include any amount in the gross spread that is paid to the manager alone and not shared with syndicate members.

TABLE 3.1   General Obligation Bond Scale

Amount	Matures	Coupon	Yield
$550,000	2004	7%	5.00%
$650,000	2005	7%	5.05%
$750,000	2006	7%	5.10%
$750,000	2007	7%	5.15%
$800,000	2008	7%	5.20%

Awarding the Issue

After the issuer meets with its attorneys and accountants to analyze each bid, it awards the municipal bond issue to the syndicate that offers to underwrite the bonds at the lowest **net interest cost (NIC)** or **true interest cost (TIC)** to the issuer. The second best bid is known as the **cover bid**. If the winning bid is disallowed for any reason, the award goes to the syndicate with the cover bid.

Net interest cost is the most common calculation used for comparing bids and awarding the bond issue. It combines the amount of proceeds the issuer receives with the total coupon interest it pays. True interest cost provides the same type of cost comparison adjusted for the time value of money. If the bond is sold at a premium, the premium is added to the NIC. If the bond is sold at a discount, the discount is subtracted from the NIC.

In split-rate bids (with more than one interest rate), the interest is determined by the lowest average interest cost to the issuer. If each bid calls for one rate for the whole issue, the award goes to the syndicate with the lowest rate.

When the issuer makes its choice, it announces the successful bidder and returns the good faith deposits to the remaining syndicates. The unsuccessful syndicate managers must return good faith deposits to syndicate members within two business days. The successful syndicate has a firm commitment to purchase the bonds from the issuer and reoffer them to the public at the offering price the members agreed on. The issuer keeps the successful bidder's good faith deposit to ensure that the syndicate carries out its commitment.

Syndicate Account

The syndicate account is created when the issue is awarded. The syndicate manager is responsible for keeping the books and managing the account. All sale proceeds are deposited to the syndicate account, and all expenses are paid out of the account.

Breakdown of the Spread

The price at which the bonds are sold to the public is known as the **reoffering price** (or **reoffering yield**). The syndicate's compensation for underwriting the new issue is the **spread**, the difference between the price the syndicate pays the issuer and the reoffering price. Each participant in the syndicate is entitled to a portion of the spread, depending on the role each member plays in the underwriting. Figure 3.2 illustrates how the portions of a spread might be allocated.

Syndicate Manager's Fee. The syndicate manager receives a per-bond fee for its work in bringing the new issue to market. As an example, the manager might receive $3 as a management fee from a total spread of $20.

Underwriting Fee. Each syndicate member contributes a share of the spread to cover underwriting fees. Any money not spent is distributed to the members in proportion to their participation in the underwriting.

✓ *For Example:* A syndicate member that committed to 10 percent participation would receive 10 percent of the total underwriting fee after expenses are paid. The managing underwriter would be entitled to its percentage of the underwriting fee *in addition to* the management fee it receives.

Takedown. The portion of the spread that remains after subtracting the manager's and syndicate fees (which represent $7 of the $20 in Figure 3.2) is called the *takedown*. The takedown ($13 of the $20 in Figure 3.2) is the discount at which a syndicate member buys bonds from the syndicate. Members buy the bonds from the syndicate *at the takedown*.

A member that has purchased bonds at the takedown can either sell its bonds to customers at the offering price or sell them to a dealer in the selling group below the offering price.

Selling Concession and Reallowance. Using Figure 3.2, a syndicate member can buy bonds from the syndicate for $987, sell them to the public for $1,000 and earn the $13 takedown. If the firm chooses instead to sell bonds to another dealer, it does so at a price less than $1,000, in this case $992.50. The discount the dealer receives from the syndicate member is called the **concession**—$7.50 in Figure 3.2. Dealers buy bonds from syndicate members *at the concession*.

The concession can be considered a part of the total takedown. When the member does not sell the bonds directly to the public, it *concedes* a portion of

FIGURE 3.2 How a Spread Is Allocated

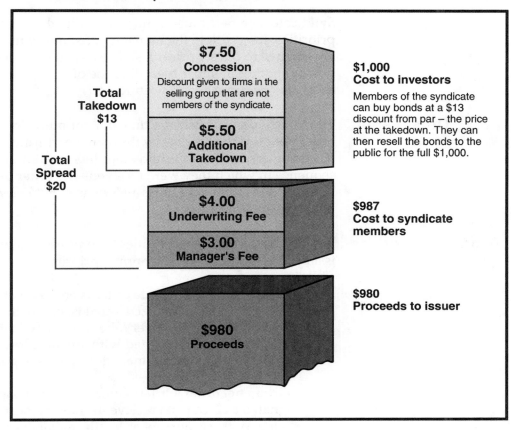

the takedown to the seller. The member keeps the remainder, called the **additional takedown**.

Order Allocation

Municipal bond orders are allocated according to priorities the syndicate sets in advance. The Municipal Securities Rulemaking Board (MSRB) requires syndicates to establish priority allocation provisions for orders. The managing underwriter must submit these provisions to all syndicate members in writing. Normally, the manager includes allocation priorities and confirmation procedures in the syndicate agreement.

The syndicate must establish a definite sequence in which orders will be accepted and may not simply state that the order priority will be left to the manager's discretion. The syndicate may include a provision in its agreement that allows the syndicate manager to deviate from the established priority on a case-by-case basis, but this exception is made *only* if such action is in the syndicate's best interest. The burden of proof for these exceptions to the stated order priority lies with the syndicate manager.

Syndicate members must signify in writing their acceptance of the allocation priorities. In addition, the manager must notify the members in writing of any change to the set priorities. If any syndicate member requests information of another member regarding the offering, the requested information must also be furnished in writing.

Order Period   The MSRB has established a time line for municipal underwritings. The order period is the time set by the manager during which the syndicate solicits customers for the issue and all orders are allocated without regard to the sequence in which they were received. The order period usually runs a few hours or days following the issue's award, but before the issuer delivers the bonds to the syndicate.

Allocation Priorities   A syndicate's allocation priorities become especially important when a bond issue is oversubscribed. The normal priority follows:

1. **Presale order**. A presale order is entered before the bond's pricing terms have been finalized—that is, before the order period. A presale order takes priority over other types of orders. Individual syndicate members are not credited with any takedown on presale orders. The entire spread, less the manager's fee, is deposited in the syndicate account.
2. **Group net order**. Orders entered during the order period that are designated as group net receive the next highest priority in allocating the issue. With a group net order, the member credits the sale to the entire syndicate (rather than to itself) to help ensure that the order will be filled. A syndicate member that wants a customer's order to receive priority enters the order as a group net order. The takedown on a group net order is deposited in the syndicate account, and upon completion of the underwriting, it is split among all syndicate members according to participation.
3. **Designated order**. The next highest priority for orders received during the order period is assigned to designated orders. One syndicate member submits a designated order for a customer, but the customer specifies that more than one member receive credit (and a percentage of the takedown) for the order.
4. **Member order**. The next priority for orders received during the order period goes to member orders. A member firm enters such an order for its own customer and receives the entire takedown.
5. **Member-related order**. The lowest priority orders are those for dealer-related accounts, such as for a dealer-sponsored unit investment trust (UIT).

The easiest way to remember the priority of the various types of orders is that the highest priority is given to those orders that benefit the most members. The lowest priority is given to orders that benefit a single member.

Within two business days after the sale date, the syndicate manager must send a written summary of how orders were allocated to the other syndicate members.

Disclosure of Orders

Certain disclosures may be required of a municipal securities dealer regarding the buyer of a new issue.

Disclosure of Capacity. Every municipal securities dealer that submits an order to a syndicate or syndicate member must make a disclosure of capacity. The disclosure identifies whether securities are being purchased for an account the dealer controls or has a financial interest in, including:

- its dealer account
- a related portfolio account
- a municipal securities investment trust it sponsors
- an accumulation account

Disclosure of Group Net Orders. When a muni dealer submits a group order, it must disclose the identity of the person for whom it submits the order. The dealer must also disclose the:

- aggregate face amount of each maturity for which it places the order; and
- maturity date of any municipal security that is the subject of such an order.

Broker's Broker

Some municipal brokers specialize in trading only with institutional customers such as banks and other municipal brokers, not with the retail public. These firms are called *brokers' brokers* because their business focuses on helping other muni dealers place unsold portions of new bond issues. A broker's broker must comply with the best execution requirement and occasionally acts as a principal in a transaction to protect the customer's or the other broker's identity. The broker's broker may hold securities in its own investment account, but does not keep an inventory of securities to sell at a later date.

Sale Date

After the issuer awards the offering, the managing underwriter notifies the syndicate members. The **underwriting period**, or **order period**, begins when the syndicate purchases the bonds from the issuer—the **date of sale**—or when the syndicate receives the first purchase order, whichever comes first. During the order period, the syndicate manager fills orders received according to the priority established in the syndicate letter. Each buyer of the issue then receives an initial, or **when issued (WI)**, confirmation of the purchase from the syndicate manager if the order was for a syndicate member's account or from a syndicate member if it was not.

Payment and Delivery

New municipal bond issues are usually sold on a when issued basis, meaning the securities are authorized, but not yet issued. After awarding an issue to a syndicate, the issuer has the bond certificates printed and finalizes any other legal matters. If the bonds are to be eligible for automated comparison and clearing, the managing underwriter must register the securities with a registered clearing agency, providing the agency with notice of the securities' coupon rate and settlement date as soon as they are known.

When the bonds are ready, the syndicate manager gives the syndicate members three business days' notice of the settlement date. The syndicate members, in turn, give notice of the settlement date to the purchasers. On the settlement date, the newly issued bonds are delivered to the underwriters with a final legal opinion, and the underwriters pay for the bonds on delivery.

The manager must return members' good faith deposits within two business days after settlement with the issuer.

Confirmations of Sales to Customers. On or before the completion of the transaction (settlement date), final (second) confirmations are mailed to investors who purchased bonds from the underwriters. The investors' confirmations disclose the purchase price and settlement date for the transaction. The underwriters then deliver the bonds, accompanied by the legal opinion, to the investors.

The settlement date should not be confused with the dated date the issuer assigns to the bond issue. The dated date is the date on which interest begins to accrue. An investor must pay any interest that has accrued from the dated date up to, but not including, the settlement date The buyer starts receiving interest on the settlement date.

Transmission and Maintenance of Payments. A municipal securities dealer may accept payment from public customers for securities when the firm participates in the distribution *only* if:

- it is a firm commitment underwriting;
- the money is promptly transmitted to the persons entitled to it; or
- the distribution is being done all or none and the money is promptly deposited in a separate bank (or escrow) account and held pending the appropriate event or contingency.

MSRB rules prohibit any other receipt of payment for participation in a distribution.

Representations A muni dealer is prohibited from making misleading representations in order to encourage an investor to purchase a municipal security.

All or None. When a muni dealer solicits indications of interest for a municipal securities offering, it may not claim that the underwriting is being done on an all or none basis unless the securities actually are part of such an offering. An all or none underwriting states that the entire issue must be sold; otherwise, the offering is canceled. This does not apply when an underwriter has made a firm commitment to purchase all the securities being offered.

At-the-Market Offers. A muni dealer participating in a syndicate distribution of municipal bonds may not claim that the securities are being sold or offered "at-the-market" unless the dealer knows or believes that a market for the securities exists other than that the syndicate makes, creates or controls.

Final Syndicate Settlement

Books and Records The managing underwriter must maintain a complete record of syndicate transactions showing:

- the securities' description and aggregate par value;
- each member's name and percentage participation;
- the terms and conditions governing the syndicate's formation and operation;
- all orders received;
- all allotments of securities and their prices;
- the date and amount of any good faith deposit;
- the date of settlement with the issuer; and
- the date of closing the account.

Reconciliation of Profits and Expenses

Within 60 days after delivery of the securities, the syndicate manager must distribute profits and make final settlement of the syndicate account. At this time, the syndicate manager must also supply a detailed record of the account to all syndicate members.

The syndicate account records must summarize how and to whom orders were allocated. They must also contain an itemized statement of all expenses incurred on behalf of the syndicate. If the underwriter includes a "miscellaneous expenses" category, the amount that appears there must not be disproportionately large compared to the other expenses.

Official Statement

Any municipal securities dealer involved in the sale of a new issue must furnish a final official statement to every customer who has purchased part of that new issue, including other muni dealers. If the final official statement is not ready when the bonds are delivered, the dealer may send the preliminary official statement or may prepare and send a summary or an abstract of the official statement. When the final official statement is ready, the dealer must send it to customers and any industry member that requests it. If the issuer does not prepare an official statement, customers must be informed of that fact.

A typical official statement includes all of the following information:

- offering terms;
- summary statement;
- purpose of issue;
- authorization of bonds;
- security of bonds;
- description of bonds;
- description of issuer, including organization and management, area economy and a financial summary;
- construction program;
- project feasibility statement;
- regulatory matters;
- specific provisions of the indenture or resolution, including funds and accounts, investment of funds, additional bonds, insurance and events of default;
- legal proceedings;
- tax status; and
- appropriate appendixes, including consultant reports, the legal opinion and financial statements.

Negotiated Underwriting.   In a negotiated underwriting, the dealer must provide the official statement and identify the amount of the underwriting spread, the amount of any fee the municipal securities dealer receives as agent for the issuer, and the initial offering price of each maturity. On or before the transaction's completion, the dealer must disclose to all customers in writing:

- the dealer's participation as an underwriter of the new issue;
- any financial advisory relationship existing between the broker-dealer and the issuer, including arrangements in which advice is given for a fee, for other compensation or for expectation of compensation; and
- any control relationship between the broker-dealer and the issuer (for instance, if the president of the broker-dealer is an official of the issuing authority).

The Municipal Bond Counsel

A law firm is employed during the underwriting process to serve as the issuer's bond counsel and to give written legal opinions as to the issue's legality. The bond counsel, or bond attorney, is a disinterested party offering certain legal assurances to the issuer and investors, including assurances that the issuer is authorized to issue the bonds, that the bonds have been properly announced and that the bond certificates are properly printed.

The Legal Opinion. One reason the issuer retains independent bond counsel is to provide an opinion on the offering's validity. The bond counsel states that the bonds are a binding debt of the issuer and can be legally issued by the municipal authority. The legal opinion also describes the bonds, any tax limitation of the issuer and any call provision of the issue.

An **unqualified legal opinion** is the most desirable because it states that the opinion is given without question or restriction—that is, without qualification. A **qualified legal opinion** expresses reservations about the issue. For instance, a qualified opinion might state that the issuer has acquired property, but may not have clear title to it.

The legal opinion also provides the bond attorney's written opinion that the interest on the bond issue is exempt from federal or state and local taxes. To meet the MSRB's requirements for good delivery, the legal opinion must be attached to or printed on the back of each bond certificate.

Some issuers, normally smaller municipalities, choose not to obtain a legal opinion. In such a case, the bond certificate must clearly state that the bonds are "ex-legal." The ex-legal designation allows a bond to meet good delivery requirements without an attached legal opinion.

The Underwriter's Counsel. The managing underwriter may choose to employ another law firm as underwriter's counsel. This firm is not responsible for the legal opinion and is employed to represent the underwriter's interests.

Advertising

Any material designed for use in the public media is considered advertising. This includes abstracts and summaries of the official statement, offering circulars, reports, market letters, form letters, professional advertisements, product advertisements and new issue advertisements. A municipal securities principal or general securities principal of the dealer must approve all advertising before use, and a copy of each advertisement must be kept on file for three years.

Preliminary and final official statements are not considered advertising because they are prepared by or on behalf of an issuer.

The Broker-Dealer as Financial Adviser

Financial Advisers The MSRB has established ethical standards and disclosure requirements for municipal securities dealers that act as financial advisers to municipal securities' issuers. A financial advisory relationship exists when a muni dealer provides financial advisory or consulting services to an issuer with respect to a new issue for a fee or other compensation. This includes advice regarding the structure, timing and terms of, as well as other matters concerning, the issue or issuer. Any customer that purchases a new municipal security from a dealer with a financial advisory relationship with the issuer must be informed of the relationship before the purchase and in writing before the transaction's completion.

A financial advisory relationship does not exist when the dealer, acting as an underwriter, advises an issuer about structure, timing, terms and similar matters concerning the new issue.

Basis of Compensation. Each financial advisory relationship must be documented in writing before, upon or promptly after its inception. This document establishes the basis of compensation for the advisory services to be rendered and includes:

- an explanation of how fees will be paid;
- provisions relating to the deposit of funds;
- use of fiduciary or agency services the broker-dealer offers; and
- use of services offered by a person controlling, controlled by or under common control with the broker-dealer.

Use of Ownership Information. In a financial advisory, fiduciary or agency capacity for an issuer, a municipal securities dealer often obtains confidential information about its bondholders. The dealer cannot use this information to solicit purchases or sales of municipal securities or to pursue other financial gain without the issuer's consent.

Examples of fiduciary and agency capacities include, but are not limited to, acting as paying agent, transfer agent, registrar or indenture trustee for an issuer or acting as clearing agent, safekeeping agent or correspondent for another dealer.

Conflicts of Interest Potential conflicts of interest arise if a firm acts as both underwriter and financial adviser for the same issue. Consequently, the MSRB requires the following:

- A firm consulting with a municipal issuer for a fee must describe the advisory relationship in writing and disclose the amount of compensation.
- Before submitting a competitive bid, a firm acting as financial adviser to an issuer must have the issuer's consent.

- Before submitting a negotiated bid, the adviser must receive the issuer's consent and terminate the advisory relationship in writing. The broker-dealer must also inform the issuer of the possible conflict and disclose the source and amount of money it anticipates receiving for participating in the issue.
- Purchasers of the securities must be informed if an advisory relationship exists or once existed.

Prohibited Transactions. In general, a dealer that has a financial advisory relationship with a municipal securities issuer cannot underwrite a new issue for that issuer. Whether the dealer acts alone or as part of a syndicate, or whether it acts directly or indirectly, it cannot acquire the securities. The dealer also cannot arrange for purchases by a control person. This applies to any municipal securities dealer controlling, controlled by or under common control with the dealer that has a financial advisory relationship.

Allowable Transactions. In the case of a competitive bid, a dealer that has a financial advisory relationship with the issuer can purchase all or part of the new issue if the issuer has consented in writing before the bid to such acquisition or participation.

In a negotiated sale, a muni dealer that has a financial advisory relationship can purchase all or part of a new issue if it meets the following conditions:

- it expressly discloses in writing to the issuer at or before the termination of the relationship that a conflict of interest may exist; and the issuer expressly acknowledges in writing to the broker-dealer receiving such disclosure; or
- the broker-dealer discloses in writing at or before termination the source of the anticipated amount of all remuneration to the broker-dealer with respect to the issue, in addition to compensation received for financial advisory services, and the issuer acknowledges in writing receiving such disclosure.

Control Relationships. The limitations and requirements of the above rules apply to any broker-dealer controlling, controlled by or under common control with the broker-dealer having a financial advisory relationship.

Assistance with Official Statement. As part of its financial advisory services to an issuer, a municipal securities dealer may help prepare the final official statement for a new issue. If it prepares the official statement, the financial adviser must make a copy of that statement available to the managing underwriter promptly after the award is made and at least two days before the syndicate manager delivers the securities to the syndicate members.

Municipal Trading and Taxation

Quotations

Municipal bonds are bought and sold in the over-the-counter (OTC) market. Most large brokerages maintain trading departments that deal exclusively in municipal bonds. Many of the rules governing the trading of other OTC securities also apply to municipal bond transactions.

Muni dealers are called upon regularly to provide current quotations for municipal securities. The term "quotation" means any bid for or offer of municipal securities. Any indication of interest or solicitation by a muni dealer (such as "bid wanted" or "offer wanted") would be considered a quotation request.

Municipal bonds are usually priced and offered for sale on a **yield to maturity (YTM)** basis rather than a dollar price. This is called a **basis quote**.

✔ *For Example:* A dealer might publish a bid for a 6 percent coupon bond at 6.10 basis, indicating that the bond is selling at a discount.

Dollar Bonds. Some municipal revenue bonds are quoted on a percentage of par dollar basis rather than YTM. Such bonds are commonly called *dollar bonds*. Dollar bonds are usually term bonds callable before maturity. A dollar bond may be offered by a muni dealer for 104.

Bona Fide. If a muni dealer gives, distributes or publishes a quotation for a security, that quote must be bona fide. For a quote to be considered bona fide, or firm, the dealer must be prepared to trade the security at the price specified in the quote and under the conditions and restrictions (if any) accompanying the quote. A bona fide quote:

- *must* reflect the dealer's best judgment and have a reasonable relationship to the fair market value for that security; and
- *may* reflect the firm's inventory and expectations of market direction.

In other words, a quotation need not represent *only* the security's fair market value but it must have at least a *reasonable* relationship to fair market value. A quotation may take into consideration such other factors as the dealer's inventory position and any anticipated market movement.

If the dealer distributes or publishes the quotation on behalf of another dealer, it must have reason to believe that the quote is bona fide and based on the other dealer's best judgment of fair market value. Dealers cannot knowingly misrepresent a quote another municipal securities dealer makes.

Quotations are always subject to prior sale or change in price. Any means of communication, including print, voice and electronic media, can be used to disseminate, distribute or publish quotations.

Types of Quotations.　A municipal securities dealer can give several types of quotations in addition to firm quotes. The most common follow:

- A **workable indication** reflects a bid price at which a dealer will purchase securities from another dealer. A dealer giving a workable indication is always free to revise its bid for the securities as market conditions change.
- A **nominal** (or **subject**) **quotation** indicates a dealer's *estimate* of a security's market value. Nominal quotations are provided for informational purposes only and are permitted if the quotes are clearly labeled as such. The rules on nominal quotes apply to all municipal bond quotes distributed or published by any dealer.

Holding a Quote.　A municipal securities dealer may quote a bond price that is firm for a certain period of time.

✔ **For Example:**　A dealer may give an **out-firm quote** that is firm for one hour with five-minute recall. Within that hour, if another interested buyer seeks a quote for the same bond, he is given a **subject quote**, signifying that the dealer has given out a firm quote to another buyer. The dealer may then call the first buyer back and give him five minutes to confirm his order or lose his right to buy the bond at the price quoted.

Reports of Sales　MSRB rules prohibit dealers from distributing or publishing any report of a municipal security's purchase or sale unless they know or have reason to believe that the transaction actually took place. Broker-dealers reporting the sale must believe that the reported trade was real and not fictitious, fraudulent or deceitful.

Municipal securities dealers must report trades with other dealers to the National Securities Clearing Corporation (NSCC). The report must include the two executing firms' names and the amount of accrued interest, if known.

Broker-Dealer Regulation

Reciprocal Dealings (Antireciprocal Rule)　A dealer cannot solicit trades in municipal securities for an investment company in return for sales by the dealer of shares or units in the investment company.

For instance, if NavCo Municipal Bond Fund makes a large number of trades every month in its portfolio, a muni dealer *cannot* be selected to execute the fund's portfolio trades based only on the firm's promise that its account executives will increase sales of NavCo shares. The firm *can* be selected to execute those trades based on the services the dealer offers to the fund, such as prompt execution and research.

Customer Recommendations   MSRB rules require municipal securities brokers and dealers to make suitable recommendations to customers. Before making a recommendation, a municipal securities firm must make a reasonable effort to learn the customer's financial status, tax status and investment objectives. The suitability test applies to discretionary accounts as well as to other accounts. The practice of increasing commissions through excessive trading, or **churning**, is specifically prohibited.

Protecting Customer Accounts. Municipal securities dealers cannot misuse securities or funds held for another person. Dealers also may not guarantee customers against loss (put options and repurchase agreements are *not* considered guarantees against loss) or share in the profits or losses of a customer's account. An exception to this rule applies in the case of an associated person who establishes a personal joint account with a customer and obtains written permission from the firm. In this situation, the associated person may share in the account's profits and losses *only in proportion to* the amount of capital contributed to the account.

In general, a muni dealer that receives a fee from a customer for securities advice cannot enter a transaction for that customer in any security that the dealer helps underwrite or in which it has a financial interest. However, a transaction is allowed if the firm discloses the potential conflict of interest to the customer in writing. The disclosure must be made at or before the transaction settlement date.

Disclosure of Control. A municipal securities firm that has a control relationship with respect to a municipal security is subject to additional disclosure requirements. A control relationship exists if the dealer controls, is controlled by or is under common control with that security's issuer. This includes a dealer that underwrites a new issue of securities or has some other financial interest in a new issue. The dealer must disclose the control relationship to the customer before it can effect any transaction in that security for that customer. While initially this disclosure can be verbal, the dealer must make a written disclosure must be made at or before the transaction's completion. If the transaction is for a discretionary account, the customer must give express permission before the transaction can be executed.

Markups and Commissions

A dealer acts as an **agent** when it arranges trades for customers and charges commissions. A dealer acts as a **principal** when it buys and sells securities for its own inventory. The dealer charges a **markup** for principal transactions when it sells securities and a **markdown** when it buys securities.

Principal Transactions

Each principal transaction is executed at an **aggregate price**, which includes the markup or markdown. Some of the factors taken into consideration include the:

- dealer's best judgment of fair market value;
- expense of effecting the transaction;
- fact that the dealer is entitled to a markup or markdown, or "profit";
- total dollar amount of the transaction; and
- value of any security exchanged or traded.

Agency Transactions

Each agency transaction is executed for a commission that is not in excess of a fair and reasonable amount, considering all relevant factors. For an agency commission calculation, a dealer takes into consideration the:

- security's availability;
- expense of executing the order;
- value of services the dealer renders; and
- amount of any other compensation received or to be received in connection with the transaction.

Best Execution. When executing an order as an agent, a dealer must make a reasonable effort to obtain a fair and reasonable price.

Confirmations

A customer must receive a written confirmation of each municipal securities transaction she has entered. The confirmation must describe the security; list the trade date, settlement date and amount of accrued interest; state the firm's name, address and phone number; and indicate whether the firm acted as agent or principal in the trade. A confirmation that does not include the time of execution must indicate that this information will be provided if the customer requests it.

Disclosing Yield

The MSRB requires that a confirmation for a dollar bond trade include the price and indicate the lowest potential yield the customer might receive. The lowest yield could be yield to call or yield to maturity. A confirmation for a trade involving callable securities must include a statement indicating that the yield shown may be affected by the exercise of a call provision and that the dealer will provide information concerning the call provision upon request. This does not apply to bonds that have a catastrophic call provision only.

A bond quoted or sold on a yield basis must also disclose the lowest potential yield. If the bond is sold at a premium, the dealer must show the bond's yield to the first call date. If the bond is sold at a discount, the dealer must show the yield to maturity. In short, the customer must always be informed of the lowest potential yield on a bond.

Variable-Rate Municipal Securities. Some municipal bonds and notes are issued with variable, or "floating," rates of interest. A variable-rate municipal bond offers interest payments that are tied to the movements of another specified interest rate. Confirmations for variable-rate bonds and notes must disclose that both the rates of interest and the yields to maturity are variable.

Zero-Coupon Municipal Securities. A zero-coupon bond is issued at a deep discount from par and pays no current interest. The confirmation must indicate an interest rate of 0 percent and state that accrued interest is not calculated.

Municipal Collateralized Mortgage Obligations (CMOs). A municipal CMO receives a share of interest and principal payments made on a pool of mortgages. Because interest rate trends affect the amount of interest and principal the mortgage pool receives, the rate of return to the CMO holder is not guaranteed. The confirmation for a CMO purchase must state that yield varies according to the payments received on the underlying mortgages. The confirmation must also indicate that information about the factors that affect yield will be provided to the investor upon written request.

Required Information on Confirmations

Each confirmation must also include the following information:

- in an agency transaction, the name of the party on the other side of the transaction and the source and amount of any commission (the name of the other party must be disclosed on request if it is not listed on the confirmation);
- the dated date if it affects the interest calculation;
- whether the securities are fully registered, registered as to principal only or available in book-entry form;
- whether the securities are called or prerefunded, as well as the date of maturity fixed by the call notice and the amount of the call price;
- the certificate denomination of any municipal note and, for municipal bonds, any denomination other than standard units ($1,000 or $5,000 par value);
- any special qualification or factor that might affect payment of principal or interest; and
- whether the bond interest is taxable or subject to the alternative minimum tax (AMT).

Since 1983, any confirmation sent to a customer must include the security's Committee on Uniform Securities Identification Procedures (CUSIP) number, a unique identification assigned to every security.

If the trade is done on a principal basis, the muni dealer need not disclose the source or amount of any markup or markdown.

Taxation of Municipal Issues

Tax-exempt Interest Payments

The Tax Reform Act of 1986 restricted the federal income tax exemption of interest for municipal bonds to **public purpose bonds,** bonds issued to finance projects that benefit citizens in general rather than particular private interests. If a bond channels more than 10 percent of its proceeds to private parties, it is considered a private activity bond and is not automatically granted tax exemption.

Calculating Tax Benefits

An investor considering the purchase of a tax-exempt bond should compare its yield carefully with that of taxable securities. Because of the tax savings, the tax-free bond may be more attractive than a taxable bond with a higher interest rate. This depends, in part, on the investor's tax bracket: the higher the tax bracket, the greater the tax exemption's value.

To determine a municipal bond investment's tax benefit, an investor must calculate the **tax-equivalent yield**. To do so, divide the tax-free yield by 100 percent *less* the investor's tax rate.

$$\frac{\text{Tax-free yield}}{100\% - \text{Tax rate}} = \text{Tax-equivalent yield}$$

✓ *For Example:* Assume that two investors, one in a 15 percent tax bracket and one in a 30 percent tax bracket, consider purchasing $10,000 worth of a new municipal bond with a 7 percent coupon. Comparable corporate bonds are currently being issued at 8.5 percent.

The investor in the 15 percent tax bracket would receive a tax-equivalent yield of 8.2 percent. To calculate this, divide 7 percent by 100 percent minus his tax rate of 15 percent, or 7 percent divided by 85 percent (.85), which equals 8.2 percent. The municipal bond would not be a good choice for this investor because he could get a higher rate of return by investing in corporates.

The investor in the 30 percent tax bracket would receive a tax-equivalent yield of 10 percent (7 percent divided by 100 percent minus his 30 percent tax rate, or 7 percent divided by 70 percent) and, therefore, would receive a higher after-tax yield from the municipal.

✎ *Take Note:* To determine the after-tax yield for a corporate bond, simply reduce the taxable yield by the appropriate tax bracket. A 10 percent taxable bond would provide a 7 percent after-tax return to someone in the 30 percent tax bracket.

Bond Swaps   Swapping bonds is a technique investors use to generate current tax losses, improve yields or quality, or change the maturity of their portfolios. An investor swaps by selling bonds he owns and buying other bonds that better meet his investment objectives.

To create a tax loss with a bond swap, an investor sells bonds he holds at a loss and buys similar bonds.

> ✓ **For Example:** An investor holding 20 AA Kenosha, WI GO 10s of 2008 that he bought at par and that are now selling for 92 could do a bond swap and lock in a capital loss by selling these and buying 20 AA Racine, WI GO 10s of 2011 at 91 as a replacement. The result of the swap would be a tax loss of $80 per bond in exchange for bonds with the same coupon and a slightly longer maturity.

To avoid having the IRS classify a legitimate bond swap as a **wash sale**, in which case the loss would be disallowed for tax purposes, the replacement bonds purchased must differ in some significant respect from those sold. A tax loss is disallowed if the investor sells a bond at a loss and purchases the same or a substantially identical bond within 30 days before or after the trade date establishing the loss. The sale at a loss and the repurchase within this period is a wash sale. The IRS will not consider a bond swap a wash sale if the new bonds represent a change in issuer, maturity date or coupon.

Bond swaps take a considerable amount of research and attention to the market if they are to be accomplished successfully. Because there will probably be a difference between the yields or prices of the bonds sold and the bonds bought, the investor must be willing to accept bonds with a later maturity, lower coupon rate or lower rating than that of the bonds sold. An investor unwilling to accept some such change in his investment must be prepared to invest additional funds.

Analysis of Municipal Securities

Different criteria are used to evaluate the merits of general obligation and revenue municipal bonds. When analyzing GOs, investors assess the municipality's ability to raise enough tax revenue to pay its debt. Revenue bond debt service depends on the income generated from a specific facility to cover its operating costs and pay its debt.

Analyzing the Official Statement

Analysts study the documents included in the official statement to determine the issuer's financial condition at the present and in the foreseeable future.

Future Financial Needs. The municipality's financial statements should be scrutinized for signs of future debt requirements. The municipality might need to issue more debt if:

- its annual income is not sufficient to make the payments on its short-term (or floating) debt;
- principal repayments are scheduled too close together;
- sinking funds for outstanding term bonds are inadequate;
- pension liabilities are unfunded; or
- it plans to make more capital improvements soon.

Issuing more debt in the near future could damage an issuer's credit rating, which would cause the current issue to trade at a lower price.

The Debt Statement. The debt statement includes the estimated full valuation of taxable property, the estimated assessed value of property and the assessment percentage, and the estimated population.

To evaluate the municipality's debt structure, an analyst calculates **total debt**, the sum of all bonds issued by the municipality, and subtracts **self-supporting debt** from this figure. Although revenue bond debt is included in total debt, it is backed by revenues from the facility it financed and is not a burden on the municipality's taxpayers.

The result is the municipality's **net direct debt**, which includes GOs and short-term notes issued in anticipation of taxes or for interim financing. To net direct debt the analyst adds **overlapping debt**.

Overlapping debt disclosed on the debt statement is the city's proportionate share of the county's, school district's, park district's and sanitary district's debts. The city's **net total debt**, also called **net overall debt**, is the sum of the overlapping debt and the net direct debt.

Calculating a Municipality's Net Total Debt. A municipality's net total debt can be calculated as follows:

	Total debt
minus	Self-supporting debt
minus	Sinking fund debt
equals	Net direct debt
plus	Overlapping debt
equals	Net total debt

General Obligation Bonds

General Wealth of the Community. Because GOs are backed primarily by tax revenues, their safety is determined by the community's general wealth, which includes its:

- property values
- retail sales per capita
- local bank deposits and bank clearings
- diversity of industry in its tax base
- population growth or decline

A GO issuer's taxing power enables it to make principal and interest payments through all but the most unusual economic circumstances.

Characteristics of the Issuer. A **quantitative analysis** focuses on objective information regarding a municipality's population, property values and per capita income.

✓ *For Example:* The city of Mineral Point announces it will sell a GO issue. The issue's official statement will note that Mineral Point is incorporated and has a year-round population of 50,000. Within the city limits are 10,000 single-family homes and apartments. The county assessor estimates that the market value of all nongovernmental property in the city is $1 billion. The average value of each parcel of real property is $140,000. All of this quantitative information would be considered in an analysis of the issuer.

A **qualitative analysis** focuses on subjective factors that affect a municipality's securities. The community's attitude toward debt and taxation, population trends, property value trends, and plans and projects being undertaken in the area are all relevant considerations.

Debt Limits. To protect taxpayers from excessive taxes, statutory limits may be placed on the overall amount of debt a municipality can have. If a city's total debt is limited to 5 percent of the estimated market value of all taxable property within the city limits, this is the city's **constitutional debt limit**. A bond's official statement discloses how close total outstanding debt, including newly issued debt, comes to its constitutional debt limit.

A state constitution or city charter can also limit the purposes for which a city may issue bonds. Often, a city may issue bonds to finance capital improvements only if those bonds mature within the expected lifetimes of the improvements. This provision ensures that the city will not owe money on a facility when it becomes obsolete.

A municipality's citizens control the city's GO debt. Because their taxes service such debt, voters must approve each issue through referendum.

Overlapping Debt. Overlapping debt occurs when more than one issuer can draw tax revenues from the same source. If property taxes finance a bond issue, for instance, the investor needs to know how many other issuers have a claim on those taxes.

Income of the Municipality. The primary sources of municipal income follow:

- Income and sales taxes are major sources of state income.
- Real property taxes are the *principal* income source of counties, school districts and cities.
- Real property taxes are the *largest* source of city income.
- City income can include fines, license fees, assessments, sales taxes, hotel taxes, city income taxes, utility taxes and any city personal property tax.

Ad Valorem Taxes. Property taxes are based on a property's assessed valuation, which is a percentage of the estimated market value. That percentage is established by each state or county and varies substantially. The market value of each piece of property in a county is determined by the county assessor, who relies on recent sale prices of similar properties, income streams, replacement costs and other information.

Because the real property tax is based on the property's value, it is said to be an ad valorem, or **per value**, tax. The tax is a lien on the property, which means the property can be seized if the tax is not paid. GOs, backed by the power to tax and seize property, are considered safer than revenue bonds of the same issuer and, therefore, can be issued with a lower interest rate.

Revenue Bonds

Revenue bonds are rated according to a facility's potential to generate sufficient money to cover operating expenses and principal and interest payments. Because revenue bonds are not repaid from taxes, they are not subject to statutory debt limits. Revenue bonds are meant to be self-supporting, and if the facility they finance does not make enough money to repay the debts, the bondholders, not the taxpayers, bear the risk. When assessing the quality of revenue bonds, an investor should consider the following factors:

- **Economic justification.** The facility being built should be able to generate revenues.
- **Competing facilities.** A facility should not be placed where better alternatives are easily available.
- **Sources of revenue.** Sources of revenue should be dependable.
- **Call provisions.** With callable bonds, the higher the call price, the more attractive a bond is to an investor.

- **Flow of funds**. The revenues generated must be sufficient to pay all of the facility's operating expenses and to meet debt service obligations.

As part of its due diligence research, a revenue bond underwriter performs a feasibility study to determine whether the project makes economic sense and whether it is sufficiently funded. This study is included in the official statement.

Applications of Revenues

Principal and interest on revenue bonds are paid almost exclusively from money generated by the facility the issue finances. The issuer pledges to pay expenses in a specific order, called the *flow of funds*. The flow of funds is detailed in the feasibility study.

In most cases, a **net revenue pledge** is used, meaning operating and maintenance expenses are paid first. The remaining funds, or net revenues, are used to pay debt service and meet other obligations.

Flow of Funds in a Net Revenue Pledge

In a net revenue pledge, total receipts from operating the facility are usually deposited in the **revenue fund**, and the funds are disbursed in the following order:

1. **operations and maintenance**—used to pay current operating and maintenance expenses; remaining funds are called *net revenues;*
2. **debt service account**—used to pay the interest and principal maturing in the current year and serving as a sinking fund for term issues;
3. **debt service reserve fund**—used to hold enough money to pay one year's debt service;
4. **reserve maintenance fund**—used to supplement the general maintenance fund;
5. **renewal and replacement fund**—used to create reserve funds for major renewal projects and equipment replacements; and
6. **surplus fund**—used for a variety of purposes, such as redeeming bonds or paying for improvements.

If the issuer has not pledged to pay operating and maintenance expenses first, debt service is the priority expense. When debt service is paid first, the flow of funds is called a **gross revenue pledge**.

The debt service includes current principal and interest due, plus any sinking fund obligations. If revenues exceed operating and other obligations, the money is usually placed in a **surplus fund**.

Gross Revenue Pledge	*Net Revenue Pledge*
Issuer pays debt service first, from gross revenues.	Issuer pays expenses first, from gross revenues.
User pays operations and maintenance.	Issuer pays debt service second, from net revenues.

Municipal Debt Ratios

A community's ability to meet its general obligation debt service is reflected in the following mathematical ratios based on information in the debt statement and other documents:

- **Net debt to assessed valuation.** A ratio of 5 percent ($5,000 of debt per $100,000 of assessed property value) is considered reasonable for a municipality.
- **Net debt to estimated valuation.** Because assessed valuation varies among municipalities, most analysts prefer to use estimated valuation of property.
- **Taxes per person or per capita.** This ratio equals the city's tax income divided by the city population; it is used to evaluate the population's tax burden.
- **Debt service to annual revenues.** This ratio indicates whether the community is overburdened with debt service expenses.
- **Debt per capita.** Larger cities can assume more debt per capita because their tax bases are more diversified.
- **Debt trend.** This number indicates whether the ratios are rising or falling. Because bonds can be long-term investments, it is important to anticipate the community's future financial position.
- **Collection ratio.** The collection ratio equals the taxes collected divided by the taxes assessed. The ratio can help detect deteriorating credit conditions.
- **Coverage ratio.** The coverage ratio, also called the *times interest earned ratio*, shows how many times annual revenues will cover debt service. A coverage of 2:1 is considered adequate for a typical municipal revenue bond. For utility revenue bonds (sewer, water and electricity), a coverage of 5:4 (125 percent) of fixed charges is considered adequate.

Other Sources of Information for Municipal Bond Analysis

Interest Rate Comparisons In addition to issuer-specific information, the value of any bond is affected by trends in the overall bond market. Municipal bond prices tend to fluctuate more than government and corporate bond prices because each issue is unique and may have few regular market makers. Because fewer market makers exist in the municipal bond market than exist in the OTC equity market, the market for any specific municipal bond is typically thinner than the market for comparable corporate or government bonds.

Municipal Bond Insurance
Municipal bond issuers can insure their securities' principal and interest payments by buying insurance from the Municipal Bond Investors Assurance Corp. (MBIA), AMBAC Indemnity Corporation (AMBAC) or Financial Guaranty Insurance Company (FGIC). Insured bonds can be issued with lower coupon rates because investors will accept lower rates of return for the added safety insurance affords. AMBAC-insured and MBIA-insured bonds are typically rated AAA.

Municipal Securities Rules and Regulations

The Securities Act of 1933 is intended to protect investors considering the purchase of new issue securities. According to this federal law, issuers must meet registration requirements, and municipal securities dealers must comply with antifraud provisions. Among the provisions of the 1933 act are:

- the requirement that all new issues to be distributed interstate be registered;
- the requirement that an issuer provide full and fair disclosure about itself and the offering;
- the requirement that an issuer make available all material information necessary for an investor to judge the issue's merit;
- regulations concerning the underwriting and distribution of primary and secondary issues; and
- provisions for criminal penalties for fraud in the issuance of new securities.

Municipal and government securities are exempt from the registration requirements of the Securities Act of 1933. Municipal issuers, underwriters, brokers and dealers are, however, always subject to the antifraud provisions of the acts of 1933 and 1934.

Municipal Securities Rulemaking Board

The Securities Acts Amendments of 1975 established the Municipal Securities Rulemaking Board as an independent self-regulatory organization (SRO). The MSRB governs the issuing and trading of municipal securities. The rules require municipal securities underwriters and dealers to protect investors' interests, to be ethical in offering advice, and to be responsive to complaints and disputes. The MSRB rules apply to all firms and individuals engaged in the conduct of municipal securities business.

The Rulemaking Process. When the MSRB revises, amends or creates a rule, it files the rule with the Securities and Exchange Commission (SEC). The SEC reviews the proposed rule and publishes it in the *Federal Register* to solicit comments from the public and the industry. The MSRB also submits the proposal to federal bank regulatory agencies for their review. The rule becomes effective after SEC clearance.

The MSRB does not have to seek comments or prior SEC approval of a rule that relates solely to its administration or the fees charged its members. Such rules becomes effective on filing with the SEC, although the SEC has 60 days to rescind them.

Rule Enforcement. The MSRB has no authority to enforce the rules it makes. The rules concerning municipal securities dealers are enforced by the National Association of Securities Dealers (NASD) and the SEC; the Office of the Comptroller of the Currency enforces those rules that apply to national banks. The Federal Reserve Board (FRB) enforces MSRB rules governing any non-national banks that are members of the Federal Reserve System. The Federal Deposit Insurance Corporation (FDIC) enforces MSRB rules for non-national banks that are not members of the Federal Reserve System. The MSRB has no authority over municipal issuers.

Finances. Like the NASD and NYSE, the MSRB is a self-supporting SRO. Annual fees of $200 charged to each municipal securities dealer, supplemented by fees paid for each municipal bond underwritten, provide the funds necessary to run the MSRB.

General Regulations

The three categories of MSRB rules include (1) rules that provide consistent legal definitions of terms used in the business of trading municipal securities, (2) administrative rules that cover the organization and functions of the MSRB itself and (3) general rules and regulations that describe MSRB policies. The following sections provide more information on MSRB rules. (Note: for exam purposes, it is not necessary to remember the rule numbers.)

Rule G-1. A bank that has a *separately identifiable* department or division engaged in any activity related to the municipal securities business is classified as a municipal securities dealer and must comply with the MSRB. A separately identifiable division is one under direct supervision of the bank officer responsible for day-to-day conduct of municipal securities business.

Municipal securities–related activity includes underwriting, trading or selling municipal securities or serving as an issuer's financial adviser. A firm that provides research or advisory services for municipal securities investors or that communicates with the public in any way about investing in municipal securities is considered a municipal securities dealer as well.

Rule G-2. People who work in the industry must meet MSRB qualification standards. No dealer may engage in any municipal securities business unless that firm and all persons associated with it are qualified in accordance with MSRB rules.

Rules G-2 and G-3. Those who must qualify by examination under MSRB rules include municipal securities principals, financial and operations principals, and municipal securities representatives. A municipal securities rep is any person who gives financial advice to municipal securities issuers or investment advice to investors. Anyone who communicates with the public about municipal securities acts as a representative.

A person must pass the Municipal Securities Representative Qualification Exam (Series 52) or the General Securities Registered Representative Exam (Series 7) to be qualified as a municipal securities representative. To qualify as a municipal securities principal, a person must pass the Municipal Securities Principal Qualification Exam (Series 53).

If a new municipal rep has not passed the appropriate exam within 180 days, he must stop performing all functions of a municipal rep.

A 90-day apprenticeship is required of people entering the industry, and during this period they may not engage in any municipal securities business with the public. An apprentice may engage in municipal business with other dealers, but may not receive commissions for such transactions, although the apprentice can receive a salary during this period. The MSRB counts time spent as a general securities representative toward the 90-day requirement.

Rule G-4. Brokers, dealers and representatives are disqualified from membership if they have been expelled or suspended from any securities exchange or another SRO, if they have been convicted of any securities-related crime or if they have violated any part of any securities legislation.

Rule G-5. Anyone engaged in the municipal securities business must follow the rules of the SEC, any SRO to which he belongs and the MSRB. Violation of these rules is cause for disciplinary action.

Rule G-6. The MSRB requires municipal broker-dealers to maintain blanket fidelity bonds as mandated by the SRO to which a broker-dealer belongs. The dollar amount of coverage required varies according to the firm's size. Banks are not affected by this rule.

Rule G-7. A municipal securities dealer must obtain and keep on file specific information about its associated persons. Most of the required information, such as employment history, disciplinary actions, residence and personal data, is contained on the U-4 and U-5 forms.

Rule G-8. Municipal securities dealers must maintain books and records of original entry (blotters); account records; securities records; subsidiary records; records of put options; repurchase agreements; records of agency, principal and syndicate transactions; copies of customer confirms; financial records; customer account information; customer complaints; records concerning the delivery of official statements; and records of those persons responsible for firm recordkeeping.

Rule G-9. Record maintenance requirements specify the length of time various records must be kept. A firm's articles of incorporation or partnership agreement, minutes of board meetings and records of stock certificates must be kept for the firm's lifetime.

A firm must keep the following records for at least *six years*:

- blotters (the original entries of trades and various accounts);
- records showing separate positions for each municipal security;
- records of all transactions the firm makes while acting as a member of various syndicates;
- written customer complaints and the firm's responses; and
- detailed account records for each customer—that is, buy and sell transactions and money deposited in or withdrawn from the account.

A firm must keep the following records for at least *three years:*

- records of securities that have been transferred, borrowed or loaned and transactions that were not complete on the settlement dates;
- put options and repurchase agreements;
- transactions in which the firm acted as an agent (broker);
- transactions in which the firm acted as a dealer (principal); and
- copies of confirmations.

Account records must be kept for *six years* after the account is closed. Basic customer account holder information, which must be kept for *three years*, includes:

- the customer's name and address;
- whether the customer is an adult or a minor;
- the customer's Social Security number or corporate or partnership tax ID number;
- the customer's occupation, with the employer's name and address;
- the signature of the representative who introduced the account and of the representative's supervisory principal who accepted the account;
- in a discretionary account, the customer's written authorization; and
- in a margin account, a signed hypothecation agreement, if applicable.

All required records must be kept in an *easily accessible place for at least two years*. After that, the time and effort needed to access them must be reasonable.

Rule G-10. Any time a municipal securities firm receives a written complaint from a customer, the firm must enter the complaint in a complaint file, indicating what action, if any, the firm has taken, and it must deliver a copy of the MSRB's investor brochure to that customer.

Rule G-11. During the underwriting period, a syndicate must establish a priority for allocating orders and identify any conditions that might alter the priority. The managing underwriter sets the priority and informs the syndicate. Every member that submits a group order must disclose the identity of the party for whom the member submits the order. A syndicate member must inform the manager whether an order it submits is for its own account or a related account.

The syndicate manager must give syndicate members a statement of expenses the syndicate has incurred. The syndicate manager must also prepare a statement showing the aggregate par values and prices of all bonds sold from the syndicate account.

Rule G-12. This rule outlines the procedures (uniform practices) for settling transactions between municipal securities firms. Included in the MSRB uniform practices are regulations regarding settlement dates, which are the same for municipal securities firms as they are for the rest of the securities industry:

- Cash trades settle on the trade date.
- Trades done regular way settle on the third business day after the trade date.
- When-, as- and if-issued trades settle on the date on which both parties agree, but not sooner than three business days after the confirmation (indicating that the settlement date is set).

Confirmations for trades between dealers are sent on the trade date or on the next business day. Confirmations between municipal broker-dealers must include essentially the same information as confirms sent to public customers (see Rule G-15). In addition, the concession amount, if any, must be shown. Any instruction for nonstandard delivery must be stated. Good delivery also requires that the seller provide a delivery ticket, which contains much of the information disclosed on the confirm.

Rule G-12 explains how municipal securities firms should handle confirmations they do not recognize. Don't Know (DK) procedures help resolve the problem.

Rule G-12 discusses good delivery requirements. Securities that are not in good delivery form are *rejected* (the buyer does not accept delivery) or *reclaimed* (the buyer accepts delivery only to find the bonds are not good delivery). This does not invalidate the trade—the seller is still obligated to sell the securities.

Delivery is made in denominations of $1,000 or $5,000 for bearer bonds. Registered bonds are delivered in multiples of $1,000 par value, with a maximum par value on any one certificate of $100,000. Bonds issued in both registered and bearer form may be delivered in bearer form unless both parties agree otherwise.

Mutilated certificates are not good delivery unless the transfer agent or some other acceptable official of the issuer validates the security. The issuer or a commercial bank must endorse mutilated coupons for them to be considered good delivery. Coupon bonds must have all unpaid coupons attached in proper order.

In the case of an issue's partial call, the called securities are not good delivery unless they are identified as *called* when traded. Municipal securities without legal opinions attached are not good delivery unless it is specified on the trade date that the transaction is ex-legal.

Rule G-12 also discusses the settlement of a new issue syndicate account. The managing underwriter must provide the registered clearing agency with notice of the settlement date as soon as the settlement date is known. The syndicate manager returns good faith deposits to the syndicate members within two business days of settling with the issuer. Final settlement of the syndicate account must be made within 60 days after the manager delivers the securities to the members. If a customer has designated a credit to be paid to a particular member, it must be delivered within 30 business days after delivery of the securities to the customer. In general, municipal securities transactions are settled in clearinghouse funds, unlike U.S. government securities transactions, which settle in federal funds.

Rule G-13. Dealers can publish quotations only for bona fide bids or offers. Nominal quotes (informational only) are permissible if identified as such. No dealer participating in a joint account may distribute a quotation indicating more than one market for that security.

Rule G-14. Municipal securities dealers must report transactions in a timely manner. The dealers must report only those transactions they know or have reason to believe actually took place. No fictitious, deceptive or manipulative reports are allowed.

Rule G-15. Confirmations of trades must be sent or given to customers at or before a transaction's completion. Each confirm must include the following information:

- broker-dealer's name, address and telephone number;
- customer's name;
- detailed description of the security, including issuer, interest rate and maturity, whether it is callable, etc.;
- trade date and time of execution;
- settlement date;
- CUSIP number, if any;
- yield and dollar price;

- amount of accrued interest;
- extended principal amount (the total principal of all securities the information covers);
- total dollar amount (the extended principal plus any accrued interest);
- whether the firm acted as broker or dealer (if it acted as broker, the name of the person on the other side of the trade must be given, if requested, and the dollar amount of commission earned from both parties must be disclosed);
- dated date, if it affects the interest calculation and the first interest payment date;
- level of registration of the security (fully registered, registered as to principal only or book-entry);
- whether the bonds are called or prerefunded; and
- any other special fact about the security traded (escrowed to maturity, ex-legal trade, federally taxable, odd denominations, etc.).

Rule G-16. Each municipal broker-dealer must be examined at least every 24 months to ensure that the firm is in compliance with MSRB regulations, SEC rules and the Securities Exchange Act of 1934. Because the MSRB does not enforce its own rules, it does not examine municipal securities firms. The appropriate enforcement agency (NASD, FDIC, Comptroller of the Currency, FRB) administers the examinations.

Rule G-17. Municipal securities dealers must deal fairly with everyone in transacting municipal securities business and must not engage in deceptive, dishonest, unfair or manipulative practices.

Rule G-18. Dealers must try to obtain prices for customers that are reasonable and fairly related to the market. This rule also applies to brokers' brokers, which regularly effect trades for the accounts of other municipal brokers and dealers.

Rule G-19. A municipal securities firm, through its reps, must obtain extensive financial, personal and investment information about a client to ensure suitable recommendations and transactions. A rep must obtain and use as much information as possible when making recommendations and must have reasonable grounds for recommending any particular security or transaction. The MSRB prohibits broker-dealers from recommending municipal securities to a customer if a broker-dealer has not obtained the customer's financial information, tax status and investment objectives, even if the broker-dealer has reasonable grounds to believe that the recommendation is suitable for the customer.

The MSRB makes an exception to the suitability rule in the case of unsolicited transactions. A municipal broker-dealer may execute an unsolicited transaction for a customer without making a suitability determination. In an unsolicited transaction, the customer requests a specific bond and provides the rep with all of the material facts to identify the bond.

✓ *For Example:* If a customer identified the issuer, coupon and maturity of a bond he wished to buy, the transaction would be unsolicited.

A customer must authorize a discretionary account in writing. In addition, the customer must to provide all relevant suitability information. The firm's principal must approve the opening of such an account, review and approve each trade, and check the account frequently for any possible abuse of discretionary authority. Churning is prohibited.

Rule G-20. Municipal securities dealers cannot give gifts valued at more than $100 to any person in one year other than their own employees. Payments for services rendered are allowed. Gifts of occasional meals or tickets to sporting events or concerts (not season passes) are permitted. Sponsorship of legitimate business functions is also permissible.

Rule G-21. Municipal securities firms must be truthful in their advertising. They must not publish advertisements that are false or misleading in regard to their services, skills or products. An advertisement for a new issue can show the original reoffering price, even though it may have changed, if the advertisement contains the sale date. A firm's municipal or general securities principal must approve each advertisement in writing before first use.

Rule G-22. Clients must be informed if a control relationship exists between a municipal firm and an issuer. A control relationship means the dealer or one of its officers is in a position to influence the issuer or is in a position to be influenced by the issuer. The phrase "controls, is controlled by or is under common control with" allows the broadest interpretation of the term "control."

✓ *For Example:* A city official who controls the selection of the underwriter for a bond issue is considered to be in a control relationship if he is also a principal for a dealer underwriting the issue.

Although the rule does not prohibit control relationships, it requires that broker-dealers in control situations inform their customers in writing before settlement of trades. If a control relationship exists, a broker-dealer cannot execute a transaction in a discretionary account without the customer's specific authorization.

Rule G-23. To avoid a conflict of interest in a situation where a municipal securities firm acts as a financial adviser, then becomes an underwriter for an issuer, the firm must disclose the advisory relationship and compensation to customers in writing. If a firm agrees to give financial advice, or contracts for a fee to consult for an issuer about a new issue of municipal securities, the firm has a financial advisory relationship with the issuer. It must disclose the compensation for this service to customers who purchase that issuer's securities.

If a firm acting in a financial advisory capacity wants to participate in the issue on which it has advised, it must get written consent from the issuer to submit a competitive bid. For a negotiated bid, the advisory contract must be terminated in writing, and the issuer must give written consent. The former financial adviser must tell the issuer of the possible conflict of interest and disclose to the issuer the source and anticipated amount of money received, if participating in the issue. Also, if a financial advisory relationship exists or did exist between the dealer and issuer, the dealer must inform buyers of the securities of this fact.

A broker-dealer with a financial advisory relationship can buy newly issued securities for its own trading account or a customer's account provided it has followed certain procedures.

Rule G-24. In the normal course of business, dealers gain access to confidential, nonpublic information about their customers. Municipal securities firms may not use this confidential information to solicit trades of municipal securities except with an issuer's express consent.

Rule G-25. Like other types of broker-dealers, municipal securities firms and their representatives may not misuse securities or money held for other people. They must not guarantee a customer against loss or share in the profits or losses of a customer's account, although joint accounts in a private capacity are allowed. Bona fide put options and repurchase agreements are not considered guarantees against loss.

Rule G-26. Rule G-26 covers the procedures a municipal securities dealer must follow when a customer requests the transfer of his account to another broker-dealer. Both the old firm and the new firm must communicate and coordinate their procedures to make sure that the transfer happens smoothly.

Rule G-27. Each municipal securities firm must designate a principal to supervise the firm's representatives and must create and maintain a written supervisory procedures manual. The designated principal for the firm must approve in writing:

- the opening of new customer accounts
- every municipal securities transaction
- actions taken on customer complaints
- correspondence regarding municipal securities trades

Every broker-dealer, but not bank-dealers, must have a financial and operations principal (FinOp) who maintains the financial books and records required by Rules G-8 and G-9.

Rule G-28. If a municipal securities dealer employee opens an account with another municipal securities firm, MSRB rules require the firm opening the account to notify the employer in writing and to send duplicate confirmations to the employer. The firm opening the account must comply with any other requests the employer makes. This rule also applies when a firm opens an account for the spouse or minor child of an employee of another firm, if this information is known.

Rule G-29. Every municipal securities dealer's office must keep a copy of MSRB regulations so that it may provide a copy of these rules for review to any customer upon request.

Rule G-30. The markups or markdowns municipal securities dealers charge must be fair and reasonable, taking into account all characteristics of a trade, such as:

- fair market value of the securities at trade time
- total dollar amount of the transaction
- any special difficulty in doing the trade
- the fact that the dealer is entitled to a profit

Unlike the NASD rules, the MSRB rules have no 5 percent guideline for markups or markdowns.

Rule G-31. A municipal securities broker-dealer may not solicit business from an investment company based on the broker-dealer's record of sales of the investment company's shares.

Rule G-32. When a new issue of municipal securities is delivered to a customer, a copy of the official statement must accompany or precede the delivery. If it is not yet completed, a preliminary official statement is acceptable with the delivery. A summary or an abstract of the official statement is also permitted; however, these two documents are considered to be advertising and must be approved by a principal of the firm before either can be distributed. A final official statement must be delivered to all buyers when it is made available.

If the issue is a negotiated underwriting, the municipal firm must disclose in writing to the customer the amount of the spread, the amount of any fee received if the firm acted as an agent in the sale, and the initial offering price for each maturity in the issue.

It is the underwriter's responsibility to supply offering documents upon request to any broker-dealer to which it sells new municipal securities.

Rule G-33. Municipal dealers must calculate accrued interest when a municipal security trades "and interest." Municipal bonds, like corporates, use a 360-day year with 30-day months.

Rule G-34. A municipal securities firm that is managing an underwriting for a new issue must, in most cases, apply for CUSIP numbers for the securities to be issued. An issue is eligible for CUSIP numbers if the issuer has filed appropriate documentation (i.e., official statements, notices of sales, legal opinions) with CUSIP.

CUSIP numbers are not required for local assessment bonds or for notes that mature in one year or less.

Rule G-35. The MSRB arbitration rule covers disputes between participants in the municipal securities business.

Rule G-36. The underwriter of a new municipal securities offering must send two copies of the official statement to the MSRB, along with two copies of Form G-36 no later than 10 days after the issue is awarded to the underwriter. If the issue is canceled after the MSRB has been sent the official statement, it must be notified of the cancellation.

Rule G-37. A broker, dealer or municipal securities dealer cannot conduct municipal securities business with an issuer for two years when political contributions to an official of that issuer exceed $250. Contributions include those made by the firm, a municipal finance professional associated with the firm, a political action committee controlled by the firm or a municipal finance professional. The rule applies to contributions made to any federal, state or local official who awards municipal securities business or appoints the officials who do so, whether the recipient is a candidate, an official-elect or an incumbent.

The rule defines a municipal finance professional as any associated person, supervisor or officer of a firm. Contributions include any gift, subscription, loan, advance, money or item of value. When contributions exceed the $250 maximum, the firm cannot participate in a negotiated underwriting or private placement of a new issue and cannot act as a financial adviser for a new issue. The firm may participate in a competitive bid underwriting.

Rule G-38. Municipal securities firms that engage consultants must have written agreements with the consultants and disclose the consulting arrangements to issuers and to the MSRB. A consultant is any person a dealer pays to obtain or retain municipal securities business by communicating with an issuer on the dealer's behalf. Associated persons and professionals paid for legal advice, accounting services or engineering services are not considered consultants as long as these professionals do not perform "finder" activities.

Rule G-39. Telemarketers calling on behalf of a firm may not call a person before 8:00 a.m. or after 9:00 p.m. in the called person's time zone. The caller must disclose his name and the firm's name, the firm's telephone number or address, and the fact that he is calling to solicit the purchase of municipal bonds or investment services. The requirements do not apply if the person called is an established customer who has an account and has made a transaction within the previous year. Calls made to other broker or dealers are also exempt.

Tracking Municipal Securities

Tax-exempt bonds are listed in financial publications such as *The Blue List*, *The Bond Buyer* and *The Wall Street Journal*. Figure 3.3 is an example of municipal bond quotations as reported by *The Bond Buyer*.

Take, for example, the Kenton County, Kentucky Airport bond. The name of the bond appears in the left column under "Issue." The entries in the "Coupon" and "Maturity" columns indicate that the bond pays 6.300 percent interest and matures on March 1, 2015. The bond was traded at 95¼, or $952.50 per $1,000 bond. The price represents a half-point ($5) decrease from the last trade, as reported under the "Chg" (change) column. The 6.71 yield is the bid yield and the yield to maturity. Because the bond is selling at a discount, the yield to maturity is higher than the coupon yield.

FIGURE 3.3 Tax-Exempt Bond Transactions

Tax-Exempt Bonds

Representative prices for tax-exempt revenue and GO bonds based on institutional trades. Changes rounded to nearest 1/8th. Yield is YTM.

Issue	Coupon	Maturity	Price	Chg	Bid Yld
Alaska Hsg Fin Corp	6.600	12-01-23	97 1/2	- 1/4	6.79
Cal Dept of Wtr Res	6.125	12-01-13	95 3/4	- 1/2	6.50
Charlotte Hosp Auth	6.250	01-01-20	95 3/8	+ 1/2	6.62
Farmington NM Util Sys	5.750	05-15-13	91 1/4	- 1/8	6.53
Ill State Toll Hwy Auth	6.375	01-01-15	96	+ 3/8	6.72
Kenton Co KY Airport	6.300	03-01-15	95 1/4	- 1/2	6.71

Summary

Municipal securities offer investors a relatively safe means of investing for tax-free income. Because the interest municipal securities pay is not taxable by the federal government, the yield is lower than that of taxable corporate or government bonds.

The two primary types of municipal securities are general obligation bonds, which are almost always issued in a competitive bid offering, and revenue bonds, which are normally issued in a negotiated offering. The principal and interest payments for general obligation bonds are paid for by tax receipts and other forms of income the issuer generates. Principal and interest payments for revenue bonds are paid for by the revenues generated by the facility that the bonds were issued to finance.

Once issued, municipal securities trade in the over-the-counter market. As fixed-income investments, municipal bond prices fluctuate with interest rates: as interest rates rise, bond prices fall, and vice versa. Because municipal bonds tend to be suitable for long-term investors and many issues are relatively small, the trading for a given issue can be very thin.

Key Concepts

To prepare for your license exam, you should learn the following concepts.

In addition to studying these key concepts, use the Municipal Securities Hot Sheet on page 635 for further review.

agreement among underwriters
bid form
bond counsel
bond swap
competitive bidding
coterminous
doctrine of reciprocal immunity
due diligence
Eastern account
feasibility study
general obligation bond (GO)
Glass-Steagall Act of 1933
good faith deposit
indenture
limited tax bond
Municipal Securities Rulemaking
    Board (MSRB)
Munifacts

negotiated underwriting
net interest cost (NIC)
official notice of sale
official statement (OS)
public purpose bond
qualified opinion
red herring
revenue bond
spread
tax-equivalent yield
The Blue List
The Bond Buyer
true interest cost (TIC)
underwriting syndicate
unqualified opinion
visible supply
Western account
workable indication

Review Questions

1. Municipal bonds are issued for all of the following EXCEPT

   A. sewers
   B. GNMAs
   C. hospitals
   D. capital improvements

2. In safety of principal, municipal bonds are considered second only to

   A. preferred stock
   B. common stock
   C. U.S. government agency bonds
   D. FNMA securities

3. A general obligation bond is backed by

   A. tolls
   B. special taxes
   C. public housing
   D. the full faith and credit of the issuing municipality

4. If interest rates rise, municipal bond prices should

   A. rise
   B. decline
   C. fluctuate
   D. stay the same

5. If a municipality appoints an underwriter to offer a new issue, the underwriting is

   A. negotiated
   B. a competitive bid
   C. proportionate
   D. an Eastern agreement

6. A legal opinion on a municipal bond is prepared by

   A. the underwriter
   B. the trustee
   C. the municipality
   D. an independent bond attorney

7. All of the following are short-term, tax-exempt municipal issues EXCEPT

   A. BANs
   B. RANs
   C. AONs
   D. TANs

8. Short-term municipal notes normally have all the following characteristics EXCEPT that they

   A. mature in less than one year
   B. are issued in anticipation of a bond sale
   C. pay interest every six months
   D. pay interest that is exempt from federal taxation

9. The manager of a municipal syndicate is a dealer that will

   A. act for the underwriting group
   B. take the largest position
   C. act for the issuing authority
   D. provide the legal opinion

10. In a municipal securities underwriting, which of the following sign(s) the agreement among underwriters?

   A. Members of the syndicate
   B. Issuer
   C. Bond counsel
   D. Trustee

Answers & Rationale

1. **B.** This is an "except" question. Remember that "GNMA" stands for Government National Mortgage Association, a government agency.

2. **C.** In the ranking of investments by safety of principal, municipal securities are considered second only to U.S. government and U.S. government agency securities.

3. **D.** A general obligation (GO) bond is backed by the full faith and credit of the issuing municipality.

4. **B.** Remember the inverse relationship of bonds: if interest rates rise, bond prices decline.

5. **A.** When a municipality appoints an underwriter to offer a new issue, this is always a negotiated bid. When a municipality requests bids, this is a competitive bid. Competitive bids are used primarily for GO offerings.

6. **D.** For a legal opinion, the issuer retains and pays an independent bond attorney to provide an opinion on the validity of the offering.

7. **C.** The initials stand for bond anticipation notes (BANs), revenue anticipation notes (RANs) and tax anticipation notes (TANs). "AON" (all or none) is a type of underwriting agreement.

8. **C.** This is an "except" question. Short-term municipal notes do not pay interest every six months; they pay the interest at maturity because they mature in less than a year.

9. **A.** The manager of the syndicate acts on behalf of the underwriting group when dealing with the issuer.

10. **A.** Members of the syndicate formalize their relationship by signing a syndicate letter (in a competitive bid) or a syndicate contract or an agreement among underwriters (in a negotiated underwriting.)

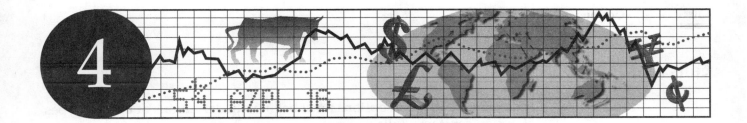

Options

OVERVIEW

Option contracts offer investors a means to invest for income or capital gain, to speculate on individual securities, markets, foreign currencies and other instruments, or to protect investment positions.

Because an option contract's value is derived from the value from another instrument, such as a stock, stock index or foreign currency, options are **derivative securities**.

The Option Contract

An option is simply a contract that establishes a price and time frame for the purchase or sale of a particular investment instrument. Two parties are involved in the contract: One party receives the right to exercise the contract to buy or sell the underlying security; the other is obligated to fulfill the terms of the contract.

Listed option contracts are issued in standardized formats by the Options Clearing Corporation (OCC) and traded on the Chicago Board Options Exchange (CBOE) or other exchanges. Because the CBOE and other exchanges provide forums to trade, and the OCC stands behind option contracts in the event of a firm failure, options are easily tradeable.

Underlying Instruments. In theory, options can be created on any item with a fluctuating market value. The most familiar options are those issued on common stocks; they are called **equity options**. This lesson will focus on equity and certain nonequity options.

Calls and Puts

A discussion of equity options must begin with definitions of the two types of option contracts: calls and puts.

- A **call** option is the right to buy a stock for a specific price within a specified timeframe. A call buyer buys the *right to buy* a specific stock, and a call seller takes on the *obligation to sell* the stock.
- A **put** option is the right to sell a stock for a specific price within a specified timeframe. A put buyer buys the *right to sell* a specific stock, and a put seller takes on the *obligation to buy* the stock.

Each stock option contract covers 100 shares (a round lot) of stock. An option's cost is called the **premium**. Premiums are quoted in dollars per share. Because a contract covers 100 shares, a premium of $3 means $3 for each share times 100 shares, which equals $300.

Exercise Prices

An option's **exercise** or **strike price** is the price at which the option owner is entitled to buy or sell the underlying security and the price at which the option seller has agreed to sell or buy the security.

✓ **For Example:** An RST May 60 call indicates a strike price of $60.

The OCC sets strike prices, which usually range from 10 to 20 points below to 10 to 20 points above the underlying stock's market price. Most exercise prices are set at $5 intervals; however, strike prices at intervals of $2.50, $10 or $20 are sometimes used as well. If a stock's price moves enough, the OCC establishes additional strike prices. Table 4.1 illustrates a sample listing of strike prices and the call and put premiums for RST options.

TABLE 4.1   Sample Call and Put Strike Prices and Premiums

Stock and Price	Strike Price	Call Premium	Put Premium
RST $58	50	9 1/4	1 1/4
	55	6	2 1/2
	60	3 1/4	5 1/8
	65	2	8 1/2
	70	1 1/8	13 3/4

FIGURE 4.1   Option Table

CHICAGO BOARD

Option & NY Close	Strike Price	Calls-Last			Puts-Last		
		Jan	Feb	Mar	Jan	Feb	Mar
Adm Fam	40	1 3/8	3 5/8	r	3/16	7/8	1 1/4
41 1/8	45	1/2	1 1/2	2 1/8	3 7/8	r	5 1/4
41 1/8	50	r	3/8	5/8	s	s	12
ALFA, Inc.	30	7 7/8	9 1/8	11	r	r	1/8
37 7/8	35	3 1/8	4 1/2	6 3/4	r	1/4	1/8
37 7/8	40	3/4	1 5/8	3	3/4	7/8	r
All Swel	25	1/4	1 3/8	2	1/8	1	1 5/8
25 1/4	30	r	1/8	7/8	3 3/4	4 5/8	7
Bulln Bar	20	r	r	r	r	r	7/8
24	22 1/2	1	r	r	r	r	r
24	25	5/16	1	2 1/4	r	r	2 5/8

Total call vol 1,240,086   Call open int 3,038,532
Total put vol   105,755   Put open int   941,395

r - Not Traded. s - No Option.

Although most strike prices are initially designated in $5 increments, they are adjusted for stock splits and dividends. Options are not adjusted for ordinary cash dividends.

The option tables printed in many newspapers offer most of the relevant information about a stock's options. The number immediately below the stock's name is the price at which the stock closed the day before. The option strike prices currently available are listed under the heading "Strike Price." The prices listed under the headings "Calls—Last" and "Puts—Last" are the last premiums at which the option traded the previous day. Figure 4.1 provides a sample newspaper option table.

Leverage.   Because an option's cost is normally much less than the underlying stock's cost, option contracts provide investors with leverage: relatively little money allows an investor to "control" an investment that would otherwise require a much larger capital outlay.

✓ *For Example:* An investor can buy RST for $58, investing $5,800, or buy an RST 55 call for $6, for an investment of $600. If RST's price increases to $70, the stock investor will see little more than a 20 percent profit ($12 profit ÷

$58 investment), while the option investor, with the call worth a minimum of $15 ($70 – $55), will have more than doubled his money ($15 ÷ 6 = 250%).

Expiration

An option, such as an RST 60 call, is available in several expiration months. These include the two nearest calendar months and two or three months farther out, up to nine months. Equity option contracts expire on the Saturday following the third Friday of the expiration month; they cease trading on the third Friday of the expiration month.

 For Example: All RST options with an August expiration will not trade after the third Friday of August. The following Monday, a new expiration month will open for trading.

Type, Class and Series

Options are categorized by type, class and series, as shown in Figure 4.2:

- **Type.** The two types of options are calls and puts.
- **Class.** All options of the same type on the same underlying security are of the same class regardless of strike price or expiration month. For example, all ALF calls are one class of options; all ALF puts are another class.
- **Series.** All options of the same class, exercise price and expiration month are in the same series. For instance, all Jan 45 ADM puts are one series of options; all Jan 50 ADM puts are another series.

Premiums

As stated earlier, an option's price is known as the *premium*. Option premiums are quoted in terms of bid and ask prices, such as 3¼ bid, 3½ offered. An option buyer pays the ask price, and an option seller sells for the bid price.

 For Example: Assume the quote for an RST Aug 50 call is 9⅛–9½. An investor who wants to establish a long position pays 9½, or $950, to buy the call. An investor who wants to establish a short position receives 9⅛, or $912.50, for selling the call.

Payment and Settlement

Options cannot be bought on margin and have no loan value, although they may be bought or sold in a margin account. Each option transaction must be fully paid for on the next business day after the transaction is executed.

Exercise Style

All options are exercisable either **American style** or **European style**. American style exercise means an option contract may be exercised any time up to

FIGURE 4.2   Option Types, Classes and Series

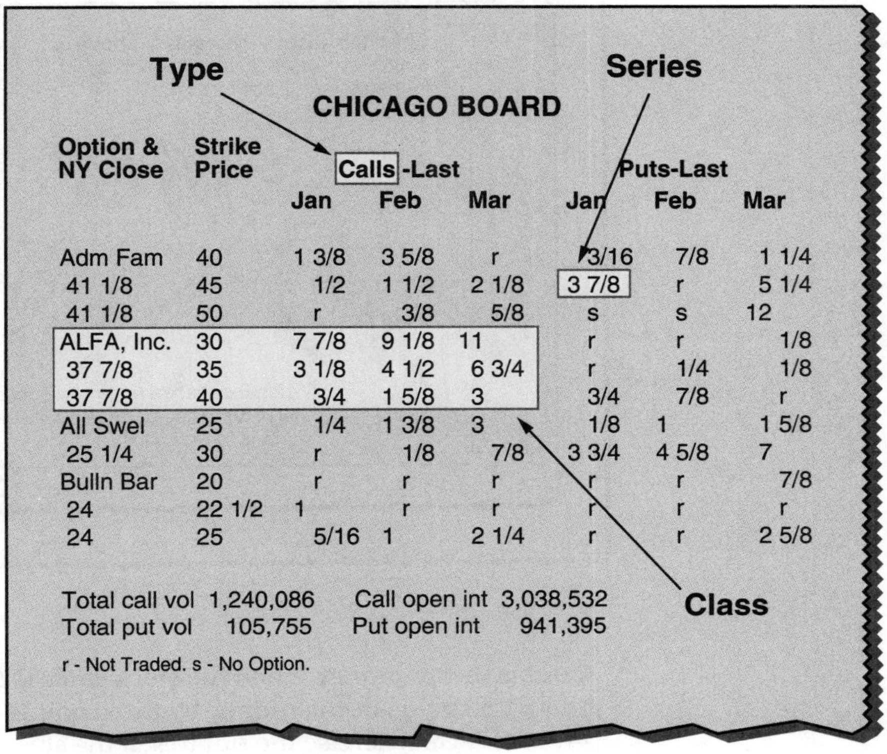

Type   **Series**

CHICAGO BOARD

Option & NY Close	Strike Price	Calls-Last			Puts-Last		
		Jan	Feb	Mar	Jan	Feb	Mar
Adm Fam	40	1 3/8	3 5/8	r	3/16	7/8	1 1/4
41 1/8	45	1/2	1 1/2	2 1/8	3 7/8	r	5 1/4
41 1/8	50	r	3/8	5/8	s	s	12
ALFA, Inc.	30	7 7/8	9 1/8	11	r	r	1/8
37 7/8	35	3 1/8	4 1/2	6 3/4	r	1/4	1/8
37 7/8	40	3/4	1 5/8	3	3/4	7/8	r
All Swel	25	1/4	1 3/8	3	1/8	1	1 5/8
25 1/4	30	r	1/8	7/8	3 3/4	4 5/8	7
Bulln Bar	20	r	r	r	r	r	7/8
24	22 1/2	1	r	r	r	r	r
24	25	5/16	1	2 1/4	r	r	2 5/8

Total call vol   1,240,086   Call open int   3,038,532   **Class**
Total put vol   105,755   Put open int   941,395

r - Not Traded. s - No Option.

the expiration date. European style exercise means a contract is exercisable only at expiration. Most equity options are American style exercise. Foreign currency options may be either American style or European style.

Value of an Option   The option buyer, like the buyer of any investment, hopes to profit from his position. An option's price, or premium, changes as the:

- underlying security's market price changes—the more volatile the underlying security, the more volatile the premium tends to be;
- option's intrinsic value increases or decreases; and
- time remaining until the option's expiration date grows nearer.

A call option is **in-the-money** when the stock's price is *above* the option's strike price. For example, an RST 50 call is in-the-money by seven points if RST stock is $57 because the call owner can exercise the option to buy the stock for $50 and sell it in the market for $57 for an immediate gain of $7 per share.

FIGURE 4.3   Comparison of In–, At– and Out-of-the-Money Options

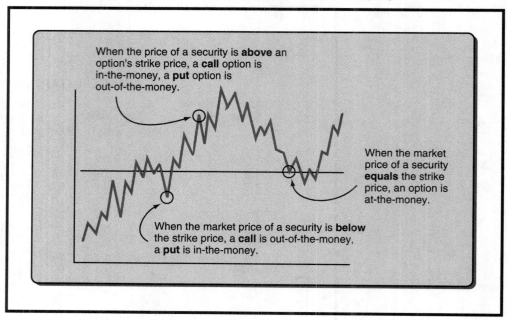

A put is in-the-money when the stock price is *below* the option's strike price. An RST 60 put is in-the-money by three points if RST stock is $57 because the put owner can exercise the put to sell the stock for $60 when the stock's market price is $57.

A call option is **out-of-the-money** when the stock price is *below* the exercise price. No investor will exercise an RST 60 call to buy RST for $60 if she can buy RST in the market for $57.

A put is out-of-the-money if the stock price is *above* the exercise price. No investor will exercise an RST 50 put to sell the stock for $50 if she can sell RST in the market for $57.

✎ *Take Note:* The terms "in-the-money" and "out-of-the-money" refer to the relationship between an option's strike price and the underlying stock's price. They *do not* refer to the investor's profit or loss. An option's premium is not relevant when determining whether the option is in-the-money or out-of-the-money.

An option is **at-the-money** when the underlying stock is trading at the option's strike price. Investors are unlikely to exercise at-the-money options.

Figure 4.3 compares in-the-money, at-the-money and out-of-the-money options.

Option premiums reflect two types of value:

- **intrinsic value**—the amount by which an option is in-the-money; and
- **time value**—the amount by which the premium exceeds intrinsic value.

Intrinsic Value. If an option is in-the-money, its premium reflects, at a minimum, the difference between the strike price and the stock's price. This difference is known as *intrinsic value*. Intrinsic value is the amount by which an option is in-the-money.

An out-of-the-money option has no intrinsic value.

Time Value. If an option's premium exceeds its intrinsic value, the option has time value. An option expires on a preset date; the farther away that date is, the more time remains for a change in the underlying stock's price, and therefore the greater the time value. Time value diminishes as an option's expiration date approaches. At expiration, when no time remains, the option premium equals its intrinsic value, if any. An option premium equal to its intrinsic value is at **parity**.

Options are **wasting assets**; that is, the passage of time depletes their value.

Table 4.2 illustrates the intrinsic values and time values of premiums.

TABLE 4.2   Intrinsic and Time Value of Premiums

Stock and Price	Strike Price	Call			Put		
		Premium	Intrinsic Value	Time Value	Premium	Intrinsic Value	Time Value
RST $58	50	9 1/4	8	1 1/4	1 1/4	0	1 1/4
	55	6	3	3	2 1/2	0	2 1/2
	60	3	0	3	5 1/8	2	3 1/8
	65	2	0	2	8 1/2	7	1 1/2
	70	1 1/8	0	1 1/8	13 3/4	12	1 3/4

Before You Go On: RST is trading for $54. What are the intrinsic values and time values of the following options?

1. RST September 50 call for 6
2. RST October 55 call for 2¼
3. RST September 60 put for 7¼
4. RST October 50 put for 1⅛

Answers: 1. $4 intrinsic; $2 time; 2. No intrinsic; $2¼ time. 3. $6 intrinsic; $1¼ time. 4. No intrinsic; $1⅛ time.

Basic Option Transactions

Because two types of options exist (calls and puts) and two types of transactions exist (purchases and sales), four basic strategies are available to an option investor (see Figure 4.4):

- buy calls
- sell calls
- buy puts
- sell puts

Option buyers are *long* the positions; option sellers are *short* the positions.

FIGURE 4.4   The Four Basic Option Transactions

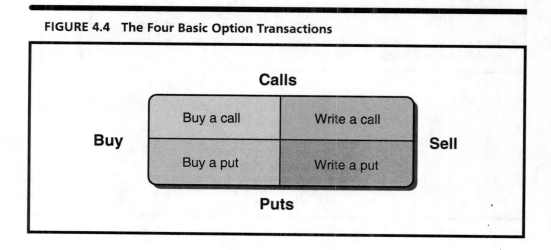

Disposing of an Option

The owner of a put or call option contract has three choices:

1. **exercise** the option to buy or sell the security specified in the contract
2. let the option **expire**
3. **sell** the option contract before the expiration date

✍ **Before You Go On:** When RST is trading for $57, an investor believes it will trade above $60 soon. He buys 1 Nov 60 call for $3 on September 1 in an opening transaction. On October 10, the stock is trading for 66¾ and the call is quoted at 7¾–8. What alternatives are available to the investor?

Answer: He can sell the call in a closing transaction for 7¾ ($775), for a gain of $475, exercise the call to buy the stock for $60, or wait until expiration to see whether the stock continues to trade higher.

Opening and Closing Transactions

Because an option conveys rights and obligations for a short period of time, each transaction has a beginning and an end—an open and a close. An option position opened by an investor buying a call, for instance, is closed when the call is exercised, is sold or expires. An option position opened by an investor selling a call is closed when the call is exercised, is bought or expires.

When a customer first buys a call or put, the order ticket and confirmation are marked "opening purchase." Once bought, an option may be sold any time before it expires. The second transaction is known as a *closing sale,* and the ticket and confirmation are marked "closing sale." A customer who originally sold an option in an opening sale transaction may buy it back any time before expiration in a closing purchase, and the ticket and confirmation are marked "closing purchase."

To close an option position, an investor enters the transaction opposite of her opening transaction.

✍ **Before You Go On:** An investor enters an opening purchase transaction for an RST 55 call for 6. If he decides to sell the call, what must he do?

Answer: He must enter a closing sale transaction.

Buying and Selling Calls and Puts

Option positions are typically either **bullish** or **bearish** on the underlying stock (see Figure 4.5). The primary reason for buying or selling options is to profit from or protect against price movement in the underlying security.

A bullish investor may buy calls or write puts and profit if prices rise. A bearish investor can write calls or buy puts and profit if prices decline.

FIGURE 4.5 Bullish and Bearish Option Positions

	Long	**Short**
Calls	Right to buy Bullish	Obligation to sell Bearish
Puts	Right to sell Bearish	Obligation to buy Bullish
	(Buyer, Holder, Owner)	(Seller, Writer, Grantor)

Buying Calls   Call buyers expect the underlying stock to increase in value. By buying a call, an investor can profit from the increase in the stock's price while investing a relatively small amount of money.

✔ *For Example:* An investor believes the price of RST, trading for $58, will trade into the mid 60s. He can buy 1 RST Nov 60 call for $3 (a total investment of $300) in an opening transaction. The option conveys the right to buy 100 shares of RST at $60 per share before the November expiration. If the stock trades for $65 in October, the investor can exercise the option and buy 100 RST shares for $6,000 or sell the option in a closing transaction for a profit. If the stock price remains below $60, the investor can sell the option, most likely at a loss, or allow it to expire, losing the $300 (see Figure 4.6).

Long options allow investors to profit from a stock's movement while investing as little cash as possible. In the example above, the investor bought one option for $300, allowing him to profit from the price change of 100 shares of RST. To buy 100 shares would have required $5,800.

The option investor can lose the entire $300 purchase price, but no more. The stock investor may lose money as well—as much as $5,800 if the stock price falls to zero. The stock buyer has the advantage of time, however, because he has no set timeframe within which he needs to see the price change.

Maximum Gain. Theoretically, the potential gains available to call owners are unlimited because there is no limit on a rise in stock price. In practice, of course, stock prices do not rise infinitely.

Maximum Loss. On a long call, an investor risks losing 100 percent of the premium paid. This happens if the stock's market price is below the option's exercise price at expiration, making the option worthless.

FIGURE 4.6   Gain, Loss and Breakeven on a Long Call

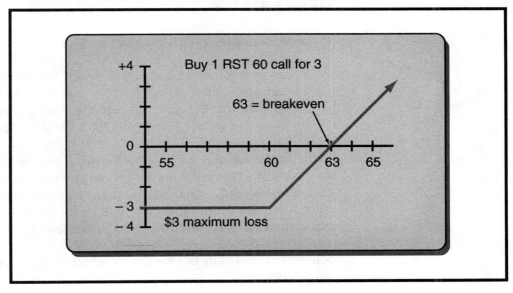

Breakeven Point. Because the call buyer pays a premium, he breaks even when the underlying stock's market price equals the sum of the strike price and the premium paid.

Figure 4.6 illustrates how the option call buyer will make money, break even or lose money.

✍ *Before You Go On:* At what price on the underlying stock does each of the following call transactions break even?

1. DCB 25 call for 2½
2. SRQ 45 call for 3
3. XEO 910 call for 23½

Answers: 1. DCB at $27½; 2. SRQ at $48; 3. XEO at $933½.

Writing Calls   A neutral or bearish investor can write a call and collect the premium. An investor who believes a stock's price will stay the same or decline can write a call to:

- generate income from the option premium;
- *partially* protect his position if he owns the stock by offsetting any loss on the sale of the stock by the premium amount; or
- speculate on the decline in the stock price.

If the stock price increases, the call may be exercised. The writer will be paid the strike price for the stock, in addition to the premium he received for writing the call.

✔ **For Example:** If RST is trading for $58:

- an investor who owns 100 shares of RST and wants to generate income can write 1 Nov 60 call for $3 and receive the $300 premium; and
- an investor who does not own the stock and believes it will decline in price can write 1 Nov 60 call for $3 and receive the $300 premium.

In the first example, the investor writes a **covered** call: if the stock is called, the investor's risk is covered by shares owned. The second investor's position is **uncovered**, or **naked**, because he does not own the stock. If the stock price increases dramatically, he will be forced to buy stock at the market price, then sell it for the $60 strike price (see Figure 4.7).

Selling covered calls is a means by which many investors increase an investment's return.

Maximum Gain. An uncovered call writer's maximum gain is the premium he receives. The writer earns the maximum gain when the stock's price is below the exercise price at expiration. The call expires unexercised, allowing the writer to keep the premium.

Maximum Loss. An uncovered call writer's maximum loss is unlimited if she does not own the underlying stock. The writer could be forced to buy the stock at an infinitely higher price to sell at the strike price.

Breakeven Point. An uncovered call writer breaks even when the stock's market price equals the sum of the strike price and the premium received. This is identical to the call buyer's breakeven.

Figure 4.7 illustrates how the uncovered call writer will make money, break even or lose money.

✍ **Before You Go On:** What are the maximum gains and losses for the following short calls?

1. DCB 25 call for 2½
2. SRQ 45 call for 3
3. XEO 910 call for 23½

Answers: 1. Maximum gain: $250 (2½); maximum loss: unlimited; 2. Maximum gain: $300 (3), maximum loss: unlimited; 3. Maximum gain: $2,350 (23½), maximum loss: unlimited.

FIGURE 4.7   Gain, Loss and Breakeven on an Uncovered Short Call

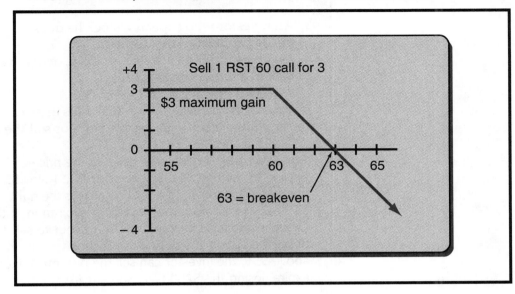

✍ *Before You Go On:* Identify whether the following situations are covered or uncovered positions, as well as the maximum gains, losses and breakevens.

1. Investor A buys 500 shares of SRQ for $50 and writes 5 SRQ Oct 50 calls for $3.
2. Investor B, convinced a market decline is imminent, writes 10 SRQ Oct 45 calls for $7.

Answers: 1. The option is covered because he owns 500 shares. If the option is exercised, his maximum gain is the $3 premium times 500 shares, or $1,500. His breakeven is $47 on the stock: the stock price ($50) minus premium received ($3). His maximum loss is $47 per share: the stock price minus the premium received, should the stock decline to zero. 2. The option is naked because he does not own the stock. His maximum gain is the $7 premium received times 10 contracts, or 1,000 shares, for $7,000. His maximum loss is unlimited. His breakeven occurs when the stock trades for $52 ($45 strike + $7 premium).

Buying Puts   A put buyer acquires the right to sell 100 shares of the underlying stock at the strike price before the expiration date. Because he expects the underlying security to decline in value, a put buyer is generally bearish.

Puts can be used to speculate on or *fully* protect against a decline in a stock's value in the following ways:

- An investor who expects a stock he does not own to decline can buy a put to profit from the decline.
- An investor who expects a stock he owns to decline can buy a put to lock in a minimum sale price.

If a put owner is correct and the stock falls in price, he could exercise the put option to sell the stock at the strike price or sell the put at a profit.

✓ **For Example:** An investor believes the price of RST, trading for $58, will decline to the mid 40s. She can buy 1 RST Nov 55 put for $2½ ($250) in an opening transaction. The option conveys the right to sell 100 shares of RST at $55 per share before the November expiration. If the stock trades for $45 in October, the investor can exercise the put to sell 100 RST shares for $5,500 or sell the option in a closing transaction for a profit. If the stock price remains above $55, the investor can sell the put, most likely at a loss, or allow it to expire, losing the $250 (see Figure 4.8).

Maximum Gain. The maximum gain for a long put is the option's strike price less the premium paid. The maximum gain occurs if the underlying stock price declines to zero.

Maximum Loss. A put buyer's maximum loss is the premium paid for the option. On all long options, the worst that can happen is that an option expires worthless.

Breakeven Point. The put buyer breaks even when the stock's market price is below the strike price by the amount of the premium paid.

Figure 4.8 illustrates the maximum gain, loss and breakeven point for a put buyer.

✍ **Before You Go On:** At what price on the underlying stock does each of the following long put transactions break even?

1. DCB 25 put for 1¾
2. SRQ 45 put for 2½
3. XEO 910 put for 19¼

Answers: 1. DCB at $23¼; 2. SRQ at $42½; 3. XEO at $890¾.

FIGURE 4.8   Gain, Loss and Breakeven on a Long Put

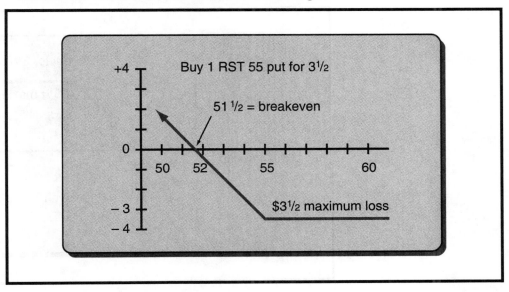

Writing Puts   Generally, investors who write puts believe the stock's price will rise.

A put writer is obligated to buy stock at the exercise price if the put buyer puts it to the put writer. If a stock's price is above the put strike price at expiration, the put expires unexercised, allowing the put writer to keep the premium.

Some investors write puts with the intent of having the options exercised against them. Writing a put is a means to buy stock at a reduced price because the premium received, in effect, reduces the cost of the stock. If the put is not exercised, the writer keeps the premium.

✓ *For Example:* An investor believes the price of RST, trading for $58, will trade into the mid 60s. He can sell 1 RST Nov 55 put for $3½ ($350) in an opening transaction. By selling the put option, the investor takes on the obligation to buy 100 shares of RST at $55 per share if the option is exercised. If the stock trades for $45 in October, the put will be exercised and the investor will have to buy 100 RST shares for $5,500. If the stock remains above $55 and the put expires, the investor keeps the $350 (see Figure 4.9).

Maximum Gain. A put writer's maximum gain is the premium received. The maximum gain occurs when the stock price is above the exercise price at expiration. The put expires worthless, and the writer keeps the premium.

Maximum Loss. A put seller's maximum loss is the put's strike price less the premium received; it occurs if the stock price drops to zero. At that point, the put seller must buy worthless stock for the exercise price.

FIGURE 4.9 Gain, Loss and Breakeven on a Short Put

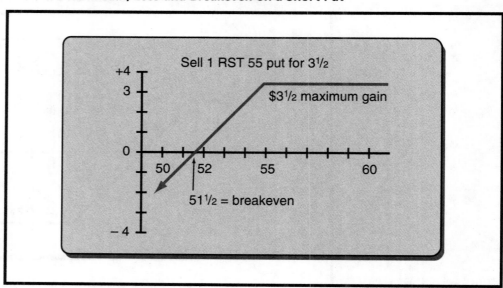

Breakeven Point. The put seller breaks even when the stock's market price is below the strike price by the premium received.

Figure 4.9 illustrates the maximum gain, loss and breakeven point for a put seller.

 Before You Go On: What are the maximum gain and loss on the following short puts?

1. DCB 25 put for 1¾
2. SRQ 45 put for 2½
3. XEO 910 put for 19¼

Answers: 1. Maximum gain: $175 (1¾); maximum loss: $2,325 ($2,500 – $175) if the stock price declines to zero; 2. Maximum gain: $250 (2½); maximum loss: $4,250 ($4,500 – $250) if the stock price declines to zero; 3. Maximum gain: $1,925 (19¼); maximum loss: $89,075 ($91,000 – $1,925) if the stock price declines to zero.

Take Note: A call writer's potential loss is unlimited if it's naked. A put writer's potential loss equals the option's strike price less the premium received should the underlying stock price decline to zero.

FIGURE 4.10   **Breakeven, Gain and Loss on Uncovered Positions**

Position	Breakeven	Maximum Gain	Maximum Loss
Long Call	Strike price plus premium	Unlimited	Premium
Short Call	Strike price plus premium	Premium	Unlimited
Long Put	Strike price minus premium	Strike price minus premium	Premium
Short Put	Strike price minus premium	Premium	Strike price minus premium

Summary of Breakevens, Gains and Losses

Figure 4.10 summarizes breakeven points, maximum gains and maximum losses on single option positions. Note the following:

- Both the long and short, or uncovered, positions have the same breakeven point.
- The maximum loss when buying an option is the premium paid.
- The maximum gain when writing an option is the premium received.
- The uncovered writer's potential loss is the buyer's potential gain.

Long-Term Equity Options

The CBOE's Long-term Equity AnticiPation Securities, or LEAPS®, are options with long-term expiration dates. Expiration dates of up to 39 months are authorized, but the LEAPS currently available expire within two years.

LEAPS contracts expire in January. As currently issued, LEAPS offer a choice of two expiration years. An investor considering an option purchase in December 1998, for example, could purchase a traditional option with a January 1999 expiration or a LEAPS contract with a January 2000 or January 2001 expiration.

LEAPS premiums are higher than traditional option premiums due to the long expiration's greater time value. When LEAPS are within nine months of their expiration dates, they become traditional options, and their prices are listed in newspapers with traditional options prices.

For transaction purposes, LEAPS are identical to traditional options: bulls buy calls or sell puts; bears buy puts or sell calls.

Using Options to Protect a Position

An investor with an established position in a stock can use options to change the position's risk and reward characteristics. Normally, investors seek either to increase potential rewards or to reduce potential loss.

Long Stock and Long Puts

An investor who owns a stock can protect against a decline in market value by buying a put. Doing so allows the investor to sell the stock by exercising the put if the stock price declines before expiration, or selling the put at a profit, which will offset the decline in the stock price.

Any profits in the stock are offset by the cost of the put premiums.

✔ **For Example:** An investor buys 100 shares of RST at $53 and buys 1 RST 50 put at 2. The maximum gain is unlimited. Should the stock price fall below the strike price of 50, the investor will exercise the put to sell the stock for 50. The investor loses $3 per share on the stock and has spent $2 per share for the put. The total loss equals $500. The breakeven point is reached when the stock rises by the amount paid for the put; in this case, 53 plus 2 equals 55.

Long Stock and Short Calls (Covered Call Writing)

A covered call is a call written on a stock an investor owns. The covered call writer reduces the risk of his long stock position *and generates income* with the dollars he receives in premiums from selling the call.

If the call is not exercised, the call writer keeps the premium. If the call is exercised, the covered call writer can deliver the stock he owns. The covered call writer limits his upside potential in exchange for the partial protection against a loss.

Partial Protection. By writing a covered call and receiving the premium, an investor, in effect, reduces the stock cost by the premium amount. If the stock price falls below the purchase price minus the premium received, the investor incurs a loss. Should the stock price rise dramatically, the stock will likely be called.

✔ **For Example:** An investor buys 100 shares of RST at 53 and writes 1 RST 55 call for 2. In effect, the premium offsets the stock price. The maximum gain equals $400: if the stock price rises above 55, the call will be exercised; thus, the investor will sell the stock for a gain of $200, in addition to the $200 premium received. The maximum loss is $5,100 should the stock become worthless. The breakeven point is reached when the stock falls by the amount of the premium received. Therefore, 53 minus 2 equals 51.

✎ **Take Note:** A covered call is partial protection that generates income and reduces the stock's upside potential. Buying puts provides nearly total downside protection that costs money and does not reduce the stock position's upside potential.

Short Stock and Long Calls

An investor who sells a stock short sells borrowed stock, expecting the price to decline. The short seller must buy stock to repay the stock loan and hopes to do so at a lower price. Just as a long stock investor can buy puts to protect against a price decline, a short seller can buy calls to protect against a price rise.

 For Example: An investor sells short 100 shares of RST at 58 and buys an RST 60 call for 3. The investor's maximum gain is $5,500: if the stock becomes worthless, the investor gains $5,800 from the short sale minus the $300 paid for the call.

The maximum loss is $500: if the stock price rises above $60, the investor will exercise the call to buy the stock for 60, incurring a $200 loss on the short sale, in addition to the $300 paid for the call. The breakeven point is the stock's sale price minus the premium paid—in this case, $58 minus 3, or $55.

Short Stock and Short Puts

A short stock position can be partially protected by selling puts, known as *writing a covered put*. At a certain point, however, the potential loss can be unlimited. An investor who sells a stock short, then sells a put, also limits his potential profit.

 For Example: A customer sells short 100 RST at 55 and writes an RST 55 put for 2½ for partial protection. The maximum gain is $250. If the stock declines to zero and the put is exercised against him, the customer is obligated to pay $5,500 to buy the stock, losing $5,500. However, he receives a $5,500 gain from the short sale. Because he received the $250 premium, the stock can increase to 57½, the breakeven point, before the short stock position generates a loss, which is potentially unlimited.

Ratio Call Writing

Ratio call writing involves selling more calls than the long stock position covers. The ratio writer is subject to the same risks and gains as a covered writer on the covered position and as a naked writer on the uncovered position(s). If the owner of 100 shares of RST writes 2 RST 60 calls for 3, the customer has established one covered call and one uncovered call. The call options were written on a 2-to-1 (2:1) ratio against the stock. The stockholders uses ratio writing to increase premium income.

Multiple Option Transactions

Investors can simultaneously buy or sell more than one option contract on opposite sides of the market. Multiple option positions, such as **spreads**, **straddles** and **combinations**, can be used to speculate on a security's price movement, as well as to limit position costs or risks.

Spreads   A spread is the simultaneous purchase and sale of two options of the same class. A **call spread** is a long call and short call. A **put spread** is a long put and short put. The two options in a spread have different strike prices, expiration dates or both.

Types of Spreads

An investor can buy or sell three types of spreads.

Price Spread. A price spread, or **vertical spread**, is one in which the option bought and the option sold have the same expiration date and *different strike prices*. It is called a *vertical spread* because option tables report prices vertically.

> ✓ *For Example:* An investor could buy an RST Nov 50 call for $7 and sell an RST Nov 60 call for $3, for a net cost of $4.

Time Spread. A time spread, or **calendar spread,** includes option contracts with *different expiration dates*. The investor hopes to profit from the different rates at which the time values of the two options' premiums will erode. A time spread is also called a **horizontal spread** because expiration months are arranged horizontally on option tables.

> ✓ *For Example:* In October, an investor could sell an RST Nov 60 call for $3 and buy an RST Jan 60 call for $5, for a net cost of $2.

Diagonal Spread. A diagonal spread is one in which the options differ in both price and time. It's called a *diagonal spread* because a line drawn between the two options on option tables would be diagonal.

> ✓ *For Example:* An investor could sell an RST Nov 60 call for $3 and buy an RST Jan 55 call for $6, for a net cost of $3.

Figure 4.11 illustrates the three types of spreads.

Credit Spreads and Debit Spreads   When the option sold in a spread goes for a price lower than that of the option purchased, the investor pays money; therefore, it is known as a **debit spread**. When the option bought in a spread goes for a price lower than that of the option sold, the investor receives money; therefore, it is known as a **credit spread**.

The premiums for options with different strike prices always are different. The more a put or call is in-the-money, the higher the option premium. The more an option is out-of-the-money, the lower the premium.

FIGURE 4.11   The Three Types of Equity Spreads

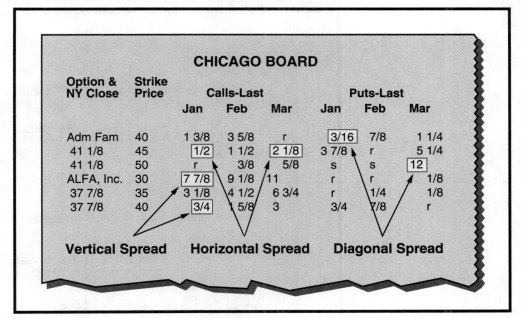

Take Note: When comparing the prices of two call options, the *call with the lower strike price **always has** a higher premium* than one with a higher strike price. When comparing the prices of two put options, the *put with the higher strike price **always has** a higher premium* than one with a lower strike price.

The greater an option's intrinsic value, the higher the premium. If a stock sells for $60, a call with a strike price of 50 has more intrinsic value than a 55 call and still more than a 60 call. A put with a strike price of 70 has more intrinsic value than a 65 put and still more than a 60 put. The more remote the liklihood an option will ever have any intrinsic value, the lower its premium will be.

The term "spread" is sometimes used to refer to the difference between the premiums of the two options rather than the difference between the strike prices. Strike prices do not change; premiums do. Whether investors who establish spreads want the premiums closer together or farther apart depends on whether a position is a credit or debit spread. Investors want the premium of debit spreads to be wider and credit spreads to be narrower.

For many people, a T chart is a useful tool in tracking multiple option transactions. Figure 4.12 illustrates a T chart.

FIGURE 4.12   Using the T Chart to Find Debits and Credits

The T Chart

Minus side of the transaction   Plus side of the transaction
(debit record, or DR)   (credit record, or CR)

	Paid (DR)	Received (CR)
Buy 1 DWQ 25 call at 4	– 4	
Write 1 DWQ 30 call at 1		+ 1
Net:	– 3	

This is a **debit** spread. Money is flowing **out** of the account.

	Paid (DR)	Received (CR)
Buy 1 DWQ 35 call at 2	– 2	
Write 1 DWQ 30 call at 6		+ 6
Net:		+ 4

This is a **credit** spread. Money is flowing **into** the account.

Debit Call Spread (Bull Call Spread)

A debit call spread requires the purchase of a call with a low strike price and the sale of a call with a higher strike price. Because a call with a low strike price is worth more than one with a high strike price, the investor pays for the spread, hence the name *debit spread*.

The debit call spread investor reduces the cost and potential profit of the long call position by selling the call with the higher strike price.

✓ **For Example:** An investor believes the price of RST, trading for $58, will trade into the mid 60s. He can buy 1 RST Nov 55 call for 6 and sell 1 Nov 60 call for 3, for a debit of $300. The two transactions give the investor the right to buy RST for 55 and the obligation to sell for 60. If the stock trades above $55 but below $60 at expiration, he can exercise the 55 call and the 60 call will expire unexercised. If the stock trades above 60, both calls will be exercised, and he will buy RST for $55, sell it for $60 and realize a $500 profit. After the $300 cost of the spread, the investor's net profit is $200. If the stock price remains below $55, both options will expire and the investor will lose the $300 debit (see Figure 4.13).

Maximum Gain. The maximum gain for a debit call spread is the difference between the options' two strike prices less the net premium (the net debit from the purchase and sale transactions). If the stock's market price is above the higher option's strike price, the investor can buy stock at the low strike, sell at the high strike and keep the difference between the two prices, less the net premium.

In the example above, the $5 difference between the two strike prices less the $3 premium paid equals the investor's maximum gain—$2.

Maximum Loss. If a stock's price is less than the lower option's strike price at expiration, both calls will expire worthless. The maximum loss on any debit spread is the net premium.

Breakeven. A debit call spread's breakeven point lies between the two options' strike prices. Breakeven occurs when the stock's market price is above the lower strike price by the net premium amount. The breakeven point on a call spread is the lower strike price plus the net premium.

In the example above, the breakeven point is the lower strike price, $55, plus the $3 net premium, which equals $58. At any price above $58, the investor makes money; at any price below, the investor begins to lose money.

Figure 4.13 illustrates the maximum gain, loss and breakeven point for a debit call spread.

✎ *Take Note:* In determining the breakeven point, **C**alls **A**dd to the **L**ower— **CAL**.

✍ *Before You Go On:* Calculate the net debit, maximum gain, maximum loss and breakeven point for each of the following debit call spreads.

1. With DCB trading for 26, Larry Long opens a debit spread by buying a Mar 25 call at 2½ and selling a Mar 30 call at ¾.
2. With SRQ trading for 45, Linda Long opens a debit spread by buying a Mar 45 call at 3¾ and selling a Mar 50 call at 1¾.
3. With XEO trading for 910, Lyle Long opens a debit call spread by buying a Mar 905 call at 22 and selling a Mar 915 call at 16.

Answers: 1. Larry's net debit is $175 (2½ − ¾ = 1¾); the maximum gain is $325 (30 − 25 = 5; 5 − 1¾ = 3¼); the maximum loss is the premium paid, which is $175 (1¾); the breakeven is 26¾ (25 + 1¾ = 26¾). 2. Linda's net debit is $200 (3¾ − 1¾ = 2); the maximum gain is $300 (50 − 45 = 5; 5 − 2 = 3); the maximum loss is the premium paid, which is $200 (2); the breakeven is $47 (45 + 2). 3. Lyle's net debit is $600 (22 − 16 = 6); the maximum gain is $400 (915 − 905 = 10; 10 − 6 = 4); the maximum loss is the premium paid, which is $600 (6); the breakeven is $911 (905 + 6).

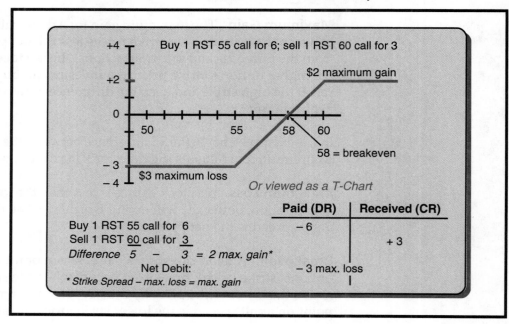

FIGURE 4.13   Gain, Loss and Breakeven on a Debit Call Spread

Credit Call Spread (Bear Call Spread)

A credit call spread requires buying a call with a high strike price and selling a call with a lower strike price. A call with a high strike price has a lower premium than a call with a low strike price, so the investor pays less for the purchase than he receives for the sale, creating a credit in the account.

A bearish investor sells a call spread, expecting the underlying stock's price to decline below the lower strike price. If it does, both options expire worthless and the investor keeps the net premium.

If the investor is wrong and the stock price increases, the investor's losses are limited. The long option can be exercised to buy the stock, which will then have to be delivered against the short option. The investor loses the difference between the two options' strike prices, but keeps the net premium.

✔ **For Example:** An investor believes the price of RST, trading for $58, will decline. He can sell 1 RST Nov 55 call for 6 and buy 1 Nov 60 call for 3, for a credit of $300. The two transactions convey the obligation to sell RST for 55 and the right to buy RST for 60. If the stock trades above $55 but below $60 at expiration, the 55 call will be exercised, the investor will have to sell the stock for 55, and the 60 call will expire.

If the stock trades above 60, both calls will be in-the-money. The owner of the 55 call would force the investor to sell 100 shares of stock at 55. This investor,

FIGURE 4.14   Gain, Loss and Breakeven on a Credit Call Spread

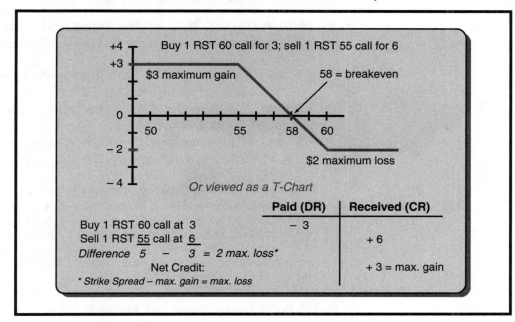

however, is long a 60 call and can buy the stock for 60, for a net cost of $500. After the $300 credit he received, his net loss is $200.

If the stock price remains below $55, both options will expire and the investor will keep the $300 credit (see Figure 4.14).

Maximum Gain. The most an investor can gain in a credit call spread, as with any credit position, is the net premium. The maximum gain occurs when the stock price is below the lower strike price.

In the example above, if RST closes below $55 at expiration, neither call will be exercised, allowing the option seller to keep the net premium.

Maximum Loss. A credit call spread reduces risk substantially compared with naked call writing. A credit call spread's maximum loss is the difference between strike prices less the net premium. The maximum loss occurs when the stock's price is at or above the higher strike price.

Breakeven. An investor breaks even when the stock's market price equals the lower strike price plus the net premium. The breakeven is the same for the credit spread as it is for the debit spread.

Figure 4.14 illustrates the maximum gain, loss and breakeven for a credit call spread.

✎ **Take Note:** Whether it is a credit or a debit spread, **C**alls **A**dd to the **L**ower—
CAL.

✍ **Before You Go On:** Calculate the net credit, maximum gain, maximum loss
and breakeven for each of the following call spreads.

1. With DCB trading for 26, Sean Short opens a credit spread by selling a Mar
   25 call at 2½ and buying a Mar 30 call at ¾.
2. With SRQ trading for 45, Sue Short opens a credit spread by selling a Mar
   45 call at 3¾ and buying a Mar 50 call at 1¾.
3. With XEO trading for 910, Sam Short opens a credit call spread by selling
   a Mar 905 call at 22 and buying a Mar 915 call at 16.

Answers: 1. Sean's net credit is $175 (2½ − ¾ = 1¾); the maximum gain is the net credit of
$175 (1¾); the maximum loss is $325 (30 − 25 = 5; 5 − 1¾ = 3¼); the breakeven is 26¾ on
the stock (25 + 1¾ = 26¾). 2. Sue's net credit is $200 (3¾ − 1¾ = 2); the maximum gain is
the net credit of $200 (2); the maximum loss is $300 (50 − 45 = 5; 5 − 2 = 3); the breakeven
is 47 on the stock (45 + 2 = 47). 3. Sam's net credit is $600 (22 − 16 = 6); the maximum gain
is the net credit of $600 (6); the maximum loss is $400 (915 − 905 = 10; 10 − 6 = 4); the
breakeven is 911 on the stock (905 + 6).

Debit Put Spread (Bear Put Spread)

A debit put spread requires buying a put with a high strike price and selling
one with a lower strike price. A put with a high strike price is worth more
than one with a lower strike price, so money flows out of the account.

A bearish investor who establishes a debit put spread reduces the put's cost
and limits her potential gain by selling the put with the lower strike price.

✓ **For Example:** An investor believes the price of RST, trading for $58, will
decline. He can buy 1 RST Nov 60 put for 5 and sell 1 Nov 55 put for 2½, for
a debit of $250. The two transactions convey the right to sell RST for 60 and
the obligation to buy RST for 55. If the stock trades below $60 but above $55
at expiration, the investor can exercise the 60 put to sell the stock for 60 and
the 55 put will expire. If the stock trades below 55, both puts will be exercised, and he will sell RST for $60, buy it for $55, and take in $500. After the
$250 debit he paid, his net gain is $250. If the stock price is above $60 at
expiration, both puts will expire and the investor will lose the $250 debit (see
Figure 4.15).

Maximum Gain. The maximum gain for a debit put spread occurs when the
stock's price is at or below the lower option's strike price at expiration. As
with debit call spreads, the maximum gain is the difference between the two
strike prices less the premium paid.

Maximum Loss. If the stock's price is above the higher option's strike price
at expiration, both puts will expire worthless. The maximum loss on a debit
spread, put or call, is the net premium paid.

FIGURE 4.15   **Gain, Loss and Breakeven on a Debit Put Spread**

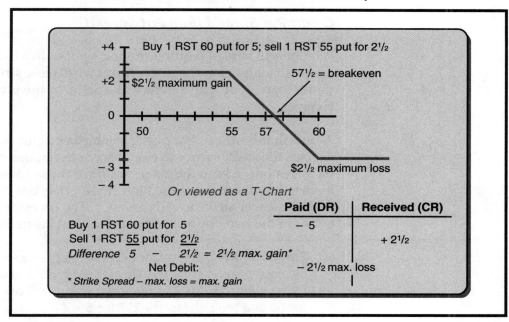

Breakeven. An investor breaks even when the stock's market price is below the higher strike price by the amount of the net premium paid. The breakeven point on a put spread is the higher strike price minus the net premium.

Figure 4.15 illustrates the maximum gain, loss and breakeven point for a debit put spread.

Take Note: In calculating the breakeven for a put spread, **P**uts **S**ubtract from the **H**igher—**PSH**.

Before You Go On: Calculate the net debit, maximum gain, maximum loss and breakeven for each of the following put spreads.

    1. With DCB trading for 25½, Dave Debit opens a debit put spread by buying a Mar 30 put at 5¼ and selling a Mar 25 put at 2¼.

    2. With SRQ trading for 45, Donna Debit opens a debit put spread by buying a Mar 50 put at 4¼ and selling a Mar 45 put at 1¾.

    3. With XEO trading for 910, Dan Debit opens a debit put spread by buying a Mar 915 put at 18 and selling a Mar 905 put at 14.

Answers: 1. Dave's net debit is $300 (5¼ – 2¼ = 3); the maximum gain is $200 (30 – 25 = 5; 5 – 3 = 2); the maximum loss is the premium paid, which is $300 (3); the breakeven is 27 on the stock (30 – 3). 2. Donna's net debit is $250 (4¼ – 1¾ = 2½); the maximum gain is $250 (50 – 45 = 5; 5 – 2½ = 2½); the maximum loss is the premium paid, which is $250 (2½); the breakeven is 47½ on the stock (50 – 2½ = 47½). 3. Dan's net debit is $400 (18 – 14 = 4); the maximum gain is $600 (915 − 905 = 10; 10 − 4 = 6); the maximum loss is the premium paid, which is $400 (4); the breakeven is 911 on the stock (915 − 4 = 911).

Credit Put Spread (Bull Put Spread)

A credit put spread requires buying a put with a low strike price and selling one with a higher strike price. A put with a low strike price has a lower premium than a put with a high strike price, so the investor pays less than he receives.

A bullish investor sells a put or establishes a put credit spread because she expects the stock's price to rise. If so, both options can expire worthless and the investor can keep the net premium. If the stock declines, the investor may have to buy the stock at the high strike price, but can then exercise the put with the lower strike to sell the stock. The investor loses the difference between the two options' strike prices, but keeps the net premium.

✓ **For Example:** An investor believes the price of RST, trading for $58, will increase. He can sell 1 RST Nov 60 put for 5 and buy 1 Nov 55 put for 2½, for a credit of $250. The two transactions convey the obligation to buy RST for 60 and the right to sell RST for 55.

If the stock trades below $60 but above $55 at expiration, the 60 put will be exercised, the investor will have to buy the stock for 60, and the 55 put will expire.

If the stock trades below 55, both puts will be exercised and he will buy RST for $60, then sell it for $55, a $500 loss. After the $250 credit he received, his net loss is $250. If the stock price is above $60 at expiration, both options will expire and the investor will keep the $250 credit (see Figure 4.16).

Maximum Gain. A credit put spread's maximum gain is the net premium received. The maximum gain occurs when the stock price is at or above the higher strike price.

Maximum Loss. A credit put spread's maximum loss is the difference between strike prices minus the net premium. The maximum loss occurs when the stock's market price is at or below the lower strike price.

Breakeven. A credit put spread's breakeven point is the higher strike price minus the net premium.

Figure 4.16 illustrates the maximum gain, loss and breakeven point for a credit put spread.

✎ **Take Note:** Remember, **P**uts **S**ubtract from the **H**igher—**PSH**.

FIGURE 4.16   Gain, Loss and Breakeven on a Credit Put Spread

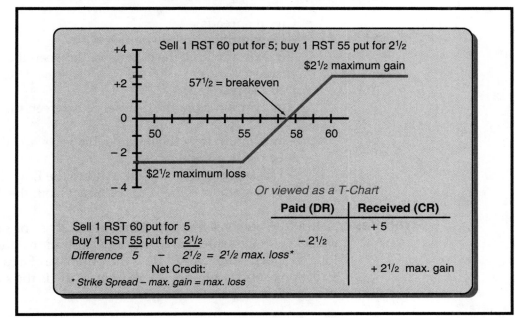

✍ *Before You Go On:* Calculate the net credit, maximum gain, maximum loss and breakeven for each of the following put spreads.

1. With DCB trading for 25½, Clyde Credit opens a credit put spread with a Mar 30 put at 5¼ and a Mar 25 put at 2¼.
2. With SRQ trading for 45, Carmine Credit opens a credit put spread with a Mar 50 put at 4¼ and a Mar 45 put at 1¾.
3. With XEO trading for 910, Calvin Credit opens a credit put spread with a Mar 915 put at 18 and a Mar 905 put at 14.

Answers: 1. Clyde's net credit is $300 (5¼ – 2¼ = 3); the maximum gain is the net credit, which is $300 (3); the maximum loss is $200 (30 – 25 = 5; 5 – 3 = 2); the breakeven is 27 on the stock (30 – 3 = 27). 2. Carmine's net credit is $250 (4¼ – 1¾ = 2½); the maximum gain is the net credit, which is $250 (50 – 45 = 5; 5 – 2½ = 2½); the maximum loss is $250 (2½); the breakeven is 47½ on the stock (50 – 2½ = 47½). 3. Calvin's net credit is $400 (18 – 14 = 4); the maximum gain is the net credit, which is $400 (4); the maximum loss is $600 (915 – 905 = 10; 10 – 4 = 6); the breakeven is 911 on the stock (915 – 4 = 911).

Rules of Thumb for Risk and Reward on Spreads

✎ *Take Note:* Here is a quick way to identify bull spreads and bear spreads: if the position is long the lower strike price, the position is bullish; if it is short the lower strike, the position is bearish.

Following are the rules to remember to determine gains, losses and breakeven points for spreads:

- Credit spreads
  - maximum gain: the initial credit
  - maximum loss: the difference between the strike prices minus the credit
- Debit spreads
  - maximum gain: the difference between the strike prices minus the debit
  - maximum loss: the initial debit
- Breakeven points
  - call spreads: CAL—Calls Add to the Lower
  - put spreads: PSH—Puts Subtract from the Higher

Straddles   A straddle involves the simultaneous purchase or sale of a call and a put on a stock with the same strike price and expiration date. Straddles can be either long or short. A **long straddle** is the purchase of a call and put with the same strike price and expiration. A **short straddle** is the sale of a call and put with the same strike price and expiration.

Long Straddle

An investor who uses a long straddle expects the stock's price to be volatile, but is unsure which direction the price will take. Because both options in a straddle have the same strike price, sufficient price movement *in either direction* can make a long straddle profitable for an investor.

✓ **For Example:** An investor believes the price of RST, trading for $60, will move either up or down dramatically. He can buy 1 RST Nov 60 put for 3¼ and buy 1 Nov 60 call for 3½, for a total cost of $675 (6¾). The two transactions convey the right to sell RST for 60 and the right to buy RST for 60. If the stock trades below $60 at expiration, the 60 put can be exercised to sell the stock for 60 and the call will expire.

If the stock trades above 60, the call can be exercised to buy the stock for 60 and the put will expire. If the stock trades above or below 60 by an amount greater than the total cost, 6¾, either the put or the call can be exercised at a profit. If the stock trades above or below 60 by an amount less than 6¾, either the put or the call can be exercised, but the proceeds will be less than the straddle's cost and the strategy will realize a loss.

If the stock trades for $60 at expiration, both the put and the call will expire worthless, generating the maximum loss on the straddle—6¾ (see Figure 4.17).

Maximum Gain. The maximum gain for a long straddle is determined by how far up or down the stock price moves. Because the potential gain on the

FIGURE 4.17   Gain, Loss and Breakeven on a Long Straddle

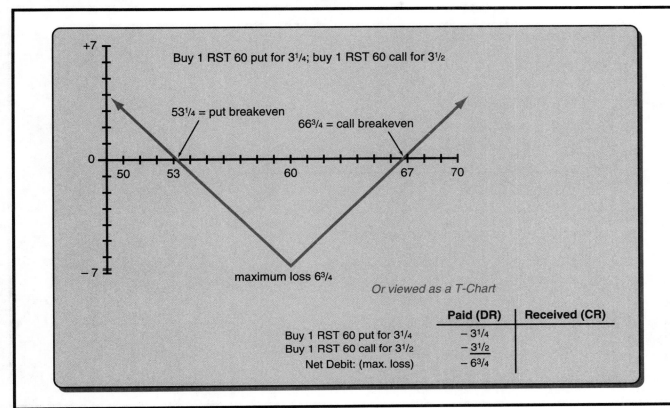

Buy 1 RST 60 put for 3¼; buy 1 RST 60 call for 3½

53¼ = put breakeven

66¾ = call breakeven

maximum loss 6¾

Or viewed as a T-Chart

	Paid (DR)	Received (CR)
Buy 1 RST 60 put for 3¼	− 3¼	
Buy 1 RST 60 call for 3½	− 3½	
Net Debit: (max. loss)	− 6¾	

long call is unlimited, the potential gain for a straddle is unlimited. The potential gain on the put option is the strike price less the premium paid, which occurs if the underlying stock price declines to zero. The maximum gain for a long straddle, therefore, is unlimited.

Maximum Loss. The entire premium is lost when the stock sells for the strike price at expiration because neither option is worth exercising.

Breakeven. If the stock price is between the strike price plus or minus the total premium, a long straddle loses some money. Long straddles have two breakeven points: one on the call strike price plus both premiums; the other on the put strike price minus both premiums. The call breakeven is the strike price plus the total premiums; the put breakeven is the strike price minus the total premiums paid.

Short Straddle

An investor who writes a straddle believes the stock's price will not change much and will not move outside the breakeven points.

FIGURE 4.18   Gain, Loss and Breakeven on a Short Straddle

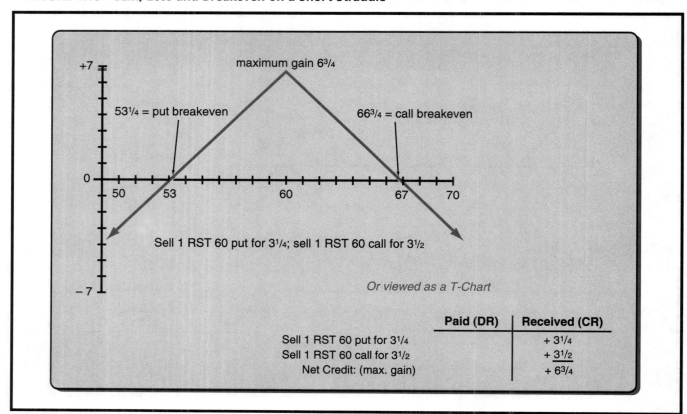

maximum gain 6¾

53¼ = put breakeven

66¾ = call breakeven

Sell 1 RST 60 put for 3¼; sell 1 RST 60 call for 3½

Or viewed as a T-Chart

	Paid (DR)	Received (CR)
Sell 1 RST 60 put for 3¼		+ 3¼
Sell 1 RST 60 call for 3½		+ 3½
Net Credit: (max. gain)		+ 6¾

✓ **For Example:** An investor believes the price of RST, trading for $60, will move neither up nor down in the near future. He can sell 1 RST Nov 60 put for 3¼ and sell 1 Nov 60 call for 3½, for a net premium of $675 (6¾). The two transactions convey the obligation to sell RST for 60 and the obligation to buy RST for 60.

If the stock trades below $60 at expiration, the 60 put will be exercised, the investor will have to buy the stock for 60, and the call will expire. If the stock trades above 60, the call will be exercised, he will have to sell the stock for 60, and the put will expire.

If the stock trades above or below 60 by an amount greater than the total premiums received, 6¾, either the put or the call will be exercised, creating a loss on the stock transaction that is more than the premiums received.

If the stock trades above or below 60 by an amount less than 6¾, either the put or the call can be exercised, but the proceeds will be less than the straddle premiums, giving the investor a profit. If the stock trades for $60 at expiration, both the put and the call will expire worthless, generating the maximum gain—6¾ (see Figure 4.18).

Maximum Gain. The maximum potential gain for a short straddle is the initial premiums received.

Maximum Loss. If the stock price is above or below the option's strike price by more than the combined premium amount, a short straddle loses money. The maximum potential loss for the short call is unlimited; therefore, the maximum loss for a short straddle is unlimited.

Breakeven. Short straddles have the same two breakeven points as long straddles: the call breakeven is the strike price plus the two premiums; the put breakeven is the strike price minus both premiums.

Combinations Combinations are similar to straddles. Unlike a straddle, however, a combination involves options with different strike prices, expiration dates or both.

A **long combination** is the purchase of a call and a put on the same stock with different strike prices or expiration dates. A **short combination** is the sale of a call and a put on the same stock with different strike prices or expiration dates.

Long Combination

An investor uses a long combination instead of a long straddle when she expects a sharp movement in the market. Long combinations are usually cheaper to establish than long straddles because most long combinations are established when both contracts are out-of-the-money.

✓ *For Example:* An investor believes the price of RST, trading for $58, will move either up or down in the near future. He can buy 1 RST Nov 55 put for 2½ and buy 1 Nov 60 call for 3, for a net premium of $550 (5½). The two transactions convey the right to sell RST for 55 and the right to buy RST for 60.

If the stock trades below 55 at expiration, the 55 put can be exercised to sell the stock for 55 and the call will expire.

If the stock trades above 60, the call can be exercised to buy the stock for 60 and the put will expire. If the stock trades below 55 or above 60 by an amount greater than the total premiums paid, 5½, either the put or the call can be exercised at a profit for the combination.

If the stock trades between 55 and 60, neither the put nor the call is worth exercising and both will expire worthless.

Maximum Gain. Because the maximum gain for the long call in a combination is limitless, the maximum gain for a long combination is limitless.

Maximum Loss. If the stock price remains between 55 and 60, both sides of the combination will expire unexercised and the investor will lose the premiums paid. The maximum loss on a long combination, as with any long position, is the premiums paid.

Breakeven. The breakeven points for a combination are the call strike price plus the total premiums, and the put strike price minus the total premiums.

Short Combination

An investor uses a short combination instead of a short straddle when she expects no movement in the market. The writer collects the premiums and keeps them if both sides expire unexercised. The maximum loss potential is unlimited because the short call is uncovered. The breakeven points for a short combination are the same as those for a long.

✍ *Before You Go On:* With RST trading for 58, identify which of the following transactions has(have) unlimited risk.

1. Sell an RST 65 call.
2. Enter a short combination on RST with a 55 put and a 65 call.
3. Sell short 100 shares of RST and sell an RST 65 put.
4. Enter a short straddle on RST with a 60 put and a 60 call.

Answer: Each position exposes the investor to unlimited risk.

Nonequity Options

Nonequity options function, for the most part, the same as equity options: bulls buy calls or sell puts; bears buy puts or sell calls. Because the underlying instruments are not stocks, nonequity options have different contract sizes and delivery and exercise standards. This section covers the basic characteristics of index, interest rate and foreign currency options.

Index Options   Options on stock indexes are relatively new, but stock indexes that measure the movements of markets or market segments have been around for decades. The two primary types of indexes are described below:

- **Broad-based indexes** reflect the movement of the market as a whole. Options are available on the S&P 100, the S&P 500 and the Dow Jones Industrial Average, all broad-based indexes.
- **Narrow-based indexes** track the movements of market segments, such as a group of stocks in one industry. Narrow-based indexes include the Technology Index and the Pharmaceutical Index, among others.

Options on Indexes. Indexes are not securities; they are measures of the overall market or market segments. Investors cannot buy or sell an index. Because indexes track groups of investments with changing values, investors can speculate on the direction, degree and timing of such changes by buying or selling options on the indexes. Index options can be used to speculate on or protect against market movements.

Contract Specifications

Quotation Multiplier. Indexes normally use a multiplier of $100 to convert the strike prices and the premiums into dollar values. An S&P 500 Index (SPX) Jun 940 call at 12 represents a cash value of $94,000 and a premium of $1,200.

✎ *Take Note:* Think of an index option as a stock option with a very high price—in the example above, an option on a $940 stock.

Exercise and Settlement. Index options settle in cash rather than in the delivery of a security. If an option is exercised, the writer delivers cash equal to the intrinsic value—the in-the-money amount—to the buyer.

✓ *For Example:* The writer of an SPX 980 call would have to deliver $1,000 in cash if the SPX is 990 at expiration. The writer of an SPX 980 put would have to deliver $1,000 if the SPX is 970 at expiration.

Cash settlement creates a special risk because it means that all short calls on indexes are naked unless hedged with spreads. A writer cannot cover a call by owning the index, as a stock option writer can cover a call by owning the underlying stock.

If an index option is exercised, its settlement price is based on the *closing value* for the S&P 100 the day of exercise, *not* the value at the time of exercise. This is a significant risk for the option holder because an option exercised in the morning for a significant gain may lose money if the market changes direction in the afternoon.

Dates and Times. Trading in index options takes place between 9:30 a.m. and 4:15 p.m. EST for broad-based indexes and until 4:02 p.m. EST for narrow-based indexes. The daily exercise cut-off occurs at 4:15 p.m. EST. Settlement occurs one business day after exercise. In Figure 4.19, the expiration months are May, June and July. The expiration date is the Saturday following the third Friday of the expiration month.

Position and Exercise Limits. The number of index option contracts investors can establish and exercise is limited, to prevent investors from influencing the market. Some index options have a position limit of 25,000 contracts on the same side of the market and an exercise limit of 15,000 contracts in five

FIGURE 4.19   Index Option Transactions

Options
Chicago Board

S&P 100 Index – $100 times index

Strike Price	Calls–Last			Puts–Last		
	May	Jun	Jul	May	Jun	Jul
350	....	....	....	3/8	1 7/16	2 5/8
355	....	....	....	1/2	1 13/16	3 3/8
360	24 1/4	....	....	11/16	2 3/8	4 1/8
365	21 1/4	....	....	15/16	3	5 1/4
370	17 1/4	18	19 7/8	1 3/8	4 1/4	5 3/4
375	12 5/8	14 5/8	....	2 1/8	5 1/8	7 7/8
380	8 1/2	12	14 3/4	3 1/4	6 5/8	8 5/8
385	5 1/4	9 1/8	11 1/2	5 1/8	8 1/2	10 1/2
390	2 15/16	6 3/8	8 5/8	7 7/8	11 1/8	13
395	1 1/2	4 1/4	5 3/8	12	16	....
400	3/4	2 11/16	4	16	20 1/4	....

Total call volume 112,492   Total call open interest 291,317
Total put volume 117,237   Total put open interest 318,021
The index: High 386.25; Low 381.70; Close 386.24; +1.62

S&P 500 Index – $100 times index

Strike Price	Calls–Last			Puts–Last		
	May	Jun	Jul	May	Jun	Jul
350	....	....	....	....	11/16	....
355	....	....	....	....	13/16	....
360	....	....	....	....	1 1/8	....
365	....	....	....	7/16	....	....
370	39	....	....	5/8	....	....
375	34	37 1/4	....	5/8	2 1/16	....
380	31 3/8	....	....	5/8	2 1/4	....
385	....	....	....	1 1/8	2 5/8	....
390	20	....	....	1 1/8	3 1/2	5 7/8
395	15 3/8	....	....	1 5/8	4 1/2	6 5/8
400	13 1/8	16 1/2	....	2 3/8	5 5/8	....

Total call volume 12,524   Total call open interest 317,476
Total put volume 29,314   Total put open interest 481,160
The index: High 391.60; Low 386.86; Close 386.90; +1.79

days on the same side of the market. The position limits are subject to change and vary with different types of options.

✓ **For Example:** When the position limit is 25,000 contracts, an investor with 10,000 long calls could not be short more than 15,000 puts because long calls and short puts are both on the bullish side of the market.

Capped Index Options

Capped index options have a "capped" price set by the exchange that triggers automatic exercise of the options when the capped price is reached. Capped index calls and puts are listed initially with the strike price nearest to the value of the underlying index. The **cap interval** is normally set at 30 points above the strike price for a call and 30 points below the strike price for a put. When the index hits or goes through the capped price, the option is automatically exercised. If a capped index option is not automatically exercised before the expiration date, it can be exercised at expiration. The index multiplier of $100 is used to convert strike prices and premiums into dollars.

✓ **For Example:** If the SPX index is 940, capped SPX calls would be listed with a strike price of 940 and a capped price of 970, and capped SPX puts would be listed with a strike price of 940 and a capped price of 910.

Because capped index options limit a position's risk and potential gain, they are similar to spreads.

Capped index options on both the S&P 100 and the S&P 500 are traded on the CBOE.

Index Options Summary

Buying calls or puts on indexes allows an investor to:

- speculate on the direction of the market without the selection risk associated with equity options;
- protect a portfolio or generate income for the portfolio; or
- hedge against systemic risk (sometimes called "systematic risk").

Interest Rate Options

Interest rate options allow investors to speculate on or protect against fluctuations in interest rates. The two types of interest rate options are price based and yield based.

Price-Based Options

Price-based interest rate options, as the name implies, are options on the price changes of U.S. government debt securities caused by interest rates movements. The contract size for an interest rate option is $100,000 for Treasury notes and bonds and $1 million for Treasury bills.

The value of Treasury bills, notes and bonds moves inversely with interest rates: as interest rates rise, bond prices fall. Therefore, an investor who expects interest rates to decline and bond values to rise would buy price-based calls or sell puts. An investor who expects interest rates to increase and bond prices to decline would buy price-based puts or sell calls.

FIGURE 4.20 Interest Rate Option Table

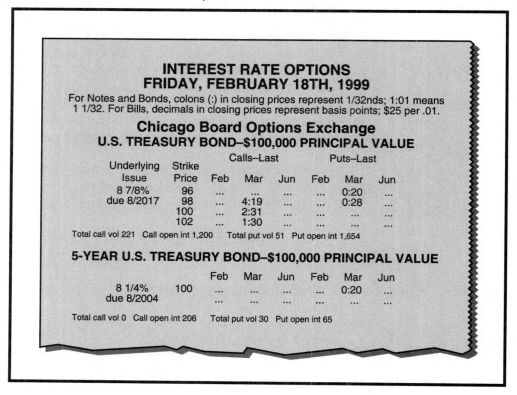

Treasury Notes and Bonds. Treasury notes are issued for maturities of 1 to 10 years and pay semiannual interest. Bonds are issued with maturities of 10 or more years. An option on either a note or a bond represents a specific underlying security with a face value of $100,000. Upon an option's exercise, the owner of a put or the writer of a call must deliver a specific note or bond.

Strike prices for options on notes and bonds are quoted as percentages of face value. In Figure 4.20, an option on the 8⅞ percent bond has a strike price of 102. The owner of a Mar call on the bond can exercise the option to purchase the bond for 102 percent of face value, or $102,000.

One point of premium equals 1 percent of the note's or bond's face value, or $1,000. In Figure 4.20, Mar 98 puts on the 8⅞ percent bonds are trading at a premium of :28. The premium quotes are expressed in 1/32 of a point, as are Treasury note and bond quotes. A premium of :28, then, equals 28/32 of 1 percent of the bond's face value, or $875. The premium for a Mar 102 call on the 8⅞ percent bond is 1:30, equal to $1,000 plus 30/32 of $1,000, or $1,937.50. Table 4.3 illustrates how to calculate note and bond option premiums.

TABLE 4.3   Premiums on Note and Bond Options

The contract's face value	$100,000
has a one-point premium	x 1% (.01)
or	= $1,000
Since quotes are in 32nds,	$1,000 ÷ 32 = 31.25
then	:28
equals	(1 ÷ 32) x 28
or	= .875 or $875
Therefore, a quote of	1:30
is equal to	$1,000
plus	(1 ÷ 32) x 30
or	+ $937.50
which equals	= $1,937.50

Expiration and Exercise. Expiration of interest rate options is the Saturday following the third Friday of the month. Two business days after the option's exercise, the call writer or put buyer must deliver the underlying note or bond. The investor who receives the security must pay the exercise price plus accrued interest, as in a normal bond transaction.

Treasury Bills. T bills are sold at a discount from par value and do not pay interest. One T bill option represents $1 million worth of a future issue of the 13-week bill rather than the current T bill. Therefore, an investor cannot write a covered call on a T bill because the deliverable bills are not yet issued.

Because the T bill has not been issued, an investor who writes a T bill call does not know the price at which the bill will be issued. Rather, the investor expects the T bills issued closest to expiration to be trading at a price lower than the strike price, just as a call writer on a stock wants the stock to trade below the exercise price. If an option is exercised, settlement takes place on the Thursday following exercise.

The premium is an annualized percentage of the face value, $1 million. Although 1 percent of $1 million is $10,000, the T bill's life span is 13 weeks, one-fourth of a 52-week year. Each point, therefore, equals $2,500, one-fourth of $10,000. To turn a T bill premium quote into a dollar figure, multiply it by $2,500. An investor interested in purchasing a T bill call quoted at a premium of .5 would pay $1,250.

✓ *For Example:* A portfolio manager believes that interest rates will fall, thus causing bond prices to rise. The manager would, therefore, buy price-based interest rate call options.

Yield-Based Options

Yield-based options allow an investor to profit from or protect against the *change in yield* of Treasury securities. Traded on the CBOE, interest-based options are available on the most recently issued:

- 13-week Treasury bill
- 5-year and 10-year Treasury notes
- 30-year Treasury bond

Investors use yield-based options for the same purpose as price-based debt options—to speculate on or protect against interest rate risk. However, yield-based options have a contract size multiplier of $100 and settle in cash rather than in delivery of the underlying security.

A yield-based option's strike price reflects the underlying security's annualized yield to maturity. A strike price of 65 equals a yield of 6.5 percent. Yield-based options are exercised European style, on the trading day prior to expiration.

Whereas debt securities' *prices* have an *inverse* relationship to interest rates, their *yields* have a *direct* relationship. When interest rates rise, yields rise. Thus, an investor expecting interest rates to increase buys yield-based calls.

✓ *For Example:* An investor who believes interest rates are rising buys a yield-based call with a strike price of 65. Interest rates rise to 7.5 percent, and the investor receives, in cash, the difference between the strike price of 65 and the exercise settlement value of 75, times the multiplier of 100, or a total of $1,000.

In the same way, an investor who expects rates to decline buys yield-based puts.

✓ *For Example:* An investor who believes interest rates are declining buys a yield-based put with a strike price of 75. If interest rates decline to 6.5 percent, the investor, upon exercise, receives, in cash, the difference between the strike price of 75 and the exercise settlement value of 65. The investor's profit is the difference between the strike price and the exercise settlement value, less the premium paid. If the strike price is 75 and the exercise settlement value is 65, the difference equals 10. Multiply this by $100 to calculate the settlement amount, which equals $1,000. If the premium cost 3¼, the put buyer's profit is $1,000 minus $325, which equals $675.

FIGURE 4.21 Inverse Relationship Between Two Currencies

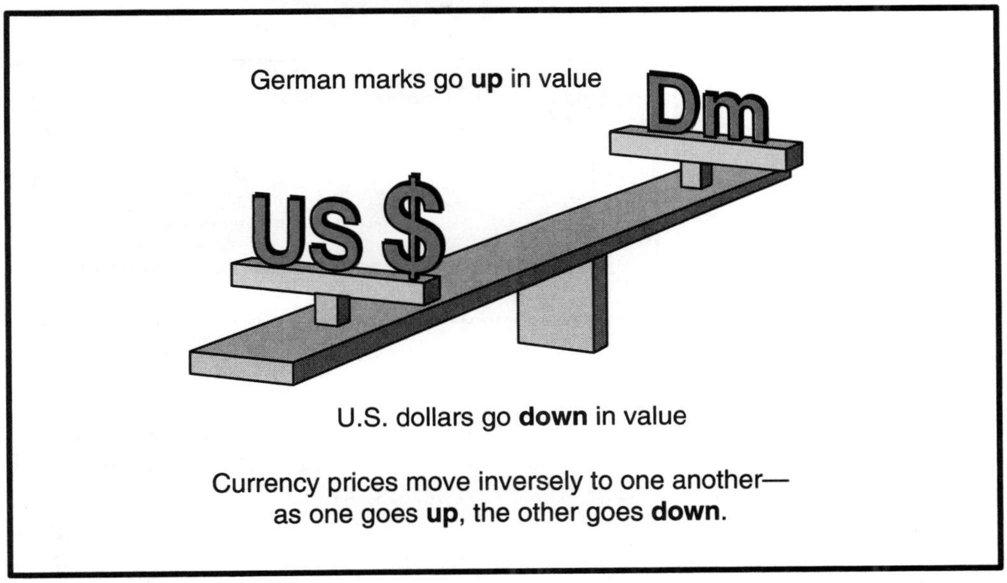

German marks go **up** in value

U.S. dollars go **down** in value

Currency prices move inversely to one another—
as one goes **up**, the other goes **down**.

Foreign Currency Options A currency's value fluctuates relative to other world currencies based on supply and demand.

✓ *For Example:* If $1 can be exchanged for 2 German marks, it could also be said that it takes $.50 to buy 1 German mark.

A multitude of economic and political factors can affect the stability of a particular currency's value at any given time. As a result, currencies constantly fluctuate in value relative to other currencies. Because the U.S. dollar is the predominant currency of international trade, currency fluctuations are measured relative to the dollar. No options are traded on the U.S. dollar in the domestic securities markets.

✓ *For Example:* If it now takes $.60 to buy 1 German mark, it takes more dollars to buy marks. The mark is said to be strong against the dollar, or the dollar weak relative to the mark. If it takes $.40 to buy 1 mark, it takes fewer dollars to buy marks. The mark is said to be weak against the dollar, or the dollar strong relative to the mark.

An inverse relationship exists between the exchange rates of two currencies: as one rises, the other falls (see Figure 4.21).

Investors can use foreign currency options (FCOs) to speculate on or protect against fluctuating currency exchange rates.

FIGURE 4.22 Currency Contract Specifications

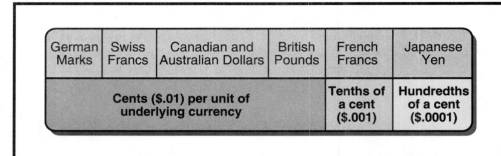

German Marks	Swiss Francs	Canadian and Australian Dollars	British Pounds	French Francs	Japanese Yen
Cents ($.01) per unit of underlying currency				Tenths of a cent ($.001)	Hundredths of a cent ($.0001)

Currency Risk. Currency exchange rate fluctuation is a significant risk for companies that do business in foreign countries. U.S. corporations with contracts to buy or sell goods in Germany for marks, for instance, can use currency options to protect against changes in the exchange rate between the dollar and the mark.

Characteristics of Foreign Currency Options. Foreign currency options are traded on the Philadelphia Stock Exchange (PHLX). Each FCO contract represents a specific amount of foreign currency. The exchange sets the amount. The options' strike prices are stated in U.S. dollars, with each contract representing the right to buy or sell the foreign currency for the specified dollar amount.

If the foreign currency rises, requiring more dollars to buy it, a call owner can purchase the currency at the cheaper strike price. The owner of a foreign currency call option, therefore, can lock in a certain exchange rate for a period of time, just as the owner of a stock option can lock in the stock's purchase price for a period of time.

✓ *For Example:* In March, $.56 buys 1 German mark. USA Imports, Inc., contracts to buy $5.6 million in goods from a German supplier. Payment for the goods is to be made in 10 million German marks and is due in three months. To lock in the current exchange rate of $.56 to 1 mark, USA Imports buys calls on the German mark. By doing so, it locks in the exchange rate.

Underlying Currencies. Currency options are available on British pounds, Canadian dollars, German marks, French francs, Japanese yen, Swiss francs and others, and all are based on the currency's value relative to the U.S. dollar. Therefore, no options are traded in domestic markets on the U.S. dollar. Figure 4.22 illustrates the different contract quote characteristics for the most common currency option contracts.

✎ *Take Note:* You need not memorize the chart. Just be familiar with it so you're not surprised to see these numbers on the exam.

FIGURE 4.23   Foreign Currency Option Table

Foreign Currency Options
Philadelphia

Thursday, May 22, 1998

Option & Underlying	Strike Price	Calls–Last			Puts–Last		
		May	Jun	Jul	May	Jun	Jul
50,000 Australian Dollars-cents per unit.							
ADollr	75	r	r	r	0.26	0.49	r
76.33	76	0.25	r	r	0.47	1.18	r
31,250 British Pounds–European Style.							
BPound	167 1/2	r	r	r	r	0.55	r
31,250 British Pounds–cents per unit.							
BPound	157 1/2	r	r	r	r	0.05	r
176.28	167 1/2	r	r	r	r	0.58	r
176.28	170	r	r	r	r	1.08	3.60
176.28	172 1/2	r	r	r	0.56	r	r
62,500 German Marks–cents per unit.							
DMark	56	r	r	r	r	r	0.59
60.14	57 1/2	2.66	r	s	r	0.28	s
60.14	58	r	r	r	0.12	r	1.23
60.14	58 1/2	r	r	s	0.20	0.48	s
6,250,000 Japanese Yen-100ths of a cent per unit.							
JYen	70	r	r	r	r	0.07	r
74.58	71	r	r	r	r	0.12	0.55
74.58	72	r	r	r	r	0.26	r
74.58	73	r	r	s	0.20	r	1.16

Price of the Underlying Currency. The sample currency option table in Figure 4.23 lists current exchange rates in U.S. currency per unit of the underlying currency. Exchange rates are quoted in U.S. cents per unit of the underlying currency, with two exceptions: French francs trade in 1/10 of a cent per franc; Japanese yen trade in 1/100 of a cent per yen.

✓ **For Example:** The British pound was trading at 176.28 at the end of the trading day on Thursday, May 22. Therefore, a U.S. importer could exchange 176.28 cents American ($1.76 plus 28/100 of a cent) for 1 British pound. On the same day, Japanese yen closed at 74.58 (.7458 cents, or $.007458 per yen).

Contract Sizes. Because FCOs are designed to meet the needs of institutions, one option contract covers a large amount of currency. In Figure 4.23, contract sizes are listed in the left-hand column, just above the exchange rate for the previous day. A call on British pounds on the PHLX represents a contract for 31,250 pounds, for instance.

Premium quotes use the same units of U.S. currency employed in quoting exchange rates on the underlying instruments. To calculate both exchange rates and premium values, multiply the value per unit by one unit's equivalent stated in dollar terms. For instance, one cent equals $.01. One one-hundredth of a cent, as in the yen contract, equals $.0001.

The premium on the May 172½ put on the British pound was .56. Because the premiums are quoted in U.S. cents, the writer receives .56 cents per British pound in the contract, or $.0056. Because each contract represents 31,250 pounds, the writer receives $175 ($.0056 × 31,250). Table 4.4 illustrates how to calculate the premium value for the German mark.

Expiration Date and Last Trading Day. All FCOs expire on the Friday preceding the third Wednesday of the month. Trading ceases at 1:30 p.m. EST on the expiration date. The PHLX trades FCOs from 2:30 a.m. until 2:30 p.m. EST, and the trading hours are likely to be extended to meet the growing demands of the global markets.

Position and Exercise Limits. On the PHLX, position and exercise limits are 200,000 contracts on the *same side* of the market.

Exercise Settlement. All PHLX options can be exercised either American style, at any time up to and including the last business day before expiration, or European style, at expiration only. When an FCO is exercised, the owner of the put or writer of the call must deliver the specified foreign currency.

TABLE 4.4   Calculating Currency Option Contract and Premium Values

The strike price is U.S. cents per foreign currency unit (dollar to mark)	$.575
multiplied by the contract size	x 62,500
equals the value of one contract	= $35,937.50
Likewise:	
The premium price in U.S. cents per foreign currency unit (dollar to mark)	.28 (28/100 of 1 cent)
converted to dollars per unit	x .01
or	.0028
multiplied by the contract size	x 62,500
equals the cost of one option premium	= $175.00

How the Options Market Functions

Options trade on the major U.S. exchanges and the over-the-counter (OTC) market. Exchange-traded options, known as **listed options**, have standardized strike prices and expiration dates.

Unlike listed options, options traded OTC are not standardized. Each option contract is normally created by a hedger (someone protecting a position) and an OTC dealer. The writer and the buyer determine the contract terms. Because the contract is not standardized, little secondary market activity exists in OTC options.

Trading and Settlement. Listed stock options and narrow-based index options are traded between 9:30 a.m. and 4:02 p.m. EST. Broad-based index options, such as the S&P 100, trade until 4:15 p.m. EST. Listed option transactions settle on the next business day.

Options Trading Personnel

Options are bought and sold on an exchange floor in a double-auction market. Certain individuals have key roles in maintaining an orderly options market.

Order Book Official. The CBOE employs **order book officials (OBOs)**, or **board brokers**, to ensure that the auction process runs smoothly. The OBOs keep track of limit orders and maintain orderly markets; they cannot trade for their own accounts.

Each OBO maintains a record of all limit orders on a particular class of options in his order book.

Market Maker. A market maker is an individual registered with an exchange who acts as an options dealer, trading at his own risk for his own account.

Each market maker helps maintain a fair and orderly market in at least one underlying security's options. The market maker may hold a position in the option, either long or short, and stands ready to buy or sell the option. The market maker is not required to support a falling market by continuously purchasing the option for his own account.

Summary of Options Trading Personnel. Other personnel with options trading authority include floor brokers and registered options traders. Figure 4.24 shows which options trading personnel are present on each major options exchange.

FIGURE 4.24   Option Trading Personnel by Exchange

	Specialist	Market Maker	Floor Broker	Reg. Options Trader	Order Book Official	Board Broker
AMEX/NYSE	✓	✓	✓	✓		
CBOE		✓	✓		✓	✓
PSE		✓	✓		✓	
PHLX	✓		✓	✓		

Trading Rotations

The exchanges use trading rotations to open trading each day. During these time periods, bids and offers are accepted for one option series at a time. When trading is completed in one series, it rotates to the next in sequence, beginning with the nearest expiration month and lowest strike price for calls or highest strike price for puts, moving in order until all series are opened for trading. Market orders have priority over limit orders at the opening. Orders for option spreads have priority over equal but separate bids and offers. This is known as the *spread priority rule*.

Expiration closing rotations take place on the third Friday of each month. If trading is halted in the underlying stock, the options automatically cease trading as well. Rotation is used to reopen the options when trading resumes.

In a fast market, where two exchange floor officials believe the market is becoming disorderly, an exchange can impose rotation to restore order.

Order Routing Systems

Broker-dealers often use computerized order routing systems to handle customer option transactions. An order sent through a computerized system ordinarily is routed from the broker-dealer to the floor broker who presents it in the trading crowd. If the order is executed, notice of the execution is relayed to the broker-dealer, which notifies the registered rep and the customer.

For small market orders and small, executable limit orders, the routing system may select automatic execution. In such a case, the system bypasses the commission house communication booth and floor broker and sends the order directly to the trading post. Each order is executed against an order on the limit order book or a market maker's quote, and the notice of execution is sent directly to the broker-dealer.

Options Clearing Corporation

Created and owned by the exchanges that trade options, the Options Clearing Corporation standardizes option contracts, guarantees performance of the contracts and issues options.

The OCC designates the standardized strike prices and expiration months for exchange-traded options. The market determines premiums. The OCC issues an option contract *without a certificate* the day after the order is executed. The investor's proof of option ownership is the trade confirmation.

The OCC provides investors with a ready means of closing open option positions. An investor long an option closes the position by entering a closing sale of an identical contract. An investor who is short an option closes the position by making a closing purchase of an identical contract.

In each case, the OCC takes the opposite side of the trade. This is possible because the options the OCC creates are interchangeable with others of their kind. As an example, all ALF May 70 puts are interchangeable, as are all ACM Apr 40 calls. This is known as *fungibility*.

OCC Options Disclosure Document. To satisfy the 1933 act's prospectus requirement, the OCC publishes an options disclosure document called *Characteristics and Risks of Standardized Options.* An investor must receive this document from the broker-dealer upon or prior to receiving approval for options trading.

Option Contract Adjustments

Options are adjusted for stock splits, reverse stock splits, stock dividends and rights offerings.

Stock Splits. When a stock splits, the option also splits.

✓ **For Example:** If ALF stock splits two-for-one, each ALF 60 call becomes 2 ALF 30 calls, and an ALF 65 put becomes 2 ALF 32½ puts. The option owner has twice as many contracts as before, and each contract's exercise price is half of the original exercise price. The total exercise value remains the same. Therefore, 1 ALF 60 call represents a contract for 100 shares at $60 each—$6,000 worth of ALF stock. After the split, the investor holds two calls with a strike price of $30—still $6,000 worth of stock.

When stock splits do not create even round lots, the option strike price and number of shares represented can be adjusted accordingly.

✓ **For Example:** If RST splits three-for-two, each RST 60 option becomes 1 RST 40 with 150 shares in the contract. The exercise price is adjusted down to two-thirds of the presplit strike, and the number of shares is adjusted up so that each contract's aggregate value remains the same. The option holder originally owned one option on 100 shares at $60–a $6,000 value. The new option controls 150 shares at $40 per share, still a $6,000 value.

Stock Dividends. When a company declares a stock dividend, the OCC normally adjusts the strike price and the number of shares in the contract.

✔ *For Example:* If LMN declared a 5 percent stock dividend, a holder of 100 shares at a market price of $20 would receive five new shares and the shares' market price would be approximately $19. An LMN 20 call would be adjusted after the dividend to 105 shares with a strike price of $19.

Cash Dividends. The OCC does not adjust the strike price of standardized options for ordinary cash dividends.

Rounding. Adjustments to exercise prices are rounded to the nearest eighth or sixteenth, and adjustments in the number of underlying shares are rounded down to the next whole share.

Position and Exercise Limits

The exchanges limit the number of options an individual investor can control on the same side—bullish or bearish—of the market. The exchanges adjust these limits frequently. As of August 1997, investors are limited to 25,000 equity option contracts on the same side of the market for the most heavily traded stocks.

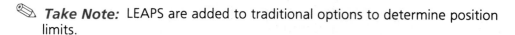 *Take Note:* LEAPS are added to traditional options to determine position limits.

✔ *For Example:* One investor could be long 25,000 calls and 25,000 puts or short 25,000 calls and 25,000 puts. An investor long 15,000 calls, however, could be short no more than 10,000 puts because both long calls and short puts are bullish.

Under the exercise limits system, investors may not exercise more than the allowed number of contracts within *five consecutive business days.* For stock options, the exercise limit is the same as the position limit. When a stock splits, position limits are normally adjusted accordingly.

Position and exercise limits apply to individuals, individuals *acting in concert* and reps acting for discretionary accounts, among others. A group of investors may not split a large order so as to exceed the limits.

Expiration and Exercise

The OCC sets specific times at which options must cease trading the day before expiration:

- 4:02 p.m. EST (3:02 p.m. CST) on the third Friday of the month of expiration—listed equity options cease trading;
- 5:30 p.m. EST on the third Friday of the month of expiration—holders can no longer exercise their options; and
- 11:59 p.m. EST on the Saturday following the third Friday of the expiration month—options expire. The hours between 5:30 p.m. the previous business day and 11:59 p.m. on Saturday allow firms time to clear their books of option transactions by giving proper notice to the OCC.

Automatic Exercise. Unless otherwise instructed, the OCC will exercise certain in-the-money contracts so they don't expire. Public customer contracts that are at least ¾ of a point in-the-money and those members own that are at least ¼ of a point in-the-money are normally exercised automatically.

Assignment of Exercise. When notified, the OCC randomly selects a firm to which it assigns an exercise. The broker-dealer can assign the exercise to one of its customers randomly or on a "first in, first out" (FIFO) basis. It may not assign on the basis of who has the largest position or can best afford it.

Sales Practice Rules   **Options Public Communication.** A compliance registered options principal (CROP) must approve advertising, educational or sales literature before its use with the public. Strictly educational material is not considered sales literature, according to the options exchanges; it must, however, tell the investor where to obtain information about the risks of investing in options.

Options Agreement. A registered options principal (ROP) must approve an investor for options trading before the first trade in the account, and the broker-dealer's CROP must promptly review and approve the investor for trading. A broker-dealer must obtain a signed options agreement from any customer who intends to invest in options. It must receive the agreement within 15 days of approving the account for trading regardless of when the customer intends to trade options.

Tax Rules for Options

Trading options generates profits and losses, which are taxable events.

Call or Put Option Expires. A standard option that expires unexercised results in a short-term capital loss for the person who bought it. A long-term option, such as a LEAPS contract, can result in a long-term capital loss if the investor holds it for more than 12 months. The writer of a standard option or a LEAP contract realizes a short-term capital gain from the premium if the option remains unexercised at expiration.

Close an Open Position. A closing purchase or sale generates a capital gain or loss if the option's sale price differs from the purchase price.

Option Exercise. When an option is exercised, one investor buys and another sells the stock. The option premium affects the cost basis if the stock is being purchased or the sale proceeds if the stock is being sold.

When a call is exercised, the option holder buys the stock. Because the investor paid a premium for the call, the total cost basis for the stock includes the premium and the strike price.

Because the call writer received the premium, his cost basis is reduced by the premium amount.

When a long put is exercised, the option premium is subtracted from the sale proceeds of the stock.

Determining Gains or Losses. To determine whether an option exercise generates a gain or loss, compare the total cost or revenue from the option and stock transactions with the original cost basis of the stock.

Effect of Options on Stock Holding Periods

Long Stock and Put. The IRS has ruled that the purchase of a put on stock held *12 months or less* automatically caps that stock's holding period at 12 months. Thus, any gain on that stock is treated as short term.

If the investor sells the put in a closing transaction, the stock's holding period restarts as of the put sale date.

If the stock was held more than 12 months before the put purchase, the holding period is unaffected. To the IRS, the fact that the holding period is already long term is adequate proof that the investor is not attempting to turn a short-term gain into a long-term gain through purchasing a put.

Covered Call. The IRS has ruled that the sale of a deep in-the-money call on stock held 12 months or less suspends the holding period on the stock position. Thus, any gain is treated as short term. If the position is closed with a purchase, the stock's holding period resumes.

If the investor writes an out-of-the-money call, or if the stock was held more than 12 months before the call's sale, the holding period is unaffected.

TABLE 4.5   Possible Tax Consequences of Option Strategies

Investment Strategy	Option Expires	Option Exercised	Position Closed at Intrinsic Value
Buy a call	Capital loss	Strike price + Premium = Cost basis	Capital gain or loss
Sell a call	Capital gain	Strike price + Premium = Sale proceeds	Capital gain or loss
Buy a put	Capital loss	Strike price – Premium = Sale proceeds	Capital gain or loss
Sell a put	Capital gain	Strike price – Premium = Cost basis	Capital gain or loss

LEAPS.   Because a LEAPS buyer can maintain their position for up to two and one-half years, gains or losses can be long term for tax purposes.

Nonequity Options   Investors holding nonequity option positions on December 31 are taxed as if the option positions were closed out.

Summary of the Tax Consequences of Option Strategies

Table 4.5 summarizes the tax consequences of option strategies.

Tracking Options

Options are listed in publications such as *Barron's* and *The Wall Street Journal*. Figure 4.25 is an example of stock option quotations as reported by the Chicago Board Options Exchange and reprinted in the financial press.

Look down the left column entitled "Option & NY Close" for the ALFA, Inc. options. The name of the underlying stock appears first, and the price at which that stock closed in the previous day's trading on the NYSE appears below it. The next column lists the option strike prices currently available on ALFA common stock, which include strike prices of 30, 35 and 40.

The numbers under each available option represent the current premium for that option. The ALFA Feb 35 call, for instance, is currently trading at 4½ ($450) and the ALFA Mar 35 put is trading at ⅛ ($12.50). The premium is quoted in dollars per share; one option normally represents a round lot (100 shares) of the underlying security.

FIGURE 4.25   Option Transactions

CHICAGO BOARD

Option & NY Close	Strike Price	Calls-Last			Puts-Last		
		Jan	Feb	Mar	Jan	Feb	Mar
Adm Fam	40	1 3/8	3 5/8	r	3/16	7/8	1 1/4
41 1/8	45	1/2	1 1/2	2 1/8	3 7/8	r	5 1/4
41 1/8	50	r	3/8	5/8	s	s	12
ALFA, Inc.	30	7 7/8	9 1/8	11	r	r	1/8
37 7/8	35	3 1/8	4 1/2	6 3/4	r	1/4	1/8
37 7/8	40	3/4	1 5/8	3	3/4	7/8	r
All Swel	25	1/4	1 3/8	2	1/8	1	1 5/8
25 1/4	30	r	1/8	7/8	3 3/4	4 5/8	7
Bulln Bar	20	r	r	r	r	r	7/8
24	22 1/2	1	r	r	r	r	r
24	25	5/16	1	2 1/4	r	r	2 5/8

Total call vol 1,240,086   Call open int 3,038,532
Total put vol   105,755   Put open int   941,395

r - Not Traded. s - No Option.

If an "r" is listed for an option instead of a premium, it means that the option was not traded on that day. If an "s" appears, no option is available because the CBOE has not yet issued one.

Summary

An option is a two-party contract that conveys a right to the buyer and an obligation to the seller.

- A call option buyer has the right to purchase the underlying security for a specified price within a specified timeframe.
- A call option seller is obligated to sell the underlying security for a specified price within a specified timeframe.

- A put option buyer has the right to sell the underlying security for a specified price within a specified timeframe.
- A put option seller is obligated to purchase the underlying security for a specified price within a specified timeframe.

The terms of option contracts are standardized by the Options Clearing Corporation, which allows them to be traded easily on an exchange such as the Chicago Board of Options Exchange.

The underlying security for which an option contract is created may be a stock, a stock market index, a foreign currency, an interest rate or a government bond.

Because of the leverage option contracts offer investors, they may be used to protect investment portfolio positions or to speculate on the direction of the underlying security.

An option contract has a relatively short life span. The time remaining to expiration is important in determining the option's value. The amount by which the contract is in-the-money is also critical. Initial transactions in options are "opening" purchases or sales. Once a position is established, a "closing" sale or purchase-offsetting transaction, or the expiration of the contract, ends the position.

Option transactions may be straightforward, such as the opening purchase or sale of a call or put. They may be coupled with other portfolio securities or other option contracts in order to use more complicated investment strategies.

Finally, the major point of concern for the Series 7 exam is the ability to determine maximum gain, loss and breakeven points for option transactions. For the four basic option transactions these are:

- Long call
  - maximum gain: unlimited
  - maximum loss: premium paid
  - breakeven: strike price plus premium
- Short call
  - maximum gain: premium received
  - maximum loss: unlimited
  - breakeven: strike price plus premium
- Long put
  - maximum gain: strike price minus premium paid
  - maximum loss: premium paid
  - breakeven: strike price minus premium
- Short put
  - maximum gain: premium received
  - maximum loss: strike price minus premium received
  - breakeven: strike price minus premium

Key Concepts

To prepare for your license exam, you should learn the following concepts.

In addition to studying these key concepts, use the Options Hot Sheet on pages 636 and 637 for further review.

at-the-money	intrinsic value
bearish	nonequity option
breakeven point	option contract
bullish	Options Clearing Corporation (OCC)
call	order book official (OBO)
call buyer	out-of-the-money
call writer	premium
class	put
combination	put buyer
covered call writing	put writer
credit spread	series
debit spread	spread
equity option	straddle
exercise price	strike price
expiration date	time value
foreign currency option (FCO)	type
index option	underlying instrument
in-the-money	

Review Questions

1. As the underlying stock price increases, the premium of a call option will generally

   A. increase
   B. decrease
   C. remain the same
   D. fluctuate

2. Which of the following investors will purchase stock if the option is exercised?

   I. Owner of a call
   II. Owner of a put
   III. Writer of a call
   IV. Writer of a put

   A. I and II
   B. I and IV
   C. II and III
   D. III and IV

3. Which of the following investors will sell stock if the option is exercised?

   I. Owner of a call
   II. Owner of a put
   III. Writer of a call
   IV. Writer of a put

   A. I and II
   B. I and IV
   C. II and III
   D. III and IV

4. Who issues a listed option?

   A. Member firm of the option writer
   B. Exchange on which the option is purchased
   C. Investor who writes the option
   D. Options Clearing Corporation

5. All the following are characteristics of non-standardized options EXCEPT

   A. negotiated exercise prices
   B. active secondary trading
   C. premiums determined by the market
   D. negotiated expiration dates

6. A call is in-the-money when the market price of the underlying stock is

   A. equal to the strike price
   B. above the strike price
   C. below the strike price
   D. equal to the strike price plus or minus the premium

7. COD stock is trading at 25¾. COD Jul 25 calls are trading at a premium of 2. What is the intrinsic value of these calls?

   A. $0
   B. $75
   C. $125
   D. $200

8. DWQ stock is trading at 25¾. DWQ Jul 25 calls are trading at a premium of 2. What is the time value of the Jul 25 calls?

   A. $0
   B. $75
   C. $125
   D. $200

9. Which of the following investors are bearish?

   I. Buyer of a call
   II. Writer of a call
   III. Buyer of a put
   IV. Writer of a put

   A. I and II
   B. I and IV
   C. II and III
   D. III and IV

10. Which of the following investors has the greatest potential risk if the price of GIZ goes up?

    A. Angus, long 10 calls on GIZ
    B. Karen, short 10 calls on GIZ
    C. Adam, long 10 puts on GIZ
    D. Belle, short 10 puts on GIZ

Answers & Rationale

1. **A.** The premium of an option changes as the market price of the underlying security moves; therefore, if the stock price increases the premium will also increase.

2. **B.** Remember the following definitions:
   - Call buyers have the right to buy.
   - Call sellers are obligated to sell.
   - Put buyers have the right to sell.
   - Put sellers are obligated to buy.

3. **C.** Remember the following definitions:
   - Call buyers have the right to buy.
   - Call sellers are obligated to sell.
   - Put buyers have the right to sell.
   - Put sellers are obligated to buy.

4. **D.** The Options Clearing Corporation (OCC) is the entity that standardizes option contracts, guarantees performance of the contracts and issues options.

5. **B.** This is an "except" question. There is no active secondary trading in the nonstandard options.

6. **B.** A call is in-the-money when the market price of the underlying stock is above the strike price. Think of it as: Is it worth exercising the option contract?

7. **B.** Intrinsic value is the difference between the option's strike price (25) and the price of the underlying stock (25¾). $25\frac{3}{4} - 25 = .75$; $.75 \times 100 = \$75.00$.

8. **C.** Time value is the difference between the premium (2) and the intrinsic value of the contract ($25\frac{3}{4} - 25 = .75$). $2 - .75 = 1.25$; $1.25 \times 100 = \$125.00$.

9. **C.** Remember, buyers of calls and writers of puts are bullish and buyers of puts and writers of calls are bearish.

10. **B.** The greatest potential risk that an investor can take is to be short naked calls.

5

Customer Accounts

OVERVIEW

The customer account serves as a repository for cash and securities and as a record of a customer's investment activity.

The customer's investment objectives, approach and account trading authority determine which of the several types of accounts available the rep opens for the customer.

Every account type has its own recordkeeping requirements. Some accounts help track customers' daily transactions; others are required by the Securities and Exchange Commission (SEC), self-regulatory organizations (SROs) or various government agencies.

New Accounts

A completed new account form is *required for every account* opened. Other forms have specific applications, including:

- customer agreements
- loan consent agreements
- IRA contracts
- Keogh forms
- partnership agreements
- corporate charters
- simplified employee pension plan (SEP) applications
- annuity contracts

- trust documents
- mutual fund applications
- full or limited powers of attorney

Classification of Accounts

Account Ownership. Procedures and regulations vary according to the type of account ownership. The principal types of ownership are:

- individual
- joint
- corporate
- partnership

Trading Authorization. At times, persons other than an account owner may be authorized to buy and sell securities on behalf of the owner. The primary types of trading authorization follow:

- **Discretionary.** After receiving written authority from the customer, the registered representative enters trades without having to consult the customer before each trade.
- **Fiduciary.** The individual given fiduciary responsibility enters the trades for the account.
- **Custodial.** The custodian for the beneficial owner enters all trades.

Payment Method. Customers may pay for securities with cash or on margin. In cash accounts, customers must pay the full purchase price of securities by the transaction settlement date. Margin accounts allow customers to borrow part of a security's purchase price from the broker-dealer.

Opening New Accounts

Generally, any competent person of age may open an account. Any person declared legally incompetent may not. Fiduciary or custodial accounts may be opened for minors or legally incompetent individuals.

Required Information. According to NYSE Rule 405 ("Know Your Customer"), exchange members must attempt to learn essential facts about every customer and account. General guidelines suggest a registered rep should know a customer's present holdings, financial situation, risk tolerance, needs and objectives.

Payment and Delivery Instructions. After opening an account, the customer and the registered rep establish payment and delivery instructions.

Although these instructions may be changed for individual transactions, the customer selects any of the following:

- **Transfer and ship.** Securities are registered in the customer's name and shipped to him.
- **Transfer and hold in safekeeping.** Securities are registered in the customer's name, and the broker-dealer holds them in safekeeping.
- **Hold in street name.** Securities are registered in the broker-dealer's name and held by the broker-dealer. Although the broker-dealer is the securities' nominal owner, the customer is their beneficial owner.
- **Delivery vs. payment.** Delivery vs. payment (DVP) securities are delivered to a bank or depository against payment. Normally used for institutional accounts, this is a cash on delivery (COD) settlement. The broker-dealer must verify the arrangement between the customer and the bank or depository, and the customer must notify the bank or depository of each purchase or sale.

In addition, the customer designates whether the broker-dealer should hold or forward any cash balance.

Approval and Acceptance of an Account   A partner or a principal of the firm must approve every new account in writing on the account form before or promptly after the completion of the first transaction in the account.

Documenting New Accounts

New account form. A registered rep must fill out a new account form for each account opened. Figure 5.1 shows a typical new account form. The rep must attempt to enter the following identification details and suitability information on the form for each customer who will have access to the account:

- full name;
- address and telephone number (business and residence);
- Social Security or tax identification number;
- occupation, employer and type of business;
- citizenship;
- whether the customer is of legal age;
- estimated income and net worth;
- investment objectives;
- bank and brokerage references;
- whether the customer is an employee of a member broker-dealer;
- how the account was acquired;
- name and occupation of the person(s) with authority to make transactions in the account; and

FIGURE 5.1   New Account Form

Greenback Securities, Inc.

Staking Your Financial Future
12654 Futurity Blvd.
Belmont, CA 99462

NEW ACCOUNT FORM

TAXPAYER ID NUMBER	☐ SSN ☐ TAX ID	AGE	BRANCH#	RR#	ACCOUNT#	DATE

LEGAL NAME(S) AND MAILING ADDRESS	☐ HOME ☐ BUS

ACCOUNT TYPE ☐ CASH ☐ OPTION
☐ MARGIN ☐ COMMODITY

MARITAL STATUS ☐ MARRIED ☐ SINGLE
☐ DIVORCED ☐ WIDOWED

ACCOUNT REGIS. ☐ SINGLE ☐ JTWROS
☐ JTIC ☐ INV CLUB
☐ CORP ☐ PARTNER
☐ RETIRE ☐ OTHER

TELEPHONE NO.	☐ HOME ☐ BUS	TELEPHONE NO.	☐ HOME ☐ BUS	DIVIDENDS ☐ HOLD ☐ MAIL	U.S. CITIZEN?	☐ YES ☐ NO _____

IS THE CUSTOMER OR SPOUSE EMPLOYED BY, OR RELATED ☐ YES DUPLICATE ☐ YES   **ATTACH SPECIAL INSTRUCTIONS**
TO AN EMPLOYEE OF, ANY FINANCIAL INSTITUTION?   ☐ NO   CONFIRMS? ☐ NO

EMPLOYMENT

EMPLOYER'S NAME	YEARS EMPLOYED	DOCUMENTATION			OTHER (DESCRIBE)
		MARGIN AGR	☐ PEND	☐ RCVD	_____
ADDRESS		JOINT ACCT	☐ PEND	☐ RCVD	_____
		TRADING AUTH	☐ PEND	☐ RCVD	_____
		CORP/PART AGR	☐ PEND	☐ RCVD	_____
TYPE OF BUSINESS	CLIENT'S OCCUPATION	RETIRE ACCT	☐ PEND	☐ RCVD	_____
		SIG CARD	☐ PEND	☐ RCVD	_____

REFERENCE

BANK NAME AND ADDRESS	☐ CHECKING ☐ VERIFIED ☐ SAVINGS ☐ NOT VERIFIED

DOES CLIENT HAVE AN ACCOUNT   ☐ YES   IF YES, WITH WHAT FIRM?
WITH ANOTHER BROKERAGE FIRM? ☐ NO

SPOUSE

NAME	OCCUPATION	AGE
EMPLOYER	ADDRESS	ANNUAL INCOME

INVESTMENT EXPERIENCE	DOES CLIENT OR SPOUSE HAVE ANOTHER ACCOUNT WITH US? ☐ YES ☐ NO IF YES, LIST:	HOW WAS ACCOUNT ACQUIRED? ☐ WALK IN ☐ REFERRAL ☐ PHONE IN ☐ PROSPECT ☐ OTHER ☐ ACQUAINTANCE	OPTION TRADES ANTICIPATED ☐ BUY ONLY ☐ STRADDLES ☐ COV CALLS ☐ SPREADS ☐ COV PUTS ☐ COMBINS ☐ UNC OPTS ☐ OTHER

INVESTMENT OBJECTIVES
☐ GROWTH ☐ SPECULATION
☐ INCOME ☐ RETIREMENT
☐ GRO/INC ☐ TAX

IS CLIENT NOW OR HAS CLIENT EVER BEEN A CORPORATE OFFICER OR OWNER OF 10% OF ANY CORPORATION'S SECURITIES?
☐ YES   ☐ NO
IF YES, NAME:

INITIAL TRANSACTION
☐ BUY   DESCRIBE:
☐ SELL
☐ OTHER
INITIAL DEPOSIT

IS CLIENT FAMILIAR WITH OPTIONS?
☐ YES   ☐ NO
HAS CLIENT RECEIVED OCC PROSPECTUS?
☐ YES DATE _____
HAS CLIENT PREVIOUSLY TRADED OPTIONS?
☐ YES   ☐ NO
ARE OPTIONS SUITABLE?
☐ YES   ☐ NO

HOME ☐ OWN ☐ RENT
NO. OF DEPENDENTS _____
ANNUAL INC _____
NET WORTH _____

DISCRETIONARY AUTHORIZATION
☐ FULL ☐ LIMITED ☐ NONE

RR SIGNATURE	AGENT'S NAME AND ADDRESS
BRANCH MGR APPROVAL DATE	ROP SIGNATURE (OPTIONS APPROVAL)

- signatures of the representative opening the account and a principal of the firm (the customer's signature is not required on a new account form).

NYSE and NASD rules require the items listed above. The Municipal Securities Rulemaking Board (MSRB) requires the registered rep to specify the customer's tax status as well.

Even if a customer refuses to provide all of the information requested, a firm may open the account if it believes the customer has the financial resources to carry it.

Customer information should be updated periodically as situations change. Sometimes a customer wants to place a transaction that a registered rep considers unsuitable or that the rep has not recommended. In this case, the registered rep should mark the order ticket "unsolicited." If the ticket is not marked, the trade will be assumed to be solicited.

Mailing Instructions. A customer gives specific mailing instructions when opening a new account. Statements and confirms may be sent to someone who holds power of attorney for the customer if the customer requests it in writing or if duplicate confirms are also sent to the customer. A member firm may hold a customer's mail for up to two months if the customer is traveling in the United States and for up to three months if the customer is abroad.

Cash Accounts and Margin Accounts

A customer can open either a cash account or a margin account, depending on how she chooses to pay for securities.

Cash Accounts   A cash account is the basic investment account. Anyone eligible to open an investment account can open a cash account. In a cash account, a customer pays in full for any securities purchased.

Certain accounts may be opened *only* as cash accounts, such as personal retirement accounts (individual retirement accounts—IRAs—Keoghs and tax-sheltered annuities—TSAs), corporate retirement accounts and custodial accounts (Uniform Gifts to Minors Act accounts—UGMAs).

Margin Accounts   A margin account allows a customer to borrow money for investing. The term "margin" refers to the minimum amount of cash or marginable securities a customer must deposit to buy securities.

A margin account allows a customer to control an investment for less money than he would need were he to buy the securities outright. Margin also is a potential source of cash. If a customer has fully paid securities in an account and needs cash, a firm normally lends money against those securities up to the margin limit the Federal Reserve Board (FRB) sets. A customer can have both a cash and a margin account.

When a customer borrows money to invest, she **leverages** her own investment funds. Leverage, in this case through buying securities on margin, allows a person to magnify the gains or losses generated on the dollars she personally invests. The interest rate charged on margin accounts is based on the **broker call rate**, also known as the **broker loan rate**, typically less than rates banks charge. Several rules apply to margin accounts due to the risks of investing borrowed money.

The Federal Reserve Board's Regulation T

The Securities Exchange Act of 1934 grants the Federal Reserve Board authority to regulate credit extended for the purchase of securities. The FRB established Regulation T, which specifies the equity requirements for securities transactions in a margin account. Regulation T also stipulates which securities may be purchased on margin. Although the FRB establishes the regulations governing margin accounts, the SEC enforces the regulations.

Opening a Margin Account

A customer who opens a margin account must meet certain minimal financial requirements. The customer may then buy and sell securities on margin and pay interest on the borrowed funds. The securities purchased are held in street name as collateral for the margin loan.

Documenting a Margin Account. When opening a margin account, the customer signs a **margin agreement**, which includes a credit agreement, a hypothecation agreement and an optional loan consent:

- The **credit agreement** discloses the terms under which credit is extended. SEC **Rule 10b-16** requires that the firm disclose the annual rate and method of computing interest and the conditions under which interest rates and charges will be changed. The firm also must send the customer an assurance that statements accounting for interest charges will be sent at least quarterly.
- The **hypothecation agreement** gives the firm permission to pledge, or hypothecate, securities held on margin. The hypothecation agreement is a mandatory part of the margin agreement.
- The **loan consent agreement** gives the firm permission to lend securities held in the margin account to other brokers, usually for short sales. It is not mandatory for the customer to sign the loan consent agreement.

Options Agreement

If a customer wishes to trade options, she must sign an options agreement. By signing the agreement, the customer acknowledges having read the OCC Options Disclosure Document published by the Options Clearing

Corporation, which explains the risks and requirements of option trading, and claims to understand the risks associated with options.

Initial approval for options accounts may come from the branch manager. In offices with more than three reps producing options business, the manager is a registered options principal (ROP). If the manager is not a ROP, the manager's signature must be approved by a ROP, senior ROP (SROP) or compliance ROP (CROP) within a reasonable time. When approving an account for options, a registered rep must:

- ascertain the customer's investment history and financial status;
- ascertain the customer's investment objectives and needs;
- provide the customer with the OCC Options Disclosure Document; and
- obtain the customer's signature on a customer options agreement within 15 days after the customer opens the account. The agreement states that the investor will abide by OCC guidelines and option exchange regulations.

Retirement Accounts Each type of personal and corporate retirement account has its own forms and applications. The most important are those that establish the firm's custodial relationship with the retirement account owner, necessary for Internal Revenue Service (IRS) reporting purposes.

Business Accounts When a registered rep opens a business account of any type, he must establish three items:

1. the business's legal right to open an investment account;
2. an indication of any limitations that the owners, the stockholders, a court or any other entity has placed on the investments in which the business can invest; and
3. who will represent the business in transactions involving the account.

A copy of the legal documents that established the business usually contains this information and must be kept on file with the other account forms.

Trading Authorization/ Power of Attorney A power of attorney or a discretionary power allows a party other than the account owner to make investment decisions for the account without consulting the account owner. When such authority has been established for an account, a signed copy of the document must be kept on file.

Special Account Situations Sometimes, account owners request that their accounts be handled in a special manner. The most commonly requested situations are discussed below.

Numbered Accounts. At a customer's request, his account may be identified by only a number or symbol. The customer must sign a form certifying that he owns the account(s) identified by the number or symbol and must supply other information identifying the customer as the owner. In most cases, institutions use numbered accounts to preserve anonymity.

Multiple Accounts. A customer who has both a cash and a margin account is considered to have only one account. If a customer wishes to open more than one individual account with a broker-dealer, the representative must get a statement from the customer attesting that no one else has any interest in the second and subsequent accounts and that each account unreservedly guarantees the others. These are sometimes called *guaranteed accounts*.

Account Transfers. To transfer a customer's account from one broker-dealer to another, the customer submits transfer instructions to the new broker-dealer. If any of the assets in the account cannot be transferred, the customer must instruct the rep whether they should be liquidated, retained for the customer by the original broker-dealer or transferred to the customer.

The transfer instructions are then sent to the firm currently carrying the account. The firm has *three business days* either to validate or to take exception to the transfer instructions. The firm may take exception to the transfer instructions if it has no record of the account, the instructions are not valid or the account contains no transferable assets. The firm may not take exception solely because of a dispute about the value of the cash or securities in the account.

The transfer instructions are validated when the current firm returns them to the new firm together with an attachment detailing the customer's securities positions, securities held in street name, cash balances and outstanding Regulation T calls. The account is then frozen, except for options expiring within seven days.

The new firm reviews the attachment and may reject the account *in its entirety* if it does not meet the firm's minimum account size requirements or credit policies.

 For Example: If a customer's credit and debit balances do not meet house margin requirements, the new firm may not reject the portion of the account that is not in compliance with credit policies while accepting the remainder. The account transfer must be completed within *four business days after validation*.

Account Records

A registered rep is responsible for maintaining records for each customer's account, including each securities holding. All customer transactions are posted daily and maintained at the branch and main offices. The required information includes the following:

- customer's name, address and phone number
- type of account and account number
- investment objective
- list of all securities deposited with the firm
- list of all transactions

Opening Accounts for Employees of Other Brokers

The National Association of Securities Dealers (NASD), the New York Stock Exchange (NYSE) and MSRB require broker-dealers to give permission or written notification to other broker-dealers regarding the establishment of accounts for certain individuals, including:

- employees of broker-dealers
- spouses or minor children of broker-dealer employees

NYSE Requirements. The NYSE requires prior written approval from the employer broker-dealer before an employee of a member firm can open a cash or margin account with another firm. If the account is approved, the transacting firm must send duplicate statements and confirmations to the employer broker-dealer. NYSE employees also need the employer's written permission.

NASD Requirements. NASD rules do not require an employee of one NASD member firm to get his employer's permission to open an account with another NASD member, but do require the firm opening the account to notify the customer's employer. The employee is responsible for disclosing that he is an associated person of an NASD member when opening the account. Duplicate confirmations and statements must be sent to the employer broker-dealer if the employer requests them.

MSRB Requirements. Like the NASD, the MSRB does not require an employee of a member firm to obtain prior permission from the employer to open an account with another firm. The broker-dealer must notify the employer in writing, however, that the account is being opened and must supply the employer with duplicate confirmations unless requested in writing not to do so.

Summary of SRO Notification and Confirmation Requirements. Table 5.1 shows the account forms and confirms needed for employees of each SRO.

TABLE 5.1   SRO Notification and Confirmation Requirements

Employed By:	Margin Account	Cash Account	Duplicate Confirm
NASD member	Notification (not permission)	Notification (not permission)	Upon request
NYSE member	Prior permission	Prior permission	Yes
MSRB member	Notification (not permission)	Notification (not permission)	Yes

Types of Accounts

When an account is opened, it is registered in the name(s) of one or more persons. They are the account owners and the only individuals who are allowed access to and control of the investments in the account.

Single Accounts   A single account has one beneficial owner. The account holder is the only person who can:

- control the investments within the account
- request distributions of cash or securities from the account

Joint Accounts   In a joint account, two or more adults are named on the account as co-owners, with each allowed some form of control over the account.

In addition to the appropriate new account form, a joint account agreement must be signed, and the account must be designated as either joint tenants in common (JTIC) or joint tenants with right of survivorship (JTWROS).

The account forms for joint accounts require the signatures of all owners. Both types of joint account agreements provide that any or all tenants may transact business in the account. Checks must be made payable to the names in which the account is registered and must be endorsed for deposit by all tenants, although mail need be sent to only a single address. To be in good delivery form, securities sold from a joint account must be signed by all tenants.

Joint Tenants in Common. JTIC ownership provides that a deceased tenant's fractional interest in the account is retained by that tenant's estate and is not passed to the surviving tenant(s).

For Example: If a JTIC agreement provides for 60 percent ownership interest by one owner and 40 percent ownership interest by the other, that fraction of the account would pass into the deceased owner's estate if he died. The JTIC agreement may be used by more than two individuals.

Joint Tenants with Right of Survivorship. JTWROS ownership stipulates that a deceased tenant's interest in the account passes to the surviving tenant(s).

✎ **Take Note:** Joint tenants in common can own unequal interests in the account, as opposed to joint tenants with rights of survivorship, which always share equally.

Partnership Accounts

A partnership is an unincorporated association of two or more individuals. Partnerships frequently open cash, margin, retirement and other types of accounts necessary for business purposes. The partnership must provide a partnership agreement stating which of the partners can make transactions for the account. If the partnership opens a margin account, the partnership must disclose any investment limitations.

Corporate Accounts

A corporate account must include a corporate resolution identifying which members of the corporation may trade in the account. The resolution, signed by the secretary of the corporation, identifies officers authorized to make transactions.

In addition to the documentation required for all margin accounts, a corporate margin account requires a certified copy of the corporate charter and bylaws that authorize the margin account. A **certificate of incumbency**, which empowers the officers to trade the account, must be obtained within 60 days of opening the account.

Figure 5.2 compares the forms needed to open various types of accounts.

Fiduciary and Custodial Accounts

When securities are placed in a fiduciary, or custodial, account, a person other than the owner initiates trades. The most familiar example of a fiduciary account is a trust account. Money or securities are placed in trust for one person, often a minor, but someone else manages the account. The manager or trustee is a fiduciary.

In a fiduciary account, the investments exist for the owner's beneficial interest, yet the owner has little or no legal control over them. The fiduciary makes all of the investment, management and distribution decisions and must manage the account in the owner's best interests. The fiduciary may not use the account's contents for his own benefit, although he may be reimbursed for reasonable expenses incurred in managing the account.

Securities bought in a custodial account must be registered in such a way that the custodial relationship is evident.

FIGURE 5.2   Forms Needed to Open an Account

Form	Individual		Joint		Partnership		Corporate	
	Cash	Margin	Cash	Margin	Cash	Margin	Cash	Margin
New account form	✓	✓	✓	✓	✓	✓	✓	✓
Margin agreement		✓		✓		✓		✓
Joint account agreement			✓	✓				
Corporate charter and bylaws								✓
Partnership agreement					✓	✓		
Corporate/partnership resolution					✓	✓	✓	✓
Discretionary authorization	As needed							
Power of attorney	As needed							
Options agreement	As needed							

✓ **For Example:** In the case of an account where Marilyn Johnson, the donor, has appointed her daughter's aunt, Barbara Woodward, as custodian for the account of her minor daughter, Alexis, the account and the certificates would read "Barbara Woodward as custodian for Alexis Johnson." The beneficial owner's Social Security number is used on the account.

A fiduciary is any person legally appointed and authorized to represent another person, act on his behalf and make whatever decisions are necessary to the prudent management of his account. Fiduciaries include:

- **trustee** designated to administer a trust;
- **executor** designated in a decedent's will to manage the affairs of the estate;
- **administrator** appointed by the courts to liquidate the estate of a person who died intestate—that is, without a will;
- **guardian** designated by the courts to handle a minor's affairs until the minor reaches the age of majority or to handle an incompetent's affairs;
- **custodian** of an UGMA account;
- **receiver** in a bankruptcy; and
- **conservator** for an incompetent.

Any trades the fiduciary enters must be compatible with the trust's investment objectives.

Opening a Fiduciary Account. Opening a fiduciary account may require a court certification of the individual's appointment and authority. An account for a trustee must include a trust agreement detailing the limitations placed on the fiduciary. No documentation of custodial rights or court certification is required for an individual acting as the custodian for an UGMA. The registered rep for a fiduciary account must be aware of the following rules:

- Proper authorization must be given (the necessary court documents must be filed with and verified by the broker-dealer).
- Speculative transactions generally are not permitted.
- Margin accounts are permitted only if the legal documents establishing the fiduciary accounts authorize them.
- The **prudent man rule** requires fiduciaries to make wise and safe investments.
- Many states publish a **legal list** of securities approved for fiduciary accounts.
- No authority may be delegated (a power of attorney cannot be accepted for a fiduciary account).
- A fiduciary may not share in an account's profits, but may charge a reasonable fee for services.

Power of Attorney

If a person not named on an account will have trading authority, the customer must file written authorization with the broker-dealer giving that person access to the account. This trading authorization usually takes the form of a power of attorney. Two basic types of trading authorizations are full and limited powers of attorney.

Full Power of Attorney

A full power of attorney allows someone who is not the owner of an account to:

- deposit or withdraw cash or securities
- make investment decisions for the account owner

Custodians, trustees, guardians and other people filling similar legal duties are often given full powers of attorney.

Limited Power of Attorney

A limited power of attorney allows an individual to have some, but not total, control over an account. The document specifies the level of access the person may exercise.

Discretionary Accounts

An account set up with preapproved authority for a registered rep to make transactions without having to ask for specific approval is a discretionary account. "Discretion" is defined as the authority to decide:

- what security
- the number of shares or units
- whether to buy or sell

Discretion does not apply to decisions regarding the timing of an investment or the price at which it is acquired. An order from a customer worded "Buy 100 shares of Microscam for my account whenever you think the price is right" is not a discretionary order.

Discretionary Authority. A customer can give discretionary power over his account(s) only by filing a trading authorization or a limited power of attorney with the broker-dealer. No transactions of a discretionary nature can take place without this document on file. Once authorization has been given, the customer is legally bound to accept the registered rep's decisions, although the customer may continue to enter orders on his own.

The customer may give discretion for the account only to a specific individual. If the registered rep leaves the firm or in any other way stops working with the account, the discretionary authority ends immediately.

Regulation of Discretionary Accounts. In addition to requiring the proper documentation, discretionary accounts are subject to the following rules:

- Each discretionary order must be identified as such at the time it is entered for execution.
- An officer or a partner of the brokerage house must approve each order promptly and in writing, not necessarily before order entry.
- A record must be kept of all transactions.
- No excessive trading may occur in the account, relative to the size of the account and the customer's investment objectives.
- To safeguard against the possibility of churning, a designated supervisor or manager must review all trading activity frequently and systematically.

Disclosure of Control. The NASD and MSRB require the customer to give specific authorization for the purchase of a security for the account if a control relationship exists between the broker-dealer and the security's issuer.

Death or Incompetence of an Account Holder

If a customer dies or a court declares her incompetent, the registered rep and the principal must obtain the necessary legal documents (e.g., death certificate, affidavit of domicile and letters testamentary) and aid the executor in dissolving the account.

All trading authorizations cease upon an account owner's death or declaration of incompetency.

Single Accounts

If the owner of a single account dies or is declared incompetent, all pending transactions and outstanding orders must be *canceled immediately*. Depending on the laws of the state in which the account is held, the registered rep may need to obtain a copy of the death certificate, the document appointing the estate's executor or certificate of incompetency. Once an executor has provided a firm with the necessary forms establishing his legal right to manage the account, the executor of the estate instructs the registered rep regarding the account disposition.

Joint Accounts

The handling of a joint account upon the death or declaration of incompetency of one of the owners varies according to the type of joint account involved.

Joint Tenants with Right of Survivorship

Each JTWROS account owner has an *equal and undivided interest* in the cash and securities in the account. Upon the death or declaration of incompetency of any or all of the account owners, account ownership passes to the survivor(s)—a "right of succession" occurs.

Joint Tenants in Common

Each JTIC account owner has a *separate title* but an *undivided interest* in the cash and securities in the account. Ownership of a JTIC account may be divided unequally. At the death or declaration of incompetency of one of the account owners, that person's proportionate share of the cash and securities in the account is distributed according to the instructions in the decedent's will.

If one joint tenant in common dies or is declared incompetent, all pending transactions and outstanding orders must be canceled immediately.

Custodial Accounts

If the beneficial owner of a custodial account dies, any securities or cash in the account goes to the owner's estate, not the custodian or custodian's estate. If the custodian dies, a new custodian must be named to manage the account.

Partnership Accounts   If one of the partners in a partnership account dies or is declared incompetent, all pending transactions and outstanding orders must be canceled and the account frozen. The rep may need to obtain forms similar to those required at the death or declaration of incompetency of the owner of a personal investment account. Once the firm has obtained the necessary forms, the executor of the partner's estate instructs the rep regarding the account disposition.

Uniform Gifts to Minors Act Accounts

Uniform Gifts to Minors Act and Uniform Transfers to Minors Act (UTMA) accounts require an adult or a trustee to act as custodian for a minor (the beneficial owner). Any kind of security—cash, life insurance, annuity contracts and other forms of property—may be given to the account without limitation.

Donating Securities   When a person makes a gift of securities to a minor under the UGMA laws, that person is the **donor** of the securities. A gift under UGMA conveys an **indefeasible title**; that is, the donor may not take back the gift, nor may the minor return the gift until she has reached the age of majority. Once the gift is donated, the donor gives up all rights to the property. When the minor reaches the specified age, the property in the account is transferred into her name.

Custodian   Any securities given to a minor through an UGMA account are managed by a custodian until the minor reaches the age of majority. The custodian has full control over the minor's account and can:

- buy or sell securities
- exercise rights or warrants
- liquidate, trade or hold securities

The custodian may also use the property in the account in any way he deems proper for the minor's support, education, maintenance, general use or benefit. However, the account is not normally used to pay expenses associated with raising a child because the parents can incur negative tax consequences.

Registered representatives must be aware of the following rules regarding UGMA custodial accounts:

- An account may have only one custodian and one minor or beneficial owner.

- A minor can be the beneficiary of more than one account and a person may serve as custodian for more than one UGMA as long as each account benefits only one minor.
- The donor of securities can act as custodian or can appoint someone else to do so.
- Unless acting as custodians, parents have no legal control over an UGMA account or the securities in it.

A registered representative is not responsible for determining whether an appointment is valid or whether a custodian's activities are appropriate.

Opening an UGMA Account

When opening an UGMA account, a rep must ensure that the account application contains the custodian's name, the minor's name and Social Security number, and the state in which the UGMA is registered.

Registration of UGMA Securities

Any securities in an UGMA account are registered in the custodian's name for the benefit of the minor; they *cannot* be registered in street name. Typically, the securities are registered to "Joan R. Smith as custodian for Brenda Lee Smith," for example, or a variation of this form. When the minor reaches the age of majority, all of the securities in the account will be registered in her name.

The gift of securities is considered complete when this registration has been completed.

Fiduciary Responsibility

An UGMA custodian is charged with fiduciary responsibilities in managing the minor's account. Certain restrictions have been placed on what is deemed to be proper handling of the investments in an UGMA. The most important limitations follow:

- UGMAs may be opened and managed as cash accounts only.
- A custodian may not purchase securities in an account on margin or pledge them as collateral for a loan.
- A custodian must reinvest all cash proceeds, dividends and interest within a reasonable period of time. Cash proceeds from sales or dividends may be held in a noninterest-bearing custodial account for a reasonable period, but should not remain idle for long.
- Investment decisions must take into account a minor's age and the custodial relationship; commodities futures, naked options and other high-risk securities are examples of inappropriate investments. Options may not be bought in a custodial account because no evidence of ownership is issued to an options buyer. Covered call writing is normally allowed.
- Stock subscription rights or warrants must be either exercised or sold.
- A custodian for an UGMA may not grant trading authority to a third party.
- A custodian may loan money to an account, but may not borrow from it.

A custodian may be reimbursed for any reasonable expenses she incurs in managing the account unless the custodian is also the donor.

Taxation The minor's Social Security number appears on an UGMA account, and the minor must file an annual income tax return and pay taxes on any income exceeding $1,400 (1998) produced by the UGMA at *the parent's top marginal tax rate*, regardless of the source of the gift, until the minor reaches the age of 14. Exclusions are available, and they are indexed for inflation.

✓ *For Example:* In 1998, the first $700 of a minor's earnings is tax free and the next $700 is taxed at the minor's rate, usually 15 percent, for a total of $1,400; earnings exceeding $1,400 are taxed at the parent's top rate.

When the minor reaches age 14, the account will be taxed at the minor's tax rate.

Although the minor is the account's beneficiary and is responsible for any and all taxes on the account, in most states it is the custodian's responsibility to see that the taxes are paid.

Death of the Minor If the beneficiary of an UGMA dies, the securities in the account pass to the minor's estate, not to the parents' or custodian's estate. In the event of the custodian's death or resignation, either a court of law or the donor must appoint a new custodian.

Summary

The customer account serves as the repository for the customer's cash and securities. In addition, the account serves as a record of the customer's investment objectives and activity.

There are numerous types of account, each requiring its own documentation, and in some instances, authorization. All new accounts must be accepted on behalf of the firm by a principal.

Accounts can be differentiated by ownership or decision authority, or by investment approach. Accounts differentiated by ownership or decision authority include:

- individual (including retirement)
- joint
  - joint tenants in common
  - joint tenants with rights of survivorship
- corporate

- partnership
- fiduciary or custodial
  - UGMA
  - discretionary
  - power of attorney

Accounts differentiated by investment approach or payment method are:

- cash
- margin
- option

Strict adherence to documentation and recordkeeping is required of the registered rep and the firm in maintaining customer accounts. This information is also to be kept in strict confidence. In addition, no one except specifically authorized individuals may make investment decisions for an account.

Key Concepts

To prepare for your license exam, you should learn the following concepts.

In addition to studying these key concepts, use the Customer Accounts Hot Sheet on page 638 for further review.

administrator
cash account
corporate account
credit agreement
custodial account
custodian
delivery vs. payment (DVP)
discretionary account
donor
executor
fiduciary account
full power of attorney
guardian
hypothecation agreement
indefeasible title
joint account
joint tenants in common (JTIC)
Joint tenants with right of
   survivorship (JTWROS)

limited power of attorney
loan consent agreement
margin account
new account form
numbered account
options account
partnership account
Regulation T (Reg T)
retirement account agreement
single account
special cash account
third party
trading authorization
trustee
Uniform Gifts to Minors Act
   (UGMA)
Uniform Transfers to Minors Act
   (UTMA)

Review Questions

1. A brokerage firm can open an account for all of the following EXCEPT a(n)

   A. pension fund
   B. insurance company
   C. estate
   D. third party without written authorization to do so

2. An employee of another NASD member broker-dealer would like to open an account with your firm. All of the following statements regarding the employee and the account are true EXCEPT the

   A. employer must receive duplicate copies of all transactions made in the account if requested
   B. employer must be notified of the opening of the account
   C. opening member must notify the employee in writing that the employer will be notified of the employee's intent to open the account
   D. broker-dealer holding the account must approve each transaction made by the person before entry of the order

3. A customer wishes her account designated by a number, not by her name. The registered representative

   A. can open the account with a written statement of ownership from the customer
   B. can open the account with a written statement of approval from an authorized delegate of the customer
   C. can open the account without additional documentation
   D. cannot open the account in this manner

4. All of the following customer information is required on a new account form EXCEPT

   A. name
   B. date of birth
   C. Social Security number
   D. occupation

5. Which of the following customer information should the registered rep normally attempt to obtain when opening a new account?

   I. Occupation
   II. Financial condition
   III. Investment objective

   A. I and II only
   B. I and III only
   C. II and III only
   D. I, II and III

6. An account is owned by three partners, one of whom dies. The registered rep

   A. may continue to trade the account once a letter is received stating that the partner has died
   B. must freeze the account's assets
   C. must close out the account and all outstanding orders because the death of a partner dissolves the partnership
   D. may continue to trade the account only after receiving a certified copy of the partner's death certificate

7. Which of the following persons are considered fiduciaries?

   I. Executor of an estate
   II. Administrator of a trust
   III. Custodian of an UGMA/UTMA account
   IV. Conservator for a legally incompetent person

   A. I and II only
   B. I, II and III only
   C. III and IV only
   D. I, II, III and IV

8. A customer would like to open a custodial UGMA/UTMA account for his nephew, a minor. The uncle

   A. can open the account provided the proper trust arrangements are filed first
   B. can open the account and name himself custodian
   C. needs a legal document evidencing the nephew's parents' approval of the account
   D. can be custodian for the account only if he is also the minor's legal guardian

9. Which of the following characteristics describe a joint tenants with right of survivorship account?

   I. Orders may be given by either party.
   II. Checks must be made out in the name of the account.
   III. Mail may be sent to either party.
   IV. In the event of the death of one of the tenants, the surviving party assumes control of the entire account.

   A. I and IV only
   B. II and III only
   C. III and IV only
   D. I, II, III and IV

10. All of the following statements regarding customer accounts are true EXCEPT

   A. stock held in a custodial account may not be held in street name
   B. the customer who opens a numbered account must sign a statement attesting to ownership
   C. stock held under JTWROS goes to the survivor in the event of the death of one of the tenants
   D. margin trading in a fiduciary account does not require any special consideration

Answers & Rationale

1. **D.** Broker-dealers are prohibited from opening third-party accounts without written permission.

2. **D.** The broker-dealer has no obligation to approve every transaction prior to entry.

3. **A.** The customer can have her account listed in any manner she wishes as long as she has filed a written statement of ownership.

4. **B.** The registered rep must ascertain that the customer is of legal age in that state, but is under no obligation to determine an exact birth date.

5. **D.** When opening a new account, the registered rep would normally obtain information on, among other things, the customer's occupation, financial condition and investment objectives.

6. **B.** As soon as a registered rep learns that an owner of a partnership account has died, the account must be frozen immediately and all pending transactions canceled.

7. **D.** All of the persons listed have fiduciary responsibilities because of the authority with which they are entrusted.

8. **B.** No documentation of custodial status is required to open an UGMA account.

9. **D.** In a JTWROS account, any party named on the account may enter orders for the account but distributions from the account must be sent in the names of all of the owners.

10. **D.** Trading on margin is prohibited to fiduciary accounts except under special circumstances and with the appropriate prior permission and documentation.

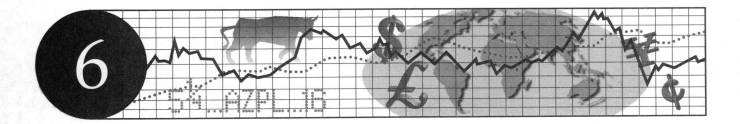

6

Margin Accounts

OVERVIEW

In the 1930s, Congress identified excessive borrowing to buy securities as one of the causes of the stock market crash of 1929. Buying securities with a down payment of less than their full market value is called *buying on margin*. Congress, through the Securities Exchange Act of 1934, gave the Federal Reserve Board (FRB) authority to regulate margin buying.

Extension of Credit in the Securities Industry

Buying on margin is common in the securities business and, essentially, it means buying stock or other securities on credit.

A margin account is a collateralized loan account in which a customer increases his trading capital by borrowing money from a brokerage house. In all cases, the stock or other securities purchased in a margin account are held by the brokerage house in street name as collateral for the outstanding loan. As with any loan, the customer pays interest on the borrowed money until it is repaid.

Though not as common a practice, stock can also be sold short in a margin account, enabling the customer to profit from a decline in value. In fact, short sales are always executed and accounted for in a margin account.

Advantages of a Margin Account

Advantages and risks are associated with margin accounts for both customers and broker-dealers.

Advantages of a Margin Account to a Customer.   A margin account offers a customer two distinct advantages:

1. The customer can purchase more securities with a lower initial cash outlay.
2. By borrowing a portion of the purchase price, the customer can **leverage** an investment, meaning the customer who buys on margin magnifies his gain or loss compared with the customer who pays for securities in full.

✓ *For Example:* An investor buys 1,000 shares of COW for $10 per share, or $10,000, in a cash account. The stock then increases to $15 per share. The customer's position is worth $15,000, representing a $5,000 gain, or 50 percent return. By contrast, if the customer bought on margin and put up only $5,000 (having borrowed $5,000 from the broker), he would realize a return of 100 percent on the initial $5,000 cash outlay. Therefore, the customer's return is magnified by leveraging the investment in a margin account (100 percent versus 50 percent).

Of course, the stock's price could just as easily decline, in which case a margin account customer would have a magnified loss.

Advantages of a Margin Account to a Broker-Dealer.   From a broker-dealer's viewpoint, margin accounts are profitable for two reasons:

1. Margin account loans generate interest income for the firm.
2. With borrowed capital added to the customers' own capital, margin customers typically trade bigger positions, resulting in increased commission revenue for the firm.

Significant Downside Risk. For the broker-dealer, the primary risk in a margin account is that the securities securing a loan might decline in value to the point where the loan (customer's debit balance) is no longer fully collateralized. While customers are legally responsible for repaying their loans in full, regardless of what happens to the securities' market value, some will inevitably default.

Relationship between Customer and Broker. A margin account changes the relationship between customer and broker-dealer. The firm becomes the customer's creditor, so all securities purchased on margin are registered in street name. The brokerage firm is called the *nominal owner* of the securities. The customer is known as the *beneficial owner*.

Regulation T

Under **Regulation T (Reg T)**, the Federal Reserve Board sets the minimum amount a customer must deposit when purchasing securities on margin or when selling securities short. This amount, known as the *Reg T call, initial margin requirement, initial margin call* or *federal call*, is currently 50 percent of the market value for marginable securities and 100 percent of the market value for nonmarginable securities. Therefore, at 50 percent margin, for every $10,000 worth of securities purchased or sold short, the customer must deposit $5,000 and the broker dealer advances the other $5,000 as a loan against the securities.

The 50 percent requirement represents the *minimum* amount a customer must deposit; he can always pay a larger percentage of the purchase price.

✓ **For Example:** A customer buying on margin could deposit 80 percent of the value of the securities and borrow 20 percent from the broker-dealer.

Marginable Securities

Reg T also identifies which securities are eligible for purchase on margin.

Eligible Securities. A brokerage firm may lend money to help a customer purchase marginable securities or may accept such securities as collateral for loans for other purchases. Marginable securities include:

- stocks and bonds listed on an exchange;
- stocks quoted on the Nasdaq National Market (NNM) as eligible for trading in the NNM;
- certain over-the-counter (OTC) securities the FRB designates; and
- warrants (for listed and designated securities only).

Noneligible Securities. According to Reg T, the following nonmarginable securities cannot be used as collateral for loans and must be paid for in full:

- put and call options
- common and preferred OTC stocks not designated by the FRB
- rights
- insurance contracts (not securities)
- new issues

✎ **Take Note:** Mutual funds and new issues may not be purchased on margin, but both may be used as collateral in a margin account when owned and paid in full for 30 days.

Exempt Securities. Securities exempt from Reg T are:

- U.S. Treasury bills, notes and bonds
- government agency securities

- municipal securities
- corporate straight debt (nonconvertible) securities

These securities can be bought or sold in a margin account, subject to an initial payment the broker-dealer sets. The firm is free to determine the initial loan value for exempt securities, subject to the NYSE and NASD minimum margin maintenance requirements.

Initial Requirements

A customer must open a margin account to use margin for any transactions. All margin transactions are handled in a margin account, regardless of the types of securities involved.

To open a margin account, the NASD/NYSE requires a minimum deposit of $2,000 if any borrowing is involved. If the 50 percent Reg T initial requirement is larger, the larger deposit is required.

✓ *For Example:* If an investor buys 200 shares of stock for $12 per share, even though the Reg T requirement is $1,200, he would be required to deposit $2,000.

However, if the initial transaction in a margin account is a purchase for less than $2,000, the customer need not deposit more than the transaction's total cost.

✓ *For Example:* If an investor buys 100 shares of stock for $12 per share, he would be required to deposit $1,200.

✎ *Take Note:* Margin requirements have varied widely over the years; they have been as high as 90 percent and as low as 10 percent. Though it is subject to change, the current 50 percent requirement has been in place for more than 20 years, and throughout this course a 50 percent margin requirement is assumed in all margin illustrations and calculations

When Issued Securities

Purchases of when issued, or when distributed, securities are subject to the same Reg T and NASD/NYSE requirements as other securities purchases. If the when issued security is part of a new issue (within the first 30 days of issue), the customer must deposit 100 percent of the purchase price. Otherwise, Reg T margin requirements apply. When issued exempt securities, such as municipal bonds, are not subject to these credit requirements, and individual firms may set their own requirements.

Deadlines for Meeting Margin Calls

Reg T requires all margin account customers to meet initial margin deposits not later than the *fifth business day* after the trade date—that is, two business days after the regular way settlement date—the same as in cash accounts. The deposit can be in cash or marginable securities.

TABLE 6.1   Summary of Initial Requirements and Loan Values

Securities	Reg T Initial Requirement	Loan Value
Listed equity securities, OTC margin securities, listed warrants	50% of the purchase cost or 50% of the proceeds of the short sale	100% minus the current Reg T requirement (e.g., 50% if Reg T is 50%, 30% if Reg T is 70%)
U.S. government obligations	Exempt (no Reg T requirement)	Set by NASD/NYSE
Municipal bonds	Exempt (no Reg T requirement)	Set by NASD/NYSE
Nonconvertible bonds	Treated as exempt from the Reg T requirement	Set by NASD/NYSE
Listed convertible bonds with and without warrants	50% of the purchase cost	50%

Payment Extensions for Margin Customers. As it may do with cash account customers, a broker-dealer may apply to its designated examining authority for permission to extend credit beyond the fifth business day to margin account customers late in meeting margin calls.

Forced Sell-Outs. If a margin customer does not meet a Reg T initial margin call by the fifth business day and no extension has been granted, the broker-dealer must liquidate enough securities in the account to satisfy the call in full. In addition, the firm must *freeze the account for 90 days*. During this period, it may extend no credit to the customer. For amounts less than $1,000, the broker-dealer can choose to take no action. However, although not required to send a funds due notice in these cases, most broker-dealers overlook small amounts due only for large or well-established customers.

Table 6.1 summarizes the Reg T initial requirements and loan values.

Margin Definitions

The use of margin involves certain concepts and terminology that are unfamiliar to most people. As you read the remainder of this lesson, it may be helpful to understand the terms listed below.

Buying Power (BP). The amount of fully margined securities a customer could buy without any additional deposits by using the cash and securities available in her account.

Credit Balance (or Credit Register/CR). The amount of money a brokerage firm owes a customer.

Creditor. Any broker or dealer, member of a national securities exchange, or person associated with a broker or dealer who has loaned money or securities.

Customer. Any person who would be considered a customer of a broker-dealer according to the ordinary usage of the term in the industry, especially a person for whom the broker-dealer arranges, extends or maintains credit.

Debit Balance (or Debit Register/DR). The amount of money a customer owes a brokerage firm. The customer pays the firm interest on any outstanding debit balance, and any unpaid interest increases the customer's debit balance.

Equity (EQ). A customer's net worth in a margin account. It equals what the customer owns minus what he owes.

Excess Equity (EE). The amount by which the equity in a customer's margin account exceeds the Regulation T requirement.

Hypothecation. The pledging of securities as collateral. The term is usually used in reference to securities purchased in a margin account.

Long Purchase. The purchase (ownership) of stock.

Marginable Security. Any exchange-traded security, OTC marginable security or NNM security.

Market Value. Securities in a margin account are valued at the current market price, also referred to as the **current market value (CMV)**. The term "long market value (LMV)" or "short market value (SMV)" may also be used, depending on the position.

Marking to Market. The practice of checking a security's market price, recording it in the margin account and adjusting the value of the securities held in the account accordingly. This is typically done every day based on the closing prices and affects the equity in the account.

OTC Margin Stock. Any security that (1) meets certain quality standards, and (2) has been designated by the Federal Reserve Board as eligible for trading on margin. These stocks appear in the FRB's published list of OTC margin stocks.

Rehypothecation. The practice of a broker-dealer pledging a customer's margined securities to a bank as collateral for a loan to carry the customer's margin account. The bank grants the broker-dealer a loan known as a *call loan* or *call money loan*. Call loans carry floating interest rates, known as *call money rates*, and do not have stated maturities.

Short Sale. The sale of borrowed stock.

Margin Accounting

Calculating Initial Requirements

The concept of a margin account is analogous to a home with an outstanding mortgage. A typical homeowner has a house with a market value, a debt (the amount of the mortgage left to pay) on which he pays interest, and equity (the difference between the house's market value and the mortgage balance). A customer with a margin account has current market value (the securities), debt (the margin loan from the broker-dealer) on which he pays interest, and equity (the difference between the market value and the loan balance).

Initial Transaction and Reg T Initial Margin

If a customer buys 1,000 shares of AMF stock at $50 per share, a $50,000 debit exists in the account. Within five business days, the customer must deposit $25,000 to meet the 50 percent Reg T requirement, which leaves a $25,000 debit balance, the amount the firm has loaned for the purchase.

The customer's margin account now has 1,000 shares of AMF with a market value of $50,000, no cash, a debit balance (loan) of $25,000 and equity of $25,000. The account would look like this:

Account's long market value (LMV)	$ 50,000
Debit register (DR)	− 25,000
Equity (EQ)	$ 25,000

Equity in the account does not represent a cash balance; it represents that portion of the securities in the account that the customer fully owns. Margin account balances are calculated each day, a process known as *marking to the market*. Once an account balance is marked to market, a customer's equity is compared to the securities' current market value, using the percentage specified in Reg T as a benchmark. When equity is above 50 percent of the market value, the customer has **excess equity**; if the equity falls below 50 percent of the market value, the account becomes **restricted**.

In the example above, the customer has no excess equity:

LMV	$50,000
DR	−25,000
EQ	$25,000
50% of LMV	−25,000
EE	$0

Tracking an Initial Transaction

Lets take another look at this example and examine the account's status as we move through the transaction. Assume Jerry opens an account and buys 1,000 shares of AMF at $50 per share. The status of the account before any money is deposited follows:

LMV	$50,000
DR	−50,000
EQ	$0

The first step the firm takes is to issue a Reg T margin call for $25,000 (50 percent of the stock cost). Jerry promptly deposits the required $25,000 in cash, resulting in the following account status:

LMV	$50,000
DR	−25,000
EQ	$25,000
50% of LMV	−25,000
EE	$0

At this point, Jerry's account is 50 percent margined: his equity in the account equals half the account's market value.

Using Securities for Margin Requirements

Fully paid securities may be used instead of cash to purchase stock in a margin account. To meet margin requirements using securities, a customer must deposit securities with a loan value equal to the debit in the account. The stock's loan value is the complement of Reg T—50 percent of the stock's current market value. (If the Reg T requirement were 60 percent, the loan value would be 40 percent; if Reg T were 70 percent, the loan value would be 30 percent.) Therefore, with Reg T at 50 percent, the customer must have on deposit $2 worth of fully paid securities for each $1 of margin debit.

In the illustration above, Jerry bought $50,000 worth of AMF. Instead of depositing $25,000 in cash to meet the initial margin requirement, he could deposit $50,000 worth of fully paid stock, an amount equal to the purchase. His account would look like this:

LMV	$100,000
DR	−50,000
EQ	$50,000
50% LMV	−50,000
EE	$0

✎ *Take Note:* When using securities to meet a margin requirement, the dollar value of the securities deposited must equal the dollar value of the securities purchased. The margin requirement value of securities is twice the cash requirement.

Excess Equity   As noted earlier, excess equity in a margin account is the amount of equity exceeding the initial margin requirement:

$$EQ - 50\% \text{ of LMV} = EE$$

Excess equity generates **buying power**. The customer can use the excess equity to buy more securities, or he can withdraw the excess equity in cash. The value of an account's buying power is calculated as the excess equity multiplied by 2 (EE × 2 = BP).

In a margin account, any deposit of cash that is not needed to meet a margin call—a customer's additional cash payments, for instance, or a dividend payment—is applied to pay off part of the debt. Anything that reduces debt increases equity.

✓ *For Example:* A $500 dividend would reduce the debit by $500 and would increase equity by $500. It would not affect the account's current market value.

If a dividend of $2 per share is paid on the 1,000 shares of Jerry's AMF stock, the result is a $2,000 decrease in his debit balance and a $2,000 increase in equity:

	Before	Dividend (applied to debt)	After
CMV	$50,000		$50,000
DR	−25,000	$2,000	−23,000
EQ	$25,000		$27,000
50% LMV	−25,000		−25,000
EE	$0		$2,000
			× 2
BP	$0		$4,000

The increase in equity does not represent more cash in the account (cash exists only when there is no debit balance), but rather becomes equity exceeding the 50 percent requirement.

Conversely, new debits not related to purchases of additional securities, such as interest charges and account fees, increase the debit balance in the account and decrease equity.

Increase in Market Value   As a stock's market value increases, equity in the account increases; and as the market value falls, equity decreases. The debit balance remains the same until the customer deposits or withdraws cash from the account.

If Jerry's 1,000 shares of AMF appreciate from $50 to $55 per share, the account's CMV increases by $5,000, to $55,000. The debit remains $25,000— the amount initially borrowed to buy the stock does not change. What does change is the equity—it increases by $5,000:

CMV	$55,000
DR	−25,000
EQ	$30,000
50% of LMV	−27,500
EE	$2,500

If Jerry's account value rises by an additional $5 a share, or $5,000, his account would look like this:

LMV	$60,000
DR	−25,000
EQ	$35,000
50% LMV	−30,000
EE	$5,000

The account now has $5,000 in excess equity. Jerry can withdraw this amount in cash from the account, use it to buy $10,000 worth of additional securities or leave it in the account.

As noted earlier, recalculating a customer's equity position, as illustrated above, is called *marking to the market*. Margin accounts are marked to the market each business day to determine a customer's equity and buying power. Excess equity is recorded daily in a **special memorandum account (SMA)**, as discussed later in this lesson.

Using Excess Equity to Purchase Stock

Using excess equity to purchase stock is common. In our illustration, Jerry has $5,000 in excess equity. Because the Reg T requirement is 50 percent, he can use the $5,000 to buy $10,000 worth of stock. The broker would loan him the full amount of the purchase. If Jerry buys $10,000 worth of MCS stock, his account would look like this:

LMV	$70,000
DR	−35,000
EQ	$35,000
50% LMV	−35,000
EE	$0

Withdrawing Excess Equity in Cash

A margin account customer may also use excess equity to take cash withdrawals. Because no actual cash exists in a margin account, the customer that does so borrows money against his securities' increased loan value. When a customer withdraws money from a margin account, he increases his margin loan's debt balance.

Rather than buy more stock, if Jerry withdraws his $5,000 in excess equity in cash, the transaction would change his account status as illustrated here:

	Before	Withdraw $5,000 from Excess Equity (Adds to Debit)	After
LMV	$60,000		$60,000
DR	−25,000	+ $5,000	−30,000
EQ	$35,000		$30,000
50% LMV	−30,000		−30,000
EE	$5,000	− $5,000	$0

Decrease in Market Value

If the stock in a margin account declines in value, the equity in the account falls dollar for dollar with the stock's market value. The debit balance dollar amount does not change; it is a record of money borrowed and cash flowing into and out of the account. However, as the CMV decreases, the debit balance becomes a larger percentage of the CMV.

Suppose that two weeks after Jerry's last transaction—the $5,000 withdrawal—the market moves against him. As a result, his margin securities decline in value $10,000, from $60,000 to $50,000. His account status would be as follows:

LMV	$50,000
DR	−30,000
EQ	$20,000
50% LMV	−25,000
Restricted	$<5,000>

Reg T does not require that the account be kept at a 50 percent margin; it requires the 50 percent deposit only for the initial purchase. A decrease in market value that brings equity below the Reg T requirement does not necessarily require an additional deposit of cash or securities. If no deposit is made, however, the account's status changes and it becomes a **restricted account**.

 Take Note: Declines in market value reduce a customer's equity dollar for dollar: a $10,000 loss in market value, for instance, results in a $10,000 loss in equity. Declines in market value do not change the debit balance amount owed to the broker-dealer.

Restricted Accounts   The term "restricted account" is somewhat misleading because it implies that activity is limited. When used in conjunction with a margin account, "restricted" means that the percentage of equity in the account is less than the Reg T initial requirement.

✓ **For Example:** When the market moved against Jerry, his account's equity changed:

CMV	$50,000	(100%)
DR	−30,000	(60%)
EQ	$20,000	(40%)

Current Reg T requirements do not mandate that a margin account be kept at 50 percent equity; therefore, a decrease in market value that brings equity below the Reg T initial requirement does not necessarily require an additional cash deposit by the customer. In fact, the customer can undertake the same types of transactions in a restricted account as he can in an account that has 50 percent equity.

In a restricted account, a customer may purchase or sell securities:

- If the customer wants to purchase additional shares in a restricted account, he must meet the Reg T requirement for an initial transaction, either by depositing 50 percent of the securities' value in cash or 100 percent of the value in securities.
- If the customer sells securities in a restricted account, any sale proceeds are credited to the customer's debit balance, decreasing the amount he owes the broker-dealer. However, under Reg T retention requirements, 50 percent of the proceeds of any sale must be retained in the account to be applied toward the debit balance, and a maximum of 50 percent may be made available for withdrawal by the customer.

If a customer would like to withdraw 100 shares of COD with a $6,000 CMV from his restricted margin account, the retention requirement states that he must deposit $3,000 either in cash or 100 percent in securities with a loan value of $3,000.

✓ **For Example:** Assume Jerry sells $10,000 worth of securities from his restricted account. His account status would look like this:

	Before Sale	*After Sale*
CMV	$50,000	$40,000
DR	−30,000	−20,000
EQ	$20,000	$20,000

Now Jerry can withdraw cash up to 50 percent of the proceeds of the sale, or $5,000. Keep in mind that the withdrawal is essentially another loan.

	After Sale		After $5,000 Cash Withdrawal
CMV	$40,000		$40,000
DR	−20,000	+ $5,000	−25,000
EQ	$20,000	− $5,000	$15,000

Withdrawals Not Involving Securities Transactions

Customers can make withdrawals from their accounts without selling securities. Two types of withdrawals that do not involve selling securities are cash withdrawals and stock withdrawals.

Cash Withdrawals. Whether or not an account is restricted, a customer can withdraw cash dividends and interest. A dividend or an interest payment the account receives reduces the debit. A $500 dividend, for instance, reduces the debit by $500 without affecting CMV. If the customer withdraws that amount, the debit increases by $500 and the account is back where it was before it received the dividend, as if nothing happened.

For any other cash withdrawal, a customer with a restricted account must either deposit additional marginable securities with a loan value equal to the amount of the cash withdrawn, or have SMA, which will be discussed later. The customer, in effect, borrows against the new securities deposited.

If a customer wants to withdraw $20,000 from a restricted margin account, she can deposit other fully paid securities in her margin account as collateral. With Reg T at 50 percent, the maximum loan available from the broker is 50 percent of the securities' market value:

$$CMV \times 50\% = \text{Loan value of securities deposited}$$

Stock Withdrawals. If a customer wants to withdraw stock from his account, he must deposit cash equal to the retention requirement. Because the retention requirement is 50 percent, he must deposit cash equal to half the value of the securities withdrawn.

Instead of depositing cash, a customer can withdraw stock by depositing fully paid stock held elsewhere. He must deposit new stock with a loan value equal to 50 percent of the value of the stock withdrawn. In effect, with Reg T at 50 percent this is a dollar-for-dollar substitution—for example, $10 worth of one stock for $10 worth of another.

Maintenance Requirements

Once a customer has met the initial margin requirement, she must meet NASD/NYSE margin maintenance requirements when the market moves adversely, whether it's a decline in a long position's value or an increase in a short position's value. A margin maintenance call is a demand that the customer make additional payment on her loan (debit balance) promptly. If payment is not made, the broker-dealer liquidates the customer's securities.

Maintenance Calls

The NASD/NYSE maintenance requirement for stock purchased on margin is 25 percent of the current market value. In other words, a customer must maintain a level of equity equal to at least 25 percent of his account's current market value. If equity drops below this amount, a maintenance call is sent. A maintenance call is a request for a deposit of cash or marginable securities to bring the equity up to the required level.

✓ **For Example:** If the value of Jerry's account declines by 25 percent, it would look like this:

	Before Decline	After Decline
CMV	$50,000 (100%)	$37,500 (100%)
DR	−30,000	−30,000
EQ	$20,000 (40%)	$7,500 (20%)
NASD/NYSE req.	$12,500 (25%)	$9,375 (25%)

As you can see, the decline in the value of Jerry's account brought his equity below the required minimum by $1,875. In this situation, Jerry will receive a maintenance call from his broker-dealer for $1,875, which he must meet by depositing cash or marginable securities or by liquidating securities in his account promptly.

Calculating Minimum Maintenance

The formula used to calculate the market value of securities that represents the minimum maintenance level follows:

$$DR \div 75\% = LMV \text{ at minimum maintenance}$$

Using Jerry's account as an example, we can see that the current market value can decline to $40,000 before equity falls below the 25 percent minimum:

$$\$30,000 \text{ DR} \div 75\% = \$40,000$$

At $40,000, his account status would be as follows:

CMV	$40,000 (100%)
DR	−30,000 (75%)
EQ	$10,000 (25%)

TABLE 6.2   NASD/NYSE Maintenance Margin Requirements

Security or Transaction	NASD/NYSE Maintenance Requirement
Equity securities—long	25% of CMV
Equity securities—short:	
1. Selling at more than $5	Greater of $5 per share or 30% of CMV
2. Selling at $5 or less	Greater of $2.50 per share or 100% of CMV
Corporate bonds—long	Greater of 7% of principal or 20% of CMV
Corporate bonds—short	Greater of 5% of principal or 30% of CMV
Municipal bonds	Greater of 7% of principal or 15% of CMV
U.S. government and agency securities	1% to 6% of par value

House Maintenance Requirements

It should be noted that most broker-dealers impose higher margin maintenance requirements than those set by the NYSE and NASD. On long positions, the house maintenance might be 30 percent rather than 25 percent. Some firms raise their maintenance requirements during volatile market conditions.

Broker-dealers can set house requirements higher than both the Reg T initial requirement and NASD/NYSE initial and minimum maintenance requirements, but never lower. House maintenance calls are due promptly, but most firms allow a reasonable period of time for payment.

Table 6.2 summarizes the maintenance requirements for different types of securities.

Short Sales and Margin Requirements

Selling short is a strategy an investor uses to profit from a decline in a stock's price. Short sellers sell shares of stock they do not own. They initially borrow stock from a broker-dealer, then sell the stock at the market. Because they are obligated to buy the stock later to replace the borrowed shares, they anticipate that the stock price will decline enough to allow them to replace the borrowed shares at a lower price. A short seller profits when she can buy back the stock at a lower price than the price that she sold it for. Selling short is always done in a margin account.

Sources of Borrowed Stock

A customer does not borrow money for short sales, he borrows securities to sell and makes margin deposits to cover his risks—actions that put money in the account. The resulting credit balance represents actual cash—the sales proceeds plus the margin deposit requirement—which is available when the customer wants to purchase the securities to close the short position. Equity in a short account equals the amount by which the credit balance exceeds the current short market value (SMV) of the securities in the account.

Reg T Requirements

A customer who sells stock short must deposit cash in a margin account as assurance that he will be able to purchase the stock needed to cover the short position in the event of a price increase. The current Reg T requirement is the same for short sales as it is for long purchases: 50 percent.

✔ **For Example:** If a client sells short 100 shares of stock with a market value of $50, he would have to deposit $2,500, or 50 percent of the sale proceeds.

When defining its requirements, Reg T uses the phrase "150 percent of the security's current market value" to indicate that the full amount (100 percent) of the sale proceeds *plus* an additional 50 percent initial margin on the position must be on deposit in the account by the fifth business day, as shown in the example below:

Transaction	Price	Sale Proceeds	+	Reg T 50%	=	CR
Short 100 shares GIZ	60	$6,000	+	$3,000	=	$9,000
Short 500 shares COD	20	$10,000	+	$5,000	=	$15,000

As is true with long purchases, Reg T initial margin on short sales can be met either with cash or through the deposit of marginable securities with a loan value equal to the call amount. The deposit is expected promptly, but is required within five business days.

NASD/NYSE Minimum Deposit on Short Sales

When opening a long margin account, a client must deposit a minimum of $2,000 or 100 percent of the securities' market value, whichever is less. When establishing a short margin account, on the other hand, a client must always deposit a minimum of $2,000. Even if a client sells short only $100 worth of stock, he must deposit at least $2,000.

Margin Maintenance Calls on Short Sales

NASD/NYSE margin maintenance requirements on short positions is 30 percent, compared to 25 percent for long positions. House maintenance requirements on short positions can be higher still.

When the market increases and a short sale position moves adversely, minimum requirement rules require enough equity in the account to cover 100 percent of the higher current market value, plus 30 percent of the current market value.

To illustrate the working of a short margin account, assume that Sherry opens a margin account and sells short 100 shares of RST at 70, or $7,000, which is credited to her account. The broker-dealer then issues an initial Reg T call for $3,500 (50 percent of the sale proceeds) which she promptly deposits. Her account would look like this:

SMV	$7,000	(100%)
50% req.	+3,500	(50%)
CR	$10,500	(150%)

To determine the equity in a short position, subtract the securities' value from the total amount credited to the account:

$$CR - SMV = EQ$$

In a short account, the customer *owes* the securities; therefore, the short market value is subtracted from the credit balance. Thus, we can see that the equity in Sherry's account—the amount by which the credit balance ($10,500) exceeds the current market value of the securities short in the account ($7,000)—is $3,500:

CR	$10,500
SMV	−7,000
EQ	$3,500

A decline in a security's short market value below the original short sale price may produce excess equity in a customer's margin account.

✔ **For Example:** If the price of Sherry's RST declines to 60, the SMV goes from $7,000 to $6,000, resulting in $1,500 excess equity:

CR	$10,500
SMV	−6,000
EQ	$4,500
50% SMV	−3,000
EE	$1,500

As with long accounts, excess equity generates buying power, which can be preserved as SMA if not used.

In contrast, a rise in a security's current market value above the original short sale price reduces the customer's equity.

✓ **For Example:** If the price of Sherry's RST increases to $80, the SMV rises from $7,000 to $8,000, resulting in $2,500 equity:

CR	$10,500
SMV	−8,000
EQ	$2,500

At this point, with the securities' value above the selling price and equity less than half the SMV, Sherry's account becomes restricted. However, the brokerage firm does not have to take action until and unless the equity in the account drops below 30 percent of the current market value. When this happens, a maintenance call will be issued.

Margin Maintenance Calls on Short Sales

As noted earlier, the NASD/NYSE margin maintenance requirement on short positions is 30 percent. The maximum market value to which a short sale position can increase before a margin maintenance call is issued can be determined with the following formula:

Total credit balance ÷ 130% = Maximum market value

Applying this formula to the current example, the maximum market value to which Sherry's short position could advance would be $8,077:

$10,500 ÷ 130% = $8,077

It should be noted that the brokerage firm can set its own maintenance requirement at a level higher than 30 percent. In addition, the NASD/NYSE margin maintenance requirement on short positions in stocks less than $5 per share is the greater of $2.50 per share or 100 percent of market value.

✓ **For Example:** A customer who sells short 1,000 shares of a $2 stock must deposit $2,500 to comply with the initial margin requirement.

Combined Accounts

A client who has a margin account with both long and short positions in different securities is said to have a *combined (mixed) account*. In combined accounts, equity and margin requirements are determined by calculating the long and short positions separately and combining the results.

Determining Customer Equity

The equity in a combined account equals the equity for the long position (LMV – DR) plus the equity for the short position (CR – SMV).

Initial Margin Requirement

To calculate the Reg T initial margin requirement for a combined account, determine the requirements for the long and short positions separately, then combine them.

LMV	$18,000	×	50%	=	$9,000	
SMV	$6,000	×	50%	=	$3,000	
Combined	$24,000	×	50%	=	$12,000 Reg T	

Maintenance Requirement

To determine the maintenance requirement for a combined account, calculate the long and short positions separately, because each has a different requirement. For a long position, the NASD/NYSE requirement is 25 percent of the CMV. For a short position, the NASD/NYSE requirement is 30 percent of the CMV. The combined maintenance requirement is determined as follows:

LMV	$18,000	×	25%	=	$4,500
SMV	$6,000	×	30%	=	$1,800
NASD/NYSE minimum maintenance				=	$6,300

Buying Power

The formula for calculating buying power in a combined account is determined in the same way as in a long account. When Reg T is 50 percent, any excess equity in the account has buying power of 2 to 1.

Withdrawing Cash. As with ordinary margin accounts, customers may withdraw cash from combined accounts to the extent that excess equity exists in the account.

Special Memorandum Account

Any margin account in which the customer's equity exceeds 50 percent of the current market value of the securities in the account has excess equity. A margin account typically acquires excess equity from securities' price increases. The customer may withdraw this excess equity or use it to buy additional securities.

Excess equity also can be credited to a separate part of the margin account called the **special memorandum account**. No real funds, cash or securities are actually transferred to an SMA; it is simply a line of credit, a limit on the amount of money a customer could borrow now or in the future. It is similar to the credit limit placed on a credit card. The term "SMA" applies to both the special account itself and the value of the line of credit it represents.

A customer may withdraw funds against her SMA just as she might withdraw funds from a credit line at a bank or take out a cash advance on a credit card. When the customer does withdraw or use SMA, she is actually borrowing *more* money from the broker-dealer, thereby increasing the debit balance in her account. When this occurs, interest is charged on any amount withdrawn or borrowed.

A customer can always use the balance in her SMA unless the transaction—withdrawal of cash or securities or purchase of securities—will cause the account equity to drop below the minimum maintenance (or the $2,000 minimum) requirement.

The most important characteristics of SMA covered in this section follow:

- SMA increases as the excess equity in a margin account increases.
- SMA does not decrease as the result of market value decreases.
- SMA may be more than excess equity or may exist even if no excess equity is in the account.

Generating SMA   An SMA balance can be generated when excess equity is credited to SMA. Any of the following also could generate SMA:

- **Nonrequired cash deposits.** If a customer's cash deposit is not required to meet a margin call, the full amount reduces the debit and is also credited to SMA.
- **Dividends and interest earned.** Dividends and interest received on securities in a margin account are added to SMA. The customer can always withdraw the entire amount, even if the account is restricted.
- **Loan value.** If a customer makes a nonrequired deposit of marginable stocks, that stock's loan value is credited to SMA.

Excess Equity

If a customer buys 200 shares of stock at $100 and deposits cash to meet the 50 percent Reg T requirements, his margin account will look like this:

CMV (200 × $100)	$20,000
DR	−10,000
EQ	$10,000
Reg T (50%)	−10,000
EE	$0
SMA	$0

If the stock increases in market value to $110 per share, this creates excess equity in the customer's account. Excess equity can be borrowed, used to purchase additional securities or left in the account to be credited to SMA. The increase in market value would affect the account as follows:

CMV	$22,000
DR	−10,000
EQ	$12,000
Reg T	−11,000
EE	$1,000
SMA	$1,000

If the stock's price subsequently drops to $95, the CMV declines, the debit remains unchanged, equity decreases and excess equity decreases, but SMA remains the same. Once SMA is credited to a customer's account, only the customer's use of it can deplete it. Market or broker actions cannot take away the SMA line of credit. The stock's price drop would affect the account as follows:

CMV	$19,000
DR	−10,000
EQ	$9,000
Reg T	−9,500
EE	$0
SMA	$1,000

Selling Securities. As mentioned earlier, the Reg T retention requirement allows an investor to withdraw or use for additional purchases 50 percent of the proceeds of any sale in a margin account. If the investor does not use the amount immediately, it is credited to SMA. When stock is sold in a margin account, you can calculate the new SMA balance by adding 50 percent of the sale proceeds to the existing SMA amount.

Depleting SMA   An SMA balance is depleted by all of the following:

- **Cash withdrawals from a margin account.** This includes the withdrawal of dividends.
- **New margin purchases.** A customer may use the balance in an SMA to meet the Reg T requirement for purchases.
- **Withdrawals of securities.** This reduces the SMA balance by 50 percent of the market value of the securities withdrawn. The SMA, in this case, may be used to meet a retention requirement.

Using SMA to Buy Stock. Because SMA is a line of credit, the investor can use it to meet the margin requirements on stock purchases. SMA gives the investor buying power. The following equation calculates SMA's buying power:

$$\text{SMA} \div \text{Reg T requirement} = \text{Buying power}$$

For every dollar of SMA, the investor can purchase two dollars of securities when Reg T is 50 percent ($1 ÷ 50 percent = $2). Consider the following example of an investor who uses the available SMA to buy stock:

	Before Purchase	The Purchase	After Using SMA
CMV	$10,000	$6,000	$16,000
DR	−2,000	−6,000	−8,000
EQ	$8,000		$8,000
Reg T (50%)	−5,000		
SMA	$3,000	$0	$0

The investor borrowed the new security's entire purchase price from the firm, as always happens initially. She uses the SMA to meet the initial call, but because it does not represent an actual cash deposit, but rather is a line of credit, the SMA increases the customer's debit balance. Because the investor has deposited no more cash, her equity remains the same as before the purchase.

Withdrawing Cash. Customers also may use SMA to withdraw (that is, borrow) money from their margin accounts.

✓ *For Example:* If a customer's margin account has a market value of $10,000 and $2,000 in SMA, and he wants to withdraw cash equal to the entire SMA balance, the customer's CMV would remain unchanged. However, the debit balance would increase, equity would decrease by the amount borrowed and the SMA would be depleted, as shown next:

	Before	After
CMV	$10,000	$10,000
DR	−5,000	−7,000
EQ	$5,000	$3,000
SMA	$2,000	$0

An investor may not make a withdrawal if it would bring the equity below $2,000 or the minimum maintenance requirement, whichever is greater. To determine how much SMA can be used without going below the 25 percent minimum requirement, calculate the difference between the existing equity and the minimum equity; that is the maximum amount that may be withdrawn.

 Take Note: Because SMA is not cash, and using SMA for cash withdrawals increases the debit balance and reduces equity, SMA may not be used to meet a maintenance call.

SMA and Restricted Accounts   A customer must meet the 50 percent Reg T retention requirement when withdrawing securities from a restricted account. This can be done with *SMA* unless doing so violates maintenance requirements. For example:

CMV	$8,000
DR	−4,200
EQ	$3,800
SMA	$900

Notice that the above account is restricted by $200. This customer has $3,800 in equity instead of the $4,000 Reg T requires. When withdrawing securities, the customer must deposit 50 percent of the market value in cash or use SMA to meet the Reg T requirement. To calculate how much market value of securities the customer can withdraw, divide the SMA balance by the retention requirement (50 percent):

SMA ÷ Retention requirement = CMV of withdrawable securities

Therefore, $900, in this case, divided by 50 percent equals $1,800.

After the customer withdraws the securities, the account is restricted even further, but the equity still meets the minimum requirements. The account looks like this:

CMV $6,200
DR   −4,200
EQ $2,000
SMA $0

Same-Day Substitution of Stock. A customer can sell one stock and buy an equivalent amount of another stock without incurring a Reg T call, resulting in a same-day substitution. A same-day substitution works much the same way as a stock withdrawal. Assuming the customer's account is restricted and the cost of the stock purchased exceeds the value of the stock sold, the difference between the two positions' costs is subject to Reg T requirements.

✓ *For Example:* If the customer sells stock for $10,000 and buys stock for $12,000, the $2,000 net difference is subject to a Reg T call of $1,000 (50 percent of the excess purchase).

If the proceeds of the stock sold exceed the cost of the stock purchased, the difference in a restricted account is still subject to the 50 percent retention requirement.

✓ *For Example:* If the customer sells stock for $12,000 and buys stock for $10,000, the amount of cash the customer could withdraw would be $1,000, or 50 percent (50 percent retention requirement × net proceeds of $2,000).

Summary of Effects on SMA

Table 6.3 shows the effects on SMA of various account activities.

Pledging Customer Securities for Loans

When a customer purchases securities on margin, the securities are pledged to the broker-dealer as collateral for the loan. This process is called **hypothecation** of the securities. A broker-dealer lends money to margin account customers from its own working capital. As a means of replenishing this working capital, the broker-dealer borrows from banks, using customer margin account securities as collateral. When a broker-dealer borrows money from a bank using customer securities to finance customer debit balances, the process is called **rehypothecation**.

Commingling of Customer Securities. SEC **Rule 15c2-1** prohibits a broker-dealer from commingling one customer's securities with another customer's securities as joint collateral for a bank loan unless the customers specifically

TABLE 6.3   Effects of Various Account Activities on SMA

Activity	Effect on SMA	Remarks
Rise in market value	Increase	Only if the new excess equity is higher than the old SMA.
Sale of securities	Increase	The client is entitled to excess equity in the account after the sale, or to 50% of the sale proceeds, whichever is greater.
Deposit of cash	Increase	The full amount of the deposit is credited to SMA unless a margin call has been issued.
Deposit of marginable securities	Increase	Increased by the loan value of the securities deposited, as prescribed by Reg T at the time of deposit.
Dividends or interest	Increase	100% of a cash dividend or interest (a nonrequired deposit) is credited to SMA.
Purchase of securities	Decrease	The margin requirement on new purchases is deducted from SMA. If SMA is insufficient to meet the margin requirement, a cash deposit is required.
Withdrawal of cash	Decrease	The full amount of the cash withdrawal is deducted from SMA. Equity must remain higher than the NASD/NYSE or house equity requirement.
Withdrawal of marginable securities	Decrease	Decreased by the retention requirement of the withdrawn stock.
Fall in market value	No effect	After the SMA balance is established, it is not affected by a fall in market value.
Interest charges	No effect	SMA remains the same.
Stock dividend or split	No effect	SMA remains the same.

give written authorization. The **customer hypothecation agreement** on a standard margin agreement provides this authorization.

Broker-dealers are always prohibited from commingling customer securities with firm securities and pledging them jointly as collateral for a bank loan. If this occurred, then a firm defaulted on its portion of the loan, a **cross lien** would be created on the customer securities.

Liens. Loans a broker-dealer enters into for firm business may be collateralized only by securities the firm owns. The lender cannot place a lien on customer securities that may be pledged separately. The only liens permitted against securities pledged as customer collateral are liens a lender places for loans that benefit customers. A broker-dealer may, however, pledge its own securities to protect customer loans. In such instances, a **one-way lien** is permitted against the broker's securities. The lender has no claim on customer securities for this loan, only on the firm's securities.

Notice and Certification Requirements. A broker-dealer cannot rehypothecate customer securities to a lender unless, at the time of the pledge, the lender is given written notice that the broker-dealer carries the securities for a customer's account and the pledge does not violate Rule 15c2-1. Day loans are exempt from this requirement.

Borrowing Limits. In addition, the maximum amount that a broker-dealer can borrow using customer securities as collateral is limited to 100 percent of the customer's debit balance. The broker-dealer cannot pledge customer securities to borrow an amount that exceeds the customer's total indebtedness.

140 Percent Hypothecation Rule. The maximum amount of customer securities that a broker-dealer can pledge as collateral, or hypothecate, is 140 percent of the customer's debit balance. The broker-dealer is limited to pledging 140 percent of the customer's debit balance to secure a loan that is a maximum of 100 percent of the customer's debit balance.

Customer Protection, Reserves and Customer Securities

The SEC requires that a customer's fully paid securities and excess margin securities—securities valued in excess of 140 percent of the customer's debit balance—must be segregated (physically set aside) and kept safely. Each firm must also keep a reserve bank account for customers' funds.

Customers and Customer Securities. A customer is any person who has an account with a broker-dealer, who is not a broker-dealer, or a partner or an officer of a broker-dealer, and who is not a subordinated lender. A broker-dealer that has an omnibus account with a clearing broker-dealer is considered a customer. Omnibus accounts are master accounts in which cash and securities are held for many individual customers of another broker-dealer on an unidentified, undisclosed basis. **Customer securities** are any securities received by, held for, sold to or bought for a customer's account.

Fully Paid Securities. Fully paid securities are held for a customer in an account in which the customer has no debit balance. All fully paid securities must be delivered to the customer upon request.

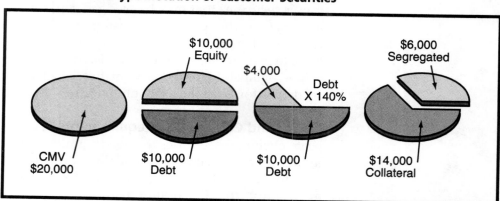

FIGURE 6.1 **Rehypothecation of Customer Securities**

Margin Securities. Those securities in a margin account that have a market value of up to 140 percent of the account's net debit balance are known as *margin securities*. The net debit balance is all margin debits less all cash balances. Credits from short sales of securities are excluded. Margin securities are available to broker-dealers to use for financing customer debit balances.

Excess Margin Securities. All of the securities in a margin account exceeding 140 percent of the account's net debit balance are known as *excess margin securities*. Customers' fully paid and excess margin securities a broker-dealer holds must be segregated from the firm's own accounts and earmarked as the customer's property. They cannot be commingled with the firm's inventory and may not be loaned to other customers for short sales.

✓ *For Example:* If a customer has a $10,000 net debit balance in a margin account and $20,000 CMV of securities, the firm may rehypothecate up to $14,000 worth of the customer's margined securities ($14,000 is 140 percent of $10,000). The other $6,000 worth of securities ($20,000 – $14,000) are considered excess margin securities; they must be segregated and cannot be used as loan collateral. Figure 6.1 illustrates this example.

Summary

Buying securities on margin is a common means by which investors leverage their investment dollars. In margin accounts, investors borrow money to purchase securities from brokerage firms by pledging securities they own as collateral.

The leverage that margin provides serves to magnify the potential gain or loss from investment positions. As a result, the Federal Reserve Board regulates margin transactions.

The FRB specifies which securities may be marginable. It also specifies, through Reg T, the initial equity requirements for purchases and short sales in a margin account. The SROs require maintenance of a minimum level of equity after the initiation of the transaction.

In studying for the Series 7 exam, pay particular attention to calculating the initial and maintenance margin requirements for margin transactions.

Key Concepts

To prepare for your license exam, you should learn the following concepts.

In addition to studying these key concepts, use the Margin Accounts Hot Sheet on page 639 for further review.

buying power
credit register (CR)
current market value (CMV)
debit register (DR)
equity (EQ)
excess equity (EE)
exempt security
house maintenance
hypothecation
long position
maintenance call
margin

margin call
margin maintenance call
mark to the market
market value
Reg T call
Regulation T (Reg T)
rehypothecation
restricted account
short position
special memorandum account
 (SMA)

Review Questions

1. When stock held in a margin account appreciates, which of the following increase(s)?

   I. Current market value
   II. Debit balance
   III. Equity

   A. I only
   B. I and III only
   C. II only
   D. I, II and III

2. A customer chooses to leave a dividend payment in a margin account; as a result

   I. equity increases
   II. equity decreases
   III. debit balance increases
   IV. debit balance decreases

   A. I and III
   B. I and IV
   C. II and III
   D. II and IV

3. Selling a security held long in a margin account

   I. decreases the debit balance
   II. decreases the current market value
   III. decreases the equity
   IV. increases the equity

   A. I and II
   B. I, II and IV
   C. I and III
   D. II and III

4. A customer opens a margin account and signs a loan consent, hypothecation and credit agreement. Which of the following statements are true?

   I. The customer's stock will be kept in street name.
   II. A portion of the stock may be pledged for a loan.
   III. The customer will be required to pay interest on the money loaned (debit balance).

   A. I and II only
   B. I and III only
   C. II and III only
   D. I, II and III

5. A customer purchases stock in a cash account and requests that the stock be held in street name. The registered rep should inform the customer that the

   A. firm can use the stock as collateral for a loan
   B. firm may hypothecate the securities
   C. customer can have the stock registered in his name at any time
   D. firm can loan the stock to another customer for a short sale transaction

6. A customer has a margin account with $23,000 in securities and a debit of $12,000. Which of the following statements are true?

   I. The account is restricted.
   II. The customer will receive a margin call for $500.
   III. The customer may withdraw securities if he deposits 50 percent of the securities' value in cash.
   IV. The account has excess equity of $5,250.

   A. I and II only
   B. I and III only
   C. III and IV only
   D. I, II, III and IV

7. A customer has a margin account with market value of $300,000 and equity of $100,000. The stock drops $20,000 in value. The customer will receive a maintenance call for

    A. $0
    B. $20,000
    C. $75,000
    D. $100,000

8. A customer has a margin account with market value of $300,000 and equity of $100,000. The market value drops $35,000 in value. The customer will receive a maintenance call for

    A. $0
    B. $1,250
    C. $1,600
    D. $35,000

Answers & Rationale

1. **B.** The debit balance changes when securities are purchased or sold; it does not change when a stock's price appreciates or depreciates.

2. **B.** A dividend received into an account results in an increased equity balance and a decreased debit balance. If the dividend is subsequently paid out, equity will decrease and debits will increase.

3. **A.** When a security that is held long in an account is sold, the proceeds from the sale decrease both the debit balance and the total market value of the account.

4. **D.** In order for a customer to borrow money through a margin account to purchase securities, she must (1) agree to allow the broker-dealer to pledge those securities, (2) pay interest on the loan, and (3) leave the stock in the broker-dealer's safekeeping, registered in street name.

5. **C.** Customers retain the right to have fully paid stock registered in any manner they wish.

6. **B.** When an account is restricted, the customer must deposit the Reg T initial margin requirement (currently 50 percent) in order to make new purchases or withdraw stock.

7. **A.** At this point, the customer has equity of $80,000, a CMV of $280,000 and a debit balance of $200,000. The maintenance requirement for the stock at a CMV of $280,000 is $70,000 ($280,000 × 25%), so the customer is still $10,000 above the point at which he would be issued a maintenance call.

8. **B.** At this point, the customer has equity of $65,000, a CMV of $265,000 and a debit balance of $200,000. The maintenance requirement for the stock at a CMV of $265,000 is $66,250 ($265,000 × 25%), so the customer will be issued a maintenance call for $1,250.

7

Issuing Securities

OVERVIEW

In general, securities are bought either as new issues from a corporation, municipality or federal government or in the secondary market as trades between investors. This lesson introduces the market for newly issued securities, including the process of registering a new securities offering and the role an investment bank plays in various types of offerings.

The Regulation of New Issues

The Legislative Framework

After the stock market crash of 1929, Congress examined the causes of the debacle and passed several laws meant to prevent its recurrence. This legislation included the Securities Act of 1933 and the Securities Exchange Act of 1934, among others.

The Securities Act of 1933. The Securities Act of 1933 regulates new issues of corporate securities sold to the public and requires securities issuers to provide enough information for investors to make fully informed buying decisions. This information must be registered with the federal government and published in a prospectus. The act prohibits any fraudulent activity in connection with the underwriting and issuing of all securities.

The Securities Exchange Act of 1934. The Securities Exchange Act of 1934 addresses secondary trading of securities, personnel involved in secondary trading and fraudulent trading practices. It also created the Securities and Exchange Commission (SEC) to oversee the industry.

In 1938, the act was amended by the **Maloney Act,** which provides for the establishment of a self-regulatory body to help police the industry. Under Maloney Act provisions, the National Association of Securities Dealers (NASD) regulates over-the-counter (OTC) trading in much the same way as the exchanges regulate their members.

The Trust Indenture Act of 1939. The Trust Indenture Act of 1939 was created to provide the same sort of protection to the purchasers of debt securities as is afforded to investors in equities. The act prohibits the sale of any corporate debt security exceeding $5 million with a maturity of more than nine months unless it has been issued under a **trust indenture**. The trust indenture is a contract that gives a trustee the powers necessary to enforce the issuer's obligations and the debt holders' rights. In addition to providing full disclosure about the nature of the debt issue and the issuer, the trust indenture identifies the trustee's rights and responsibilities.

Registration of Securities

The Securities Act of 1933 is also referred to as the *Full Disclosure Act*, the *New Issues Act*, the *Truth in Securities Act* and the *Prospectus Act*. The act's main purpose is to ensure that the investing public is fully informed about a security and its issuing company when the security is first sold in the **primary market**.

The 1933 act protects investors who buy new issues by:

- requiring registration of new issues to be distributed interstate;
- requiring an issuer to provide full and fair disclosure about itself and the offering;
- requiring an issuer to make available all material information necessary for an investor to judge the issue's merit;
- regulating the underwriting and distribution of primary and secondary issues; and
- providing *criminal penalties* for fraud in the issuance of new securities.

An issuer must file with the SEC a **registration statement** disclosing material information about the issue. Part of the registration statement is a prospectus, which must be provided to all purchasers of the new issue. The registration statement must contain:

- a description of the issuer's business;
- the names and addresses of company officers and directors, their salaries and a five-year business history of each;
- the amount of corporate securities company officers and directors own, and identification of investors who own 10 percent or more of the company;
- the company's capitalization, including its equity and debt;

- a description of how the proceeds will be used; and
- whether the company is involved in any legal proceedings.

The underwriter may assist the issuer in preparing and filing the registration statement and prospectus. The registration statement must be signed by the issuer's chief executive officer, chief financial officer and chief accounting officer, as well as a majority of the issuer's board of directors.

State Registration. State securities laws, also called **blue-sky laws**, require state registration of new issues, broker-dealers and registered reps. According to the Uniform Securities Act, an issuer or investment banker may blue-sky an issue by one of the following three methods:

1. **Qualification.** Typically used for interstate offerings, the issue is registered with the state independent of federal registration, and it meets all state requirements.
2. **Coordination.** Typically used for initial public offerings (IPOs), the issuer registers simultaneously with the state and the SEC. Both registrations become effective on the same date.
3. **Filing.** Certain states allow some new issues to be blue-skied by having the issuer notify the state of the issue's SEC registration. In this case, the state requires no registration statement, although certain other information must be filed.

Most states exempt securities from individual registration if they meet one or more other requirements—typically, listing on a regional or national stock exchange or qualifying as a National Association of Securities Dealers Automated Quotation system (Nasdaq) or Nasdaq National Market (NNM) stock.

Each state has its own registration requirements not only for securities, but also for the registration of broker-dealers, investment advisers and registered reps. A person or broker-dealer usually must be registered in any state in which it sells or attempts to sell securities.

The Prospectus   After an issuer files a registration statement with the SEC, a 20-day **cooling-off** period begins.

Cooling-off Period

After the issuer (with the underwriter's assistance) files with the SEC for registration of the securities, the cooling-off period ensues before the registration becomes effective. The registration can become effective as early as the 20th calendar day following the date the SEC receives it. In practice, however, the cooling-off period is seldom 20 days; the SEC usually takes longer to clear registration statements. If it finds that the registration statement needs revision or expansion, the SEC may suspend the review and issue a **deficiency letter**. The 20-day cooling-off period resumes when the issuer submits a corrected registration statement.

Because of the time it takes to make additions and corrections, the cooling-off period can, in fact, last several months. The SEC sometimes issues a **stop order** which demands that all underwriting activities cease. This may be done if requirements of the 1933 act have not been met or if fraud is suspected.

The preliminary prospectus can be used as a prospecting tool, allowing underwriters and selling group members to gauge investor interest and gather **indications of interest**.

An indication of interest is a broker-dealer's or an investor's declaration that he might be interested in purchasing some of the security from the underwriter after the security comes out of registration. A broker-dealer's or an investor's indication of interest is *not* a commitment to buy because sales are prohibited until after the registration becomes effective (the **effective date**).

Due Diligence

Near the end of the cooling-off period, the underwriter holds a **due diligence meeting**. The preliminary studies, investigations, research, meetings and compilation of information about a corporation and a proposed new issue that go on during an underwriting are known collectively as **due diligence**.

The underwriter must conduct a formal due diligence meeting to provide brokers with information about the issue, the issuer's financial background and the intended use of the proceeds. Representatives of the issuer and the underwriter attend these meetings and answer questions from brokers, securities analysts and top institutional accounts.

As part of the due diligence process, the investment banker must:

- examine the use of the proceeds
- perform financial analysis and feasibility studies
- determine the company's stability
- determine whether the risk is reasonable

The Final Prospectus

When the registration statement becomes effective, the issuer amends the preliminary prospectus and adds information, including the final offering price and the underwriting spread for the final prospectus. Registered representatives may then take orders from those customers who indicated interest in buying during the cooling-off period.

A copy of the final prospectus must precede or accompany all sales confirmations. The prospectus should include all of the following information:

- description of the offering
- offering price
- selling discounts
- offering date
- use of the proceeds
- description of the underwriting, but not the actual contract
- statement of the possibility that the issue's price may be stabilized
- history of the business
- risks to the purchasers
- description of management
- material financial information
- legal opinion concerning the formation of the corporation
- SEC disclaimer

SEC Review

The SEC reviews the prospectus to ensure that it contains the necessary material facts, but it does not guarantee the disclosures' accuracy. Furthermore, the SEC does not approve the issue, but simply clears it for distribution. Implying that the SEC has approved the issue violates federal law. Finally, the SEC does not pass judgment on the issue's investment merit. The front of every prospectus must contain a clearly printed SEC disclaimer specifying the limits of the SEC's review procedures. A typical SEC disclaimer clause reads as follows:

> These securities have not been approved or disapproved by the Securities and Exchange Commission or by any State Securities Commission nor has the Securities and Exchange Commission or any State Securities Commission passed upon the accuracy or adequacy of this prospectus. Any representation to the contrary is a criminal offense.

The information supplied to the SEC becomes public once a registration statement is filed.

The three phases of an underwriting are illustrated in Figure 7.1.

Preliminary Prospectus. The preliminary prospectus, also known as the **red herring**, must be made available to any customer who expresses interest in the securities between the SEC registration filing date and the effective date.

48-hour Rule. If the issuer is *not* an SEC-reporting company, a preliminary prospectus must be sent to all interested customers and must arrive at least 48 hours before the mailing of a customer purchase confirmation.

FIGURE 7.1   The Three Phases of an Underwriting

Aftermarket Sales by Prospectus. The SEC requires that all sales of public offering stock listed on an exchange or traded on Nasdaq be accompanied by a prospectus for a specified time period following the public offering. During this period, a broker-dealer must furnish a final prospectus with every sale of the newly issued security. Specified time periods include:

- 90 days for an initial public offering
- 40 days for an additional issue not listed on an exchange or quoted on Nasdaq
- 25 days for an additional issue listed on an exchange or quoted on Nasdaq

The 25-day sale-by-prospectus requirement applies to anyone who participates in the public distribution—that is, underwriters and selling group members.

Advertising a New Issue

Advertising and sales literature include any notice, circular, advertisement, letter or other communication published or transmitted to any person. The only advertising allowed during the cooling-off period is a **tombstone**, a simple statement of facts regarding the issue. The tombstone announces a new issue, but does not offer the securities for sale.

Advertising copy and other sales materials qualify as tombstones, not a prospectus, meaning they need not be filed with the SEC as part of the registration statement.

The tombstone may appear before or after the effective date. Issuers are not required to publish tombstones.

The Underwriting Process

Investment Banking

A business or municipal government that plans to issue securities usually works with an **investment bank,** a securities broker-dealer that may also specialize in underwriting new issues.

An investment bank's functions may include:

- advising corporations on the best ways to raise long-term capital
- raising capital for issuers by distributing new securities
- buying securities from issuers and reselling them to the public
- distributing large blocks of stock to the public and to institutions
- helping issuers comply with securities laws

Participants in a Corporate New Issue

The main participants in a new issue are the company selling the securities and the broker-dealer acting as the underwriter.

The Issuer. The issuer, the party selling the securities to raise money, is responsible for:

- filing the registration statement with the SEC;
- filing a registration statement with the states in which it intends to sell securities (also known as *blue-skying the issue*); and
- negotiating the securities' price and the amount of the spread with the underwriter.

The Underwriter. The underwriter assists with the registration and distribution of the new security and may advise the corporate issuer on the best way to raise capital. Among other things, the underwriter considers the following matters:

- **Whether to offer stock or bonds**. If bonds are currently selling with high coupon rates, the company may choose to issue stock. Determining the cheapest cost of capital is a very important role of the investment bank.
- **Tax consequences of the offering**. The interest a corporation pays on its bonds is tax deductible; cash dividends to stockholders are paid out of after-tax profits.
- **Money market financing**. Money market instruments are a short-term financing mechanism, typically one year or less.
- **Capital market financing**. The capital markets represent long-term financing for secured bonds, debentures, preferred stock or common stock. Normally, these securities require registration and sale by prospectus.

Types of Offerings

A new stock offering is identified by whom is selling the securities as well as by whether or not the company is already publicly traded.

New Issues

The new issue market is composed of companies going public by selling common stock to the public for the first time in an **initial public offering**.

Additional Issues

The additional issue market is made up of new securities issued by companies that are already publicly owned. These companies increase their equity capitalization by issuing more stock and having an underwriter either distribute the stock in a public offering or arrange for the shares to be sold in a private placement.

In addition to being classified as new or additional issues of stock, offerings can be classified by the final distribution of their proceeds.

Primary Offering

In a primary offering, the underwriting proceeds go to the issuing corporation. The corporation increases its capitalization by selling stock, in either a new or an additional issue. It may do this at any time and in any amount, provided the total stock outstanding does not exceed the amount authorized in the corporation's bylaws.

Secondary Offering

In a secondary offering, one or more major stockholders in the corporation sell all or a major portion of their holdings. The underwriting proceeds are paid to the stockholders rather than to the corporation itself.

Table 7.1 compares primary and secondary offerings.

Split Offering (or Combined Distribution)

A split offering simply combines a primary and a secondary offering. The corporation issues some of the stock offered; present corporation stockholders hold the rest.

Shelf Offering (Rule 415)

Through a **shelf offering**, an issuer can register a new securities issue without selling the entire issue at once. The issuer can sell portions of a registered shelf offering over a two-year period without having to reregister the

TABLE 7.1   Offerings and Markets

	New Issue (IPO) Market	Additional Issue Market
Primary Offering	Company is going public; underwriting proceeds go to the company.	Company is already public; underwriting proceeds go to the company.
Secondary Offering	Company is going public; underwriting proceeds go to the selling stockholders.	Company is public; underwriting proceeds go to the selling stockholders.

security, but it must file a supplemental prospectus before each sale. Shelf registration can be used for both equity and debt offerings.

Public Offerings and Private Placements

Corporate securities are sold to investors through **public offerings** or **private placements**. In a public offering, securities are sold to the investing public through one or more broker-dealers.

A private placement occurs when the issuing company, with the assistance of its investment bank, sells securities to private investors, as opposed to the general investing public. Although private placement buyers tend to be institutional investors, securities can be sold to small groups of wealthy individuals—especially in conjunction with the distribution of limited partnership program securities. Private placements are generally exempt from the registration requirements of the Securities Act of 1933.

Underwriting Sequence

Forming the Syndicate

The syndicate and selling group may be assembled before or after the issue is awarded to the underwriter. In a competitive bidding, the syndicate is assembled first and syndicate members work together to arrive at the bid. In a negotiated underwriting, the syndicate may be formed after the issuer and underwriting manager have negotiated the terms of the offering.

Pricing the New Issue

The underwriter advises the issuing corporation on the best price at which to offer shares to the public. The variables below may be considered when pricing new issues:

- indications of interest from the underwriter's book;
- prevailing market conditions, including recent offerings, and the prices of similar new issue stocks recently issued (hot issues or overpriced);
- price the syndicate members will accept;
- price-earnings (PE) ratios of similar companies and the company's most recent earnings report (at what price must the shares be offered so that the PE ratio is in line with the PEs of other similar publicly traded stocks); and
- company's dividend payment record and financial health.

An issue's price is determined by the effective date of the registration. The effective date is when the security begins to trade.

Stabilizing Price

When considerably less demand than supply exists for a new issue, the price in the public offering aftermarket is likely to fall when the offering closes. Under these circumstances, the underwriter can **stabilize** the security by bidding for shares in the open market. The managing underwriter can enter or can appoint a syndicate member to enter stabilizing bids for the security until the end of the offering period.

Stabilizing bids must *not* be made at a price higher than the public offering price (POP). Stabilization is not illegal; however, if the stabilization bid is made at a price higher than the public offering price, it is called *pegging*, or *fixing*, and is prohibited by the SEC.

If public buying interest does not increase, the managing underwriter may have no choice but to abandon the POP, pull the stabilizing bid and let the stock find its own level.

The Underwriting Syndicate

Corporate underwriting normally takes the form of a negotiated agreement between the issuer and investment banker. This negotiated agreement, known as the **underwriting agreement**, is signed before the effective date.

Depending on the offering size, the underwriter may want to form a syndicate, or a joint account for the purposes of the underwriting. The underwriting syndicate includes a syndicate manager and an association of underwriters.

Underwriting Manager. The investment banker that negotiates with the issuer is known as the *underwriting manager* or *syndicate manager*. The underwriting manager directs the entire underwriting process, including signing the underwriting agreement with the issuer and directing the due diligence meeting and distribution process. A syndicate may have more than one manager, acting as co-managers.

Syndicate. Underwriting syndicate members make a financial commitment to help bring the securities public. In a firm commitment offering, all syndicate members commit to distribute an agreed-on amount of the issue (their participation, or bracket).

Syndicate members sign a syndicate agreement, or syndicate letter, that describes the participants' responsibilities and allocates syndicate profits.

Syndicate Account

The *agreement among underwriters* details each underwriter's commitment and liability—particularly for any shares that remain unsold at the underwriting syndicate's termination.

Forming the Selling Group

Although the members of an underwriting syndicate agree to underwrite an entire offering, they frequently enlist other firms to help distribute the securities as members of the **selling group**. Selling group members act as agents with no commitment to buy securities.

The managing underwriter is normally responsible for determining whether to use a selling group and, if so, which firms to include. If the securities to be issued are attractive, broker-dealers will want to participate. If the securities are not attractive, the manager may have to be persuasive to get broker-dealers to join.

Selling group members sign a **selling group agreement** with the underwriters, which typically contains the following terms:

- statement that the manager acts for all of the underwriters;
- amount of securities each selling group member will be allotted and the tentative public offering price at which the securities will be sold (this price is firmed up just before the offering date);
- provisions as to how and when payment for shares is to be made to the managing underwriter; and
- legal provisions limiting each selling group member's liability in conjunction with the underwriting.

Types of Underwriting Commitments

Different types of underwriting agreements require different levels of commitment from underwriters. This results in different levels of risk.

Firm Commitment

The **firm commitment** is the most widely used type of underwriting contract. Under its terms, the underwriter contracts with the issuing corporation, selling stockholders or both to buy the securities at a specified price and quantity range, on or about a given date. The terms are detailed in a **letter of intent (LOI)** signed by the underwriter and the issuer.

The underwriter commits to buy securities from the issuer and pay the underwriting proceeds to the company. Under a firm commitment contract, any losses incurred due to unsold shares are prorated among the underwriting firms according to their participation.

Market-Out Clause

In a firm commitment underwriting, the underwriter assumes substantial financial risk for the underwriting. To limit its risks, a market-out clause in the underwriting agreement specifies conditions under which the offering may be canceled.

Risks Beyond the Underwriter's Control. Underwriters may suspend or abort an offering if a *material, adverse event* occurs that affects the issuing corporation and impairs the investment quality of the securities to be offered. The sudden death of the company president might be such an event.

Risks that the Underwriter Must Assume. Underwriters may not exercise market-out provisions if a *nonmaterial, adverse event* occurs that affects the issuing company, but does not impair the securities' investment quality. A nonmaterial, adverse event could be a Federal Reserve policy shift that leads to a general market decline before the offering. This would not qualify as a material event.

Negotiated

In a negotiated underwriting, the issuer and the investment banker negotiate the offering terms, including the amount of securities to be offered, the offering price and the underwriting fees.

Negotiated underwritings are standard in underwriting corporate securities because of close business relationships between issuing corporations and investment banking firms.

Competitive Bid   Competitive bid arrangements are the standard for underwriting most municipal securities and are often required by state law. In a competitive bid, a state or municipal government invites investment bankers to bid for a new issue of bonds. The issuer awards the securities to the underwriter(s) whose bid results in the lowest net interest cost to the issuer.

All or None   In an all or none (AON) underwriting, the issuing corporation determines that it wants an agreement that the underwriter must sell all of the shares or cancel the underwriting. Because of the uncertainty over the outcome of an AON offering, any funds collected from investors during the offering period must be held in escrow pending final disposition of the underwriting.

Prohibitions. Underwriters and others engaged in an AON distribution are prohibited from deceiving investors by stating that all of the securities in the underwriting have been sold if it is not the case.

Best Efforts   In a best efforts arrangement, the underwriter acts as agent for the issuing corporation, contingent on the underwriter's ability to sell shares in either a public offering or a private placement.

✔ *For Example:* If a corporation plans to issue 100,000 shares of common stock at $20 per share, but—after exerting best efforts—the underwriter can distribute only 80,000 shares, the extent of the underwriter's commitment is limited to 80,000 shares.

Mini-Max   A mini-max offering is a best efforts underwriting with a floor and a ceiling on the dollar amount of securities the issuer will sell. The underwriter must locate enough interested buyers to support the minimum (floor) issuance requirement. Once the minimum is met, the underwriter can expand the offering up to the maximum (ceiling) amount of shares the issuer specified. Mini-max underwriting terms are most frequently found in limited partnership program offerings.

Standby   When a company's current stockholders do not exercise their preemptive rights in an additional offering, a corporation usually has an underwriter standing by to purchase the unused rights, exercise them and sell the shares.

Firm Commitment. The standby underwriter *unconditionally agrees* to buy all shares current stockholders do not subscribe to at the subscription price.

Rights Market-Making Activity. The standby underwriter also agrees to maintain a trading market in the subscription rights, buying rights from any present stockholders who choose to sell.

Underwriter Exercises Rights. At the end of the subscription period, the standby underwriter uses the rights acquired in the open market and any rights abandoned by stockholders to buy the unsubscribed portion of the offering at the subscription price minus an underwriting fee.

Public Offering. The standby underwriter then offers the stock to the general public at the original subscription price, which now becomes the public offering price.

Underwriting Compensation

The price at which underwriters buy stock from issuers always differs from the price at which they offer the shares to the public. The price the issuer receives is known as the *underwriting proceeds*, and the price investors pay is the public offering price. The underwriting spread, the difference between the two prices, consists of the:

- **manager's fee**, for negotiating the deal and managing the underwriting and distribution process;
- **underwriting fee**, for assuming the risk of buying securities from the issuer without assurance that the securities can be resold; and
- **selling concession**, for placing the securities with investors.

Industry Standard Practices

The industry norm for allocating the spread for corporate equity issues is as follows:

Underwriting Component	Fee Range
Syndicate manager's fee	10% to 20%
Underwriting syndicate fee	20% to 30%
Selling concession	50% to 60%

The NASD's Committee on Corporate Finance relies on these guidelines when evaluating underwriting spreads for fairness and reasonableness.

Figure 7.2 illustrates a sample spread distribution for an IPO of 1 million shares at $10 per share with a spread of $.65 per share.

The $.65 spread is allocated as follows:

- **Syndicate manager's fee.** This is compensation for the manager's role in the underwriting—in this case, $.12 per share, or $120,000 for 1 million shares. The manager's fee is typically the smallest portion of the spread.
- **Underwriting fee.** This portion of the spread compensates syndicate members for the risk they assume in the underwriting. The underwriting fee—in this case, $.13 per share—is allocated to syndicate members based on their participation.
- **Selling concession.** The largest portion of the spread is the selling concession, the amount received by any member that sells the shares.

FIGURE 7.2 Who Gets What in an Underwriting

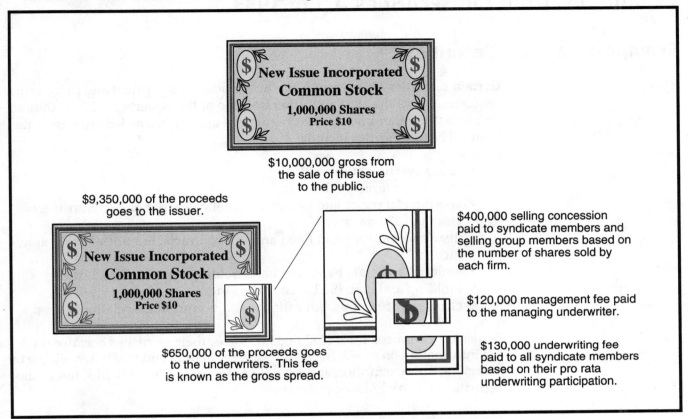

New Issue Incorporated Common Stock
1,000,000 Shares
Price $10

$10,000,000 gross from
the sale of the issue
to the public.

$9,350,000 of the proceeds
goes to the issuer.

New Issue Incorporated Common Stock
1,000,000 Shares
Price $10

$650,000 of the proceeds goes
to the underwriters. This fee
is known as the gross spread.

$400,000 selling concession
paid to syndicate members and
selling group members based on
the number of shares sold by
each firm.

$120,000 management fee paid
to the managing underwriter.

$130,000 underwriting fee
paid to all syndicate members
based on their pro rata
underwriting participation.

The amount of the spread varies by issue and can be influenced by any of the following:

- **Type of commitment.** A firm commitment earns a larger spread than a best efforts agreement due to the risks the underwriter assumes.
- **Security's marketability.** A triple-A (AAA) bond has a smaller spread than a speculative stock.
- **Issuer's business.** A stable utility stock usually has a smaller spread than a more volatile stock.
- **Offering size.** In a very large offering, the underwriter can spread costs over a larger number of shares; thus, the per-share cost may be lower.

Exemptions from the Securities Act of 1933

Exempt Issuers and Securities

Certain securities are exempt from the registration statement and prospectus requirements of the 1933 act, either because of the issuer's creditworthiness or because another government regulatory agency has jurisdiction over the issuer. These securities include:

- U.S. government securities;
- state and municipal bonds;
- commercial paper and bankers' acceptances that have maturities of less than 270 days;
- insurance policies and fixed annuity contracts, but not variable annuities;
- national and state bank (not bank holding company) securities;
- building and loan (S&L) securities; and
- charitable, religious, educational and nonprofit association issues.

Banks are exempted from SEC registration of their securities because they file information on new issues with bank regulators and make it available to investors. This exemption applies only to the securities of banks, not to the securities of bank holding companies.

Insurance policies are not included in the definition of "security"; however, variable annuities, variable life insurance and variable universal life insurance are funded by separate accounts and must be registered as securities with the SEC.

Exempt Transactions

Securities offered by industrial, financial and other corporations may qualify for exemption from the registration statement and prospectus requirements of the 1933 act under one of the following exclusionary provisions:

- **Regulation A**: corporate offerings of less than $5 million
- **Regulation D**: private placements
- **Rule 147**: securities offered and sold exclusively intrastate

In addition, other exempt transactions include Rule 144, Rule 144a and Rule 145.

Regulation A: Small Offerings

Regulation A (Reg A) permits issuers to raise up to $5 million in a 12-month period without full registration. This allows a small company access to the capital market to raise a small amount of money without incurring prohibitive costs.

In a Reg A offering, the issuer files an abbreviated notice of sale, or **offering circular**, with the regional SEC office. Investors are provided with the offering circular rather than a full prospectus. The cooling-off period is 20 days between the filing date and effective date, and the issuer need not provide audited financial information. The Regulation A exemption is not available for investment companies or for oil and gas limited partnerships.

Regulation D: Private Placements

The SEC does not require registration of an offering if it is privately placed with:

- officers or other insiders of the issuer;
- financial institutions or **accredited investors** that do not need SEC protection; or
- a maximum of 35 individual (nonaccredited) investors. This is detailed according to Rule 506 of Regulation D.

An accredited investor is one who:

- has a net worth of $1 million or more; or
- has had an annual income of $200,000 or more in each of the two most recent years (or $300,000 jointly with a spouse) and who has a reasonable expectation of reaching the same income level in the current year.

The purchasers must have access to the same type of information they would receive if the securities were being sold under prospectus in a registered offering. The amount of capital that can be raised under Rule 506 is not limited.

A private placement investor must sign a letter stating that he intends to hold the stock for investment purposes only. Private placement stock is referred to as **lettered stock** due to this investment letter. The certificate may bear a legend indicating that it cannot be transferred without registration or exemption; therefore, private placement stock is also referred to as **legend stock**.

Rule 147: Intrastate Offerings

Under Rule 147, offerings that take place entirely in one state do not fall under the SEC's jurisdiction. They are, instead, the responsibility of the state commissioner of securities. SEC Rule 147 exempts such an offering from registration when:

- the issuer has its principal office and receives at least 80 percent of its income in the state;
- at least 80 percent of the issuer's assets are located within the state;
- at least 80 percent of the offering proceeds are used within the state;

- the broker-dealer acting as underwriter is a resident of the state and has an office in the state; and
- all purchasers are residents of the state.

Purchasers of an intrastate issue may not resell the stock to any resident of another state for at least *nine months* after the underwriting.

Rule 144 Rule 144 regulates the sale of control and restricted securities, stipulating the holding period, quantity limitations, manner of sale and filing procedures.

Control securities are owned by directors, officers or persons who own or control 10 percent or more of any type of a company's outstanding securities. Individuals who have a control relationship with an issuer are considered **affiliated persons**.

Restricted securities are those acquired through some means other than a registered public offering. A security purchased in a private placement is a restricted security.

Restricted securities may not be sold until they have been held fully paid for one year. According to Rule 144, the total sales of stock over any 90-day period must not exceed the greater of:

- 1 percent of the total outstanding shares of the same class at the time of sale; or
- the average weekly trading volume in the stock over the past four weeks on all exchanges or as reported through Nasdaq.

Sales in amounts not exceeding 500 shares or $10,000 in sale proceeds are permitted without the filing of Form 144. Current information about the company must be made available to the buyer. This can be accomplished by verifying that the company is a reporting company that regularly files 10K and 10Q reports with the SEC.

Rule 144a Rule 144a, which covers nonregistered foreign and domestic securities sold to institutional investors in the United States, has no holding period requirement. To qualify under a Rule 144a exemption, the seller must determine that the purchaser is a **qualified institutional buyer (QIB)**. Securities bought in a Rule 144a transaction are restricted.

Rule 145 Rule 145 of the 1933 act is intended to protect stockholders of any company that proposes to reorganize its ownership structure, acquire another company or merge with another company. Any such proposition requires stockholder approval. Rule 145 requires that stockholders be sent a full disclosure document—that is, a **proxy statement**—to inform them of the proposition.

Transactions Covered by Rule 145. Transactions Rule 145 covers are reclassifications, mergers or consolidations, and transfers of assets:

- **Reclassification**—when one class of securities is to be exchanged internally for another class in a way that shifts ownership control.
- **Merger or consolidation**—when stockholders in a target company are offered securities in another company in exchange for the surrender of their stock.
- **Transfer of assets**—when all or some of one company's business assets are exchanged for another company's securities. Stockholders thus solicited are being asked to approve their company's dissolution.

Antifraud Regulations of the Acts of 1933 and 1934

Although a security might be exempt from the registration and prospectus requirements, *no offering is exempt from the antifraud provisions* of the Securities Act of 1933 or any other securities act, including the Securities Exchange Act of 1934. The antifraud provisions of the act of 1933 apply to all new securities offerings, whether exempt from registration or not. Issuers must provide accurate information regarding any securities offered to the public.

Freeriding and Withholding: Hot Issues

Hot issues are public offering securities that sell or have the potential to sell at an *immediate premium* over the POP in the secondary market.

A member's failure to make a bona fide offering at the POP is considered **freeriding and withholding** under the NASD's Conduct Rules. Any NASD member firm engaged in distributing a stock that proves to be a hot issue must:

- make a bona fide public offering of the securities at the announced POP (the member firm must not withhold stock in its investment or trading accounts—or in any other account—for the purpose of selling it later at a higher price in the open market);
- not sell the stock to any employee or officer of the member firm under any circumstances; and
- not sell the stock to any individual customer with a restricted account unless he can demonstrate that his normal investment practice includes the purchase of similar securities.

Prohibited Accounts. It violates NASD rules for any underwriter or selling group member—or any broker-dealer buying public offering securities from an underwriter or a selling group member—to sell any hot issue security to any individual listed below:

- the underwriters;
- any NASD member broker-dealer;
- any person associated with an NASD member;
- supported family members of a person associated with an NASD member; or
- any person financially dependent on a person associated with an NASD member.

Exceptions   Under certain circumstances, limited amounts of a hot issue may be sold to the following people.

Nonsecurities Persons Associated with the Underwriting. This category includes any person who acts in a business or professional capacity in connection with a public offering, such as a finder, an accountant, an attorney, a financial consultant or another person performing a fiduciary service for the managing underwriter, and any person who is supported financially by a person in this category. A person in this category should not be allowed to purchase a hot issue unless it can be proved that she regularly and routinely buys similar public offering securities. In other words, it is the person's normal investment practice.

Officers and Certain Employees of Financial Institutions. This category includes senior officers of banks, savings and loans, insurance companies, investment companies, investment advisers and other types of institutional investors, as well as any person who is supported financially by a person in this category.

Immediate Family Members. A family member who is *not* materially supported by any securities industry personnel may buy a hot issue if he purchases the issue from a broker-dealer that does not employ the restricted person and if the:

- family member has a history of purchasing similar securities;
- purchase size is consistent with his normal investment practice;
- sale is of an insubstantial amount compared to the total amount available; and
- total of all sales of the security to all classified accounts is not disproportionate to the amount the dealer has available for sale.

The NASD focuses on certain measurements when monitoring sales of hot issues to people in the restricted categories defined above to determine whether a violation of the freeriding and withholding rule has occurred.

Normal Investment Practice. "Normal investment practice" refers to an account's investment history, usually over the previous year, but sometimes longer. Specifically, a hot issue can be sold to a restricted individual if that type of security is consistent with the individual's investment patterns.

Insubstantiality. "Insubstantiality" refers to sales to restricted accounts that total less than 10 percent of the member firm's allotment, but that are concentrated in only one or a few accounts. If no concentration exists, the NASD most likely will rule that no violation has occurred (on the basis that the amount of stock involved is insubstantial).

Summary

New securities are sold in the primary market.

The new issue market is regulated primarily by the Securities Act of 1933. The act of 1933 requires issuers of securities to provide sufficient information to the investing public in a prospectus so that investors may make informed investment decisions. The information must be registered with the SEC before an issue can be offered to the public.

The act of 1933 strictly prohibits fraudulent information or activity in connection with the underwriting and distribution of new issues.

A new issue of publicly traded securities may be an initial offering, in which the securities are being offered for the first time, or an additional issue, in which the company is already publicly traded. In addition, the offering may be a primary offering, in which the company issuing the securities receives all of the proceeds, or a secondary offering, in which one or more stockholders sell their stock and receive the proceeds.

The issuer will enlist the help of an underwriter, a broker-dealer that specializes in investment banking and the distribution of new issues. The underwriter will often advise the issuer regarding the best financing mechanism, equity or debt, in light of current market conditions and tax considerations.

The underwriter will also normally form an underwriting syndicate, a group of other broker-dealers, to assist in the distribution of the new issue.

An underwriter may commit to distribute a new issue in several different ways, each involving a different degree of risk to the underwriter. The degree of risk the underwriter assumes in the distribution of a new issue, along with other factors, will affect the level of compensation they receive for the underwriting.

In a firm commitment underwriting, the most frequently used, members of the underwriting syndicate commit to distribute a certain portion of the shares and are financially liable for shares they are unable to distribute.

When a new issue is a hot issue, members involved in the distribution are prohibited from:

- withholding shares from the public at the offering price in order to profit in the firm's account;
- selling the stock to employees or family members of employees; and
- selling the stock to restricted accounts without meeting certain criteria.

Certain issues of new securities are exempt from the registration requirement with the SEC. Exemptions generally occur because the issuer is subject to other regulations or the securities are not offered to the general public. Institutional investors take part in such private transactions involving unregistered securities.

Key Concepts

To prepare for your license exam, you should learn the following concepts.

In addition to studying these key concepts, use the Issuing Securities Hot Sheet on page 640 for further review.

all or none (AON)	preliminary prospectus
best effort	primary offering
competitive bid underwriting	private placement
cooling-off period	public offering price (POP)
due diligence	red herring
Eastern (undivided) account	registration statement
firm commitment	secondary offering
freeriding and withholding	Securities Act of 1933
Glass-Steagall Act of 1933	Securities Exchange Act of 1934
hot issue	selling group
indications of interest	shelf offering
investment banker	split offering
letter of intent (LOI)	syndicate manager
Maloney Act	tombstone
mini-max offering	underwriting
negotiated underwriting	Western (divided) account
new issue market	

Review Questions

1. Which of the following are types of under-writings?

    I. Firm commitment
    II. All or none
    III. Standby
    IV. Best efforts

    A. I and II only
    B. I, III and IV only
    C. II and III only
    D. I, II, III and IV

2. In a best efforts offering, an underwriter

    A. makes no guarantee that an offering will be sold
    B. makes a best efforts attempt to reduce the underwriting spread
    C. guarantees a minimum price and makes a best efforts attempt to increase that price
    D. makes a best efforts attempt to bring the security to market within the cooling-off period

3. A standby underwriting is used

    A. by a company going public for the first time
    B. in a secondary offering
    C. in a best efforts underwriting
    D. in a rights offering

4. ALFA Enterprises has filed an offering of 425,000 shares of common stock. One-third of the shares are being sold by existing stockholders, and the balance is new shares. Which of the following statements are true?

    I. ALFA Enterprises will receive the proceeds from the entire sale.
    II. This offering is a combined distribution.
    III. The selling stockholders will receive some of the proceeds.
    IV. This offering is an exchange distribution.

    A. I and II
    B. I and IV
    C. II and III
    D. II, III and IV

5. The principal functions of an investment banker are to

    I. distribute securities to the public
    II. provide a secondary market
    III. provide financing for an individual
    IV. advise the issuer about alternatives in raising capital

    A. I and II
    B. I and IV
    C. II and III
    D. III and IV

6. All of the following acts are prohibited during the cooling-off period EXCEPT

    A. promising a certain amount of the issue to a customer
    B. soliciting indications of interest
    C. taking an order
    D. accepting a check from a customer to purchase the issue

7. The red herring typically includes all of the following information EXCEPT

    A. a list of company officers
    B. the price of the issue
    C. a list of principal underwriters
    D. the number of shares

8. The Securities Act of 1933 does all the following EXCEPT

    A. require SEC registration of most new issues of securities
    B. require publication of material information about the issue
    C. provide for the establishment of self-regulatory organizations
    D. exempt certain types of securities from registration

9. Which of the following best describes the underwriting manager?

    A. Employee who supervises the underwriting activities of an investment banker
    B. Broker-dealer that supervises the activity of the issuer on authority of the SEC
    C. Broker-dealer that publishes the offering prospectus
    D. Broker-dealer that supervises the activity of the underwriting syndicate and selling group

10. Which of the following are considered by an underwriter when establishing the offering price?

    I. Projected earnings for the company
    II. Likely dividends to be paid over the coming years
    III. Demand for the security by the investing public
    IV. Earnings multiples for other companies in the market in the same industry

    A. I only
    B. I and III only
    C. II and IV only
    D. I, II, III and IV

Answers & Rationale

1. **D.** All four choices are types of underwriting. They differ as to the level of commitment by the broker-dealer to sell all or part of the issue. In a firm commitment underwriting, the broker-dealer purchases all the securities and then resells them. In an all or none underwriting, the broker-dealer tries to sell the entire issue. If the entire issue is not sold, the offering is canceled.

2. **A.** In a best efforts underwriting, the firm sells as much as it can with no obligation to purchase any part of the unsold offering.

3. **D.** In a standby commitment, a firm agrees to purchase any part of an issue that has not been subscribed to through a rights offering.

4. **C.** Because existing stockholders are receiving some of the proceeds, this characterizes the offering as a combined distribution. In a combined distribution (or split offering) part of the proceeds go to the issuer with the rest going to stockholders. That part of the proceeds going to stockholders is considered a secondary offering.

5. **B.** The primary roles of a broker-dealer are to distribute securities to the public and advise issuers on the best ways to raise capital. Broker-dealers do not have to provide a secondary market for any security. Providing individual financing is the role of commercial banks and other lending institutions.

6. **B.** The only action that can be taken during the cooling-off period is to determine investor interest in the security.

7. **B.** The offering price of the issue is one of the last details to be determined. As a result, the issue's price will not be known until much closer to the time the issue actually comes to market.

8. **C.** The 1933 act was designed to protect investors considering the purchase of new issues. Beginning with the Securities Exchange Act of 1934, legislation was enacted to provide for industry self-regulatory organizations.

9. **D.** In addition to negotiating with the issuer, the underwriting manager directs the entire underwriting process from registration to directing the sales process with the other firms in the syndicate and selling group.

10. **D.** All of the choices listed are important when determining an offering price. The offering price has to appeal to investors and should reflect as fair and reasonable a market value as is possible considering the competitiveness of the securities markets.

8

Trading Securities

OVERVIEW

Stocks and bonds are bought and sold on exchanges in a two-way auction process. The major exchanges include:

- the New York Stock Exchange (NYSE)
- the American Stock Exchange (AMEX)
- regional stock exchanges

Other trades take place in the nationwide network of broker-dealers known as the *over-the-counter (OTC) market*. This lesson introduces the terminology and language of trading securities.

The Regulation of Trading

As the Securities Act of 1933 regulates primary issues of securities, the Securities Exchange Act of 1934 regulates secondary trading.

The Securities Exchange Act of 1934

The 1934 act, known as the **Exchange Act**, formed the SEC and gave it the authority to regulate the securities exchanges and the OTC markets to maintain a fair and orderly market for the investing public.

The Securities Exchange Act of 1934 requires exchange members, broker-dealers that trade securities OTC and on exchanges, and individuals who make securities trades for the public to be registered with the SEC.

267

The Securities Exchange Act of 1934 addresses the:

- creation of the SEC
- regulation of exchanges
- regulation of credit by the Federal Reserve Board (FRB)
- registration of broker-dealers
- regulation of insider transactions, short sales and proxies
- regulation of trading activities
- regulation of client accounts
- customer protection rule
- regulation of the OTC market
- net capital rule

The Securities and Exchange Commission

Composed of five commissioners appointed by the President of the United States and approved by the Senate, the SEC enforces the 1934 act by regulating the securities markets and behavior of market participants.

Registration of Exchanges and Firms

The 1934 act requires national securities exchanges to file registration statements with the SEC. By registering, exchanges agree to comply with and help enforce the rules of this act. Each exchange gives the SEC copies of its bylaws, constitution and articles of incorporation. An exchange must disclose to the SEC any amendment to exchange rules as soon as it is adopted.

The act of 1934 also requires companies that list their securities on the exchanges and certain firms traded OTC to register with the SEC. An SEC–registered company must file quarterly and annual reports (Form 10Q and 10K, respectively) informing the SEC of its financial status and providing other information.

Financial Statements Sent to Customers

Every broker-dealer must provide its customers with copies of its financial statements. A **customer** is any person for whom the broker-dealer holds funds or securities or anyone who has made a securities transaction at any time up to one month before the date of a financial statement. Other broker-dealers, partners or officers of broker-dealers, and subordinated lenders are not considered customers.

Regulation of Credit

The act of 1934 authorized the FRB to regulate margin accounts, the credit extended for the purchase of securities. Within FRB jurisdiction are:

- Regulation T—regulates the extension of credit by broker-dealers
- Regulation U—deals with the extension of credit by banks

Securities Markets and Broker-Dealers

Securities Markets

A market is the exchange on which securities are traded. The market in which securities are bought and sold is also known as the *secondary market*, as opposed to the *primary market* for new issues. All securities transactions take place in one of four trading markets.

Exchange Market

The exchange market is composed of the NYSE and other exchanges on which *listed* securities are traded. The term "listed security" refers to any security listed for trading on an exchange.

Over-the-Counter Market

The OTC market is an interdealer market in which *unlisted* securities—that is, securities not listed on any exchange—trade.

In the OTC market, securities dealers across the country are connected by computer and telephone. Thousands of securities are traded OTC, including stocks, bonds and all municipal and U.S. government securities.

Third Market (OTC–Listed)

The third market is a trading market in which *exchange-listed* securities are traded in the OTC market. Broker-dealers registered as OTC **market makers** in listed securities arrange third market transactions.

All securities listed on the NYSE and AMEX and most securities listed on the regional exchanges are eligible for OTC trading as long as the trades are reported on the **Consolidated Tape** within 90 seconds of execution.

Fourth Market

The fourth market is a market for institutional investors in which large blocks of stock, *both listed and unlisted*, trade in privately negotiated transactions unassisted by broker-dealers. Most of these transactions take place through the **INSTINET** service.

Registered with the SEC as a broker-dealer, INSTINET includes a large number of mutual funds and other institutional investors among its subscribers. All INSTINET members are linked by computer terminals.

Trading Hours   Both the NYSE and AMEX trade between 9:30 a.m. and 4:00 p.m. EST each business day.

Normal hours for retail OTC trading are the same as those of the NYSE.

To accommodate institutional investors in the third market, NASD members functioning as registered market makers in listed securities may remain open until 6:30 p.m. EST.

Comparison of Listed and OTC Markets   Differences between the listed and OTC markets affect a transaction's cost and execution. As computers play an increasingly critical role in executing transactions on all markets, however, the differences should diminish.

Listed Markets

Each stock exchange requires companies to meet certain criteria before it will allow their stock to be listed for trading on the exchange.

Location. Listed markets, such as the NYSE and AMEX, have central marketplaces and trading floor facilities.

Pricing System. Listed markets operate as **double-auction markets**. Floor brokers compete among themselves to execute trades at prices most favorable to the public.

Price Dynamics. When a floor broker representing a buyer executes a trade by taking stock at a current offer price higher than the last sale, a plus tick occurs (market up); when a selling broker accepts a current bid price below the last sale price, a minus tick occurs (market down).

Major Force in the Market. The **specialist** maintains an orderly market and provides price continuity. He fills limit and market orders for the public and trades for his own account to either stabilize or facilitate trading when imbalances in supply and demand occur.

Transactions Away from the Main Market. Customer orders are routed to an exchange trading floor for execution, and the originating firm charges a commission for services rendered.

OTC Markets

Historically, the criteria a company was required to meet to have its stock traded in the OTC market were rather loose. In recent years, however, the quality of companies that trade OTC has improved substantially.

Location. No central marketplace facilitates OTC trading. Trading takes place over the phone, over computer networks and in trading rooms across the country.

Pricing System. The OTC market works through an **interdealer network**. Registered market makers compete among themselves to post the best bid and ask prices. The OTC market is a negotiated market.

Price Dynamics. When a market maker raises its bid price to attract sellers, the stock price rises; when a market maker lowers its ask price to attract buyers, the stock price declines.

Major Force in the Market. Market makers post the current bid and ask prices. The best price at which the public can buy (best ask) and the best price at which the public can sell (best bid) are called the **inside market**.

Transactions Away from the Main Market. Many dealers maintain inventories in OTC stocks without registering as market makers. Such firms can fill customer orders either as principal or agency trades, but may not act as both principals and agents in the same transaction.

Trading Halts

If a trading halt is called for a security, all trading in the security stops in the market where the halt was declared. During the halt, however, open orders may be canceled and options may be exercised. Moreover, a trading halt in a security in one market does not automatically affect trading of the security in other markets. Whenever a market halts or suspends trading in an eligible security, NASD members may continue to trade it in the OTC market during the halt or suspension and report all last sale prices for display on the Consolidated Tape.

If the NASD initiates an OTC trading halt in a security, members may not trade the security until the NASD removes the trading halt.

Role of the Broker-Dealer

Firms engaged in buying and selling securities for the public must register as broker-dealers. Most firms act both as brokers and dealers, but not in the same transaction.

Brokers. Brokers are agents that arrange trades for clients and charge commissions. Brokers do not buy shares, but simply arrange trades between buyers and sellers.

Dealers. Dealers, or principals, buy and sell securities for their own accounts, often called **position trading**. When selling from their inventories, dealers charge their clients markups rather than commissions. A markup is the difference between the current interdealer offering price and the actual price charged the client. When a price to a client includes a dealer's markup, it is called the *net price*.

Filling an Order. A broker-dealer may fill a customer's order to buy securities in any of the following ways:

- The *broker* may act as the client's agent by finding a seller of the securities and arranging a trade.
- The *dealer* may buy the securities from a market maker, mark up the price and resell them to the client.
- If it has the securities in its own inventory, the *dealer* may sell the shares to the client from that inventory.

Broker-Dealer Role in Transactions. A firm cannot act as both a broker and a dealer in the same transaction.

✓ *For Example:* A firm cannot make a market in a stock, mark up that stock and add an agency commission. If the firm acts as a broker, it may charge a commission. If it acts as a dealer, it may charge a markup or markdown. Violation of this practice is called *making a hidden profit.*

The following chart compares brokers and dealers:

Broker	*Dealer*
Acts as an agent, transacting orders on the client's behalf.	Acts as a principal, dealing in securities for its own account and at its own risk.
Charges a commission.	Charges a markup or markdown.
Is not a market maker.	Makes markets and takes positions (long or short) in securities.
Must disclose its role to the client and the amount of its commission.	Must disclose its role to the client, but not necessarily the amount or source of the markup or markdown.

An easy way to remember these relationships is to memorize the letters "BAC/DPP," which stand for "**B**rokers act as **A**gents for **C**ommissions/**D**ealers act as **P**rincipals for **P**rofits."

The New York Stock Exchange

The NYSE is the most widely known stock exchange. Although exchanges are called "stock" markets, other securities may trade there as well.

Often called the *Big Board*, the NYSE handles roughly three-fourths of all exchange transactions. Stocks listed on the NYSE can also be listed on regional exchanges, such as the Chicago Stock Exchange, but not on the AMEX. The

NYSE's primary objectives are to monitor operations and to facilitate an orderly market and prevent fraudulent practices. The Exchange itself does not buy and sell stocks.

Securities traded on the NYSE, known as **listed securities**, must satisfy the Exchange's listing requirements. The Exchange itself does not influence or determine prices.

Exchange Listing Requirements

The initial requirements for any corporation that wants its stock listed on the NYSE follow:

- At least 1.1 million shares must be publicly held.
- Two thousand stockholders must each hold 100 shares or more (2,000 round-lot owners).

Delisting. A company may request that its stock be delisted. To receive the Exchange's permission to delist, it must have approval from the holders of a substantial percentage of its shares and must not have received any objections from a substantial percentage of its stockholders. A decision by the board of directors alone is not sufficient justification for delisting.

Trading on the Floor of the Exchange

Only NYSE members, individual seat owners, can trade on the floor. The four types of traders follow:

1. **Commission house broker.** Also called *floor brokers*, commission house brokers (CHBs) execute orders for clients and for their firms' accounts.
2. **Two-dollar broker.** When commission brokers are too busy to execute all of their firms' orders, they call on two-dollar brokers to execute orders for them. Two-dollar brokers charge commissions for their services.
3. **Registered trader.** Registered traders are members of the Exchange who trade primarily for their own accounts. If they accept a public customer's order from a floor broker, they must give that order priority. They may not execute their own trades while holding an unfilled public order.
4. **Specialist.** Specialists facilitate trading in specific stocks. Their chief function is to maintain a fair and orderly market in those stocks. In fulfilling this function, they act as both brokers and dealers. They act as dealers when they execute orders for their own accounts and as brokers when they execute orders other members leave with them.

Auction Market   Exchange securities are bought and sold in an **auction market**. Exchange markets are also sometimes referred to as **double auction markets** because both buyers and sellers call out their best bids and offers in an attempt to transact business at the best possible price. To establish the best bid, a buying broker-dealer must announce a bid at least ⅟₁₆ of a point higher than the current best bid. The best offer by a selling broker-dealer must be at least ⅟₁₆ of a point lower than the current best offer.

Several bids at the same price and several offers at the same price may occur. To provide for the orderly transaction of business on the floor, the highest bids and lowest offers always receive first consideration.

Priority, Precedence and Parity. When more than one broker enters the same bid or offer, the specialist awards the trade in the following order:

1. **priority**—first order in
2. **precedence**—largest order of those submitted
3. **parity**—random drawing

Volatile Market Conditions   The NYSE has adopted rules 80A and 80B intended to protect against rapid, uncontrolled drops in the market. The specific point change in the Dow Jones Industrial Average (DJIA) required to initiate market restrictions is subject to change over time.

In the past, and likely as it appears on the exam, if the Dow Jones Industrial Average increased or decreased by 50 points in one day, the NYSE restricts **program trading** and **index arbitrage** transactions. If the DJIA falls 250 points within one day, the NYSE halts trading on the Exchange for one hour. If the DJIA then continues to decline to 400 points below the previous day's close, trading is halted for an additional two hours.

 Take Note: A decline of 10 percent will cause a 1-hour trading halt, 20 percent a 2-hour halt, and 30 percent a halt for the rest of the day. The NASD will reflect these changes on the exam when it chooses.

Arbitrage

Arbitrage is a trading strategy specialized traders called **arbitrageurs** use to profit from temporary price differences between markets or securities. Several types of transactions are called *arbitrage*. In general, arbitrageurs look for ways to profit from temporary price disparities in the same or equivalent securities.

Market Arbitrage. Some securities trade in more than one market—on two exchanges, for instance—creating the possibility that a security may sell for two different prices at the same time. When that happens, arbitrageurs buy at the lower price in one market and sell at the higher price in the other.

Convertible Security Arbitrage. Arbitrage trades are also possible in equivalent securities—convertible bonds and the underlying stock, for instance. If conditions are right, an arbitrageur may be able to convert bonds to stock and sell the stock for a profit.

Risk Arbitrage. Risk arbitrage becomes possible in proposed corporate takeovers. Arbitrageurs buy the stock in the company being acquired and sell short the acquiring company's stock. They do so believing that the merger will raise the acquisition's stock price and lower the acquirer's stock price.

Nine Bond Rule

The nine bond rule requires that special attention be given to orders for fewer than 10 bonds. These orders must be shown on the Exchange floor before being traded OTC, where most bonds trade. The trade may be done OTC if the price is better there or if the customer requests it. Bonds that must be redeemed within 12 months are exempt from the nine bond rule.

The Specialist

Role of the Specialist on the Exchange

The specialist's chief function is to maintain a fair and orderly market in the stocks for which he is responsible. A secondary function is to minimize price disparities that may occur at the opening of daily trading. He does this by buying or selling, as a dealer, stock from his own inventory only when a need for such intervention exists. Otherwise, the specialist lets public supply and demand set the market's course.

Market Maker. Because maintaining a market in a stock requires considerable financial resources, the specialist must have enough capital to maintain a substantial position in the security.

Agent and Principal. The specialist is both agent and principal. On the Exchange floor, specialists can act in the following ways:

- As agents, or brokers' brokers, specialists execute all orders other brokers leave with them. Specialists accept certain kinds of orders from members, such as limit and stop orders, and execute these as conditions permit. Specialists receive commissions for such transactions.

- As principals, or dealers, specialists buy and sell in their own accounts to make markets in assigned stock. They are expected to maintain continuous, fair and orderly markets—that is, markets with reasonable price variations. A specialist, however, may not buy stock for his own account at a price that would compete with the current market.

Responsibilities of the Specialist. A specialist must abide by certain NYSE floor rules in the daily conduct of his business:

- He must work to maintain a fair and orderly market.
- He must stand ready to buy and sell for his own account, if necessary, to maintain a fair and orderly market.
- He is expected to transact business for his own account in such a way as to maintain price continuity and minimize temporary price disparities attributable to supply and demand differences.
- He must avoid transacting business for his own account at the opening or reopening of trading in a stock if this would upset the public balance of supply and demand.
- He must file the reports and keep the books and records the Exchange requires.
- He may trade for his own account in between the current bid and ask quotes in his book.

Trading Posts   Each stock listed with the Exchange is traded at a particular horseshoe-shaped trading post surrounded by computer terminals. The specialist positioned at this post has been assigned responsibility for a certain number of issues. The specialist does not participate in every transaction in the stocks in which she specializes, but any transactions in a stock must take place in front of the specialist assigned to it.

✓ *For Example:* A commission house broker takes a buy or sell order to the post designated for that security. Around the post, the broker finds a crowd interested in trading the security. The "crowd" may be as small as one specialist or as large as two specialists and a group of interested traders. The commission house broker may execute the order in the crowd at the best available price, leave the order with the specialist to execute when the price is right or hand the order to a two-dollar broker to trade.

A specialist cannot accept orders in stocks in which he specializes from anyone except a member on the floor or a commission house broker.

Order Book   A specialist's **order book** records limit and stop orders the specialist holds for execution, as well as market orders received after the close. The book's contents are confidential; the specialist need not disclose entries to anyone.

The specialist must always get the best possible price for a limit order.

Specialist Quotations

Figure 8.1 is an excerpt from a specialist's book in ALFA Enterprises stock. The specialist enters buy orders on the left, sell orders on the right.

Quote. A current quote for ALF would be "51⅛ to ½," meaning market orders to buy can be executed immediately at 51½ and market orders to sell can be executed immediately at 51⅛. The current quote on a stock includes the highest bid limit order and the lowest offer because market orders are

FIGURE 8.1 Excerpt from a Specialist's Book

BUY	ALF	SELL
1 ML		
1 PW	**51**	
1 AGE		
4 Pru	1/8	
3 Ray James STOP	1/4	
	3/8	
		2 Smith Barn STOP
	1/2	4 Oppen
		2 Tucker Anth
		3 Piper
	5/8	
		2 DWR
	3/4	
		5 Bear Stearns
	7/8	

executed immediately at those prices. Stop orders are not included in the quote because no order has been triggered yet and they cannot be executed.

 For Example: Each of the following situations reflects quotes of the highest bid and lowest offer:

- Floor Broker X offers to sell ALF stock at 51⅛. Although the specialist already has offers to sell at 51½, the quote in ALF will be 51⅛ bid and 51⅜ offered.
- If there is more than one specialist in a stock, the specialists may compete against each other. The resulting quotation on a particular stock would be composed of the highest bid and the lowest offer from all the specialists' books combined.
- The specialist may offer a different quotation in an attempt to get a better price for the orders in the book.

Size. The specialist can reveal the number of shares available in a current quote, but cannot reveal the number of shares or prices above or below the current quote. Upon request, the specialist provides a quote and size:

- The quote "51⅛ to ½, 5 by 9" means 500 shares bid for at 51⅛, 900 shares offered at 51½.
- The quote and size are good only for the moment they are given; however, they provide some indication of supply and demand.
- The quote and size are from the specialist's book only and may or may not include any indications from the crowd.

Stopping Stock

To guarantee that a market order will be filled at the current bid or offer, a specialist **stops stock**. This allows the commission house broker who originated the order time to go into the crowd and try to find a better price. The commission house broker is thus assured of not missing the market while trying to find a better bid or offer for the client. A specialist may stop stock only for the benefit of a public order and does not require the Exchange's permission to do so. If the price in the crowd moves beyond the stopped price, the specialist automatically executes the order.

Crossing Orders

If a member receives two market orders for the same stock—one an order to buy 1,000 shares, the other to sell 1,000 shares—the member may **cross** the two orders and use one order to fill the other.

Before crossing the orders, however, the member must offer the stock in the trading crowd surrounding the specialist's post at a price higher than the bid by the minimum variation. This broker then goes to the post at which the stock trades and asks the specialist for a quote.

 For Example: A specialist's quote is 63⅛ to 63⅜. If the member wants to cross the orders at 63¼, he offers the 1,000 shares to the crowd at 63⅜. If no takers come forth, the member crosses the two orders at 63¼.

Types of Orders

Numerous types of orders are available to customers. Orders that restrict the price of the transaction include:

- **market**—executed immediately at the market price;
- **limit**—limits the amount paid or received for securities;
- **stop**—becomes a market order if the stock reaches or goes through the stop price; and
- **stop limit**—entered as a stop order and changed to a limit order if the stock hits or goes through the trigger price.

Orders based on time considerations include:

- **day**—expires if not filled by the end of the day;
- **good till canceled**—does not expire until filled or canceled;
- **at-the-open and market-on-close**—executed at the opening of trading the day after the order is placed or as close as possible to the close of trading on the day the order is placed;
- **not held**—gives the floor broker discretion on price and time of execution;
- **fill or kill**—must be executed immediately in full or be canceled;
- **immediate or cancel**—must be executed immediately in full or in part; any part of the order that remains unfilled is canceled;
- **all or none**—must be executed in full, but not immediately; and
- **alternative**—provides two alternatives, such as sell a stock at a limit or sell it on stop.

The most frequently used orders are discussed in more detail below.

Market Orders

A market order is sent immediately to the floor for execution without restrictions or limits. It is executed immediately at the current market price and has priority over all other types of orders. A market order to buy is executed at the lowest offering price available; a market order to sell is executed at the highest bid price available. As long as the security is trading, a market order guarantees execution.

Limit Orders

In a limit order, a customer limits the acceptable purchase or selling price. A limit order can be executed only at the specified price or better.

If the order cannot be executed at the market, the commission house broker leaves the order with the specialist, who writes down the trade in the order book and executes the order if and when the market price meets the order limit.

Risks and Disadvantages of Limit Orders. A customer who enters a limit order risks missing the chance to buy or sell, especially if the market moves away from the limit price. The market may never go as low as the buy limit price or as high as the sell limit price.

Sometimes limit orders are not executed, even if a limit price is met. Two possible explanations for this follow:

1. **Stock ahead.** Limit orders on the specialist's book for the same price are arranged according to when they were received. If a limit order at a specific price was not filled, chances are another order at the same price took precedence; that is, there was stock ahead.
2. **Plus (up) tick.** Limit orders to sell short may be executed only on plus ticks or zero-plus ticks. This means that even if you see a sale on the NYSE Tape at your price, your limit order to sell short might not be executed because a plus tick did not occur.

Stop Orders

A stop order, also known as a *stop loss order*, is designed to protect a profit or prevent a loss if the stock begins to move in the wrong direction.

The stop order becomes a market order once the stock trades at or moves through a certain price, known as the **stop price**. Stop orders are usually left with and executed by the specialist. No guarantee exists that the executed price will be the stop price, unlike the price on a limit order.

A trade at the stop price *triggers* the order, which then becomes a market order. A stop order takes two trades to execute:

1. **Trigger.** The trigger transaction at or through the stop price activates the trade.
2. **Execution.** The stop order becomes a market order and is executed at the market price, completing the trade.

Buy Stop Order. A buy stop order, always entered at a price above the current offering price, is triggered when the market price touches or goes through the buy stop price. An investor would place a stop order to "buy 100 COD at 42¼ stop" when the market is at 40 if she believes 42 represents a technical resistance point, above which the stock price will continue to rise. Demonstrating this point, Figure 8.2 illustrates the trading pattern of COD over a period of time.

Sell Stop Order. A sell stop order protects a profit or limits a loss in a long stock position. (A sell stop is also called a **stop loss**). A buy stop order limits the risk of a short sale. It makes sense, then, that a buy stop order is placed

FIGURE 8.2   Buy Stop Order

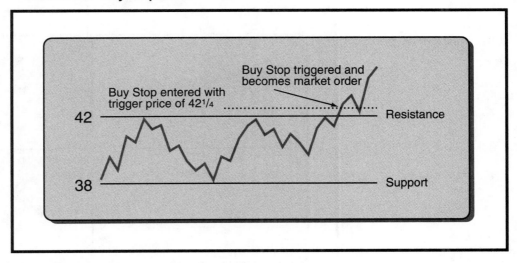

above the market and a sell stop is placed below the market, as illustrated in Figure 8.3.

If the market is at 40, a customer who purchased the stock at a lower price might place an order to "sell 100 COD at 37¾ stop" if she believes 38 represents a technical support level, below which the stock price will continue to fall.

If a large number of stop orders are triggered at the same price, a flurry of trading activity takes place as they become market orders. This activity may

FIGURE 8.3   Sell Stop Order

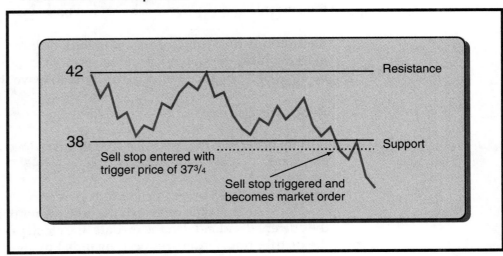

FIGURE 8.4   Stop and Limit Orders

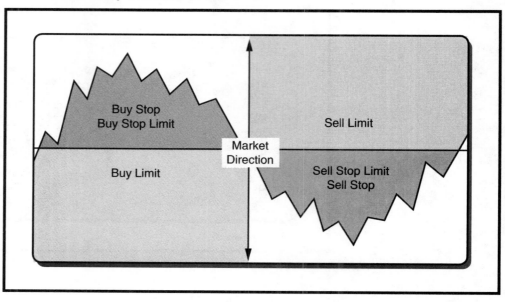

accelerate the advance or decline of the stock price, which can subvert the stop order's intent to curtail a loss or protect a profit.

Stop Limit Order. A stop limit order is a stop order that, once triggered, becomes a limit order instead of a market order.

 For Example: An order that reads "sell 100 COD at 52 stop, 51½ limit" means that the stop will be activated at or below 52. Because a 51½ limit exists, the order to sell cannot be executed below 51½.

Buy stop, buy stop limit and sell limit orders are entered *above* the current market price. Buy limit, sell stop and sell stop limit orders are entered *below* the current market price, as shown in Figure 8.4.

Restrictions on Stop Orders. Stop limit orders are not allowed in the OTC market unless the stop price and the limit price are the same because there is no equivalent of a specialist with whom to leave the orders.

Reducing Orders

Certain orders on the specialist's book are reduced when a stock goes ex-dividend.

All orders entered below the market are reduced on the ex-dividend date, or ex-date—the first date on which the new owner of stock does not qualify for the current dividend. On the ex-date, the stock price drops by the amount of the distribution. Orders reduced include buy limits, sell stops and sell stop limits. Without this reduction, trading at the lower price on the ex-dividend date could cause execution. This is illustrated in the following chart:

Dividend Value	*Reduction (Equiv. Fraction)*	*Order Price Less Reduction*	*Order Price after Reduction*
\$.20	\$.25 (¼)	35⅛ – ¼	= 34⅞
\$.52	\$.62½ (⅝)	35⅛ – ⅝	= 34½
\$.02	\$.12½ (⅛)	35⅛ – ⅛	= 35

The stop or limit price is reduced by the next greatest increment of trading; that is, the dividend amount is rounded to the next highest 1⁄16.

Do Not Reduce (DNR). A DNR order is not reduced by an ordinary cash dividend. It is reduced for other distributions, such as after a stock dividend or when a stock trades ex-rights.

Reductions for Stock Splits (Proportional Reductions). To calculate an open order's price reduction after a stock split, divide the market price by the fraction that represents the split.

✓ ***For Example:*** If a buy stop order has been entered for a stock at \$100 and it is the ex-date for a 5-for-4 stock split, the \$100 order price is divided by the fraction 5⁄4 to find the adjusted order price of \$80.

Calculating Order Adjustments for Stock Splits

Order price: \$100
Stock split: 5 for 4
5⁄4 = 1.25
\$100 ÷ 5⁄4 = \$80
Adjusted order price = \$80

Order price: \$100
Stock split: 2 for 1
2⁄1 = 2.00
\$100 ÷ 2⁄1 = \$50
Adjusted order price = \$50

Order price: \$100
Stock split: 3 for 2
3⁄2 = 1.50
\$100 ÷ 3⁄2 = \$66.67
Adjusted order price = \$66.625 (66⅝)

Table 8.1 compares order characteristics.

TABLE 8.1   Comparison of Order Characteristics

Order Type	Description	Exchange Orders	OTC Orders
Market	Buy or sell at the best available market price.	Most common order type on all exchanges.	Most common OTC order type.
Limit	Minimum price for sell orders; maximum price for buy orders.	Handled by specialist floor broker as a day or GTC order.	Acceptable on either a day or GTC basis.
Stop	Buy orders entered above the market; sell orders entered below the market.	Acceptable on all major exchanges as day or GTC orders.	Not currently acceptable OTC.
Stop Limit	Stop order that becomes a limit order once the stop price has been reached or exceeded.	Acceptable on all exchanges.	Not currently acceptable OTC.

Time-Sensitive Orders

The most frequently used orders that specify a time period in which to execute the transaction are discussed below.

Day Orders. Unless marked to the contrary, an order is assumed to be a day order, valid only until the close of trading on the day it is entered. If the order has not been filled, it is canceled at the close of the day's trading.

Good Till Canceled (GTC) Orders. GTC orders, or **open orders**, are valid until executed or canceled. However, regardless of when GTC orders are entered, the specialist cancels all GTC orders on the last business day of April and October unless customers renew them at that time. Individual firms may clear out GTC orders as frequently as monthly. This clears the specialists' books of obsolete orders and reduces the risk of executing trades that customers have forgotten.

A GTC order that has been properly renewed or confirmed retains its original position on the specialist's book. If a GTC order is not renewed or confirmed at the appropriate time, it is canceled and must be reentered as a new order.

At-the-Open and Market-on-Close Orders. At-the-open orders are executed at the opening of the market. Partial executions are allowable. They can be either market or limit orders, but must reach the post by the open of trading in that security or else they are canceled. Market-on-close orders are executed at or as near as possible to the closing price. If an at-the-open or a market-on-close order does not reach the post in time, the order is canceled.

Not Held (NH) Orders. A market order coded "NH" indicates that the customer agrees not to hold the floor broker or broker-dealer firm to a particular time and price of execution. This provides the floor broker with discretion to decide the best time and price at which to execute the trade. Market not held orders may not be placed with the specialist.

Fill or Kill (FOK) Orders. The commission house broker is instructed to fill an entire FOK order immediately at the limit price or better. A broker that cannot fill the entire order immediately cancels it and notifies the originating branch office. The commission house broker will not leave the order with the specialist.

Immediate or Cancel (IOC) Orders. IOC orders are like FOK orders except that a partial execution is acceptable. The portion not executed is canceled.

All or None (AON) Orders. AON orders must be executed in their entirety or not at all. AON orders can be day or GTC orders. They differ from the FOKs in that they do not have to be filled immediately.

Long and Short Sale Rules

A purchase order is normally a straight-forward transaction. Certain rules apply to short sales, however.

Long Sale. When an investor buys shares of a stock, she is *long* the position. When she sells share of stock owned, it is a long sale—the sale of stock held long in the account.

Short Sale. Selling short is a technique to profit from the decline in a stock's price. The short seller initially borrows stock from a broker-dealer to sell at the market. The investor expects the stock price to decline enough to allow him to buy shares at a lower price and replace the borrowed stock at a later date. Unless the stock price declines to zero, the short seller is obligated to buy the stock and replace the borrowed shares to close the short position.

Short sales are risky because if the stock price rises instead of falls, the investor still must buy the shares to replace the borrowed stock. In addition, a stock's price can rise without limit. Therefore, the position has unlimited risk.

Comparison of Long and Short Sales. Ultimately, every investment involves the purchase and eventual sale of the investment. The following chart compares long and short sales:

	Long Position	*Short Position*
First transaction	Buy low	Sell high (borrow securities and sell them)
Second transaction	Sell high	Buy low (buy back securities to replace those borrowed)

The following are points to remember about short sales:

- Short sales are always executed and accounted for in a customer's margin account and are subject to Reg T 50 percent initial margin requirements.
- Short sales always entail the delivery of borrowed stock to the buy side of the trade.
- Short sales are subject to higher NASD/NYSE minimum margin maintenance requirements than long purchases in a margin account.

Exchange Short Sale Rules

SEC and exchange plus tick rules are designed to block a short seller from feeding orders into a declining market to drive a stock's price lower. An order to sell a listed security short may be executed on either a **plus tick** or a **zero-plus tick**. A plus tick is a price higher than the last different price—for instance, from 30 to 30⅛. A zero-plus tick occurs when the last trade for the security was made at the same price as the trade before, but that trade was higher than the previous trade. The plus or minus tick carries over from the previous day's trading.

✓ **For Example:** A trade at 30⅛ after a trade at 30 is a plus tick; if the next trade is also at 30⅛, it is a zero-plus tick.

Look at the sequence of prices in the chart that follows. According to the up tick rule, an order to sell short could be executed on the third, fourth and fifth trades.

			30 1/8	30 1/8		
30		30			30	30
	29 7/8					
Opening sale.	Down tick. Short sales not permitted.	Plus tick. Short sales permitted.	Plus tick. Short sales permitted.	Zero plus tick. Short sales permitted.	Down tick. Short sales not permitted.	Zero down tick. Short sales not permitted.

OTC Short Sale Rules

Nasdaq's short sale rule prohibits entering a short sale in a Nasdaq National Market (NNM) security at or below the current inside bid whenever that bid is lower than the previous inside bid. In the OTC market, the inside bid is the best (highest) bid price at which the customer can sell the stock.

A short sale on a "down bid" (equivalent to the exchange's minus tick) is permitted if the sale is at least $\frac{1}{16}$ above the current inside bid. An opening bid is a down bid if it is lower than the previous day's closing bid or the same as the previous day's closing bid if that closing bid was a down bid.

Exemptions from the Nasdaq short sale rule include sales by any:

- member in which a sell order is marked "long" and the member has no reason to know that the sale is actually short;
- member to offset odd lot customer orders;
- member to liquidate a long position that is less than a round lot; and
- person in a special arbitrage or special international arbitrage account.

Short Sale Regulations

The Securities Exchange Act of 1934 prohibits directors, officers and principal stockholders (insiders) from selling short stock in their own companies.

Sell Order Tickets

A person is long a security if he:

- has title to it;
- has purchased the security or has entered into an unconditional contract to purchase the security, but has not yet received it;
- owns a security convertible into or exchangeable for the security and has tendered such security for conversion or exchange; or
- has an option to purchase the security and has exercised that option.

Unless one or more of these conditions are met, the SEC considers any sale of securities a short sale.

Sell Orders Must be Identified. The SEC requires that all sell orders be identified as either "long" or "short." No sale can be marked "long" unless the security to be delivered is in the customer's account or is owned by the customer and will be delivered to the broker by the settlement date. If a security the customer owns will not be delivered to complete the sale, the customer goes **short against the box.**

Shorting Bonds

Securities, such as listed stocks, have many equivalent securities trading at any time. It is easy to short 100 shares of GM because an equivalent 100 shares of GM can be purchased on the NYSE at any time. It is not easy to cover shorts for most municipal and many corporate bonds because the limited number of bonds available in each issue could make it very difficult to buy in the short position.

Other Domestic and International Exchanges

American Stock Exchange

The American Stock Exchange, a private, not-for-profit corporation located in New York City, handles about one-fifth of all of the listed securities trades in the United States.

The AMEX, also known as the *curb*, is organized and operates in much the same manner as the NYSE. To execute trades on the exchange floor, brokerage firms must be members of the exchange. The AMEX is governed by a board of 25 governors consisting of 12 exchange members, 12 public representatives and one chair.

Specialists operate as market makers on the AMEX much the same way as they operate on the NYSE and on other exchanges that employ the specialist system.

Regional Exchanges

In addition to the national stock exchanges, other stock exchanges serve the financial communities in different regions of the country. Regional exchanges include the Boston Stock Exchange, the Chicago Stock Exchange, the Cincinnati Stock Exchange, the Pacific Stock Exchange and the Philadelphia Stock Exchange.

Regional exchanges tend to focus on the securities of companies within their regions, although they also offer trading in many securities listed on the NYSE or AMEX. Listing requirements on regional exchanges are often less stringent than those of the national exchanges, and the companies they list are usually among the smallest and newest in their industries.

International Markets

Foreign companies' stocks trade on the major stock exchanges in the financial centers of Europe and Asia. As a result of increasing global economic interdependence and the instant access to information available through telecommunications, events in London or Tokyo can have a dramatic effect on U.S. markets, and vice versa. Traders in the United States monitor foreign markets closely to detect trends and events that will affect the prices of securities around the world.

Computerized Order Routing

In addition to the electronic systems each exchange develops, automated **order routing systems** link the specialists from each exchange through the **Intermarket Trading System (ITS)**.

New York Stock Exchange SuperDot

Nearly 75 percent of the orders the NYSE receives each day are processed through a computerized trading and execution system called **SuperDot** (Super Designated Order Turnaround). Broker-dealers use this computerized order routing system to choose an order's destination. An order can be routed directly to the appropriate specialist or sent to the brokerage firm's house booth for handling by the commission broker. Once the specialist or commission broker receives the order, it is presented in the auction market.

Orders can be sent through the system either preopening or postopening. The computer automatically pairs preopening orders received before the opening of trading with other orders and executes them at the opening market. Any order that cannot be matched before the opening is given to the specialist to handle. If an order is received postopening, it is sent directly to the specialist post and presented to the crowd. All NYSE–listed stocks are eligible for trading on SuperDot, subject to the following limits:

- preopening market orders—up to 30,099 shares per order
- postopening market orders—up to 2,099 shares per order
- pre- and postopening limit orders—up to 99,999 shares per order

National Association of Securities Dealers SOES

The NASD's Small Order Execution System (SOES) is an automatic order execution system designed to facilitate the trading of small public market and executable limit orders of up to 1,000 shares. Any Nasdaq or NNM security with at least one active SOES market maker is eligible for trading through SOES.

INSTINET

The **INSTINET Corporation** is a privately operated computerized system to facilitate fourth market trades between institutions. Institutional investors subscribing to the service can enter bids and offers and trade directly with other institutions. Trades are reported to the Consolidated Tape. Round lot orders of up to 2,099 shares are also sent through the SuperDot system.

The Consolidated Tape

How the Tape Works   The Consolidated Tape system, also known as the *Consolidated Ticker Tape,* is an NYSE service designed to deliver real-time reports of securities transactions to subscribers as they occur on the various exchanges. Subscribers to the Tape can choose to receive transaction reports through their quote terminals or their ticker lines.

The Tape reports are distributed over two networks. **Network A** reports transactions in NYSE–listed securities wherever they are traded. As an example, a trade involving NYSE–listed IBM on the Pacific Stock Exchange would be reported on Network A. **Network B** limits its coverage to AMEX–listed and regional exchange transactions. Each network reports transactions within 90 seconds of the trades.

How to Read the Consolidated Tape

The Tape prints volumes and prices of securities transactions within seconds of their execution. On the high-speed line, the transactions are reported with market identifiers, letters identifying the exchanges or markets on which the transactions took place. The market identifiers currently used on the high-speed line follow:

AMEX	**A**	Boston	**B**	Cincinnati	**C**
Chicago	**M**	NYSE	**N**	INSTINET	**O**
Pacific	**P**	NASD	**T**	Philadelphia	**X**

Quotations and Administrative Messages

The Tape reports a variety of transaction information. The ticker abbreviation (trading symbol for the stock, warrant, right and so on) appears on the upper line of the Tape. The number of shares sold, the price and any other necessary information are printed immediately below the trading symbol.

Number of Shares. The Tape reports a sale of a single round lot (100 shares) of stock by listing the trading symbol and the price at which the transaction occurred, but with no quantity. A report of "T 25¼" means that 100 shares of AT&T traded at 25¼. Sales of multiples of a round lot are indicated by printing the number of round lots followed by the letter "s" and the price. A report of "AEP6s39¾" indicates that 600 shares of American Electric Power traded at 39¾.

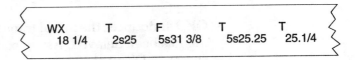

```
    WX        T         F           T            T
   18 1/4    2s25     5s31 3/8    5s25.25     25.1/4
```

If a transaction is executed for 10,000 shares or more, the entire amount is printed ("T 14,000s25" indicates 14,000 shares of AT&T traded at 25).

Stocks sold in 10-share units have their numbers abbreviated, like round lots, and are followed by the symbol § (a trade of 50 shares of T at 24 would appear as "T5 § 24").

✔ *For Example:* The first three transactions listed in the above Tape, reading from left to right, show trades of 100 shares of WX (Westinghouse Electric) at 18¼, 200 shares of T (AT&T) at 25, followed by 500 shares of F (Ford) at 31⅜.

If two similar trades for the same security occur consecutively, the report prints them under the same trading symbol and separates them with a dot. The transaction "T5s25.25" on the Tape above indicates trades of 500 shares of AT&T at 25 followed by 100 shares at 25. The "T25.¼" indicates two 100-share trades of AT&T, one at 25 and one at 25¼. The dot can also indicate that one trade has been split, such as might occur if two different brokers buy 100 shares of a 200-share sell order.

Active Markets. At times, the market and exchanges can be so active that trade information can be inaccurate or out of sequence. Several **delete information modes** have been established to abbreviate reports and keep the Tape from running late. The following notations indicate information will be omitted:

- **DIGITS & VOL DELETED.** When this message appears, both the first digit of the price and the volume will be dropped. A trade for 200 shares of IBM at 92½ will appear as "IBM2½." DIGITS & VOL RESUMED appears when trading activity slows.
- **REPEAT PRICES OMITTED.** This message indicates that the Tape will show only transactions that differ in price from the previous reports.
- **MINIMUM PRICE CHANGES OMITTED.** If necessary, the Tape will print only those trades that differ by more than ⅛ of a point from the last reports printed.

Other Messages. Other messages that may appear on the Tape include:

- SLD indicates that the exchange did not report a sale on time, so it is out of sequence on the Tape. For example, a customer who sees "AEP25" on the Tape followed by "AEP.SLD2s25⅛" might believe that AEP's price is going up. In reality, however, the price may be going

down: the 25⅛ is out of sequence and should have appeared before the 25.
- OPD announces the initial transaction in a security for which the opening has been delayed. As an example, the delayed opening of 1,200 shares of DWQ at 42 would appear as "DWQ.OPD12s42."
- HALT means that trading in a security has been halted.
- "W" over "I" designates when-issued stock resulting from a stock split or stock trading when issued.
- "R" over "T" designates rights.
- WS designates warrants.
- Pr designates preferred stock.

The Over-the-Counter Market

The oldest securities market is the over-the-counter market in which broker-dealers negotiate trades directly with one another. The OTC market is a highly sophisticated telecommunications and computer network connecting broker-dealers across the country. OTC trading is regulated by both the SEC and the NASD, the self-regulatory organization (SRO) for the OTC market.

The computerized information system that tracks OTC trading is called **Nasdaq**—the National Association of Securities Dealers Automated Quotation service.

Securities that can be traded in the OTC market include, but are not limited to:

- American depositary receipts (ADRs);
- common stocks, especially of banks and insurance and technology companies;
- most corporate bonds;
- municipal bonds;
- U.S. government securities;
- preferred stock;
- equipment trust certificates; and
- closed-end investment companies.

The differences between the OTC and NYSE markets are summarized below:

OTC	NYSE
Securities' prices determined through negotiation.	Securities' prices determined through auction bidding.
Regulated by the NASD.	Regulated by the NYSE.
Broker-dealers must register with both the SEC and NASD.	Broker-dealers must be registered with the SEC and must be Exchange members.
Traded at many locations across the country.	Traded only on the NYSE floor.

Negotiated Market

The OTC market is a negotiated market in which market makers may bargain during a trade. A negotiated market is competitive: a firm competes against other brokerage firms, each trading for its own inventory. Dealers communicate by phone, and when a customer wants to buy or sell a security, a firm calls one or more market makers in that security to negotiate a price.

OTC Market Makers

Specialists on an exchange act as market makers and stand ready, willing and able to trade in specified securities. The OTC market has no specialists. But some OTC dealers make a market in certain securities. They buy and sell these securities for their own inventories, for their own profit and at their own risk. A broker-dealer acting as a market maker, buying and selling for its own account rather than arranging trades, acts as a principal, not an agent.

Quotations

Bids, Offers and Quotes

A quote is a dealer's current bid and offer on a security. The current bid is the highest price at which the dealer will buy, and the current offer is the lowest price at which the dealer will sell. The difference between the bid and ask is known as the **spread**.

A typical quote might be expressed as "bid 63–offered 63$\frac{1}{16}$." The highest purchase price the dealer will pay is 63, and the lowest selling price the dealer will accept is 63$\frac{1}{16}$. The spread is $\frac{1}{16}$ of a point between the bid and ask. The broker could also say "63 bid–63$\frac{1}{16}$ ask" or "63 to $\frac{1}{16}$." The following chart illustrates the customer's and the broker-dealer's relationship to the quote:

	Bid–63	Ask/Offer–63¹⁄₁₆
Quoting dealer	Buys	Sells
Customer	Sells	Buys

When a customer buys a stock from a firm acting as principal, the broker marks up the ask price to reach the net price to the customer. Likewise, when a customer sells stock to a firm acting as principal, the dealer marks down from the bid price to reach the net proceeds to the customer. If WXYZ is quoted as "43¼ to ½," for instance, and the dealer wants a half-point for the trade, a customer buying would pay 44 net and a customer selling would receive 42¾ net.

 Take Note: To identify the net cost or proceeds of a principal trade, mark up the ask (buy) and mark down the bid (sell).

Firm Quote   A firm quotation is the price at which a market maker or broker-dealer stands ready to buy or sell at least one trading unit—100 shares of stock or five bonds—at the quoted price with other NASD member firms. When an OTC firm makes a market in a security, the broker-dealer must be willing to buy or sell at least one trading unit of the security at its firm quote. All quotes are firm quotes unless otherwise indicated.

As is true of market order executions on an exchange floor, an OTC trader may attempt to negotiate a better price with a market maker by making a counter offer or a counter bid—especially if the spread between the market maker's bid and ask is fairly wide. However, the only way to guarantee an immediate execution is to buy stock at the market maker's ask price or sell at the bid price.

In a typical transaction, a trader at one broker-dealer calls a trader at another broker-dealer (a market maker) to buy XYZ. A market maker might give another broker-dealer a quote that is firm for an hour with five-minute recall. This is a firm quote that remains good for an hour. If, within that hour, the market maker receives another order for the same security, the trader calls the broker-dealer back and gives it five minutes to confirm its order or lose its right to buy that security at the price quoted.

Backing Away. A market maker can revise a firm quote in response to market conditions and trading activity, but a market maker that refuses to do business at the price(s) quoted backs away from the quote. Backing away is contrary to NASD trading rules.

Recognized Quotation. A recognized quotation under NASD/NYSE rules is any public bid or offer for one or more round lots or other normal trading units. Any bid for less than a round lot must state the amount of the security for which it is good.

If the bid or offer is made for multiple round lots, it must also be good for a smaller number of units. For example, if the bid is for 1,000 shares of stock, the bidder must buy any round lots offered of 100 or more at the same price.

Subject Quote   A subject quote is one in which the price is tentative, subject to reconfirmation by the market maker. When the market maker knows the transaction size, the broker-dealer either firms up the subject quote or gives a replacement quote.

Some typical expressions used to denote subject and firm quotes are shown in the chart below. Note that firm quotes are absolute statements, whereas subject quotes are hedged:

Subject or Workout Market	*Firm Market*
"It is around 40–41."	"The market is 40–41."
"Last I saw, it was 40–41."	"It is currently 40–41."
"It is 40–41 subject."	
"40 to 42½ work out."	

Qualified Quotes   A quote will often be given with qualifiers intended to allow the broker-dealer to back away if market conditions change.

Workout Quote. This term is usually reserved for situations in which a market maker knows that special handling will be required to accommodate a particular trade. Either the order size is too big for the market to absorb without disruption, or the market might be too thin or temporarily unstable. A workout quote is an approximate figure used to provide the buyer or seller with an indication of price, not a firm quote. Block positioners use workout quotes frequently.

Nominal Quote. A nominal quote is someone's assessment of where a stock might trade in an active market. Nominal quotes may be used to give customers an idea of the market value of an inactively traded security, but they are not firm quotes. Nominal quotes in print must be clearly labeled as such.

Quotation Spread and Size

Spread. The difference between a security's bid and asked prices is known as the *spread*. Many factors influence a spread's size, including the:

- issue's size
- issuer's financial condition

- amount of market activity in the issue
- market conditions

Size. Unless otherwise specified, a firm quote is always good for one round lot (100 shares). For example, a firm quote of 8¼–½ means the market maker stands ready to buy 100 shares of stock from another broker-dealer at the 8¼ bid price or sell 100 shares to anyone at the 8½ ask price.

Reporting Quotes

As quotes change throughout the day, they are displayed on brokers' computer terminals. Quotes at the end of trading are reported for the public.

The Nasdaq National Market List

The NASD Information Committee compiles a list of securities for which it supplies quotations for dissemination to the media from the ranks of all qualifying Nasdaq securities. It provides this **National List** to newspapers and other news services for daily publication.

Pink Sheets

Each afternoon, OTC market makers send their interdealer quotations to the National Quotation Bureau for publication. The quotations, printed weekly on pink paper, are known as the *Pink Sheets*.

Although *Pink Sheet* quotes are subject, a dealer that publishes a quote on a security in the *Pink Sheets* must be ready to quote a firm price for 100 shares of that security. The *Pink Sheets* list all OTC market makers' quotes from the previous day. The National Quotation Bureau also publishes corporate bond quotations called the *Yellow Sheets*.

Manipulative and Deceptive Practices

The Conduct Rules mandate that any quote given must represent a real bid or offer. No fictitious quotes are allowed.

NASD 5 Percent Markup Policy

The NASD adopted the 5 percent markup policy to ensure that the investing public receives fair treatment and pays reasonable rates for brokerage services in the OTC markets. It is considered *a guideline only* and is not a firm rule for markups and markdowns. A firm charging a customer more or less than a 5 percent markup may or may not be in violation of fair and equitable trade practices. The markup may be considered excessive once all of the relevant factors are taken into account.

A broker-dealer can fill a customer order in the OTC market in two ways:

1. If the broker-dealer is a market maker in the security, it can, as principal, buy from or sell to the customer, charging a markup or markdown.
2. If the firm is not a market maker in the security, it can fill the order as agent, without taking a position in the security, and charge a commission for its execution services.

Markup Based on Representative Market Prices

In OTC principal transactions, the 5 percent markup is based on the price *representative of prevailing (inside) market prices* at the time of a customer transaction.

The NASD 5 percent markup policy applies to all transactions in nonexempt OTC securities regardless of whether the transactions are executed as agency or principal trades. Although the NASD Conduct Rules do not apply to government and municipal securities, the NASD investigates and bases charges of markup violations on SEC and MSRB rules and regulations.

Fixed Public Offering Price Securities

The 5 percent markup policy does not apply to mutual funds, variable annuity contracts or securities sold in public offerings—all of which are sold by a prospectus.

Dealer's Inventory Costs

If a customer's buy order is filled from a broker-dealer's inventory, the net price to the customer is based on the prevailing market price regardless of whether the broker-dealer selling to the customer is also making a market in the stock and regardless of what the firm's own quote might be.

The price at which the broker-dealer acquired the stock being sold to the customer has no bearing on the net price to the customer; the price to the customer must be reasonably related to the current market.

Riskless and Simultaneous Transactions

A riskless and simultaneous transaction is an order to buy or sell stock that a broker-dealer does not carry in its trading inventory. The dealer can buy or sell for its own account, then buy or sell to the customer as principal, charging a markup or markdown subject to the 5 percent policy:

The customer confirmation for a riskless and simultaneous transaction must disclose the markup or markdown for the trade.

Proceeds Transactions. When a customer sells securities and uses the proceeds to purchase other securities in a proceeds transaction, the broker-dealer's combined commissions and markups must be consistent with the NASD's 5 percent markup policy.

Markup Policy Considerations

In assessing the fairness of a broker-dealer's commission and markup practices, the NASD considers the following factors.

Type of Security. In general, more market risk is associated with making markets and trading common stocks than is associated with dealing in bonds. The more risk a broker-dealer assumes, the greater the justification for higher markups.

Inactively Traded Stocks. The thinner the market for a security, the more volatile the stock and the greater the market risk to anyone dealing in the stock. Thus, a broker-dealer is justified in charging higher markups on inactively traded stocks.

Selling Price of Security. Commission and markup rates should decrease as a stock's price increases.

Dollar Amount of Transaction. Transactions involving relatively small dollar amounts generally warrant higher markups than large-dollar transactions.

Nature of the Broker-Dealer's Business. This standard pertains to full-service brokers versus discount brokers. In most cases, the NASD accepts the fact that a general securities firm has higher operating costs than an introducing broker and, thus, may justify higher commissions and markups.

Pattern of Markups. Although the NASD is concerned primarily with detecting cases where broker-dealers have established patterns of excessive markups, a single incident could still be considered an unfair markup.

Disclosure. Even in unique situations involving unusual securities or special transactions where little or no precedent exists for determining a commission's or markup's fairness, broker-dealers must keep their fees reasonable and fair.

Markups on Inactive Stocks (Contemporaneous Cost). For inactive stocks and situations where no prevailing market quotes are available, a broker-dealer may base a markup on its cost in the stock. This is the only instance in which a broker-dealer's own cost has any bearing whatsoever on the net price charged to a customer, and the broker-dealer must disclose the markup to the customer.

NASD Automated Quotation System

Nasdaq Quotation Service

Nasdaq provides a computer link between broker-dealers that trade OTC. The system provides three levels of stock quotation service to the securities industry (see Figure 8.5):

- **Level 1.** Nasdaq Level 1 is available to registered reps through a variety of public vendors. Level 1 displays the inside market only: the highest bids and the lowest asks for securities included in the system. Because of normal market price fluctuations, a registered rep cannot guarantee a Level 1 price to a client.
- **Level 2.** Nasdaq Level 2 is available to NASD approved subscribers only. Level 2 provides the current quote and quote size available from each market maker in a security in the system. To list a quote on Level 2, a market maker must guarantee that the quote is firm for at least 100 shares.
- **Level 3.** Nasdaq Level 3 provides subscribers with all of the services of Levels 1 and 2 and allows registered market makers to update their quotes on any securities in which they make a market. A selling broker-dealer must update its quotes within 90 seconds of any change.

Generally, the Nasdaq system does not provide up-to-the-minute volume in each security, nor does it provide the last sale price in each security. It does, however, give the volume in each security at the end of the day.

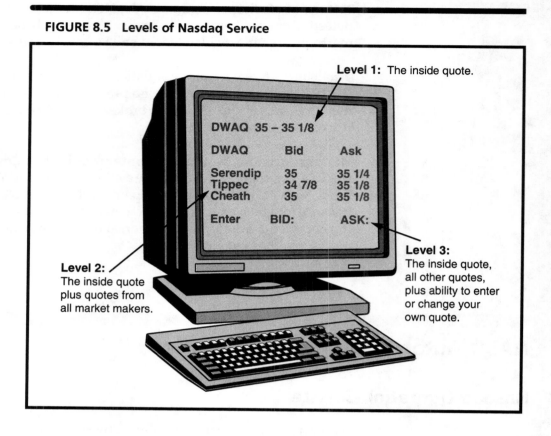

FIGURE 8.5 Levels of Nasdaq Service

Level 1: The inside quote.

DWAQ 35 – 35 1/8

DWAQ	Bid	Ask
Serendip	35	35 1/4
Tippec	34 7/8	35 1/8
Cheath	35	35 1/8

Enter   BID: ASK:

Level 2:
The inside quote
plus quotes from
all market makers.

Level 3:
The inside quote,
all other quotes,
plus ability to enter
or change your
own quote.

Nasdaq Market Maker Requirements

Market Maker Reports Registered market makers must transmit reports of last sales made during designated transaction-reporting hours. These reports must include a security's Nasdaq symbol, the number of shares, the transaction price and whether the trade was a buy, sell or cross.

90-Second Reporting. Market maker transactions must be reported *within 90 seconds* after a trade's execution. Any transactions executed outside of normal trading hours must be reported weekly to Nasdaq.

Volume Reports. Registered market makers must make daily reports to Nasdaq of their total daily volume in all securities for which they are registered market makers. If no activity has occurred in a security that day, the market maker must report "zero volume."

Members do not have to report odd lot trades, new issue transactions, purchases or sales resulting from option exercises, or **Computer Assisted Execution System (CAES)** transactions.

Table 8.2 summarizes the Nasdaq system: who interacts with the system at each level and the kinds of information input and output those participants need.

The Inside Market   The inside market is the best bid (highest) price at which stock can be sold in the interdealer market and the best ask (lowest) price at which the same stock can be bought.

For example, four OTC dealers making a market in Microscan may quote the stock as follows:

Market Maker	Bid	Ask
Wallace Capital Group	10	11
ALFA Securities	10⅛	10¾
Greenspring Securities	10¼	11
White, Winter Capital	10⅛	10⅞

The inside bid, in this case, belongs to Greenspring Securities; its 10¼ bid is the highest of the four. The inside ask belongs to ALFA; its 10¾ ask is the lowest of the four. The inside market of 10¼–10¾ will be released to the quotation vending services as the market in Microscan.

OTC traders across the country will look first to Greenspring and ALFA Securities as the lead markets, the firms to contact if they want to buy or sell Microscan. If the other market makers merely adjust their quotes to match

TABLE 8.2   Features of the Nasdaq System

Level 1	Level 2	Level 3
Registered reps and the investing public.	OTC trading room staff and institutional accounts.	Registered market makers and head traders.
Quote monitoring only.	Quote monitoring only.	Quote monitoring and input.
Representative bid and ask prices currently quoted.	Full display of all market makers' quotes and size.	Full display of all market makers' quotes and size. Update, change or delete quotes and size of quotes.

the current inside market, the stock's price level does not change. If one of them quotes a better market price and a trade occurs at the better price, the price level changes.

Whichever broker-dealer makes the inside market will account for most of the trading in the interdealer market until competing market makers adjust their own market quotes.

NASD rules require that customer transactions be based on the inside market quotation, even when no business is transacted with the firm(s) making the inside market.

Quote Machines

To provide registered reps and market makers with as much information as possible, the information the Consolidated Tape provides is condensed into a series of symbols and numbers when it appears on a quote machine. For example, the current market and trading data for Datawaq might appear as follows:

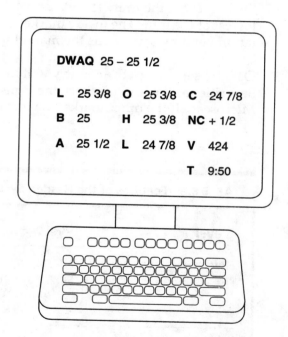

The abbreviations that appear on the previous screen translate to:

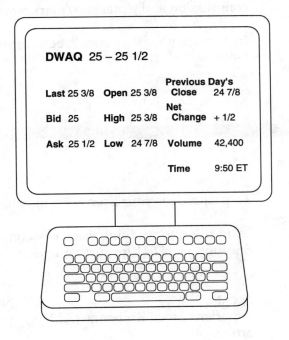

Summary

The trading of securities in the secondary market is regulated by the Securities Exchange Act of 1934. The act of 1934 created the Securities and Exchange commission and gave it the authority to regulate securities exchanges and the over-the-counter market.

Exchanges, such as the New York Stock Exchange, operate as double-auction markets where stocks listed on the exchange are traded. A specialist maintains an orderly market in the stocks in which he specializes, and will buy or sell from his own account or on behalf of others to do so.

The over-the-counter market is an inter-dealer computer and telephone network where market makers in stocks show the bid and ask price for stocks in which they make a market.

Brokers charge a commission for agency trades, usually for listed stock transactions, while dealers charge a mark-up or mark-down for principal trades, usually for OTC stocks in which they make a market. A broker-dealer may act as either a broker or a dealer in a transaction, but may not charge both a commission and a markup/markdown.

In preparing for the Series 7, be sure you understand the Key Concepts listed below.

Key Concepts

To prepare for your license exam, you should learn the following concepts.

In addition to studying these key concepts, use the Trading Securities Hot Sheet on page 641 for further review.

agent
American Stock Exchange (AMEX)
arbitrage
ask
auction market
bid
broker
commission house broker (CHB)
Consolidated Quotation System
Consolidated Tape
dealer
exchange market
fourth market
INSTINET
limit order
listed security
long sale
market maker
market order

National Association of Securities
    Dealers Automated Quotation
    (Nasdaq) System
Nasdaq National Market (NNM)
New York Stock Exchange (NYSE)
Order Routing System (ORS)
over-the-counter (OTC) market
parity
precedence
principal
priority
short sale
Small Order Execution System (SOES)
specialist
stop order
SuperDot
third market
trading halt
two-dollar broker

Review Questions

1. The New York Stock Exchange serves investors by

   A. offering securities for sale
   B. buying securities for members
   C. both of the above
   D. none of the above

2. Which of the following statements about the NYSE are true?

   I. The NYSE is a corporation operated by a board of directors.
   II. Membership on the Exchange is fixed at 1,000.
   III. Allied members can trade on the floor of the Exchange.
   IV. NYSE auction procedures are based on rules of priority, precedence and parity.

   A. I and II
   B. I and IV
   C. II and III
   D. III and IV

3. Which of the following brokers would be allowed to trade on the NYSE?

   I. Registered representative
   II. Specialist
   III. Registered trader
   IV. Commission broker

   A. I and II only
   B. I and III only
   C. II, III and IV only
   D. I, II, III and IV

4. All of the following are used in awarding trades on the NYSE EXCEPT

   A. priority
   B. parity
   C. premium
   D. precedence

5. Which of the following reasons justifies selling a stock short?

   A. To cut losses on a long position
   B. To benefit from a decline in the price of the stock
   C. To benefit from a rise in the price of the stock
   D. To seek a modest potential reward with limited risk

6. The over-the-counter market is a(n)

   A. negotiated market
   B. auction market
   C. transfer market
   D. double-auction market

7. Which of the following statements are true regarding the OTC market?

   I. It facilitates the trading of stock not listed on an exchange.
   II. It is a connection of broker-dealers via computers and phones.
   III. Stocks of banks and insurance companies typically trade in the over-the-counter market.

   A. I and II only
   B. I and III only
   C. II and III only
   D. I, II and III

8. An over-the-counter trader attempting to buy stock is given a quote of "16–17 work out." This indicates that the quote is

   A. $16 with a suggested broker-dealer markup of $1
   B. firm
   C. bona fide
   D. approximate

9. All of the following are usually traded over the counter EXCEPT

   A. mutual fund shares
   B. foreign securities and ADRs
   C. exchange-listed stocks
   D. closed-end investment company securities

10. Which of the following orders would NOT be reduced by the specialist on the ex-dividend date?

   I. Buy limit orders
   II. Open sell stop orders
   III. Buy stop orders
   IV. Sell limit orders

   A. I and II
   B. I and IV
   C. II, III and IV
   D. III and IV

Answers & Rationale

1. **D.** The primary objective of the NYSE is to provide a central location for the transaction of its members' business and the trading of securities.

2. **B.** The NYSE is a corporation operated by a board of directors. Membership is fixed at 1,366 and allied members are not allowed to trade on the Exchange floor. The Exchange has established trading procedures based on the rules of priority, precedence and parity in order to facilitate orderly trading.

3. **C.** The NYSE permits only specialists, registered traders and commission brokers to trade on the Exchange floor. Registered representatives deal with the investing public and initiate orders that are transmitted for execution to the Exchange floor.

4. **C.** The NYSE does not allow premiums to be used in order to award the purchase or sale of a security.

5. **B.** Investors sell a stock short with the expectation that the price will decline in the future. If, however, the stock's price rises, the investor is exposed to a potentially large risk.

6. **A.** The OTC market is not an auction market like the NYSE. Prices are negotiated between broker-dealers.

7. **D.** All three statements are true of the OTC. Some stocks cannot meet the NYSE listing requirements so they trade over the counter. Bank and insurance company stocks typically trade in this market because many of them have only regional interest rather than national interest. The OTC market is a system of telephone and computer connections between broker-dealers.

8. **D.** A workout quote is usually given as a range of prices within which the dealer or broker thinks it can make the trade. A firm quote would be "The market is 16–17," or, "It is currently 16–17."

9. **A.** Because mutual fund shares are redeemed by the issuer, there is no secondary market trading.

10. **D.** Buy stop orders and sell limit orders would not be reduced on the ex-dividend date because these market orders are placed above the underlying stock's current market price. Buy limit orders and open sell stop orders would be reduced because these orders are placed below the stock's current market price. They are adjusted downward to avoid execution after a dividend has been declared.

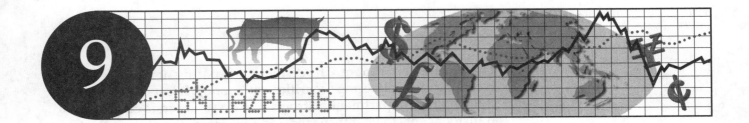

9

Brokerage Office Procedures

OVERVIEW

Registered representatives and principals are responsible for maintaining accurate and thorough information regarding customer transactions. Some of the procedures they follow are particular to their firms, while others are required by securities regulations such as the NASD's Uniform Practice Code.

Brokerage Support Services

Processing an Order

Several steps are involved in processing a securities transaction. The process begins when a client places an order with a registered representative. The representative enters the transaction on his computer or writes an order ticket. The order is routed through the following departments:

- **Order department (wire room, order room).** This department transmits orders to the proper markets for execution. Completed trade tickets are sent to the registered reps who initiated the trades and to the purchase and sales department.
- **Purchases and sales department.** The P&S department records all transactions in a client's accounts and handles all billing. It mails trade confirmations, which specify commission and total cost.
- **Margin or credit department.** This department handles activities involving credit for cash and margin accounts. It computes the dates on which clients must deposit money and the deposit amount.

- **Cashiering department**. The cashiering department is responsible for receiving and delivering securities and money. It issues payment only if the margin department instructs it to do so. It sends certificates to transfer agents to be transferred and registered, then forwards the certificates to clients.

A clearing corporation, such as the National Securities Clearing Corporation (NSCC), can simplify this process by providing specialized comparison clearance and settlement services. A clearinghouse acts as a bookkeeper for a number of broker-dealers.

Other departments involved in customer transactions follow:

- **Reorganization department**. The reorganization department handles any transaction that represents a change in the securities outstanding. This includes exchanging or transmitting customer securities involved in tender offers, bond calls, redemptions of preferred stock, mergers and acquisitions.
- **Dividend department**. This department credits customer accounts with dividends and interest payments for securities held in the firm's name.
- **Proxy department**. The proxy department sends proxy statements to customers whose securities are held in the firm's name. It also sends out financial reports and other publications received from the issuer for its stockholders.
- **Stock record department**. This department maintains the ledger that lists each stock owner and the certificate's location.

Figure 9.1 illustrates the route a typical order takes through a broker-dealer.

Transactions and Trade Settlement

Receipt and Delivery of Securities

When a representative accepts a buy or sell order from a customer, the rep must be assured that the customer can pay for or deliver the securities. If the customer claims the securities are being held in street name at another firm, the rep must verify this before executing a sale for the customer.

Order Memorandum

To enter a customer order, the registered rep traditionally has filled out an **order ticket** (see Figure 9.2). Increasingly, reps are entering orders electronically on computers. Orders are sent to the wire room. The wire room transmits each order to the proper market for execution. A registered rep must prepare the order ticket, and a principal must approve it on the day of the trade.

A customer order is most susceptible to error at two points: communication of the order between customer and broker; and transmission of the order from broker to wire operator.

FIGURE 9.1   Route of an Order

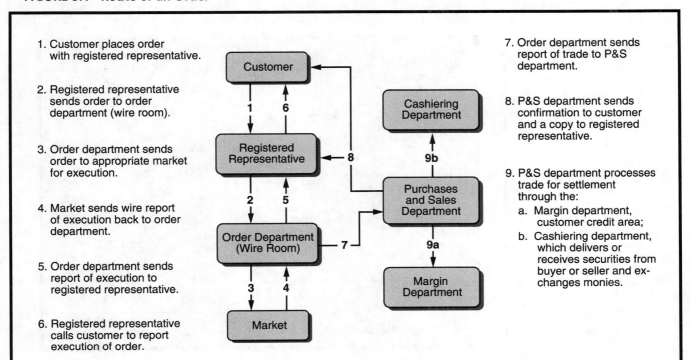

1. Customer places order with registered representative.

2. Registered representative sends order to order department (wire room).

3. Order department sends order to appropriate market for execution.

4. Market sends wire report of execution back to order department.

5. Order department sends report of execution to registered representative.

6. Registered representative calls customer to report execution of order.

7. Order department sends report of trade to P&S department.

8. P&S department sends confirmation to customer and a copy to registered representative.

9. P&S department processes trade for settlement through the:
   a. Margin department, customer credit area;
   b. Cashiering department, which delivers or receives securities from buyer or seller and exchanges monies.

Breakdowns in communication in the ordering process most often occur because of inaccurate information on a ticket. The following information is required on the order ticket:

- customer account number
- registered rep identification number
- description of the security (symbol)
- number of shares or bonds to be traded
- where the security is traded
- action (buy, sell long, sell short)
- options (buy, write, covered, uncovered, opening, closing)
- price qualifications (market, GTC, day order, etc.)
- type of account (cash, margin)
- settlement instructions
- security instructions
- payment instructions
- location of certificates sold

FIGURE 9.2 Order Ticket

					NYSE Spec. Handling	Other	Seq. No. & Off.
1	NEX ☐ BND ☐ OTC ☐ PBW☐ ASE☐						
2	**BUY**	**SELL**	**SS**	**OTHER**		Dupe. or Orig. Seq. No.	
3	Quantity	Symbol or Description		Suffix	Price/MKT	Other than LMT/MKT	
4	Add'l info. - GTC - AON - NH - DNR - Cash - etc.			**Account Name**			
4a	CXL - OR - BUY - SL - SHORT		Price Chg.				
4b	Quantity	Symbol or Description	Suffix	**Mgr/VP OK** _____			
4c	Add'l former order info., if any		Sol. ☐ Unsol. ☐	☐ Phone ☐ Long ☐ Letter ☐ Deliver ☐ Person ☐ Convert ☐ Power ☐ Borrow ☐ Other ☐ COD/DVP			
5	**Office**	Account No.		**AE No.**			
ALFA Financial Services, Inc.			Entered by:			Date:	

Report of Execution

A registered rep receives a report after a trade is executed. He first checks the execution report against the order ticket to make sure that everything was done as the customer requested. If everything is in order, he reports the execution to the customer. If an error exists, the rep should report it to a supervisor or manager immediately.

Erroneous Reports. Sometimes the details of a trade are reported to a customer incorrectly. Despite the mistaken report, the actual trade is binding on the customer. However, if an order is executed outside the customer's limit, the trade is not binding.

Route of an Order

When a customer places an order, it typically takes the following route:

1. The client places the order with the registered rep.
2. The registered rep writes the order ticket.
3. The order department receives the ticket and transmits the order to the proper market for execution.
4. The market or exchange receives the order. If the order is executed, it is reported back to the firm's order department.
5. The P&S department computes and records the transaction and handles the billing and confirmation.

6. The Margin department computes the amount the customer must deposit and transmits this information to her.
7. The cashiering department receives and delivers the securities and money. It issues payment as instructed by the margin department.

Trade Confirmations

A confirmation is a printed document that confirms a trade, its settlement date and the amount of money due from or owed to the customer (see Figure 9.3). For each transaction, a customer must be sent or given a written confirmation of the trade *at or before the completion of the transaction*, the **settlement date**. An exception to this rule is made for wire order purchases of mutual funds, for which selling agents may send confirmation as late as the day after the settlement date. A registered rep receives a copy of a customer's confirmation and checks its accuracy against the order ticket.

The trade confirmation includes the following information:

- **Trade Date**—day on which the transaction is executed. The settlement date is usually the third business day after the trade date.
- **Account No.**—branch office number followed by an account number.
- **AE No.**—account executive's identification number.

FIGURE 9.3 **Customer Confirmation**

Confirmation of your order:

Order	No.	Description	Price	Amount	Inter. or Tax	Reg. Fee	Commission
BOT	100	G. Heileman	28 7/8	2887.50	.00	.10	87.20

| Trade Date | 5/13/99 |
| Settlement | 5/16/99 |

Account No.	AE No.	AE Name
453-01243-1	27	Walker

Odd-lot Diff.
00.00

Net Amount
2974.80

Customer Name/Address:

Ms. Jaxson Pollac
5047 W. Kenneth Ave.
Chicago, IL 60699-3287

PLEASE NOTE: On odd-lot orders (orders for other than 100-share lots) on all exchanges purchases are executed at the round-lot price plus a premium (odd-lot differential). Sales are executed at the round-lot price less a discount.

Payment for securities bought and delivery of securities sold are due promptly and in any event on or before the end of payment period in order to comply with federal Regulation T and to avoid interest or premium charges.

ALFA Financial Services, Inc.

Please keep a copy of this confirmation for your records.

- **BOT** (bought) or **SLD** (sold)—indicates the customer's role in the trade.
- **No.** (or **Quantity**)—number of shares of stock or the par value of bonds bought or sold for the customer.
- **Description**—specific security bought or sold for the customer.
- **Yield**—indicates that the yield for callable bonds may be affected by the exercise of a call provision.
- **CUSIP Number**—applicable Committee on Uniform Securities Identification Procedures (CUSIP) number, if any.
- **Price**—price per share for stock or bonds before any charge or deduction.
- **Odd-lot Differential**—extra fee the broker-dealer adds for executing a trade of less than a round lot of an exchange-traded security. No odd-lot differential is added to OTC trades.
- **Amount**—price paid or received before commissions and other charges, also referred to as **extended principal** for municipal securities transactions.
- **Commission**—added to buy transactions and subtracted from sell transactions completed on an agency basis. A commission will not appear on the confirmation if a markup has been charged in a principal transaction.
- **Inter. or Tax**—interest portion of a bond transaction added to or the state tax subtracted on sales of stock in certain states.
- **Reg. Fee**—SEC registration fee subtracted from the sales made on exchanges and postage.
- **Net Amount**—obtained on purchases by adding expenses (commissions and postage) to the principal amount. Whether the transaction is a purchase or sale, interest is always added whenever bonds are traded with accrued interest.

Disclosure of Capacity. The confirmation must also show the capacity in which the broker-dealer acts, agency or principal. The markup or markdown is generally not disclosed unless the broker-dealer acts as a principal in a Nasdaq trade or riskless and simultaneous transaction.

Timely Mailing of Confirmations. Customer confirmations must be sent no later than *at or before the completion of the transactions.* It is unlawful to make settlement without first sending or giving a customer a trade confirmation.

Customer Account Statements

At a minimum, firms must send each customer a quarterly statement, although most firms send customers monthly statements. A statement shows:

- all activity in the account since the previous statement
- securities positions, long or short
- account balances, debit or credit

If a customer's account has a cash balance, the firm may hold it in the account. However, the statement must advise the customer that these funds are available on request.

Disclosure of Financial Condition

Upon written request, a member firm must deliver a copy of its most recently prepared balance sheet to:

- any customer with securities or cash held by the member; or
- a member firm with cash or securities on deposit or transacting business with the member.

Charges for Services Performed

A member broker-dealer's fees and charges must be reasonable, must relate to the work performed, transaction entered or advisory services given, and must not be unfairly discriminatory between customers. Most broker-dealers print fee and service charge schedules on each customer's monthly statement.

A "reasonable" fee is one that is not excessive when compared to the fees other broker-dealers or investment advisers charge for similar services.

Transaction Settlement Dates and Terms

Settlement date is the date on which ownership changes between buyer and seller. It is the date on which broker-dealers are *required* to exchange the securities and funds involved in a transaction and the date on which customers are *requested* to pay for securities bought and deliver securities sold. The Uniform Practice Code (UPC) standardizes the dates and times for each type of settlement.

Regular Way Settlement

Regular way settlement for most securities transactions is the *third business day* following the trade date, also known as T+3. As an example, if a trade occurs on a Tuesday (trade date), it would settle regular way on Friday. If a trade takes place on a Thursday, it would settle the following Tuesday.

If the seller delivers before the settlement date, the buyer may either accept the security or refuse it without prejudice.

U.S. government note and bond transactions settle regular way the *next business day*. Money-market securities transactions settle the *same day*.

Cash Settlement

Cash settlement, or **same day settlement**, requires delivery of securities from the seller and payment from the buyer on the same day a trade is executed.

Stock or bonds sold for cash settlement must be available on the spot for delivery to the buyer.

Cash trade settlement occurs no later than 2:30 p.m. EST if the trade is executed before 2:00 p.m. If the trade occurs after 2:00 p.m., settlement is due within 30 minutes.

Seller's Option Contracts

This form of settlement is available to customers who want to sell securities, but cannot deliver the physical securities in time for regular way settlement. A seller's option contract lets a customer lock in a selling price for securities without having to make delivery on the third business day. Instead, the seller can settle the trade up to 60 calendar days from the trade date. Or, if the seller elects to settle earlier than originally specified, the trade can be settled on any date from the 4th business day through the 60th calendar day, provided the buyer is given a one-day written notice.

A buyer's option contract works the same way, with the buyer specifying when settlement will take place.

When-, As- and If-Issued Contracts

When issued trades occur through corporate stock splits and new issue municipal bonds. After a stock split is announced and before it is distributed, an investor who owns shares and wants to sell can either sell the old stock with a due bill—that is, a promise to deliver the split stock when it is distributed—or sell the stock from the split on a when issued basis. The NASD's Uniform Practice Committee determines the final settlement date of when issued trades, normally three business days after issuance.

Typically, new municipal bond issues are sold to investors before the bonds are physically printed. An investor receives a when issued confirmation describing the bonds. The confirmation does not include a total dollar amount or settlement date because until the settlement date is known, the accrued interest can't be calculated to determine the total dollar amount. Once the bonds are printed, the investor receives a new confirmation stating the purchase price and settlement date. A when issued transaction confirmation must include:

- an adequate description of the security, with the contract price;
- designation of the NASD or another self-regulatory organization (SRO) whose rules will govern settlement of the contract; and
- provision for marking the contract to the market.

Because the delivery date is unknown, a when issued confirm for bonds and other interest-bearing obligations must include accrued interest computed up to the settlement date due to the bond issuer.

TABLE 9.1   Summary of Contracts and Settlement Dates

Type of Security	Delivery Contract	Delivery Time
Corporate and Municipal Securities	Cash	By 2:30 pm on the same day as the trade.
	Regular way	On the third business day after the trade date.
	Seller's/buyer's option	No sooner than the fourth business day after the trade date but no later than 60 calendar days after the trade date.
	When issued	Exempt from regular way settlement; normally settle three business days after the securities are ready for delivery.
	COD/DVP	No sooner than regular way settlement but no later than 35 calendar days.
Government Securities	Cash	By 2:30 pm on the same day as the trade.
	Regular way	On the first business day following the trade date.
	Seller's/buyer's option	No sooner than the second business day after the trade date but no later than 60 calendar days after the trade date.
	When issued	One business day after the securities are ready for delivery.
	COD/DVP	No sooner than regular way settlement but no later than 35 calendar days.

Table 9.1 compares the settlement dates of various securities transactions.

Reg T Payment   Reg T specifies the date customers are *required* to pay for purchase transactions. The settlement date, however, is the date customers are *requested* to deliver cash or securities involved in transactions. Under Reg T, payment is due two business days after regular way settlement. Customer payment is due one calendar week after the trade date.

✓ ***For Example:*** Because regular way settlement of a security is three business days, customer payment under Reg T is five business days (three business days plus two business days). If a trade occurs on a Tuesday (trade date), it would settle regular way on Friday (T+3) and Reg T payment would be due the following Tuesday. If a trade occurs on a Thursday, it would settle the following Tuesday and Reg T payment would be due on Thursday.

Extensions. If a buyer cannot pay for a trade within five business days from the trade date, the broker-dealer may request an extension from its designated examining authority (DEA) before the fifth business day. The broker-dealer has the option of ignoring amounts of less than $1,000 without violating Reg T requirements. If the customer cannot pay by the end of the extension, the broker-dealer sells the securities in a close-out transaction. After the close-out, the account is restricted for 90 days. A restricted account must have sufficient cash before a buy transaction may be executed.

Frozen Accounts. If a customer buys securities in a cash account and sells them before paying for the buy side by the fifth business day, the account is frozen. Any additional buy transactions require full payment in the account, and sell transactions need securities on deposit. Frozen account status continues for *90 calendar days*.

Dividend Department

The dividend department collects and distributes cash dividends for stocks held in **street name**. In addition to processing cash dividends, the department handles registered bonds' interest payments, stock dividends, stock splits, rights offerings, warrants and any special distributions to a corporation's stockholders or bondholders.

Dividend Disbursing Agent

Stockholders are sent cash, property or stock dividends, or new shares after a split or a reverse split. If the broker-dealer holds the securities in street name, the **dividend disbursing agent** (DDA, in the case of dividends) or the **transfer agent** (in the case of stock splits) makes the appropriate distributions or transfers directly to the broker-dealer. The broker-dealer's dividend department then distributes the dividends or additional shares to the appropriate accounts.

If a stockholder has possession of the shares, the DDA or the transfer agent contacts him directly.

Dividend Disbursing Process

Declaration Date. When a company's board of directors approves a dividend payment, it also designates the payment date and the **dividend record**

date. The SEC requires any corporation that intends to pay cash dividends or make other distributions to notify the NASD or the appropriate exchange at least 10 business days before the record date. This enables the NASD or exchange to establish the ex-date.

Ex-Dividend Date. Based on the dividend record date, the NASD Uniform Practice Committee or the exchange, if the stock is listed, posts an **ex-date**. The ex-date is *two business days* before the record date. Because most trades settle regular way—three business days after the trade date—a customer must purchase the stock three business days before the record date to qualify for the dividend.

On the ex-date, the stock's opening price drops to compensate for the fact that customers who buy the stock that day or later do not qualify for the dividend. Trades executed regular way on or after the ex-date do not settle until after the record date.

The customer who buys the stock before the ex-date receives the dividend, but pays a higher price for the stock. The customer who buys the stock after the ex-date does not receive the dividend, but pays a lower price for the stock.

Dividend Record Date. The stockholders of record on the record date receive the dividend distribution.

Payable Date. Three or four weeks after the record date, the dividend disbursing agent sends dividend checks to all stockholders whose names appeared on the books as of the record date.

Cash Trades. Cash trades settle the same day, so they go ex-dividend on the day after the record date because no lag occurs between the trade date and the transaction settlement.

Late Receipt of Information. If the Uniform Practice Committee does not receive the necessary declaration date information in time to schedule a normal ex-date, it sets as the ex-date the first practical date in view of all surrounding circumstances.

Ex-date and Record Date Relationship

The NASD sets an ex-date for trading purposes two business days before the record date. If RST declares a cash dividend of $.75 payable to stockholders of record on Wednesday, June 21, the ex-date is Monday, June 19.

✓ *For Example:* On Friday, June 16, a transaction in RST stock is executed with regular way settlement on June 21, the record date. The stock's market price on June 16 includes the $.75 upcoming dividend payment.

On the settlement date, the buyer's name replaces the seller's on the company's books and the buyer receives the dividend.

On June 19, the ex-date, another transaction is executed with regular way settlement, this time on June 22, one day after the record date. The seller receives the dividend, even though he has sold the stock. To compensate both parties, the stock's market price on the ex-date dropped by $.75.

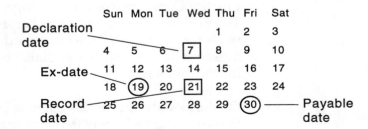

June

	Sun	Mon	Tue	Wed	Thu	Fri	Sat
Declaration date					1	2	3
	4	5	6	7	8	9	10
Ex-date	11	12	13	14	15	16	17
	18	19	20	21	22	23	24
Record date	25	26	27	28	29	30	Payable date

In adjusting a stock's opening price on the ex-date, the value of the dividend deducted must conform to the minimum price variation of ¹⁄₁₆ of a point. If the dividend amount falls between two standard price variations, the higher price variation is used as the price markdown.

✓ **For Example:** If the cash dividend is $.40, between ⅜ and ½, the markdown will be $.50.

Rights and Warrant Distributions

Rights are distributed in connection with stock subscription offerings. The ex-rights date is the first business day after the SEC registration statement's effective date. **Warrant distributions** are treated in the same manner as dividends. The ex-warrant date is the same as the ex-dividend date, which is two business days before the record date.

Stock Dividends and Splits

Normal stock dividends are handled the same as cash dividends. A stock distribution of up to 25 percent or more of the shares outstanding is subject to special handling. The same is true of stock splits where total shares outstanding increase by 25 percent or more. The ex-date on stock dividends exceeding 25 percent and stock splits of 5 for 4 or better is the *first business day* following the payable date.

For cash settlement transactions, the ex-date is the next business day after the record date. Thus, anyone who buys for cash on the record date becomes a stockholder of record.

Normally, if a corporation issues subscription rights to its stockholders, the ex-rights date is the first business day after the registration statement's effective date.

Due Bills

A due bill is a printed statement showing a seller's obligation to deliver securities, rights or cash to the purchaser. If securities are sold before the ex-date, but delivered too late for the buyer's name to be put on the books by the

TABLE 9.2   Summary of Significant Dates

Event	Definition	Duration/Expiration
Trade date	Date on which the transaction occurs.	Initiation date for all types of payment contracts. Due date for cash settlement.
Settlement date	Date on which payment must be received under NASD, NYSE or MSRB rules.	Varies according to type of delivery contract: same day for cash; three business days for regular way; 60 days for seller's or buyer's option.
Record date	Date that determines who is eligible to receive dividends or rights distributions. Fixed by the issuing corporation.	The investor must have settled the transaction to be considered the stockholder of record on the record date.
Ex-date (Ex-dividend date)	Date set by the Uniform Practice Committee after being informed of the distribution declaration by the issuer. Stock is sold without (ex-) the right to receive the dividend.	One-day period dictated by the record date for distributions. Normally two business days before the record date. Stock trades without (ex-) rights or dividends.
Ex-rights date	Date on which the seller of the underlying security is entitled to receive the stock rights.	First business day after registration's effective date.
Ex-warrant date	Date on which the seller of the underlying security is entitled to receive the warrants.	Second business day preceding the expiration of the warrant.

record date, a due bill accompanies the securities. The seller owes the buyer the amount of the dividend, right or warrant received.

Bonds Traded Flat   Bonds traded "flat" (income bonds and bond issues with interest in arrears) have an ex-date and record date if the issuer declares an interest payment.

Summary of Ex-Dates

The ex-date determines whether a security's buyer or seller is entitled to a distribution. Table 9.2 compares types of transaction dates.

Proxy Department

The Proxy.   A corporation's stockholders usually vote by means of a **proxy,** like an absentee ballot. A proxy is a limited power of attorney that a stockholder gives to another person, transferring the right to vote on the stockholder's behalf.

A proxy is revoked if the stockholder attends the shareholder meeting. A proxy may also be revoked by another proxy the stockholder executes at a later date.

Proxy Solicitation. Stockholders can receive multiple proxy solicitations for controversial company proposals.

If proxies are solicited, the SEC requires a company to give stockholders information about the items to be voted on. The company must allow the SEC to review the information before it sends the proxies to stockholders. In a **proxy contest**, everyone who participates must register with the SEC. Also, anyone who is not a direct participant but who provides stockholders with unsolicited advice must register as a participant.

Forwarding Proxies and Other Materials

Member firms must forward all proxies and other corporate materials to customers whose securities it holds in street name. Instructions from customers to the contrary cannot be honored. Member firms must vote street name stock in accordance with customer wishes. If a customer does not return a proxy within 10 business days, the member firm can vote the shares if the issue is of minor importance. If the issue is important and involves a proxy contest, the member firm cannot vote the customer's shares.

SEC rules require that the proxy issuer reimburse the costs a member firm incurs in handling proxy material.

Don't Know Procedures

When one broker-dealer confirms a transaction, the contra broker-dealer must also confirm the transaction within *four business days* of the trade date. After the fourth business day, the confirming party can demand that the contra party either confirm or **don't know (DK)** the trade in question within the next four business days. If the confirming broker-dealer receives no response from the contra party within that time limit, the confirming party may assume that the contra party has "DK'ed" the transaction. At that point, the confirming party is free to disown the trade as well.

Tender Offers

A tender is an offer to buy securities. The buyer may want an unlimited amount of stock or just enough stock to gain control.

✓ **For Example:** Colorado Interstate Corporation offers to buy 10 million shares of Texas Gas common stock at $45 per share. The offer is not contingent on a minimum number of shares being tendered. Although an expiration date is set for the tender offer, Colorado Interstate can extend the offer.

A tender offer can have restrictions allowing the offer to be canceled for a number of reasons. For instance, Colorado Interstate's offer to buy 10 million shares of Texas Gas might be contingent on at least 8 million shares being tendered or else the whole offer is canceled.

An **exchange offer** is a tender offer where one party offers to exchange its own securities for those of another party.

✓ *For Example:* Colorado Interstate may offer Texas Gas stockholders one share of its own stock for each share submitted.

Accrued Interest Calculations

Most bonds trade "and interest," meaning a buyer pays a seller a bond's market price, plus any accrued interest since the last interest payment. The buyer receives the full amount of the next interest payment, including interest that accrued while the seller owned the bond.

Most bonds pay interest every six months on either the 1st or the 15th of the specified months. The payment dates are known as *coupon dates*. Some examples follow.

If the interest dates are. . .	*The bonds are known as. . .*
January 1 and July 1	J&J bonds
May 1 and November 1	M&N bonds
February 15 and August 15	F&A 15 bonds
June 15 and December 15	J&D 15 bonds

Accrued interest affects bond transactions when settlement occurs between coupon dates.

✓ *For Example:* If a J&J bond trades in March, the buyer collects six months of interest in July from the issuer even though he owned the bond for only three months of that period. Therefore, the buyer pays the accrued interest to the seller and receives the full interest payment on the next coupon date.

Accrued Interest and the Dated Date. For a new bond issue, the date from which interest accrual begins is called the **dated date**.

✓ *For Example:* A new municipal bond issue's preliminary official statement indicates the bond is "dated September 1." Even if the bonds are issued late in September, they begin to accrue interest on September 1.

Corporate and Municipal Bonds Unless the settlement date on a bond transaction coincides with the bond's most current interest payment date, the bond cost to the buyer and the proceeds to the seller include **accrued interest**. Accrued interest increases the bond cost to the buyer and the proceeds to the seller.

Accrued interest is calculated from the last interest payment date up to, but not including, the settlement date. The buyer owns the bond on the settlement date, which means that the interest for that day belongs to the buyer.

✓ *For Example:* An investor sells 10 J&J 7 percent bonds on Monday, February 15. The transaction settles on Thursday, February 18. The buyer is entitled to the interest from February 18 through July 1. The seller is entitled to the interest from January 1 through February 17.

Accrued Interest Calculations

Two methods are used to calculate accrued interest. The 30-day-month (360-day-year) method is used on all corporate and municipal bonds:

The actual-calendar-days (365-day-year) method is used on all U.S. government bonds.

Accrued Interest Calculation: 360-Day-Year. Accrued interest on corporate and municipal bonds is calculated for a 360-day-year of 30-day months.

Principal × Interest rate × Elapsed days ÷ 360 days = Accrued bond interest

If an F&A municipal bond is traded regular way on Monday, March 5, the number of days of accrued interest would be calculated as follows:

February	30 days
March 5 trade	7 days (settles March 8)
Days of accrued interest	37 days

Because the trade settles on March 8, seven days of interest accrue for March.

If an A&O corporate or municipal bond is bought or sold in a cash trade on August 16, the number of days of accrued interest would be calculated as follows:

April	30 days
May	30 days
June	30 days
July	30 days
August	<u>15 days</u> (day before trade date)
	135 days

✓ *For Example:* A corporate bond pays an 8 percent coupon on January 1 and July 1. On Tuesday, July 5, a customer sells 10 of the bonds. Regular way settlement occurs on Friday, July 8, the third business day from the July 5 trade date.

The selling customer is entitled to seven days' accrued interest (July 1 through July 7). Using the 360-day-year interest formula presented earlier, accrued interest on this transaction is $15.55:

$$\$10,000 \times 8\% \times 7 \text{ days} \div 360 \text{ days} = \$15.55$$

Accrued Interest Calculation: 365-Day-Year

For calculating time elapsed since the most recent interest payment on a government bond, an actual-days-elapsed method is used instead of the 30-day-month, 360-day-year method used for corporate and municipal bonds.

$$\text{Coupon rate} \div 365 = \text{Interest per day}$$

$$\text{Therefore, } 8\% \div 365 = .0219 \text{ (IPO)}$$

$$\$10,000 \times .0219 \times 7 = \$15.34, 7 \text{ days interest}$$

If an F&A government bond is traded regular way on Monday, March 5, the number of days of accrued interest would be calculated as follows:

February	28 days	
March	<u>5 days</u>	
	33 days	(up to but not including the March 6 settlement date)

If an A&O government bond is traded for cash on August 16, the number of days of accrued interest would be calculated as follows:

April	30 days
May	31 days
June	30 days
July	31 days
August	15 days

137 days (actual days elapsed)

✍️ *Before You Go On:* Assume a U.S. government bond with an 8 percent coupon pays interest semiannually on January 1 and July 1. Using the calendar below, assume that today's date is Friday, May 14, and that a customer has entered an order to sell $10,000 worth of these bonds for regular way settlement.

When will this transaction settle?
How many days of accrued interest are involved?

Answer: The transaction will settle on Monday, May 17, the next business day after Friday, May 14. Remember that regular way settlement for government securities is the next business day, not the third business day, after the trade date. Accrued interest runs up to but does not include the settlement date, which, in this case, is through Sunday, May 16.

Calendar Month	Accrued Interest, Actual Days
January	31
February	28
March	31
April	30
May	16
	136

The actual number of calendar days from the last coupon interest date (January 1) to May 16 is 136 days.

Table 9.3 summarizes accrued interest calculation rules.

Rules of Good Delivery

A security must be in **good delivery** form before it can be delivered to a buyer. It is the registered rep's responsibility to ensure that a security is in good delivery when a customer sells it.

"Good delivery" describes the physical condition of, signatures on, attachments to and denomination of the certificates involved in a securities transaction. Good delivery is normally a back-office consideration between

TABLE 9.3   Summary of Accrued Interest Calculations

	Corporate or Municipal Bonds	U.S. Government Bonds
Regular way settlement	Third business day from trade date.	Next business day after trade date.
Monthly interest days	30-day months (including February).	Actual calendar days per month.
Accrued interest meter starts	Last interest payment date is Day One for accrued interest purposes.	Same.
Accrued interest meter stops	Bond interest accrues up to, but does not include, settlement date.	Same.

buying and selling brokers. In any broker-to-broker transaction, the delivered securities must be accompanied by a properly executed **uniform delivery ticket**. The transfer agent is the final arbiter of whether a security meets the requirements of good delivery.

Registered and Bearer Bonds. Normal delivery, dealer to dealer, is $1,000 or $5,000 bearer bonds. If it is revealed at the time of the trade that the bonds being sold are registered and this is acceptable to the purchaser, then registered bonds are good delivery. If nothing is said and registered bonds are delivered, the delivery is not good.

Overdelivery and Underdelivery. In settling customer sell transactions in which the securities delivery matches the exact number of shares or bonds sold, the first rule of good delivery is met. But if the customer overdelivers or underdelivers, the transaction is not good delivery.

- Example of overdelivery: A customer sells 300 shares and brings in one certificate for 325 shares.
- Example of underdelivery: A customer sells 100 shares and brings in one certificate for 80 shares.

Partial Delivery. A broker-to-broker partial delivery must be accepted if the remainder of the delivery constitutes a round lot or multiple thereof.

FIGURE 9.4   Irrevocable Power on Back of Certificate

ALFA Enterprises, Incorporated

The Company will furnish without charge to each stockholder who so requests the powers, designations, preferences and relative, participating optional or other special rights of each class of stock or series thereof of the Company, and the qualifications, limitations or restrictions of such preferences and/or rights. Such request may be made to the Office of the Secretary of the Company or to the Transfer Agent.

The following abbreviations, when used in the inscription on the face of this certificate, shall be construed as though they were written out in full according to the applicable laws or regulations:

TEN COM	– as tenants in common	
TEN ENT	– as tenants by entireties	
JT TEN	– as joint tenants with right of survivorship	

UNIFORM GIFT MIN ACT

_____ Custodian _____
(Cust)   (Minor)

under Uniform Gifts to Minors Act of

(State) _____

For value received _____ *hereby sell, assign and transfer unto*

PLEASE INSERT SOCIAL SECURITY NUMBER OR OTHER IDENTIFYING NUMBER OF ASSIGNEE

_____

_____

_____
Please type or print name of assignee

Shares of the capital stock represented by the within Certificate and do hereby irrevocably constitute and appoint _____

_____

_____

Attorney to transfer the said stock on the books of the within-named Company with full power of substitution in the premises.

Dated: _____   X _____
                                             Sign here

                                        X _____
                                        If joint account, both parties must sign

Good Delivery Clearing Rule (100-Share Uniform Units). When one broker-dealer delivers stock to another broker-dealer, single round lots and odd lots are cleared separately. However, odd lot certificates can be used to clear round lot trades provided the odd lot certificates add up to single round lots (100 shares).

Missing Coupons. If coupons are missing from a bond, the general practice is to deduct the missing coupons' cash value from the sale proceeds to the customer.

If an issuer is in default on a coupon bond, all of the unpaid coupons must be attached for it to be good delivery.

Partially Called Bonds. If a partial call of a bond issue occurs, no bonds in the issue are good delivery between brokers. However, if the entire bond issue has been called, normal good delivery rules apply. The same is true of partially called preferred stock.

Certificate Negotiability

Assignment. Each stock and bond certificate must be **assigned** (endorsed by signature) by the owner(s) whose name is registered on the certificate's face. Certificates registered in joint name require all owners' signatures.

Endorsement by a customer may be made on the back of a certificate on the signature line or on a separate **stock power**. One stock or bond power can be used with any number of certificates for one security, but a separate power is required for each security.

If an alteration or a correction has been made to an assignment, a full explanation of the change signed by the person or firm who executed the correction must be attached.

Figure 9.4 illustrates a stock power on the back of a certificate. Figure 9.5 illustrates a stock power that is separate from the certificate.

Signature Guarantee. All customer signatures must be guaranteed by a party acceptable to the transfer agent, such as an NYSE member or a national bank.

Signature Requirements. A customer's signature must match exactly the name registered on the face of a security.

Legal Transfer Items. Any form of registration other than individual or joint ownership may require supporting guarantees or documentation to render a certificate negotiable.

FIGURE 9.5   Separate Irrevocable Power

IRREVOCABLE STOCK OR BOND POWER

FOR VALUE RECEIVED, the undersigned do(es) hereby sell, assign and transfer to

_____

_____

Social Security Number
or Tax Identification Number

IF STOCK,   _____ shares of the _____ stock of _____
COMPLETE   _____ represented by certificate(s)
THIS PORTION   No.(s) _____ inclusive standing in the name of the under-
signed on the books of said company.

IF BONDS,   _____ bonds of _____
COMPLETE   in the principal amount of $ _____ No.(s) _____
THIS PORTION   inclusive standing in the name of the undersigned on the
books of said company.

The undersigned do(es) hereby irrevocably constitute and appoint

_____

_____

_____

Attorney to transfer said stock or bonds as the case may be on the books of said Company with full power of substitution in the premises.

Dated: _____

X   _____

X   _____

(Person[s] executing this Power sign[s] here)

IMPORTANT NOTICE – READ CAREFULLY

The signature(s) to this Power must correspond with the name(s) as written upon the face of the certificate(s) or bond(s) in every particular without alteration or enlargement or any change whatever. Signature guarantee should be made by a member or a member organization of the New York Stock Exchange, members of other Exchanges having signatures on file with transfer agents or by a commercial bank or trust company having its principal office or correspondent in the City of New York.

For business registrations involving sole proprietorships or partnerships, a simple guarantee by a broker-dealer is usually sufficient.

For corporate registrations and certificates in the names of fiduciaries, a transfer agent may require a corporate resolution naming the person signing a certificate as authorized to do so. Fiduciaries must supply either a certified copy of a trust agreement or a copy of a court appointment, depending on the type of fiduciary involved.

Invalid Signatures. If a broker-dealer guarantees a forged signature, such as of a deceased person, the firm becomes liable. The executor or administrator of the estate must either endorse the certificate or furnish stock power and must transfer the securities to the name of the estate before they can be sold.

Minors' signatures are invalid for securities registration purposes.

Good Condition of Security. If a certificate is mutilated or appears to be counterfeit, appropriate authentication must be obtained before a transfer agent can accept the security for replacement. If the damage is so extensive that the transfer agent doubts the certificate's authenticity, it will require a surety bond.

NASD CUSIP Regulations

CUSIP numbers are used in all trade confirmations and correspondence regarding specific securities. A separate CUSIP number is assigned to each issue of securities; if an issue is subdivided into classes with differing characteristics each class is assigned a separate CUSIP number.

Legal Opinion: Municipal Securities

Unless a municipal bond is traded and stamped "ex-legal" (without the legal opinion), the legal opinion must be printed on or attached to the bond as evidence of the bond's validity. Securities traded ex-legal are in good delivery condition without the legal opinion.

Fail to Deliver

A **fail to deliver** situation occurs when the broker-dealer on the sell side of a contract does not deliver the securities in good delivery form to the broker-dealer on the buy side on or before settlement. As long as a fail to deliver exists, the seller will not receive payment.

In a fail to deliver situation, the buying broker-dealer may buy in the securities to close the contract and may charge the seller for any loss caused by changes in the market.

Summary

It is important to know the general roles of the various departments involved in processing customer orders and disbursing dividends and stock splits.

Most records must be maintained for three years, and it is the principal's responsibility to ensure that records are accurate.

Note that the Reg T settlement date and regular way settlement dates are different. Unless specified otherwise, always assume regular way settlement.

You should be comfortable calculating accrued interest for bond transactions. Keep in mind that government bonds use a 365-day-year for accrued interest whereas corporate and municipal bonds use a 360-day-year.

Key Concepts

To prepare for your license exam, you should learn the following concepts.

In addition to studying these key concepts, use the Brokerage Office Procedures Hot Sheet on page 642 for further review.

assignment	order department
cashiering department	order memorandum
clearing corporation	proxy contest
confirmation	purchases and sales department
CUSIP number	regular way
declaration date	round lot
dividend disbursing agent (DDA)	settlement date
don't know (DK)	stock power
due bill	tender offer
ex-date	trade date
failure to deliver	transfer agent
frozen account	Uniform Practice Code (UPC)
good delivery	when issued (WI)
margin department	wire room

Review Questions

1. Which department in a brokerage firm would handle all credit transactions for a customer?

   A. Margin
   B. Cashiering
   C. Purchases and sales
   D. Reorganization

2. Once orders are received, in what sequence do they flow through a brokerage firm?

   I. Wire room
   II. Purchases and sales department
   III. Margin department
   IV. Cashier

   A. I, II, III, IV
   B. I, IV, II, III
   C. II, I, IV, III
   D. III, IV, II, I

3. According to regulations, a statement for an inactive account should be sent to each customer

   A. weekly
   B. monthly
   C. quarterly
   D. immediately after each trade

4. A customer purchases a Treasury bond in a regular way transaction on Monday, April 4. Settlement will be on

   A. Monday, April 4
   B. Tuesday, April 5
   C. Wednesday, April 6
   D. Thursday, April 7

5. A customer purchases a Treasury bond in a regular way transaction on Monday, April 4. The bond is a J&J bond. How many days of accrued interest will the seller receive?

   A. 79
   B. 80
   C. 94
   D. 96

6. A bond is dated June 1, 1995. The first interest payment is on January 1, 1996. How many months will the first and second interest payments cover?

   A. One month for the first, five months for the second
   B. One month for the first, six months for the second
   C. Seven months for the first, five months for the second
   D. Seven months for the first, six months for the second

7. As long as a fail to deliver situation exists, the seller

   A. will have all accounts frozen
   B. must conduct all transactions on a cash basis
   C. will not receive payment
   D. will not receive accrued interest on bonds

8. A buy-in occurs when the seller of a security fails to complete the contract according to its terms. TRUE or FALSE (circle one).

9. To be considered in good delivery form, certificates must be

   A. accompanied by a preliminary prospectus
   B. called for redemption by the issuing body
   C. accompanied by an assignment or a stock power
   D. in the name of the deceased person, if he died after the trade date

10. Your customer has a certificate registered in his own name. To be a good delivery, the certificate must be accompanied by

    A. a properly executed assignment to the brokerage firm on the reverse side of the certificate
    B. the promise that it has not been called for redemption
    C. a buyer's option
    D. the legal opinion unless the customer is selling municipal bonds

Answers & Rationale

1. **A.** The credit that a broker-dealer extends to its customers is handled by its margin department.

2. **A.** Orders are received by the wire room and then are sent to the appropriate market. When the wire room receives back the transaction report, it sends the report to the Purchases and Sales department. The P&S department sends a confirmation to the customer, and then sends notice of the trade to the margin department. The margin department then notifies the cashier of any balance due to or from the customer.

3. **C.** Broker-dealers are required to send quarterly statements to customers with inactive accounts.

4. **B.** Transactions in U.S. government securities settle on the next business day.

5. **C.** The seller will receive 94 days of interest (actual days) from the previous payment date up to, but not including, the settlement date of April 5.

6. **D.** Interest is paid semiannually on most debt securities. The bond's dated date is the date on which the bond begins to accrue interest. The first payment date is scheduled for seven months later. Thereafter the bond will pay interest at six-month intervals.

7. **C.** Until the seller delivers the securities sold, he will not receive payment for them.

8. **True.** If a seller fails to deliver securities sold in a transaction, the buying broker-dealer will initiate a buy-in to cover the deficiency.

9. **C.** One of the requirements for good delivery is that the security be accompanied by a proper assignment or stock power.

10. **A.** When a customer sells a security, he must execute the assignment on the back of the certificate or on a separate stock or bond power, assigning the security to the broker-dealer.

10

Investment Company Products

OVERVIEW

An investment company is a corporation or a trust through which individuals invest in large, diversified portfolios of securities by pooling their funds with other investors' funds. By investing through an investment company, individuals gain some of the advantages large investors enjoy, such as diversification of investments, lower transaction costs, professional management and more.

This lesson describes the different types of investment companies and the distinguishing characteristics of each. The areas to be highlighted include:

- how investment companies are established and governed
- how they are structured
- what features and corresponding benefits they offer investors

Investment Company Offerings

An investment company pools investors' money and invests in securities for them. Investment company management attempts to invest and manage funds for people more effectively than the individual investors could themselves. Investment companies operate and invest these pooled funds as a single large account jointly owned by every investor in a company.

Investment Company Purpose

Like corporate issuers, investment companies raise capital by selling shares to the public. Investment companies must abide by the same registration and prospectus requirements imposed by the Securities Act of 1933 on every other issuer. Investment companies are also subject to regulations regarding how their shares are sold to the public. The Investment Company Act of 1940 provides for SEC regulation of investment companies and their activities.

People often invest in investment companies because they believe a professional money manager should be able to outperform the average investor in the market.

Types of Investment Companies

The Investment Company Act of 1940 classifies investment companies into three broad types: face-amount certificate companies (FACs); unit investment trusts (UITs); and management investment companies. Figure 10.1 breaks down the various classifications of investment companies.

Face-Amount Certificate Companies A face-amount certificate is a contract between an investor and an issuer in which the issuer guarantees payment of a stated (or fixed) sum to the investor at some set date in the future. In return for this future payment, the investor agrees to pay the issuer a set amount of money either as a lump sum or in periodic installments. If the investor pays for the certificate in a lump sum, the investment is known as a *fully paid face-amount certificate*. Issuers of these investments are called, naturally enough, *face-amount certificate companies*. Very few face-amount certificate companies operate today because tax law changes have eliminated their tax advantages.

Unit Investment Trusts A UIT is an investment company organized under a trust indenture. The primary characteristics follow:

- They do not have boards of directors.
- They do not employ investment advisers.
- They do not actively manage their own portfolios (trade securities).

A UIT functions as a holding company for its investors. UIT managers typically purchase other investment company shares or government and municipal bonds. They then sell redeemable shares, also known as *units* or *shares of beneficial interest*, in this portfolio of securities. Each share is an undivided interest in the underlying portfolio. Because UITs are not managed, when any securities in the portfolio are liquidated, the proceeds must be distributed.

A UIT may be fixed or nonfixed. A fixed UIT typically purchases a portfolio of bonds and terminates when the bonds in the portfolio mature. A nonfixed

FIGURE 10.1   Classification of Investment Companies

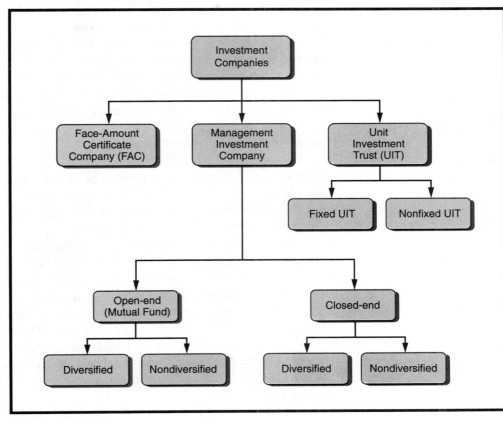

UIT purchases shares of an underlying mutual fund. Under the act of 1940, the trustees of both fixed and nonfixed UITs must maintain secondary markets in the units, thus guaranteeing a measure of liquidity to shareholders.

Management Investment Companies   The most familiar type of investment company is the management investment company, which actively manages a securities portfolio to achieve a stated investment objective. A management investment company is either closed-end or open-end. Initially, both closed- and open-end companies sell shares to the public; the difference between them lies in the type of securities they sell and where investors buy and sell their shares—in the primary or secondary market.

Closed-End Investment Companies

When a closed-end investment company wants to raise capital to invest, it conducts a common stock offering. For the initial offering, the company registers a fixed number of shares with the SEC and offers them to the public for a limited time through an underwriting group. The fund's capitalization is fixed unless an additional public offering is made. Closed-end investment companies can issue bonds and preferred stock as well.

Closed-end investment companies are commonly known as *publicly traded funds*. After the stock is distributed, anyone can buy or sell shares in the secondary market, either on an exchange or over the counter (OTC). Supply and demand determine the bid price (price at which an investor can sell) and the ask price (price at which an investor can buy). Closed-end fund shares may trade at a premium or discount to the shares' underlying value.

Open-End Investment Companies

An open-end investment company, or **mutual fund**, does not specify the exact number of shares it intends to issue. It registers an open offering with the SEC. With this registration type, the open-end investment company can raise an unlimited amount of investment capital by continuously issuing new shares. Conversely, when investors liquidate holdings in a mutual fund, the fund's capital shrinks because the fund redeems its shares. The offering never "closes" because the number of shares the company can offer is unlimited. Any person who wants to invest in the company buys shares directly from the company or its underwriters at the public offering price (POP). A mutual fund's POP is the net asset value (NAV) per share plus a sales charge. A mutual fund's NAV is calculated by deducting the fund's liabilities from its total assets. NAV per share is calculated by dividing the fund's NAV by the number of shares outstanding. Calculating NAV will be covered in detail later in this lesson.

The shares an open-end investment company sells are known as *redeemable securities*. When an investor sells shares, the company redeems them at their NAV. For each share an investor redeems, the company sends the investor money for the proportionate share of the company's net assets. Therefore, a mutual fund's capital shrinks when investors redeem shares.

Table 10.1 compares open-end and closed-end investment companies.

Diversified and Nondiversified

Diversification provides risk management that makes mutual funds popular with many investors. But not all investment companies feature diversified portfolios.

Diversified. Under the Investment Company Act of 1940, an investment company qualifies as a diversified investment company if it meets the following **75-5-10** test:

- *75 percent* of total assets must be invested in securities issued by companies other than the investment company itself or its affiliates. Cash on hand and cash equivalent investments (short-term government and

TABLE 10.1 Comparison of Open-End and Closed-End Investment Companies

Characteristic	Open-End	Closed-End
Capitalization	Unlimited; continuous offering of shares.	Fixed; single offering of shares.
Issues	Common stock only; no debt securities; permitted to borrow.	May issue common, preferred and debt securities.
Shares	Full or fractional.	Full only.
Offerings and Trading	Sold and redeemed by the fund only. Continuous primary offering. Must redeem shares.	Initial primary offering. Secondary trading OTC or on an exchange. Does not redeem shares.
Pricing	NAV plus sales charge. Selling price is determined by a formula found in the prospectus.	CMV plus commission. Price is determined by supply and demand.
Shareholder Rights	Dividends (when declared), voting.	Dividends (when declared), voting, preemptive.
Ex-date	Set by board of directors.	Set by the exchange or the NASD.

money-market securities) are counted as part of the 75 percent required investment in outside companies.

- No more than *5 percent* of total assets can be invested in any one corporation's securities.
- The investment company can own no more than *10 percent* of an outside corporation's voting class securities (common stock).

Nondiversified. A nondiversified investment company fails to meet the 75-5-10 test.

An investment company that specializes in an industry is not necessarily a nondiversified company. Some investment companies choose to concentrate their assets in an industry or a geographic area, such as health care or technology stocks. These are known as *specialized* or *sector funds*. An investment company that invests in a single industry can still be considered diversified as long as it meets the 75-5-10 test.

Investment Company Registration

A company must register with the SEC as an investment company if:

- the company is in the business of investing in, reinvesting in, owning, holding or trading securities; or
- 40 percent or more of the company's assets are invested in securities. (Government securities and securities of majority-owned subsidiaries are not used in calculating the 40 percent limitation.)

A company must meet certain minimum requirements before it may register as an investment company with the SEC. An investment company cannot issue securities to the public unless it has:

- private capitalization (seed money) of at least $100,000
- 100 investors
- clearly defined investment objectives

If the investment company does not have 100 shareholders and $100,000 in assets, it can still register a public offering with the SEC if it can meet these requirements within 90 days of registration.

The company must clearly define an investment objective under which it plans to operate. Once defined, the objective may be changed only by a majority vote of the company's outstanding shares.

Open-End Companies. In addition, the act of 1940 requires open-end companies to have:

- no more than one class of security
- a minimum asset-to-debt ratio of 300 percent

Because open-end investment companies may issue only one class of security (common stock), they are permitted to borrow from banks as long as a company's asset-to-debt ratio is not less than 3-to-1—that is, debt coverage by assets of at least 300 percent, or no more than one-third of assets from borrowed money.

SEC Registration and Public Offering Requirements

Investment companies must file registration statements with the SEC, provide full disclosure and generally follow the same public offering procedures required of other corporations when issuing securities. In filing for registration, an investment company must identify:

- the type of investment company it intends to be (i.e., open-end or closed-end);
- any plans the company has to raise money by borrowing;

- the company's intention, if any, to concentrate its investments in a single industry;
- any plans for investing in real estate or commodities;
- conditions under which investment policies may be changed by a vote of the shareholders;
- the full name and address of each affiliated person; and
- a description of the business experience of each officer and director during the preceding five years.

The investment company is considered registered when the SEC receives its notification of registration. Once registered, an investment company is strictly prohibited from:

- seeking to gain control of other companies;
- acting in the capacity of a broker by trading securities for commissions;
- acting as a bank, an insurance company or a savings and loan; and
- operating with fewer than 100 shareholders or less than $100,000 in assets.

These guidelines have exceptions. Under the act, the following corporations are exempt from registration as investment companies with the SEC, even if more than 40 percent of their assets are invested in securities:

- underwriters and brokers
- banks, insurance companies and bank investment advisory accounts
- mortgage bankers
- security holders protective committees
- real estate investment trusts (REITs)

Continuous Public Offering Securities

The SEC treats the sale of open-end investment company shares as a continuous public offering of shares, which means all sales must be accompanied by a prospectus. The financial information in the prospectus must be dated not more than 16 months prior to the sale. With closed-end funds, only the initial public offering of stock is sold with a prospectus.

Purchasing Mutual Fund Shares on Margin. Because a mutual fund is considered a continuous primary offering, Regulation T prohibits the purchase of mutual fund shares on margin. Margin is the use of money borrowed from a brokerage firm to purchase securities. Mutual fund shares may be used as collateral in a margin account, however, if they have been held fully paid for more than 30 days.

Registration of Investment Company Securities

After filing as an investment company under the act of 1940, the investment company must register with the SEC any securities it intends to sell. The registration of shares takes place under the Securities Act of 1933.

Registration Statement and Prospectus

The registration statement an investment company must file consists of two parts. Part 1 is the prospectus that must be furnished to every person to whom the company offers the securities. Part 1 is also called an **N1-A prospectus** or a **summary prospectus**. Part 2 is the document containing information that need not be furnished to every purchaser, but must be made available for public inspection. Part 2 is called the **statement of additional information (SAI)**. The prospectus must contain any information that the SEC decides should be revealed. The fact that all publicly issued securities must be registered with the SEC does not mean that the SEC in any way approves the securities. For that reason, every prospectus must contain a disclaimer similar to the following on its front cover:

> These securities have not been approved or disapproved by the Securities and Exchange Commission nor has the Commission passed on the accuracy or adequacy of this prospectus. No state has approved or disapproved this offering. Any representation to the contrary is a criminal offense.

Restrictions on Operations

The SEC prohibits a mutual fund from engaging in the following activities unless the fund meets stringent disclosure and financial requirements:

- making securities purchases on margin;
- selling securities short;
- participating in joint investment or trading accounts; and
- acting as distributor of its own securities, except through an underwriter.

The fund must specifically disclose these activities, and the extent to which it plans to engage in these activities, in its prospectus.

Shareholders' Right to Vote

Before any change can be made to a fund's published bylaws or objectives, shareholder approval is mandatory. In voting matters, it is the majority of shares voted for or against a proposition that counts, not the majority of people voting. Thus, one shareholder holding 51 percent of all the shares outstanding can determine a vote's outcome.

Among the changes that require a majority vote of the shares outstanding are:

- changes in borrowing by open-end companies;
- issuing or underwriting other securities;
- purchasing or underwriting real estate;
- making loans;
- changing subclassification (for example, from open-end to closed-end or from diversified to nondiversified);
- changing sales load policy (for example, from a no-load fund to a load fund);
- changing the nature of the business (for example, ceasing business as an investment company); and
- changing investment policy (for example, from income to growth or from bonds to small capitalization stocks).

In addition to the right to vote on these items, shareholders retain all rights that stockholders normally possess.

Management of Investment Companies

Five parties work together to help an investment company operate: board of directors, investment adviser, custodian, transfer agent and underwriter.

Board of Directors

Like publicly owned corporations in general, a management investment company has a CEO, a team of officers and a board of directors (BOD), all in place to serve the interests of its investors. The officers and directors concern themselves with policy and administrative matters. They *do not* manage the investment portfolio. As with other types of corporations, the shareholders of an investment company elect the board of directors to make decisions and oversee operations.

A management investment company's board of directors pulls together the different parts of a mutual fund:

- It defines the type of fund(s) to offer, such as growth, income, combination or sector.
- It defines the fund's objective.
- It approves and hires the transfer agent, custodian and investment adviser.

The act of 1940 restricts who may sit on an investment company's board of directors. The act requires at least 40 percent of the directors to be independent or noninterested persons. A noninterested person is unaffiliated with the investment company except in her capacity as a director. A noninterested person is unaffiliated with the investment company's investment adviser, transfer agent and custodian bank. This means that no more than 60 percent of the board members may be interested persons, including attorneys on retainer, accountants and any persons employed in similar capacities with the company.

Also, no one who has been convicted of a felony of any type or a misdemeanor involving the securities industry may serve on a board of directors, nor may any person who has been either temporarily or permanently barred from acting as an underwriter, a broker, a dealer or an investment company by any court.

Affiliated and Interested Persons

The act of 1940 and its amendments identify certain categories of individuals and entities that have control over or may influence investment company's operations. The identification of these persons is critical, as the act regulates and restricts their activities. The act broadly defines two classes of persons: affiliated and interested.

An **affiliated person** is anyone who could have any type of control over an investment company's operations. The act prohibits affiliated persons from using the control they have for their personal benefit.

The designation **interested person** broadens the category of people whose actions the SEC restricts or regulates to include broker-dealers, legal counselors and the immediate families of affiliated persons, as well as anybody else the SEC wishes to designate as such.

An affiliated or interested person cannot:

- borrow money from the investment company; or
- sell any security or other property to the investment company or to any company the investment company controls.

Investment Adviser

An investment company's board of directors contracts with an outside investment adviser or portfolio manager to invest the cash and securities held in the fund's portfolio, implement investment strategy, identify the tax status of distributions made to shareholders and manage the portfolio's day-to-day trading. Naturally, the adviser must adhere to the objective stated in the fund's prospectus. The adviser cannot transfer the responsibility of portfolio management to anyone else.

The investment adviser earns a management fee for his services, typically a set annual percentage of the portfolio asset value, which is paid from the fund's net assets. In addition, if the investment adviser consistently outperforms a specified market performance benchmark, he usually earns an incentive bonus.

An investment company cannot contract with an investment adviser who has been convicted of a securities-related felony unless the SEC has granted an exemption. In addition, an investment company cannot lend money to its investment adviser.

Custodian

To protect investors' assets, the act of 1940 requires each investment company to place its securities in the custody of a bank or a stock exchange member broker-dealer. The bank or broker-dealer performs an important safekeeping role as custodian of the company's securities and cash, and it receives a fee for its services. Often, the custodian handles most of the investment company's clerical functions. The custodian may, with the consent of the investment company, deposit the securities it is entrusted to hold in one of the systems for the central handling of securities established by the NASD or the NYSE. These systems make it easier to transfer or pledge securities. Once securities are placed in the system, most such transfers can be accomplished with a simple bookkeeping entry rather than physical delivery of the securities.

Once an investment company designates a custodian and transfers its assets into the custodian's safekeeping, the custodian must:

- keep the investment company's assets physically segregated at all times;
- allow withdrawal only under SEC rules; and
- restrict access to the account to certain officers and employees of the investment company.

Transfer Agent (Customer Services Agent)

The transfer agent's functions include issuing, redeeming and canceling fund shares, handling name changes for the fund and sending customer confirmations and fund distributions.

The transfer agent can be the fund custodian or a separate service company. The fund pays the transfer agent a fee for its services.

TABLE 10.2 Investment Company Operators

Board of Directors	Investment Adviser	Custodian	Transfer Agent	Underwriter
Administrative matters	Makes investment decisions	Holds assets	Transfers shares and funds	Distributes shares
Elected by shareholders	Paid a percentage of NAV	Paid a fee by the fund	Paid a fee by the fund	Paid from charges
		Clerical duties	Issues and redeems shares	

Underwriter

A mutual fund's underwriter, often called the **sponsor** or **distributor**, is appointed by the board of directors and receives a fee for selling and marketing the fund shares to the public. The open-end investment company sells its shares to the underwriter at the current NAV, but only as the underwriter needs the shares to fill customer orders. The underwriter is prohibited from maintaining an inventory of open-end company shares. The underwriter is compensated by adding a sales charge to the share's NAV when it makes sales to the public.

In general, a mutual fund may not act as its own distributor or underwriter.

✓ *For Example:* The distributor for the JH Mutual Fund must be a separate and distinct entity from the JH Mutual Fund even though it may be called JH Distributors. Section 12b-1 of the 1940 act provides an exception to this prohibition and allows a fund to charge a fee to cover its expenses for acting as its own distributor.

Table 10.2 defines the roles of the various investment company operators.

Information Distributed to Investors

Investors must be provided with specific information when purchasing and tracking mutual funds.

Prospectus The prospectus must be distributed to an investor before or during any solicitation for sale. The prospectus contains information on the fund's objective, investment policies, sales charges and management expenses, and services offered. It also discloses the 1-, 5- and 10-year performance histories. The statement of additional information typically contains the fund's consolidated financial statements, including the balance sheet, statement of operations, income statement and portfolio list at the time the statement was compiled.

Financial Reports   The act of 1940 requires that shareholders receive financial reports at least semiannually (twice per year). One of these must be an audited annual report. The reports must contain:

- the investment company's balance sheet;
- a valuation of all securities in the investment company's portfolio on the date of the balance sheet (a portfolio list);
- the investment company's income statement;
- a complete statement of all compensation paid to the board of directors and to the advisory board; and
- a statement of the total dollar amount of securities purchased and sold during the period.

In addition, the company must send a copy of its balance sheet to any shareholder who requests one in writing at any time between semiannual reports.

Additional Disclosures   The SEC also requires the fund to include in its prospectus or annual reports the following:

- a discussion of those factors and strategies that materially affected its performance during its most recently completed fiscal year;
- a line graph comparing its performance to that of an appropriate broad-based securities market index; and
- the name(s) and title(s) of the person(s) who is primarily responsible for the fund portfolio's day-to-day management.

Characteristics of Mutual Funds

A mutual fund is a pool of investors' money invested in various securities as determined by the fund's objective. Mutual funds have several unique characteristics.

The Mutual Fund Concept

A mutual fund must redeem shares at the net asset value. Unlike other securities, mutual funds offer guaranteed marketability: there is always a willing buyer for the shares.

Each investor in the mutual fund's portfolio owns an undivided interest in the portfolio. All investors in an open-end fund are mutual participants. No one investor has a preferred status over any other investor because mutual funds issue only one class of common stock. Each investor shares mutually with other investors in gains and distributions derived from the investment company portfolio.

Each investor's share in the fund's performance is based on the number of shares owned. Mutual fund shares may be purchased in either full or fractional units, unlike corporate stock, which may be purchased in full units only. Because mutual fund shares can be fractional, the investor can think in terms of dollars rather than number of shares owned.

✓ **For Example:** If NavCo Mutual Fund shares are $15 per share, a $100 investment purchases 6.666 shares ($100 ÷ $15 = 6.666).

An investment company portfolio is elastic. Money is constantly being invested or paid out when shares are redeemed. The mutual fund portfolio's value and holdings fluctuate as money is invested or redeemed and as the value of the securities held by the portfolio rises and falls. The investor's account value fluctuates proportionately with the mutual fund portfolio's value.

Other mutual fund characteristics include the following:

- A professional investment adviser manages the portfolio for investors.
- Mutual funds provide diversification by investing in many different companies.
- A custodian holds a mutual fund's shares to ensure safekeeping.
- Most funds allow a minimum investment, often $500 or less, to open an account, and they allow additional investment for as little as $25.
- An investment company may allow investments at reduced sales charges by offering breakpoints, for instance, through a letter of intent or rights of accumulation.
- An investor retains voting rights similar to those extended to common stockholders, such as the right to vote for changes in the board of directors, approval of the investment adviser, changes in the fund's investment objective, changes in sales charges and liquidation of the fund.
- Many funds offer automatic reinvestment of capital gains and dividend distributions without a sales charge.
- An investor can liquidate a portion of his holdings without disturbing the investment's balance or diversification.
- Tax liabilities for an investor are simplified because each year the fund distributes a 1099 form explaining taxability of distributions.
- A fund may offer various withdrawal plans that allow different payment methods at redemption.

Table 10.3 compares common stock and mutual fund shares.

TABLE 10.3 Comparison of Common Stock and Mutual Fund Shares

Common Stock	Mutual Fund Shares
Dividends from corporate profits	Dividends from net investment income
Price of stock determined by supply and demand	Price of share determined by forward pricing - the next price calculated as determined by the fund's pricing policy
Traded on an exchange or the OTC market	Purchased from and redeemed by the investment company; no secondary trading
Sold in full shares only	Can purchase full or fractional shares
First security issued by a public corporation	Only security issued by a mutual fund
Carries voting rights	Carries voting rights
May carry preemptive rights	Does not carry preemptive rights
Ex-dividend: 2 business days prior to record date	Ex-dividend: typically the day after record date as set by the board of directors

Investment Objectives

Once a mutual fund defines its objective, the portfolio is invested to match it. The objective must be clearly stated in the mutual fund's prospectus and can be changed only by a majority vote of the fund's outstanding shares.

Stock Funds

Common stock is normally the growth component of any mutual fund that has growth as a primary or secondary objective. Bonds, preferred stock and blue chip stocks are typically used to provide the income component of any mutual fund that has income as a primary or secondary objective.

Growth Funds. Growth funds invest in stocks of companies whose businesses are growing rapidly. Growth companies tend to reinvest all or most of their profits for research and development rather than pay dividends. Therefore, growth funds are focused on generating capital gains rather than income.

Income Funds. An income fund stresses current income over growth. The fund's objective may be accomplished by investing in the stocks of companies with long histories of dividend payments, such as utility company stocks, blue chip stocks and preferred stocks.

Combination Funds. A combination fund, also called a *growth and income fund*, may attempt to combine the objectives of growth and current yield by diversifying its portfolio among companies showing long-term growth potential and companies paying high dividends.

Specialized (Sector) Funds. Many funds attempt to specialize in particular economic sectors or industries. Usually, the funds have a minimum of 25 percent of their assets invested in their specialties. Examples include gold funds (gold mining stock), technology funds and low-grade (noninvestment-grade) bond funds, among others.

Special Situation Funds. Special situation funds buy securities of companies that may benefit from a change within the companies or in the economy. Takeover candidates and turnaround situations are common investments.

Sector funds offer high appreciation potential, but may also pose higher risks to the investor.

Index Funds. Index funds invest in securities to mirror a market index, such as the S&P 500. An index fund buys and sells securities in a manner that mirrors the composition of the selected index. The fund's performance tracks the underlying index's performance.

Turnover of securities in an index fund's portfolio is minimal. As a result, an index fund generally has lower management costs than other types of funds.

Foreign Stock Funds. Foreign stock funds invest mostly in the securities of companies that have their principal business activities outside the United States. Long-term capital appreciation is their primary objective, although some funds also seek current income.

Balanced Funds

Balanced funds invest in stocks for appreciation and bonds for income. In a balanced fund, different types of securities are purchased according to a pre-set formula. For example, a balanced fund's portfolio might contain 60 percent stocks and 40 percent bonds.

Asset Allocation Funds

Asset allocation funds split investments between stocks for growth, bonds for income and money-market instruments or cash for stability. Fund advisers switch the percentage of holdings in each asset category according to the performance, or expected performance, of that group.

A fund may have 60 percent of its investments in stock, 20 percent in bonds and the remaining 20 percent in cash. If the stock market is expected to do well, the adviser may switch from cash and bonds into stock. The result may be a portfolio of 80 percent in stock, 10 percent in bonds and 10 percent in cash. Conversely, if the stock market is expected to decline, the fund may invest heavily in cash and sell stocks.

Bond Funds

Bond funds have income as their primary investment objective. Some funds invest solely in investment-grade corporate bonds. Others, seeking enhanced safety, invest in government issues only. Still others pursue capital appreciation by investing in lower rated issues that may be upgraded in the future.

Tax-free (Tax-exempt) Bond Funds. Tax-exempt funds invest in municipal bonds or notes that produce income exempt from federal income tax. Tax-free funds can invest in municipal bonds and tax-exempt money-market instruments.

U.S. Government and Agency Security Funds. U.S. government funds purchase securities issued by the U.S. Treasury or an agency of the U.S. government, such as Ginnie Mae. Investors in these funds seek current income and maximum safety.

Dual-Purpose Funds

Dual-purpose funds are closed-end funds that meet two objectives: Investors seeking income purchase income shares and receive all the interest and dividends the fund's portfolio earns. Investors interested in capital gains purchase the gains shares and receive all gains on portfolio holdings. The two types of shares in a dual fund are listed separately in the financial pages.

Money-Market Funds

Money-market funds are usually no-load, open-end mutual funds that serve as temporary holding tanks for investors' money. "No-load" means investors pay no sales or liquidation fees. A fund manager invests the fund's capital in money-market instruments that pay interest and have short maturities. Interest rates on money-market funds are not fixed or guaranteed and change often. The interest these funds earn is computed daily and credited to customers' accounts monthly. Many funds offer check-writing privileges;

however, checks normally must be written for amounts of $500 or more. The largest expense to investors is the management fee, which is usually around .5 percent.

The net asset value of money-market funds is set at $1 per share. Although this price is not guaranteed, a fund is managed in order not to "break the buck" regardless of market changes. Thus, the price of money-market shares does not fluctuate in response to changing market conditions.

Many market funds have a low **beta coefficient**. Beta is a measure of the volatility of a security or a portfolio of securities in comparison with the stock markets as a whole. The stock market beta is always one. Money-market funds have a beta less than one, which means that they are less volatile than the overall market.

Restrictions on Money-Market Funds. SEC rules limit the investments available to money-market funds and require certain disclosures to investors. Restrictions include the following:

- The front cover of every prospectus must prominently disclose that an investment in a money-market fund is neither insured nor guaranteed by the U.S. government and that an investor has no assurance the fund will be able to maintain a stable NAV. This statement must also appear in all literature used to market the fund.
- No more than 5 percent of a fund's assets may be invested in any one issuer's securities.
- Investments are limited to securities with remaining maturities of not more than 13 months, with the average portfolio maturity not exceeding 90 days.
- Investments are limited to eligible securities determined to have minimal risk. Eligible securities are defined as those rated by nationally recognized rating organizations (Standard & Poor's, Moody's, etc.) in one of the top two categories. (No more than 5 percent of the portfolio may be in the second tier of ratings.) Comparable unrated securities must adhere to the definition of safety as provided by the rating organizations. (Tax-exempt money-market funds are exempt from certain parts of the requirement to invest only in rated securities.)

Comparing Mutual Funds

When comparing mutual funds, an investor should select funds that match her personal objectives. The investor will find many such investment companies.

When comparing funds with similar objectives, the investor should review information regarding the funds':

- performance
- costs
- taxation
- portfolio turnover
- services offered

Performance   Securities law requires that each fund disclose the average annual total returns for 1, 5 and 10 years or since inception. The manager's track record in keeping with the fund's objectives as stated in the prospectus is important as well.

> ✓ **For Example:** A growth fund with a high dividend payout has not followed its investment objective.

Costs   Sales loads, management fees and operating expenses reduce an investor's returns because they diminish the amount of money invested in a fund.

Sales Loads

Historically, mutual funds have charged front-end loads of up to 8.5 percent of the money invested. This percentage serves as a form of sales commission to a sales force. Many *low-load* funds charge between 2 percent and 5 percent. Additionally, funds may charge a *back-end* load when funds are withdrawn. Some funds charge ongoing fees under section 12b-1 of the Investment Company Act of 1940. These funds deduct annual fees to pay for marketing and distribution costs. Sales loads are covered in detail later in this lesson.

Expense Ratio

A fund's expense ratio relates the management fees and operating expenses to the fund's net assets. All mutual funds, load and no-load, have expense ratios. The expense ratio is calculated by dividing a fund's expenses by its average net assets. An expense ratio of 1.72 percent means that the fund charges $1.72 per year for every $100 invested. Typically, more aggressive funds have higher expense ratios.

> ✓ **For Example:** An aggressive growth fund's expense ratio is usually higher than a AAA bond fund's expense ratio because more trading occurs in the growth fund's portfolio.

Stock funds generally have expense ratios between 1 percent and 1.5 percent of a fund's average net assets. For bond funds, the ratio is typically between .5 percent and 1 percent.

Taxation   Mutual fund investors pay taxes on capital gains the fund receives. These taxes are based on how long the fund owned the security it sold. Because tax rates for long-term gains are capped, it is better for an investor in a high tax bracket to receive a long-term gain than a short-term gain.

Portfolio Turnover   The costs of buying and selling securities, including commissions or mark-ups and markdowns, are reflected in the portfolio turnover ratio. It is not uncommon for an aggressive growth fund to reflect an annual turnover rate of 100 percent or more. A 100 percent turnover rate means the fund replaces its portfolio annually. If the fund achieves superior returns, the strategy is working; if not, the strategy is subjecting investors to undue costs.

The portfolio turnover rate reflects a fund's holding period. If a fund has a turnover rate of 100 percent, it holds its securities, on average, for less than one year. Therefore, all gains are likely to be short term and subject to the maximum tax rate. On the other hand, a portfolio with a turnover rate of 25 percent has an average holding period of four years, and gains are likely taxed at the long-term rate.

Services Offered   The services mutual funds offer include retirement accounts, investment plans, check-writing privileges, telephone transfers, conversion privileges, combination investment plans, withdrawal plans and others. However, an investor should always weigh the cost of services provided against the value of the services to the investor.

Mutual Fund Marketing and Pricing

Mutual fund shares may be marketed in several ways; however, mutual fund shares are priced according to a set formula.

Marketing Mutual Fund Shares

A fund can use any number of methods to market its shares to the public. A discussion of some of the marketing methods various firms use follows.

Fund to Underwriter to Dealer to Investor

An investor gives an order for fund shares to a dealer. The dealer then places the order with the underwriter. To fill the order, the fund sells shares to the underwriter at the current NAV. The underwriter sells the shares to the dealer at the NAV plus the underwriter's concession (another way to say this is the public offering price less the dealer's reallowance or discount). The dealer sells the shares to the investor at the full POP.

Fund to Underwriter to Investor

The underwriter acts as the dealer and uses its own sales force to sell shares to the public. An investor gives an order for fund shares to the underwriter. To fill the order, the fund sells shares to the underwriter at the current NAV. The underwriter then adds the sales charge and sells the shares to the investor at the POP. The sales charge is split among the various salespeople.

Fund to Investor

Some funds sell directly to the public without using an underwriter or a sales force and without assessing a sales charge. If an open-end investment company distributes shares to the public directly—that is, without the services of a distributor—and the fund offers its shares with no sales charge, the fund is called a **no-load fund**. The fund pays all sales expenses.

Fund to Underwriter to Plan Company to Investor

Organizations that sell contractual plans for the periodic purchase of mutual fund shares are called *plan companies*. Such a company purchases fund shares and holds them in trust for an individual purchasing the shares under a periodic payment plan.

Sales at the POP Any sale of fund shares to a customer must be made at the public offering price. The NASD defines a customer as anyone who is *not* an NASD member. The route the sale takes is not important—the nonmember customer must be charged the POP. Only an NASD member acting as a dealer or an underwriter may purchase the fund shares at a discount from the issuer.

Determining the Value of Mutual Fund Shares

Mutual funds must calculate the NAV of fund shares at least once per business day because purchase and redemption prices are based on the NAV. Most funds wait until after the NYSE closes (4:00 p.m. EST) before making their NAV calculations. The price of purchase or redemption orders for mutual fund shares is determined at the next NAV calculation after an order is entered. This is known as **forward pricing**.

Net Asset Value per Share When a customer buys mutual fund shares, she is charged the public offering price. The POP equals the NAV per share plus the sales charge. When a customer sells, the liquidation price always equals the current NAV.

To determine the fund's total NAV, the custodian totals the value of all assets and subtracts all liabilities.

Assets (Cash + Current value of securities) – Liabilities = Fund's NAV

The NAV per share is determined by dividing the total net assets by the number of shares outstanding.

$$\frac{\text{Fund's NAV}}{\text{Number of shares outstanding}} = \text{NAV per share}$$

✓ **For Example:** Assume that a mutual fund has $47.6 million in total assets and $7 million in total liabilities, with 2.5 million shares outstanding. The NAV per share would be $16.24 ([$47.6 million − $7 million] ÷ 2.5 million shares = $16.24).

In working with NAV calculations, a fund's total assets include everything of value the fund owns, not just the investment portfolio.

Changes in NAV The NAV can change daily because of changes in the market value of a fund's portfolio. The events discussed below may change a fund's NAV per share:

- NAV per share *increases* when portfolio securities increase in value or when the portfolio receives investment income.
- NAV per share *decreases* when portfolio securities decrease in value or when portfolio income and gains are paid to shareholders.
- NAV per share *does not change* when shares are sold or redeemed or when portfolio securities are bought or sold. In these circumstances, the fund exchanges securities for cash so that the total net assets remain unchanged.

Sales Charges

The NASD prohibits its members from assessing sales charges *in excess of 8.5 percent* of the POP on customers' mutual fund purchases. However, members selling mutual fund contractual plans may not assess sales charges *in excess of 9 percent* of the POP over the life of a fund. Broker-dealers are free to charge lower rates *if they specify these rates in the prospectus.*

Closed-End Funds

Closed-end funds do not carry sales charges. An investor pays a brokerage commission in an agency transaction or pays a markup or markdown in a principal transaction.

Open-End Funds

All sales commissions and expenses are paid from the sales charges collected. Sales expenses include commissions for the managing underwriter, dealers, brokers and registered representatives, as well as all advertising and sales literature expenses.

Mutual fund distributors use three different methods to collect the fees for the sale of shares:

1. front-end loads (difference between POP and net NAV)
2. back-end loads (contingent deferred sales loads)
3. 12b-1 sales charges (asset-based fees)

Front-End Loads

Front-end sales loads are the charges included in a fund's public offering price. The charges are added to the NAV at the time an investor buys shares. Front-end loads are the most common way of paying for the distribution services a funds underwriter provides.

Back-End Loads

A back-end sales load, also called a *contingent deferred load*, is charged at the time an investor redeems mutual fund shares. The sales load, a declining percentage charge that is reduced annually (for instance, 8 percent the first year, 7 percent the second, 6 percent the third, etc.), is applied to the proceeds of any shares sold in that year. The back-end load is usually structured so that it drops to zero after an extended holding period. The sales load schedule is specified in a fund's prospectus.

12b-1 Asset-Based Fees

Mutual funds cannot act as distributors for their own fund shares except under Section 12b-1 of the Investment Company Act of 1940. This section permits a mutual fund to collect a fee for promoting, selling or undertaking related activity in connection with the distribution of its shares. The fee is determined annually as a flat dollar amount or as a percentage of the fund's average total NAV during the year and is charged quarterly. The fee is disclosed in the fund's prospectus. Requirements include the following:

- The percentage of net assets charged must be reasonable—typically ½ percent of net assets. This annual fee cannot exceed 8.5 percent of the offering price per share.
- The fee must reflect the anticipated level of distribution services.

The payments represent fees that would have been paid to an underwriter if sales charges had been negotiated for sales, promotion and related activities.

Approval. The 12b-1 plan must be approved initially and reapproved at least annually by a majority of the outstanding shares, the board of directors and those directors who are noninterested persons.

Termination. The 12b-1 plan may be terminated at any time by a majority vote of the noninterested directors or by a majority vote of outstanding shares.

Misuse of No-Load Terminology. A fund that has a deferred sales charge or an asset-based 12b-1 fee of more than .25 percent of average net assets may not be described as a no-load fund. To do so violates the NASD's Conducct Rules; the violation is not alleviated by disclosures in the fund's prospectus.

Classes of Fund Shares

Mutual funds may offer several classes of shares to allow investors to select how they pay the sales charges. The following is a typical method by which firms may classify fund shares by fee type, referred to as Class A, B, C and D shares.

- **Class A** shares have a *front-end load*, so an investor pays the charge at the time of purchase.
- **Class B** shares have a *back-end load*, which declines over time so an investor pays the charge at redemption.
- **Class C** shares have a *level load*, so an investor pays the asset-based fee annually.
- **Class D** shares have both an *asset-based fee* and a *back-end load*.

The class of shares determines the type of sales charge only. All other rights associated with mutual fund ownership remain the same across each class.

Computing the Sales Charge Percentage

When the NAV and the POP are known, the sales charge percentage can be determined as shown below:

$$POP - NAV = \text{Sales charge (\$ amount)}$$

$$\frac{\text{Sales charge (\$ amount)}}{POP} = \text{Sales charge \%}$$

✓ *For Example:* If the POP is $19.67 and the NAV is $18 per share, the sales charge percentage is calculated as follows:

$$\$19.67 - \$18.00 = \$1.67 \text{ (Sales charge \$ amount)}$$

$$\frac{1.67}{19.67} = 8.49\%$$

If the dollar amounts for the NAV and sales charges are specified, the formula for determining the POP of mutual fund shares is:

$$NAV + \text{Sales charge (\$)} = POP \text{ (\$)}$$

A mutual fund prospectus must contain a formula that explains how the fund computes the NAV and how the sales charge is added. Note that the sales charge is always based on the POP, not on the NAV. To determine the POP, divide the NAV by 100 percent minus the sales charge. The formula is as follows:

$$\frac{NAV}{100\% - \text{Sales charge } \%} = POP$$

✓ **For Example:** To calculate the POP when a fund's NAV is $10 per share and the sales charge is 7 percent, divide the NAV by 100 percent minus the sales charge (100% – 7% = 93%, or .93). An NAV of $10 divided by 93 percent equals a POP of $10.75.

Because of the possible high front-end sales charge, mutual funds should be recommended for long-term investing.

Reductions in Sales Charges

The maximum permitted sales charge is reduced from 8½ percent to 6¼ percent if an investment company does not offer certain features. To qualify for the maximum 8½ percent sales charge, the investment company must offer all of the following:

- breakpoints—a scale of declining sales charges based on the amount invested;
- automatic reinvestment of distributions at NAV; and
- rights of accumulation.

Breakpoints The schedule of discounts a mutual fund offers is called the fund's **breakpoints**. Breakpoints are available to any person. For a breakpoint qualification, "person" includes married couples, parents and their *minor* children, and corporations. Investment clubs or associations formed for the purpose of investing do *not* qualify for breakpoints. The following table illustrates a breakpoint schedule:

Purchase	Sales Charge
$1 to $9,999	8½%
$10,000 to $24,999	7½%
$25,000 to $49,999	7%
$50,000 plus	6½%

An investor can qualify for breakpoints in several ways. A large lump-sum investment is one method. Mutual funds offer additional incentives for an investor to continue to invest and qualify for breakpoints through a **letter of intent** or **rights of accumulation**.

Breakpoint Sales. The NASD prohibits registered reps from making higher commissions by selling investment company shares in a dollar amount just below the point at which the sales charge is reduced. This is known as a *breakpoint sale*.

The NASD considers this practice contrary to just and equitable principles of trade. It is the responsibility of all parties concerned, particularly the principal, to prevent such practices.

Letter of Intent

A person who plans to invest more money with the same mutual fund company may decrease his overall sales charges by signing a **letter of intent (LOI)**. In the LOI, the investor informs the investment company that he intends to invest the additional funds necessary to reach the breakpoint within 13 months.

The LOI is a one-sided contract binding on the fund only. The customer must complete the investment to qualify for the reduced sales charge. The fund holds the extra shares purchased from the reduced sales charge in escrow. If the customer deposits the money to complete the LOI, he receives the escrowed shares. Appreciation and reinvested dividends do not count toward the LOI.

Referring back to the sample breakpoint schedule, you see that a customer investing $9,000 is just short of the $10,000 breakpoint. In this situation, the customer might sign a letter of intent promising an amount that will qualify for the breakpoint within 13 months from the date of the letter. An additional $1,000 within 13 months qualifies the customer for the reduced sales charge. Each investment is charged the appropriate sales charge at the time of purchase.

If the customer has not completed the investment within 13 months, she will be given the choice of sending a check for the difference in sales charges or cashing in escrowed shares to pay the difference.

Backdating the Letter. A fund often permits a customer to sign a letter of intent as late as the 90th day after an initial purchase. The LOI may be backdated by up to 90 days to include prior purchases, but may not cover more than 13 months in total. This means that if the customer signs the LOI after 60 days, he has 11 months to complete the letter.

Rights of Accumulation

Rights of accumulation, like letters of intent, allow an investor to qualify for reduced sales charges. The major differences are that rights of accumulation:

- are available for subsequent investment and do not apply to initial transactions;
- allow the investor to use prior share appreciation to qualify for break points; and
- do not impose time limits.

The customer may qualify for reduced charges when the total value of shares previously purchased and shares currently being purchased exceeds a breakpoint. For the purpose of qualifying customers for breakpoints, the mutual fund bases the quantity of securities owned on:

- the current value of the securities at either NAV or POP;
- total purchases of the securities at the actual offering price; or
- the higher of current NAV or the total of purchases made to date.

✓ **For Example:** A customer who originally invested $10,000 has seen her investment grow to $15,000. She now wishes to invest an additional $10,000. Under rights of accumulation, the customer is charged 7 percent on the additional $10,000 investment because the total NAV meets the $25,000 threshold. The original sales charge on the initial investment is not adjusted. Most funds do not limit the amount of time during which an investor can qualify for breakpoints under rights of accumulation.

Combination Privilege

A mutual fund sponsor frequently offers more than one fund and refers to these multiple offerings as its **family of funds**. An investor seeking a reduced sales charge may be allowed to combine separate investments in two or more funds within the same family to reach a breakpoint.

✓ **For Example:** Joe Smith has invested $15,000 in the ACE Growth Fund for retirement and $10,000 in the ACE Income Fund for his children's education. The sponsor may view the two separate expenditures as one investment totaling $25,000 when calculating the sales charge.

Exchanges within a Family of Funds

Many sponsors offer **exchange** or **conversion** privileges within their families of funds. Exchange privileges allow an investor to convert an investment in one fund for an equal investment in another fund in the same family, often without incurring an additional sales charge.

✎ **Take Note:** Any exchange of funds is considered a sale for tax purposes. Any gains or losses are fully reportable at the time of the exchange.

Mutual funds may be purchased at NAV under a no-load exchange privilege. Certain rules apply:

- Purchase may not exceed the proceeds generated by the redemption of the other fund.

- The redemption may not involve a refund of sales charges.
- The exchange must take place within 30 days after the redemption.
- The sales personnel and dealers must receive no compensation of any kind from the reinvestment.

Redemption of Fund Shares

A mutual fund must redeem shares within seven days of receiving a written request for redemption. If the customer holds the fund certificates, the mutual fund must redeem shares within seven days of the date the certificates and instructions to liquidate arrive at the custodian bank. The customer's signature on the written request must be guaranteed. The price at which shares are redeemed is the NAV; it must be calculated at least once per business day. The redemption requirement may be suspended when:

- the NYSE is closed other than for a customary weekend or holiday closing;
- trading on the NYSE has been restricted;
- an emergency exists that would make disposal of securities owned by the company not reasonably practical; or
- the SEC has ordered the suspension of redemptions for the protection of the company's securities holders.

Otherwise, the fund must redeem shares upon request.

Forward Pricing. A mutual fund share's purchase or redemption price is determined by the next NAV calculation after the mutual fund receives the order. This is known as **forward pricing**.

✓ *For Example:* If, on Friday, a fund receives a request to redeem shares, it would hold the request until the next time the fund calculates the NAV per share. If the fund received the request after it had made Friday's calculation, the redemption would occur at the next calculation on Monday (or Tuesday if Monday is a holiday). Forward pricing applies to the purchase and redemption of fund shares.

Cancelation of Fund Shares

Because an open-end mutual fund is a continuous initial public offering, after a mutual fund share has been redeemed the share is destroyed. Unlike other corporate securities, mutual fund shares cannot be transferred to other owners. An investor purchasing mutual fund shares receives new shares.

Mutual Fund Distributions and Taxation

Distributions from mutual funds are derived from income received from portfolio securities or gains from the sale of portfolio securities. Whether taken in cash or reinvested, distributions are taxable.

Distributions from Mutual Funds

Mutual fund distributions are taxed according to the conduit theory, as described below.

The Conduit Theory   Because an investment company is organized as a corporation or trust, you might assume its earnings are subject to tax. Consider, however, how an additional level of taxation shrinks a dividend distribution's value. Assume GEM Fund owns shares of Mountain Brewing Co. First, Mountain Brewing is taxed on its earnings before it pays a dividend. Then GEM Fund pays tax on the amount of the dividend it receives. Finally, the investor pays income tax on the distribution from the fund.

Triple taxation of investment income may be avoided if the mutual fund qualifies under Subchapter M of the Internal Revenue Code (IRC). If a mutual fund acts as a conduit, or pipeline, for the distribution of net investment income, the fund may qualify as a regulated investment company, subject to tax only on the amount of investment income the fund retains. The investment income distributed to shareholders escapes taxation at the mutual fund level.

Subchapter M requires a fund to distribute at least 90 percent of its net investment income to shareholders. The fund then pays taxes only on the undistributed 10 percent. If the fund distributes 89 percent, it pays taxes on 100 percent of net investment income.

Dividend Distributions   A mutual fund may pay dividends to each shareholder in the same way corporations pay dividends to stockholders. Dividends are paid from the mutual fund's net investment income.

Net investment income includes gross investment income—dividend and interest income from securities held in the portfolio—minus operating expenses. Advertising and sales expenses are *not* included in a fund's operating expenses when calculating net investment income. Dividends from net investment income are taxed as ordinary income.

Capital Gains Distributions   The appreciation or depreciation of portfolio securities is called unrealized capital gain or loss if the fund does not sell the securities. Therefore, shareholders experience no tax consequences. When the fund sells the securities, the gain or loss is **realized** and affects shareholder taxes.

Capital gains distributions are derived from realized gains. If the fund has held the securities for at least one year, the gain is a long-term capital gain, taxed at the long-term capital gains rate. The mutual fund may reinvest the gain or distribute it to shareholders. A long-term capital gains distribution may not be made more than once per year.

Any gains distribution from a mutual fund is long term. A short-term gain is identified, distributed and taxed as an income distribution.

Calculating Fund Yield

To calculate fund yield, divide the dividend paid from net investment income by the current offering price. Yield quotations must disclose the:

- general direction of the stock market for the period in question
- fund's NAV at the beginning and the end of the period
- percentage change in the fund's price during the period

Current yield calculations may be based only on income distributions for the preceding 12 months. Gains distributions may *not* be included in yield calculations.

Most mutual funds distribute dividends quarterly. A mutual fund must disclose the source of a dividend payment if it is from other than retained or current income.

Ex-Dividend Date

Unlike the ex-dividend date for other corporate securities, the ex-dividend date for mutual funds is set by the board of directors. Normally, the ex-dividend date for mutual funds is the day after the record date.

Selling Dividends

If an investor purchases fund shares just before the ex-dividend date, the fund shares' market value decreases by the distribution amount. The investor is also taxed on the distribution. A registered representative may not encourage investors to purchase fund shares before a distribution because of this tax liability. Doing so is **selling dividends**, a violation of NASD rules.

Reinvestment of Distributions

Dividends and capital gains are distributed in cash. However, a shareholder may elect to reinvest distributions in additional mutual fund shares. The automatic reinvestment of distributions is similar to compounding interest. The reinvested distributions purchase additional shares, which may earn dividends or gains distributions.

Customers may systematically reinvest dividends and capital gains at less than the POP and can use them to purchase full and fractional shares as long as:

- shareholders who are not already participants in the reinvestment plan are given a separate opportunity to reinvest each dividend;
- the plan is described in the prospectus;
- the securities issuer bears no additional costs beyond those that it would have incurred in the normal payout of dividends; and
- all shareholders are notified of the availability of the dividend reinvestment plan at least once every year.

A mutual fund may apply a reasonable charge against each dividend reinvestment.

If a company wishes to establish a plan through which investors can reinvest their capital gains distributions, as opposed to their dividends, at a discount to the POP, the following rules apply:

- The plan must be described in the prospectus.
- All participants must be given a separate opportunity to reinvest capital gains at each distribution.
- All participants must be notified at least once every year of the availability of the distribution reinvestment plan.

Taxation of Reinvested Distributions

Distributions are taxable to shareholders whether the distributions are taken in cash or reinvested. The fund must disclose whether each distribution is from income or capital tax transactions. Form 1099, which is sent to shareholders after the close of the year, details tax information related to distributions for the year.

Fund Share Liquidations to the Investor

When an investor sells mutual fund shares, he must establish his **cost base**, or **basis**, in the shares to calculate the tax liability. A simple definition of cost base is the amount of money invested. Upon liquidation, cost base represents a return of capital and is not taxed again.

Valuing Fund Shares

The cost base of mutual fund shares includes the shares' total cost, including sales charges, plus any reinvested income and capital gains. For tax purposes, the investor compares cost base to the amount of money received from selling the shares. If the amount received is greater than the cost base, the investor reports a taxable gain. If the amount received is less than the cost base, the investor reports a loss.

Calculate the gain or loss on mutual fund shares as illustrated below.

$$\text{Total value of fund shares} - \text{Cost base} = \text{Taxable gain or loss}$$

 Take Note: The investor does not receive a separate tax form from the mutual fund identifying the cost base of the shares sold. Recordkeeping for purchases and sales is the shareholder's responsibility.

Calculating Net Gains and Losses

To calculate tax liability, taxpayers must first add all capital gains for the year. Then, they separately add all capital losses. Finally, they offset the totals to determine the net capital gain or loss for the year. Net capital losses are deductible against earned income up to a maximum of $3,000 per year. Any capital losses not deducted in a year may be carried forward indefinitely to be used in future years.

Accounting Methods

If an investor decides to liquidate shares, he determines the cost base by electing one of three accounting methods: "first in, first out" (FIFO), share identification or average basis. If the investor fails to choose, the IRS assumes the investor liquidates shares on a FIFO basis.

First In, First Out

When FIFO shares are sold, the cost of the shares held the longest is used to calculate the gain or loss. In a rising market, this method normally creates adverse tax consequences.

Share Identification

When using the share identification accounting method, the investor keeps track of the cost of each share purchased and uses this information when deciding which shares to liquidate. He then liquidates the shares that provide the desired tax benefits.

Average Basis

The shareholder may elect to use an average cost basis when redeeming fund shares. The shareholder calculates average basis by dividing the total cost of all shares owned by the total number of shares. The shareholder may not change his decision to use the average basis method without IRS permission.

Other Mutual Fund Tax Considerations   Mutual fund investors must consider many tax factors when buying and selling mutual fund shares.

Withholding Tax

If an investor neglects or fails to include her tax ID number when purchasing mutual fund shares, the fund must withhold 31 percent of the distributions to the investor as a withholding tax.

Cost Basis of Shares Transferred

The cost basis of inherited property is either stepped up or stepped down to its fair market value (FMV) at the date of the decedent's death.

✓ **For Example:** June Polar inherited $10,000 worth of mutual fund shares from her father. At her father's death, the shares' NAV was $11,500. June's basis in the shares is the FMV, or $11,500.

Dividend Exclusions

Corporations that invest in other companies' stock may deduct 70 percent of the dividend received from taxable income. No similar exclusion exists for individual investors.

Taxation of Investment Returns

The taxation of investment returns can be summarized as follows:

Income distributions:	Taxed as ordinary income
Capital gains distributions:	Taxed at investor's capital gains tax rate
Profit or loss on sale:	Short- or long-term gain or loss depending on length of holding period and cost basis

Exchanges within a Family of Funds

Even though exchange within a fund family incurs no sales charge, the IRS considers a sale to have taken place, and if a gain occurs, the customer is taxed. This tax liability can be significant, and shareholders should be aware of this potential conversion cost.

Mutual Fund Purchase and Withdrawal Plans

Mutual fund investors can select from among several methods by which to purchase mutual fund shares or withdraw money from the mutual fund account.

Types of Mutual Fund Accounts

When an investor opens an account with a mutual fund, he makes an initial deposit of at least the minimum required by the fund, and he specifies whether fund share distributions are to be made in cash or reinvested. If the customer elects to receive distributions in cash rather than reinvesting them, his proportionate interest in the fund is reduced each time a distribution is made. The customer can make additional investments in an open account at any time and in any dollar amount; that is, the law sets no minimum requirement, although each fund may set its own.

Accumulation Plans   Mutual funds have established several accumulation plans that allow investors to use the dollar cost averaging strategy.

Voluntary Accumulation Plan

A voluntary accumulation plan allows a customer to deposit regular periodic investments on a voluntary basis. The plan is designed to help the customer form regular investment habits while still offering some flexibility.

Voluntary accumulation plans may require a minimum initial purchase and minimum additional purchase amounts. Many funds offer automatic withdrawal from customer checking accounts to simplify contributions. If a customer misses a payment, the fund does not penalize him because the plan is voluntary. The customer may discontinue the plan at any time.

Dollar Cost Averaging. One method of purchasing mutual fund shares is called *dollar cost averaging*, where a person invests regular amounts over time. This form of investing allows the individual to purchase more shares when prices are low and fewer shares when prices are high. In a fluctuating market that trends upward, over a period of time *the average cost per share is lower than the average price of the shares*. However, dollar cost averaging does not guarantee profits in a declining market because prices may continue to decline for some time. In this case, the investor buys more shares of a sinking investment.

The following example illustrates how average price and average cost may vary with dollar cost averaging:

Month	Amount Invested	Price per Share	No. of Shares
January	$600	$20	30
February	$600	$24	25
March	$600	$30	20
April	$600	$40	15
Total	$2,400	$114	90

The average *cost* per share equals $2,400 (the total investment) divided by 90 (the total number of shares purchased), or $26.67 per share, while the average *price* per share is $28.50 ($114 ÷ 4).

Withdrawal Plans   In addition to lump-sum withdrawals where customers sell all of their shares, mutual funds offer **systematic withdrawal plans**. Withdrawal plans are normally a free service. Not all mutual funds offer withdrawal plans, but those that do may offer plans that include the following.

Fixed Dollar

A customer may request the periodic withdrawal of a fixed dollar amount. Thus, the fund liquidates enough shares each period to send that sum. The amount of money liquidated can be more or less than the account earnings during the period.

Fixed Percentage or Fixed Share

Under a fixed-percentage or fixed-share withdrawal plan, either a fixed number of shares or a fixed percentage of the account is liquidated each period.

Fixed Time

Under a fixed-time withdrawal plan, customers liquidate their holdings over a fixed period of time.

✓ **For Example:** If a customer wants to receive account proceeds monthly for 10 years, the fund sends an initial check equal to $\frac{1}{120}$ of the current account value. Because the customer has fixed the time, this type of withdrawal plan is considered self-exhausting. The customer's account will be liquidated in 10 years.

Most mutual funds require a customer to invest a minimum amount of money before a withdrawal plan may begin. Additionally, most funds discourage continued investment once withdrawals start.

Withdrawal Plan Disclosures Withdrawal plans are not guaranteed. With fixed-dollar plans, only the dollar amount to be received each period is fixed. All other factors, including the number of shares liquidated and a plan's length, are variable. For a fixed-time plan, only the period of time is fixed; the amount of money the investor receives varies each period. Because withdrawal plans are not guaranteed, the registered rep must:

- never promise an investor a guaranteed rate of return;
- stress to the investor that it is possible to exhaust the account by over-withdrawing;
- state that during a down market it is *possible* that the account will be exhausted if the investor withdraws even a small amount; and
- never use charts or tables unless the SEC specifically clears their use.

Tracking Investment Company Securities

Investment company prices, like those for individual securities, are quoted daily in the financial press. However, because of the various methods used to calculate sales charges, as described below, the financial press provides several footnotes to explain the type of sales charge a mutual fund issuer uses. A registered representative must understand the presentation and meaning of the footnotes associated with investment company quotes so that he can accurately describe the quotes to the investing public. An example of mutual fund quotations and associated footnotes is shown in Figure 10.2.

Most newspapers carry daily quotes of the NAVs and offer prices for most major mutual funds. A mutual fund's NAV is its bid price. The offer price, also called the *public offering price* or *POP*, is the ask price; it is the NAV plus the *maximum* sales charge, if any. The "NAV Chg." column reflects the change in NAV from the previous day's quote.

Look at the family of funds called ArGood Mutual Funds. ArGood Growth Fund is a part of this group; its net asset value, offering price and the change in its net asset value per share are listed. As stated previously, when a difference exists between the NAV and the offering price, the fund is a load fund. A no-load fund is usually identified by the letters "NL" in the "Offer Price" column. Look at the Best Mutual funds; they are a family of no-load funds.

FIGURE 10.2   Mutual Fund Quotations

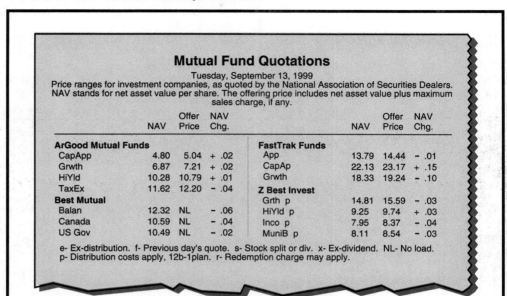

Mutual Fund Quotations

Tuesday, September 13, 1999

Price ranges for investment companies, as quoted by the National Association of Securities Dealers. NAV stands for net asset value per share. The offering price includes net asset value plus maximum sales charge, if any.

	NAV	Offer Price	NAV Chg.		NAV	Offer Price	NAV Chg.
ArGood Mutual Funds				**FastTrak Funds**			
CapApp	4.80	5.04	+ .02	App	13.79	14.44	– .01
Grwth	6.87	7.21	+ .02	CapAp	22.13	23.17	+ .15
HiYld	10.28	10.79	+ .01	Grwth	18.33	19.24	– .10
TaxEx	11.62	12.20	– .04	**Z Best Invest**			
Best Mutual				Grth p	14.81	15.59	– .03
Balan	12.32	NL	– .06	HiYld p	9.25	9.74	+ .03
Canada	10.59	NL	– .04	Inco p	7.95	8.37	– .04
US Gov	10.49	NL	– .02	MuniB p	8.11	8.54	– .03

e- Ex-distribution. f- Previous day's quote. s- Stock split or div. x- Ex-dividend. NL- No load. p- Distribution costs apply, 12b-1plan. r- Redemption charge may apply.

The final column shows the change in a share's net asset value since the last trading date. A plus (+) indicates an upward move, and a minus (–) indicates a downward turn.

From this information, you can calculate any mutual fund's sales charge. For example, find the FastTrak group of funds in Figure 10.2. The first entry is App.

Remember the formula for calculating the sales charge:

Public offering price – NAV = Sales charge

Therefore, in this case, the calculation is:

$14. 44 – $13.79 = $.65

To calculate the sales charge percentage, use the following formula:

Sales charge ÷ Public offering price = Sales charge %

In this case, the calculation follows:

$.65 ÷ $14.44 = 4.5%

You can also watch the movements of the fund's share value.

FIGURE 10.3 **Standard & Poor's Mutual Fund Summary**

Fund	Prin. Obj.	Type	Dec 31, 1998 Total Net Assets (MILS)	Cash & Equiv (MILS)	Net Assets per Share % Chg. from Prev. Dec. 31 At Dec. 31 1996	1997	1998	Min. Unit	Max. Sales Chg. %	$10,000 Invested 12-31-88 Now Worth	Price Record 1998 High	Low	NAV Per Sh as of 12-31-98 NAV per Shr.	Offer Price
Acorn	G	C	525.8	47.0	+ 3.9	+30.1	+15.4	$4,000	None	29,603	47.71	37.61	47.71	47.71
ALFA Securities	G	C	672.6	22.9	+33.5	+41.1	+21.6	$1,000	None	32,518	24.75	19.62	24.47	24.47
Alliance Fund	G	C	948.2	19.0	- 5.2	+29.5	+ 8.9	$250	5.5	24,661	9.67	6.96	9.45	10.00
Alliance Tech	G	C	200.8	10.0	- 16.4	+26.1	+12.0	$250	5.5	....	36.47	23.44	34.24	36.23
Amer Balanced	IS	B	202.0	24.0	+ 7.7	+27.1	+15.8	$500	8.5	27,889	12.61	10.92	12.32	13.46
Amer Cap Corp Bond	IS	BD	136.0	16.0	+ 9.2	+24.6	+10.8	$500	8.5	23,457	7.51	7.12	7.12	7.48
Amer Cap Mun Bond	I	TF	187.0	7.0	+10.0	+22.0	+15.9	$500	4.75	22,897	21.74	18.53	19.14	20.09
Analytic Opt Equity	GI	C	85.7	11.7	+ 6.6	+15.5	+10.2	$5,000	None	20,662	15.59	13.88	15.45	15.45
Axe-Houghton Bond	SIR	B	204.5	4.0	+ 5.8	+31.6	+21.5	$1,000	None	27,766	12.16	10.26	11.93	11.93
Axe-Houghton Stock	G	C	93.4	2.0	- 15.0	+31.1	+10.8	$1,000	None	28,394	11.46	8.25	11.13	11.13

Principal Objective: G-Growth; I-Income; R-Return on Capital; S-Stability; E-Objectives treated Equally; P-Preservation of Capital; Listed in order of importance. Type: B-Balanced; BD-Bond; C-Common; CV-Conv Bond and Prefd Stock; FL-Flexible; GB-Long-term Gov't; GL-Global; H-Hedge; L-Leverage; P-Preferred; PM-Precious Metals; O-Options; SP-Specialized; TF-Tax Free; ST-Short-term investments.

Stock guides such as Standard & Poor's include summaries of mutual funds for the year. Figure 10.3 shows a portion of a table taken from a *Standard & Poor's Stock Guide;* you can use it to evaluate mutual funds. To the right of the third fund listed on the table, Alliance Fund, the following information is listed:

- **Principal objective of the fund.** "G" means Alliance is a growth fund. Other objectives might be income, return on capital and stability; they are listed in the footnotes below the table.
- **Type of fund.** Alliance Fund is a "C" or common stock fund. Other types of funds are listed in the footnotes. They include the following:

B	– balanced		FL	– flexible
BD	– bond		H	– hedge
C	– common		L	– leverage
CN	– Canadian		P	– preferred
CT	– common		SP	– specialized
CV	– convertible bond and preferred stock		TF	– tax free

- **Total net assets.** This column lists total net assets at market value—that is, assets minus liabilities. Alliance Fund has total net assets of $948.2 million.
- **Cash and equivalents.** This column includes cash and receivables, short-term government securities and other money-market instruments less current liabilities. Cash and equivalents are part of the total net assets.
- **Percentage change in net assets per share.** These columns show a fund's performance over a specific period—in this case, from the previous December 31. For example, on December 31, 1997, Alliance Fund had a 29.5 percent increase in net asset value per share since December 31, 1996.
- **Minimum unit.** This is the minimum initial purchase of shares. For Alliance Fund, it is $250.
- **Maximum sales charge.** Alliance Fund charges 5.5 percent. If a fund is a no-load fund, it levies no sales charge.
- **Current worth of $10,000 invested December 31, 1988.** This column provides a gauge of a fund's performance over several years. In this case, $10,000 invested in Alliance Fund on December 31, 1988, would have more than doubled, growing to $24,661.
- **Price record.** From these columns, you can learn a share's percentage of appreciation from its low price of the year. To determine the percentage, subtract the low price from the latest NAV per share, then divide the difference by the low price. For example, during 1998 Alliance Fund sold at a low of 6.96. If on June 30, 1998 (the current date), its NAV per share was 9.67, the appreciation would be computed as follows:

$$
\begin{array}{lr}
\text{NAV} & 9.67 \\
\text{Low} & -\underline{6.96} \\
& 2.71
\end{array}
$$

$$2.71 \div 6.96 = 38.93\% \text{ Appreciation}$$

- **NAV per share.** This column shows the current NAV per share, as well as the current POP.

Summary

Investment companies offer investors a means to invest in large, diversified portfolios of securities. Doing so allows an investor to take advantage of professional portfolio management and many other services, as well as save on transaction costs.

Investment companies are either closed-end or open-end. Closed-end investment companies are sold by prospectus in an initial public offering. Once the stated amount of capital is raised, the fund is closed and its shares trade on a stock exchange or OTC, like any other stock.

Open-end investment companies are a continuous public offering and thus are always sold by prospectus. Shares are bought through a broker or directly from the fund at their public offering price. The public offering price may be the share's net asset value in the case of a no-load fund, or the NAV plus a sales charge in the case of a load fund. When an investor decides to sell his shares, he redeems them directly to the fund company for the NAV.

Open-end fund transactions are based on forward pricing, meaning the share price is based on the next NAV calculation after the transaction is entered.

Distributions from a mutual fund are classified as either income or capital gains. In addition, the sale of fund shares is a taxable event. The tax consequences are determined by the investor's cost basis in the fund shares, which it is the investor's responsibility to determine.

Key Concepts

To prepare for your license exam, you should learn the following concepts.

In addition to studying these key concepts, use the Investment Company Procedures Hot Sheet on page 643 for further review.

asset allocation fund	money-market fund
balanced fund	mutual fund
bond fund	nondiversified company
breakpoint	open-end investment company
closed-end investment company	preferred stock fund
combination fund	publicly traded fund
diversification	sales load
dual-purpose fund	75-5-10 test
expense ratio	specialized (sector) fund
face-amount certificate (FAC)	tax-free bond fund
family of funds	U.S. government fund
fixed dollar plan	underwriting group
growth fund	unit investment trust (UIT)
income fund	withdrawal plan
management company	

Review Questions

1. "Mutual fund" is a popular name for

    A. all investment companies
    B. open-end investment companies
    C. closed-end investment companies
    D. any company that invests pooled funds

2. What kind of investment company has no provision for redeeming outstanding shares?

    A. Open-end company
    B. Closed-end company
    C. Unit investment trust
    D. Mutual fund

3. The essential difference between an open-end fund and a closed-end fund is

    A. the method of determining book value
    B. closed-end funds are closed to secondary trading
    C. capitalization
    D. There is no difference.

4. An investor looking for current income would be LEAST interested in

    A. bond funds
    B. preferred stock funds
    C. common stock funds
    D. gains shares in a dual-purpose fund

5. Money-market funds usually offer which of the following?

    I. Daily interest calculations
    II. Check-writing privileges
    III. No-load funds
    IV. Long-term growth potential

    A. I and II
    B. I, II and III
    C. I and IV
    D. III and IV

6. The custodian of a mutual fund usually does which of the following?

    A. Approves changes in investment policy
    B. Holds the fund's cash and securities and performs related clerical functions
    C. Manages the fund
    D. Cleans the fund's properties and carries out related duties

7. Which type of mutual fund is sold at net asset value?

    A. Open-end
    B. Closed-end
    C. Front-end load
    D. No-load

8. For a company to charge the maximum sales charge of 8½ percent, it must offer all of the following EXCEPT

    A. automatic reinvestment of dividends and capital gains at NAV
    B. breakpoints
    C. automatic reinvestment at POP
    D. rights of accumulation

9. If a mutual fund is quoted at $16.56 NAV and $18 POP, the sales charge percentage is

    A. 7½ percent
    B. 7¾ percent
    C. 8 percent
    D. 8½ percent

10. A no-load fund may be redeemed at

    A. NAV minus sales charge
    B. POP minus sales charge
    C. NAV plus sales charge
    D. NAV

Answers & Rationale

1. **B.** The term "mutual fund" is used exclusively for open-end investment companies.

2. **B.** Closed-end investment companies do not redeem their own shares. Once a closed-end fund has sold all of its shares in its initial public offering, investors can buy and sell shares only in the open market.

3. **C.** A closed-end fund issues a set number of shares in an initial public offering to raise capital. An open-end fund raises capital through an open-ended offering in which it continuously issues new shares.

4. **D.** A dual-purpose fund issues two types of shares—income shares and gains shares. Owners of income shares receive any income the fund distributes. Owners of gains shares receive the benefits of the fund's capital gains.

5. **B.** Money-market funds invest in short-term debt instruments that do not offer potential for long-term growth or capital gains.

6. **B.** The bank or other financial institution the fund hires to act as its custodian is charged with all of the clerical functions related to holding the fund's cash and securities.

7. **D.** No-load funds are sold at their net asset values—that is, without sales charges or commissions.

8. **C.** A firm that offers automatic reinvestment at the public offering price does not give its investors any special advantage.

9. **C.** The sales charge is calculated as a percentage of the public offering price.

10. **D.** A no-load fund is bought and sold at its net asset value.

Retirement Plans

OVERVIEW

An important goal for many investors is to provide themselves with retirement income. Many individuals accomplish this through corporate retirement plans, others set up their own plans, and some have both individual and corporate retirement plans.

Nonqualified Corporate Retirement Plans

A nonqualified plan does not allow tax deductibility of contributions. Earnings, however, accumulate on a tax-deferred basis. A nonqualified plan need not comply with nondiscrimination rules that apply to qualified plans. The employer can make nonqualified benefits available to key employees and exclude others.

Nonqualified plans are not subject to the same reporting and disclosure requirements as qualified plans. However, nonqualified plans still must be in writing and communicated to the plan participants.

Taxation Contributions to nonqualified plans are not exempt from current income tax. The tax is paid on the amount of contribution in the year the contribution is made, whether it is made by the employer or the employee. The corporation cannot deduct company contributions made on behalf of the participant until paid to the participant; contributions are not taxable to the employee until she receives the benefit.

Contributions to nonqualified plans that have already been taxed make up the investor's cost base. When the investor withdraws money from the nonqualified plan, the cost base is not taxed. However, earnings are taxed when withdrawn.

Types of Plans   Two types of nonqualified plans are payroll deduction plans and deferred compensation plans.

Payroll Deduction Plans

A payroll deduction program involves a deduction from an employee's check on a weekly, monthly or quarterly basis as authorized by the employee. The money is deducted after taxes are paid and may be invested in any number of investment vehicles at the employee's option.

 Take Note: For NASD testing purposes, 401(k) plans are considered *qualified salary reduction* plans, not *payroll deduction* plans. Assume all payroll deduction plans are nonqualified.

Deferred Compensation Plans

A deferred compensation plan is a contractual agreement between a firm and an employee in which the employee agrees to defer receipt of current compensation in favor of a payout at retirement when it is assumed that the employee will be in a lower tax bracket. The agreement underlying a deferred compensation plan usually includes the following:

- conditions and circumstances under which some or all of the benefits may be forfeited, such as if the employee moves to a competing firm;
- statement to the effect that the employee is not entitled to any claim against the employer's assets until retirement, death or disability; and
- disclaimer that the agreement may be void if the firm suffers a business failure or bankruptcy.

Company directors are not considered employees for the purpose of establishing eligibility for a deferred compensation plan and, as a result, may not participate in the plan.

Business Failure. Generally, an employee enjoys no benefits from a deferred compensation program until retirement. If the business fails, the employee is a general creditor of the business with no guarantee he will receive the deferred payment.

Funding. Deferred compensation plans are typically unfunded, in which case the deferred compensation is paid from the firm's operating assets. If the plan is funded, the employer sets up a specific account to fund the program.

Table 11.1 compares qualified and nonqualified plans.

TABLE 11.1   Qualified vs. Nonqualified Plans

Qualified Plans	Nonqualified Plans
Contributions currently tax deductible	Contributions are not currently tax deductible
Plan approved by the IRS	Plan does not need IRS approval
Plan cannot discriminate	Plan can discriminate
Tax on accumulation is deferred	Tax on accumulation is deferred
All withdrawals taxed	Excess over cost base taxed

Individual Retirement Accounts

Individual retirement accounts (IRAs) were created to encourage people to save for their retirement. All employed individuals may open and contribute to an IRA. Four types of IRAs are available, with different contribution, tax and distribution characteristics:

- Traditional IRA
- SEP IRA
- Roth IRA
- Education IRA

Traditional IRAs. A traditional IRA allows a maximum *tax-deductible* annual contribution of $2,000 per individual or $4,000 per couple. The income and capital gains earned in the account are tax deferred until the funds are withdrawn. The tax deductibility of contributions to traditional IRAs is phased out as income increases.

Distributions without penalty may begin after age 59½ and must begin by April 1 of the year following the year an individual turns 70½. Distributions before age 59½ are subject to a 10 percent penalty as well as regular income taxes, and contributions after age 70½ are not allowed.

The early withdrawal penalty is waived if the distribution is made to a first-time homebuyer for the purchase of a principal residence (subject to a lifetime maximum of $10,000) or for education expenses for the taxpayer or a spouse, child or grandchild.

SEP IRAs. Self-employed individuals and corporations may contribute the lesser of 15 percent of their postcontribution incomes or $30,000 in tax-deductible dollars each year to IRAs established by their employees. All other characteristics are the same as those of traditional IRAs.

Roth IRAs. Created in 1997, Roth IRAs allow *after-tax* contributions of up to $2,000 per individual, $4,000 per couple, per year. Contributions to other IRAs reduce the $2,000 limit. Income and capital gains are not taxed as they accrue nor when distributed from an account. Normal distributions may begin after the money has been in an account for five taxable years and the IRA owner reaches age 59½, dies, becomes disabled or purchases a home for the first time.

Required minimum distributions do not apply to Roth IRAs. The 10 percent penalty for distributions before age 59½ is waived for first-time homebuyers if they use the funds to purchase a principal residence.

Education IRAs. Created in 1997 along with Roth IRAs, education IRAs allow after-tax contributions of up to $500 per student per year for children younger than age 18. Distributions are tax free as long as the funds are used for higher education expenses. If a student's account is not depleted by the age of 30, the funds must be distributed to the individual, subject to income tax and 10 percent penalty, or rolled into an education IRA for another family member beneficiary.

The early withdrawal penalties for all IRAs are waived in the event of death or disability.

Because Roth and education IRAs, as well as the homebuyer and education expense penalty waivers, were features introduced in late 1997, it is uncertain when the NASD will include test questions relating to these topics. The balance of this discussion focuses on traditional and SEP IRAs.

Tax Benefits   IRA participants may deduct contributions to their IRAs from their taxable income. The deductibility limits are lowered for individuals who are eligible for other qualified plans. The portion deductible declines gradually and is eliminated entirely for single filers whose adjusted gross income (AGI) exceeds $40,000 or married couples whose combined AGI exceeds $60,000. These AGI limits will increase every year beginning in 1998. Individuals who are ineligible to participate in qualified plans may deduct IRA contributions regardless of income level.

Income and capital gains earned from investments in an IRA account are not taxed until the funds are withdrawn.

Participation in an IRA   Any taxpayer younger than age 70½ reporting earned income for a given tax year may contribute to an IRA. Passive income from investments is not earned income. Contributions to an IRA may be made up to April 15 of the year following the tax year.

IRA Custodians   Taxpayers can appoint IRA custodians of their choice, selecting from securities broker-dealers, banks and savings institutions, insurance carriers, credit unions and mutual fund distributors.

IRA Contributions   The maximum annual IRA contribution is $2,000 or 100 percent of earned income, whichever is less, for an employed individual and $2,000 for his spousal IRA, whether or not the spouse is employed.

The deductibility of an individual's contribution is reduced or eliminated if she participates in an employer-sponsored retirement plan or earns more than a specified amount. IRA tax deductions are summarized in Table 11.2.

✓ *For Example:* A married couple who are both ineligible to participate in a qualified plan and whose combined income is $120,000 may contribute and deduct a total of $4,000. A married couple who are both eligible to participate in a qualified plan and whose combined income is $55,000 may contribute $4,000, but may deduct only $2,000 because of income limits imposed on eligible participants.

IRA owners are entitled to withdraw any or all of their accounts at any time, although the funds attributable to earnings and pretax contributions are subject to income tax and may be subject to early withdrawal penalties.

TABLE 11.2   Tax-Deductible IRA Contributions for Eligible Employees (1998)

Tier	Taxpayer's Adjusted Gross Income (AGI)	Allowable Tax Deduction
1	Single, less than $30,000 Married, less than $50,000	Contribution is 100% tax deductible.
2	Single, from $30,000 to $40,000 Married, from $50,000 to $60,000	Allowable deduction reduces at the rate of 10% per $1,000 income over $30,000 ($50,000 if married).
3	Single, more than $40,000 Married, more than $60,000	No portion of the contribution is tax deductible.

Excess Contributions. Annual IRA contributions exceeding the maximum allowed are subject to a 6 percent penalty tax if the excess is not removed by the time the taxpayer files a tax return. In some instances, the excess may be applied toward future contributions. The 6 percent penalty applies for each year the money remains in the account, until corrected. The only way to avoid the 6 percent penalty is to remove the excess.

IRA Investments   Depending on where a person is in his earnings cycle and how close his projected retirement date, growth-oriented stocks and mutual funds may be the best choices even though they carry with them the higher risks associated with investments in the stock market.

Permissible Investments. Funds in an IRA account may be used to buy stocks, bonds, mutual funds, UITs, limited partnerships, government securities, U.S. government-issued gold and silver coins, annuities and many others.

IRA investments should be relatively conservative and should reflect the investor's age and risk tolerance profile. Because an IRA serves as a source of retirement funds, it is important that the account be managed for adequate long-term growth.

Ineligible Investments. Collectibles, including antiques, gems, rare coins, works of art and stamps, are not acceptable IRA investments. Life insurance contracts, such as cash value, term and decreasing term insurance with no cash surrender value, may not be purchased in an IRA. Tax-free municipal bonds are also inappropriate for an IRA because their yields are typically lower than those of other similar investments and the income generated is taxable upon withdrawal.

Ineligible Investment Practices. No short sales of stock, speculative option strategies or margin account trading is permitted in an IRA or any other retirement plan. Covered call writing is allowed.

IRA Withdrawals   Withdrawals may be made in lump sums, in varying amounts or in regular installments and are taxable as ordinary income. Withdrawals exceeding basis before age 59½ are subject to a 10 percent early withdrawal penalty unless they are due to death or disability. Withdrawals must begin by April 1 of the year following the year in which the account owner reaches age 70½, and they must meet minimum Internal Revenue Code (IRC) distribution requirements or incur a 50 percent penalty.

✓ *For Example:* If an IRA owner reaches age 70½ on January 1, 1999, he would have to begin withdrawals by April 1, 2000.

All distributions are treated as taxable income in the year in which received. IRA distributions can be made to the account owner or jointly to the owner and her spouse. If the account owner dies, payments are made to a designated beneficiary.

Nondeductible Capital Withdrawals. IRA investors who contribute after-tax dollars to an IRA are not taxed on those funds when they are withdrawn from the account, but they are taxed at the ordinary income tax rate when they withdraw funds resulting from investment gains or income.

Moving IRAs

Individuals may move their funds and investments from one qualified plan to another qualified plan through a rollover or transfer.

Rollovers. An IRA account owner may take temporary possession of the account funds in order to move the retirement account to another custodian. The account owner may do so only once per 12-month period, and the rollover must be completed within *60 calendar days* of the funds' withdrawal from the original plan. However, 100 percent of the account value must be rolled into the new account or be subject to income tax and, if applicable, early withdrawal penalty.

A participant in a qualified plan may move his plan assets to an IRA if he leaves the company. If the rollover is made directly from the qualified plan to an IRA, the participant never takes possession of the funds. If the participant does take possession of the funds, he must complete the rollover within *60 calendar days* of withdrawing the funds from the qualified plan. In addition, when the participant takes possession of the funds from a qualified plan to make a rollover, the payor of the distribution must, by law, withhold 20 percent of the distribution as a withholding tax. The participant must, nonetheless, roll over 100 percent of the plan distribution, including the funds withheld, or be subject to income tax and, if applicable, early withdrawal penalty.

✓ *For Example:* A 50-year-old individual with $100,000 in his company retirement plan changes employers. His pension plan may be distributed to him as a rollover in a lump-sum payment, minus the mandatory 20 percent withholding of $20,000. He must then deposit $100,000 in an IRA rollover account within 60 days. Any portion not rolled over, including the $20,000 withholding, is considered a distribution subject to ordinary income tax and early withdrawal penalty. If he deposits the entire $100,000 into the IRA, he must apply on his next income tax return for a refund of the $20,000 withheld.

Transfers. In a direct transfer of an IRA or a qualified retirement plan, all account assets are sent directly from one IRA custodian to another, and the account owner never takes possession of the funds. The number of IRA transfers an account owner may make is unlimited.

Simplified Employee Pensions (SEP-IRAs)

Simplified employee pension plans (SEPs) offer self-employed persons and small businesses easy-to-administer pension plans. A SEP is a qualified plan that allows an employer to contribute money to SEP-IRAs its employees set up to receive employer contributions.

Eligibility. To be eligible, an employee must be at least 21 years of age, have performed services for the employer during at least three of the last five years and have received at least $400 in compensation from the employer in the current year (the annual compensation figure is indexed for inflation).

Participation. SEP rules require the employer and *all eligible employees* to participate.

Funding. A SEP allows the employer to contribute from 0 percent to 15 percent of an employee's salary to the employee's SEP-IRA each year, up to a maximum of $30,000 per employee per year. The employer determines the level of contributions each year and must contribute the same percentage for each employee, including the employer. An employee older than age 70½ must receive a SEP contribution if one is made.

An employee may also use the SEP-IRA for his own annual IRA contribution, subject to the $2,000 limit. Participation in the SEP or any other qualified plan reduces the personal IRA contribution's deductibility if income limits are surpassed.

Vesting. Participants in a SEP are fully vested immediately, meaning all the money deposited in an employee's SEP-IRA belongs to the employee.

Taxation. Employer contributions are tax deductible to the employer. Contributions are not taxable to an employee until withdrawn, and earnings in the account are tax deferred. The same rules for early withdrawal from IRAs apply to SEP-IRAs.

Keogh (HR-10) Plans

Keogh plans are qualified plans intended for self-employed persons and owner-employees of unincorporated businesses or professional practices filing Schedule C with the IRS.

As with all qualified plans, only earned income, not passive income from investments or other unearned sources, is eligible. Owner-employees of businesses or professional practices must show a gross profit to qualify for a tax-deductible contribution to a Keogh plan. If a business does not profit, no contribution is allowed.

Contributions
The 25 percent contribution limit for a business owner or self-employed person is based on the individual's income remaining *after* she makes the contribution (20 percent of pre-contribution income).

The Keogh contribution limit for employees of a self-employed person is the same as the employer's after-contribution percentage, but is applied to an employee's gross income. The contribution limit range is the lesser of 25 percent of gross income or $30,000. The Keogh contributions for the employer and the employee must be the same percentage. If an employer's own Keogh contribution is 15 percent of after-contribution income, he must make a 15 percent contribution of gross income for each eligible employee.

Nontax-Deductible Contributions

In addition to tax-deductible contributions, a Keogh plan participant may make nondeductible contributions. The income and capital gains accumulate tax free until the owner withdraws them. However, if the voluntary contribution results in a total contribution that exceeds the annual maximum, the excess may be subject to a 10 percent penalty tax.

Eligibility
Employee participation in a Keogh plan is subject to the following eligibility rules:

- **Full-time employees**. All employees who receive compensation for at least 1,000 hours of work per year.
- **Tenured employees**. All employees who have completed one or more years of continuous employment or who have been employed continuously from the Keogh plan's start-up date if less than three years have elapsed.
- **Adult employees**. All employees 21 years and older.

Vesting Requirements
Vesting refers to the period an employee must work before employer contributions become the employee's property. In general, an employee must be fully vested after five years of full-time service.

Comparison of IRAs and Keogh Plans
Keogh plans and IRAs are designed to encourage individuals to set aside funds for retirement income. Although both IRAs and Keoghs are considered qualified plans, an IRA does not involve employer contributions and, thus, is not a plan qualified by the Employee Retirement Income Security Act of 1974 (ERISA).

The principal similarities between Keoghs and IRAs follow:

- **Tax deferral of income contributed to plans**. Taxes are deferred on contributions until the individual receives distributions.
- **Tax-sheltered**. Investment income and capital gains are not taxed until withdrawn.

TABLE 11.3 Differences Between Keogh Plans and IRAs

Characteristic	Keogh Plans	IRAs
Source of contributions	Employer; employee may also make nondeductible contributions.	Employee.
Permissible investments	Most equity and debt securities, U.S. government-minted precious-metal coins, annuities and cash-value life insurance.	Most equity and debt securities, U.S. government-minted precious-metal coins and annuities.
Nonpermissible investments	Term insurance and collectibles.	Term insurance, collectibles and cash-value life insurance.
Change of employer	Lump-sum distribution can be rolled over into an IRA within 60 days.	Does not apply.
Penalty for excess contribution	10% penalty.	6% penalty.
Taxation of distributions	Taxed as ordinary income.	Taxed as ordinary income.

- **Contributions.** Only cash may be contributed to a plan. In the event of a rollover or transfer, cash and securities from the old account can be deposited.
- **Distributions.** Distributions without penalty can begin as early as age 59½.
- **Penalties for early withdrawal.** The individual pays income tax on the total amount withdrawn, plus a 10 percent penalty. Early withdrawals without penalty are permitted in the event of death or disability.
- **Rollovers and transfers.** Accounts may be rolled over once every 12 months, and rollovers must be completed within 60 days. The number of direct transfers is not limited.
- **Payout options.** Distributions may be in lump sums, eligible for five-year income averaging, or regular, periodic payments. Five-year averaging will be eliminated after 1999.
- **Beneficiary.** Upon the planholder's death, payments are made to a designated beneficiary(ies).

The differences between Keoghs and IRAs are shown in Table 11.3.

Tax-Sheltered Annuities

Qualified annuity plans offered under Sections 403(b) and 501(c)3 of the Internal Revenue Code, sometimes referred to as *tax-sheltered annuities* (*TSAs*), are designed for long-term savings only. To ensure this objective, TSAs (like IRAs and other retirement plans) are subject to tax penalties if savings are withdrawn before a participant retires.

Tax Advantages   TSAs are entitled to the following tax advantages:

- Contributions to a TSA are excluded from a participant's gross income.
- Participant's earnings in a TSA accumulate tax free until distribution.

Income Exclusion. If an eligible employee elects to make annual contributions to a TSA, those contributions are excluded from the employee's gross income for that year. The amount of the contribution is not reported as income, resulting in lower current income taxes.

Tax-Free Accumulation. Earnings in a TSA accumulate tax free and do not increase the participant's taxable income until the total dollars are withdrawn at retirement, usually when that person is in a lower tax bracket than during her working years.

Investments

Tax-sheltered annuity plans offer mutual funds, stocks, bonds and CDs as investment vehicles. Because of the range of investments, banks, brokerage houses, savings and loans and credit unions may offer these plans.

Eligibility Requirements   To be eligible to establish a TSA, an employer must qualify as one of the following:

- public educational 403(b) institution
- tax-exempt 501(c)3 organization
- church organization

Public Educational 403(b). To qualify as a public educational institution, an organization must be state supported or a political subdivision or an agency of a state. Private school systems have a separate set of qualifying rules, as explained in the next section. State-run educational systems include:

- elementary schools
- secondary schools
- colleges and universities
- medical schools

Individuals employed by the above school systems in the following job classifications may enroll in a TSA plan:

- teachers and other faculty members;
- administrators, managers, principals, supervisors and other members of the administrative staff;
- counselors;
- clerical staff and maintenance workers; and
- individuals who perform services for the institution, such as doctors or nurses.

Tax-Exempt 501(c)3. As stated earlier, 501(c)3 organizations are tax-exempt entities specifically cited in the IRC as being eligible to establish TSAs for their employees. Typical 501(c)3 organizations include:

- private colleges and universities
- trade schools
- parochial schools
- zoos and museums
- research and scientific foundations
- religious and charitable institutions
- private hospitals and medical schools

Definition of an Employee

Only employees of qualified employers are eligible to participate in a TSA plan. Independent contractors are not eligible. It is the employer's responsibility to determine an individual's status or definition.

Eligibility. Similar to other qualified plans, all TSAs, whether employer contribution or employee elective deferral, must be made available to each employee who has both:

- reached age 21
- completed one year of service

Plan Requirements A TSA must meet two plan requirements:

1. The plan must be in writing, through a plan instrument, a trust agreement or both.
2. The employer must remit plan contributions to an annuity contract, a mutual fund or another approved investment.

Employee Elective Deferrals. Under an employee elective deferral TSA program, the employer makes no contributions. The employer and employee must enter into a written agreement that specifies the amount or percentage of pay to be deducted, the timing of the deductions (e.g., weekly, monthly, quarterly), and whether the deductions constitute a salary reduction or an agreement to forego a pay increase.

The salary reduction agreement between the employer and employee must be in writing and legally binding on both parties. Compensation covered under the agreement must be earned after the date of the agreement and can cover a period of one year only. The employer and employee must enter into a new agreement each year. Additionally, the employee is not allowed to contribute personal funds to the TSA. All employee contributions must result from salary reductions, per the agreement.

Contribution Limits   An employer can make contributions to a TSA solely on behalf of the covered employee or in conjunction with an employee deferral.

Personal Contributions. Elective employee deferrals to a TSA cannot exceed $9,500 per year. This $9,500 limit applies to the total amount of all elective deferrals if an individual participates in two or more TSA plans.

Employer Contributions. Employer contributions to a TSA are subject to the same maximums that apply to all defined contribution plans: the lesser of 25 percent of the participant's compensation or $30,000 per year.

Taxation of Distributions from a TSA   Distributions from a TSA must follow the same rules as distributions from all qualified plans. Because the employee's TSA contributions are made with pretax dollars, any distribution is subject to ordinary income tax rates in the year it is received. A normal distribution can start at age 59½. A premature distribution is subject to a 10 percent penalty tax unless the distribution is made for an allowable reason. Delayed distributions must start by April 1 of the year following the year in which the participant reaches age 70½ or they will be subject to the excess accumulation tax. Once delayed distributions begin, they must be paid annually by December 31 of each tax year following the initial distribution.

Corporate Retirement Plans

All corporate pension and profit-sharing plans must be established under a trust agreement. A trustee is appointed for each plan and has a fiduciary responsibility for the plan and the beneficial owners—the planholders.

Defined Contribution and Defined Benefit   All qualified retirement plans fall into one of two categories. Those that shelter contributions of current taxable income are called **defined contribution plans**. Those that promise a specific retirement benefit but do not specify the level of current contributions are called **defined benefit plans**. It is important to understand the distinctions between these two approaches.

Defined Contribution Plans. Defined contribution plans include profit-sharing plans, money-purchase pension plans, thrift plans, 401(k) plans, stock bonus plans and target benefit pension plans, though target benefit plans have many characteristics in common with defined benefit plans.

Defined contribution plan participants' funds accumulate until a future event, generally retirement, when the funds may be withdrawn. The ultimate account value depends on the total amount contributed, along with interest and capital gains from the investments. In this type of plan, the plan participant assumes the investment risk.

Defined Benefit Plans. Defined benefit plans are designed to provide specific retirement benefits for participants, such as fixed monthly income. Regardless of investment performance, the promised benefit is paid under the contract terms. Under a defined benefit plan, the plan sponsor assumes the investment risk.

Contributions and Benefit Limitations

Both defined contribution and defined benefit corporate retirement plans are subject to contribution and benefit limits.

Defined Contribution Plans

Employer contributions to a defined contribution plan are limited to the lesser of 25 percent of the plan participants' compensation or $30,000.

Defined Benefit Plans

A defined benefit pension plan provides a specified or formulated benefit at normal retirement age. The benefit may be expressed as a flat or fixed dollar amount, such as $1,000 per month for life, or a percentage of compensation, such as a monthly income equal to 70 percent of the participant's highest five consecutive years' average earnings. The contribution amount is based on a stated formula that considers the participant's age, years of service and amount of compensation. An actuarial calculation determines the contribution.

Taxation

Distributions are taxed at the employee's ordinary income rate at the time of distribution. A qualified plan participant may elect to receive a lump-sum distribution and pay tax based on five-year income averaging. Under five-year averaging rules, the participant pays tax on the lump sum in the year she receives it as if the participant received the sum in five equal annual installments. The result may be lower tax liability because the taxpayer is not subject to the higher rate that would apply if the entire distribution were included in one tax year. Five-year averaging will be eliminated after 1999.

Profit-Sharing Plans

A profit-sharing plan established by an employer allows employees to participate in the business's profits. The benefits may be paid directly to the employee or deferred into an account for future payment, such as retirement, or a combination of both. This discussion concerns profit-sharing plans that defer benefits toward retirement.

Profit-sharing plans need not have a predetermined contribution formula. Plans that do include such a formula generally express contributions as a fixed percentage of profits. In either event, to be qualified, a profit-sharing plan must have "substantial and recurring" contributions, according to the Internal Revenue Code. The maximum contribution is the lesser of 15 percent of a participant's salary or $30,000.

Profit-sharing plans are popular because they offer the greatest amount of investment and contribution flexibility. The ability to skip contributions in years of low profits appeals to small and medium-sized corporations. They are also relatively easy to install, administer and communicate to employees.

Thrift and 401(k) Plans

An employee who participates in a 401(k) plan directs her employer to contribute a percentage of her salary to her retirement account.

Thrift and 401(k) plans permit an employer to make matching contributions up to a set percentage of the employee-directed contributions. All contributions are made with pretax dollars.

Employee Retirement Income Security Act of 1974

ERISA protects participants in corporate pension plans across the country against the abuse and misuse of pension funds. ERISA guidelines for the regulation of retirement plans include the following:

- **Participation.** If a company offers a retirement plan, employees must be covered within a reasonable time, defined by ERISA as no more than three years.
- **Funding.** Funds contributed to the plan must be segregated from other corporate assets. The plan's trustees have a fiduciary responsibility to invest prudently and manage funds in a way that represents the best interests of all participants.
- **Vesting.** Employees must be entitled to their entire retirement benefit amounts within a certain time period, even if they no longer work for the employer.
- **Communication.** The retirement plan must be in writing, and employees must be kept informed of plan benefits, availability, account status and vesting procedure.
- **Nondiscrimination.** A uniformly applied formula determines all employees' benefits and contributions. Such a method ensures equitable and impartial treatment.

ERISA is often referred to as the *Pension Reform Act*, but it actually regulates almost all types of employee benefit plans and personal retirement plans.

Summary

Qualified retirement plans allow contributions of tax-deductible dollars to an investment account. The income and gains are not taxed until withdrawn. Withdrawals before the age of 59½ are subject to penalties in most cases, in addition to the normal income tax.

Nonqualified retirement plan contributions are not tax deductible, but the income plan investments generate is not taxed until funds are withdrawn.

Qualified plans may be established by individuals in an IRA, or by a company on behalf of its employees through 401(k), SEP or Keogh (HR-10) plans, or through tax-sheltered annuities. The investment options available in such plans cover a wide spectrum.

Corporate retirement plans are either defined contribution or defined benefit plans. A defined contribution plan provides for a specific contribution amount and may include a matching employer contribution. In addition, the employee assumes the investment risk. A defined benefit plan, on the other hand, provides a specific retirement benefit, based on a formula, for the participant, and the plan sponsor assumes the investment risk.

Key Concepts

To prepare for your license exam, you should learn the following concepts.

In addition to studying these key concepts, use the Retirement Plans Hot Sheet on page 644 for further review.

deferred compensation plan
defined benefit plan
defined contribution plan
Employee Retirement Income
   Security Act of 1974 (ERISA)
individual retirement account (IRA)
Keogh plan

payroll deduction plan
Pension Reform Act
profit-sharing plan
qualified plan
rollover
spousal IRA
vesting

Review Questions

1. Each of the following is an example of a qualified retirement plan EXCEPT a(n)

    A. deferred compensation plan
    B. individual retirement account
    C. pension and profit-sharing plan
    D. defined benefit plan

2. Under ERISA, payments upon retirement can go to the

    I. employee only
    II. employee jointly with the employee's spouse
    III. employee, and at the employee's death, to a designated beneficiary
    IV. employee's designated beneficiary

    A. I only
    B. I, II and III only
    C. IV only
    D. I, II, III and IV

3. Which of the following plans requires an actuary's services?

    A. Profit-sharing
    B. Defined benefit
    C. Defined contribution
    D. 401(k)

4. Regulations regarding how contributions are made to tax-qualified plans relate to which of the following ERISA requirements?

    A. Vesting
    B. Funding
    C. Nondiscrimination
    D. Reporting and disclosure

5. A qualified profit-sharing plan has all of the following features EXCEPT the

    A. contribution is tax deductible to the employee
    B. employer reports the contribution
    C. contribution is taxable upon payment at retirement
    D. beneficiary may average out the income at retirement

6. Which of the following determines the amount paid into a defined contribution plan?

    A. ERISA-defined contribution requirements
    B. Trust agreement
    C. Employer's age
    D. Employer's profits

7. Which of the following statements is true when an employee's contribution to an employer-sponsored qualified pension plan is distributed to the employee?

    A. It is returned tax free.
    B. It is taxed at a reduced rate.
    C. It is taxed at the beneficiary's ordinary tax rate.
    D. It is taxed at the current capital gains rate.

8. Corporate pension plans have all of the following features EXCEPT that payments

    A. cannot exceed Social Security benefits
    B. can be tied to Social Security benefits
    C. depend on length of service and salary
    D. depend on an employee's value to the company

9. A corporate profit-sharing plan must be in the form of a(n)

    A. trust
    B. conservatorship
    C. administratorship
    D. beneficial ownership

10. Under Keogh plan provisions, a full-time employee would be defined as one working at least how many hours per year?

    A. 100
    B. 500
    C. 800
    D. 1,000

Answers & Rationale

1. **A.** A deferred compensation plan is considered a nonqualified plan because no IRS approval is required to initiate such a plan for employees. All qualified retirement plans need IRS approval.

2. **D.** Under ERISA, benefits do not die with the employee, but can be passed on to a beneficiary.

3. **B.** Because the payout is set and the contributions must cover the benefits adequately, an actuary performs the calculations based on the employee's life expectancy.

4. **B.** "Vesting" describes how quickly rights to a retirement account turn over to the employee. "Nondiscrimination" refers to employee coverage by a plan. All retirement plans must meet ERISA's fiduciary responsibility reporting and disclosure requirements. Only "funding" covers how an employer contributes to or funds a plan.

5. **A.** Qualified retirement plans are tax deductible to the employer, not to the employee.

6. **B.** The retirement plan's trust agreement contains a section explaining the formula(s) used to determine the contributions to a defined contribution plan.

7. **A.** Employee contributions to a qualified retirement plan are made with after-tax dollars. Therefore, because the employee already paid taxes on this money, it is returned tax free. All earnings attributable to those dollars, as well as all employer-contributed money, are taxed at the employee's ordinary income rate at the time of distribution.

8. **A.** Payments made to an employee at retirement can be of any amount and are not limited by Social Security payments. All of the other statements are true.

9. **A.** All corporate pension and profit-sharing plans must be set up under a trust agreement. A plan's trustee has fiduciary responsibility for the plan.

10. **D.** "Full-time" is defined as 1,000 hours or more per year, regardless of the number of days, weeks or months worked. In other words, to be considered full time, a person must work at least 50 percent of the 2,000 hours that a typical employee works in a year.

12

Variable Annuities

OVERVIEW

An annuity is a contract between an individual and an insurance company, usually purchased for retirement income. An investor, called an **annuitant**, contributes money to the plan either in a lump sum or as periodic payments. At a future date, the annuitant begins receiving regular income distributions.

An annuity combines certain elements of both retirement accounts and mutual funds. An annuity may be established by an individual looking for tax-deferred income or by a corporation to serve as a retirement plan for its employees.

An owner of a variable annuity, like the owner of a mutual fund share, has the right to vote on changes in investment policy and the right to vote for the investment adviser every two years. The annuitant elects a board of managers to oversee the portfolio's management as well.

Types of Annuity Contracts

Annuity contracts are classified into three kinds, depending on the type of payment the annuity makes:

1. fixed annuities
2. variable annuities
3. combination and other annuities

Fixed Annuities

A fixed annuity has a guaranteed rate of return. When the individual elects to begin receiving income, the payout is determined by the account's value and the annuitant's life expectancy based on mortality tables. A fixed annuity payment remains constant throughout the annuitant's life. Because the insurance company guarantees the return in a fixed annuity and the annuitant bears no risk, a fixed annuity is considered an insurance product. Therefore, a salesperson must have an insurance license to sell fixed annuities.

Although principal and interest are not at risk, a fixed annuity risks loss of purchasing power because of inflation.

 For Example: An individual who annuitized a contract in 1960 may have been guaranteed monthly payments of $375. Decades later, this amount may provide insufficient income on which to live.

Variable Annuities   The investor who wants to minimize inflation risks associated with fixed annuities can purchase a variable annuity contract. The money deposited in a variable annuity is invested primarily in a stock portfolio, which has a better chance of keeping pace with inflation than fixed-income investments. The greater potential gain of a variable annuity involves more potential risk because it invests in equity securities rather than bonds. Payouts may vary considerably as an annuity unit's value fluctuates with the securities' value.

Comparison of Fixed and Variable Annuities

Table 12.1 compares the principal features of fixed and variable annuities.

TABLE 12.1 Comparison of Fixed and Variable Annuities

Fixed	Variable
Guaranteed fixed payments	Variable payments
Guaranteed interest rate	Variable rate of return
Investment company risk assumed by insurance company	Investment risk assumed by annuitant
Portfolio of fixed-income securities	Portfolio of equities, debt or money-market instruments
General account	Separate account
Vulnerable to inflation	Resistant to inflation
Subject to insurance regulation	Subject to insurance and securities regulation

Separate Account

The contributions investors make to a variable annuity are kept in a **separate account** from the insurance company's general funds. The separate account may begin operations as long as the insurance company has a net worth of $1 million or the separate account has a net worth of $1 million. The separate account is identified as a:

- **management investment company** under the Investment Company Act of 1940 if the funds in the account are used to purchase securities directly; or a
- **unit investment trust (UIT)** under the act of 1940 if the funds in the account are used to purchase shares in a mutual fund managed by someone other than the variable annuity's issuer.

Because the investor rather than the insurance company bears the risk, each variable annuity must be registered under the Investment Company Act of 1940. Variable annuity salespeople must be registered with the SEC and NASD in addition to having an insurance license.

Direct and Indirect Investment. If the annuity money is invested directly into a separate account operated as a mutual fund, the separate account must register as a mutual fund. The value of a contract holder's investment in the separate account is an undivided interest in the securities held in the separate account, called **accumulation units**.

With an **indirect investment**, the separate account holds mutual fund shares purchased in trust for the contract holder's benefit and does not manage the securities. With **direct investment**, the contract holder's money is invested in a portfolio of individual securities actively managed by the separate account.

Comparison of Mutual Funds and Variable Annuities

Table 12.2 compares the principal features of mutual funds and variable annuities.

Combination Annuities

A combination annuity attempts to provide guaranteed payments as well as payments that keep pace with inflation. An investor contributes to both a fixed account and a variable account for a combination annuity. The result is a guaranteed return on the fixed annuity portion and a potentially higher return on the variable annuity portion.

Figure 12.1 shows how combination annuity investments may be split into the separate and general accounts.

TABLE 12.2 Comparison of Mutual Funds and Variable Annuities

Mutual Funds	Variable Annuities
Investment company	Insurance company
Shares	Units
Redeemed by issuer	Redeemed by issuer
Price based on formula	Price based on formula
Investment objectives varied	Investment objectives primarily growth and income
Board of directors	Board of managers
No guarantees	Few guarantees

Purchasing Annuities

Insurance companies offer a number of purchase options to make it easy for annuity owners to accumulate money.

Deferred Annuity. An annuity may be purchased with a single lump-sum investment, with payment of benefits deferred until the annuitant elects to receive them. This type of investment is referred to as a **single-premium deferred annuity**.

Periodic Payment Deferred Annuity. A periodic payment deferred annuity allows a person to make periodic payments over a period of time. The contract holder can invest money on a monthly, a quarterly or an annual basis.

Immediate Annuity. An investor may also purchase an immediate annuity. In an immediate annuity contract, an investor purchases the annuity by depositing a single lump sum. The insurance company then begins to pay out the annuity's benefits immediately (usually within 60 days).

FIGURE 12.1   Investing Variable Annuity Premium Dollars

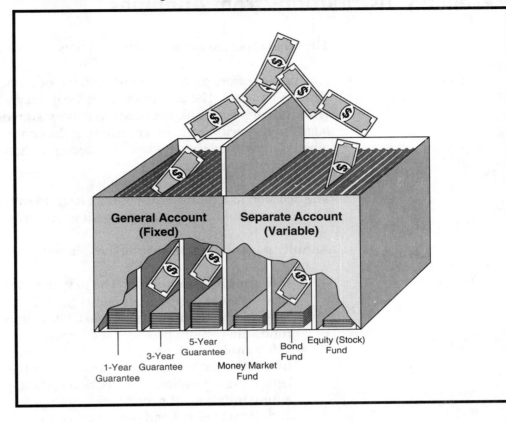

General Account (Fixed)

Separate Account (Variable)

1-Year Guarantee

3-Year Guarantee

5-Year Guarantee

Money Market Fund

Bond Fund

Equity (Stock) Fund

Accumulation Stage

The pay-in period for an annuity is known as the **accumulation stage**. During the accumulation stage of an annuity contract, the contract terms are quite flexible. If an investor misses a periodic payment, she is in no danger of forfeiting any of the preceding contributions. The client can terminate the contract at any time during the accumulation stage. To discourage termination of contracts, insurance companies often allow contract holders to borrow from an account without having to cancel the contract.

Accumulation Units

An accumulation unit is an accounting measure that represents an investor's share of ownership in the separate account. An accumulation unit's value is determined in the same way as that of mutual fund shares. The unit value changes with the value of the securities held in the separate account and the total number of accumulation units outstanding.

Sales Charges on Variable Annuities

Although variable annuities are subject to slightly different rules and restrictions on sales charges, they are administered in basically the same manner as mutual funds and UITs. In general, the maximum sales charge cannot exceed 8.5 percent of the total payments.

Receiving Distributions from Annuities

The payout period for an annuity is known as the **annuity stage**.

Annuity Payout Options

An annuity offers several payout options for money accumulated in the annuity contract. The investor can let the money accumulate in the annuity, withdraw the accumulated funds in a lump sum or withdraw the accumulated funds periodically by **annuitizing** the contract. Annuitizing occurs when the investor changes from the accumulation (pay-in) stage to the distribution (payout) stage.

The decision to annuitize the contract locks in the specified payment option. The contract holder may not change it in any way in the future.

Annuity payout options include the following:

- **Life annuity/straight life.** The payout is structured so that the annuitant receives periodic payments (usually monthly) over his lifetime. No added options or benefits exist, therefore, for a given amount of funds, this option provides the largest periodic payment.
- **Life annuity with period certain.** An annuitant receives payments for life, with a certain period of time guaranteed. If the annuitant dies before the expiration of the period certain, payments continue to the annuitant's named beneficiary until the period certain expires. If the annuitant lives beyond the period certain, payments continue until the annuitant's death. For instance, assume a client purchases a life annuity with a 10-year period certain. The insurance company guarantees payments for the life of the annuitant or for 10 years, whichever is longer. If the annuitant lives for only one year after payments begin, the company continues to make payments to the annuitant's beneficiary for nine more years. If the annuitant dies after receiving payments for 13 years, payments cease at death.
- **Joint life with last survivor annuity.** With this option, the annuity covers two or more people and payment is conditioned on both (all) lives. A husband and wife, for instance, might own an annuity jointly with a last survivor clause. The contract pays benefits as long as one of the annuitants remains alive. The payment may be the same as when both were alive, or it may be reduced for the surviving annuitant, depending on the contract. If this option includes more than two annuitants, payments would cease at the last survivor's death.
- **Life contingency annuity.** This is an annuity with a death benefit that applies during the accumulation stage. A full contribution will be made to the account if the owner dies and the payout will be made to the beneficiary.

TABLE 12.3 Effects of Investment Returns on Annuity Payouts

IF the realized rate of return:	THEN the value of the annuity unit:	AND the payout in relation to the previous payout:
Increases above AIR	Increases	Increases
Decreases below AIR	Decreases	Decreases
Stays the same as AIR	Stays the same	Stays the same

Annuity Units

When a contract is annuitized, accumulation units become annuity units. An annuity unit is a measure of value used only during an annuitized contract's payout period. It is an accounting measure that determines the amount of each payment to the annuitant.

The number of annuity units is calculated when the owner annuitizes the contract. The number of annuity units does not change, but each unit's value fluctuates with the separate account portfolio's value. The number of units credited to the annuitant's account is based on the initial annuity unit value and other variables, such as the payout option selected, accumulated value of the annuitant's account, individual's age and sex, and assumed interest rate.

Assumed Interest Rate

The assumed interest rate (AIR) is a basis for projecting earnings for a variable annuity. The rate provides an earnings target for the separate account and is usually estimated conservatively.

An AIR is used to project the value of an account through the annuitant's age at death, as forecasted by mortality tables. Based on this value, the insurance company projects its distributions to the annuitant. The AIR is also used when determining the number of annuity units. The higher the AIR, the higher the projected value of units and the greater the initial payment. The reverse, of course, is also true.

Effects of Investment Returns on Annuity Payouts. The AIR does not guarantee a rate of return. It is a tool for adjusting an annuity unit's value to reflect changes in the investment return of the separate account portfolio. An annuity unit's change in value alters the amount of annuity payments. The annuitant always receives a payment equal to the value of one annuity unit times the number of units in the annuitant's account. Table 12.3 shows the effect of investment returns on annuity payouts.

Variable Annuity Payments

Although variable annuity payments are not fixed, they are determined initially by mortality tables and the value of the securities in an annuitant's portfolio. Variable annuity plans do not guarantee the payment amount because the insurance company cannot guarantee the separate account's performance.

Initial payout is used to determine the number of annuity units in the account; future payouts are determined by the fluctuating value of the annuity units.

✓ **For Example:** An investor who annuitized a variable annuity in 1960 and began with monthly payments of $375 may now receive $1,275 per month.

Fluctuating Payments. After the insurance company determines the number of annuity units used in calculating the payment, the amount of each payment equals the number of units multiplied by the annuity unit's current value. The number of annuity units used to calculate future payment remains the same. However, because the units' value depends on the performance of the separate account, the annuitant's payments may fluctuate if the units' value fluctuates.

If an insurance company chooses an AIR that is too high, subsequent payments continually decrease because the projections are not met by actual portfolio performance. If the AIR is too low, payments most likely continually increase as projected returns are surpassed.

Mortality Guarantee. The annuity company guarantees payments for as long as annuitants live. If for any reason a sudden change occurs in life expectancy and annuitants live longer than originally anticipated, the insurance company assumes the increased mortality cost. This is known as the *mortality guarantee*.

Operating Expense Guarantee. When calculating the amount that the annuity company can pay out to a customer, the insurance company must project its own expenses for administering the plan. If for any reason the costs of operation increase, the company sets a ceiling for expenses charged to the separate account, and if the actual cost is greater, the company pays the difference. This is known as the *operating expense guarantee*.

Taxation of Annuities

Contributions to an annuity that is not part of an employer-sponsored retirement plan are made with after-tax dollars. Because contributions have already been taxed, the total contribution amount is not taxable when the account is annuitized. As with other investments, the money invested in an annuity represents the investor's cost basis. The primary advantage of an annuity as an investment is that the tax on interest, dividends and capital gains is deferred until the owner withdraws money from the contract. On withdrawal, the amount exceeding the investor's cost basis is taxed as ordinary income.

Lump-sum withdrawals are taken out using LIFO (last in, first out). This means earnings are removed before contributions. If an investor receives a lump-sum withdrawal before age 59½, the earnings portion withdrawn is taxed as ordinary income and is subject to an additional 10 percent penalty. The penalty does not apply if the funds are withdrawn after age 59½, are withdrawn due to death or disability or are part of a life-income option plan with fixed payments.

✓ *For Example:* A contract with a $100,000 value consists of $40,000 in contributions and $60,000 in earnings. If the investor withdraws all $100,000 at once, the $60,000 in earnings is taxed and the $40,000 cost basis is returned tax-free.

Random withdrawals also use LIFO. Distributions are taxed until all earnings have been distributed.

Annuitized payments for a nonqualified plan have a cost basis determined by the contract's initial value divided by the number of years of life expectancy. That dollar figure is considered the nontaxable amount of each year's payments. Distributions exceeding the cost basis are taxable at ordinary income rates.

Summary

A variable annuity is a contract with an insurance company, and it is similar to a mutual fund. Annuities and mutual funds are subject to the same regulations.

Like a retirement account, an annuity is a mechanism used primarily to invest for retirement. Taxes on income and capital gains are deferred until the funds are withdrawn. Unlike a retirement account, however, an annuity does not restrict the amount of funds that may be invested, and the funds invested are not tax deductible.

The guarantee feature and the lifetime payout option make annuities very popular with investors.

Key Concepts

To prepare for your license exam, you should learn the following concepts.

In addition to studying these key concepts, use the Variable Annuities Hot Sheet on page 645 for further review.

accumulation stage

accumulation unit

annuity unit

combination annuity

fixed annuity

joint with last survivor payout option

life contingency payout option

mortality risk

period certain payout option

periodic payment annuity

separate account

straight life payout option

Review Questions

1. Which of the following information must be included in a prospectus describing variable life insurance to clients?

    I. Summary explanation in nontechnical terms of the policy's principal features
    II. Statement of the separate account's investment policy
    III. Statement of the separate account's net investment return for the past 10 years
    IV. Statement of the deductions and charges against the gross premium, including all commissions paid to agents for each policy year the commissions are to be paid

    A. I and II only
    B. I, II and III only
    C. III and IV only
    D. I, II, III and IV

2. If a variable annuity has an assumed investment rate of 5 percent and the separate account's annualized return is 4 percent, which of the following statements are true?

    I. The accumulation unit's value will rise.
    II. The annuity unit's value will rise.
    III. The accumulation unit's value will fall.
    IV. The annuity unit's value will fall.

    A. I and II
    B. I and IV
    C. II and III
    D. III and IV

3. Which of the following factors may determine the amount of payout from a variable annuity?

    I. Company's mortality experience
    II. Annuitant's age and sex
    III. Annuitant's insurability
    IV. Separate account's rate of return

    A. I, II and IV only
    B. II only
    C. III and IV only
    D. I, II, III and IV

4. An annuity may be purchased under which of the following methods?

    I. Single payment deferred annuity
    II. Single payment immediate annuity
    III. Periodic payment deferred annuity
    IV. Periodic payment immediate annuity

    A. I and II only
    B. I, II and III only
    C. III and IV only
    D. I, II, III and IV

5. Joe Kuhl has just purchased an immediate variable annuity. Which of the following statements describe Joe's investment?

    I. It was a lump-sum purchase.
    II. Distribution of dividends occurs during the accumulation period.
    III. Accumulation and payment of dividends occur during the payout period.

    A. I and II only
    B. I and III only
    C. II and III only
    D. I, II and III

Answers & Rationale

1. **D.** All of the information listed here must be presented in the prospectus distributed to clients.

2. **B.** The accumulation unit will increase in value because the portfolio earned 4 percent; however, the annuity unit's value will decrease because the portfolio's actual return of 4 percent was less than the assumed interest rate of 5 percent necessary to maintain payments.

3. **A.** Mortality experience, age, sex and rate of return all have a bearing on the size of payout. The annuitant's insurability has no bearing.

4. **B.** A periodic payment immediate annuity would be rather difficult to provide. As the annuitant is contributing, he would also be receiving.

5. **B.** An immediate annuity has no accumulation period. A single lump-sum investment is made, and payments begin immediately. During payout, the principal and earnings are distributed.

13

Direct Participation Programs

OVERVIEW

Direct participation programs (DPPs), sometimes called *tax shelters*, are businesses organized in such a way as to enable them to pass all of their income, gains, losses and tax benefits directly to their owners. The businesses themselves pay no tax directly because tax liability is apportioned among the investors. Most DPPs, which are usually structured as limited partnerships, invest in real estate or oil and gas operations.

Characteristics of Limited Partnerships

Limited partnerships are direct participation programs that allow the economic consequences of the businesses to flow through to investors. Unlike corporations, limited partnerships pay no dividends. Rather, they pass income, gains, losses, deductions and credits directly to investors.

Limited partnerships offer investors limited liability. Should a limited partnership default on its loans, investors could lose their entire investments, which might include a specific share of partnership debt, but they are not personally liable for other partnership debts. Partnerships usually borrow money in **nonrecourse** loans, meaning the general partners, not the limited partners, assume responsibility for repayment of the loan. In this regard, partnerships resemble corporations.

A **recourse** loan is one where the limited partners assume responsibility for loan repayment.

Units of ownership in a partnership are called *interests*, rather than *shares*.

Private Placements. In a private placement limited partnership, a small number of limited partners each contributes a large amount of money, such as $100,000 or more. Private placements are offered to **accredited investors** —wealthy investors with substantial investment experience—not the general public.

Public Offerings. In a public offering limited partnership, a larger number of investors each makes a relatively small contribution of capital to the business, such as $1,000 to $5,000. These partnerships can be publicly advertised, are relatively large and may attract investors with smaller budgets and less investment sophistication. Typically, they are more tightly regulated and subject to more stringent federal registration and prospectus requirements than private placements.

Advantages and Disadvantages of the Limited Partnership

The DPP investor enjoys several advantages:

- an investment managed by others
- flow-through of income and certain expenses
- limited liability

Liquidity Risk. The greatest disadvantage is lack of liquidity. Because the secondary market for DPPs is limited, investors who want to sell their interests frequently cannot locate buyers.

Legislative Risk. When Congress changes tax laws, new rules can cause substantial damage to limited partners (LPs), who may be locked into illiquid investments that lose their tax advantages.

Tax Reporting for Partnerships

Partnership losses are often apportioned among investors, enabling them to claim those losses as deductions on their personal tax returns. If the partnership's operations result in taxable income, that amount is divided proportionally among the partners. Each investor adds that amount to his personal taxable income.

Under current tax law, LPs are classified as **passive investors**. Any income they receive from a partnership is passive income and any loss passed through to them is a passive loss. Investors can deduct passive losses against passive income only. Unused passive losses can be carried forward to the next year and used to offset future passive income. Dividend and interest income and wages are not passive income.

 Take Note: An investor may use a tax loss from a partnership to offset income from another passive investment only.

Maintaining Partnership Status

The Internal Revenue Code (IRC) is the final determinant as to whether an organization qualifies for tax treatment as a corporation or a limited partnership. Under IRS regulations, corporations may have any or all of the characteristics in the list below without affecting their tax status. Limited partnerships, however, may have no more than four of these six corporate characteristics and still qualify for the special tax treatment afforded partnerships.

In order of ease of avoidance, the six corporate characteristics follow.

1. **Continuity of life.** This is the easiest of the corporate characteristics for a limited partnership to avoid. The partnership agreement usually sets a date on which the partnership will be dissolved.
2. **Free transferability of interests.** Most limited partnerships can avoid this characteristic. Transfer of interests to nonpartners must be approved by one or more limited partners (LPs) and at least one general partner (GP) and usually requires payment of a fee.
3. **Limited liability.** A limited partnership can avoid this characteristic easily. GPs must make nonpartnership assets available to creditors. The limited partners' liability is limited to their investment.
4. **Centralization of management.** Hard to get around for a limited partnership, management centralization can be avoided only if the GP holds more than a 20 percent interest in capital or profits. Avoidance may conflict with state laws requiring LPs to have no role in management.
5. **Division of profits.** This is impossible for a limited partnership to avoid because it is one of the reasons the partnership was formed.
6. **Business associates.** It is impossible for a limited partnership to avoid having business associates. A partnership must have associates because the law requires at least one GP and one LP per partnership. Without a limited partner, no limited partnership exists; without an active general partner, no one is running the business.

Forming a Limited Partnership

Syndication and Underwriting

The syndicator, or syndicate manager, is the individual or firm designated to work with a limited partnership's general partners. The syndicator's duties include preparing the paperwork needed to register the limited partnership with the SEC, organizing and overseeing the selling syndicate and selling group, and promoting the partnership.

Documentation

Subscription Agreement. An investor interested in purchasing a limited partnership unit completes and signs a subscription agreement, which includes a statement of the investor's net worth and annual income and a power of attorney appointing the GP as the agent of the partnership. It is the registered rep's responsibility to make certain that the information the potential investor provides in the subscription agreement is complete and accurate.

The subscription agreement, with the subscriber's money, is merely an offer to buy. The GP may decline the subscriber's offer if the offering has sold out or if the subscriber's net worth or income is insufficient.

✎ *Take Note:* The subscription agreement becomes effective only when the GP accepts and signs it.

Certificate of Limited Partnership. To be legally recognized as a limited partnership, a business organization must file a certificate of limited partnership in its home state, usually with the office of the secretary of state. The primary purpose of the certificate is to let creditors know which partners are liable for the partnership's debts (the GPs) and which partners have limited liability (the LPs). Unless a certificate is filed, all partners may be treated as GPs; that is, investors may be denied limited liability. The certificate of limited partnership includes the following information:

- partnership's name;
- partnership's business;
- principal place of business;
- amount of time the partnership expects to be in business;
- size of each LP's investment and any additional investment expected;
- when each investor's contribution will be returned, if a time has been set;
- each LP's share of the profits or other compensation;
- whether and under what conditions an LP can assign (sell or donate) an interest;
- whether LPs may admit additional LPs;
- whether some LPs will have priority over others in contributions or compensation;
- whether, upon a GP's death or incapacity, remaining GPs may continue the business; and
- if granted, an LP's right to request compensation in property instead of cash.

Partnership Agreement. The partnership agreement is a contract that provides guidelines for operating the partnership and describes the general and limited partners' roles, including each party's rights and responsibilities. Each partner receives a copy of the partnership agreement.

Table 13.1 summarizes the documents necessary to establish a partnership.

TABLE 13.1 Partnership Documents

Document	Purpose
Subscription Agreement	Finalizes the sale of a partnership interest. Grants power of attorney to the general partners.
Certificate of Limited Partnership	To inform creditors and to comply with state statutes. Includes identification of the partnership, contributions of the members, the sharing arrangement, the partnership's term and provisions for changes in membership.
Partnership Agreement	Establishes guidelines for the partnership. Defines the role of the general and limited partners.

Dissolving a Limited Partnership

In most cases, a limited partnership is liquidated on the date specified in the partnership agreement. Sometimes a partnership closes down before the specified date, however. Early shutdown may occur if the LPs holding a majority interest endorse a decision to dissolve the partnership or if the partnership sells or otherwise disposes of all assets.

Dissolution of Partnership and Settlement of Accounts.   When the partnership dissolves, the GP must cancel the certificate of limited partnership and settle accounts in the following order:

1. secured lenders;
2. other creditors;
3. limited partners, first for their claims to a share of profits and second for their claims to a return of contributed capital; and
4. general partners, first for fees and other claims not involving profits or capital, second for a share of profits and third for capital return.

Investors in a Limited Partnership

A limited partnership must have at least one general partner and one limited partner. A certificate of limited partnership filed with the secretary of state lists the status of each investor as a limited or general partner.

General Partner The GPs are the active investors in a limited partnership and assume responsibility for all aspects of the partnership's operations. A GP does all of the following:

- makes decisions that bind the partnership
- buys and sells property for the partnership
- manages the partnership property and money
- supervises all aspects of the partnership's business
- maintains a minimum 1 percent financial interest in the partnership

During a limited partnership's operating phase, a GP earns money by charging a management fee, acting as partnership or property manager for a fee, or earning commissions on the purchase or sale of partnership property.

Unlike LPs, who have limited liability, GPs have unlimited liability and are, therefore, personally liable for all partnership business losses and debts. A partnership's creditors may seek repayment from the GPs and may go after their personal assets.

A GP has a fiduciary relationship to the LPs. That is, the GP has been entrusted with the LPs' capital and is morally and legally bound to use that capital in the investors' best interests. The GP must manage the business in the partnership's best interest and avoid the appearance of improper use of assets and conflicts of interest. The GP cannot borrow from the partnership, compete with the partnership or commingle personal funds with partnership funds.

Limited Partner Along with one or more GPs, a limited partnership must include one or more LPs. LPs are passive investors with no management or decision making responsibilities; therefore, they usually are not held personally responsible for the partnership's indebtedness.

LPs may receive cash distributions and capital gains from partnerships. The total yield of a partnership investment takes into account all potential rewards: tax deductions, cash distributions and capital gains.

Like corporate stockholders, LPs have limited liability. That is, if the business fails, investors may lose only their investments, including any money borrowed on behalf of the partnership for which they are personally liable.

Rights and Responsibilities. An LP's basic obligation is to provide capital. The LP has the right to:

- vote on changes to partnership investment objectives
- vote on the admission of a new GP
- sue the GP(s)
- vote on the sale or refinancing of partnership property
- inspect partnership books and records

TABLE 13.2 Responsibilities, Rights and Limitations of General and Limited Partners

Characteristic	General Partner	Limited Partner
Responsibilities	Organizes and manages the partnership business; acts on behalf of the LPs.	Provides capital for the partnership's business.
Rights	Can legally bind the partnership.	Can: • receive justified returns; • monitor the partnership; • sue or remove a GP; • petition a court to dissolve the partnership.
Limitations	Can receive only the compensation specified in the agreement. Cannot: • prevent the ordinary flow of partnership business; • assign or possess partnership property for purposes other than those of the partnership; • compete against the partnership for personal gain; • admit new GPs or LPs or continue the partnership after the loss of a GP unless specified in the partnership agreement.	Cannot: • participate in the management of partnership business; • act on behalf of the partnership; • knowingly sign a certificate containing false information; • have his name appear as part of the partnership's name.

In special circumstances, the LPs may be required to vote, an act called *exercising the partnership democracy*. A vote may be taken to permit the GP(s) to act contrary to the limited partnership agreement or confess a judgment against the partnership. Table 13.2 summarizes the responsibilities, rights and limitations of general and limited partners.

Restrictions on Limited Partner Activities. As already mentioned, LPs have limited liability, like corporate stockholders. If, however, a limited partner takes part in managing the partnership's business, she loses her limited liability status and has unlimited liability.

Selling a Limited Partnership

Limited partnerships can be structured as managed or nonmanaged offerings. In a managed offering, a securities firm handles the sale of interests and acts as principal underwriter. In a nonmanaged offering, the general partner(s) works directly through registered representatives at different firms or hires a wholesaler to contact the representatives.

The limit on underwriting compensation, including the costs of wholesaling, is 10 percent of the gross dollar amount of securities sold. This 10 percent limit applies to all compensation paid to underwriters and wholesalers for their services in the offering process. (The NASD currently is considering a lower fee structure.)

The NASD specifically forbids firms to participate in offerings that provide more than a fair and reasonable compensation to those who sell or organize a partnership. The NASD also disapproves of certain types and undue amounts of underwriting compensation.

 For Example: Compensation with an indeterminate value is forbidden. In general, any sort of interest in the future proceeds or profits of the business is not, in the NASD's view, reasonable underwriting compensation.

Types of Limited Partnership Programs

Limited partnerships can be formed to run any type of business. Three of the most common types are real estate, oil and gas, and equipment-leasing businesses.

Real Estate Limited Partnerships   Real estate limited partnerships may provide capital growth potential through the appreciation of property. Partnerships may also distribute cash income, which can be sheltered from taxes by deductions for mortgage interest and depreciation. Depreciation is a tax deduction that accounts for the "wearing out" of the building and any capital improvements.

Three types of real estate programs are: new construction, existing property and raw land.

New Construction. A new construction program builds new property. The principal advantage of such a program is the potential for appreciation. The disadvantages of new construction are potential cost overruns, no established track record for the new property, the difficulty of finding permanent financing and an inability to deduct current expenses during the construction period.

TABLE 13.3 Comparison of the Various Types of Oil and Gas Programs

Characteristic	Exploratory	Developmental	Income
Cost of mineral rights	Low	Medium	High
IDCs	High	Medium	None
Tangible costs	High	Medium	None
Risk/reward	High	Medium	Low
Immediate tax write-offs	High	High	Low

Existing Property. Programs based on existing property with track records are generally less risky than new construction programs. Income and expenses are easier to estimate, and cash flow can begin immediately. Potential disadvantages include greater maintenance or repair expenses than for new construction, expiring leases that may not be renewed and less than favorable existing rental arrangements.

Raw Land. A limited partnership based on raw land is the most speculative type of real estate limited partnership. Its main attraction is the appreciation potential of the property. Because undeveloped land offers neither income nor depreciation deductions, it is not a tax shelter. If the purchase is leveraged, the partnership loses money to debt service and taxes. All of the benefits of owning raw land are delayed until the sale of the property.

Oil and Gas Limited Partnerships

Oil and gas programs include speculative drilling programs and income programs that invest in producing wells. Table 13.3 compares the three types of oil and gas programs, which are discussed next.

Exploratory Drilling. Exploratory drilling programs, also known as *wildcat programs,* attempt to locate undiscovered reserves of oil and gas. Exploratory wells are drilled based on the speculation that oil is present. Exploratory drilling programs offer high risks and high rewards: few wells actually produce, but if one does, it can be very profitable.

The principal tax advantage of exploratory drilling programs is the write-off of intangible drilling costs (IDCs). Normally, 100 percent of these write-offs are taken in the first year of operation. IDCs are the noncapitalized costs associated with drilling a well, such as wages, supplies and geological surveys.

Developmental Drilling. Developmental drilling programs target areas of proven reserves and plan new well drilling near existing fields. In general, developmental programs offer less risk and less reward potential than exploratory programs. Both share the same potential tax advantages.

Income Programs. An oil and gas income program is geared toward investors who seek income because the program attempts to provide immediate, reliable cash flow. The partnership buys the value of the oil in the ground, with the expectation that the partnership can sell it and receive income sheltered by depletion allowances that enable investors to recover costs of mineral rights.

A depletion allowance is a tax deduction that compensates the partnership for the decreasing supply of oil or gas. The depletion allowance is typically based on a percentage of the revenues received from the sale of the oil and gas produced.

Income programs are the least risky of the three types of oil and gas programs.

Combination Program. A combination program splits its investment between drilling for oil and acquiring producing wells.

Sharing Arrangements

Limited partnerships use different methods of sharing the costs and revenues associated with oil and gas programs. The LP's objective is to bear as little cost and get as many benefits as possible, consistent with providing the GP(s) with an incentive for improving a partnership's profitability. This is accomplished through various sharing arrangements.

Overriding Royalty Interest. A person with a royalty interest takes no risks, but receives a share of the revenues. The landowner who sells mineral rights to a partnership, for example, commonly retains a royalty interest. The landowner with a royalty interest does not participate in the business or share risks, but does receive a portion of the income from a successful well. The GP who holds an overriding royalty interest incurs no costs (the LPs bear all deductible and nondeductible costs), but receives a specified percentage of oil revenue. Unlike the landowner with a royalty interest, the GP with an overriding royalty interest is involved in the business and stands to lose money if the venture fails.

Reversionary Working Interest. The GP bears none of the program's costs (the LPs bear all deductible and nondeductible costs), but does not receive his share of revenues until the LPs have recovered their capital.

Net Operating Profits Interest.   The GP bears none of the program's costs (the LPs bear all deductible and nondeductible costs), but is entitled to a percentage of net profits (revenues less expenses). The net profits interest is figured before deducting the depletion allowance.

Disproportionate Sharing.   The GP bears a relatively small percentage of expenses and is entitled to a relatively large percentage of revenues.

Carried Interest.   The GP shares tangible drilling costs with the LPs, but pays no part of the IDCs. In a sense, it is advantageous to bear intangible, rather than tangible, costs. IDCs generate current deductions, whereas tangible costs must be depreciated over the property's life.

Functional Allocation.   This is the most common sharing arrangement. The GP bears tangible costs—capitalized expenses such as the cost of building an oil rig—and the LPs bear IDCs. Revenues are shared.

Equipment-Leasing Limited Partnerships

Some DPPs purchase equipment that they then lease to other businesses. Each investor receives a share of the income from the lease payments and a proportional share of operating expenses, interest expense and depreciation.

Because equipment rarely appreciates, tax-sheltered income is the primary objective of these programs.

Analysis and Evaluation of Direct Participation Programs

The total yield of a partnership investment takes into account tax deductions, cash distributions and capital gains. An investor should choose a limited partnership because:

- it is economically viable;
- the general partner(s) has demonstrated management ability and expertise in running similar programs;
- the program's objectives match the investor's objectives, and does so within a time frame that meets the investor's needs; and
- the start-up costs and projected revenues are in line with the start-up costs and revenues of similar ventures.

Promoters structure DPPs to meet various objectives. When a promoter's tax stance is too aggressive or is without economic purpose in the view of the IRS, the program is considered an abusive tax shelter. If the IRS judges the program to be abusive, it disallows deductions; assesses back taxes, interest and penalties; and, in some cases, charges the promoter with criminal intent to defraud.

Investors should try to match their current and future objectives with a program's stated objectives.

✓ *For Example:* A person seeking taxable passive income should not invest in an oil and gas exploratory drilling program.

Because DPPs are illiquid, investors must commit money for a long time.

Summary

Direct participation programs are illiquid investments that pass income, gains, losses and tax benefits, such as depreciation allowances, directly to the limited partners.

A general partner(s) runs the partnership business and assumes certain liabilities with regard to the partnership's commitments. Limited partners are not allowed to be actively involved in business decisions, and so are afforded limited liability in the event of a business failure.

Most LPs invest in real estate, oil and gas, or equipment-leasing programs.

Limited partnership programs are either private placements, offered to wealthy accredited investors who make substantial investments, or public programs requiring much smaller investments.

Under current tax law, limited partnerships generate passive income and losses. Passive losses may be used to shelter passive income only.

Key Concepts

To prepare for your license exam, you should learn the following concepts.

In addition to studying these key concepts, use the Direct Participation Programs Hot Sheet on page 646 for further review.

agreement of limited partnership	limited partner (LP)
certificate of limited partnership	limited partnership
direct participation program (DPP)	oil and gas limited partnership
equipment leasing	passive income
general partner (GP)	real estate limited partnership
intangible drilling cost (IDC)	subscription agreement
limited liability	

Review Questions

1. "DPP" stands for which of the following?

   A. Direct placement program
   B. Directed profits program
   C. Direct participation program
   D. Directors' and principals' program

2. Which of the following forms of business involves the greatest risk to the owner?

   A. Sole proprietorship
   B. General partnership
   C. Corporation
   D. Limited partnership

3. Which of the following assumes the greatest liability?

   A. General partner
   B. Limited partner
   C. Corporate stockholder
   D. Trustee

4. The person who organizes and registers a partnership is known as a(n)

   A. syndicator
   B. property manager
   C. program manager
   D. underwriter

5. Raw land is which of the following types of investment?

   A. Speculative
   B. Conservative
   C. Balanced
   D. Income-producing

6. All of the following could be benefits of a long-term equipment-leasing direct participation program EXCEPT

   A. steady income from rental payments
   B. operating expenses to offset revenues
   C. cost recovery deductions
   D. capital appreciation

7. Which of the following would NOT generate IDCs in an oil-drilling program?

   A. Labor costs
   B. Cost of casing the well
   C. Fuel costs
   D. Geologist's fees

8. An investor should consider which of the following to be a potential source of conflict of interest for the sponsor of an oil and gas program?

   I. Underdeveloped adjacent sponsor lease
   II. Loan by the program to the sponsor
   III. Sponsor's compensation rates
   IV. Commingling of program funds

   A. I only
   B. I, II and IV only
   C. III only
   D. I, II, III and IV

Answers & Rationale

1. **C.** The initials "DPP" stand for "direct participation program."

2. **A.** In a sole proprietorship the owner is personally liable for all business debts. Therefore, the sole proprietorship is the riskiest form of business.

3. **A.** The general partner (GP) has unlimited liability and is, therefore, personally liable for all partnership losses and debts.

4. **A.** The individual who organizes and registers the partnership is the syndicator.

5. **A.** Raw land is the most speculative of these investments. The partnership can actually lose money to debt service and taxes because raw land offers neither income nor depreciation deductions.

6. **D.** Unlike real estate or undeveloped mineral reserves, equipment ordinarily does not appreciate.

7. **B.** The cost of casing a well is a tangible cost and, therefore, does not qualify for intangible drilling cost (IDC) write-offs.

8. **D.** All of the choices listed are potential conflicts of interest for the sponsor in a DPP.

14

Economics and Analysis

OVERVIEW

Economic activity reflects the overall health of a country's economy. In particular, economists attempt to measure and predict the economy's cycles and the effect on various industries and corporations.

Economics is the study of supply and demand. When people want to buy an item that is in short supply, the item's price rises. When people do not want to buy an item that is in plentiful supply, the price declines. This simple notion, the foundation of all economic study, is true for bread, shoes, cars, clothes, stocks, bonds and money.

Economics

The economic climate has an enormous effect on the conditions of individual companies and, therefore, the securities markets. In addition to a company's earnings and business prospects, business cycles, changes in the money supply, Federal Reserve Board (FRB) actions and a host of complex international monetary factors affect securities prices and trading.

Business Cycles Throughout history, periods of economic expansion have been followed by periods of economic contraction in a pattern called the **business cycle**. Business cycles go through four stages:

1. expansion
2. peak
3. contraction
4. trough

FIGURE 14.1 The Four Stages of the Business Cycle

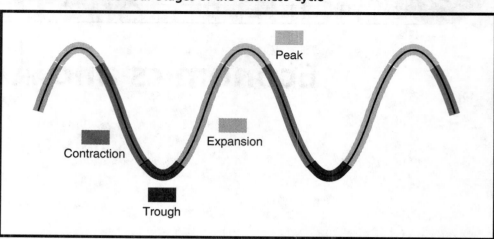

Expansion is characterized by increased business activity—increasing sales, manufacturing and wages—throughout the economy. For a variety of reasons, an economy can expand for only so long; when it reaches its upper limit, it has reached its **peak**. When business activity declines from its peak, the economy is **contracting**. Economists call mild short-term contractions **recessions**. Longer, more severe contractions are **depressions**. When business activity stops declining and levels off, it is known as a **trough**. Figure 14.1 illustrates the four stages of the business cycle.

According to the U.S. Commerce Department, the economy is in a recession when a decline in real output of goods and services—the **gross domestic product (GDP)**—lasts for six months or more. It defines a depression as a severe downturn lasting for several years, with unemployment rates greater than 15 percent.

In the normal course of events, some industries or corporations prosper as others fail. So to determine the economy's overall direction, economists consider many aspects of business activity. Expansions are characterized by:

- increased consumer demand for goods and services
- increases in industrial production
- rising stock markets
- rising property values
- increasing GDP

Downturns in the business cycle tend to be characterized by:

- rising numbers of bankruptcies and bond defaults
- higher consumer debt

- falling stock markets
- rising inventories (a sign of slackening consumer demand in hard times)
- decreasing GDP

Gross Domestic Product A nation's annual economic output—all of the goods and services produced within the nation—is known as its *gross domestic product*. The United States' GDP includes personal consumption, government spending, gross private investment, foreign investment and the total value of exports.

Price Levels **Consumer Price Index.** The most prominent measure of general price changes is the Consumer Price Index (CPI). The CPI measures the rate of increase or decrease in a broad range of consumer prices, such as food, housing, transportation, medical care, clothing, electricity, entertainment and services. The CPI is computed each month.

Inflation. When comparing the economic output of one period with that of another, analysts must account for changes in the relative prices of products that have occurred during the intervening time. Economists adjust GDP figures to **constant dollars** rather than compare actual dollars. This allows the economists and others who use GDP figures to compare the actual purchasing power of the dollars rather than the dollars themselves.

Inflation is a general increase in prices. Mild inflation can encourage economic growth because gradually increasing prices tend to stimulate business investments. High inflation reduces a dollar's buying power, which hurts the economy.

Increased inflation drives up interest rates of fixed-income securities, which drives down bond prices. Decreases in the inflation rate have the opposite effect: as inflation declines, bond yields decline and prices rise.

Deflation. Though rare, deflation is a general decline in prices. Deflation usually occurs during severe recessions when unemployment is on the rise.

Economic Indicators Certain aspects of economic activity serve as barometers, or **indicators**, of business cycle phases.

Leading Indicators. Leading indicators are slices of business activity that reliably *predict* trends in the economy. Positive changes in these indicators suggest economic improvement. Negative changes suggest economic contraction. Leading indicators used most often include:

- money supply
- building permits (housing starts)
- average weekly initial claims for state unemployment compensation
- average work week in manufacturing
- new orders for consumer goods

- slowdowns in deliveries by vendors
- contracts and orders for plants and equipment
- changes in inventories of durable goods
- changes in sensitive materials prices
- stock prices
- changes in business and consumer borrowing

Not all of the indicators move in tandem. Positive changes in a majority of leading indicators point to increased spending, production and employment. Negative changes in a majority of indicators can forecast a recession.

Coincident Indicators. Leading indicators reflect where the economy is going; coincident indicators confirm where it is. Coincident indicators are those measurable factors that vary directly and simultaneously with the business cycle. Widely used coincident indicators include:

- nonagricultural employment
- personal income
- industrial production
- manufacturing and trade sales

Lagging Indicators. Lagging indicators are those factors that change *after* the economy has begun a new trend, but serve as confirmation of the new trend. Lagging indicators help analysts differentiate long-term trends from short-term reversals that occur in any trend. Lagging indicators include:

- average duration of unemployment
- labor cost per unit of output (manufacturing)
- ratio of inventories to sales
- commercial and industrial loans outstanding
- corporate profits
- ratio of consumer installment credit to personal income

Economic Theories and the Business Cycle

Keynesian Theory   The economist John Maynard Keynes held that active government involvement in the economy was vital to the health and stability of a nation's economy. Keynesians believe that *demand* for goods ultimately controls employment and prices. Insufficient demand for goods causes unemployment; too much demand causes inflation. Keynes believed that it was the government's right and responsibility to manipulate overall demand, and therefore artificially manipulate the economy, by changing its own levels of spending and taxation.

The Government's Role in Keynesian Economics

According to Keynes, a government's **fiscal policies** determine the country's economic health. Fiscal policy involves adjusting the level of taxation and government spending. The government is expected to intervene in the economy as a major force in creating prosperity by engaging in activities that affect aggregate demand.

Government affects individual levels of spending and saving by adjusting taxes and its spending. Increasing taxes removes money from the private sector, which discourages private sector demand and spending. Government spending puts money back into the economy. To increase private sector demand for goods, the government reduces taxes, which increases people's disposable dollars; to reduce demand, it increases taxes, which reduces disposable dollars.

Monetarist Theory

Milton Friedman is considered the originator of monetarist economic theory. Monetarists believe the quantity of money, the **money supply**, is the major determinant of price levels. Too many dollars chasing too few goods leads to inflation, and too few dollars chasing too many goods leads to deflation. Monetarists believe a well-controlled, moderately increasing money supply leads to price stability. Price stability allows business managers, more efficient allocators of resources than the government, to plan and invest, which in turn keeps the economy healthy.

Supply Side Economics

Supply-side economics holds that government should allow market forces to determine prices of all goods, such as housing. Supply siders believe the federal government should reduce government spending as well as taxes. This way, sellers of goods will price them at a rate which allows them to meet market demand and still sell them profitably.

The Laffer Curve

Economist Arthur Laffer studied government revenues as a function of tax rates to find the tax rate that produces the most revenue for the government. At a tax rate of 20 percent, governments take in greater revenues than at either a higher or lower tax rate. This is because at this rate, businesses' profits can be reinvested to create more jobs and products, which increases the size of the pie from which the government draws its tax slice.

Economic Policy

In a nutshell, the difference between Keynesians and monetarists is their perspectives toward the government's role in the economy. Keynesians believe

FIGURE 14.2 The Parts of the Money Supply

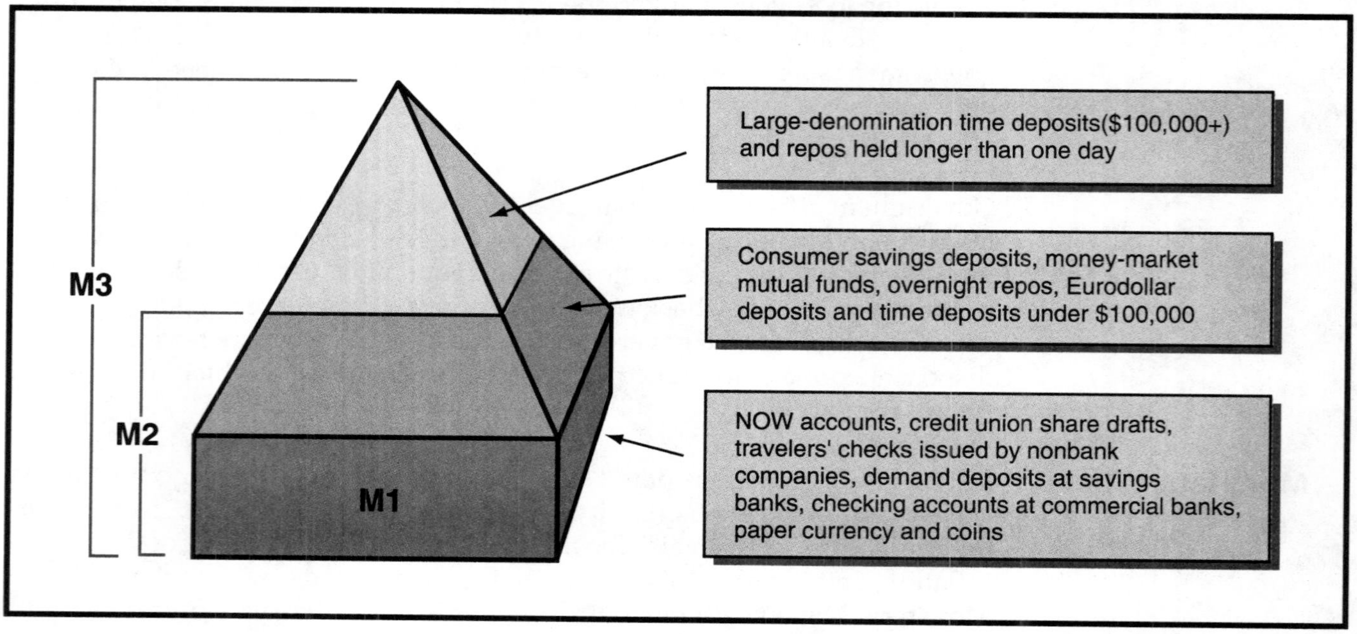

M3

M2

M1

Large-denomination time deposits($100,000+) and repos held longer than one day

Consumer savings deposits, money-market mutual funds, overnight repos, Eurodollar deposits and time deposits under $100,000

NOW accounts, credit union share drafts, travelers' checks issued by nonbank companies, demand deposits at savings banks, checking accounts at commercial banks, paper currency and coins

the government, through its fiscal policies, should be a driving force in determining the level and allocation of economic resources. Monetarists, on the other hand, believe the private sector allocates resources much more efficiently, and the government's role is to provide a stable monetary environment within which private sector decisions can be made.

Monetary Policy

Definition of Money   Most people think of "money" as cash in their pockets. An economist takes a much broader view and includes loans, credit and an assortment of other liquid instruments. Economists divide money into three categories (see Figure 14.2):

1. **M1.** The most readily available type of money, M1 consists of currency and demand deposits that can be converted to currency immediately. This is the money consumers use for ordinary purchases of goods and services.
2. **M2.** In addition to M1, M2 includes some time deposits that are fairly easy to convert into demand deposits. These time deposits include savings accounts, money-market funds and overnight repurchase agreements.

3. **M3.** In addition to M1 and M2, M3 includes time deposits of more than $100,000 and repurchase agreements with terms longer than one day.

Most money (M1) is in demand deposits—that is, checking accounts. M1 is the largest and most liquid component of the money supply.

The Federal Reserve Board

The Federal Reserve consists of 12 regional Federal Reserve Banks and hundreds of national and state banks that belong to the system. The FRB determines monetary policy and takes actions to implement its policies, including:

- acting as an agent of the U.S. Treasury;
- regulating the U.S. money supply;
- setting reserve requirements for members;
- supervising the printing of currency;
- clearing fund transfers throughout the system; and
- examining members to ensure their compliance with federal regulations.

Because the FRB determines how much money is available for businesses and consumers to spend, its decisions are a critical aspect of the U.S. economy. The FRB affects the money supply through its use of three policy tools:

1. open-market operations (buying and selling bonds)
2. changes in the discount rate (on loans to member banks)
3. changes in reserve requirements

Open-Market Operations

The Fed buys and sells U.S. government securities in the open market to expand and contract the money supply. The **Federal Open Market Committee (FOMC)** meets regularly to direct the government's open-market operations.

When the FOMC buys securities, it increases the supply of money in the banking system, and when it sells securities, it decreases the supply.

When the Fed wants to expand, or loosen, the money supply, it buys securities from banks. The banks receive direct credit in their reserve accounts. The increase of reserves allows banks to make more loans and effectively lowers interest rates. Thus, by buying securities, the Fed pumps money into the banking system, expanding the money supply.

When the Fed wants to contract, or tighten, the money supply, it sells securities to banks. Each sale is charged against a bank's reserve balance. This reduces the bank's ability to lend money, which tightens credit and effectively raises interest rates. By selling securities, the Fed pulls money out of the system, contracting the money supply.

Discount Rate

The Fed can also adjust the money supply by raising or lowering the **discount rate**—the interest rate the Fed charges its members for short-term loans.

To compensate for shortfalls in its reserve requirement, a bank may borrow money directly from the Fed at its discount rate or borrow the **excess reserves** (federal funds) from another member bank. The interest rate banks charge each other for such loans is called the **federal funds rate**.

The federal funds rate fluctuates daily and is among the most volatile interest rates. A rising rate usually indicates that member banks are more reluctant to lend their funds and, therefore, want a higher rate of interest in return. A higher rate usually results from a shortage of funds to lend and probably indicates that deposits, in general, are shrinking. A falling federal funds rate generally means that the lending banks are competing to loan money and are trying to make their own loans more attractive by lowering their rates. A lower rate often results from an excess of deposits.

Lowering the discount rate reduces the cost of money to banks, which increases the demand for loans. Raising the discount rate increases the cost of money and reduces the demand for loans.

Reserve Requirements

Commercial banks must deposit a certain percentage of their depositors' money with the Federal Reserve. This is known as the **reserve requirement**. All money commercial banks deposit at Federal Reserve Banks, including money exceeding the reserve requirement, is known as **federal funds**.

When the Fed raises the reserve requirement, banks must deposit more funds with the Fed and, thus, have less money to lend. Reducing the reserve requirement has the opposite effect.

Table 14.1 summarizes the Fed's official tactics to implement its monetary policy.

Fiscal Policy

Fiscal policy refers to governmental budget decisions, which can include increases or decreases in:

- federal spending
- money raised through taxes
- federal budget deficits or surpluses

TABLE 14.1 Federal Reserve Policy Tactics

To expand credit during a recession to stimulate a slow economy:	To tighten credit to slow economic expansion and prevent inflation:
Buy U.S. government securities in the open market	Sell U.S. government securities in the open market
Lower the discount rate	Raise the discount rate
Lower reserve requirements	Raise reserve requirements

Fiscal policy is based on the assumption that the government can control unemployment levels and inflation by adjusting overall demand for goods and services.

The political process determines fiscal policy. Therefore, it takes time for conditions and solutions to be identified and implemented. Because of the time and negotiations involved, fiscal policy is an inefficient means to solve short-term economic problems.

The Stock Market

Fiscal and monetary policies have considerable influence on the stock market. If the FRB eases interest rates, the money supply increases, making credit easier to obtain. This increases overall liquidity.

Similarly, lower tax rates can stimulate spending by leaving more spendable dollars in the hands of individuals and businesses. Like easier credit, lower tax rates are bullish for the stock market. Raising taxes has the opposite effect, reducing the amount of money available to businesses and consumers for spending and investment.

Interest Rates

A loan's interest rate is the cost of the money. In large measure, the supply and demand of money determines interest rates. When the money supply exceeds demand, interest rates fall. When the FRB tightens the money supply, interest rates rise. The Fed influences the money supply in several ways, which directly or indirectly affect interest rate levels.

Disintermediation

When a person deposits money with a bank, she earns interest on her funds. The bank, in turn, acts as an intermediary by lending the money at a higher interest rate that allows it to pay the depositor and earn a profit. Disintermediation is the flow of money from traditional, low-yielding savings accounts to higher yielding investments in the marketplace without a bank acting as an intermediary or a middleman. Disintermediation often takes place when the FRB tightens the money supply and interest rates rise.

International Monetary Factors

Balance of Payments   The flow of money between the United States and other countries is known as the **balance of payments**.

The balance of payments may be a surplus (more money flowing into the country than out) or a deficit (more money flowing out of the country than in). A deficit may occur when interest rates in another country are high because money flows to where it earns the highest return.

Debit Items	*Credit Items*
Imports	Exports
U.S. spending abroad	Foreign spending in the U.S.
U.S. investments abroad	Foreign investments in the U.S.
U.S. bank loans abroad	
U.S. foreign aid	

The largest component of the balance of payments is the **balance of trade**—the export and import of merchandise. On the U.S. credit side are sales of American products to foreign countries. On the debit side are American purchases of foreign goods that cause American dollars to flow out of the country. When debits exceed credits, a deficit in the balance of payments occurs; when credits exceed debits, a surplus exists.

 For Example: If the U.S. imports $5 billion in Toyotas from Japan and exports $4 billion of wheat to Japan, a $1 billion trade deficit occurs.

Technical Analysis

Both technical and fundamental analysis attempt to predict the supply and demand of markets and individual stocks. Technical analysis attempts to predict the direction of prices based on historic price and trading volume patterns when laid out graphically on charts. Fundamental analysts concentrate on broad-based economic trends, current business conditions within an industry, and the quality of a particular corporation's business, finances and management.

Market Averages and Indexes

Stock prices tend to move, or **trend**, together, although some move in the opposite direction. The average stock, by definition, tends to rise in a bull market and decline in a bear market. Technical analysts chart the daily prices and volume movements of individual stocks and market indexes to discern patterns that allow them to predict the direction of market price movements.

Trading Volume. Market trading volume that is substantially above normal signifies or confirms a pattern in the direction of prices. If overall volume has been listless for months and suddenly jumps significantly, a technical analyst views that as the beginning of a trend.

Advances/Declines. The number of issues closing up or down on a specific day reflects **market breadth**. The number of advances and declines can be a significant indication of the market's relative strength. When declines outnumber advances by a large amount, the market is bearish even if it closed higher. In bull markets, advances substantially outnumber declines. Technical analysts plot daily advances and declines on a graph to produce an **advance/decline line** that gives them an indication of market breadth trends.

Charting Stocks

In addition to studying the overall market, technical analysts attempt to identify patterns in the prices of individual stocks.

Trendlines

While a stock's price may spike up or down daily, over time its price tends to move in one direction.

Technical analysts identify patterns in the trendlines of individual stocks from graphs as they do patterns in the overall market. They base their buy or sell recommendations on a stock's price trendline. An upward trendline is bullish; a downward one is bearish.

A trendline (see Figure 14.3) connects the reaction lows in an uptrend and the rally highs in a downtrend. Three common patterns in stock price trendlines are consolidations, reversals, and support and resistance levels.

Consolidations. If a stock's price stays within a narrow range, it is said to be *consolidating*. When viewed on a graph, the trendline is horizontal and moves sideways, neither up nor down.

Reversals. A reversal indicates that an upward or a downward trendline has halted and the stock's price is moving in the opposite direction. In between the two trendlines, a period of consolidation occurs, and the stock price levels off.

A genuine reversal pattern can be difficult to recognize because trends, as you can see in Figure 14.3, are composed of many rises and declines, which may occur at different rates and for different lengths of time.

Because of its gently curving shape, an easily identifiable reversal pattern is called a *saucer* (reversal of a downtrend) or an *inverted saucer* (reversal of an uptrend). A similar reversal pattern is the head-and-shoulders pattern, named for its resemblance to the human body. Figure 14.4 illustrates head and shoulders top and head and shoulders bottom patterns.

The head and shoulders top pattern depicted in Figure 14.4 indicates the beginning of a bearish trend in the stock. First, the stock price rises, then it reaches a plateau at the neckline (left shoulder). A second advance pushes the price higher, but then the price falls back to the neckline (head). Finally, the stock price rises again, but falls back to the neckline (right shoulder) and continues downward, indicating a reversal of the upward trend.

When reversed, this pattern is called a *head and shoulders bottom*, or *an inverted head and shoulders*, and indicates a bullish reversal.

FIGURE 14.3   Upward and Downward Trendlines

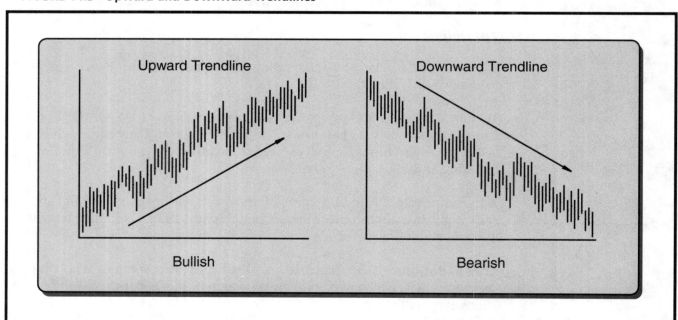

FIGURE 14.4 Head and Shoulders Top and Bottom Trendlines

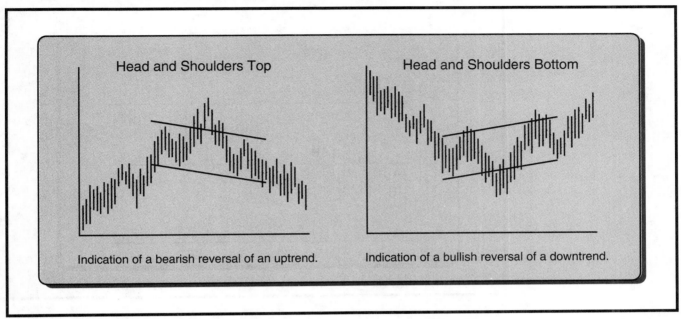

Head and Shoulders Top

Head and Shoulders Bottom

Indication of a bearish reversal of an uptrend.

Indication of a bullish reversal of a downtrend.

Support and Resistance Levels. Stock prices may move within a narrow range for months or even years. The bottom of this trading range is known as the **support level**; the top of the trading range is called the **resistance level**.

When a stock declines to its support level, the low price attracts buyers, whose buying supports the price and keeps it from declining further. When a stock increases to its resistance level, the high price attracts sellers, whose selling hinders a further price rise. Stocks may fluctuate in trading ranges for months, testing their support and resistance levels (see Figure 14.5).

If a particular stock's price penetrates either the support or the resistance level, the change is considered significant. A decline through the support level is called a **bearish breakout**; a rise through the resistance level is called a **bullish breakout**. Breakouts usually signal the beginning of a new upward or downward trend.

FIGURE 14.5   Support and Resistance Levels

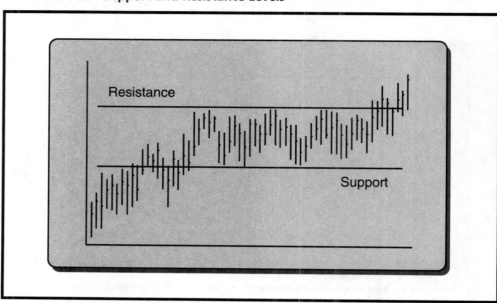

Technical Market Theories

Technical analysts follow various theories regarding market trends. Some of them are outlined below.

Dow Theory. Analysts use the Dow theory to confirm the end of a major market trend. According to the theory, the three types of changes in stock prices are primary trends (one year or more), secondary trends (3 to 12 weeks) and short-term fluctuations (hours or days).

In a bull market, the primary trend is upward. But stock prices may still drop in a secondary trend within the primary upward trend, even for as long as 12 weeks. The trough of the downward secondary trend should be higher than the trough of the previous downward trend. In a bear market, secondary upward trends may occur, but the highs reached during those secondary upward movements are successively lower.

According to the Dow theory, the primary trend in a bull market is a series of higher highs and higher lows. In a bear market, the primary trend is a series of lower highs and lower lows. Daily fluctuations are considered irrelevant.

Figure 14.6 shows a primary upward trend interrupted by secondary downward movements. Note that the chart illustrates a series of successively higher highs and lows, conforming to the definition of a primary upward trend.

FIGURE 14.6   Dow Theory of Market Trends

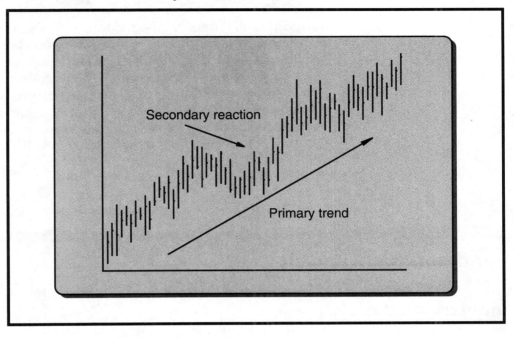

Any change in direction is considered deceptive unless the Dow Jones Industrial and Transportation Averages reflect the change. This method lacks precision and is sometimes slow in confirming changes in market trends.

Odd Lot Theory. Typically, small investors engage in odd lot trading. Followers of the odd lot theory believe that these small investors invariably buy and sell at the wrong times. When odd lot traders buy, odd lot analysts are bearish. When odd lot traders sell, odd lot analysts are bullish.

Short Interest Theory. "Short interest" refers to the number of shares that have been sold short. Because short positions must be repurchased eventually, some analysts believe that short interest reflects mandatory demand, which creates a support level for stock prices. High short interest is a bullish indicator, and low short interest is a bearish indicator.

Other Market Theories

Modern Portfolio Theory. Instead of emphasizing particular stocks, modern portfolio theory (MPT) focuses on the relationship of all the investments in a portfolio. The theory holds that analysts' ability to predict price movements is of no value. Adherents to MPT believe securities markets are efficient markets, meaning securities prices react so quickly to most investment information that no analyst is likely to outsmart the market as a whole. MPT portfolio managers select a general mix of investments weighted to emphasize economic trends.

Random Walk Theory. The random walk theory is an academic theory maintaining that the direction of stock or market prices is unpredictable. This hypothesis is based on the **efficient market theory**, which holds that the stock market is perfectly efficient, with prices reflecting all known information at any given time. It is impossible, therefore, to "beat the market" using fundamental or technical analysis. Throwing darts at the stock listings is as good a method as any for selecting stocks for investment. Many people have become wealthy investing in stocks, but none has done so using the random walk theory.

Fundamental Analysis

Industry Analysis

Fundamental analysis is the study of the business prospects of an individual company within the context of its industry and the overall economy. Because business cycle phases have different effects on different industries, fundamental analysts look for companies in industries that offer better-than-average opportunities in the context of the business cycle. It is useful to distinguish between the four types of industries and investments: defensive, cyclical, growth and special situation.

Defensive Industries. Defensive industries are least affected by normal business cycles. Companies in defensive industries generally produce non-durable consumer goods such as food, pharmaceuticals, tobacco and energy. Public consumption of such goods remains fairly steady throughout the business cycle.

During recessions and bear markets, stocks in defensive industries generally decline less than stocks in other industries. During expansions and bull markets, defensive stocks may advance less. Investments in defensive industries tend to involve less risk and, consequently, lower investment returns.

Cyclical Industries. Cyclical industries are highly sensitive to business cycles and inflation trends. Most cyclical industries produce durable goods such as heavy machinery, raw materials like steel, and automobiles. During recessions, the demand for such products declines as manufacturers postpone investments in new capital goods and consumers postpone purchases of automobiles. **Counter-cyclical industries**, on the other hand, tend to turn down as the economy heats up and to rise when the economy turns down.

Growth Industries. Every industry passes through four phases during its existence: introduction, growth, maturity and decline. An industry is considered in its growth phase if the industry is growing faster than the economy as a whole because of technological changes, new products or changing consumer tastes. Computers and bioengineering are current growth industries. Because many growth companies retain nearly all of their earnings to finance their business expansion, growth stocks usually pay little or no dividends.

Special Situation Stocks. Special situation stocks are stocks of a company with unusual profit potential due to nonrecurring circumstances, such as new management, the discovery of a valuable natural resource on corporate property or the introduction of a new product.

Corporate Analysis

After considering the state of the economy and the health of various industries, fundamental analysts study a company's position within its industry, prospects for growth and stability, and financial strength.

Fundamental analysts also look at a firm's quality of management and its historical earnings trends. They compare the level and stability of its projected growth with that of its competitors. Analysts also examine the structure of a corporation's capitalization and use of working capital.

Financial Statements   A corporation's financial statements provide a fundamental analyst with the raw material needed to assess that corporation's profitability, financial strength and operating efficiency. By examining how certain static numbers from the statement relate to one another and how the resulting ratios relate to the company's competitors, the analyst can determine how financially viable the company is.

Companies issue quarterly and annual financial reports to their stockholders. Among other items, these include a company's balance sheet and income statement.

Balance Sheet

The balance sheet provides a snapshot of a company's financial position at a specific point in time. It identifies the value of the company's assets (what it owns) and its liabilities (what it owes). The difference between these two figures is the corporation's equity, or net worth. Figure 14.7 illustrates the balance sheet equation.

A corporation can be compared to a homeowner who borrows money to buy a home. The homeowner's equity is the difference between the mortgage balance (liability) and the home's market value (asset value). A corporation can buy assets using borrowed money (liabilities) and equity raised by selling

FIGURE 14.7   The Balance Sheet Equation

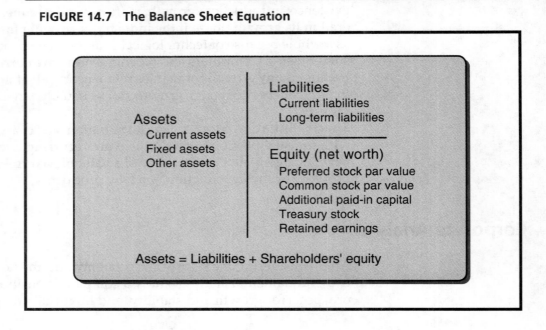

stock. The value of its assets must equal (balance with) the value of its liabilities and equity, as illustrated in Figure 14.7.

While useful in determining a company's current value, the balance sheet cannot tell the analyst whether the company's business is improving or deteriorating.

Figure 14.8 shows a sample balance sheet for Amalgamated Widget.

Balance Sheet Components

The balance sheet gets its name from the fact that its two sides must balance. The balance sheet equation mathematically expresses the relationship between the two sides of the balance sheet.

Assets

Assets appear on the balance sheet in order of liquidity, the ease with which they can be turned into cash. Those most readily convertible into cash are listed first, followed by less liquid assets. Balance sheets commonly identify three types of assets: current assets (cash and assets easily convertible into cash); fixed assets (physical assets that could eventually be sold); and other assets (usually intangible and only of value to the corporation that owns them).

FIGURE 14.8 Sample Balance Sheet

Balance Sheet
Amalgamated Widget
as of Dec. 31, 1999

ASSETS

Current assets	Cash and equivalents	$ 5,000,000	
	Accounts receivable	15,000,000	
	Inventory	19,000,000	
	Prepaid expenses	1,000,000	
	Total Current Assets		$ 40,000,000
Fixed assets	Buildings, furniture and fixtures		
	(including $10,000,000 depreciation)	$40,000,000	
	Land	15,000,000	
	Total Fixed Assets		$ 55,000,000
Other (intangibles, goodwill)			$ 5,000,000
Total Assets			$100,000,000

LIABILITIES AND NET WORTH

Current liabilities	Accounts payable	$ 5,000,000	
	Accrued wages payable	4,000,000	
	Current portion of long-term debt	1,000,000	
	Total Current Liabilities		$ 10,000,000
Long-term liabilities	8% 20-year convertible debentures		$ 50,000,000
Total Liabilities			$ 60,000,000
Net worth	Preferred stock $100 par ($5 noncum		
	conv, 200,000 shares issued)	$20,000,000	
	Common stock $1 par (1,000,000 shares)	1,000,000	
	Capital in excess of par	4,000,000	
	Retained earnings	15,000,000	
Total Net Worth			$ 40,000,000
Total Liabilities and Net Worth			$100,000,000

Current Assets. Current assets include all cash and other items expected to be converted into cash within the next 12 months, including:

- **cash and equivalents**—cash and short-term safe investments, such as money-market instruments, that can be sold readily, as well as other marketable securities;

- **accounts receivable**—amounts due from customers for goods delivered or services rendered, reduced by the allowance for bad debts;
- **inventory**—the cost of raw materials, work in process and finished goods ready for sale; and
- **prepaid expenses**—items a company has already paid for, but has not yet benefited from, such as prepaid advertising, rents, taxes and operating supplies.

Fixed Assets. Fixed assets are typically property, plant and equipment. Unlike current assets, they are not easily converted into cash. Fixed assets, such as factories, have limited useful lives because wear and tear eventually reduce their value. For this reason, their cost can be **depreciated** over time, deducted from taxable income in annual installments to compensate for loss in value. Note that on the Amalgamated Widget balance sheet (Figure 14.8), depreciation has reduced fixed assets by $10 million.

Other Assets. Intangible assets are nonphysical properties, such as formulas, contract rights and trademarks. Goodwill, also an intangible asset, is a company's value over and above its book value. This extra sum is paid for the corporation's reputation and relationship with its clients. Note that Amalgamated Widget reported $5 million in other assets, including intangible assets and goodwill.

Liabilities

Total liabilities on a balance sheet represent all financial claims by creditors against the corporation's assets. Balance sheets usually include two main types of liabilities: **current liabilities** (debts due within 12 months) and **long-term liabilities** (debts maturing in more than 12 months).

Current Liabilities. Current liabilities are corporate debt obligations due for payment within the next 12 months. For Amalgamated Widget, these include:

- **accounts payable**—amounts owed to suppliers of materials and other business costs;
- **accrued wages payable**—unpaid wages, salaries, commissions and interest; and
- **current long-term debt**—any portion of long-term debt due within 12 months.

A balance sheet might also include as current liabilities:

- **notes payable**—the balance due on equipment purchased on credit or cash borrowed; and
- **accrued taxes**—unpaid federal, state and local taxes.

Long-Term Liabilities. Long-term debts are financial obligations due for payment after 12 months. Examples of long-term debts are mortgages on real property, long-term promissory notes and outstanding corporate bonds. Funded debt is any long-term debt payable in five years or more.

Shareholders' Equity

Shareholders' equity, also called *net worth* or *owners' equity*, is the stockholders' claims on a company's assets after all of its creditors have been paid. Shareholders' equity equals total assets less total liabilities. On a balance sheet, three types of shareholders' equity are identified: capital stock at par, capital in excess of par and retained earnings.

Capital Stock at Par. Capital stock includes preferred and common stock, listed at par value. Par value is the total dollar value assigned to stock certificates when a corporation's owners, the stockholders, first contributed capital. Par value of common stock is an arbitrary value with no relationship to market price.

Capital in Excess of Par. Capital in excess of par, often called **additional paid-in capital**, is the amount of money over par value that a company received for selling stock.

✓ *For Example:* Amalgamated Widget's balance sheet indicates that it issued 1 million shares of common stock with a par value of $1, for a total value of $1 million. It also has $4 million of capital in excess of par ($4 per share above the par value). Therefore, it sold the stock for $5 per share in its initial public offering.

Retained Earnings. Retained earnings, sometimes called *earned surplus*, are profits that have not been paid out in dividends. Retained earnings represent the total of all earnings held since the corporation was formed less dividends paid to stockholders. Operating losses in any year reduce the retained earnings from prior years.

Capitalization

A company's capitalization is the combined sum of its long-term debt and equity accounts. The capital structure is the relative amounts of debt and equity that compose a company's capitalization. Some companies finance their business with a large proportion of borrowed funds; others can finance their growth with retained earnings from normal operations and little or no debt.

Liquidity

Working capital is the amount of capital or cash a company has available. Working capital is, therefore, a measure of a firm's liquidity, its ability to quickly turn assets into cash to meet its short-term obligations. The formula for working capital follows:

$$\text{Current assets} - \text{Current liabilities} = \text{Working capital}$$

Liquidity is important because it is the measure of a company's ability to pay the expenses associated with running the business. A company that can't pay its expenses does not stay in business.

Changes that Affect the Balance Sheet

Balancing the Balance Sheet. Balance sheets, by definition, must balance. Every financial change in a business requires two offsetting changes on the company books, known as *double-entry bookkeeping*.

✔ **For Example:** A company that buys an asset for cash increases the value of its *fixed asset* balance sheet account and reduces the value of its *cash* balance sheet account by the asset's cost. If Amalgamated Widget buys a stamping machine for $500,000 in cash, the company's assets increase by $500,000 and its cash decreases by $500,000.

Depreciating Assets. Because fixed assets, such as buildings, equipment and machinery, wear out as they are used, they decline in value over time. This decline in value is called *depreciation*. A company's tax bills are reduced each year the company depreciates fixed assets used in the businesses.

Depreciation affects the balance sheet in two ways: accumulated depreciation reduces the value of fixed assets, and the depreciation deduction reduces tax liability by the same amount. The two changes balance out so that total assets continue to equal the sum of liabilities and net worth on the balance sheet.

Capital Structure

A corporation builds its capital structure with four elements:

1. long-term debt
2. capital stock (both common and preferred)
3. capital in excess of par
4. earned surplus (retained earnings)

The total capitalization for Amalgamated Widget (see Figure 14.8) is $90 million ($50 million in long-term debt, $20 million in preferred stock and $20 million in common shareholders' equity). Note that capital stock plus capital in excess of par plus earned surplus equals shareholders' equity (net worth).

✓ **For Example:** If Amalgamated Widget changes its capitalization by issuing stock or bonds, the effects will show up on the balance sheet.

Issuing Securities. The Amalgamated Widget balance sheet indicates the company issued 1 million shares of $1 par common stock. If it issues another 1 million shares, the net worth (shareholders' equity) will increase by the additional capital raised and the amount of cash on the asset side of the balance sheet will increase.

Convertible Securities. When a stockholder converts one of Amalgamated Widget's convertible bonds into shares of common stock, the amount of liabilities decreases and equity increases. The changes are on the same side of the balance sheet, so the bottom line is unchanged.

Bond Redemption. When bonds are redeemed, liabilities on the balance sheet are reduced—by $50 million for Amalgamated Widget. The offsetting change would be a decrease of $50 million in cash on the asset side of the balance sheet. Amalgamated Widget would have $50 million less debt outstanding, but it would also have $50 million less cash.

Dividends. When a cash dividend is *declared*, retained earnings are lowered and current liabilities are increased. The declaration of a cash dividend establishes a current liability until it is paid. Once *paid*, it reduces cash in current assets and also reduces current liabilities.

Distribution of stock dividends has no effect on corporate assets or liabilities, nor does it change the stockholders' proportionate equity in the corporation. The number of shares each stockholder owns increases, but each single share represents a smaller slice of ownership in the corporation.

Stock Splits. Like a stock dividend, a stock split does not affect shareholders' equity. On the balance sheet, only the par value per share and number of shares outstanding change.

Financial Leverage

Financial leverage is a company's ability to use long-term debt to increase its return on equity. A company with a high ratio of long-term debt to common stock is said to be *highly leveraged*.

Stockholders benefit from leverage if the return on borrowed money exceeds the debt service costs. But leverage is risky because increases in debt raise the possibility of default in a business downturn.

As a rule of thumb, industrial companies with debt-to-equity ratios of 30 percent or higher are considered highly leveraged. Traditionally, utilities, with their relatively stable earnings and cash flows, can be more highly leveraged without subjecting stockholders to undue risk.

FIGURE 14.9   Sample Income Statement

Income Statement **Amalgamated Widget** **Jan 1 – Dec 31, 1999**		
Net sales		$60,000,000
Cost of goods sold	$10,000,000	
General operating expenses (including $2,000,000 depreciation)	$30,000,000	$40,000,000
Operating income		$20,000,000
Interest expense		$ 4,000,000
Pretax income		$16,000,000
Taxes		$ 6,000,000
Net income after taxes		$10,000,000
Preferred dividends		$ 1,000,000
Earnings available to common		$ 9,000,000

Income Statement

The income statement summarizes a corporation's revenues and expenses for a fiscal period, usually quarterly, year to date or the full year. It compares revenue against costs and expenses during the period. Figure 14.9 provides an income statement for Amalgamated Widget.

Fundamental analysts use the income statement to judge the efficiency of a company's operation, as well as its profitability. Table 14.2 illustrates typical entries on an income statement.

Components of the Income Statement

The various operating and nonoperating expenses on the income statement are discussed below.

Operating Income. Operating income, also called *operating profit, operating margin* or earnings before interest and taxes (EBIT), is a company's profits from business operations.

Interest Expense. Interest payments on a corporation's debt is not considered an operating expense. Interest payments reduce the corporation's taxable income. Pretax income, the amount of taxable income, is operating income less interest payment expenses.

TABLE 14.2 Income Statement Entries

	Net Sales
minus	Cost of goods sold (COGS)
minus	Operating costs (including depreciation)
equals	Operating profit
plus	Nonoperating income
equals	Operating income (earnings before interest and taxes)
minus	Interest expenses
equals	Taxable income
minus	Taxes
equals	Net income after taxes
minus	Preferred dividends
equals	Earnings available to common
minus	Common dividends
equals	Retained earnings

Net Income After Taxes. If dividends are paid to stockholders, they are paid out of net income, after taxes have been paid. After preferred dividends have been paid, the remaining income is available to invest in the business or pay dividends to common stockholders.

 Take Note: Interest payments reduce a corporation's taxable income, while dividend payments to stockholders are paid with after-tax dollars. Because they are taxable as income to stockholders, dividends are taxed twice, while interest payments are taxed once, as income to the recipient.

Earnings Per Share (EPS). Earnings per share is what remains after payment of interest, taxes and preferred dividends. Dividing net income after taxes, interest and payment of preferred dividends by the number of common shares outstanding determines earnings per share.

Retained Earnings. Retained earnings, or earned surplus, is earnings not paid out in dividends.

Financial Ratios

Analyzing Corporate Equity

Figures from the balance sheet or income statement can be expressed as ratios. Financial ratios allow an analyst to compare a company's performance to its past performance and to the performances of other companies within its industry. Such comparisons provide a more thorough understanding of a company's financial strengths and weaknesses.

✓ **For Example:** Companies A and B are in the same business, and both have total sales of $1 million. If company A earns $100,000, its profit margin is 10 percent (100,000 ÷ 1,000,000). If company B's net profit is $300,000, its profit margin is 30 percent and it is three times as profitable as company A.

Capitalization Ratios   Analysts can assess the risk of a company going bankrupt by studying the amount of leverage (the proportionate amount of long-term debt) in its overall capitalization (long-term debt plus equity).

When assessing a company's capitalization, analysts use ratios that express the percentage of capitalization composed of long-term debt, common stock and preferred stock. The following four ratios are commonly used to assess the stability of a corporation's capitalization:

Debt-to-equity ratio = Total long-term debt ÷ Total shareholders' equity

Bond ratio (debt ratio) = Long-term liabilities ÷ Total capitalization

Common stock ratio = Common shareholders' equity ÷ Total capitalization

Preferred stock ratio = Preferred stock ÷ Total capitalization

Leverage. Leverage is the use of long-term debt financing to increase earnings. The debt-to-equity ratio provides a common measure of leverage.

More debt can lead to greater EPS, but can also increase risk to the common stockholders. A company with a disproportionately high amount of debt may not be able to meet its interest obligations during a business downturn. Low debt-to-equity ratios are considered more conservative than high debt-to-equity ratios. The debt-to-equity ratio is similar to the bond ratio, which compares total long-term debt to total capitalization rather than to shareholders' equity.

The bond ratio, or debt ratio, measures the percentage of total capitalization provided by long-term debt financing. The common stock ratio measures the percentage of total capitalization contributed by common stockholders, including the stock's par value, amount paid for the stock in excess of par, and retained earnings. The preferred stock ratio measures the percentage of total capitalization from preferred stock.

Liquidity Ratios   Liquidity ratios measure a firm's ability to meet its current financial obligations. Working capital, though not a ratio, is the amount of liquid assets available to pay for short-term obligations. It is calculated as follows:

$$\textbf{Working capital} = \text{Current assets} - \text{Current liabilities}$$

Because working capital is a dollar amount, it does not, by itself, allow analysts to compare companies. The current ratio, on the other hand, compares current assets with a company's current financial obligations, regardless of the company's size or business:

$$\textbf{Current ratio} = \text{Current assets} \div \text{Current liabilities}$$

Another measure of liquidity is quick assets, which subtracts unsold inventory, a current asset, from other current assets because inventory is not as liquid (as quick to convert to cash) as cash or securities. Analysts use quick assets instead of current assets to calculate the acid-test ratio. The acid-test ratio, also called the *quick ratio*, is a more stringent measure of a company's liquidity than its current ratio. The quick assets and acid-test ratio equations look like this:

$$\textbf{Quick assets} = \text{Current assets} - \text{Inventory}$$

$$\textbf{Acid-test ratio} = \text{Quick assets} \div \text{Current liabilities}$$

Debt Service Ratio. The debt service ratio reflects a company's ability to meet the principal and interest payments on its bonds. It looks like this:

$$\textbf{Debt service ratio} = \text{EBIT} \div (\text{Annual interest} + \text{Principal payments})$$

Book Value Per Share. In a liquidation, a company sells its tangible assets and uses the proceeds to pay creditors and stockholders. Potential investors want to know how the value of tangible assets, also known as **net tangible asset value**, compares to the size of the company's debt and equity.

The book value of a company's assets (the amount at which they are carried on the books) is determined by deducting all liabilities and preferred stock from the company's total tangible assets. Dividing this figure by the number of shares of common stock shows how much a company's assets are worth (assuming they can be sold for their book value) per share. The equation looks like this:

$$(\text{Assets} - \text{Liabilities} - \text{Intangibles} - \text{Par value of preferred stock})$$
$$\div \text{Shares of common stock outstanding} = \text{Book value per share}$$

Valuation Ratios   Valuation ratios are used by analysts to compare companies within an industry as well as in different industries.

Earnings Per Share. Among the most widely used statistics is earnings per share. EPS measures the value of a company's earnings for each common share. It is calculated as follows:

EPS = Earnings available to common ÷ No. of common shares outstanding

Earnings available to common are the remaining earnings after the preferred dividend has been paid. Earnings per share relates to common stock only. Preferred stockholders have no claims to earnings beyond the stipulated preferred stock dividends.

Earnings Per Share After Dilution. If a corporation has rights, warrants, convertible preferred stock or convertible bonds outstanding, the EPS could be diluted by an increase in the number of shares of common outstanding. That is, if the same amount of earnings available to common stockholders were allocated to more shares of stock, earnings would be less for each share. EPS is sometimes called **primary earnings per share** or **basic earnings per share** to differentiate it from earnings after dilution.

EPS after dilution assumes that all convertible securities have been converted into the common. Because of tax adjustments, the calculations for figuring EPS after dilution can be complicated.

Dividends Per Share. The dividends per share is simply the dollar amount of cash dividends paid on each common share during the year. It is calculated as follows:

$$\text{Dividends per share} = \frac{\text{Annual cash dividends}}{\text{No. of common shares outstanding}}$$

Current Yield. A common stock's current yield, like the current yield on bonds, expresses the annual dividend payout as a percentage of the stock price:

$$\text{Current yield} = \frac{\text{Annual dividends per common share}}{\text{Market value per common share}}$$

Dividend Payout Ratio. The dividend payout ratio measures the proportion of earnings paid to stockholders as dividends. Its equation follows:

$$\text{Dividend payout ratio} = \frac{\text{Annual dividends per common share}}{\text{Earnings per share}}$$

In general, older companies pay out larger percentages of earnings as dividends. Utilities as a group have an especially high payout ratio. Growth companies normally have the lowest ratios because they reinvest their earnings in the businesses. Companies on the way up hope to reward stockholders with gains in the stock value rather than with high dividend income.

Price-Earnings Ratio. The widely used price-earnings (PE) ratio provides investors with a rough idea of the relationship between the prices of different common stocks compared to the earnings that accrue to one share of stock. Calculate the PE ratio as follows:

PE ratio = Current market price of common stock ÷ Earnings per share

Growth companies usually have higher PE ratios than cyclical companies. Investors are willing to pay more per dollar of current earnings if a company's future earnings are expected to be dramatically higher than earnings for stocks that rise and fall with business cycles. Companies subject to cyclical fluctuations generally sell at lower PEs; declining industries sell at still lower PEs. Investors should beware of extremely high or extremely low PEs. Speculative stocks often sell at one extreme or the other.

If you know a stock's market price and PE ratio, you can calculate the earnings per share as follows:

PE ratio = Market price ÷ EPS

Summary

Economics is the study of supply and demand. When supply exceeds demand, prices decline. If a store has an inventory of shirts it wants to move, a sale at reduced prices prompts people to buy more shirts. When demand exceeds supply, prices rise. If tickets to a playoff game have sold out, scalpers charge a premium for tickets on the black market.

Inflation is a barometer of the general direction of price levels. As such, it is a measure of the buying power of a dollar. Periods of low inflation have relatively stable prices and low interest rates and, as a result, are positive for business and the stock market. Periods of high inflation have increasing prices and high interest rates, and tend to be bad for business and the stock market. In a growing economy, there is always some amount of inflation.

Keynesian economic policy emphasizes the government's role in maintaining a balance between overall supply and demand. Taxes and spending compose fiscal policy, and are the mechanisms by which the government attempts to influence the direction of the economy.

Monetary economic policy is controlled by the Federal Reserve Board. Monetarists believe that the amount of money in the system is the major influence on economic performance. The reserve requirement, discount rate and open market operations are the tools used by monetarists to regulate the economy.

Technical analysis attempts to predict future movements in individual stocks and the stock market by observing past price patterns (supply and demand) as depicted on charts. Technical analysts pay particular attention to support and resistance levels in a price pattern

Fundamental analysis looks to the financial condition of specific companies and industries and attempts to predict the future profitability of those companies and the consequent demand for the stocks. Fundamental analysts study companies' balance sheets and income statements, and use financial ratios as a means to normalize the relative valuation and profitability comparisons of different companies in different industries.

Key Concepts

In addition to studying these key concepts, use the Economics and Analysis Hot Sheet on page 647 for further review.

acid test ratio
assets
business cycle
capitalization
coincident indicator
constant dollar
Consumer Price Index (CPI)
consumption
contraction
current assets
current ratio
cyclical industry
debt-to-equity ratio
defensive industry
deflation
demand deposit
depreciation
depression
discount rate
disintermediation
earnings per share (EPS)
expansion
federal funds rate
Federal Open Market Committee
Federal Reserve Board (FRB)
fiscal policy

fundamental analysis
gross domestic product (GDP)
growth industry
inflation
Keynesian economics
lagging indicator
leading indicator
liabilities
M1, M2, M3
monetarist theory
monetary policy
money supply
odd-lot theory
peak
price-earnings ratio
recession
recovery
reserve requirement
shareholders' equity
short interest theory
support level
technical analysis
time deposit
trendline
trough

Review Questions

1. Gross domestic product is the

   A. sum of all goods and services produced by a nation
   B. goods produced by a country
   C. household goods of a country
   D. manufactured and nonmanufactured goods

2. A fundamental analyst would be interested in all the following EXCEPT

   A. statistics of the U.S. Department of Commerce on disposable income
   B. daily trading volumes on the NYSE
   C. corporate annual reports
   D. new innovations within a particular industry

3. The balance sheet formula is

   A. assets = liabilities + equity
   B. assets + equity = liabilities
   C. assets + equity = net worth
   D. (assets − equity) × liability = net worth

4. Which of the following is the narrowest measure of the market?

   A. NYSE Composite Index
   B. *Value Line* Index
   C. DJIA
   D. Standard & Poor's 500

5. The NYSE Composite Index consists of

   A. common stocks
   B. preferred stocks
   C. certain listed bonds
   D. all of the above

6. The stock index that contains securities of 400 industrial corporations is the

   A. Dow Jones Index
   B. Nasdaq Index
   C. NYSE Composite Index
   D. Standard & Poor's 500

7. When a technical analyst says that the market is *consolidating*, the trendline is moving

   A. upward
   B. downward
   C. sideways
   D. unpredictably

8. From a chartist's (technical analyst's) viewpoint, which of the following statements is true?

   A. Once a trendline is established, the price movement of a stock usually follows the trendline.
   B. More odd-lot buying than selling is bullish.
   C. Heavy volume in a declining market is bullish.
   D. Light volume in an advancing market is bullish.

9. Proponents of which of the following technical theories assume that small investors are usually wrong?

   A. Breadth-of-market theory
   B. Short-interest theory
   C. Volume of trading theory
   D. Odd-lot theory

10. Changes in which of the following industries would be considered a leading indicator of economic growth?

    A. Unemployment
    B. Natural gas
    C. Retailing
    D. New housing

Answers & Rationale

1. **A.** The annual economic output of a nation (all of the goods and services produced by the people, businesses and government units within it) is known as its gross domestic product.

2. **B.** A fundamental analyst would be interested in evaluating the intrinsic value of a particular stock. Fundamental analysis is a study of the overall economy, industry conditions and the financial condition and management of a particular company.

3. **A.** The balance sheet formula is:

   Assets = Liabilities + Shareholders' equity

4. **C.** The narrowest measure of the market is the Dow Jones Industrial Average, which charts the performance of 30 industrial stocks.

5. **A.** The NYSE Composite Index is based on the prices of all common stocks listed on the Exchange.

6. **D.** Standard & Poor's 500 stock index is based on the prices of 400 industrial, 20 transportation, 40 financial, and 40 public utility common stocks.

7. **C.** If a market is staying within a narrow price range, it is said to be consolidating.

8. **A.** A trendline connects the reaction lows in an uptrend and the rally highs in a downtrend. Once established, trendlines are not easily halted or reversed.

9. **D.** Odd-lot trading typically is done by small investors. Followers of the odd-lot theory act on the belief that small investors invariably buy and sell at the wrong times.

10. **D.** The issuance of more building permits (new housing) is considered by most economists to be a leading indicator of economic growth.

15

Ethics, Recommendations and Taxation

OVERVIEW

Providing suitable investment recommendations for customers is a critical aspect of a registered representative's role in a customer relationship. In addition to adhering to strict ethical standards, the representative must base appropriate investment recommendations on a customer's:

- financial objectives
- financial status
- investment constraints
- tax situation

Ethics in the Securities Industry

Ethical Business Practices

The securities industry is governed by a very strong code of ethics. Unacceptable behavior is subject to sanctions ranging from fines and reprimands to expulsion from the industry or jail. Business behavior and practices are measured against clear standards for fairness and equity.

Securities industry regulators work to prevent and detect unethical behavior. Investigators regularly examine activity at all levels—from large firms to investment advisers to registered reps to individual investors. Even the most junior of employees is expected to adhere to high standards of business ethics and commercial honor in dealing with the public, customers, broker-dealer firms and the industry.

Corporate Ethics and Responsibility

The rules that guide relationships between members of the securities industry and all other participants are set by the states, the North American Securities Administrators Association (NASAA), the NASD, the SEC, the MSRB and other regulatory bodies and exchanges throughout the country. The federal securities acts, state laws, NASAA's *Statement of Policy on Unethical Business Practices of Investment Advisers*, *NASD Manual*, *NYSE Constitution and Rules* and various other legislative acts governing securities all contain guidelines for acceptable behavior. It is the responsibility of broker-dealers, investment advisers, registered reps and others in the securities industry to be familiar with and follow these guidelines.

One part of corporate responsibility for ethical behavior involves a commitment to self-regulation. It is every broker-dealer's duty to supervise all of its associated persons. Each firm must have a written procedures manual and must designate a supervisor (principal) responsible for enforcing its rules.

The principal must review and approve all correspondence and keep a record of all securities transactions and correspondence. Member firms must regularly review all branch office activities to detect and discipline any individuals who engage in unethical behavior. Member firms' compliance departments are generally at the center of such reviews.

Employee Ethics and Responsibility

The various federal and state securities regulations, the NASD Conduct Rules and other laws cover employees as well as broker-dealers. Both producer and nonproducer employees are responsible for ensuring that their activities fall within the guidelines set by regulators and by their firms.

Many firms view the regulations as minimum standards and set stricter policies for internal behavior. Employees are responsible for knowing their firms' particular policies. Even a well-intentioned employee of a broker-dealer can inadvertently violate the regulations.

 For Example: A customer requests that an employee deliver a security in person however, to by-pass the time and expense of registration and registered-mail delivery; in most firms such a delivery is strictly prohibited.

Customer Ethics and Responsibility

Practices that provide an unfair advantage to investors over the general public are strictly prohibited. Insider trading is an example. It is the individual investor's responsibility to abide by the regulations that guide customer ethics.

A customer also should make full and honest disclosure to her registered representative or investment adviser. This information is all the representative or adviser has on which to base recommendations. A customer who fails to disclose relevant information jeopardizes the representative's or adviser's career. A customer's failure to provide information is a red flag to compliance departments.

Prohibited Practices

The following practices in customer dealings are prohibited at all times.

Manipulative and Fraudulent Devices

NASD member firms are strictly prohibited from using manipulative, deceptive or other fraudulent tactics or methods to induce a security's sale or purchase. The statute of limitations under the act of 1934 is three years from the alleged is manipulation and within one year of discovering it. No dollar limit is placed on damages in lawsuits based on allegations of manipulation.

Outside Business Activity

An associated person cannot work for any business other than his member firm or engage in private securities transactions without his employing broker-dealer's knowledge and consent. The NASD's Conduct Rules define a **private securities transaction** as any sale of securities outside an associated person's regular business and his employing member. Private securities transaction are also known as **selling away**.

Notification. If an associated person wishes to enter into a private securities transaction or outside employment, that person must:

- provide prior written notice to his employer;
- describe in detail the proposed transaction;
- describe in detail his proposed role in the transaction; and
- disclose whether he has or may receive compensation for the transaction.

If the associated person wishes to enter into the transaction or business activity for compensation, the employing member may approve or disapprove the associated person's participation. If the member approves the participation, it must treat the transaction as if it is being done on its own behalf by entering the transaction on its own books and supervising the associated person during the transaction. If the member disapproves the transaction, the associated person may not participate in it.

If the associated person has not received or will not receive compensation for the private securities transaction, the employing member must acknowledge that it has received written notification and may require the associated person to adhere to specified conditions during his participation.

Transactions that the associated person enters into on behalf of immediate family members and for which the associated person receives no compensation are excluded from the definition of private securities transactions. Also excluded are personal transactions in investment company and variable annuity securities.

A passive investment, such as the purchase of a limited partnership unit, is not considered an outside business activity, even if the purchaser receives money as a result of the investment. An associated person may make a passive investment for his own account without providing written notice to or receiving written approval from the employing broker-dealer.

Recommendations

Investment recommendations must be consistent with customer needs, financial capability and objectives. Investment recommendations should be in a customer's best interest, not the broker's. Each investment should be explained fully, including its risks. At no time should the customer own an investment that could put her at risk beyond her financial capacity.

Fair Dealing

The NASD's Conduct Rules and the laws of most states require broker-dealers, registered reps and investment advisers to inquire into a customer's financial situation before making any recommendation to buy, sell or exchange securities. This includes determining the client's other security holdings, income, expenses and financial goals and objectives.

The following activities violate the fair dealing rules:

- recommending any investment that isn't suitable for the customer's financial situation and risk tolerance;
- short-term trading of mutual funds;
- setting up fictitious accounts to transact business that otherwise would be prohibited;
- making unauthorized transactions or use of funds;
- recommending purchases that are inconsistent with the customer's ability to pay; and
- committing fraudulent acts, such as forgery and the omission or mis-statement of material facts.

Excessive Trading

Excessive trading in a customer's account to generate commissions, rather than to help achieve the customer's stated investment objectives, is an abuse of fiduciary responsibility known as *churning*. Churning can take the form of either excessive frequency or excessive size of transactions.

To prevent such abuses, self-regulatory organizations require that a principal of the member firm review all accounts, especially those in which a registered rep or an investment adviser has discretionary authority.

Influencing Employees of Other Firms

Broker-dealers cannot distribute business-related compensation, either cash or noncash gifts or gratuities, to the employees of other member firms. However, an offeror may give other firms' employees some form of compensation without violating the rules if:

- the compensation is not conditional on sales or promises of sales;
- it has the employing member's prior approval; and

- the compensation's total value does not exceed the annual limit set by the NASD Board of Governors (currently $100 per year) or the MSRB (currently $100 per year).

Employment Contracts. This rule does not apply to legitimate employment contracts in which an employee of one firm supplies or performs services for another firm. The leasing of another firm's employee is acceptable provided a written employment agreement specifies the employment duties and compensation and the person's employer, the temporary employer and the employee give their written consent.

Selling Dividends

It is improper to recommend that an investor buy mutual fund shares just before a dividend distribution. The fund shares' market value will decrease by the distribution amount, and the customer will incur a tax liability on the distribution. A registered rep is forbidden to encourage an investor to purchase shares before a distribution because of this tax liability, and doing so is known as **selling dividends**.

Breakpoint Sales

In a breakpoint sale, a customer unknowingly buys investment company shares in an amount just below an amount that would qualify the investment for a reduction in sales charges. As a result, the customer pays a higher dollar amount in sales charges, which reduces the number of shares purchased and increases the cost basis per share.

Encouraging a customer to purchase in such a manner, or remaining silent when a customer unknowingly requests such a transaction, is unethical and violates the Conduct Rules.

Borrowing and Lending

Registered reps and investment advisers must not borrow money or securities from a customer unless the customer is a bank, a broker-dealer or another financial institution in the business of lending money.

Registered reps and investment advisers may not lend money or securities to a customer. This prohibition does not include broker-dealers making margin loans or investment advisers lending money as part of their normal business practices.

Misrepresentations

Registered reps and investment advisers may not misrepresent themselves or their services to clients or potential clients. Included in this prohibition are misrepresentations covering:

- qualifications, experience and education
- nature of services offered
- fees to be charged

It is a misrepresentation to either inaccurately state or fail to state a material fact regarding any of the above.

Research Reports

Research reports recommending the purchase or sale of securities must be approved by the firm's supervisory analyst. An investment adviser or a broker-dealer is prohibited from presenting to a client research reports, analyses or recommendations prepared by other persons or firms without disclosing the fact that the adviser did not prepare them. An adviser or a broker-dealer may base a recommendation on reports or analyses prepared by others, as long as these reports are not represented as the adviser's or broker-dealer's own.

Guarantees and Sharing in Customer Accounts

Broker-dealers, investment advisers and registered reps cannot guarantee any customer against a loss or guarantee that he will achieve a gain in his account. Members, advisers and representatives are also prohibited from sharing in any profits or losses in a customer's account. An exception is made if a joint account has received the member firm's prior written approval and the registered representative shares in the profits and losses only to the extent of his proportionate contribution to the account.

If the member firm authorizes such a **shared account**, any or all such sharing must be directly proportionate to the financial contributions each party makes. If a member or an associated person shares an account with a member of that person's immediate family, directly proportionate sharing of profits and losses is not mandatory.

Immediate family members include parents, mother-in-law or father-in-law, husband or wife, children and any relative to whom the officer or employee in question contributes financial support.

Misuse of Nonpublic Information

Every investment adviser must establish, maintain and enforce written policies and procedures to prevent the use of nonpublic inside information.

Fiduciary Information

During the normal course of business, employees of member firms will have access to proprietary information regarding individual customers and securities issuers. Such information is to be treated with strict propriety.

Confidentiality of Customer Information. Broker-dealer and investment adviser employees may not divulge any personal information about customers without a customer's express permission. This includes security positions, personal and financial details and trading intentions.

Numbered Accounts. A customer may have a designated account assigned a number or a letter rather than a name if the member has a signed statement from the customer claiming ownership of that account.

Confidentiality of Issuer Information. When a member broker-dealer serves an issuer as a paying agent, a transfer agent or an underwriter or in another similar capacity, the member has established a **fiduciary** relationship with that issuer. In this role, the member may obtain confidential information.

The member cannot use the information it obtains through its fiduciary role unless the securities issuer specifically asks and authorizes the member to do so.

✓ *For Example:* A member firm acting as transfer agent for a corporation's common stock cannot solicit the stock owners for its own purposes. It may contact them on behalf of the issuer if the issuer requests and authorizes such contact.

Other Unethical Trading Practices

Transactions intended to portray an artificial market for a stock are strictly prohibited.

Painting the Tape. When one party sells stock to another with the understanding that the stock will be repurchased later in the day, it is known as *painting the tape*. The intent of such transactions is to make it appear that far more interest in a stock exists than actually does.

Matching. Matching transactions in an attempt to create the impression of a hot market for a stock is prohibited. Matching involves two people working in collusion, where one customer enters an order to buy while a second person enters an order to sell the same stock, at the same time, under the same terms, through the same broker-dealer. The broker-dealer crosses the buy and sell orders and reports the trade on the Consolidated Tape, thus showing a trade where one really did not occur.

Broker-dealers must not enter orders for the purchase or sale of securities with the knowledge that contra orders for the same stock, in the same amount, at approximately the same price have been or will be placed for the same customer or for different parties working in concert.

Excessive Trading by Broker-Dealers. When a broker-dealer, acting alone or in concert with customers, suddenly increases its own trading in a particular issue, it may be accused of excessive trading. If the firm's transaction volume in a given stock is clearly out of proportion with the firm's financial resources, or is out of line with the stock's normal daily trading volume, the firm may be suspected of trading excessively to induce public trades.

Participating in Rings or Pools. Broker-dealers cannot participate directly or indirectly in any pool, ring, syndicate or other joint account venture formed for the purpose of rigging or otherwise influencing market prices.

Payments Designed to Influence Market Prices. NASD member firms are prohibited from attempting to influence the market price of securities by paying for favorable reviews, articles or other mentions in newspapers or other financial publications. This prohibition does not apply to paid advertisements placed in these publications and marked as such.

Spreading False and Misleading Information. Broker-dealers must not promote nor disseminate false or misleading information.

Front-Running. "Front-running" refers to situations in which a broker-dealer or associated person is aware of an order to buy or sell and buys or sells the same, or substantially same, security for the firm's own account on the same side of the market as the customer's order before showing the customer's order to the market.

Joint Participation in Hidden Accounts. Broker-dealers are prohibited from holding any direct or indirect interest in any joint account without disclosing the full particulars of such an account to the NASD.

Capping. Any attempt to place selling pressure on a stock to keep a price low or move it lower is known as *capping* and is prohibited.

Summary of Ethical Practices

Ethical behavior in the securities industry can be summarized as follows:

- Do not cheat or steal.
- Do not fabricate information or lie.
- Disclose any conflicts of interest.
- Know what investments are suitable for your customers' needs.

Criminal Penalties

If a person is convicted of willfully violating federal securities regulations, or of *knowingly* making false or misleading statements in a registration document, that person can be fined up to $1 million, sentenced to prison for not more than 10 years or both. The maximum fine is $2 million for other than a natural person.

Assistance to Foreign Authorities The SEC is pledged to help foreign regulatory authorities investigate any person who has violated, is violating or is about to violate any laws or rules relating to securities matters.

Know Your Customer

The NYSE requires brokers to know their customers. This implies understanding a customer's financial status (net worth and net income) and investment objectives. It is a registered rep's responsibility to perform due diligence to determine the validity of a customer's information.

In addition, the MSRB requires that the rep inquire into the customer's tax status. The Chicago Board Options Exchange (CBOE) requires the registered rep to ask into the customer's investment experience as well.

Investment Considerations

A customer's nonfinancial considerations are often at least as important as his financial concerns. Therefore, a registered rep or an investment adviser needs to know the following:

- customer's age
- customer's marital status
- number and ages of customer's dependents
- customer's employment
- employment of customer's family members
- customer's current and future financial needs

A customer's risk tolerance and investment motivation are other important considerations that will shape his portfolio. To understand a customer's aptitude for investment, the representative or adviser should ask her customer the following questions:

- What kind of risks can you afford to take?
- How liquid must your investments be?
- How important are tax considerations?
- Are you seeking long-term or short-term investments?
- What is your investment experience?
- What types of investments do you currently hold?

Customer Investment Outlook People have many reasons for investing. Some of the basic financial objectives customers may have are outlined below.

Preservation of Capital. For many people, the most important investment objective is to preserve their capital. In general, when clients speak of *safety*, they usually mean preservation of capital from losses.

Current Income. Many investors, particularly those on fixed incomes, want to generate current income from their investments. Corporate bonds, municipal bonds, government and agency securities, income-oriented mutual funds, some stocks (including utilities and real estate investment trusts—REITs), money-market funds, annuities and some direct participation programs (DPPs) are among the investments that can contribute current income through dividend or interest payments.

Capital Growth. "Growth" refers to an increase in an investment's value over time. This can come from increases in the security's value, the reinvestment of dividends and income, or both. The most common growth-oriented investments are common stock and common stock mutual funds.

Tax Advantages. Investors often seek ways to reduce their taxes. Some vehicles, like individual retirement accounts (IRAs) and annuities, allow earnings to accumulate tax deferred (an investor pays no taxes until he withdraws money from his account). Other products, like municipal bonds, offer tax-free interest income.

Portfolio Diversification. Investors with portfolios concentrated in one or a few securities or investments are exposed to much higher risks. For them, portfolio diversification can be an important objective. These customers can be retirees with large profit-sharing distributions of one company's stock or investors with all of their money invested in certificates of deposits (CDs) or U.S. government bonds.

Liquidity. Some people want immediate access to their money at all times. A product is liquid if a customer can sell it quickly at a fair market price. Stock, for instance, has varying degrees of liquidity, while DPPs, annuities and bank CDs generally are considered illiquid. Real estate is the classic example of an illiquid investment because of the time and money it takes to convert it into cash.

Speculation. A customer may want to speculate—that is, try to earn much higher than average returns in exchange for higher than average risks.

✓ *For Example:* Ed, a somewhat cautious investor, and Joe, a more speculative investor, both believe Acme Telephone Co. (ATC) stock, trading for $30, will increase to $40 over the next six months. Ed buys 100 shares of the stock and pays $3,000. Joe buys 20 calls, expiring in six months with a strike price of 35 or 1½ each, or $3,000. In six months, if ATC trades for $40, Ed's investment will be worth $40 per share, or $4,000, an increase of 33 percent on his investment. Joe's 20 calls will be worth $5 each, for a total of $10,000 ($5 x 20 calls), more than triple his original investment. Had the stock remained at $30, Ed's investment would still be worth $3,000 and Joe's would be worthless.

Figure 15.1 illustrates an investment pyramid, used to classify investor objectives and investment vehicles.

FIGURE 15.1   The Investment Pyramid

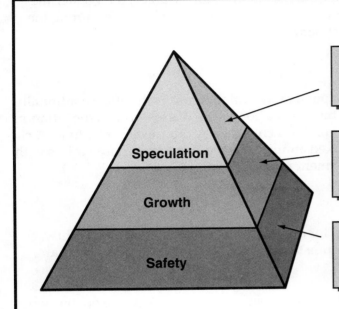

Speculative stocks and stock options, low-rated debt securities, precious metals, commodities and futures, speculative limited partnerships, speculative mutual funds

Growth and small-capitalization stocks, stock options, nonbank-grade bonds, growth-oriented limited partnerships, growth stock mutual funds, commodities funds, variable annuities

Cash, money-market funds, certificates of deposit, U.S. Treasury securities, bank-grade corporate and municipal bonds, some real estate blue-chip stocks, blue-chip stock and bond mutual funds

Analyzing Financial Risks and Rewards

Suitability

Because all investments involve trade-offs, the investment adviser's or registered rep's task is to select securities that provide the right balance between investor characteristics on the one hand and investment capabilities on the other. Selecting suitable investments to meet investor needs is both an art and a science.

Unsuitable Trades

Occasionally, a customer asks a registered rep to enter a trade that the rep feels is unsuitable. It is the rep's responsibility to explain why the trade might not be appropriate for the customer. If the customer insists on entering the transaction, the registered rep should have the customer sign a statement acknowledging that the rep recommended against the trade, and the rep should mark the order ticket "unsolicited."

Investment Risks

In general terms, the greater the risk an investor assumes, the greater the potential for reward. Several risks must be considered in determining the suitability of various investment types.

Inflation Risk

Also known as **purchasing power risk**, inflation risk is the effect continually rising prices have on investments. If a bond's yield is lower than the inflation rate, the purchasing power of the client's money diminishes over time. A client who buys a bond or a fixed annuity may be able to purchase far less with her money when the investment matures.

Capital Risk

Capital risk is the potential for an investor to lose all of his money, his invested capital, under circumstances unrelated to an issuer's financial strength.

 For Example: When an option expires out-of-the-money, the option owner loses all of his capital invested in the option even though the underlying security may be solvent.

Timing Risk

Timing can be everything. Even an investment in the soundest company with the most profit potential might do poorly simply because the investment was timed incorrectly. The risk to an investor of buying or selling at the wrong time and incurring losses or lower gains is known as *timing risk*.

Interest Rate Risk

Interest rate risk is the sensitivity of investment's value to fluctuations in interest rates. The term is generally associated with bonds because bond prices change with interest rate movements.

Reinvestment Risk

When interest rates decline, it is difficult for bond investors to invest the proceeds from redemptions to maintain the same level of income without increasing their credit or market risks.

 For Example: When interest rates decline, people with mortgages often refinance their mortgages at lower interest rates. When this happens, investors who own mortgage-backed securities receive their investment principal much sooner than they expected and cannot invest the dollars for a comparable return without accepting a greater amount of risk.

Call Risk

Related to reinvestment risk, call risk is the risk that a bond might be called before maturity and an investor will be unable to reinvest her principal at a comparable rate of return. When interest rates are falling, bonds with higher coupon rates are most likely to be called. Investors concerned about call risk should look for call protection—a period of time during which a bond cannot be called. Most corporate and municipal issuers generally provide some years of call protection.

Market Risk

Both stocks and bonds involve some degree of market risk—that is, the risk that investors may lose some of their principal due to price volatility in the overall market (known as **systematic risk**).

Bond prices fluctuate with changing interest rates, and an inverse relationship between bond prices and bond yields exists: as bond yields rise, bond prices decline, and vice versa.

Deep discount bonds are particularly responsive to changes in interest rates. Compared to other bonds, deep discount bonds tend to appreciate faster as interest rates fall and drop faster as interest rates rise. Also, the longer a bond's maturity, the more volatile it is in response to interest rate changes.

Credit Risk

Credit risk, also called **financial risk** or **default risk**, is the danger of losing all or part of one's invested principal through an issuer's failure. Credit risk varies with the investment product. Bonds backed by the federal government or municipalities have low credit risk. Long-term bonds involve more credit risk than short-term bonds because of the future's uncertainty.

Liquidity Risk

The risk that a client might not be able to sell his investment quickly at a fair market price is known as *liquidity risk*. The marketability of the securities you recommend must be consistent with the client's liquidity needs. Government bonds, for instance, are sold easily; DPPs, on the other hand are illiquid and extremely difficult to sell. Municipal securities have regional markets rather than a national market; therefore, they may be less marketable than more widely held securities.

Legislative Risk

Congress has the power to change laws affecting securities. The risk that such a change in law might affect an investment adversely is known as *legislative risk* or **political risk**. When recommending suitable investments, warn clients of any pending changes in the law that may affect those investments.

✓ *For Example:* By changing the tax consequences of passive income from DPPs, Congress destroyed many deep tax shelter investment programs.

Portfolio Management

A portfolio is an individual's or business's combined investment holdings. A portfolio of securities offers investors **diversification**.

Many things influence a portfolio's makeup, including personal and market factors. A portfolio of securities appropriate for a 25-year-old unmarried man may not be appropriate for a 45-year-old married man with two children in college or a 65-year-old woman facing retirement.

Defensive Strategies

Defensive investment strategies may have growth or income as an objective, but safety of principal tends to be the first priority. Such portfolios often are invested in blue chip stocks with moderate or low volatility and AAA or government bonds.

Aggressive Strategies

Aggressive investment strategies attempt to maximize investment returns by assuming higher risks. Such strategies include:

- selecting highly volatile stocks
- buying securities on margin
- using put and call option strategies

Balanced Strategies

Most investors adopt a combination of aggressive and defensive strategies when making decisions about the securities in their portfolios. A **balanced,** or **mixed, portfolio** holds securities of many types.

Modern Portfolio Theory

Modern portfolio theory is an approach that attempts to quantify and control portfolio risk. It differs from traditional securities analysis in that it emphasizes determining the relationship between risk and reward in the total portfolio rather than analyzing specific securities. This is derived from the **Capital Asset Pricing Model (CAPM).**

Risk Management Where investments are concerned, risk is normally associated with losing money. Investors use many techniques to reduce the potential for portfolio losses. Some of the most common are discussed below.

Diversification. Diversification—that is, buying different types of securities in various economic sectors—is a widely used investment strategy. A portfolio can be diversified in many ways, including:

- type of instrument (equity, debt, packaged and so on)
- industry
- companies within an industry
- length of maturity
- investment rating
- geography

By mixing industries and types of securities, investors spread their risk.

✓ *For Example:* If an investor's portfolio is composed predominantly of medical stocks, a government attempt to socialize medicine could devastate the portfolio's value.

Dollar Cost Averaging. Dollar cost averaging involves periodic purchases of a fixed dollar amount in one or more common stocks or mutual funds. In a fluctuating market, the average *cost* of the stock purchased in this manner is always less than the average market *price*. Dollar cost averaging does not guarantee against a loss (and it is fraudulent to imply so), but it does help control the cost of investing.

Constant Ratio Plan. In a constant ratio plan, an investor buys or sells securities in a manner that keeps the portfolio balanced between equity and debt securities. The investor initially sets an equity-to-debt ratio, such as 60 percent equity and 40 percent debt, and buys or sells stocks and bonds to maintain the ratio.

Constant Dollar Plan. The constant dollar plan's primary goal is to buy and sell securities so that a set dollar amount remains invested at all times.

✓ *For Example:* If a customer wants to keep his portfolio at a constant level of $100,000 and if his portfolio's value reaches $110,000, he will sell $10,000 worth of securities. Conversely, if his portfolio slips to $95,000, he will buy $5,000 worth of securities. This forces the investor to sell when the market is high and buy when it is low.

By using this technique, the client sells as prices rise and buys as prices fall, thus becoming the first one to sell out of a bull market and the first one to buy into a bear market.

Measuring Stock Price Volatility   Volatility is the speed and degree with which a stock's price will change. The two most common barometers of volatility analysts use in evaluating stocks are the alpha and the beta.

Alpha. A stock's alpha is a measure of its projected rate of change in price independent of market-related factors. If all other factors are equal and the market remains at the same level for a year, the price of a stock with an alpha of 1.5 could be expected to increase by 50 percent based solely on the strength of the company's business prospects.

Beta. A stock's beta is a measure of its price volatility compared to the overall market. The S&P 500 index is commonly used as the benchmark for overall market performance. Stocks with a beta of 1 move with the market; stocks with a beta greater than 1 move more than the market; stocks with a beta less than 1 move less than the market.

✓ **For Example:** If the Standard & Poor's index increases by 10 percent, a stock with a beta of 1 increases by about 10 percent; a stock with a beta of 1.5 increases by about 15 percent; and a stock with a beta of .75 increases by about 7.5 percent.

The higher the beta coefficient, the more volatile the stock. High betas imply greater profits during rising markets and greater potential losses during declining markets. High beta stocks are usually considered aggressive, and low beta stocks are considered defensive.

If the beta coefficient is. . .	The stock's return will probably. . .
exactly 1	move exactly with the market
less than 1	move less than the market moves
greater than 1	move more than the market moves

Federal and State Taxation

Regressive and Progressive Taxes

Taxes are labeled as either **regressive** or **progressive**. Regressive taxes, such as sales, excise, payroll, property and gasoline taxes, are levied equally regardless of income, thus representing a smaller portion of income for wealthy taxpayers than taxpayers with lower incomes. Because low-income families spend a larger percentage of their incomes than they save or invest, regressive taxes take a larger fraction of the income of poor people than of rich people.

Income Taxes   Progressive taxes, such as estate and income taxes, increase the tax rate as income increases. Progressive taxes affect people with high incomes more than people with low incomes.

Earned Income. Earned income includes salary, bonuses and income derived from active participation in a trade or business.

Passive Income. Passive income and losses come from rental property, limited partnerships and enterprises (regardless of business structure) in which an individual is not actively involved. For the general partner, income from a limited partnership is earned income; for the limited partner, such income is passive. Passive income is netted against passive losses to determine net taxable income. Passive losses may be used to offset passive income only.

Portfolio Income. Portfolio income includes dividends, interest and net capital gains derived from the sale of securities. No matter what the source of the income, it is taxed in the year in which it is received.

Income Tax Brackets

U.S. income tax tables are structured so that successively higher portions of a person's income are taxed at progressively higher rates.

Taxation and Investment Portfolios

Investments can generate income, capital gains or capital losses. Income and capital gains are taxed at different rates. Capital losses may offset capital gains, but if capital losses exceed capital gains, a taxpayer may use only $3,000 of net capital losses to offset income. The taxpayer may carry forward capital losses to offset capital gains in future years.

Interest Income

Interest paid on debt securities is income to the bondholder. It may or may not be taxable, depending on the type of security.

Taxable Interest Income

Corporate Bonds. Interest income from corporate bonds is taxable by federal, state and some local governments.

U.S. Government Securities. Interest income on U.S. Treasury bills, notes and bonds is exempt from state and local taxes, but is federally taxable.

Agency Issues. The interest income on most federal agency debt, like that on Treasury securities, is taxable by the federal government, but is exempt from state and local taxes. However, some issues of government agencies and government-sponsored corporations are taxable at all levels. These issues include:

- mortgage-backed securities of the Government National Mortgage Association (GNMA—Ginnie Maes);
- securities issued by the Federal National Mortgage Association (FNMA—Fannie Maes); and
- securities of the Inter-American Development Bank (IADB).

Accrued Interest. Interest income includes accrued interest an investor receives when she sells bonds between interest payment dates. The trade confirmation discloses two amounts: the amount received for the bond and the amount of accrued interest. The accrued interest is taxable income to the seller. For tax reporting, the buyer deducts the amount of accrued interest paid the seller from the total interest received to ensure that the buyer does not pay tax on that amount.

Tax-Exempt Interest Income

Municipal Securities. Interest on municipal bonds is exempt from federal taxes. Furthermore, interest from municipal obligations of U.S. territories (Puerto Rico, Guam, the Virgin Islands) is exempt from federal, state and local taxes.

Interest on a municipal bond or note normally is not taxable for residents of the state in which the bond or note is issued.

States or municipalities issue **private purpose bonds** to meet nonessential government functions. Although federally tax exempt for most taxpayers, the interest on such municipal securities is a tax preference item for the **alternative minimum tax (AMT)**, discussed later. These bonds may finance:

- single-family mortgages
- multifamily housing
- mass transit
- student loans
- water, sewer and sewage treatment facilities
- airports, docks and wharves

Taxable municipal securities may be issued to finance projects that Congress does not deem essential, such as sports arenas or convention centers. Because the interest income from such bonds is fully taxable for all taxpayers, the bonds tend to pay higher yields than other municipal securities because they have to compete with corporate bonds.

Dividend Income   Dividend income from stocks and mutual funds is taxed in the same manner as interest income from debt securities.

Dividend Income from Mutual Funds.   Owners of mutual fund shares receive dividends that represent the pass-through of dividends and interest earned on the underlying portfolio. The tax consequences depend on the types of securities in the underlying portfolio:

- Municipal bond mutual funds or unit investment trusts (UITs) distribute federally tax-free dividends to shareholders.
- Dividend distributions from taxable mutual funds are taxable in the year an investor receives them. Reinvested dividends are also taxable in the year they are distributed.

Foreign Securities

The interest and dividend income from a foreign investment, such as stock issued by a foreign corporation or bonds issued by a foreign government, is taxed by the country in which the investor is a citizen. A U.S. citizen who owns bonds or stock issued in another country is liable for state and federal taxes, but not foreign taxes, on interest and dividend income received.

If foreign tax has been withheld on a distribution of dividends or interest from a foreign security, a U.S. citizen is eligible for an income tax credit for the amount withheld. For most foreign securities transactions, the credit is 15 percent of the amount withheld.

Taxable on Receipt

Interest and dividends are taxable only in the year they are *received*. Investors do not owe taxes on dividends or interest declared or accrued until they receive the money.

Capital Gains and Losses   The sale of securities can result in a capital gain or a capital loss. A capital gain occurs when a security is sold for a price higher than the cost basis; if the selling price is lower than the cost basis, a capital loss occurs.

Adjusting Cost Basis

An investment's cost basis is used to determine whether a taxable gain or a tax-deductible loss occurs when an asset is sold. Because many things affect an asset's cost basis, the IRS allows the cost basis to be adjusted for such things as stock splits and stock dividends.

✔ **For Example:** An investor buys 100 shares of RST at $55. Later, the company declares a stock dividend, and the investor receives 10 more shares. His total investment remains $5,500, but he now owns 110 shares of RST. The investor's adjusted cost basis per share is now $50.

Capital Gains. A capital gain occurs when capital assets (securities, real estate and tangible property) are sold at prices that exceed the adjusted cost basis. Usually, computing the capital gain or loss on an asset is a simple matter of comparing the purchase price with the selling price less commissions.

Capital Losses. A capital loss occurs when capital assets are sold at prices that are less than the adjusted cost basis.

Net Capital Gains and Losses. To calculate tax liability, a taxpayer must first add all short-term capital gains and losses for the year. Then, he separately adds all long-term capital gains and losses. Finally, the taxpayer offsets the totals to determine his net capital gain or loss for the year. If the result is a net capital gain, it is included in gross income and taxed at the same rate as earned income (currently, the capital gains tax is capped at 20 percent). Net capital losses are deductible against earned income to a maximum of $3,000 per year. Any capital losses not deducted in a taxable year may be carried forward indefinitely to offset capital gains in future years.

Determining which Shares to Sell. An investor holding identical securities with different acquisition dates and cost bases may determine which shares to sell by electing one of three accounting methods: first in, first out (FIFO), last in, first out (LIFO) or share identification. If the investor fails to choose, the IRS assumes the investor liquidates shares on a FIFO basis.

Share identification is the most frequently used method of identifying per-share cost basis because it is the most flexible of the three methods. The investor keeps track of the cost of each share purchased and specifies which shares to sell based on his tax needs.

 For Example: If an investor needs to report a loss, she could sell shares with a higher cost base than the current market value; if she can use a taxable gain, she could sell lower cost base shares.

Wash Sales

An investor may not use capital losses to offset gains or income if the investor sells a security at a loss and purchases the same or a substantially identical security within 30 days before or after the trade date establishing the loss. The sale at a loss and the repurchase within this period is a wash sale. (See Figure 15.2).

The loss that was disallowed, however, is added to the repurchased shares cost basis.

 For Example: An investor purchases 100 shares for $50. One year later, the investor sells the shares for $40. Fifteen days after the sale, he repurchases 100 shares of the same stock for $42. His new cost basis is $52 because the $10 loss that was disallowed is added to the repurchase price of $42.

FIGURE 15.2   Wash Sale

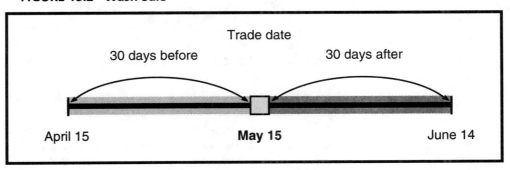

Substantially identical securities include stock rights, call options, the exercise of short-term deep in-the-money puts, warrants and convertible securities of the same issue. The IRS compares three qualities of debt securities in determining whether they are substantially identical: the maturity, coupon and issuer. A bond is substantially identical if all three qualities of the bond sold at a loss and the newly purchased bond are the same.

The wash sale rule applies only to realized losses; it does not apply to realized gains.

Adjusting the Cost Basis of Bonds

Bonds Purchased at a Premium. The investor who buys a bond at a premium, whether as a new issue or in the secondary market, must **amortize** the premium amount over the life of the bond. Amortization is the process of decreasing the investor's cost basis over time, normally on a straight-line basis. An investor usually pays a premium for a bond in the secondary market if it has a higher coupon than more recently issued bonds. The annual amount of amortization is deductible against interest received on corporate and government bonds. However, because municipal bonds pay tax-free interest, the Internal Revenue Service does not allow investors to deduct any amortization.

Any bond bought at a premium and held to maturity generates no capital loss. If a bond is sold before it matures, its cost basis must be adjusted by the amortized premium amount. While the interest on municipal bonds is tax exempt, buying and selling bonds can result in taxable capital gains or deductible capital losses.

✓ *For Example:* An investor bought a Kenosha Harbor Authority bond at 108 when the bond had 16 years to maturity. Seven years later, the investor sold the bond at 105. To determine the investor's adjusted cost basis, first calculate the annual amount of the amortized premium. The $80 premium is amortized based on a maturity of 16 years; thus, the annual amortization amount is $80 divided by 16, which equals $5. Because the investor sold the bond after seven years, only $35 (7 × $5) of the premium was amortized. The adjusted cost basis is the investor's original price of $1,080 minus the $35 amortized premium, which equals $1,045. The investor sold the bond for $1,050, resulting in a $5 capital gain per bond.

Bonds Purchased at a Discount. When bonds are issued at a discount, they are known as **original issue discount (OID)** bonds, and the difference between the discounted purchase price and the par value is **accreted**. Accretion is the process of increasing the cost basis over time. The issuer determines the annual accretion amount, normally on a straight-line basis. Owners of corporate and government OID bonds are taxed each year on the amount of the discount accreted during the year, regardless of changes in market value during the year. The amount accreted on a municipal OID bond is exempt from federal income tax.

✓ ***For Example:*** Joe bought an OID bond with 16 years to maturity for $920. Seven years later, he sold the bond at $950. To determine his adjusted cost basis, first calculate the annual amount of the accreted discount. The $80 discount is accreted based on a maturity of 16 years; thus, the annual accretion amount is $80 divided by 16, which equals $5. Because Joe sold the bond after seven years, only $35 (7 x $5) of the discount was accreted. The adjusted cost basis is Joe's original price of $920 plus the $35 accreted discount, which equals $955. He sold the bond for $950, resulting in a $5 capital loss per bond.

If an OID bond is held until maturity, 100 percent of the discount will have been accreted and the investor will have no taxable capital gain.

The cost basis of a **secondary market discount** bond—that is, one bought at a discount in the secondary market that is not an OID bond—is not adjusted. If the investor holds the bond to maturity, the discount is taxed as ordinary income. If the investor sells the bond in the secondary market, the gain or loss is determined by the difference between the bond's purchase price and sale price.

These rules do not apply to short-term debt obligations and U.S. savings bonds.

Donated (Gifted) and Inherited Securities

Gifts. When a donor makes a gift of securities, the cost basis to the recipient (the *donee*) is the donor's cost basis.

✓ ***For Example:*** In 1990, Joe Smith bought 1,000 shares of COD at $24 per share, for a total a cost of $24,000. In 1995, when COD was trading at $32.50, Joe gave those 1,000 shares to his daughter. When she sells the shares, her cost basis is Joe's cost basis on the date of his original purchase—$24 per share—not the market value on the date of the gift.

Inherited Securities. When a person dies and leaves securities to his heirs, the cost basis to the recipients is the fair market value on the date of the owner's death.

✓ *For Example:* Again, in 1990 Joe Smith bought 1,000 shares of COD at $24 per share for a total cost of $24,00. In 1995, when COD was trading at $32.50, Joe died. His daughter is Joe's sole heir and inherits the 1,000 shares upon his death. When she sells the shares, her cost basis is the fair market value on the date of Joe's death—$32.50 per share—not Joe's original purchase cost.

Margin Expenses   Margin interest is a tax-deductible expense. The one exception is interest expenses incurred in the purchase of municipal securities. Because municipal interest income is federally tax exempt, the IRS does not allow taxpayers to claim deductions for the margin interest expense on municipal securities.

Investors can deduct interest expenses for other securities to the extent they do not exceed their net investment incomes, which include interest income, dividends and all capital gains.

Alternative Minimum Tax

Congress enacted the AMT to make certain that high-income taxpayers do not escape paying taxes.

Tax Preference Items. Certain items receive favorable tax treatment. These items must be added back into taxable income for the AMT. They include:

- accelerated depreciation on property placed in service after 1986;
- certain costs associated with DPPs, such as research and development costs and intangible drilling costs;
- local tax and interest on investments that do not generate income;
- tax-exempt interest on private purpose municipal bonds issued after August 7, 1986; and
- incentive stock options exceeding their fair market value.

Corporate Taxes

Corporations are major investors in securities. Some of the Internal Revenue Code (IRC) provisions affecting corporations as investors include the following:

- **Dividend exclusion rule.** Dividends paid from one corporation to another are 70 percent exempt from taxation. A corporation that receives dividends on stocks of other domestic corporations, therefore, pays taxes on only 30 percent of the dividends received. This provision

FIGURE 15.3   Effect of the Corporate Dividend Exclusion

	Stated Return	Percentage Excluded from Taxation	Remaining Percentage that is Subject to Taxation	Tax Rate on That Amount	Net Aftertax Yield
Corporate bond	9%	0%	100%	35%	5.85%
Preferred stock ($100 par)	8%	70%	30%	35%	7.16%*

* 70% of 8% stated return is tax free	5.60%
30% of 8% is taxed at 35%, leaving an additional	
aftertax yield of 30% x 8% x 65%	1.56%
For a total aftertax yield of:	7.16%

encourages corporations to invest in common and preferred stock of other U.S. corporations. Figure 15.3 compares the effect the 70 percent dividend exclusion has on the yield a corporation receives from an investment in another corporation's stock versus its bonds.

- **Municipal securities**. Like individual taxpayers, corporations do not pay federal taxes on income received from municipal bonds.

Figure 15.3 illustrates the affect of the corporate dividend exclusion.

Summary

Ethical behavior in the securities business means keeping the customer's interests first. Any representation or misrepresentation of facts to induce a customer transaction, or any misappropriation of customer funds or securities is not ethical behavior.

Even recommendations made with the best of intentions can go wrong, and thereby be misconstrued as unethical behavior by some. All investment recommendations, therefore, must be suitable for the customer.

To make suitable recommendations, a registered rep must know his customer. This includes knowing the customer's investment objectives and history, financial position and risk tolerance levels, among other things. This also means knowing the characteristics of investment alternatives and strategies that are consistent with the customer's needs and objectives.

Tax considerations will often be an important consideration in selecting an investment. Income-oriented investors, in particular, must be aware of the after-tax returns of investment alternatives. When securities are sold, the cost basis of the original investment must be calculated to determine the true tax liability.

Key Concepts

To prepare for your license exam, you should learn the following concepts.

In addition to studying these key concepts, use the Ethics, Recommendations and Taxation Hot Sheet on page 648 for further review.

accreting
alternative minimum tax (AMT)
beta coefficient
breakpoint sales
call risk
capital gain
capital loss
capital risk
CAPM
constant dollar plan
cost basis
credit risk
dollar cost averaging
earned income
financial risk
legislative risk
liquidity risk
marketability risk

market risk
Modern Portfolio Theory
nonsystematic risk
original issue discount (OID)
passive income
progressive tax
purchasing power risk
regressive tax
reinvestment risk
risk management
selling away
selling dividends
suitability
systematic risk
tax preference item
wash sale
volatility

Review Questions

1. Which of the following characteristics best define(s) the term "growth"?

   A. Increase in the value of an investment over time
   B. Increase in principal and accumulating interest and dividends over time
   C. Investments that appreciate tax deferred
   D. All of the above

2. Credit risk involves

   A. safety of principal
   B. fluctuations in overall interest rates
   C. the danger of not being able to sell the investment at a fair market price
   D. inflationary risks

3. Which of the following investments is LEAST appropriate for a client who is primarily concerned with liquidity?

   A. Preferred stock
   B. Municipal bond mutual funds
   C. Bank savings accounts
   D. Direct participation programs

4. Bondholders face the risk that the value of their bonds may fall as interest rates rise. This is known as

   A. credit risk
   B. reinvestment risk
   C. marketability risk
   D. market risk

5. Which of the following constitutes a constant dollar plan?

   A. 60 percent equities, 40 percent fixed-income investments
   B. 40 percent equities, 60 percent fixed-income investments
   C. Fixed amount in the portfolio regardless of market price
   D. Fixed amount in fixed-income investments regardless of market price

6. Which of the following bonds are totally tax exempt?

   A. Hawaii GO bonds
   B. U.S. government bonds
   C. Puerto Rico GO bonds
   D. U.S. Steel bonds

7. Max Leveridge invests $5,000 in Ohio General Telephone 9% debentures priced at 97. The bonds are

   A. federal and state tax exempt
   B. state tax exempt
   C. federal and state tax exempt if purchased by an Ohio resident
   D. fully taxable

8. Income from all of the following securities is fully taxable at the federal, state and local levels EXCEPT

   A. Ginnie Maes
   B. Treasury bonds
   C. reinvested mutual fund dividends
   D. IADB securities

9. Losses from direct participation programs can be used to offset

   A. earned income from salary or commissions
   B. portfolio income
   C. income from limited partnerships
   D. none of the above

10. Under the Securities Exchange Act of 1934, a lawsuit alleging market manipulation must be filed within

   A. three years of the activity and one year of discovering it

   B. one year of the activity and three years of discovering it

   C. five years of the activity and three years of discovering it

   D. three years of the activity and five years of discovering it

Answers & Rationale

1. **A.** "Growth" refers to an increase in the value of an investment over time. This growth can come from increases in the value of the security, the reinvestment of dividends and income, or both.

2. **A.** Credit risk (also called financial risk or default risk) involves the danger of losing all or part of one's invested principal through failure of the issuer.

3. **D.** Direct participation programs or limited partnerships are illiquid investments because there is no immediate market for them.

4. **D.** Prices of existing bonds can fluctuate with changing interest rates. There is an inverse relationship between bond prices and bond yields: as bond yields go up, bond prices go down (and vice versa).

5. **C.** The primary goal of a constant dollar plan strategy is to buy and sell securities so that a fixed dollar amount remains invested at all times.

6. **C.** Puerto Rico GO bonds are exempt from federal, state and local taxes.

7. **D.** Ohio General Telephone Company bonds are corporate bonds, which are fully taxable.

8. **B.** Treasury bonds are not taxed at the state level.

9. **C.** Passive income and losses come from rental property, limited partnerships and enterprises in which the individual is not actively involved. Therefore, losses from direct participation programs can be used to offset income from limited partnerships.

10. **A.** According to the 1934 act, the statute of limitations extends for three years from an alleged manipulative act and for one year after the manipulative act is discovered.

16

U.S. Government and State Rules and Regulations

OVERVIEW

Federal and state securities laws require proper disclosure of information to customers and establish procedures that safeguard against fraud and misrepresentation.

The major pieces of federal legislation are the Securities Act of 1933 and the Securities Exchange Act of 1934. This lesson introduces subsequent legislation that expanded or amended these basic regulations.

The securities laws at the state level are known as *blue-sky laws*; they deal with issues such as registration requirements for securities, broker-dealers, investment advisers and representatives. The Uniform Securities Act is model legislation that most states have adopted, with each state adapting the act to its specific requirements.

Insider Trading and Securities Fraud Enforcement Act of 1988

The Securities Act of 1934 prohibits insider trading, and the act of 1988 specifies penalties for insider trading and securities fraud. The illicit use of nonpublic information by insiders (officers, directors and 10 percent shareholders) subjects the insider to liability for more than just transactions in their own accounts. An insider has a fiduciary responsibility to issuers, to stockholders and to others who might be affected by trades made with insider knowledge. Investors who have suffered monetary damage because of insider trading have legal recourse against the insider and against any other party who had control over the misuse of nonpublic information.

Inside information is any information that has not been disseminated to, or is not readily available to, the general public. To determine whether information is nonpublic, the SEC considers the method by which the information is released to the public and the timing of trades relative to the public disclosure.

An insider is any person who has access to nonpublic information about a corporation. Insiders may not use inside information as a basis for personal trading until that information has been made public. The SEC can levy a civil penalty of up to three times the amount of profit made or loss avoided if inside information is used. Any individual who is a corporate insider and owns securities in that corporation must file a statement of ownership with the SEC.

Written Supervisory Procedures. All broker-dealers must establish written supervisory procedures specifically prohibiting the use of material nonpublic information by all persons interested in, affiliated with or in any way engaged in securities-related activities. Once these procedures have been established, broker-dealers must actively enforce them.

SEC Investigations. The SEC can investigate any person suspected of violating any of the provisions of the Insider Trading Act. The Commission may require anyone suspected of a violation to file a written statement with the SEC covering all of the facts and circumstances relating to the suspected violation.

Penalties The SEC may seek civil and criminal penalties against anyone it believes has violated the Insider Trading Act. Anyone guilty of violating the act is liable for civil penalties of up to the greater of $1 million or 300 percent of profits made or losses avoided.

Contemporaneous Traders

Any person who has entered trades that have violated the insider trading regulations, or who has communicated material nonpublic information to someone who has violated these regulations, may be liable to contemporaneous traders and may be sued. A contemporaneous trader is any person who enters a trade at or near the same time and in the same security as a person who has inside information.

Civil Penalties

Statute of Limitations. A lawsuit can be filed by anyone who, at the same time as the insider, bought (if the insider sold) or sold (if the insider bought) securities of the same class. The suit may be initiated up to five years after the violation, and the damages claimed may be up to the profits the insider made or losses she avoided.

Profits Gained and Losses Avoided. When determining how much profit the inside trader made or the loss she avoided, the Commission looks at the security's market price a reasonable period after the information becomes general public knowledge. The difference between this price and the price the trader obtained is the profit or loss against which penalties are set.

Short-Swing Profits. Insiders may not retain short-swing profits (those occurring in six months or less) in securities, they must repay any such profit. Insiders cannot enter short sales in the securities of the companies in which they are insiders. Any trading of insider-owned securities must be reported to the SEC within 10 days of the trade.

Insider Trading Rules

The key elements of tipper and tippee liability under the insider trading rules are as follows:

- Does the tipper owe a fiduciary duty to a company (to its stockholders)? Has he breached it?
- Does the tipper meet the personal benefits test (even something as simple as enhancing a friendship or reputation)?
- Does the tippee know or should the tippee have known that the information was inside or confidential?
- Is the information material and nonpublic?

Given these elements, a corporate insider's innocuous comment could leave that person liable under the rules, and anyone who trades on information that she knows or should know is not public is also liable.

Chinese Wall Doctrine

The Chinese Wall doctrine describes the restrictions against sharing potentially material information between a firm's departments. Those broker-dealer departments or branches that have access to material nonpublic information (such as the legal department, the investment banking division and the various security analysts) may not disseminate this information to anyone who could conceivably trade on it. To prevent possible violations of the law, firms must erect a "Chinese wall" between those who have information and those who do not.

Securities Investor Protection Corporation

The Securities Investor Protection Corporation (SIPC) is an independent government-sponsored corporation, not an agency of the U.S. government. SIPC members pay assessments into a general insurance fund used to meet customer claims in the event a broker-dealer fails. All broker-dealers registered with the SEC must be SIPC members. Exempt from membership are:

- broker-dealers handling only open-end investment company shares or unit trusts;
- broker-dealers handling only variable annuities or insurance; and
- investment advisers.

The SIPC Fund. SIPC collects an annual assessment from each member based on a percentage of the member's gross revenues from the securities business. Any member that fails to pay its assessment to SIPC cannot engage in the brokerage business.

Protection of Customers

If the SEC or any self-regulatory organization (SRO) suspects a broker-dealer has violated its net capital requirements, it notifies SIPC immediately. If SIPC determines that the member has failed or is in imminent danger of failing, it may petition a federal court to take action by appointing a trustee to liquidate the firm and protect its customers.

The court, upon receiving SIPC's petition, issues a protective decree if the broker-dealer is, in fact, insolvent or is not in compliance with the Securities Exchange Act of 1934. The court that issues the decree has exclusive jurisdiction over all property of the broker-dealer and all suits involved in the liquidation proceeding. The court appoints a trustee for the liquidation or transfer of the broker-dealer's business. The trustee must be a disinterested party with no interests that conflict with those of the firm's customers or creditors.

Once a trustee has been appointed, the member firm cannot engage in business as a broker-dealer. It also must not attempt to conceal assets, file false statements or alter securities records to defraud the trustee, SIPC or the SEC.

Liquidation Proceedings

By law, the court-appointed trustee in a liquidation proceeding must promptly:

- deliver securities registered in a customer's name to that customer;
- assign ownership and distribute street name securities to customers;
- sell or transfer branches or other offices of the failed broker-dealer to raise capital; and
- liquidate the failed broker-dealer's business.

Notification. The appointed trustee must notify all customers of the firm by mail about the liquidation proceedings and must publish a notice of the liquidation in one or more general-circulation newspapers. Each customer must then file a statement of claim (no proof is required) with the trustee. No claim is accepted more than six months after the notice of liquidation is published.

Customer claims are based on a customer account's net equity as of the date SIPC goes to court to have a trustee appointed. The valuation date is generally the day customer protection proceedings commence. In the case of customer margin accounts, net equity is the market value of all securities in an account less the debit balances.

Payment of Customers. At this point, the trustee distributes the securities the broker-dealer holds according to the following guidelines:

- Securities registered in customer name are returned to the owners without dollar limit. If a lien has been placed against a customer's securities, the customer must pay the debt before distribution.
- Cash and securities held in street name are distributed to customers on a pro rata basis.
- After the distribution of street name securities and cash, SIPC funds are available to meet the remaining claim of each customer up to a maximum of $500,000, with cash claims not to exceed $100,000 of the $500,000 total.
- For claims exceeding $500,000, the customers become general creditors of the broker-dealer and share pro rata with all other general creditors.

Specifically Identifiable Property. For the purpose of SIPC coverage, the following securities and monies must be segregated and identified:

- all fully paid and excess margin securities in the broker-dealer's physical possession or control;
- all fully paid and excess margin securities in transfer;
- stock dividends receivable; and
- cash and qualified securities in a reserve bank account.

Other Provisions

Account Transfers. If the trustee determines that it is in the customer's best interests to do so, it may transfer customer accounts directly to another broker-dealer that is a SIPC member. It need not notify the customers first, nor does it need their permission to effect the transfers.

SIPC Cash Advances. Because the failed broker-dealer might not have enough cash and securities on hand to meet each customer's claim, the trustee can apply to SIPC for a cash advance of up to $500,000 per customer account. SIPC also can advance money to the trustee to cover claims of creditors, administrative costs of the trustee and any additional costs, as it sees fit.

Direct Payment. Under certain circumstances, SIPC can settle directly the claims of a failing broker-dealer's customers, without petitioning a court to appoint a trustee. Claims handled in this manner must be relatively small, and the cost of direct payment procedures must be less than the cost of a regular SIPC liquidation proceeding.

Customer Account Coverage	Under SIPC rules, each separate customer account is entitled to coverage up to SIPC limits.

Individuals. In general, separate customer accounts are defined as those accounts with unique beneficial owners. Usually, if an account name differs from other account names, it is considered a separate customer account and is entitled to full and separate coverage.

Claims by broker-dealers, general partners of broker-dealers, officers of broker-dealers, subordinated lenders, control persons of broker-dealers and owners of more than 5 percent of the equity of broker-dealers are not allowed.

Executors and Administrators. All accounts held on behalf of a single deceased person, even when there are different executors and estate administrators, are combined in a single account for claim purposes.

Corporate and Partnership Accounts. Each corporate and partnership account is entitled to separate customer account status—separate from the accounts of its directors, partners and owners.

Trust Accounts. If a trust is fully qualified and has all necessary trust documents on file, it is considered a separate customer account.

Joint Accounts. If two or more joint accounts exist with the same beneficial owners, all of the accounts are combined in a single account for claim purposes.

Coverage Limits. Customer accounts are covered to a maximum of $500,000, with cash claims not to exceed $100,000. Only claims for securities and cash are covered; SIPC does not cover claims resulting from open positions in commodity futures contracts. Each separate customer may enter a claim up to the $500,000 coverage limit. This limit applies to all accounts in a customer's name. For instance, John Doe's cash account and margin account are considered one account. Examples of coverage limits are shown in Table 16.1.

Advertising SIPC Membership	Broker-dealers that are SIPC members may not advertise their memberships in such a way as to imply that this coverage represents more or less than it actually is. SIPC bylaws require each member to post a sign indicating the firm's coverage under SIPC, but the term "SIPC" must not appear larger than the firm's own name, and the sign cannot imply that the member can offer SIPC benefits that other members cannot.
Fidelity Bonds	Every member firm required to join SIPC must purchase and maintain a blanket fidelity bond that indemnifies against losses due to acts such as check forgery, lost securities or fraudulent trading. The minimum coverage

TABLE 16.1 SIPC Coverage Limits

Examples of Customer Coverage Limits	
John Doe — Cash account John Doe — Margin account	1 customer = $500,000 coverage
John and Mary Doe — Joint account	1 customer = $500,000 coverage
John Doe as Custodian for Jane Doe	1 customer = $500,000 coverage

must not be less than $25,000, with substantially higher coverage amounts based on the firm's size and the scope of its business operations.

Other Federal and State Legislation

This section highlights legislation that expanded or amended the acts of 1933 and 1934.

Maloney Act

The Maloney Act created the National Association of Securities Dealers (NASD) to regulate brokers and dealers not affiliated with an exchange.

Trust Indenture Act of 1939

The Trust Indenture Act of 1939 specifies that any corporate bond issue of more than $5 million or with a maturity date of nine months or more must be issued with a trust indenture. The trust indenture contains covenants that protect the bondholders. An independent trustee is appointed to ensure that the covenants are carried out. This law requires full disclosure of information in the indenture, but because it is usually a large document, each investor does not receive a copy. Investors are entitled to review a copy at the custodian's offices.

Investment Company Act of 1940

The Investment Company Act of 1940 regulates the issuance of investment company securities. Administered by the SEC, the act sets standards for the organization and operation of investment companies, the pricing and public sale of the investments, and reporting requirements. To comply with the act of 1940, investment companies wishing to sell their shares publicly must register with the SEC. A company must state its investment objectives in the registration statement and in the prospectus.

According to the act of 1940, an investment company is any company that invests and reinvests in securities. This includes an issuer that invests 40 percent or more of its total assets. An investment company is owned by 100 persons or more and makes a public offering of its securities. A registered investment company may not publicly offer its shares unless it has a net worth of at least $100,000.

Investment Advisers Act of 1940

This act requires an individual in the business of giving investment advice for compensation to be registered as an investment adviser.

Securities Acts Amendments of 1975

The Securities Acts Amendments of 1975 established the Municipal Securities Rulemaking Board (MSRB). The MSRB regulates the issuance and trading of municipal securities.

State Securities Regulations

In addition to federal securities regulations, each state has laws that pertain to the issuance and trading of securities. State securities laws are known as **blue-sky laws**. The name "blue-sky" comes from a statement made by a U.S. Supreme Court justice, who referred to "speculative schemes that have no more basis than so many feet of blue sky." The **Uniform Securities Act (USA)** serves as model legislation that each state may follow or adapt to its own needs.

Most states require broker-dealers that do business in a state to register with the state's securities commission. Salespeople associated with a broker-dealer must also be registered in the state(s) where they do business.

Several states require that broker-dealers have a minimum net capital. In many states, broker-dealers must post fidelity bonds. The state securities administrators have the power to revoke a broker-dealer's registration or the registered representative's license if the firm or representative has violated any of a state's securities laws.

In most states, securities must be registered before they can be sold to the public. Each state has three ways to register a security:

1. **Coordination**. This is the method used most often when securities are newly issued. At the same time the issuer files with the SEC, it files with the state(s) in which the issuer wants to offer the securities. State registration is automatically effective when the federal filing becomes effective.
2. **Filing**. If an issuer meets certain criteria, it can notify the state(s) that it is about to sell a security. If the state does not reply, the registration is effective on the fifth full business day after the filing.
3. **Qualification**. If an issue cannot be registered by either coordination or filing, it might be registered by qualification. The issuer, in this case, files a registration statement with the state(s) that meets the state's requirements. This type of registration becomes effective when so ordered by the state securities administration.

Exemptions from state securities registration requirements are similar to those exempt from SEC registration. The list includes:

- securities listed on SEC–registered stock exchanges
- nonprofit organizations
- insurance companies
- banks
- private placements
- private investment companies

Under amended federal and state securities laws, registered investment companies are now exempt from state registration and regulation.

Summary

In the wake of the stock market crash of 1929, the government has taken an active interest in regulating the securities business with the intent of protecting the public. The most significant legislation covering the securities business includes the:

- Securities Act of 1933
- Securities Exchange Act of 1934
- Maloney Act
- Trust Indenture Act of 1939
- Investment Company Act of 1940
- Insider Trading Act of 1988

It is important to know the general boundaries of each law. It is also important to know what the rules and regulations are. However, the Series 7 exam does not require that you memorize specifically whether a given rule is a provision of one act as opposed to another.

Key Concepts

To prepare for your license exam, you should learn the following concepts.

In addition to studying these key concepts, use the U.S. Government and State Rules and Regulations Hot Sheet on page 649 for further review.

blue-sky laws
Chinese Wall doctrine
contemporaneous trader
fidelity bond
insider
Insider Trading Act of 1988
Investment Advisers Act of 1940
Investment Company Act of 1940

Maloney Act
Municipal Securities Rulemaking
    Board (MSRB)
Securities Acts Amendments of 1975
Securities Investor Protection
    Corporation (SIPC)
Trust Indenture Act of 1939

Review Questions

1. Tex Longhorn is in possession of material inside information about General Gizmonics, Inc. He may communicate this information to a customer

   A. if the customer knows it's inside information
   B. the day before the information is made public
   C. if the customer enters an unsolicited order
   D. under no circumstances

2. Which of the following is protected by the Securities Investor Protection Corporation?

   A. Broker-dealer failure
   B. Fraudulent transaction
   C. Issuer default
   D. Market risk

3. In the time before a registration statement becomes effective, which of the following statements would be true?

   I. No sales may be solicited.
   II. Sales literature may not be used.
   III. Unsolicited inquiries may be answered.

   A. I and II only
   B. I and III only
   C. III only
   D. I, II and III

4. According to the Uniform Securities Act, which of the following statements is true?

   A. Registered reps must register in every state.
   B. Broker-dealers must register in every state.
   C. Registered reps may not register in more than one state.
   D. Nonexempt securities must be registered in every state in which they are offered.

5. The Trust Indenture Act of 1939 was designed to

   A. protect corporate bondholders
   B. regulate investment companies
   C. establish self-regulatory organizations
   D. require the registration of investment advisers

6. In most states, the sale of securities is regulated by

   A. interstate commerce law
   B. intrastate commerce law
   C. blue laws
   D. blue-sky laws

7. The federal regulation that prohibits insider trading is the

   A. Securities Acts Amendments of 1975
   B. Trust Indenture Act of 1939
   C. Securities Exchange Act of 1934
   D. Securities Act of 1933

8. Insurance for customer accounts is provided by which federal statute?

   A. Securities Acts Amendments of 1975
   B. Securities Act of 1933
   C. Securities Exchange Act of 1934
   D. Securities Investor Protection Act of 1970

9. SIPC provides coverage up to $500,000

    A. with no more than $50,000 in cash
    B. with no more than $100,000 in cash
    C. with no more than $150,000 in cash
    D. in cash or securities

10. The Securities Investor Protection Act applies to registered broker-dealers that

    A. are members of an exchange
    B. are members of the NASD
    C. are members of both an exchange and the NASD
    D. use the mails or other instruments of interstate commerce

Answers & Rationale

1. **D.** Inside information may never be discussed until it is made public, at which point it is no longer inside information. Violations may be punished with civil penalties as well as prison sentences.

2. **A.** SIPC protects customer accounts against broker-dealer failure.

3. **D.** Before the registration becomes effective, no sales literature may be sent and no sales may be solicited, but unsolicited inquiries by an investor may be answered.

4. **D.** Blue-sky laws require issuers to register securities only in the state or states in which the securities are offered or sold. The same rule holds true for registered reps and broker-dealers: they must register with the state securities administrator in every state in which they transact business.

5. **A.** The Trust Indenture Act requires issuers of corporate debt to be bound by a trust indenture, which contains covenants that protect bondholders.

6. **D.** In addition to being registered with the SEC, an issue must be registered with the state securities administrator in each state where the underwriter wishes to sell. The state securities laws are called blue-sky laws.

7. **C.** The 1934 act prohibits insider trading.

8. **D.** The Securities Investor Protection Act of 1970 provides for the insurance of customer accounts against broker-dealer failures.

9. **B.** SIPC coverage is $500,000 per separate customer account, with coverage of cash and cash equivalents not to exceed $100,000.

10. **D.** The Securities Investor Protection Act of 1970 applies to all broker-dealers that use the mails or other instruments of interstate commerce (and, therefore, must register with the SEC).

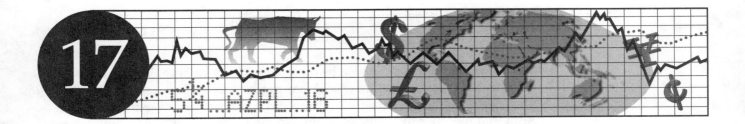

Other SEC and SRO Rules and Regulations

OVERVIEW

As an amendment to the Securities Exchange Act of 1934, the Maloney Act permitted the establishment of self-regulatory organizations (SROs) to oversee broker-dealers transacting business. The Securities and Exchange Commission (SEC) and the exchanges—the NYSE, CBOE, NASD and others—develop and enforce rules and oversee different segments of the securities industry.

Registration and Regulation of Broker-Dealers

Securities and Exchange Commission

The Securities and Exchange Commission is the securities industry's primary regulatory body. Broker-dealers that transact securities business with customers or with other broker-dealers must apply and be approved for registration with the SEC.

Broker-dealers must comply with SEC rules and regulations when conducting business. A broker-dealer that does not comply is subject to:

- censure;
- limits on activities, functions or operations;
- suspension of its registration (or one of its associated person's license to do business);
- revocation of registration;
- fine; or
- civil monetary penalties.

An associated person can also be disciplined for violating SEC rules and regulations. If the SEC bars an associated person, no broker-dealer may allow that person to associate with it without the Commission's express permission. If a member firm suspends an associated person, the firm must report the suspension to the exchanges where the firm is a member.

Although a broker-dealer must register with the SEC, the broker-dealer may not claim that this registration in any way implies that the Commission has passed upon or approved the broker-dealer's financial standing, business or conduct. Any such claim or statement is misrepresentation.

Fingerprinting

Registered broker-dealers must have fingerprint records made for all of their employees, directors, officers and partners and must submit those fingerprint cards to the U.S. attorney general for identification and processing. Certain broker-dealer employees (typically clerical) are exempt from the fingerprinting requirement if they:

- are not involved in securities sales;
- do not handle or have access to cash or securities or to the books and records of original entry relating to money and securities; and
- do not supervise other employees engaged in these activities.

Self-Regulatory Organizations

Eight self-regulatory organizations function under the SEC's oversight. Each SRO is accountable to the Commission for enforcing federal securities laws as well as supervising securities practices within an assigned jurisdiction. The largest of these SROs and their jurisdictions follow:

- **National Association of Securities Dealers (NASD).** Regulates all matters related to investment banking (securities underwriting) and trading in the over-the-counter (OTC) market and to the conduct of NASD member firms and associated persons.
- **New York Stock Exchange (NYSE).** Regulates all matters related to trading in NYSE–listed securities and to the conduct of NYSE member firms and associated persons.
- **Municipal Securities Rulemaking Board (MSRB).** Regulates all matters related to the underwriting and trading of state and municipal securities. The MSRB regulates, but does not have enforcement powers—it depends on other SROs for the enforcement of its rules.

- **Chicago Board Options Exchange (CBOE).** Regulates all matters related to trading standardized options and related contracts listed on that exchange.

The National Association of Securities Dealers

The National Association of Securities Dealers is the OTC industry's SRO. The NASD is a membership corporation—that is, the NASD does not issue capital stock. The NASD's purposes and objectives are to:

- promote the investment banking and securities business, to standardize principles and practices, to promote high standards of commercial honor and to encourage the observance of federal and state securities laws;
- provide a medium for communication among its members, and between its members, the government and other agencies;
- adopt, administer and enforce the NASD's Conduct Rules and rules designed to prevent fraudulent and manipulative practices, as well as to promote just and equitable principles of trade; and
- promote self-discipline among members and to investigate and adjust grievances between the public and members and between members.

Districts. The NASD divides the United States into eight districts to facilitate its operation. Each district elects a district committee to administer NASD rules. A committee has a maximum of 12 members who serve for three years.

Each district committee appoints a *District Business Conduct Committee (DBCC)*, which handles trade practice complaints within the district. The NASD executive committee, made up of members of the *Board of Governors*, manages NASD national affairs.

NASD Dues, Assessments and Other Charges

Assessments. The NASD is funded by assessments of member firms' registered reps and applicants and by annual fees. The annual fee each member pays includes a(n):

- basic membership fee
- assessment based on gross income
- fee for each principal and registered representative
- charge for each branch office

Failure to pay dues can result in suspension or revocation of membership.

Use of the NASD's Corporate Name

NASD members cannot use the NASD name in any manner that would suggest that the NASD has endorsed a member firm. The members may use the phrase "member of the NASD" as long as the firm places no undue emphasis on it.

NASD Manual NASD policies are specified in the *NASD Manual*. The Manual describes four sets of rules and codes by which the OTC market is regulated:

1. **Conduct Rules** (formerly the Rules of Fair Practice). These rules set out fair and ethical trade practices that member firms and their representatives must follow when dealing with the public.
2. **Uniform Practice Code**. This code established the Uniform Trade Practices, including settlement, good delivery, ex-dates, confirmations, don't know (DK) procedures and other guidelines for broker-dealers to follow when they do business with other member broker-dealer firms.
3. **Code of Procedure**. This code describes how the NASD hears and handles member violations of the Conduct Rules.
4. **Code of Arbitration Procedure**. This code governs the resolution of disagreements and claims between members, registered reps and the public; it addresses monetary claims, not violations of the Conduct Rules.

NASD Membership and Registration

The NASD's Board of Governors establishes rules, regulations and membership eligibility standards. At present, the following membership standards and registration requirements are in place.

Broker-Dealer Registration Any broker-dealer registered with the SEC is eligible and may apply for membership in the NASD. Any person who effects transactions in securities as a broker, a dealer or an investment banker also may register with the NASD, as may municipal bond firms. Application for NASD membership carries the applying firm's specific agreement to:

- comply with the Association's rules and regulations;
- comply with federal securities laws; and
- pay dues, assessments and other charges in the manner and amounts fixed by the Association.

A membership application is made to the NASD district office in the district in which the applying firm has its home office. If a district committee passes on the firm's qualifications, the firm can be accepted into NASD membership.

Associated Person Registration Any person associated with an NASD member firm who intends to engage in the investment banking or securities business must be registered with the NASD as an associated person. Anyone applying for registration with the NASD as an associated person must be sponsored by a member firm.

Qualifications Investigated. Before submitting an application to enroll any person with the NASD as a registered representative, a member firm must ascertain the person's business reputation, character, education, qualifications and experience. As part of the application process, the member firm must certify that it has made an investigation and that the candidate's credentials are in order.

Failure to Register Personnel. A member firm's failure to register an employee who performs any of the functions of a registered rep may lead to disciplinary action by the NASD.

Post-registration Rules and Regulations

Registered Persons Changing Firms. NASD registration is *nontransferable*. If a registered person leaves one member firm to join another firm, he must terminate registration at the first firm on a U-5 form and reapply for registration with the new employing member firm on a U-4 form. If a person terminates his registration with one firm, he must register with another firm within two years or he will be required to requalify for his license.

Continuing Commissions. An individual must be registered to sell securities. A registered rep who leaves a member firm—upon retirement, for instance—may continue to receive commissions on business he placed while employed. However, the rep must have a contract to this effect before he leaves the firm. A deceased representative's heirs also may receive continuing commissions on business the representative placed if a contract exists.

Notification of Disciplinary Action. A member firm must notify the NASD if any associated person in the firm's employment is subjected to disciplinary action by one of the following:

- national securities exchange or association
- clearing corporation
- commodity futures market regulatory agency
- federal or state regulatory commission

The notification must include the individual's name and the nature of the action.

A member firm also must notify the NASD of disciplinary action the firm itself has taken against an associated person and the nature of the action.

Terminations. If an associated person voluntarily ends his employment with a member, his NASD registration ceases 30 calendar days from the date the NASD receives written notice from the employing member firm. Whenever any registered person's employment is terminated, the member firm must notify the NASD and the NYSE in writing within 30 calendar days.

Terminating Reps Under Investigation. If a registered representative or another associated person is under investigation for federal securities law violations or has disciplinary action pending against him from the NASD or any other SRO, a member firm may not terminate its business relationship with the person until the investigation or disciplinary action has been resolved. However, the NASD will backdate the effective date of the person's termination as a registered representative.

Exemptions From Registration

Certain people are not required to register with the NASD as associated persons.

Foreign Associates. Non–U.S. citizens employed by NASD member firms, usually in Canadian or overseas branch offices, are not subject to registration and licensing with the Association. This does not include U.S. citizens living and working in overseas or Canadian branch offices, however. Each exempted foreign associate must agree not to engage in securities business in any country or territory under U.S. jurisdiction and not to do business with any U.S. citizen or national or resident alien.

Clerical Personnel and Corporate Officers. A member firm's clerical employees need not register with the NASD. Corporate officers who are not involved with the member's investment banking business also are exempt from registration.

Employees In Other Specific Functions. Employees registered with an exchange as floor members who work or trade only on the floor or who transact business only in exempted securities or commodities are exempt from registration.

State Registration

In addition to registering with the NASD, registered reps and broker-dealers must register with the state securities administrator in each state in which they intend to do business.

Qualifications Examinations

To become a registered representative or principal, an individual must pass the appropriate licensing examination(s).

Registered Representatives All associated persons engaged in the investment banking and securities business are considered registered representatives, including any:

- assistant officer who does not function as a principal;
- individual who supervises, solicits or conducts business in securities; and
- individual who trains people to supervise, solicit or conduct business in securities.

General Securities Representative License (Series 7)

A Series 7 general securities license allows a registered representative to sell almost all types of securities products. A general securities rep cannot sell commodities futures unless she has a Series 3 license.

Registered Principals Anyone who manages or supervises any part of a member's investment banking or securities business must be registered as a principal with the NASD. This includes people involved solely in training associated persons. Unless the member firm is a sole proprietorship, it must employ at least two registered principals, one of whom must be registered as a general securities principal.

General Securities Principal License (Series 24)

Any person actively engaged in managing a member's securities or investment banking business, including supervising, soliciting and conducting business, or in training persons associated with the member must qualify by examination and register with the NASD as a general securities principal.

A person registered as a general securities principal is not qualified to function as a municipal securities principal, a registered options principal (ROP), a financial and operations principal (FinOp) or a general securities sales supervisor. A registered general securities principal expecting to function in one or more of these areas also must be registered with the NASD in each separate field of expertise. The Series 7 is a prerequisite for the Series 24.

Limited Principal Licenses

Series 4. If a member does options business with the public, it must employ at least one ROP (Series 4) in the firm. In addition, the member must notify the Association as to which of the firm's ROPs is to be designated as a compliance registered options principal (CROP) and which as a supervisory registered options principal (SROP). No additional qualifications examinations are necessary before designation as a CROP or SROP. The Series 7 is a prerequisite for registration as a ROP.

Series 8. Each NYSE firm must have a supervisory principal overseeing sales of securities products within the firm. A person registered as a general securities sales supervisor (Series 8) may supervise the sale of all types of securities products without having to pass the individual limited principal examination for each type of security. The Series 7 is a prerequisite for registration as a general securities sales supervisor.

Series 27. In addition to having at least one general principal, each member must have at least one financial and operations principal. The FinOp is responsible for supervising the firm's financial administration and preparing, maintaining, approving and filing the reports required of general securities member firms. Currently, a person must pass no prerequisite exams before qualifying for the Series 27 principal license.

Series 53. A member that conducts municipal securities business with the public must have at least one municipal securities principal (Series 53). This license entitles the principal to manage the member's municipal and government securities business. The Series 52 or the Series 7 is a prerequisite for the Series 53 principal examination.

Ineligibility and Disqualifications

A person may not act as a registered representative or principal unless she meets the NASD's eligibility standards regarding training, experience and competence.

Statutory Disqualification.   Disciplinary sanctions by the SEC, another SRO, a foreign financial regulator or a foreign equivalent of an SRO can be cause for statutory disqualification of NASD membership. An individual applying for registration as an associated person will be rejected if he:

- has been and is expelled or suspended from membership or participation in any other SRO or from the foreign equivalent of an SRO;
- is under an SEC order or an order of a foreign financial regulator denying, suspending or revoking his registration or barring him from association with a broker-dealer; or
- has been found to be the cause of another broker-dealer or associated person being expelled or suspended by another SRO, the SEC or a foreign equivalent of an SRO.

Any of the following also can automatically disqualify an applicant for registration:

- misstatements willfully made in an application for membership or registration as an associated person;
- a felony conviction, either domestic or foreign, or a misdemeanor conviction involving securities or money within the past 10 years; and

- court injunctions prohibiting the individual from acting as an investment adviser, an underwriter or a broker-dealer or in other capacities aligned with the securities and financial services industry.

NASD Definitions

The terms below have specific meanings to the NASD.

Associated Person (AP) of a Member. Any employee, manager, director, officer or partner of a member broker-dealer or another entity (issuer, bank, etc.) or any person controlling, controlled by or in common control with that member.

Broker. (1) An individual or a firm that charges a fee or commission for executing buy and sell orders submitted by another individual or firm. (2) The role of a brokerage firm when it acts as an agent for a customer and charges the customer a commission for its services. (3) Any person engaged in the business of effecting transactions in securities for the accounts of others who is not a bank.

Completion of the Transaction. The point at which a customer pays any part of the purchase price to the broker-dealer for a security he has purchased or delivers a security he has sold. If the customer makes payment to the broker-dealer before the payment is due, completion of the transaction occurs when the broker-dealer delivers the security.

Customer. Any individual, person, partnership, corporation or other legal entity who is not a broker, dealer or municipal securities dealer—that is, the public.

Dealer. (1) The role of a brokerage firm when it acts as a principal in a particular trade. A firm acts as a dealer when it buys or sells a security for its own account and at its own risk, then charges the customer a markup or markdown. (2) Any person engaged in the business of buying and selling securities for his own account, either directly or through a broker, who is not a bank.

Member. (1) Of the NYSE: One of the 1,366 individuals owning a seat on the New York Stock Exchange. (2) Of the NASD: Any individual, partnership, corporation or other legal entity admitted to membership in the NASD.

Security. Under the act of 1934, any note, stock, bond, investment contract, variable annuity, profit-sharing or partnership agreement, certificate of deposit, option on a security or other instrument of investment commonly known as a *security*.

Codes of Procedure and of Arbitration Procedure

Code of Procedure

The NASD's Code of Procedure is a guide to settle complaints that arise between and among members and associated persons.

It is the task of the NASD Department of Enforcement to determine whether a charge or complaint is valid and, if so, to take appropriate disciplinary action against the offending member firm or associated person.

Regular Complaint Procedure

Sources of Complaints. Most complaints are filed by NASD examiners who regularly audit each member firm's books, bringing any evidence of wrongdoing to the attention of the Department of Enforcement.

When a customer, another member firm or one of the NASD's committees lodges a complaint, one of the first steps in the proceedings is to have an NASD examiner inspect the accused member's books in an effort to substantiate or discredit the complaint.

Complaint Resolution Process. The first official action occurs when the Department of Enforcement notifies the accused member (or associated person) of the specifics of the complaint, identifying who has filed the complaint and requesting a response from the accused member within 25 days of the service of the complaint. If no answer or request related to the complaint is received, a second notice is sent. A response is required within 14 days after service of the second notice.

Request for Hearing. When the regular complaint proceeding is chosen, typically the member firm either denies the charge or makes an offer of settlement. The complainant can accept the offer or demand a formal hearing.

Venue. Once a complaint has been filed, it is usually scheduled to be heard before a committee in the district in which the member has its home office or in the district in which the branch office is located.

Hearing Panels. A hearing panel is convened that consists of Department of Enforcement members, all of whom are associated persons with member firms. Hearing panels, at times, also may consist of members of the NASD's Market Regulation Committee.

Decision of the Committee. The presiding Department of Enforcement either upholds a rule violation or dismisses the complaint. Either way, the Department issues a written decision and announces the sanctions imposed on the member firm as disciplinary action. The Department's decision becomes final after 45 days.

Penalties.   If the Department of Enforcement finds that a rule violation has occurred, it may impose one or more of the following disciplinary actions:

- censure
- fine
- suspension of NASD registration
- expulsion
- barring of the associated person from association with all members

Appeal and Review.   If the Department finds in favor of the complainant, the respondent has 25 days from notification to appeal the decision to the NASD National Adjudicatory Council (NAC). The NAC may opt to review and may or may not overturn the Department's decision. The call for review by the NAC must be made within 45 days of the Department's hearing.

Settlement Procedure.   The member may offer to make a settlement at any time during the proceedings, but such offer might not be accepted.

Payment of Fines and Costs.   All fines levied as penalties for rule violations against a member firm must be paid promptly after the date of the Department of Enforcement's decision or, if that decision was appealed, after the final date of the National Adjudicatory Council's decision.

Appeal to SEC.   The complainant or the respondent can appeal to the SEC for a review of the judgement if it wishes.

Acceptance, Waiver and Consent   The acceptance, waiver and consent procedure applies to minor rule violations. If the Department of Enforcement has reason to believe a violation has occurred and the member firm or associated person does not dispute the violation, a minor rule violation letter maybe offered.

If the letter is accepted, the respondent waives the right to a hearing and any appeal. The maximum penalty that can be imposed under acceptance, waiver and consent procedure is $2,500 per respondent, plus possible public censure. If the letter is rejected, a regular complaint proceeding is initiated.

Failure to have advertisements and sales literature approved by a principal before use and failure to maintain proper books and records are among violations subject to this procedure.

Code of Arbitration Procedure

The Code of Arbitration Procedure offers participants a relatively easy method of settling disputes at a cost that is usually significantly lower than that of more formal procedures. Arbitration should not be confused with disciplinary proceedings under the Code of Procedure.

Matters Eligible For Submission. Any dispute or controversy may be submitted to the NASD's National Arbitration Committee for resolution and settlement. A claimant begins the proceedings by filing a **statement of claim**, a signed **submission agreement** and any supporting documents with the Director of Arbitration. A dispute or controversy eligible for arbitration must be submitted within six years of its occurrence.

Required Submissions. Internal disputes between member firms and between associated persons must be submitted for resolution and settlement in arbitration.

Arbitration Involving Customers. Customers are under no obligation to submit any dispute to the NASD's National Arbitration Committee. For them, arbitration is strictly optional; although a customer can take a member firm or an associated person before an arbitration panel on demand, neither a member firm nor an associated person can demand that a customer submit to arbitration. The customer must consent to arbitration in writing.

No Redress Through the Courts. All parties to an NASD arbitration proceeding forfeit any civil court proceedings while the arbitration is in progress. Findings under the Code of Arbitration are binding on all parties involved in the dispute.

NASD National Arbitration Committee. The NASD maintains a pool of arbitrators consisting of industry people and public representatives. Arbitration panels are convened as needed to hear cases.

Simplified Industry Arbitration. Disputes not involving customers can be submitted for resolution under simplified industry arbitration procedures provided a claim's dollar amount does not exceed $25,000. Claims of $25,000 or less are heard by panels of one, two or three arbitrators. The arbitrators review evidence and pleadings from both sides of the dispute and render a decision.

Simplified Customer Arbitration. As with simplified industry arbitration, the dollar amount in a simplified customer arbitration proceeding must not exceed $10,000. A single arbitrator hears such claims.

TABLE 17.1 Summary of the Codes of Arbitration and Procedure

	Code of Procedure (Disciplinary Action)	Code of Arbitration (Dispute Settlement)
Description	Used in conjunction with formal complaints that a member firm or an associated person violated specific NASD rules and regulations.	Used to resolve disputes, claims and controversies that arise in the course of business, none of which are violations of NASD rules and regulations.
Monetary Redress	Used to fine and punish a member firm or an associated person for NASD rule violations as charged in the complaint if the charges are upheld.	Used to recover monetary damages allegedly suffered by the claimant as the result of disputed acts, practices or omissions by a member firm or an associated person.
Primary Complainant or Claimant	DBCC (or Board of Governors) lodging a complaint against a member firm or an associated person based on findings of misconduct, or on reasonable grounds for same, as determined by NASD auditors/examiners.	Customer in dispute with a member firm or an associated person; associated person in dispute with a member firm or another associated person; member firm in dispute with another member firm or an associated person.
Outcome of Proceedings	Respondent has 15 days to appeal a decision.	If panel of arbitrators rules in favor of the complainant, awards for monetary damage will be made.

Arbitration Awards. The arbitration panel attempts to render decision within 30 business days.

Failure to Act Under Arbitration Procedures. Failure to participate in good faith in a matter under arbitration or failure to honor an award an arbitration panel issues violates the Conduct Rules.

Amendments to the Code of Arbitration The NASD has implemented amendments that make the Code of Arbitration Procedures uniform with other SROs' procedures. The major changes include the following:

- Disputes subject to arbitration now include the business of members as well as securities-related disputes.
- All parties have the right to challenge arbitrators, and arbitrators have the obligation to disclose potential conflicts of interest.
- When the amount in dispute exceeds $30,000, the number of arbitrators is no fewer than three nor more than five.
- Parties may agree to arrange private settlements or to withdraw from arbitration without panel approval.

Summary of the Code of Arbitration and the Code of Procedure

Table 17.1 summarizes the Code of Arbitration and the Code of Procedure.

NYSE Constitution and Rules

Organization

The NYSE is a corporation operated by a board of directors consisting of 10 Exchange members, 10 public representatives and a chairperson. The board is responsible for setting policy, supervising Exchange and member activities, listing securities, overseeing the transfer of members' seats on the Exchange and judging whether an applicant is qualified to be a specialist.

Membership The number of memberships, or **seats**, on the NYSE is fixed at 1,366. Because all of the seats are owned, to become a member one must buy a seat from a member. A seat's price is negotiated between the buyer and seller. Membership can be transferred from one person to another only with the board of directors' approval.

Only individuals can own seats on the Exchange. Many seat ownerships, however, are sponsored and funded by firms, which is where the term "**member firms**" originates.

Allied Members. Allied members are executive officers, directors or holders of more than 5 percent of a member firm's voting stock. Though allied members are responsible for supervising their organizations, they are not allowed to trade on the Exchange floor. The number of allied memberships is unlimited; they are not transferable.

Member Firms   A member organization must be open for business every day that the Exchange is open for business. Each office must display its certificate of membership with the NYSE. A member organization may not share its office with another broker-dealer except under special circumstances. The NYSE requires each member firm to undergo an annual audit by an independent accountant to verify the firm's financial health.

A member firm must obtain prior approval from the Exchange to open a branch office. If a registered representative uses his home as an office, this is considered an office of the employing firm. Every branch must be supervised by a principal who has passed the appropriate principal's examination. A very small office may be supervised by a registered representative if a principal in another office supervises the representative.

Although principals in branch offices are responsible for the business in their respective offices, the ultimate responsibility rests with the member firm's general partner or directors. The principal's supervisory duties include:

- approving new accounts;
- reviewing all correspondence, trade blotters and registered representatives' client statements;
- reviewing all transactions with clients and representatives' accounts of clients; and
- initialing all of the above items.

Commissions.   An NYSE member firm must charge a commission for acting as a broker for trades done on the Exchange, but no minimum rate is required.

Registration of Employees

Employees of NYSE member firms must be registered with the NYSE through their firms. The Exchange can deny registration to unacceptable applicants.

A registered rep cannot be employed in name only. The rep must have the intention of building a real clientele. Registered reps must, in most cases, work full time for their firms.

A registered rep may voluntarily terminate his employment. Transfer of registration is not permitted; a rep must resign from one employer and reapply for registration with the new firm. The NYSE jurisdiction over a registered rep continues for one year after a termination.

Registered reps must agree to abide by the NYSE constitution and regulations.

Employment Other Than With the Employing broker-dealer. Under NYSE rules, a registered rep must have his firm's written permission before taking a second job.

Compensation. A representative can receive compensation for securities transactions only from his employer. The registered representative can be paid a salary or a commission.

Arbitration   The NYSE Board of Arbitration hears and settles disagreements between members, allied members, member organizations and their employees. Non-members may submit voluntarily to arbitration in disputes with members or employees. The arbitrators' decisions are final; no appeal is possible.

Discipline

Disciplinary Hearing. A grievance or complaint against an employee of a member organization must be made in writing. The employee has 25 days to respond, also in writing. Then a hearing is held before an NYSE panel. The employee may have an attorney present. The panel's decision can be appealed to the NYSE board of directors, but no appeal beyond that point is possible. The board's decision is final.

Penalties and Review. If a member, an allied member or an associated person of a member is found guilty in any disciplinary hearing, the hearing panel may impose any of the following penalties:

- censure;
- fine;
- suspension of registration;
- expulsion; or
- barring of the member firm or associated person from association with any other member.

Communications with the Public

Although the general public often uses the terms interchangeably, the NASD and the NYSE expect principals and representatives to recognize the difference between "advertising" and "sales literature."

Advertising and Sales Literature

Advertising. Advertising includes copy, support graphics and other support materials intended for:

- publication in newspapers, magazines or other periodicals
- radio or television broadcast
- prerecorded telephone marketing messages and tape recordings
- videotape displays
- signs or billboards
- motion pictures and filmstrips
- electronic (computer) communication devices
- telephone directories
- any other use of the public media

Sales Literature. Sales literature is any written communication distributed to customers or to the public in general available to people upon request that does not meet the definition of "advertising." Standardized sales pitches, telephone scripts and seminar tapes are all classed as sales literature and, therefore, are subject to the same rules and regulations that apply to sales literature. Sales literature includes materials such as:

- circulars;
- research reports;
- market letters;
- form letters;
- option worksheets;
- performance reports and summaries;
- text prepared and used for educational seminars;
- telemarketing scripts;
- prepared scripts for public-interest radio and television interviews; and
- reprints and excerpts from any advertisement, sales literature or published news item or article.

Sales literature can be distributed in written, oral or electronic form. It must always be preceded or accompanied by a prospectus.

Form Letters. According to the NASD, a form letter is a sales letter that contains sections or statements identical in essence to statements made or contained in other sales letters. As with all other forms of sales literature, these must be approved in advance by the principal and maintained in a file for a period of *three years* from the date of their first use.

Generic Advertising (Rule 135a). Generic advertising promotes securities as an investment medium, but does not refer to any specific security. Generic advertising often includes information about:

- the securities investment companies offer
- the nature of investment companies
- services offered in connection with the described securities
- explanations of the various types of investment companies
- descriptions of exchange and reinvestment privileges
- where the public can write or call for further information

All generic advertisements must contain the name and address of the registered sponsor of the advertisement. A generic advertisement can be placed only by a firm that offers the type of security or service described.

✓ **For Example:** A discount brokerage firm is not permitted to advertise no-load mutual funds if it does not sell them.

Tombstones (Rule 134 Advertisements). An underwriter is limited in what it can publicly state about a security in registration. Under Rule 134, advertising copy and other sales materials need not be filed with the SEC as part of the registration statement if the body copy is limited to:

- the name of the issuer of the securities being offered;
- a brief description of the business in the offering;
- the date, time and place of the meeting at which stockholders will vote on or consent to the proposed transaction;
- a brief description of the planned transaction; or
- any legend or disclaimer statement required by state or federal law.

Advertisements that meet these restrictions are more commonly known as *tombstones* or *Rule 134 advertisements*. Any advertising copy in a tombstone must also contain the following disclaimers:

- that the issuer has filed the registration statement, but it is not yet effective;
- that the communication does not represent an offer to sell the securities described—securities are sold by prospectus only;
- the name and address of the person or firm to contact for a prospectus; and
- that a response to this advertisement does not obligate the prospect to a buying commitment of any kind.

Rule 134 also covers advertisements and other promotional materials created in support of open-end investment company securities being sold on a continuous new issue offering basis.

Approval and Filing Requirements

Approval

A registered principal of the member firm must approve each advertisement and piece of sales literature *before use* and, if applicable, *before filing with the NASD*. For advertisements or sales literature specific to options, the material must be approved by a registered options principal or compliance ROP. A supervisory analyst must approve research reports.

Filing Requirements

All advertisements and sales literature must be on file with the member for a period of three years; for the first two years, the file must be kept in an easily accessible place. This file must include the name(s) of the person(s) who prepared the material and approved its use.

If the District Business Conduct Committee determines that a member's advertising departs from the standards of fair dealing and good faith, it may require the member to file all advertising and sales literature with the Association's advertising department 10 days before use. The DBCC notifies the member in writing of the types of material to be filed and the length of time the filing requirement is in effect.

Investment Company. A member must file its advertisements and sales literature relating to investment company securities with the NASD's advertising department within 10 days of first use or publication.

Options. Any options sales literature a member sends to a customer must be preceded or accompanied by a current **Options Clearing Corporation (OCC) Options Disclosure Document.**

Direct Participation Program. A member must file its advertising and sales literature concerning direct participation programs with the NASD at least 10 days before use. The member need not file advertising and sales literature that has been filed by sponsors, the program's general partner or underwriter, or another member.

Spot Checks

Members' advertising and sales literature is subject to spot checks by the NASD. Upon written notice, a member must submit all material the NASD advertising department requests. Except for advertisements relating to municipal securities and investment companies, advertisements that have been subject to spot checks by a registered securities exchange or an SRO within the past calendar year are not subject to NASD spot checks.

Exceptions to Filing Requirements

Excluded from the filing requirements are prospectuses, preliminary prospectuses, offering circulars and similar documents used in connection with the offering of securities that have been filed with the SEC or any state. If the security is exempt from registration requirements, any sales literature or advertising need not be filed.

NASD Rules Concerning Public Communications

Securities rules and regulations protect the general public from unscrupulous investment professionals.

The two main problems the NASD's code of professionalism addresses in advertising and sales literature are omissions and distortions of material facts. In general, all communications from a member to the public must be based on principles of fair dealing and good faith. A communication should provide sound basis for evaluating the facts in regard to the product, service or industry promoted. Exaggerated, unwarranted or misleading statements are strictly prohibited.

Identification of Source. In general, sales literature—including market letters and research reports—must identify the member firm's name; the person or firm that prepared the material if copy was prepared outside the member firm; and the date the material was first used.

If the literature contains information that is not current, that fact should be stated in the material.

Customer Recommendations   A member should have reasonable grounds for believing that a security is a suitable investment for a customer before recommending its purchase.

Disclosure Requirements. Proposals and written presentations that include specific recommendations must have reasonable bases to support the recommendations, and the member firm must provide these in the proposal or other document or offer to furnish them upon request. If a recommendation includes a stock purchase, the firm must also provide the stock's current price.

When, in recommending a security to a customer, a firm uses material referring to the performance of past recommendations, it must reveal certain information:

- price or price range of the recommended security at the date and time that the recommendation is made;
- market's general direction;
- availability of information supporting the recommendation;

- any recommendations made of similar securities within the past 12 months, including the nature of the recommendations—buy, sell or hold;
- whether the firm intends to buy or sell any of the recommended security for its own account;
- whether the firm is a market maker in the recommended security;
- whether the firm or its officers or partners own options, rights or warrants to buy the recommended security;
- whether the firm managed or co-managed a public offering of the recommended security or any other of the same issuer's securities during the past three years; and
- all recommendations (gainers and losers) the firm made over the period of time in question.

The time span covered in the list of recommendations must run through consecutive periods, without skipping periods in an attempt to hide particular recommendations or negative price performance data.

A knowledgeable investor uses this type of information to determine whether a recommendation is appropriate for his situation. In addition to meeting these information requirements, the firm making the recommendation must not:

- imply that any guarantees accompany the recommendation;
- compare the recommended security to dissimilar products;
- make fraudulent or misleading statements about the recommended security; or
- make any predictions about the recommended security's future performance or potential.

Recommending Investment Company Products

When recommending mutual funds to clients as investments and when using advertisements or sales literature developed for those investments, a broker-dealer should:

- use charts or graphs showing a fund's performance over a period of time long enough to reflect variations in value under different market conditions, generally a period of at least 10 years;
- reveal the source of the graphics;
- separate dividends from capital gains when making statements about a fund's cash returns;
- not state that a mutual fund is similar to or safer than any other type of security;
- reveal a fund's highest sales charge, even if the client appears to qualify for a breakpoint; and
- not make any fraudulent or misleading statements or omissions of facts.

Periodic Payment Plans. Mutual fund plans that make periodic payments (frequently sold in this manner so investors receive the benefits of dollar cost averaging) cannot be described in advertisements or sales literature without the disclosure that:

- a profit is not assured;
- they do not provide protection from losses in a declining market;
- the plans involve continuous investments regardless of market fluctuations; and
- an investor should consider her financial ability to continue purchases during periods of declining prices.

Advertising Returns. An investor's total return from a mutual fund investment may include income distributions, gains distributions and share appreciation, minus any sales charges and fees. However, average annual total return, as defined by the SEC, assumes reinvestment of all dividends and capital gains distributions and does not deduct any sales charges or management fees. Advertisements that feature total return must also explain how the SEC calculates fund performance. If an advertisement includes any performance figures, the minimum information provided must be 1-, 5- and 10-year or life-of-fund average annual total returns.

Similarly, the SEC requires that current yield calculations be based only on income distributions for the past 12 months divided by the current per-share price:

$$\text{Annual dividend} \div \text{Current price} = \text{Current yield}$$

✓ **For Example:** If NavCo Mutual Fund has a current offering price of $10 and over the past 12 months has distributed dividends totaling $1 and capital gains totaling $.75, the current yield for this fund is 10 percent, not 17.5 percent.

Other Communication Prohibitions

Claims and Opinions Couched as Facts and Conclusions. It violates regulations to pass off opinions, projections and forecasts as guarantees of performance.

Testimonials. Testimonials and endorsements by celebrities and public opinion influencers related to specific recommendations or investment results must not mislead or suggest that past performance indicates future performance. If a member firm pays a fee or other compensation to a person for a testimonial or an endorsement, it must disclose this fact.

If a broker-dealer assembles a sales piece about a particular investment company that includes testimonials by one or more customers, the sales piece must state that:

- past performance does not indicate future performance;
- the company compensated the person who made the testimonial, if this is true; and
- the person making the testimonial has the qualifications to do so (these qualifications must be listed), if the testimonial implies that the statement is based on the customer's special experience or knowledge.

✓ *For Example:* It is improper for a member to include a testimonial by a Dr. Henderson about the investment potential of its new Medical Technology Fund if the doctor's degree is in history.

Offers of Free Service. It is unprofessional to use offers of free service if, in fact, the respondent must assume obligations of one sort or another. Reports, analyses or other services offered to the public must be furnished entirely free and without condition or obligation.

Other Rules. The following are some additional rules regarding unprofessional practices:

- A communication must not state or imply that research facilities are more extensive than they actually are.
- Hedge clauses, caveats and disclaimers must not be used if they are misleading or inconsistent with the material's content.
- Ambiguous references to the NASD or other SROs must not be made with the aim of leading people to believe that a broker-dealer acts with the endorsement and approval of the Association or one of the other SROs. If the NASD's name or logo is used in a member's sales literature, it must not appear in a typeface larger or more prominent than the one used for the member's own name.

Use of Members' Names

General Standards. No material fact is to be omitted if the omission causes the advertisement or literature to be misleading. As a result, all advertising and sales literature must:

- clearly and prominently disclose the NASD member's name;
- clearly describe the relationship between the NASD member and the named entities and products when multiple entities and products are being offered;
- clearly disclose the relationship of an individual and an NASD member when an individual is named in the communication;
- not use or refer to nonexistent degrees or designations; and
- not use degrees or designations in a misleading manner.

Fictional Names. A fictional name or DBA (doing business as) designation is permitted if the name is filed with the NASD and the SEC on Form BD and is the name used to designate the member. However, in states requiring the use of a DBA (that is, where a broker-dealer cannot file under its own name), the member must disclose that it uses the DBA in the particular state(s) for that reason and it must identify the name under which it is filed with the NASD and SEC. Whenever possible, the NASD urges the member to use a name (DBA or other) acceptable for all advertising and sales literature.

Generic Names. The NASD permits a member to use an altered version of a firm name as an "umbrella" identification for purposes of promoting name recognition. A generic, or an umbrella, name can be used as long as:

- it is displayed with the NASD member name also prominently displayed;
- its relationship with the member name is clear (i.e., the information describes the link or separation between the member and the generic name); and
- there is no implication that the generic or umbrella name is the broker-dealer.

Other Designations. A member may designate a portion of its business using a term such as "division of," "service of" or "securities offered through" only if a bona fide division exists. The member name must be clearly designated and the division be clearly identified as a division of the member.

For use by a nonmember firm, the nonmember must clearly and prominently display the member firm's name and its relationship to the member. Additionally, the securities function must be clearly identified as a function of the member, not as a nonmember function.

Recruitment Advertising

Companies that advertise to attract new registered reps are regulated by the same Conduct Rules that cover companies advertising investment products. The advertisements must be truthful, informative and fair in representing the opportunities in the industry and must not contain exaggerated or unwarranted claims.

The advertisements may not emphasize the salaries of top-paid salespeople without revealing that they are not representative, and they may not contain any other statements that may be misleading or fraudulent.

Broker-dealers are permitted, in this one instance, to run blind advertisement—that is, advertisements that do not list a company's name.

Interviews

Once a company starts interviewing potential employees, it is the principal's responsibility to see that both the industry and the job opportunity are represented honestly. Any discussions of the business must present both the upside and the downside of the position and should not misrepresent the average employee's compensation.

Review of NASD Regulations

The following summarizes the NASD regulations regarding advertising and sales literature:

- A principal must approve all advertising and sales literature before use and before filing with the NASD.
- All advertising and sales literature must be kept in a separate file for a minimum of three years.
- All advertising and sales literature concerning registered investment companies must be filed within 10 business days of first use by any member acting as a principal underwriter for the securities. With each filing, the member must provide the actual or anticipated date of first use.
- New members must file with the NASD all advertising they produce or distribute during their first year at least 10 days before first use and must provide the actual or anticipated date of first use with each filing.
- The NASD may require any member to resume filing all of its advertising and sales literature before use.

Legal Recourse of Customers

The Securities Exchange Act of 1934 and the acts of 1933 and 1940 all contain sections prohibiting the use of any fraudulent or manipulative device in the selling of securities to the public.

The rules make it unlawful for any person to use the mails or any facilities of interstate commerce to "employ, in connection with the purchase or sale of any security, any manipulative or deceptive device in contravention of such rules and regulations as the Commission may prescribe as necessary." In essence, this passage states simply that an act is unlawful if the SEC says it is, and the enforcement of the intent of the act is not to be limited by the letter of the law.

Statute of Limitations. Any client may sue for damages if he believes that a broker-dealer used any form of manipulative or deceptive practices in the sale of securities. The client must bring the lawsuit within three years of the manipulative act and within one year of his discovery of the manipulation or deception.

Telephone Communications with the Public

The Telephone Consumer Protection Act of 1991 (TCPA), administered by the Federal Communications Commission (FCC), was enacted to protect consumers from unwanted telephone solicitations. A telephone solicitation is defined as a telephone call initiated for the purpose of encouraging the purchase of or investment in property, goods or services. The act governs commercial calls, recorded solicitations from autodialers and solicitations and advertisements to facsimile machines and modems. The act requires an organization that performs telemarketing—cold calling in particular—to:

- maintain a "do-not-call list" of customers who do not want to be called and keep a customer's name on the list for 10 years from the time she makes the request;
- institute a written policy on maintenance procedures for the do-not-call list;
- train reps on using the list;
- ensure that reps acknowledge and immediately record the names and telephone numbers of customers who ask not to be called again;
- ensure that anyone making cold calls for the firm informs customers of the firm's name and telephone number or address;
- ensure that telemarketers do not call a customer within 10 years of her do-not-call request; and
- ensure that a telephone solicitation occurs only between the hours of 8:00 a.m. and 9:00 p.m. of the time zone in which the customer is located.

The act exempts calls:

- made to parties with whom the caller has an established business relationship or where the caller has prior express permission or invitation;
- made on behalf of a tax-exempt nonprofit organization;
- not made for a commercial purpose; and
- made for legitimate debt collection purposes.

Summary

The SEC was created by the Securities Exchange Act of 1934. The SEC is the primary regulatory body over the securities industry. Self-regulatory organizations, acting under authority approved by the SEC, regulate the conduct of business within particular boundaries. These include:

- New York Stock Exchange (NYSE)
- National Association of Securities Dealers, Inc. (NASD)

- Municipal Securities Rulemaking Board (MSRB)
- Chicago Board Options Exchange (CBOE)

The type and location of a security transaction determines which SRO has jurisdiction.

Key Concepts

To prepare for your license exam, you should learn the following concepts.

In addition to studying these key concepts, use the SEC and SRO Regulations Hot Sheet on page 650 for further review.

advertising
arbitration
associated person (AP)
Code of Arbitration Procedure
Code of Procedure (COP)
cold calling
Conduct Rules
District Business Conduct
   Committee (DBCC)
form letter
generic advertising

NASD Bylaws
NASD Manual
National Association of Securities
   Dealers, Inc. (NASD)
New York Stock Exchange (NYSE)
regular complaint procedure
Rule 134 advertisement
sales literature
summary complaint procedure
testimonial
Uniform Practice Code (UPC)

Review Questions

1. The NASD Uniform Practice Code was established to

   A. require that practices in the investment banking and securities industry be just, reasonable and nondiscriminatory between investors

   B. eliminate advertising and sales literature that the SEC considers to be in violation of standards

   C. provide a procedure for handling trade complaints from investors

   D. maintain similarity of business practices among member organizations in the securities industry

2. "Freeriding and withholding" refers to

   A. distributing new issues valued at amounts exceeding the cost

   B. purchasing securities with the intent of selling them before the settlement date

   C. a member of an underwriting or a selling group's failing to make a public offering of a security at the public offering price

   D. none of the above

3. A sell-out happens when which of the following occurs?

   A. The buyer of a security fails to complete the contract according to its terms, and the broker-dealer closes the contract by selling the security for the account of the buyer.

   B. The seller of a security fails to complete the contract according to its terms, and the buyer closes the contract by buying the security in the best available market and charging the seller.

   C. The party who requests the transfer of securities fails to pay the transfer agent's service charges, and the transfer agent sells the securities to cover the deficit.

   D. A season ticket holder sells a game ticket to a scalper.

4. Disciplinary decisions of the NASD Board of Governors and appellate and review procedures are matters covered in the

   A. SEC Bylaws

   B. Conduct Rules

   C. Code of Procedure

   D. Uniform Practice Code

5. The purpose of the Conduct Rules is to

   A. provide a means of handling trade complaints from investors

   B. provide a means of communication between member firms

   C. require that business practices be similar among all members

   D. promote fair and ethical trade practices for member firms to use when dealing with the public

6. The Code of Arbitration is for

   A. handling violations of the Conduct Rules
   B. ensuring just and equitable practices of fair trade
   C. establishing uniform trade practices
   D. handling disagreements and claims between member firms, registered reps and the public

7. Who is permitted to transact business on the floor of the Exchange?

   A. Members
   B. Allied members
   C. Floor clerks
   D. Floor officials

8. All of the following need permission to open a margin account with an NYSE member firm EXCEPT an employee of a(n)

   A. communications company
   B. bank
   C. broker-dealer
   D. insurance company

9. Which of the following would be considered *discretionary*?

   A. Order that specifies the size of the security but leaves the choice of price and time up to the registered rep
   B. Account in which the broker has the power to decide when and what to trade without specific customer authorization for those trades
   C. Account in which the customer has power of attorney over another individual's account
   D. Account in which an investment adviser has power of attorney over another individual's account

Answers & Rationale

1. **D.** The NASD Uniform Practice Code covers settlement, good delivery, ex-dates, confirmations and DK procedures, and contains guidelines for broker-dealers to follow when they do business with other member broker-dealers.

2. **C.** When a member firm participates in a new-issue distribution, the Conduct Rules state that the member must make a bona fide offering at the POP. Failure to do so is considered "freeriding and withholding."

3. **A.** If the buyer fails to pay for the security on time, the broker-dealer will sell the security in the open market to fulfill the buyer's contract. The buyer will be charged for all the expenses related to the sell-out (or buy-in).

4. **C.** The Code of Procedure outlines the methods for handling trade practice complaints when a violation of the Conduct Rules is involved.

5. **D.** The NASD drafted the Conduct Rules as a comprehensive set of guidelines and rules that require member firms (and registered representatives) to use just and equitable practices of trade. The main goal of the rules is to protect the customer by preventing fraud, market manipulation and unreasonable charges and commissions.

6. **D.** The Code of Arbitration provides procedures for settling disputes, claims and controversies that arise between broker-dealers, registered representatives and the public.

7. **A.** The NYSE provides a central location at which its members can transact the business of buying and selling securities.

8. **A.** To open a margin account, an employee of the Exchange or of a bank or an insurance company needs permission from his employer. An employee of a communications company could be any investor.

9. **B.** If a customer gives his registered representative written authority to decide which security to trade, what action to take (buy or sell) and how much to trade, the representative has discretion in the account; therefore, this is a discretionary account.

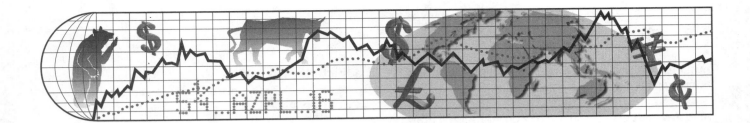

Glossary

A

Accelerated Cost Recovery System (ACRS)
See Modified Accelerated Cost Recovery System.

accordion loan A call loan that allows a brokerage firm to pledge additional securities as collateral in an existing loan account when additional credit is needed. *See also* broker's loan; call loan.

account executive (AE) *See* registered representative.

accredited investor As defined in Rule 502 of Regulation D, any institution or individual meeting minimum net worth requirements for the purchase of securities qualifying under the Regulation D registration exemption.

An accredited investor is generally accepted to be one who:
- has a net worth of $1 million or more; or
- has had an annual income of $200,000 or more in each of the two most recent years (or $300,000 jointly with a spouse) and who has a reasonable expectation of reaching the same income level in the current year.

accretion of bond discount An accounting process whereby the initial cost of a bond purchased at a discount is increased annually to reflect the basis of the bond as it approaches maturity.

When a bond is bought at a discount, the IRS requires that a portion of the difference between the discounted purchase price and the face value be taxed each year until maturity even though the gain will not be realized until maturity. *See also* amortization of bond premium; basis.

accrual accounting A method of reporting income when earned and expenses when incurred, as opposed to reporting income when received and expenses when paid. *See also* cash basis accounting.

accrued interest The interest that has accumulated since the last interest payment up to, but not including, the settlement date and that is added to a bond transaction's contract price.

There are two methods for calculating accrued interest: the 30-day-month (360-day-year) method for corporate and municipal bonds and the actual-calendar-days (365-day-year) method for government bonds. Income bonds, bonds in default and zero-coupon bonds trade without accrued interest (flat). *See also* flat.

accumulation account An account established to hold securities pending their deposit into a municipal securities unit investment trust.

accumulation stage The period during which contributions are made to an annuity account. *See also* accumulation unit; distribution stage.

accumulation unit An accounting measure used to determine an annuitant's proportionate interest in the insurer's separate account during an annuity's accumulation (deposit) stage. *See also* accumulation stage; annuity unit; separate account.

acid-test ratio A measure of a corporation's liquidity, calculated by adding cash, cash equivalents, and accounts and notes receivable, and dividing the result by total current liabilities. It is a more stringent test of liquidity than current ratio. *Syn.* quick ratio. *See also* cash assets ratio; current ratio.

acquisition fee The total charges and commissions paid by any party in connection with the selection or purchase of property by a direct participation program. Included in the total is any real estate commission, acquisition expense, development fee, selection fee or construction fee of a similar nature. The fee is added to the basis in the asset for the purpose of depreciation and calculating gain or loss.

ACRS *See* Modified Accelerated Cost Recovery System.

ACT *See* Automated Confirmation Transaction Service.

active crowd The members of the NYSE that trade actively traded bonds. *Syn.* free crowd. *See also* inactive crowd.

act of 1933 *See* Securities Act of 1933.

act of 1934 *See* Securities Exchange Act of 1934.

Additional List A list of securities for which Nasdaq will supply quotations for dissemination to the media but that do not meet the criteria for inclusion on its National List; both lists are compiled by the NASD Information Committee. *See also* National List.

adjacent acreage Producing or nonproducing oil or gas leases located within the area of an existing well site. Adjacent acreage may prove valuable for continued development of the original oil or gas prospect.

adjusted basis The value attributed to an asset or security that reflects any deductions taken on, or capital improvements to, the asset or security. Adjusted basis is used to compute the gain or loss on the sale or other disposition of the asset or security.

adjusted gross income (AGI) Earned income plus net passive income, portfolio income and capital gains. *See also* tax liability.

administrator (1) A person authorized by a court of law to liquidate an intestate decedent's estate. (2) An official or agency that administers a state's securities laws.

ADR *See* American depositary receipt.

ADS *See* American depositary receipt.

ad valorem tax A tax based on the value of real or personal property. Property taxes are the major source of revenues for local governing units. *See also* assessed value.

advance/decline line A technical analysis tool representing the total of differences between advances and declines of security prices. The advance/decline line is considered the best indicator of market movement as a whole. *See also* breadth-of-market theory.

advance refunding Refinancing an existing municipal bond issue prior to its maturity or call date by using money from the sale of a new bond issue. The proceeds of the new bond issue are used to purchase government securities, and the municipality puts the principal and interest received from these securities into an escrow account; it then uses these funds to pay off the original bond issue at the first call date. *Syn.* prerefunding. *See also* defeasance; refunding.

advertisement Any promotional material designed for use by newspapers, magazines, billboards, radio, television, telephone recording or other public media where the firm has little control over the type of individuals exposed to the material. *See also* sales literature.

advisory board Under the Investment Company Act of 1940, a board that advises an investment company on matters concerning its investments in securities, but does not have the power to make investment decisions or take action itself. An advisory board must be composed of persons who have no other connection with, and serve no other function for, the investment company.

AE *See* registered representative.

affiliate (1) A person who directly or indirectly owns, controls or holds with power to vote 10 percent or more of the outstanding voting securities of a company. (2) With respect to a direct participation program, any person who controls, is controlled by or is under common control with the program's sponsor and includes any person who beneficially owns 50 percent or more of the equity interest in the sponsor. (3) Under the Investment Company Act of 1940, a person who has any type of control over an investment company's operations, which includes anyone with 5 percent or more of the outstanding voting securities of the investment company or any corporation of which the investment company holds 5 percent or more of outstanding securities. *See also* control person; insider.

agency basis *See* agency transaction.

agency issue A debt security issued by an authorized agency of the federal government. Such an issue is backed by the issuing agency itself, not by the full faith and credit of the U.S. government (except GNMA and Federal Import Export Bank issues). *See also* government security.

agency transaction A transaction in which a broker-dealer acts for the accounts of others by buying or selling securities on behalf of customers. *Syn.* agency basis. *See also* agent; broker; principal transaction.

agent (1) An individual or a firm that effects securities transactions for the accounts of others. (2) A person licensed by a state as a life insurance agent. (3) A securities salesperson who represents a broker-dealer or an issuer when selling or trying to sell securities to the investing public; this individual is considered an agent whether he actually receives or simply solicits orders. *See also* broker; broker-dealer; dealer; principal.

aggregate indebtedness (AI) (1) An accounting of all money a broker-dealer owes to customers, other broker-dealers, banks and other lenders, business suppliers and vendors, and anyone who does business with or works for the firm. Liabilities that are excluded from aggregate indebtedness include those that are secured by fixed assets and other amounts payable that are secured by the firm's own securities. (2) Customer net margin debit balances. *See also* Rule 15c3-1.

aggressive investment strategy A method of portfolio allocation and management aimed at achieving maximum return. Aggressive investors place a high percentage of their investable assets in equity securities and a far lower percentage in safer debt securities and cash equivalents, and they pursue aggressive policies including margin trading, arbitrage and option trading. *See also* balanced investment strategy; defensive investment strategy.

AGI *See* adjusted gross income.

agreement among underwriters The agreement that sets forth the terms under which each member of an underwriting syndicate will participate in a new issue offering and states the duties and responsibilities of the underwriting manager. *See also* syndicate; underwriting manager.

agreement of limited partnership The contract that establishes guidelines for the operation of a direct participation program, including the roles of the general and limited partners.

AIR *See* assumed interest rate.

allied member A general partner of an NYSE member firm who is not an NYSE member, an owner of 5 percent or more of the outstanding voting stock of an NYSE member corporation, or a principal executive director or officer of a member corporation. Allied members do not own seats on the NYSE.

all or none order (AON) An order that instructs the floor broker to execute the entire order in one transaction; if the order cannot be executed in its entirety, it is allowed to expire.

all or none underwriting (AON) A form of best efforts underwriting in which the underwriter agrees that if it is unable to sell all the shares (or a prescribed minimum), the issuer will cancel the offering. This type of agreement may be used when the issuer requires a minimum amount of capital to be raised; if the minimum is not reached, the securities sold and the money raised are returned. Commissions are not paid unless the offering is completed. *See also* underwriting.

alpha coefficient A measure of the projected rate of change in a security's price independent of market-related factors but based instead on such indicators as the strength of the company's earnings and the expected level of sales. *See also* beta coefficient.

alternative minimum tax (AMT) An alternative tax computation that adds certain tax preference items back into adjusted gross income. If the AMT is higher than the regular tax liability for the year, the regular tax and the amount by which the AMT exceeds the regular tax are paid. *See also* tax preference item.

alternative order An order to execute either of two transactions—for example, placing a sell limit (above the market) and a sell stop (below the market) on the same stock. *Syn.* either/or order; one cancels other order.

AMBAC Indemnity Corporation (AMBAC) A corporation that offers insurance on the timely payment of interest and principal obligations of municipal securities. Bonds insured by AMBAC usually receive a AAA rating from rating services.

American depositary receipt (ADR) A negotiable certificate representing a given number of shares of stock in a foreign corporation. It is bought and sold in the American securities markets, just as stock is traded. *Syn.* American depositary share.

American Stock Exchange (AMEX) A private, not-for-profit corporation located in New York City that handles approximately one-fifth of all securities trades within the United States.

AMEX *See* American Stock Exchange.

amortization (1) The paying off of debt in regular installments over a period of time. (2) The ratable deduction of certain capitalized expenditures over a specified period of time.

amortization of bond premium An accounting process whereby the initial cost of a bond purchased at a premium is decreased to reflect the basis of the bond as it approaches maturity. *See also* accretion of bond discount.

annual compliance review The annual meeting that all registered representatives must attend, the purpose of which is to review compliance issues.

annual ROI The annual return on a bond investment, which equals the annual interest either plus the prorated discount or minus the prorated premium.

annuitant A person who receives an annuity contract's distribution.

annuitize To change an annuity contract from the accumulation (pay-in) stage to the distribution (payout) stage.

annuity A contract between an insurance company and an individual, generally guaranteeing lifetime income to the individual on whose life the contract is based in return for either a lump sum or a periodic payment to the insurance company. The contract holder's objective is usually retirement income. *See also* deferred annuity; fixed annuity; immediate annuity; variable annuity.

annuity unit An accounting measure used to determine the amount of each payment during an annuity's distribution stage. The calculation takes into account the value of each accumulation unit and such other factors as assumed interest rate and mortality risk. *See also* accumulation unit; annuity; distribution stage.

AON *See* all or none order; all or none underwriting.

AP *See* associated person of a member.

appreciation The increase in an asset's value.

approved plan *See* qualified retirement plan.

arbitrage The simultaneous purchase and sale of the same or related securities to take advantage of a market inefficiency. *See also* index arbitrage; market arbitrage; special arbitrage account.

arbitrageur One who engages in arbitrage.

arbitration The arrangement whereby the NYSE's Board of Arbitration or a designated arbitration association hears and settles disagreements between members, allied members, member organizations and their employees. Nonmembers in dispute with members or employees may submit voluntarily to arbitration. *See also* simplified arbitration.

ascending triangle On a technical analyst's trading activity chart, a pattern which indicates that the market has started to move back up; considered to be a bullish indicator. *See also* descending triangle.

ask An indication by a trader or a dealer of a willingness to sell a security or a commodity; the price at which an investor can buy from a broker-dealer. *Syn.* offer. *See also* bid; public offering price; quotation.

assessed value The value of a property as appraised by a taxing authority for the purpose of levying taxes. Assessed value may equal market value or a stipulated percentage of market value. *See also* ad valorem tax.

assessment An additional amount of capital that a participant in a direct participation program may be called upon to furnish beyond the subscription amount. Assessments may be mandatory or optional and must be called within twelve months.

asset (1) Anything that an individual or a corporation owns. (2) A balance sheet item expressing what a corporation owns.

asset allocation fund A mutual fund that splits its investment assets among stocks, bonds and other vehicles in an attempt to provide a consistent return for the investor. *See also* mutual fund.

assignee A person who has acquired a beneficial interest in a limited partnership from a third party but who is neither a substitute limited partner nor an assignee of record.

assignee of record A person who has acquired a beneficial interest in a limited partnership and whose interest has been recorded on the books of the partnership and is the subject of a written instrument of assignment.

assignment (1) A document accompanying or part of a stock certificate that is signed by the person named on the certificate for the purpose of transferring the certificate's title to another person's name. (2) The act of identifying and notifying an account holder that the option owner has exercised an option held short in that account. *See also* stock power.

associated person of a member (AP) Any employee, manager, director, officer or partner of a member broker-dealer or another entity (issuer, bank, etc.), or any person controlling, controlled by or in common control with that member. *See also* registered representative.

assumed interest rate (AIR) The net rate of investment return that must be credited to a variable life insurance policy to ensure that at all times the variable death benefit equals the amount of the death benefit. The AIR forms the basis for projecting payments, but it is not guaranteed.

at-the-close order *See* market-on-close order.

at-the-money The term used to describe an option when the underlying stock is trading precisely at the exercise price of the option. *See also* in-the-money; out-of-the-money.

at-the-opening order An order that specifies it is to be executed at the opening of the market or of trading in that security or else it is to be canceled. The order does not have to be executed at the opening price. *See also* market-on-close order.

auction market A market in which buyers enter competitive bids and sellers enter competitive offers simultaneously. The NYSE is an auction market. *Syn.* double auction market.

audited financial statement A financial statement of a program, a corporation or an issuer (including the profit and loss statement, cash flow and source and application of revenues statement, and balance sheet) that has been examined and verified by an independent certified public accountant.

authorized stock The number of shares of stock that a corporation can issue. This number of shares is stipulated in the corporation's state-approved charter and may be changed by a vote of the corporation's stockholders.

authorizing resolution The document enabling a municipal or state government to issue securities. The resolution provides for the establishment of a revenue fund in which receipts or income is deposited.

AUTOAMOS *See* Automatic AMEX Options Switch.

Automated Confirmation Transaction (ACT) Service The post-execution, on-line transaction reporting and comparison system developed by the NASD. ACT's primary purpose is to make reconciliation and matching telephone-negotiated trades easier for member firms, thereby increasing the efficiency of the firms' operations.

Automatic AMEX Options Switch (AUTOAMOS) The computerized order routing system that the American Stock Exchange uses for options orders. AUTOAMOS electronically executes trades for the four to six most active stocks of the Standard & Poor's 100 Index options, and it accepts options orders from brokers for up to 20 contracts. *See also* American Stock Exchange.

Automatic Post Execution and Reporting (AUTOPER) The computerized order routing system that the American Stock Exchange uses for equity orders. AUTOPER electronically routes day, good-till-canceled and marketable limit orders from brokers to AMEX specialists, and routes execution reports from the specialists back to the brokers. It accepts both odd-lot and round-lot equity orders from brokers for up to 2,000 shares. *See also* American Stock Exchange.

average A price at a midpoint among a number of prices. Technical analysts frequently use averages as market indicators. *See also* index.

average basis An accounting method used when an investor has made multiple purchases at different prices of the same security; the method averages the purchase prices to calculate an investor's cost basis in shares being liquidated. The difference between the average cost basis and the selling price determines the investor's tax liability. *See also* first in, first out; last in, first out; share identification.

average price A step in determining a bond's yield to maturity. A bond's average price is calculated by adding its face value to the price paid for it and dividing the result by two.

B

B Consolidated Tape market identifier for the Boston Stock Exchange.

BA *See* banker's acceptance.

back away The failure of an over-the-counter market maker to honor a firm bid and asked price. This violates the NASD Rules of Fair Practice.

back-end load A commission or sales fee that is charged when mutual fund shares or variable annuity contracts are redeemed. It declines annually, decreasing to zero over an extended holding period—up to eight years—as described in the prospectus. *Syn.* contingent-deferred sales load. *See also* front-end load.

balanced fund A mutual fund whose stated investment policy is to have at all times some portion of its investment assets in bonds and preferred stock as well as in common stock in an attempt to provide both growth and income. *See also* mutual fund.

balanced investment strategy A method of portfolio allocation and management aimed at balancing risk and return. A balanced portfolio may combine stocks, bonds, packaged products and cash equivalents.

balance of payments (BOP) An international accounting record of all transactions made by one particular country with others during a certain time period; it compares the amount of foreign currency the country has taken in to the amount of its own currency it has paid out. *See also* balance of trade.

balance of trade The largest component of a country's balance of payments; it concerns the export and import of merchandise (not services). Debit items include imports, foreign aid, domestic spending abroad and domestic investments abroad. Credit items include exports, foreign spending in the domestic economy and foreign investments in the domestic economy. *See also* balance of payments.

balance sheet A report of a corporation's financial condition at a specific time.

balance sheet equation A formula stating that a corporation's assets equal the sum of its liabilities plus shareholders' equity.

balloon maturity A repayment schedule for an issue of bonds wherein a large number of the bonds come due at a prescribed time (normally at the final maturity date); a type of serial maturity. *See also* maturity date.

BAN *See* bond anticipation note.

banker's acceptance (BA) A money-market instrument used to finance international and domestic trade. A banker's acceptance is a check drawn on a bank by an importer or exporter of goods and represents the bank's conditional promise to pay the face amount of the note at maturity (normally less than three months).

bank guarantee letter The document supplied by a commercial bank in which the bank certifies that a put writer has sufficient funds on deposit at the bank to equal the aggregate exercise price of the put; this releases the option writer from the option margin requirement.

banking act *See* Glass-Steagall Act of 1933.

bar chart A tool used by technical analysts to track the price movements of a commodity over several consecutive time periods. *See also* moving average chart; point-and-figure chart.

basis (1) The cost of an asset or security. (2) The difference between the cash price of a commodity and a futures contract price of the same commodity; basis is usually computed between the spot and the nearby futures contract.

basis point A measure of a bond's yield, equal to $\frac{1}{100}$ of 1 percent of yield. A bond whose yield increases from 5.0 percent to 5.5 percent is said to increase by 50 basis points. *See also* point.

basis quote The price of a security quoted in terms of the yield that the purchaser can expect to receive.

BD *See* broker-dealer.

bear An investor who acts on the belief that a security or the market is falling or will fall. *See also* bull.

bearer bond *See* coupon bond.

bear market A market in which prices of a certain group of securities are falling or are expected to fall. *See also* bull market.

best efforts underwriting A new issue securities underwriting in which the underwriter acts as an agent for the issuer and puts forth its best efforts to sell as many shares as possible. The underwriter has no liability for unsold shares, unlike in a firm commitment underwriting. *See also* underwriting.

beta coefficient A means of measuring the volatility of a security or a portfolio of securities in comparison with the market as a whole. A beta of 1 indicates that the security's price will move with the market. A beta greater than 1 indicates that the security's price will be more volatile than the market. A beta less than 1 means that it will be less volatile than the market.

bid An indication by an investor, a trader or a dealer of a willingness to buy a security; the price at which an investor can sell to a broker-dealer. *See also* offer; public offering price; quotation.

bid form The form submitted by underwriters in a competitive bid on a new issue of municipal securities. The underwriter states the interest rate, price bid and net interest cost to the issuer.

blind pool A direct participation program that does not state in advance all of the specific properties in which the general partners will invest the partnership's money. At least 25 percent of the proceeds of the offering are kept in reserve for the purchase of nonspecified properties. *Syn.* nonspecified property program.

block trade A trade so large that the normal auction market cannot absorb it in a reasonable time at a reasonable price. In general, 10,000 shares of stock or $200,000 worth of bonds would be considered a block trade.

blotter A book of original entry in which a broker-dealer records on a daily basis every transaction, movement of securities and cash receipt and disbursement. *Syn.* daily journal.

blue chip stock The equity issues of financially stable, well-established companies that have demonstrated their ability to pay dividends in both good and bad times.

Blue List, The A daily publication that lists current municipal bond offerings traded in the secondary market by banks and brokers nationwide.

blue-sky To register a securities offering in a particular state. *See also* blue-sky laws; registration by coordination; registration by filing; registration by qualification.

blue-sky laws The nickname for state regulations governing the securities industry. The term was coined in the early 1900s by a Kansas Supreme Court justice who wanted regulation to protect against "speculative schemes that have no more basis than so many feet of blue sky." *See also* Series 63; Series 65; Uniform Securities Act.

board of directors (1) Individuals elected by stockholders to establish corporate management policies. A board of directors decides, among other issues, if and when dividends will be paid to stockholders. (2) The body that governs the NYSE. It is composed of 20 members elected for a term of two years by the NYSE general membership.

Board of Governors The body that governs the NASD. It is composed of 27 members elected by both the NASD general membership and the Board itself.

board order An order that becomes a market order only if the market touches or breaks through the order price. Board orders to buy are placed below the current market. Board orders to sell are placed above the current market. *Syn.* market-if-touched order.

bona fide quote An offer from a broker-dealer to buy or sell securities. It indicates a willingness to execute a trade under the terms and conditions accompanying the quote. *See also* firm quote; nominal quote.

bond An issuing company's or government's legal obligation to repay the principal of a loan to bond investors at a specified future date. Bonds are usually issued with par or face values of $1,000, representing the amount of money borrowed. The issuer promises to pay a percentage of the par value as interest on the borrowed funds. The interest payment is stated on the face of the bond at issue.

bond anticipation note (BAN) A short-term municipal debt security to be paid from the proceeds of long-term debt when it is issued.

bond attorney *See* bond counsel.

bond basis book A reference book that gives yield-to-maturity tables for bonds, arranged according to coupon rates, times to maturity and prices.

Bond Buyer indexes Indexes of yield levels of municipal bonds, published daily by *The Bond Buyer*. The indexes are indicators of yields that would be offered on AA- and A-rated general obligation bonds with 20-year maturities and revenue bonds with 30-year maturities.

bond counsel An attorney retained by a municipal issuer to give an opinion concerning the legality and tax-exempt status of a municipal issue. *Syn.* bond attorney. *See also* legal opinion of counsel.

bond fund A mutual fund whose investment objective is to provide stable income with minimal capital risk. It invests in income-producing instruments, which may include corporate, government or municipal bonds. *See also* mutual fund.

bond interest coverage ratio An indication of the safety of a corporate bond. It measures the number of times by which earnings before interest and taxes exceeds annual interest on outstanding bonds. *Syn.* fixed charge coverage ratio; times fixed charges earned ratio; times interest earned ratio.

bond quote One of a number of quotations listed in the financial press and most daily newspapers that provide representative bid prices from the previous day's bond market. Quotes for corporate and government bonds are percentages of the bonds' face values (usually $1,000). Corporate bonds are quoted in increments of ⅛, where a quote of 99⅛ represents 99.125 percent of par ($1,000), or $991.25. Government bonds are quoted in ⅟₃₂nds. Municipal bonds may be quoted on a dollar basis or on a yield-to-maturity basis. *See also* quotation; stock quote.

bond rating An evaluation of the possibility of a bond issuer's default, based on an analysis of the issuer's financial condition and profit potential. Standard & Poor's, Moody's Investors Service and Fitch Investors Service, among others, provide bond rating services.

bond ratio One of several tools used by bond analysts to assess the degree of safety offered by a corporation's bonds. It measures the percentage of the corporation's capitalization that is provided by long-term debt financing, calculated by dividing the total face value of the outstanding bonds by the total capitalization. *Syn.* debt ratio.

bond swap The sale of a bond and the simultaneous purchase of a different bond in a like amount. The technique is used to control tax liability, extend maturity or update investment objectives. *Syn.* tax swap. *See also* wash sale.

bond yield The annual rate of return on a bond investment. Types of yield include nominal yield, current yield, yield to maturity and yield to call. Their relationships vary according to whether the bond in question is at a discount, at a premium or at par. *See also* current yield; nominal yield.

book-entry security A security sold without delivery of a certificate. Evidence of ownership is maintained on records kept by a central agency; for example, the Treasury keeps records of Treasury bill purchasers. Transfer of ownership is recorded by entering the change on the books or electronic files. *See also* coupon bond; registered; registered as to principal only.

book value per bond A measure of the amount of producing assets behind each corporate bond, calculated by dividing net tangible assets by funded debt. *Syn.* net tangible assets per bond.

book value per share A measure of the net worth of each share of common stock. It is calculated by subtracting intangible assets and preferred stock from total net worth, then dividing the result by the number of shares of common outstanding. *Syn.* net tangible assets per share.

BOP *See* balance of payments.

Boston Stock Exchange (BSE) The third oldest stock exchange in the United States and the first exchange to provide membership to foreign broker-dealers. *See also* regional exchange.

branch office Any location identified by any means to the public as a place where a registered broker-dealer conducts business.

breadth-of-market theory A technical analysis theory that predicts the strength of the market according

to the number of issues that advance or decline in a particular trading day. *See also* advance/decline line.

breakeven point The point at which gains equal losses.

breakout In technical analysis, the movement of a security's price through an established support or resistance level. *See also* resistance level; support level.

breakpoint The schedule of sales charge discounts a mutual fund offers for lump-sum or cumulative investments.

breakpoint sale The sale of mutual fund shares in an amount just below the level at which the purchaser would qualify for reduced sales charges. This violates the NASD Rules of Fair Practice.

broad-based index An index designed to reflect the movement of the market as a whole. Examples include the S&P 100, the S&P 500, the AMEX Major Market Index and the *Value Line* Composite Index. *See also* index.

broad tape News wires that continuously provide price and background information on securities and commodities markets.

broker (1) An individual or a firm that charges a fee or commission for executing buy and sell orders submitted by another individual or firm. (2) The role of a firm when it acts as an agent for a customer and charges the customer a commission for its services. *See also* agent; broker-dealer; dealer.

broker-dealer (BD) A person or firm in the business of buying and selling securities. A firm may act as both broker (agent) and dealer (principal), but not in the same transaction. Broker-dealers normally must register with the SEC, the appropriate SROs and any state in which they do business. *See also* agent; broker; dealer; principal.

broker fail *See* fail to deliver.

broker's broker (1) A specialist executing orders for a commission house broker or another brokerage firm. (2) A floor broker on an exchange or a broker-dealer in the over-the-counter market executing a trade as an agent for another broker. *See also* correspondent broker-dealer.

broker's loan Money loaned to a brokerage firm by a commercial bank or other lending institution for financing customers' margin account debit balances. *See also* call loan; rehypothecation; time loan.

BSE *See* Boston Stock Exchange.

bucketing Accepting customer orders without executing them immediately through an exchange. A "bucket shop" may use firm or other customer positions or orders to execute them, or may not execute them at all. Bucketing is an illegal activity.

bull An investor who acts on the belief that a security or the market is rising or will rise. *See also* bear.

bulletin board *See* OTC Bulletin Board.

bull market A market in which prices of a certain group of securities are rising or will rise. *See also* bear market.

bunching orders Combining odd-lot orders from different clients into round lots so as to save the clients the odd-lot differential.

business cycle A predictable long-term pattern of alternating periods of economic growth and decline. The cycle passes through four stages: expansion, peak, contraction and trough.

business day A day on which financial markets are open for trading. Saturdays, Sundays and legal holidays are not considered business days.

buyer's option A settlement contract that calls for delivery and payment according to a number of days specified by the buyer. *See also* regular way; seller's option.

buy-in The procedure that the buyer of a security follows when the seller fails to complete the contract by delivering the security. The buyer closes the contract by buying the security in the open market and charging the account of the seller for transaction fees and any loss caused by changes in the markets. *See also* sell-out.

buying power The amount of fully margined securities that a margin client can purchase using only the cash, securities and special memorandum account balance and without depositing additional equity.

buy stop order An order to buy a security that is entered at a price above the current offering price and that is triggered when the market price touches or goes through the buy stop price.

C

C Consolidated Tape market identifier for the Cincinnati Stock Exchange.

cabinet crowd *See* inactive crowd.

CAES *See* Intermarket Trading System/Computer Assisted Execution System.

calendar spread *See* horizontal spread.

call (1) An option contract giving the owner the right to buy a specified amount of an underlying security at a specified price within a specified time. (2) The act of exercising a call option. *See also* put.

callable bond A type of bond issued with a provision allowing the issuer to redeem the bond before maturity at a predetermined price. *See also* call price.

callable preferred stock A type of preferred stock issued with a provision allowing the corporation to call in the stock at a certain price and retire it. *See also* call price; preferred stock.

call buyer An investor who pays a premium for an option contract and receives, for a specified time, the right to buy the underlying security at a specified price. *See also* call writer; put buyer; put writer.

call date The date, specified in the prospectus of every callable security, after which the security's issuer has the option to redeem the issue at par or at par plus a premium.

call feature *See* call provision.

call loan A collateralized loan of a brokerage firm having no maturity date that may be called (terminated) at any time. The loan has a fluctuating interest rate that is recomputed daily. Generally the loan is payable on demand the day after it is contracted. If not called, the loan is automatically renewed for another day. *See also* broker's loan; time loan.

call loan rate The rate of interest a brokerage firm charges its margin account clients on their debit balances.

call money rate The rate of interest a bank or lender charges brokerage firms on stock exchange collateral.

call price The price, usually a premium over the issue's par value, at which preferred stocks or bonds can be redeemed before an issue's maturity.

call protection A provision in a bond indenture stating that the issue is noncallable for a certain period of time (5 years, 10 years, etc.) after the original issue date. *See also* call provision.

call provision The written agreement between an issuing corporation and its bondholders or preferred stockholders giving the corporation the option to redeem its senior securities at a specified price before maturity and under certain conditions. *Syn.* call feature.

call risk The potential for a bond to be called before maturity, leaving the investor without the bond's current income. As this is more likely to occur during times of falling interest rates, the investor may not be able to reinvest his principal at a comparable rate of return.

call spread An option investor's position in which the investor buys a call on a security and writes a call on the same security but with a different expiration date, exercise price, or both.

call writer An investor who receives a premium and takes on, for a specified time, the obligation to sell the underlying security at a specified price at the call buyer's discretion. *See also* call buyer; put buyer; put writer.

cancel former order (CFO) An instruction by a customer to cancel a previously entered order.

capital Accumulated money or goods available for use in producing more money or goods.

capital appreciation A rise in an asset's market price.

capital asset All tangible property, including securities, real estate and other property, held for the long term.

capital contribution The amount of a participant's investment in a direct participation program, not including units purchased by the sponsors.

capital gain The profit realized when a capital asset is sold for a higher price than the purchase price. *See also* capital loss; long-term gain.

capitalization The sum of a corporation's long-term debt, stock and surpluses. *Syn.* invested capital. *See also* capital structure.

capitalization ratio A measure of an issuer's financial status that calculates the value of its bonds, preferred stock or common stock as a percentage of its total capitalization.

capitalize An accounting procedure whereby a corporation records an expenditure as a capital asset on its books instead of charging it to expenses for the year.

capital loss The loss incurred when a capital asset is sold for a lower price than the purchase price. *See also* capital gain; long-term loss.

capital market The segment of the securities market that deals in instruments with more than one year to maturity—that is, long-term debt and equity securities.

capital risk The potential for an investor to lose all money invested owing to circumstances unrelated to an issuer's financial strength. For example, derivative instruments such as options carry risk independent of the underlying securities' changing value. *See also* derivative.

capital stock All of a corporation's outstanding preferred stock and common stock, listed at par value.

capital structure The composition of long-term funds (equity and debt) a corporation has as a source for financing. *See also* capitalization.

capital surplus The money a corporation receives in excess of the stated value of stock at the time of first sale. *Syn.* paid-in capital; paid-in surplus. *See also* par.

capped index option A type of index option issued with a capped price at a set interval above the strike price (for a call) or below the strike price (for a put). The option is automatically exercised once the underlying index reaches the capped price. *See also* index option.

capping Placing selling pressure on a stock in an attempt to keep its price low or to move its price lower; this violates the NASD Rules of Fair Practice.

carried interest A sharing arrangement in an oil and gas direct participation program whereby the general partner shares the tangible drilling costs with the limited partners but pays no part of the intangible drilling costs. *See also* sharing arrangement.

carrying broker *See* clearing broker-dealer.

carrying charge A cost associated with holding or storing a commodity, such as interest, insurance and rents.

cash account An account in which the customer is required by the SEC's Regulation T to pay in full for securities purchased not later than two days after the standard payment period set by the NASD's Uniform Practice Code. *Syn.* special cash account.

cash assets ratio The most stringent test of liquidity, calculated by dividing the sum of cash and cash equivalents by total current liabilities. *See also* acid-test ratio; current ratio.

cash basis accounting A method of reporting income when received and expenses when paid, as opposed to reporting income and expenses when incurred. *See also* accrual accounting.

cash dividend Money paid to a corporation's stockholders out of the corporation's current earnings or accumulated profits. The board of directors must declare all dividends.

cash equivalent A security that can be readily converted into cash. Examples include Treasury bills, certificates of deposit and money-market instruments and funds.

cash flow The money received by a business minus the money paid out. Cash flow is also equal to net income plus depreciation or depletion.

cashiering department The department within a brokerage firm that delivers securities and money to and receives securities and money from other firms and clients of the brokerage firm. *Syn.* security cage.

cash management bill (CMB) A debt security issued by the U.S. Treasury to meet short-term borrowing needs; a minimum of $10 million is required in order to purchase CMBs at auction.

cash market Transactions between buyers and sellers of commodities that entail immediate delivery of and payment for a physical commodity. *Syn.* cash-and-carry market; spot market.

cash trade *See* cash transaction.

cash transaction A settlement contract that calls for delivery and payment on the same day the trade is executed. Payment is due by 2:30 p.m. EST or within 30 minutes of the trade if it occurs after 2:00 p.m. EST. *Syn.* cash trade. *See also* regular way; settlement date.

catastrophe call The redemption of a bond by an issuer owing to disaster (for example, a power plant that has been built with proceeds from an issue burns to the ground).

CATS *See* Certificate of Accrual on Treasury Securities.

CBOE *See* Chicago Board Options Exchange.

CBOT *See* Chicago Board of Trade.

CD *See* negotiable certificate of deposit.

Certificate of Accrual on Treasury Securities (CATS) One of several types of zero-coupon bonds issued by brokerage firms and collateralized by Treasury securities. *See also* Treasury receipt.

certificate of deposit (CD) *See* negotiable certificate of deposit.

CFO *See* cancel former order.

change (1) For an index or average, the difference between the current value and the previous day's market close. (2) For a stock or bond quote, the difference between the current price and the last trade of the previous day.

chartist A securities analyst who uses charts and graphs of the past price movements of a security to predict its future movements. *Syn.* technician. *See also* technical analysis.

CHB *See* commission house broker.

Chicago Board of Trade (CBOT) The oldest commodity exchange in the United States; established in 1886. The exchange lists agricultural commodity futures such as corn, oats and soybeans, in addition to more recent innovations such as GNMA mortgages and the Nasdaq 100 Index.

Chicago Board Options Exchange (CBOE) The self-regulatory organization with jurisdiction over all writing and trading of standardized options and related contracts listed on that exchange. Also, the first national securities exchange for the trading of listed options. *See also* Order Routing System.

Chicago Stock Exchange (CHX) Regional exchange that provides a listed market for smaller businesses and new enterprises. In 1949, the exchange merged with the St. Louis, Cleveland and Minneapolis/St. Paul exchanges to form the Midwest Stock Exchange, but in 1993, the original name was reinstated. *See also* regional exchange.

Chinese wall A descriptive name for the division within a brokerage firm that prevents insider information from passing from corporate advisers to investment traders, who could make use of the information to reap illicit profits. *See also* Insider Trading and Securities Fraud Enforcement Act of 1988.

churning Excessive trading in a customer's account by a registered representative who ignores the customer's interests and seeks only to increase commissions. This violates the NASD Rules of Fair Practice. *Syn.* overtrading.

Cincinnati Stock Exchange (CSE) In existence since 1885, this exchange operates the National Securities Trading System, the nation's only automated auction system for unlisted securities. *See also* National Securities Trading System.

class Options of the same type (that is, all calls or all puts) on the same underlying security. *See also* series; type.

Class A share A class of mutual fund share issued with a front-end sales load. A mutual fund offers different classes of shares to allow investors to choose the type of sales charge they will pay. *See also* Class B share; Class C share; Class D share; front-end load.

Class B share A class of mutual fund share issued with a back-end load. A mutual fund offers different classes of shares to allow investors to choose the type of sales charge they will pay. *See also* back-end load; Class A share; Class C share; Class D share.

Class C share A class of mutual fund share issued with a level load. A mutual fund offers different classes of shares to allow investors to choose the type of sales charge they will pay. *See also* Class A share; Class B share; Class D share; level load.

Class D share A class of mutual fund share issued with both a level load and a back-end load. A mutual fund offers different classes of shares to allow investors to choose the type of sales charge they will pay. *See also* back-end load; Class A share; Class B share; Class C share; level load.

classical economics The theory that maximum economic benefit will be achieved if government does not attempt to influence the economy; that is, if businesses are allowed to seek profitable opportunities as they see fit.

clearing agency An intermediary between the buy and sell sides in a securities transaction that receives and delivers payments and securities. Any organization that fills this function, including a securities depository but not including a Federal Reserve Bank, is considered a clearing agency.

clearing broker-dealer A broker-dealer that clears its own trades as well as those of introducing brokers. A clearing broker-dealer can hold customers' securities and cash. *Syn.* carrying broker. *See also* introducing broker.

clearing corporation *See* clearinghouse.

clearinghouse An agency of a futures exchange, through which transactions in futures and option contracts are settled, guaranteed, offset and filled. A clearinghouse may be an independent corporation or exchange-owned. *See also* Options Clearing Corporation.

CLN *See* construction loan note.

close The price of the last transaction for a particular security on a particular day.

closed-end covenant A provision of a bond issue's trust indenture stating that any additional bonds secured by the same assets must have a subordinated claim to those assets. *See also* junior lien debt; open-end covenant.

closed-end investment company An investment company that issues a fixed number of shares in an actively managed portfolio of securities. The shares may be of several classes; they are traded in the secondary marketplace, either on an exchange or over the counter. The market price of the shares is determined by supply and demand and not by net asset value. *Syn.* publicly traded fund. *See also* dual-purpose fund; mutual fund.

closed-end management company An investment company that issues a fixed number of shares in an actively managed portfolio of securities. The shares may be of several classes; they are traded in the secondary marketplace, either on an exchange or over the counter. The shares' market price is determined by supply and demand, not by net asset value. *Syn.* publicly traded fund. *See also* dual-purpose fund.

closed-end mortgage bond A secured bond issue in which a corporation issues the maximum number of bonds authorized in the trust indenture as first-mortgage bonds. *See also* open-end mortgage bond.

closing date The date designated by the general partners in a direct participation program as the date when sales of units in the program cease; typically the offering period extends for one year.

closing purchase An options transaction in which the seller buys back an option in the same series; the two transactions effectively cancel each other out and the position is liquidated. *See also* closing sale; opening purchase.

closing range The relatively narrow range of prices at which transactions take place in the final minutes of the trading day. *See also* close.

closing sale An options transaction in which the buyer sells an option in the same series; the two transactions effectively cancel each other out and the position is liquidated. *See also* closing purchase; opening sale.

CMB *See* cash management bill.

CMO *See* collateralized mortgage obligation.

CMV *See* current market value.

COD *See* delivery vs. payment.

Code of Arbitration Procedure The NASD's formal method of handling securities-related disputes or clearing controversies between members, public customers, clearing corporations or clearing banks. Such disputes involve violations of the Uniform Practice Code rather than the Rules of Fair Practice. Any claim, dispute or controversy between member firms or associated persons must be submitted to arbitration.

Code of Procedure (COP) The NASD's formal procedure for handling trade practice complaints involving violations of the Rules of Fair Practice. The NASD District Business Conduct Committee (DBCC) is the first body to hear and judge complaints. The NASD Board of Governors handles appeals and review of DBCC decisions.

coincident indicator A measurable economic factor that varies directly and simultaneously with the business cycle, thus indicating the current state of the economy. Examples include nonagricultural employment, personal income and industrial production. *See also* lagging indicator; leading indicator.

collateral Certain assets set aside and pledged to a lender for the duration of a loan. If the borrower fails to meet obligations to pay principal or interest, the lender has claim to the assets.

collateralized mortgage obligation (CMO) A mortgage-backed corporate security. Unlike pass-through obligations issued by FNMA and GNMA, its yield is not guaranteed and it does not have the federal government's backing. These issues attempt to return interest and principal at a predetermined rate.

collateral trust bond A secured bond backed by stocks or bonds of another issuer. The collateral is held by a trustee for safekeeping. *Syn.* collateral trust certificate.

collateral trust certificate *See* collateral trust bond.

collection ratio (1) For corporations, a rough measure of the length of time accounts receivable have been outstanding. It is calculated by multiplying the receivables by 360 and dividing the result by net sales. (2) For municipal bonds, a means of detecting deteriorating credit conditions; it is calculated by dividing taxes collected by taxes assessed.

collect on delivery (COD) *See* delivery vs. payment.

combination An option position that represents a put and a call on the same stock at different strike prices, expirations or both.

combination fund An equity mutual fund that attempts to combine the objectives of growth and current yield by dividing its portfolio between companies that show long-term growth potential and companies that pay high dividends. *See also* mutual fund.

combination preferred stock A type of preferred stock that combines two or more of the following preferred stock features: participating, cumulative, convertible, callable. *See also* preferred stock.

combination privilege A benefit offered by a mutual fund whereby the investor may qualify for a sales charge breakpoint by combining separate invest-

ments in two or more mutual funds under the same management.

combined account A customer account that has cash and long and short margin positions in different securities. *Syn.* mixed account.

combined distribution *See* split offering.

commercial bank An institution that is in the business of accepting deposits and making business loans. Commercial banks may not underwrite corporate securities or most municipal bonds. *See also* investment banker.

commercial paper An unsecured, short-term promissory note issued by a corporation for financing accounts receivable and inventories. It is usually issued at a discount reflecting prevailing market interest rates. Maturities range up to 270 days.

commingling (1) The combining by a brokerage firm of one customer's securities with another customer's securities and pledging them as joint collateral for a bank loan; unless authorized by the customers, this violates SEC Rule 15c2-1. (2) The combining by a brokerage firm of customer securities with firm securities and pledging them as joint collateral for a bank loan; this practice is prohibited. *See also* cross lien; segregation.

commission A service charge an agent assesses in return for arranging a security's purchase or sale. A commission must be fair and reasonable, considering all the relevant factors of the transaction. *Syn.* sales charge. *See also* markup.

commissioner The state official with jurisdiction over insurance transactions.

commission house broker (CHB) A member of an exchange who is eligible to execute orders for customers of a member firm on the floor of the exchange. *Syn.* floor broker.

Committee on Uniform Securities Identification Procedures (CUSIP) A committee that assigns identification numbers and codes to all securities, to be used when recording all buy and sell orders.

common stock A security that represents ownership in a corporation. Holders of common stock exercise control by electing a board of directors and voting on corporate policy. *See also* equity; preferred stock.

common stock ratio One of several tools used by bond analysts to assess the degree of safety offered by a corporation's bonds. It measures the percentage of the corporation's total capitalization that is contributed by the common stockholders, and is calculated by adding the par value, the capital in excess of par and the retained earnings, and dividing the result by the total capitalization. *See also* bond ratio; preferred stock ratio.

competitive bid underwriting A form of firm commitment underwriting in which rival syndicates submit sealed bids for underwriting the issue. Competitive bidding normally is used to determine the underwriters for issues of general obligation municipal bonds, and is required by law in most states for general obligation bonds of more than $100,000. *See also* negotiated underwriting.

completion of the transaction As defined by the NASD, the point at which a customer pays any part of the purchase price to the broker-dealer for a security he has purchased or delivers a security he has sold. If the customer pays the broker-dealer before payment is due, the transaction's completion occurs when the broker-dealer delivers the security.

compliance department The department within a brokerage firm that oversees the firm's trading and market-making activities. It ensures that the firm's employees and officers abide by the rules and regulations of the SEC, exchanges and SROs.

compliance registered options principal (CROP) The principal responsible for compliance with options exchange rules and securities laws; with certain exceptions, a CROP may not have sales functions.

Composite Average *See* Dow Jones Composite Average.

Computer Assisted Execution System *See* Intermarket Trading System/Computer Assisted Execution System.

concession The profit per bond or share that an underwriter allows the seller of new issue securities.

The selling group broker-dealer purchases the securities from the syndicate member at the public offering price minus the concession. *Syn.* reallowance.

conduit theory A means for an investment company to avoid taxation on net investment income distributed to shareholders. If a mutual fund acts as a conduit for the distribution of net investment income, it may qualify as a regulated investment company and be taxed only on the income the fund retains. *Syn.* pipeline theory.

confidence theory A technical analysis theory that measures the willingness of investors to take risks by comparing the yields on high-grade bonds to the yields on lower rated bonds.

confirmation A printed document that states the trade date, settlement date and money due from or owed to a customer. It is sent or given to the customer on or before the settlement date. *See also* duplicate confirmation.

congestion A technical analysis term used to indicate that the range within which a commodity's price trades for an extended period of time is narrow.

consent to lend agreement *See* loan consent agreement.

Consolidated Quotation System (CQS) A quotation and last-sale reporting service for NASD members that are active market makers of listed securities in the third market. It is used by market makers willing to stand ready to buy and sell securities for their own accounts on a continuous basis but that do not wish to do so through an exchange. Quotation display service is available for a fee to all Nasdaq subscribers, while quotation input service is available only to those members that are registered to do business in third market stocks.

Consolidated Tape (CT) A New York Stock Exchange service that delivers real-time reports of securities transactions to subscribers as they occur on the various exchanges.

The Tape distributes reports to subscribers over two different networks that the subscribers can tap into through either the high-speed electronic lines or the low-speed ticker lines. Network A reports transactions in NYSE–listed securities. Network B reports AMEX–listed securities transactions, as well as reports of transactions in regional exchange issues that substantially meet AMEX listing requirements. *Syn.* Consolidated Ticker Tape; Tape; Ticker Tape.

Consolidated Ticker Tape *See* Consolidated Tape.

consolidation The technical analysis term for a narrowing of the trading range for a commodity or security, considered an indication that a strong price move is imminent.

constant dollar plan A defensive investment strategy in which the total sum of money invested is kept constant, regardless of any price fluctuation in the portfolio. As a result, the investor sells when the market is high and buys when it is low.

constant ratio plan An investment strategy in which the investor maintains an appropriate ratio of debt to equity securities by making purchases and sales to maintain the desired balance.

construction fee Money paid for acting as general contractor to construct improvements on a direct participation program's property.

construction loan note (CLN) A short-term municipal debt security that provides interim financing for new projects.

constructive receipt The date on which the Internal Revenue Service considers that a taxpayer receives dividends or other income.

Consumer Price Index (CPI) A measure of price changes in consumer goods and services used to identify periods of inflation or deflation.

consumption A term used by Keynesian economists to refer to the purchase by household units of newly produced goods and services.

contemporaneous trader A person who enters a trade at or near the same time and in the same security as a person who has inside information. The contemporaneous trader may bring suit against the inside trader. *See also* Insider Trading and Securities Fraud Enforcement Act of 1988.

contingent-deferred sales load *See* back-end load.

contingent order An order that is conditional upon the execution of a previous order and that will be executed only after the first order is filled.

contra broker The broker on the buy side of a sell order or on the sell side of a buy order.

contraction A period of general economic decline, one of the business cycle's four stages. *See also* business cycle.

contractionary policy A monetary policy that decreases the money supply, usually with the intention of raising interest rates and combating inflation.

contractual plan A type of accumulation plan in which an individual agrees to invest a specific amount of money in the mutual fund during a specific time period. *Syn.* penalty plan; prepaid charge plan. *See also* front-end load; mutual fund; spread load; voluntary accumulation plan.

control (controlling, controlled by, under common control with) The power to direct or affect the direction of a company's management and policies, whether through the ownership of voting securities, by contract or otherwise. Control is presumed to exist if a person, directly or indirectly, owns, controls, holds with the power to vote or holds proxies representing more than 10 percent of a company's voting securities.

control of securities A term used to indicate a broker-dealer's responsibilities with regard to securities in its possession. Under the SEC's customer protection rule, broker-dealers must maintain control procedures over customer funds and securities. Securities are considered to be under the control of or in the possession of a broker-dealer if they are in the broker-dealer's physical possession, are in an alternative location acceptable to the SEC or are in transit for a period of time that does not exceed SEC standards. *Syn.* possession of securities.

control person (1) A director, an officer or another affiliate of an issuer. (2) A stockholder who owns at least 10 percent of any class of a corporation's outstanding securities. *See also* affiliate; insider.

control security Any security owned by a director, an officer or another affiliate of the issuer or by a stockholder who owns at least 10 percent of any class of a corporation's outstanding securities. Who owns a security, not the security itself, determines whether it is a control security.

conversion parity Two securities, one of which can be converted into the other, of equal dollar value. A convertible security holder can calculate parity to help decide whether converting would lead to gain or loss.

conversion price The dollar amount of a convertible security's par value that is exchangeable for one share of common stock.

conversion privilege A feature the issuer adds to a security that allows the holder to change the security into shares of common stock. This makes the security attractive to investors and, therefore, more marketable. *See also* convertible bond; convertible preferred stock.

conversion rate *See* conversion ratio.

conversion ratio The number of shares of common stock per par value amount that the holder would receive for converting a convertible bond or preferred share. *Syn.* conversion rate.

conversion value The total market value of common stock into which a senior security is convertible.

convertible bond A debt security, usually in the form of a debenture, that can be exchanged for equity securities of the issuing corporation at specified prices or rates. *See also* debenture.

convertible preferred stock An equity security that can be exchanged for common stock at specified prices or rates. Dividends may be cumulative or noncumulative. *See also* cumulative preferred stock; noncumulative preferred stock; preferred stock.

cooling-off period The period (a minimum of 20 days) between a registration statement's filing date and the registration's effective date. In practice, the period varies in length.

coordination *See* registration by coordination.

COP *See* Code of Procedure.

corporate account An account held in a corporation's name. The corporate agreement, signed when the account is opened, specifies which officers are authorized to trade in the account. In addition to standard margin account documents, a corporation must provide a copy of its charter and bylaws authorizing a margin account.

corporate bond A debt security issued by a corporation. A corporate bond typically has a par value of $1,000, is taxable, has a term maturity and is traded on a major exchange.

corporate securities limited representative *See* Series 62.

corporation The most common form of business organization, in which the organization's total worth is divided into shares of stock, each share representing a unit of ownership. A corporation is characterized by a continuous life span and its owners' limited liability.

CORR. A message on the Consolidated Tape indicating an error in a previous report of a transaction. *See also* error report.

correspondent broker-dealer A broker-dealer that executes transactions for another broker-dealer in a market or locale in which the first broker-dealer has no office. *See also* broker's broker.

cost basis The price paid for an asset, including any commissions or fees, used to calculate capital gains or losses when the asset is sold.

cost depletion A method of calculating tax deductions for investments in mineral, oil or gas resources. The cost of the mineral-, oil- or gas-producing property is returned to the investor over the property's life by an annual deduction, which takes into account the number of known recoverable units of mineral, oil or gas to arrive at a cost-per-unit figure. The tax deduction is determined by multiplying the cost-per-unit figure by the number of units sold each year.

cost of carry All out-of-pocket costs incurred by an investor while holding an open position in a security, including margin costs, interest costs and opportunity costs.

cost-push Increasing costs of production, including raw materials and wages, that are believed to result in inflation. *See also* demand-pull.

coterminous A term used to describe municipal entities that share the same boundaries. For example, a municipality's school district and fire district may issue debt separately although the debt is backed by revenues from the same taxpayers. *See also* overlapping debt.

coupon bond A debt obligation with attached coupons representing semiannual interest payments. The holder submits the coupons to the trustee to receive the interest payments. The issuer keeps no record of the purchaser, and the purchaser's name is not printed on the certificate. *Syn.* bearer bond. *See also* book-entry security; registered; registered as to principal only.

coupon yield *See* nominal yield.

covenant A component of a debt issue's trust indenture that identifies bondholders' rights and other provisions. Examples include rate covenants that establish a minimum revenue coverage for a bond; insurance covenants that require insurance on a project; and maintenance covenants that require maintenance on a facility constructed by the proceeds of a bond issue.

coverage ratio A measure of the safety of a bond issue, based on how many times earnings will cover debt service plus operating and maintenance expenses for a specific time period.

covered call writer An investor who sells a call option while owning the underlying security or some other asset that guarantees the ability to deliver if the call is exercised.

covered put writer An investor who sells a put option while owning an asset that guarantees the ability to pay if the put is exercised.

CPI *See* Consumer Price Index.

CQS *See* Consolidated Quotation System.

CR *See* credit balance.

credit agreement A component of a customer's margin account agreement, outlining the conditions of the credit arrangement between broker and customer.

credit balance (CR) The amount of money remaining in a customer's account after all commitments have been paid in full. *Syn.* credit record; credit register. *See also* debit balance.

credit department *See* margin department.

creditor Any broker or dealer, member of a national securities exchange, or person associated with a broker-dealer involved in extending credit to customers.

credit record *See* credit balance.

credit register *See* credit balance.

credit risk The degree of probability that a bond's issuer will default in the payment of either principal or interest. *Syn.* default risk; financial risk.

credit spread A futures hedge position established when the premium received for the option sold exceeds the premium paid for the option bought. *See also* debit spread.

CROP *See* compliance registered options principal.

crossed market The situation created when one market maker bids for a stock at a higher price than another market maker is asking for the same stock, or when one market maker enters an ask price to sell a stock at a lower price than another market maker's bid price to buy the same stock. This violates the NASD Rules of Fair Practice. *See also* locked market.

crossing orders Using one customer's order to fill a second customer's order for the same security on the opposite side of the market. This practice is permitted if the security is first offered to the exchange floor at a price one tick higher than the current bid; if there are no takers, the broker may cross the orders. Crossing orders is considered manipulative, however, if the transaction is not presented or recorded with the exchange.

cross lien The pledging of customer securities as collateral for a bank loan; this practice is prohibited. *See also* one-way lien.

crossover point The point at which a limited partnership begins to show a negative cash flow with a taxable income. *See also* phantom income.

CSE *See* Cincinnati Stock Exchange.

CT *See* Consolidated Tape.

cum rights A term describing stock trading with rights. *See also* ex-rights.

cumulative preferred stock An equity security that offers the holder any unpaid dividends in arrears. These dividends accumulate and must be paid to the cumulative preferred stockholder before any dividends can be paid to the common stockholders. *See also* convertible preferred stock; noncumulative preferred stock; preferred stock.

cumulative voting A voting procedure that permits stockholders either to cast all of their votes for any one candidate or to cast their total number of votes in any proportion they choose. This results in greater representation for minority stockholders. *See also* statutory voting.

current assets Cash and other assets that are expected to be converted into cash within the next 12 months. Examples include such liquid items as cash and equivalents, accounts receivable, inventory and prepaid expenses.

current liabilities A corporation's debt obligations due for payment within the next 12 months. Examples include accounts payable, accrued wages payable and current long-term debt.

current market value (CMV) The worth of the securities in an account. The market value of listed securities is based on the closing prices on the previous business day. *Syn.* long market value. *See also* market value.

current price *See* public offering price.

current ratio A measure of a corporation's liquidity; that is, its ability to transfer assets into cash to meet current short-term obligations. It is calculated by dividing total current assets by total current liabilities. *Syn.* working capital ratio.

current yield The annual rate of return on a security, calculated by dividing the interest or dividends paid by the security's current market price. *See also* bond yield.

CUSIP *See* Committee on Uniform Securities Identification Procedures.

custodial account An account in which a custodian enters trades on behalf of the beneficial owner, often a minor. *See also* custodian.

custodian An institution or a person responsible for making all investment, management and distribution decisions in an account maintained in the best interests of another. Mutual funds have custodians responsible for safeguarding certificates and performing clerical duties. *See also* mutual fund custodian.

customer Any person who opens a trading account with a broker-dealer. A customer may be classified in terms of account ownership, trading authorization, payment method or types of securities traded.

customer agreement A document that a customer must sign when opening a margin account with a broker-dealer; it allows the firm to liquidate all or a portion of the account if the customer fails to meet a margin call.

customer ledger The accounting record that lists separately all customer cash and margin accounts carried by a firm. *See also* stock record.

customer protection rule *See* Rule 15c3-3.

customer statement A document showing a customer's trading activity, positions and account balance. The SEC requires that customer statements be sent quarterly, but customers generally receive them monthly.

cyclical industry A fundamental analysis term for an industry that is sensitive to the business cycle and price changes. Most cyclical industries produce durable goods such as raw materials and heavy equipment.

D

daily journal *See* blotter.

dated date The date on which interest on a new bond issue begins to accrue.

day order An order that is valid only until the close of trading on the day it is entered; if it is not executed by the close of trading, it is canceled.

day trader A trader in securities or commodities who opens all positions after the opening of the market and offsets or closes out all positions before the close of the market on the same day. *See also* position trader.

DBCC *See* NASD District Business Conduct Committee.

DDA *See* dividend disbursing agent.

DE *See* discretion exercised.

dealer (1) An individual or a firm engaged in the business of buying and selling securities for its own account, either directly or through a broker. (2) The role of a firm when it acts as a principal and charges the customer a markup or markdown. *Syn.* principal. *See also* broker; broker-dealer.

dealer paper Short-term, unsecured promissory notes that the issuer sells through a dealer rather than directly to the public.

debenture A debt obligation backed by the issuing corporation's general credit. *Syn.* unsecured bond.

debit balance (DR) The amount of money a customer owes a brokerage firm. *Syn.* debit record; debit register. *See also* credit balance.

debit record *See* debit balance.

debit register *See* debit balance.

debit spread A futures hedge position established when the premium paid for the option bought exceeds the premium received for the option sold. *See also* credit spread.

debt financing Raising money for working capital or for capital expenditures by selling bonds, bills or notes to individual or institutional investors. In return for the money lent, the investors become creditors and receive the issuer's promise to repay principal and interest on the debt. *See also* equity financing.

debt per capita *See* net debt per capita.

debt ratio *See* bond ratio.

debt security A security representing an investor's loan to an issuer such as a corporation, a municipality, the federal government or a federal agency. In return for the loan, the issuer promises to repay the debt on a specified date and to pay interest. *See also* equity security.

debt service The schedule for repayment of interest and principal (or the scheduled sinking fund contribution) on an outstanding debt. *See also* sinking fund.

debt service account The account used to pay a municipal revenue bond's semiannual interest and principal maturing in the current year; it also serves as a sinking fund for term issues. *See also* flow of funds.

debt service ratio An indication of the ability of an issuer to meet principal and interest payments on bonds.

debt service reserve fund The account that holds enough money to pay one year's debt service on a municipal revenue bond. *See also* flow of funds.

debt service to annual revenues ratio A ratio that indicates whether a municipality or community is overburdened with debt service expenses.

debt-to-equity ratio The ratio of total long-term debt to total stockholders' equity; it is used to measure leverage.

debt trend A method of tracking whether certain municipal debt ratios are rising or falling in order to predict a municipality's or community's financial position in the coming years.

declaration date The date on which a corporation announces an upcoming dividend's amount, payment date and record date.

declining balance depreciation An accounting procedure that allows the owner of an asset to deduct the cost of its declining value for tax purposes. The method provides a greater deduction in the early years of the asset's life, and normally a switch to straight-line depreciation occurs in order to maximize the total deductions.

decreasing debt service A schedule for debt repayment whereby the issuer repays principal in installments of equal size over the life of the issue. The amount of interest due therefore decreases and the amount of each payment becomes smaller over time. *See also* level debt service.

deduction An item or expenditure subtracted from adjusted gross income to reduce the amount of income subject to tax.

deed of trust *See* trust indenture.

default The failure to pay interest or principal promptly when due.

default risk *See* credit risk.

defeasance The termination of a debt obligation. A corporation or municipality removes debt from its balance sheet by issuing a new debt issue or creating a trust that generates enough cash flow to provide for the payment of interest and principal. *See also* advance refunding.

defensive industry A fundamental analysis term for an industry that is relatively unaffected by the business cycle. Most defensive industries produce nondurable goods for which demand remains steady throughout the business cycle; examples include the food industry and utilities.

defensive investment strategy A method of portfolio allocation and management aimed at minimizing the risk of losing principal. Defensive investors place a high percentage of their investable assets in bonds, cash equivalents and stocks that are less volatile than average.

deferred annuity An annuity contract that delays payment of income, installments or a lump sum until the investor elects to receive it. *See also* annuity.

deferred compensation plan A nonqualified retirement plan whereby the employee defers receiving current compensation in favor of a larger payout at retirement (or in the case of disability or death).

deficiency letter The SEC's notification of additions or corrections that a prospective issuer must make to a registration statement before the SEC will clear the offering for distribution. *Syn.* bedbug letter.

defined benefit plan A qualified retirement plan that specifies the total amount of money that the employee will receive at retirement.

defined contribution plan A qualified retirement plan that specifies the amount of money that the employer will contribute annually to the plan.

deflation A persistent and measurable fall in the general level of prices. *See also* inflation.

delete information mode A Consolidated Tape report from which certain information has been omitted in order to prevent the Tape from running late during periods of high market activity.

delivery The change in ownership or in control of a security in exchange for cash. Delivery takes place on the settlement date.

delivery vs. payment (DVP) A transaction settlement procedure in which securities are delivered to the buying institution's bank in exchange for payment of the amount due. *Syn.* collect on delivery (COD).

delta A measure of the responsiveness of option premiums to a change in the price of the underlying asset. Deep in-the-money options have deltas near 1; these show the biggest response to futures price changes. Deep out-of-the-money options have deltas near zero.

demand A consumer's desire and willingness to pay for a good or service. *See also* supply.

demand deposit A sum of money left with a bank (or borrowed from a bank and left on deposit) that the depositing customer has the right to withdraw immediately. *See also* time deposit.

demand-pull An excessive money supply that increases the demand for a limited supply of goods that is believed to result in inflation. *See also* cost-push.

depletion A tax deduction that compensates a business for the decreasing supply of the natural resource that provides its income (oil, gas, coal, gold or other nonrenewable resource). There are two ways to calculate depletion: cost depletion and percentage depletion. *See also* cost depletion; percentage depletion.

depreciation (1) A tax deduction that compensates a business for the cost of certain tangible assets. *See also* Modified Accelerated Cost Recovery System. (2) A decrease in the value of a particular currency relative to other currencies.

depreciation expense A bookkeeping entry of a noncash expense charged against earnings to recover the cost of an asset over its useful life.

depression A prolonged period of general economic decline.

derivative An investment vehicle, the value of which is based on another security's value. Futures contracts, forward contracts and options are among the most common types of derivatives. Institutional investors generally use derivatives to increase overall portfolio return or to hedge portfolio risk.

descending triangle On a technical analyst's trading activity chart, a pattern which indicates that the market has started to fall; considered to be a bearish indicator. *See also* ascending triangle.

designated order In a municipal bond underwriting, a customer order that is submitted by one syndicate member but that specifies more than one member to receive a percentage of the takedown. The size of the order establishes its priority for subscription to an issue. *See also* group net order; member-at-the-takedown order; presale order.

devaluation A substantial fall in a currency's value as compared to the value of gold or to the value of another country's currency.

developmental drilling program A limited partnership that drills for oil, gas or minerals in areas of proven reserves or near existing fields. *See also* explor-atory drilling program; income program; step-out well.

development fee Money paid for the packaging of a direct participation program's property, including negotiating and approving plans, undertaking to assist in obtaining zoning and necessary variances, and financing for the specific property.

diagonal spread An option hedge position established by the simultaneous purchase and sale of options of the same class but with different exercise prices and expiration dates. *See also* spread.

DIGITS & VOL DELETED A Consolidated Tape delete information mode in which the volume and the first digit of the price are omitted. A DIGITS & VOL RESUMED message appears when trading activity slows. *See also* delete information mode.

dilution A reduction in earnings per share of common stock. Dilution occurs through the issuance of additional shares of common stock and the conversion of convertible securities.

direct debt The total of a municipality's general obligation bonds, short-term notes and revenue debt.

direct paper Commercial paper sold directly to the public without the use of a dealer.

direct participation program (DPP) A business organized so as to pass all income, gains, losses and tax benefits to its owners, the investors; the business is usually structured as a limited partnership. Examples include oil and gas programs, real estate programs, agricultural programs, cattle programs, condominium securities and Subchapter S corporate offerings. *Syn.* program.

discount The difference between the lower price paid for a security and the security's face amount at issue.

discount bond A bond that sells at a lower price than its face value. *See also* par.

discount rate The interest rate charged by the 12 Federal Reserve Banks for short-term loans made to member banks.

discretion The authority given to someone other than an account's beneficial owner to make investment decisions for the account concerning the security, the number of shares or units and whether to buy or sell. The authority to decide only timing or price does not constitute discretion. *See also* limited power of attorney.

discretionary account An account in which the customer has given the registered representative authority to enter transactions at the rep's discretion.

discretion exercised (DE) The notation marked on an order placed for a discretionary account to indicate that the representative made the decision to trade. *See also* discretionary account.

discretion not exercised (DNE) The notation marked on an order placed for a discretionary account to indicate that the account owner made the decision to trade. *See also* discretionary account.

disintermediation The flow of money from low-yielding accounts in traditional savings institutions to higher yielding investments. Typically, this occurs when the Fed tightens the money supply and interest rates rise.

disposable income (DI) The sum that people divide between spending and personal savings. *See also* personal income.

disproportionate allocation One of the criteria used by the NASD to determine whether a violation of the freeriding and withholding rules has occurred. The guideline is that no more than 10 percent of a firm's allotment of hot issues should be sold to restricted accounts.

disproportionate sharing A sharing arrangement whereby the sponsor in an oil and gas direct participation program pays a portion of the program's costs but receives a disproportionately higher percentage of its revenues. *See also* sharing arrangement.

distribution Any cash or other property distributed to shareholders or general partners that arises from their interests in the business, investment company or partnership.

distribution stage The period during which an individual receives distributions from an annuity account.

Syn. payout stage. *See also* accumulation stage; accumulation unit.

District Business Conduct Committee *See* NASD District Business Conduct Committee.

diversification A risk management technique that mixes a wide variety of investments within a portfolio, thus minimizing the impact of any one security on overall portfolio performance.

diversified common stock fund A mutual fund that invests its assets in a wide range of common stocks. The fund's objectives may be growth, income or a combination of both. *See also* growth fund; mutual fund.

diversified investment company As defined by the Investment Company Act of 1940, an investment company that meets certain standards as to the percentage of assets invested. These companies use diversification to manage risk. *See also* management company; nondiversified investment company; 75-5-10 test.

diversified management company As defined by the Investment Company Act of 1940, a management company that meets certain standards for percentage of assets invested. These companies use diversification to manage risk. *See also* management company; nondiversified management company; 75-5-10 test.

divided account *See* Western account.

dividend A distribution of a corporation's earnings. Dividends may be in the form of cash, stock or property. The board of directors must declare all dividends. *Syn.* stock dividend. *See also* cash dividend; dividend yield; property dividend.

dividend department The department within a brokerage firm that is responsible for crediting client accounts with dividends and interest payments on client securities held in the firm's name.

dividend disbursing agent (DDA) The person responsible for making the required dividend distributions to the broker-dealer's dividend department.

dividend exclusion rule An IRS provision that permits a corporation to exclude from its taxable income 70 percent of dividends received from domestic preferred and common stocks. The Tax Reform Act of 1986 repealed the dividend exclusion for individual investors.

dividend payout ratio A measure of a corporation's policy of paying cash dividends, calculated by dividing the dividends paid on common stock by the net income available for common stockholders. The ratio is the complement of the retained earnings ratio.

dividends per share The dollar amount of cash dividends paid on each common share during one year.

dividend yield The annual rate of return on a common or preferred stock investment. The yield is calculated by dividing the annual dividend by the stock's purchase price. *See also* current yield; dividend.

DJIA *See* Dow Jones Industrial Average.

DK *See* don't know.

DNE *See* discretion not exercised.

DNR *See* do not reduce order.

doctrine of mutual reciprocity The agreement that established the federal tax exemption for municipal bond interest. States and municipalities do not tax federal securities or properties, and the federal government reciprocates by exempting local government securities and properties from federal taxation. *Syn.* mutual exclusion doctrine; reciprocal immunity.

dollar bonds Municipal revenue bonds that are quoted and traded on a basis of dollars rather than yield to maturity. Term bonds, tax-exempt notes and New Housing Authority bonds are dollar bonds.

dollar cost averaging A system of buying mutual fund shares in fixed dollar amounts at regular fixed intervals, regardless of the share's price. The investor purchases more shares when prices are low and fewer shares when prices are high, thus lowering the average cost per share over time.

donor A person who makes a gift of money or securities to another. Once the gift is donated, the donor gives up all rights to it. Gifts of securities to minors under the Uniform Gifts to Minors Act provide tax advantages to the donor. *See also* Uniform Gifts to Minors Act.

do not reduce order (DNR) An order that stipulates that the limit or stop price should not be reduced in response to the declaration of a cash dividend.

don't know (DK) A response to a confirmation received from a broker-dealer indicating a lack of information about, or record of, the transaction.

double auction market *See* auction market.

double-barreled bond A municipal security backed by the full faith and credit of the issuing municipality, as well as by pledged revenues. *See also* general obligation bond; revenue bond.

Dow Jones averages The most widely quoted and oldest measures of change in stock prices. Each of the four averages is based on the prices of a limited number of stocks in a particular category. *See also* average; Dow Jones Industrial Average.

Dow Jones Composite Average (DJCA) A market indicator composed of the 65 stocks that make up the Dow Jones Industrial, Transportation and Utilities Averages. *See also* average; Dow Jones Industrial Average; Dow Jones Transportation Average; Dow Jones Utilities Average.

Dow Jones Industrial Average (DJIA) The most widely used market indicator, composed of 30 large, actively traded issues of industrial stocks. *See also* average.

Dow Jones Transportation Average (DJTA) A market indicator composed of 20 transportation stocks. *See also* average; Dow Jones Composite Average; Dow Jones Industrial Average; Dow Jones Utilities Average.

Dow Jones Utilities Average (DJUA) A market indicator composed of 15 utilities stocks. *See also* average; Dow Jones Composite Average; Dow Jones Industrial Average; Dow Jones Transportation Average.

down tick *See* minus tick.

Dow theory A technical market theory that long-term trends in the stock market can be confirmed by analyzing the movements of the Dow Jones Industrial Average and the Dow Jones Transportation Average.

DPP *See* direct participation program.

DR *See* debit balance.

dry hole A well that is plugged and abandoned without being completed or that is abandoned for any reason without having produced commercially for 60 days. *See also* productive well.

dual-purpose fund A closed-end investment company that offers two classes of stock: income shares and capital shares. Income shares entitle the holder to share in the net dividends and interest paid to the fund. Capital shares entitle the holder to profit from the capital appreciation of all securities the fund holds. *See also* closed-end management company.

due bill A printed statement showing the obligation of a seller to deliver securities or rights to the purchaser. A due bill is also used as a pledge to deliver dividends when the transaction occurs after the record date.

due diligence The careful investigation by the underwriters that is necessary to ensure that all material information pertinent to an issue has been disclosed to prospective investors.

due diligence meeting A meeting at which an issuing corporation's officials and representatives of the underwriting group present information on and answer questions about a pending issue of securities. The meeting is held for the benefit of brokers, securities analysts and institutional investors.

duplicate confirmation A copy of a customer's confirmation that a brokerage firm sends to an agent or an attorney if the customer requests it in writing. In addition, if the customer is an employee of another broker-dealer, SRO regulations may require a duplicate confirmation to be sent to the employing broker-dealer. *See also* confirmation.

DVP *See* delivery vs. payment.

E

earned income Income derived from active participation in a trade or business, including wages, salary, tips, commissions and bonuses. *See also* portfolio income; unearned income.

earned surplus *See* retained earnings.

earnings per share (EPS) A corporation's net income available for common stock divided by its number of shares of common stock outstanding. *Syn.* primary earnings per share.

earnings per share fully diluted A corporation's earnings per share calculated assuming that all convertible securities have been converted. *See also* earnings per share.

Eastern account A securities underwriting in which the agreement among underwriters states that each syndicate member will be responsible for its own allocation as well as for a proportionate share of any securities remaining unsold. *Syn.* undivided account. *See also* syndicate; Western account.

economic risk The potential for international developments and domestic events to trigger losses in securities investments.

EE *See* excess equity.

EE savings bond *See* Series EE bond.

effective date The date the registration of an issue of securities becomes effective, allowing the underwriters to sell the newly issued securities to the public and confirm sales to investors who have given indications of interest.

efficient market theory A theory based on the premise that the stock market processes information efficiently. The theory postulates that, as new information becomes known, it is reflected immediately in the price of stock and therefore stock prices represent fair prices.

either/or order *See* alternative order.

elasticity The responsiveness of consumers and producers to a change in prices. A large change in demand or production resulting from a small change in price for a good is considered an indication of elasticity.

eligible security *See* margin security.

Employee Retirement Income Security Act of 1974 (ERISA) The law that governs the operation of most corporate pension and benefit plans. The law eased pension eligibility rules, set up the Pension Benefit Guaranty Corporation and established guidelines for the management of pension funds. Corporate retirement plans established under ERISA qualify for favorable tax treatment for employers and participants. *Syn.* Pension Reform Act. *See also* Title 1; Title 2; Title 3; Title 4.

endorsement The signature on the back of a stock or bond certificate by the person named on the certificate as the owner. An owner must endorse certificates when transferring them to another person. *See also* assignment.

EPS *See* earnings per share.

EQ *See* equity.

equipment bond *See* equipment trust certificate.

equipment-leasing limited partnership A direct participation program that purchases equipment for leasing to other businesses on a long-term basis. Tax-sheltered income is the primary objective of such a partnership.

equipment note *See* equipment trust certificate.

equipment trust certificate A debt obligation backed by equipment. The title to the equipment is held by an independent trustee (usually a bank), not the issuing company. Equipment trust certificates are generally issued by transportation companies such as railroads. *Syn.* equipment bond; equipment note.

equity (EQ) Common and preferred stockholders' ownership interests in a corporation. *See also* common stock; preferred stock.

equity financing Raising money for working capital or for capital expenditures by selling common or preferred stock to individual or institutional investors. In return for the money paid, the investors receive own-

ership interests in the corporation. *See also* debt financing.

equity interest The legal right or title to a share in a business or property.

equity option A security representing the right to buy or sell common stock at a specified price within a specified time. *See also* option.

equity security A security representing ownership in a corporation or another enterprise. Examples of equity securities include:
- common and preferred stock;
- interests in a limited partnership or joint venture;
- securities that carry the right to be traded for equity securities, such as convertible bonds, rights and warrants; and
- put and call options on equity securities.

See also debt security.

ERISA *See* Employee Retirement Income Security Act of 1974.

error report A message on the Consolidated Tape correcting an error in a report on a previous trade. Any necessary correction is preceded by the letters "CORR." *See also* CORR.

escrow agreement The certificate provided by an approved bank that guarantees that the indicated securities are on deposit at that bank. An investor who writes a call option and can present an escrow agreement is considered covered and does not need to meet margin requirements.

Eurobond A long-term debt instrument of a government or corporation that is denominated in the currency of the issuer's country but is issued and sold in a different country.

Eurodollar U.S. currency held in banks outside the United States.

excess equity (EE) The value of money or securities in a margin account that is in excess of the federal requirement. *Syn.* margin excess; Regulation T excess.

excess margin securities The securities in a margin account that are in excess of 140 percent of the account's debit balance. Such securities are available to the broker-dealer for debit balance financing purposes, but they must be segregated and earmarked as the customer's property.

exchange Any organization, association or group of persons that maintains or provides a marketplace in which securities can be bought and sold. An exchange need not be a physical place, and several strictly electronic exchanges do business around the world.

Exchange Act *See* Securities Exchange Act of 1934.

exchange distribution A block trading procedure in which a large number of shares of stock is crossed with offers on the floor of the exchange with no prior announcement on the broad tape.

exchange-listed security A security that has met certain requirements and has been admitted to full trading privileges on an exchange. The NYSE, the AMEX and regional exchanges set listing requirements for volume of shares outstanding, corporate earnings and other characteristics. Exchange-listed securities can also be traded in the third market, the market for institutional investors.

exchange market All of the exchanges on which listed securities are traded.

exchange offer An offer to exchange one issuer's securities for those of another, often in conjunction with a corporate takeover.

exchange privilege A feature offered by a mutual fund allowing an individual to transfer an investment in one fund to another fund under the same sponsor without incurring an additional sales charge.

exchange rate *See* foreign exchange rate.

ex-date The first date on which a security is traded that the buyer is not entitled to receive distributions previously declared. *Syn.* ex-dividend date.

ex-dividend date *See* ex-date.

executor A person given fiduciary authorization to manage the affairs of a decedent's estate. An executor's authority is established by the decedent's last will.

exempt security A security exempt from the registration requirements (although not from the antifraud requirements) of the Securities Act of 1933. Examples include U.S. government securities and municipal securities.

exempt transaction A transaction that does not trigger a state's registration and advertising requirements under the Uniform Securities Act. Examples of exempt transactions include:
- nonissuer transactions in outstanding securities (normal market trading);
- transactions with financial institutions;
- unsolicited transactions; and
- private placement transactions.

No transaction is exempt from the Uniform Securities Act's antifraud provisions.

exercise To effect the transaction offered by an option, a right or a warrant. For example, an equity call holder exercises a call by buying 100 shares of the underlying stock at the agreed-upon price within the agreed-upon time period.

exercise price The cost per share at which an option or a warrant holder may buy or sell the underlying security. *Syn.* strike price.

existing property program A real estate direct participation program that aims to provide capital appreciation and income by investing in existing construction.

ex-legal A municipal issue that trades without a written legal opinion of counsel from a bond attorney. An ex-legal issue must be designated as such at the time of the trade. *See also* legal opinion of counsel.

expansion A period of increased business activity throughout an economy; one of the four stages of the business cycle. *Syn.* recovery. *See also* business cycle.

expansionary policy A monetary policy that increases the money supply, usually with the intention of lowering interest rates and combatting deflation.

expense ratio A ratio for comparing a mutual fund's efficiency by dividing the fund's expenses by its net assets.

expiration cycle A set of four expiration months for a class of listed options. An option may have expiration dates of January, April, July and October (JAJO); February, May, August and November (FMAN); or March, June, September and December (MJSD).

expiration date The specified date on which an option buyer no longer has the rights specified in the option contract.

exploratory drilling program A limited partnership that aims to locate and recover undiscovered reserves of oil, gas or minerals. These programs are considered highly risky investments. *Syn.* wildcatting. *See also* developmental drilling program; income program.

exploratory well A well drilled either in search of an undiscovered pool of oil or gas or with the hope of substantially extending the limits of an existing pool of oil or gas.

ex-rights Stock trading without rights. *See also* cum rights.

ex-rights date The date on or after which stocks will be traded without subscription rights previously declared.

ex-warrants date The date on or after which stocks will be traded without warrants previously declared.

F

FAC *See* face-amount certificate company.

face-amount certificate company (FAC) An investment company that issues certificates obligating it to pay an investor a stated amount of money (the face amount) on a specific future date. The investor pays into the certificate in periodic payments or in a lump sum.

face value *See* par.

fail to deliver A situation where the broker-dealer on the sell side of a transaction or contract does not deliver the specified securities to the broker-dealer on the buy side. *Syn.* broker fail; fails; fails to deliver; failure to deliver.

fail to receive A situation where the broker-dealer on the buy side of a transaction or contract does not receive the specified securities from the broker-dealer on the sell side. *Syn.* fails; fails to receive; failure to receive.

Fannie Mae *See* Federal National Mortgage Association.

Farm Credit Administration (FCA) The government agency that coordinates the activities of the banks in the Farm Credit System. *See also* Farm Credit System.

Farm Credit System (FCS) An organization of 37 privately owned banks that provide credit services to farmers and mortgages on farm property. Included in the system are the Federal Land Banks, Federal Intermediate Credit Banks and Banks for Cooperatives. *See also* Federal Intermediate Credit Bank.

farm out An agreement whereby the owner of a leasehold or working interest assigns his interest in certain acreage to a third party while retaining partial interest on the condition that the drilling of one or more specific wells or some other specified task is completed.

FCA *See* Farm Credit Administration.

FCO *See* foreign currency option.

FCS *See* Farm Credit System.

FDIC *See* Federal Deposit Insurance Corporation.

Fed *See* Federal Reserve System.

Fed call *See* margin call.

federal call *See* margin call.

Federal Deposit Insurance Corporation (FDIC) The government agency that provides deposit insurance for member banks and prevents bank and thrift failures.

federal funds The reserves of banks and certain other institutions greater than the reserve requirements or excess reserves. These funds are available immediately.

federal funds rate The interest rate charged by one institution lending federal funds to another.

Federal Home Loan Bank (FHLB) A government-regulated organization that operates a credit reserve system for the nation's savings and loan institutions.

Federal Home Loan Mortgage Corporation (FHLMC) A publicly traded corporation that promotes the nationwide secondary market in mortgages by issuing mortgage-backed pass-through debt certificates. *Syn.* Freddie Mac.

Federal Intermediate Credit Bank (FICB) One of 12 banks that provide short-term financing to farmers as part of the Farm Credit System.

Federal National Mortgage Association (FNMA) A publicly held corporation that purchases conventional mortgages and mortgages from government agencies, including the Federal Housing Administration, Department of Veterans Affairs and Farmers Home Administration. *Syn.* Fannie Mae.

Federal Open Market Committee (FOMC) A committee that makes decisions concerning the Fed's operations to control the money supply.

Federal Reserve Board (FRB) A seven-member group that directs the operations of the Federal Reserve System. The President appoints board members, subject to Congressional approval.

Federal Reserve System The central bank system of the United States. Its primary responsibility is to regulate the flow of money and credit. The system includes 12 regional banks, 24 branch banks and hundreds of national and state banks. *Syn.* Fed.

FHLB *See* Federal Home Loan Bank.

FHLMC *See* Federal Home Loan Mortgage Corporation.

FICB *See* Federal Intermediate Credit Bank.

fictitious quotation A bid or an offer published before being identified by source and verified as legitimate. A fictitious quote may create the appearance of trading activity where none exists; this violates the NASD Rules of Fair Practice.

fidelity bond Insurance coverage required by the self-regulatory organizations for all employees, officers and partners of member firms to protect clients against acts of lost securities, fraudulent trading and check forgery. *Syn.* surety bond.

fiduciary A person legally appointed and authorized to hold assets in trust for another person and manage those assets for that person's benefit.

filing *See* registration by filing.

filing date The day on which an issuer submits to the SEC the registration statement for a new securities issue.

fill or kill order (FOK) An order that instructs the floor broker to fill the entire order immediately; if the entire order cannot be executed immediately, it is canceled.

final prospectus The legal document that states a new issue security's price, delivery date and underwriting spread, as well as other material information. It must be given to every investor who purchases a new issue of registered securities. *Syn.* prospectus.

Financial Guaranty Insurance Corporation (FGIC) An insurance company that offers insurance on the timely payment of interest and principal on municipal issues and unit investment trusts.

financial risk *See* credit risk.

firm commitment underwriting A type of underwriting commitment in which the underwriter agrees to sell an entire new issue of securities. The underwriter acts as a dealer, pays the issuer a lump sum for the securities and assumes all financial responsibility for any unsold shares. *See also* underwriting.

firm quote The actual price at which a trading unit of a security (such as 100 shares of stock or five bonds) may be bought or sold. All quotes are firm quotes unless otherwise indicated. *See also* bona fide quote; nominal quote.

first in, first out (FIFO) An accounting method used to assess a company's inventory, in which it is assumed that the first goods acquired are the first to be sold. The same method is used by the IRS to determine cost basis for tax purposes. *See also* average basis; last in, first out; share identification.

fiscal policy The federal tax and spending policies set by Congress or the President. These policies affect tax rates, interest rates and government spending in an effort to control the economy. *See also* monetary policy.

5 percent markup policy The NASD's general guideline for the percentage markups, markdowns and commissions on OTC securities transactions. The policy is intended to ensure fair and reasonable treatment of the investing public.

fixed annuity An insurance contract in which the insurance company makes fixed dollar payments to the annuitant for the term of the contract, usually until the annuitant dies. The insurance company guarantees both earnings and principal. *Syn.* fixed dollar annuity; guaranteed dollar annuity. *See also* annuity; variable annuity.

fixed asset A tangible, physical property used in the course of a corporation's everyday operations; it including buildings, equipment and land.

fixed charge coverage ratio *See* bond interest coverage ratio.

fixed dollar annuity *See* fixed annuity.

fixed unit investment trust An investment company that invests in a portfolio of securities in which no changes are permissible. *See also* nonfixed unit investment trust; unit investment trust.

fixing Trading in a new security for the purpose of stabilizing its price above the established public offering price; this practice is prohibited. *Syn.* pegging.

flat A term used to describe bonds traded without accrued interest. They are traded at the agreed-upon market price only. *See also* accrued interest.

flat yield curve A chart showing the yields of bonds with short maturities as equal to the yields of bonds with long maturities. *Syn.* even yield curve. *See also* inverted yield curve; normal yield curve; yield curve.

flexible premium policy A variable or whole life insurance contract that permits the holder to adjust the premium payments and death benefit according to changing needs.

floating debt An obligation payable on demand or having a very short maturity.

floor broker *See* commission house broker.

floor trader An exchange member who executes transactions from the floor of the exchange only for his own account. *Syn.* local.

flow of funds The schedule of payments disbursed from the proceeds of a facility financed by a revenue bond. The flow of funds determines the order in which the operating expenses, debt service and other expenses are paid. Typically, the priority is (1) operations and maintenance, (2) debt service, (3) debt service reserve, (4) reserve maintenance, (5) renewal and replacement, (6) surplus. *See also* debt service account; debt service reserve fund.

flow-through A term that describes the way income, deductions and credits resulting from the activities of a business are applied to individual taxes and expenses as though each incurred the income and deductions directly. *See also* limited partnership.

FNMA *See* Federal National Mortgage Association.

FOK *See* fill or kill order.

FOMC *See* Federal Open Market Committee.

forced conversion Market conditions created by a corporation to encourage convertible bondholders to exercise their conversion options. Often conversion is forced by calling the bonds when the market value of the stock is higher than the redemption price offered by the corporation. *See also* redemption.

forced sell-out The action taken when a customer fails to meet the deadline for paying for securities and no extension has been granted: the broker-dealer must liquidate enough securities to pay for the transaction.

foreign associate A non-U.S. citizen employed by an NASD member firm. Foreign associates are not subject to registration and licensing with the NASD.

However, they must not engage in the securities business in any country or territory under the jurisdiction of the United States, nor do business with any U.S. citizen, national or resident alien.

foreign currency Money issued by a country other than the one in which the investor resides. Options and futures contracts on numerous foreign currencies are traded on U.S. exchanges.

foreign currency option (FCO) A security representing the right to buy or sell a specified amount of a foreign currency. *See also* option.

foreign exchange rate The price of one country's currency in terms of another currency. *Syn.* exchange rate.

foreign fund *See* specialized fund.

Form 3 A legal document used by officers, directors and principal stockholders of a corporation to file an initial statement of beneficial ownership of equity securities. The form is filed with the exchange on which the securities trade. If the securities are listed on more than one exchange, the issuer can designate one exchange with which it will file its report.

Form 4 A legal document used to update Form 3 when there are changes in the beneficial ownership of a corporation.

Form 8K A legal document used to report events of consequence that occur in a corporation; such events include changes in control of the corporation or in its name, address, financial standing, board of directors or auditors. *Syn.* current report.

Form 10C A legal document used by an issuer of securities quoted on Nasdaq to report a change in its name and changes of more than 5 percent in the amount of securities it has outstanding.

Form 10K An annual audited report that covers essentially all the information contained in an issuing company's original registration statement. A Form 10K is due within 90 days of year end.

Form 10Q A quarterly report containing a corporation's unaudited financial data. Certain nonrecurring events that arise during the quarterly period, such as

significant litigation, must be reported. A Form 10Q is due 45 days after the end of each of the first three fiscal quarters.

form letter A sales letter sent to more than 25 persons within a 90-day period and, therefore, subject to the NASD's approval and filing requirements for sales literature. *See also* sales literature.

45-day letter *See* free-look letter.

forward pricing The valuation process for mutual fund shares, whereby an order to purchase or redeem shares is executed at the price determined by the portfolio valuation calculated after the order is received. Portfolio valuations occur at least once per business day.

401(k) plan A tax-deferred defined contribution retirement plan offered by an employer.

403(b) plan A tax-deferred annuity retirement plan available to employees of public schools and certain nonprofit organizations.

fourth market The exchange where securities are traded directly from one institutional investor to another without a brokerage firm's services, primarily through the use of INSTINET.

fractional share A portion of a whole share of stock. Mutual fund shares are frequently issued in fractional amounts. Fractional shares used to be generated when corporations declared stock dividends, merged or voted to split stock, but today it is more common for corporations to issue the cash equivalent of fractional shares.

fraud The deliberate concealment, misrepresentation or omission of material information or the truth, so as to deceive or manipulate another party for unlawful or unfair gain.

FRB *See* Federal Reserve Board.

Freddie Mac *See* Federal Home Loan Mortgage Corporation.

free credit balance The cash funds in customer accounts. Broker-dealers must notify customers of their free credit balances at least quarterly.

free-look letter A letter to mutual fund investors explaining a contractual plan's sales charge and operation. The letter must be sent within 60 days of a sale. During the free-look period, the investor may terminate the plan without paying a sales charge. *Syn.* 45-day letter. *See also* contractual plan; right of withdrawal.

freeriding Buying and immediately selling securities without making payment. This practice violates the SEC's Regulation T.

freeriding and withholding The failure of a member participating in the distribution of a hot issue to make a bona fide public offering at the public offering price. This practice violates the NASD Rules of Fair Practice. *See also* hot issue.

front-end fee The expenses paid for services rendered during a direct participation program's organization or acquisition phase, including front-end organization and offering expenses, acquisition fees and expenses, and any other similar fees designated by the sponsor.

front-end load (1) A mutual fund commission or sales fee that is charged at the time shares are purchased. The load is added to the share's net asset value when calculating the public offering price. *See also* back-end load. (2) A system of sales charge for contractual plans that permits up to 50 percent of the first year's payments to be deducted as a sales charge. Investors have a right to withdraw from such a plan, but some restrictions apply if this occurs. *See also* contractual plan; spread load.

frozen account An account requiring cash in advance before a buy order is executed and securities in hand before a sell order is executed. An account holder under such restrictions has violated the SEC's Regulation T.

Full Disclosure Act *See* Securities Act of 1933.

full power of attorney A written authorization for someone other than an account's beneficial owner to make deposits and withdrawals and to execute trades in the account. *See also* limited power of attorney.

full trading authorization An authorization, usually provided by a full power of attorney, for someone other than the customer to have full trading privileges in an account. *See also* limited trading authorization.

fully disclosed broker *See* introducing broker.

fully registered bond A debt issue that prints the bondholder's name on the certificate. The issuer's transfer agent maintains the records and sends principal and interest payments directly to the investor. *See also* registered; registered as to principal only.

functional allocation A sharing arrangement whereby the investors in an oil and gas direct participation program are responsible for intangible costs and the sponsor is responsible for tangible costs; revenues are shared. *See also* sharing arrangement.

fundamental analysis A method of evaluating securities by attempting to measure the intrinsic value of a particular stock. Fundamental analysts study the overall economy, industry conditions and the financial condition and management of particular companies. *See also* technical analysis.

funded debt All long-term debt financing of a corporation.

funding An ERISA guideline stipulating that retirement plan assets must be segregated from other corporate assets.

fund manager *See* portfolio manager.

funds statement The part of a corporation's annual report that analyzes why working capital increased or decreased.

fungible Interchangeable, owing to identical characteristics or value. A security is fungible if it can be substituted or exchanged for another security.

G

GDP *See* gross domestic product.

general account The account that holds all of an insurer's assets other than those in separate accounts. The general account holds the contributions paid for traditional life insurance contracts. *See also* separate account.

general obligation bond (GO) A municipal debt issue backed by the full faith, credit and taxing power of the issuer for payment of interest and principal. *Syn.* full faith and credit bond. *See also* double-barreled bond; revenue bond.

general partner (GP) An active investor in a direct participation program who is personally liable for all debts of the program and who manages the business of the program. The GP's duties include: making decisions that bind the partnership; buying and selling property; managing property and money; supervising all aspects of the business; and maintaining a 1 percent financial interest in the partnership. *See also* limited partner.

general partnership (GP) An association of two or more entities formed to conduct a business jointly. The partnership does not require documents for formation, and the general partners are jointly and severally liable for the partnership's liabilities. *See also* limited partnership.

General Securities Principal *See* Series 24.

General Securities Representative *See* Series 7.

General Securities Sales Supervisor *See* Series 8.

generic advertising Communications with the public that promote securities as investments, but that do not refer to particular securities. *Syn.* institutional advertising.

Ginnie Mae *See* Government National Mortgage Association.

Glass-Steagall Act of 1933 Federal legislation that forbids commercial banks to underwrite securities and forbids investment bankers to open deposit accounts or make commercial loans. *Syn.* banking act.

GNMA *See* Government National Mortgage Association.

GNP *See* gross domestic product.

GO *See* general obligation bond.

good delivery A term describing a security that is negotiable, in compliance with the contract of the sale and ready to be transferred from seller to purchaser. *See also* uniform delivery ticket.

good faith deposit A deposit contributed by each syndicate involved in a competitive bid underwriting for a municipal issue. The deposit ensures performance by the low bidder. The amount required to be deposited is stipulated in the official notice of sale sent to prospective underwriters; it is usually 2 percent to 5 percent of the bid.

good till canceled order (GTC) An order that is left on the specialist's book until it is either executed or canceled. *Syn.* open order.

goodwill An intangible asset that represents the value that a firm's business reputation adds to its book value.

Government National Mortgage Association (GNMA) A wholly government-owned corporation that issues pass-through mortgage debt certificates backed by the full faith and credit of the U.S. government. *Syn.* Ginnie Mae.

government security A debt obligation of the U.S. government, backed by its full faith, credit and taxing power, and regarded as having no risk of default. The government issues short-term Treasury bills, medium-term Treasury notes and long-term Treasury bonds. *See also* agency issue.

GP *See* general partner; general partnership.

grant anticipation note (GAN) A short-term municipal debt security issued in anticipation of receiving a funding grant, typically from a government agency.

green shoe option A provision of an issue's registration statement that allows an underwriter to buy extra shares from the issuer (thus increasing the size of the offering) if public demand proves exceptionally strong. The term derives from the Green Shoe Manufacturing Company, which first used the technique.

gross domestic product (GDP) The total value of goods and services produced in a country during one year. It includes consumption, government purchases, investments, and exports minus imports.

gross income All income of a taxpayer, from whatever source derived.

gross proceeds The total of the initial invested capital in a direct participation program contributed by all of the original and additional limited partners.

gross revenue pledge The flow of funds arrangement in a municipal revenue bond issue indicating that debt service is the first payment to be made from revenues received. The pledge is contained in the trust indenture. *See also* net revenue pledge.

gross revenues All money received by a business from its operations. The term typically does not include interest income or income from the sale, refinancing or other disposition of properties.

group net order In a municipal bond underwriting, an order received by a syndicate member that is credited to the entire syndicate. Takedowns on these orders are paid to members according to their participation in the syndicate. *See also* designated order; member-at-the-takedown order; presale order.

growth fund A diversified common stock fund that has capital appreciation as its primary goal. It invests in companies that reinvest most of their earnings for expansion, research or development. *See also* diversified common stock fund; mutual fund.

growth industry An industry that is growing faster than the economy as a whole as a result of technological changes, new products or changing consumer tastes.

growth stock A relatively speculative issue that is believed to offer significant potential for capital gains. It often pays low dividends and sells at a high price-earnings ratio.

GTC *See* good till canceled order.

guaranteed bond A debt obligation issued with a promise from a corporation other than the issuing corporation to maintain payments of principal and interest.

guaranteed dollar annuity *See* fixed annuity.

guaranteed stock An equity security, generally a preferred stock, issued with a promise from a corporation other than the issuing corporation to maintain dividend payments. The stock still represents ownership in the issuing corporation, but it is considered a dual security.

guardian A fiduciary who manages the assets of a minor or an incompetent for that person's benefit. *See also* fiduciary.

H

HALT A message on the Consolidated Tape indicating that trading in a particular security has been stopped. *See also* trading halt.

head and shoulders On a technical analyst's trading chart, a pattern that has three peaks resembling a head and two shoulders. The stock price moves up to its first peak (the left shoulder), drops back, then moves to a higher peak (the top of the head), drops again but recovers to another, lower peak (the right shoulder). A head and shoulders top typically forms after a substantial rise and indicates a market reversal. A head and shoulders bottom (an inverted head and shoulders) indicates a market advance.

hedge An investment made in order to reduce the risk of adverse price movements in a security. Normally, a hedge consists of a protecting position in a related security. *See also* long hedge; selling a hedge; short hedge.

HH savings bond *See* Series HH bond.

high The highest price a security or commodity reaches during a specified period of time. *See also* low.

holder The owner of a security. *See also* long.

holding company A company organized to invest in and manage other corporations.

holding period A time period signifying how long the owner possesses a security. It starts the day after a purchase and ends on the day of the sale.

hold in street name A securities transaction settlement and delivery procedure whereby a customer's securities are transferred into the broker-dealer's name and held by the broker-dealer. Although the broker-dealer is the nominal owner, the customer is the beneficial owner. *See also* transfer and hold in safekeeping; transfer and ship.

horizontal spread The purchase and sale of two options on the same underlying security and with the same exercise price but different expiration dates. *Syn.* calendar spread; time spread. *See also* spread.

hot issue A new issue that sells or is anticipated to sell at a premium over the public offering price. *See also* freeriding and withholding.

house maintenance call *See* margin maintenance call.

house maintenance requirement *See* margin maintenance requirement.

Housing Authority bond *See* New Housing Authority bond.

HR-10 plan *See* Keogh plan.

hypothecation Pledging to a broker-dealer securities bought on margin as collateral for the margin loan. *See also* rehypothecation.

I

IADB *See* Inter-American Development Bank.

IB *See* introducing broker.

IBRD *See* International Bank for Reconstruction and Development.

IDB *See* industrial development bond.

IDC *See* intangible drilling cost.

IDR *See* industrial development bond.

identified security The particular security designated for sale by an investor holding identical securities with different acquisition dates and cost bases.

This allows the investor to control the amount of capital gain or loss incurred through the sale.

immediate annuity An insurance contract purchased for a single premium that starts to pay the annuitant immediately following its purchase. *See also* annuity.

immediate family A parent, mother-in-law or father-in-law, husband or wife, or child or another relative supported financially by a person associated with the securities industry.

immediate or cancel order (IOC) An order that instructs the floor broker to execute it immediately, in full or in part. Any portion of the order that remains unexecuted is canceled.

inactive crowd The members of the NYSE that trade inactive, infrequently traded bonds. *Syn.* cabinet crowd; can crowd. *See also* active crowd.

incidental insurance benefit A payment received from a variable life insurance policy, other than the variable death benefit and the minimum death benefit, and including but not limited to any accidental death and dismemberment benefit, disability income benefit, guaranteed insurability option, family income benefit or fixed-benefit term rider.

income bond A debt obligation that promises to repay principal in full at maturity. Interest is paid only if the corporation's earnings are sufficient to meet the interest payment and if the board of directors declares the interest payment. Income bonds are usually traded flat. *Syn.* adjustment bond. *See also* flat.

income fund A mutual fund that seeks to provide stable current income by investing in securities that pay interest or dividends. *See also* mutual fund.

income program A limited partnership that buys and markets proven reserves of oil and gas: it buys the value of the oil in the ground. *See also* developmental drilling program; exploratory drilling program.

income statement The summary of a corporation's revenues and expenses for a specific fiscal period.

indefeasible title Ownership that cannot be declared null or void.

index A comparison of current prices to some baseline, such as prices on a particular date. Indexes are frequently used in technical analysis. *See also* average.

index arbitrage Trading a group of stocks in conjunction with stock index options or futures contracts in order to profit from incremental price differences. *See also* arbitrage.

index option A security representing the right to receive, in cash, the difference between the underlying value of a market index and the strike price of the option. The investor speculates on the direction, degree and timing of the change in the numerical value of the index. *See also* capped index option.

indication of interest (IOI) An investor's expression of conditional interest in buying an upcoming securities issue after the investor has reviewed a preliminary prospectus. An indication of interest is not a commitment to buy.

individual retirement account (IRA) A retirement investing tool for employed individuals that allows an annual contribution of 100 percent of earned income up to a maximum of $2,000. Some or all of the contribution may be deductible from current taxes, depending on the individual's adjusted gross income and coverage by employer-sponsored qualified retirement plans. *See also* Keogh plan; nonqualified retirement plan; qualified retirement plan; simplified employee pension plan.

industrial development bond (IDB) A debt security issued by a municipal authority, which uses the proceeds to finance the construction or purchase of facilities to be leased or purchased by a private company. The bonds are backed by the credit of the private company, which is ultimately responsible for principal and interest payments. *Syn.* industrial revenue bond.

industrial revenue bond (IDR) *See* industrial development bond.

industry fund *See* sector fund.

inelasticity A lack of responsiveness on the part of consumers and producers to a change in prices. *See also* elasticity.

inflation A persistent and measurable rise in the general level of prices. *See also* deflation.

inflation risk *See* purchasing power risk.

initial margin requirement The amount of equity a customer must deposit when making a new purchase in a margin account. The SEC's Regulation T requirement for equity securities is currently 50 percent of the purchase price. The NYSE and NASD's initial minimum requirement is a deposit of $2,000 but not more than 100 percent of the purchase price. *See also* margin; margin call.

initial public offering (IPO) A corporation's first sale of common stock to the public. *See also* new issue market; public offering.

in-part call The redemption of a certain portion of a bond issue at the request of the issuer. *See also* in-whole call.

inside information Material information that has not been disseminated to, or is not readily available to, the general public.

inside market The best (highest) bid price at which an OTC stock can be sold, and the best (lowest) ask price at which the same stock can be bought in the interdealer market. *See also* affiliate; control person.

insider Any person who possesses or has access to material nonpublic information about a corporation. Insiders include directors, officers and stockholders who own more than 10 percent of any class of equity security of a corporation.

Insider Trading Act *See* Insider Trading and Securities Fraud Enforcement Act of 1988.

Insider Trading and Securities Fraud Enforcement Act of 1988 Legislation that defines what constitutes the illicit use of nonpublic information in making securities trades and the liabilities and penalties that apply. *Syn.* Insider Trading Act. *See also* Chinese wall; insider.

INSTINET An electronic securities order execution system, owned by Reuters Holdings PLC, that offers institutional investors a means of trading more than 15,000 U.S. and 5,000 global securities without using a broker-dealer or going through an exchange. INSTI-NET collects price quotations from exchange-based market makers and Nasdaq and displays the best bid and asked for each security. *See also* fourth market.

institutional account An account held for the benefit of others. Examples of institutional accounts include banks, trusts, pension and profit-sharing plans, mutual funds and insurance companies.

institutional investor A person or an organization that trades securities in large enough share quantities or dollar amounts that it qualifies for preferential treatment and lower commissions. An institutional order can be of any size. Institutional investors are covered by fewer protective regulations because it is assumed that they are more knowledgeable and better able to protect themselves.

insubstantiality One of the criteria used by the NASD to determine whether a violation of the freeriding and withholding rules has taken place. Any sales to restricted accounts should not represent a significant portion of the total allocation in either total number of shares or dollar amount.

insurance covenant A provision of a municipal revenue bond's trust indenture that helps ensure the safety of the issue by promising to insure the facilities built. *See also* maintenance covenant; rate covenant.

intangible asset A property owned that is not physical, such as a formula, a copyright or goodwill. *See also* goodwill.

intangible drilling cost (IDC) In an oil and gas limited partnership, a tax-deductible cost; usually this is for a nonphysical asset, such as labor or fuel, which does not depreciate. The cost may be expensed in the year incurred, or deductions may be amortized over the life of the well. *Syn.* intangible drilling development expense.

intangible drilling development expense *See* intangible drilling cost.

Inter-American Development Bank (IADB) An institution formed to promote the social and economic development of Latin America by financing capital projects in its member countries.

interbank market An unregulated, decentralized international market in which the various major currencies of the world are traded.

interest The charge for the privilege of borrowing money, usually expressed as an annual percentage rate.

interest coverage ratio *See* bond interest coverage ratio.

interest rate option A security representing the right to buy or sell government debt securities. The federal deficit has created a large market in securities that are sensitive to changes in interest rates; the investor can profit from fluctuations in interest rates and can hedge the risks created by the fluctuations.

interest rate risk The risk associated with investments relating to the sensitivity of price or value to fluctuation in the current level of interest rates; also, the risk that involves the competitive cost of money. This term is generally associated with bond prices, but it applies to all investments. In bonds, prices carry interest risk because if bond prices rise, outstanding bonds will not remain competitive unless their yields and prices adjust to reflect the current market.

interlocking directorate Two or more corporate boards of directors that have individual directors who serve simultaneously on both boards. The concept is invoked in the Investment Company Act of 1940, which states that at least 40 percent of an investment company's board must remain independent from the investment company's operations, and no more than 60 percent of the directors may be affiliated persons, such as investment advisers, custodians or accountants.

Intermarket Trading System/Computer Assisted Execution System (ITS/CAES) An NASD service that provides a computerized link between market makers and specialists who make a market in the same security on the various exchanges. ITS/CAES market makers must maintain a continuous, two-sided market in those securities.

Internal Revenue Code (IRC) The legislation that defines tax liabilities and deductions for U.S. taxpayers.

Internal Revenue Service (IRS) The U.S. government agency responsible for collecting most federal taxes and for administering tax rules and regulations.

International Bank for Reconstruction and Development (IBRD) The international organization that finances loans for building and improving infrastructure in developing countries. The loans are guaranteed by the government of the borrowing country. *Syn.* World Bank.

interpositioning Placing a third party in the middle of a trade between a broker-dealer and a customer. The practice violates the NASD Fair Pricing Rules unless it results in a lower cost to the customer.

interstate offering An issue of securities registered with the SEC sold to residents of states other than the state in which the issuer does business.

in-the-money The term used to describe an option that has intrinsic value, such as a call option when the stock is selling above the exercise price or a put option when the stock is selling below the exercise price. *See also* at-the-money; intrinsic value; out-of-the-money.

intrastate offering An issue of securities exempt from SEC registration, available to companies that do business in one state and sell their securities only to residents of that same state. *See also* Rule 147.

intrinsic value The potential profit to be made from exercising an option. A call option is said to have intrinsic value when the underlying stock is trading above the exercise price. *See also* time value.

introduced account An account opened by an investment adviser or a broker-dealer acting on the behalf of its customers. The firm carrying the account receives full disclosure of the individual customers' account information and maintains records of statements and confirms for the individual customers. *Syn.* investment adviser's customer account. *See also* omnibus account.

introducing broker (IB) A broker-dealer that does not hold customers' money or securities; instead, it introduces customer accounts to a clearing broker-dealer, which handles all cash and securities for those accounts. *Syn.* fully disclosed broker. *See also* clearing broker-dealer.

inverted yield curve A chart showing long-term debt instruments having lower yields than short-term debt instruments. *Syn.* negative yield curve. *See also* flat yield curve; normal yield curve.

invested capital *See* capitalization.

investment adviser (1) Any person who makes investment recommendations in return for a flat fee or a percentage of assets managed. (2) For an investment company, the individual who bears the day-to-day responsibility of investing the cash and securities held in the fund's portfolio in accordance with objectives stated in the fund's prospectus.

Investment Advisers Act of 1940 Legislation governing who must register with the SEC as an investment adviser. *See also* investment adviser.

investment banker An institution in the business of raising capital for corporations and municipalities. An investment banker may not accept deposits or make commercial loans. *Syn.* investment bank.

investment banking business A broker, dealer or municipal or government securities dealer that underwrites or distributes new issues of securities as a dealer or that buys and sells securities for the accounts of others as a broker. *Syn.* investment securities business.

investment company A company engaged in the business of pooling investors' money and trading in securities for them. Examples include face-amount certificate companies, unit investment trusts and management companies.

Investment Company Act Amendments of 1970 Amendments to the Investment Company Act of 1940 requiring a registered investment company that issues contractual plans to offer all purchasers withdrawal rights and purchasers of front-end load plans surrender rights. *See also* Investment Company Act of 1940.

Investment Company Act Amendments of 1975 Amendments to the Investment Company Act of 1940 requiring, in particular, that sales charges relate to the services a fund provides its shareholders. *See also* Investment Company Act of 1940.

Investment Company Act of 1940 Congressional legislation regulating companies that invest and reinvest in securities. The act requires an investment company engaged in interstate commerce to register with the SEC.

Investment Company/Variable Contract Products Limited Principal *See* Series 26.

Investment Company/Variable Contract Products Limited Representative *See* Series 6.

investment grade security A security to which the rating services (Standard & Poor's, Moody's, etc.) have assigned a rating of BBB/Baa or above.

investment in property The amount of capital contributions allocated to the purchase, development, construction or improvement of properties acquired by a direct participation program. The amount available for investment equals the gross proceeds raised less front-end fees.

investment objective Any goal a client hopes to achieve through investing. Examples include current income, capital growth and preservation of capital.

investment pyramid A portfolio strategy that allocates investable assets according to an investment's relative safety. The pyramid base is composed of low-risk investments, the mid portion is composed of growth investments and the pyramid top is composed of speculative investments.

investment value The market price at which a convertible security (usually a debenture) would sell if it were not converted into common stock. *See also* conversion value; convertible bond; debenture.

investor The purchaser of an asset or security with the intent of profiting from the transaction.

invitation for bids A notice to securities underwriters soliciting bids for the issuing of a bond issue. These notices are published in *The Bond Buyer, Munifacts,* newspapers and journals.

in-whole call The redemption of a bond issue in its entirety at the option of the issuer, as opposed to its redemption based on a lottery held by an independent trustee. *See also* in-part call.

IOC *See* immediate or cancel order.

IOI *See* indication of interest.

IPO *See* initial public offering.

IRA *See* individual retirement account.

IRA rollover The reinvestment of assets that an individual receives as a distribution from a qualified tax-deferred retirement plan into an individual retirement account within 60 days of receiving the distribution. The individual may reinvest either the entire sum or a portion of the sum, although any portion not reinvested is taxed as ordinary income. *See also* individual retirement account; IRA transfer.

IRA transfer The direct reinvestment of retirement assets from one qualified tax-deferred retirement plan to an individual retirement account. The account owner never takes possession of the assets, but directs that they be transferred directly from the existing plan custodian to the new plan custodian. *See also* individual retirement account; IRA rollover.

IRC *See* Internal Revenue Code.

irrevocable stock power *See* stock power.

issued stock Equity securities authorized by the issuer's registration statement and distributed to the public. *See also* outstanding stock; treasury stock.

issuer The entity, such as a corporation or municipality, that offers or proposes to offer its securities for sale.

ITS *See* Intermarket Trading System/Computer Assisted Execution System.

J

joint account An account in which two or more individuals possess some form of control over the account and may transact business in the account. The account must be designated as either joint tenants in common or joint tenants with right of survivorship. *See also* joint tenants in common; joint tenants with right of survivorship.

joint life with last survivor An annuity payout option that covers two or more people, with annuity payments continuing as long as one of the annuitants remains alive.

joint tenants in common (JTIC) A form of joint ownership of an account whereby a deceased tenant's fractional interest in the account is retained by his estate. *Syn.* tenants in common. *See also* joint tenants with right of survivorship.

joint tenants with right of survivorship (JTWROS) A form of joint ownership of an account whereby a deceased tenant's fractional interest in the account passes to the surviving tenant(s). It is used almost exclusively by husbands and wives. *See also* joint tenants in common.

joint venture The cooperation of two or more individuals or enterprises in a specific business enterprise, rather than in a continuing relationship—as in a partnership.

JTIC *See* joint tenants in common.

JTWROS *See* joint tenants with right of survivorship.

junior lien debt A bond backed by the same collateral backing a previous issue and having a subordinate claim to the collateral in the event of default. *See also* closed-end covenant; open-end covenant.

K

Keogh plan A qualified tax-deferred retirement plan for persons who are self-employed and unincorporated or who earn extra income through personal services aside from their regular employment. *Syn.* HR-10 plan. *See also* individual retirement account; nonqualified retirement plan; qualified retirement plan; top-heavy rule.

Keynesian economics The theory that active government intervention in the marketplace is the best method of ensuring economic growth and stability.

know your customer rule *See* Rule 405.

L

lagging indicator A measurable economic factor that changes after the economy has started to follow a particular pattern or trend. Lagging indicators are believed to confirm long-term trends. Examples include average duration of unemployment, corporate profits and labor cost per unit of output. *See also* coincident indicator; leading indicator.

last in, first out (LIFO) An accounting method used to assess a corporation's inventory in which it is assumed that the last goods acquired are the first to be sold. The method is used to determine cost basis for tax purposes; the IRS designates last in, first out as the order in which sales or withdrawals from an investment are made. *See also* average basis; first in, first out; share identification.

leading indicator A measurable economic factor that changes before the economy starts to follow a particular pattern or trend. Leading indicators are believed to predict changes in the economy. Examples include new orders for durable goods, slowdowns in deliveries by vendors and numbers of building permits issued. *See also* coincident indicator; lagging indicator.

LEAPS® *See* long-term equity option.

lease rental bond A debt security issued by a municipal authority to raise funds for new construction with the understanding that the finished structure will be rented to the authority and that the rental payments will finance the bond payments.

legal list The selection of securities a state agency (usually a state banking or insurance commission) determines to be appropriate investments for fiduciary accounts such as mutual savings banks, pension funds and insurance companies.

legal opinion of counsel The statement of a bond attorney affirming that an issue is a municipal issue and that interest is exempt from federal taxation. Each municipal bond certificate must be accompanied by a legal opinion of counsel. *See also* ex-legal; qualified legal opinion; unqualified legal opinion.

legislative risk The potential for an investor to be adversely affected by changes in investment or tax laws.

letter of intent (LOI) A signed agreement allowing an investor to buy mutual fund shares at a lower overall sales charge, based on the total dollar amount of the intended investment. A letter of intent is valid only if the investor completes the terms of the agreement within 13 months of signing the agreement. A letter of intent may be backdated 90 days. *Syn.* statement of intention.

level debt service A schedule for debt repayment whereby principal and interest payments remain essentially constant from year to year over the life of the issue. *See also* decreasing debt service.

level load A mutual fund sales fee charged annually based on the net asset value of a share. A 12b-1 asset-based fee is an example of a level load. *See also* back-end load; Class C share; Class D share; front-end load.

Level One The basic level of Nasdaq service; through a desktop quotation machine, it provides registered representatives with up-to-the-minute inside bid and ask quotations on hundreds of over-the-counter stocks. *See also* National Association of Securities Dealers Automated Quotation System.

Level Two The second level of Nasdaq service; through a desktop quotation machine, it provides up-to-the-minute inside bid and ask quotations and the bids and askeds of each market maker for a security. *See also* National Association of Securities Dealers Automated Quotation System.

Level Three The highest level of Nasdaq service; through a desktop quotation machine, it provides up-to-the-minute inside bid and ask quotations, supplies the bids and askeds of each market maker for a security and allows each market maker to enter changes in those quotations. *See also* National Association of Securities Dealers Automated Quotation System.

leverage Using borrowed capital to increase investment return. *Syn.* trading on the equity.

liability A legal obligation to pay a debt owed. Current liabilities are debts payable within 12 months. Long-term liabilities are debts payable over a period of more than 12 months.

LIBOR *See* London Interbank Offered Rate.

license *See* Series 6; Series 7; Series 26; Series 63; Series 65.

life annuity/straight life An annuity payout option that pays a monthly check over the annuitant's lifetime.

life annuity with period certain An annuity payout option that guarantees the annuitant a monthly check for a certain time period and thereafter until the annuitant's death. If the annuitant dies before the time period expires, the payments go to the annuitant's named beneficiary.

life contingency An annuity payout option that provides a death benefit during the accumulation stage. If the annuitant dies during this period, a full contribution is made to the account, which is paid to the annuitant's named beneficiary.

LIFO *See* last in, first out.

lifting cost A cost incurred in producing and marketing oil and gas from completed wells. Lifting costs include labor, fuel, repairs, haulage of materials, supplies, utilities, ad valorem and severance taxes, insurance and casualty losses, and compensation to well operators for services rendered.

limited liability An investor's right to limit potential losses to no more than the amount invested. Equity shareholders, such as corporate stockholders and limited partners, have limited liability.

limited partner (LP) An investor in a direct participation program who does not participate in the management or control of the program and whose liability for partnership debts is limited to the amount invested in the program. *See also* general partner; participant; passive investor.

limited partnership (LP) An association of two or more partners formed to conduct a business jointly and in which one or more of the partners is liable only to the extent of the amount of money they have invested. Limited partners do not receive dividends but enjoy direct flow-through of income and expenses. *See also* flow-through; general partnership.

limited partnership agreement The contract between a partnership's limited and general partners that provides the guidelines for partnership operation and states the rights and responsibilities of each partner.

limited power of attorney A written authorization for someone other than an account's beneficial owner to make certain investment decisions regarding transactions in the account. *See also* discretion; full power of attorney.

limited principal A person who has passed an examination attesting to the knowledge and qualifications necessary to supervise a broker-dealer's business in a limited area of expertise. A limited principal is not qualified in the general fields of expertise reserved for a general securities principal; these include supervision of underwriting and market making and approval of advertising. *See also* Series 26.

limited representative A person who has passed an examination attesting to the knowledge and qualifications necessary to sell certain specified investment products. *See also* Series 6.

limited tax bond A general obligation municipal debt security issued by a municipality whose taxing power is limited to a specified maximum rate.

limited trading authorization An authorization, usually provided by a limited power of attorney, for someone other than the customer to have trading privileges in an account. These privileges are limited to purchases and sales; withdrawal of assets is not authorized. *See also* full trading authorization.

limit order An order that instructs the floor broker to buy a specified security below a certain price or to sell a specified security above a certain price. *Syn.* or better order. *See also* stop limit order; stop order.

limit order book *See* specialist's book.

liquidation priority In the case of a corporation's liquidation, the order that is strictly followed for paying off creditors and stockholders:
1. unpaid wages
2. taxes
3. secured claims (mortgages)
4. secured liabilities (bonds)
5. unsecured liabilities (debentures) and general creditors
6. subordinated debt
7. preferred stockholders
8. common stockholders

liquidity The ease with which an asset can be converted to cash in the marketplace. A large number of buyers and sellers and a high volume of trading activity provide high liquidity.

liquidity ratio A measure of a corporation's ability to meet its current obligations. The ratio compares current assets to current liabilities. *See also* acid-test ratio; current ratio.

liquidity risk The potential that an investor might not be able to sell an investment as and when desired. *Syn.* marketability risk.

listed option An option contract that can be bought and sold on a national securities exchange in a continuous secondary market. Listed options carry standardized strike prices and expiration dates. *Syn.* standardized option. *See also* OTC option.

listed security A stock, a bond or another security that satisfies certain minimum requirements and is traded on a regional or national securities exchange such as the New York Stock Exchange. *See also* over the counter.

LMV *See* current market value.

loan consent agreement An optional contract between a brokerage firm and a margin customer that permits the firm to lend the margined securities to other brokers; the contract is part of the margin agreement. *Syn.* consent to lend agreement.

loaned flat Securities loaned to short sellers without an interest charge.

loan value *See* maximum loan value.

local *See* floor trader.

Local Quotations Program A quotation dissemination service provided to the news media by the NASD Information Committee. Information on a particular security may be provided to a community based on local stockholder interest, local market conditions and the number of stockholders residing in that community.

locked market The situation created when there is no spread between the bid and the ask on the same security; that is, one market maker bids for a stock at the same price that another market maker quotes its ask price. This violates the NASD Rules of Fair Practice. *See also* crossed market.

LOI *See* letter of intent.

London Interbank Offered Rate (LIBOR) The average of the interbank-offered interest rates for dollar deposits in the London market, based on the quotations at five major banks.

long The term used to describe the owning of a security, contract or commodity. For example, a common stock owner is said to have a long position in the stock. *See also* short.

long hedge Buying puts as protection against a decline in the value of a long securities or actuals position. *See also* hedge; selling a hedge; short hedge.

long market value (LMV) *See* current market value.

long straddle An option investor's position that results from buying a call and a put on the same stock with the same exercise price and expiration month. *See also* short straddle; spread; straddle.

long-term equity option An option contract that has a longer expiration than traditional equity option contracts. The most common long-term equity option is the CBOE's Long-term Equity AnticiPation Security (LEAPS®).

long-term gain The profit earned on the sale of a capital asset that has been owned for more than 12 months. *See also* capital gain; capital loss; long-term loss.

long-term loss The loss realized on the sale of a capital asset that has been owned for more than 12 months. *See also* capital gain; capital loss; long-term gain.

loss carryover A capital loss incurred in one tax year that is carried over to the next year or later years for use as a capital loss deduction. *See also* capital loss.

low The lowest price a security or commodity reaches during a specified time period. *See also* high.

LP *See* limited partner; limited partnership.

M

M1 A category of the money supply that includes all coins, currency and demand deposits—that is, checking accounts and NOW accounts. *See also* M2; M3; money supply.

M2 A category of the money supply that includes M1 in addition to all time deposits, savings deposits and noninstitutional money-market funds. *See also* M1; M3; money supply.

M3 A category of the money supply that includes M2 in addition to all large time deposits, institutional money-market funds, short-term repurchase agreements and certain other large liquid assets. *See also* M1; M2; money supply.

maintenance call *See* margin maintenance call.

maintenance covenant A provision of a municipal revenue bond's trust indenture that helps ensure the safety of the issue by promising to keep the facility and equipment in good working order. *See also* insurance covenant; rate covenant.

maintenance requirement *See* margin maintenance requirement.

Major Market Index (MMI) A market indicator designed to track the Dow Jones industrials. It is composed of 15 of the 30 Dow Jones industrials and five other large NYSE-listed stocks. *See also* index.

make a market To stand ready to buy or sell a particular security as a dealer for its own account. A market maker accepts the risk of holding the position in the security. *See also* market maker.

Maloney Act An amendment enacted in 1938 to broaden Section 15 of the Securities Exchange Act of 1934. Named for its sponsor, the late Sen. Francis Maloney of Connecticut, the amendment provided for the creation of a self-regulatory organization for the specific purpose of supervising the over-the-counter securities market. *See also* National Association of Securities Dealers, Inc.

managed underwriting An arrangement between the issuer of a security and an investment banker in which the banker agrees to form an underwriting syndicate to bring the security to the public. The syndicate manager then directs the entire underwriting process.

management company An investment company that trades various types of securities in a portfolio in accordance with specific objectives stated in the prospectus. *See also* closed-end management company; diversified management company; mutual fund; nondiversified management company.

management fee The payment to the sponsor of a direct participation program for managing and administering the program. The fee is capped at about 5 percent of the program's gross revenues.

manager of the syndicate *See* underwriting manager.

managing partner The general partner of a direct participation program that selects the investments and operates the partnership.

managing underwriter *See* underwriting manager.

mandatory call The redemption of a bond by an issuer authorized in the trust indenture and based on a predetermined schedule or event. *See also* catastrophe call; partial call.

margin The amount of equity contributed by a customer as a percentage of the current market value of the securities held in a margin account. *See also* equity; initial margin requirement; margin call; Regulation T.

margin account A customer account in which a brokerage firm lends the customer part of the purchase price of securities. *See also* cash account; Regulation T; special arbitrage account.

margin call The Federal Reserve Board's demand that a customer deposit a specified amount of money or securities when a purchase is made in a margin account; the amount is expressed as a percentage of the market value of the securities at the time of purchase. The deposit must be made within one payment period. *Syn.* Fed call; federal call; federal margin; Reg T call; T call. *See also* initial margin requirement; margin.

margin deficiency *See* margin maintenance requirement.

margin department The department within a brokerage firm that computes the amount of money clients must deposit in margin and cash accounts. *Syn.* credit department.

margin excess *See* excess equity.

margin maintenance call A demand that a margin customer deposit money or securities when the customer's equity falls below the margin maintenance requirement set by the broker-dealer or by the NASD or NYSE. *Syn.* house maintenance call; maintenance call; NASD/NYSE maintenance call.

margin maintenance requirement The minimum equity that must be held in a margin account, determined by the broker-dealer and by the NASD or NYSE. The amount of equity required varies with the type of security bought on margin, and the broker-dealer's house requirement is usually higher than that set by the NASD or NYSE. *Syn.* house maintenance requirement; maintenance requirement; NASD/NYSE maintenance requirement.

margin of profit ratio A measure of a corporation's relative profitability. It is calculated by dividing the operating profit by the net sales. *Syn.* operating profit ratio; profit margin.

margin risk The potential that a margin customer will be required to deposit additional cash if her security positions are subject to adverse price movements.

margin security A security that is eligible for purchase on margin, including any registered security, OTC margin stock or bond or Nasdaq National Market security. A firm is permitted to lend money to help customers purchase these securities, and may accept these securities as collateral for margin purchases. *Syn.* eligible security. *See also* nonmargin security; OTC margin security.

markdown The difference between the highest current bid price among dealers and the lower price that a dealer pays to a customer.

marketability The ease with which a security can be bought or sold; having a readily available market for trading.

market arbitrage The simultaneous purchase and sale of the same security in different markets to take advantage of a price disparity between the two markets. *See also* arbitrage.

market identifier On the Consolidated Tape's high-speed line, a letter that identifies the exchange or market on which a transaction took place.

market-if-touched order (MIT) *See* board order.

market letter A publication that comments on securities, investing, the economy or other related topics and is distributed to an organization's clients or to the public. *See also* sales literature.

market maker A dealer willing to accept the risk of holding a particular security in its own account to facilitate trading in that security. *See also* make a market.

market NH *See* not held order.

market not held order *See* not held order.

market-on-close order An order that specifies it is to be executed at, or as near as possible to, the close of the market or of trading in that security, or else it is canceled. The order does not have to be executed at the closing price. *Syn.* at-the-close order. *See also* at-the-opening order.

market order An order to be executed immediately at the best available price. A market order is the only order that guarantees execution. *Syn.* unrestricted order.

market-out clause The standard provision of a firm commitment underwriting agreement that relieves the underwriter of its obligation to underwrite the issue under circumstances that impair the investment quality of the securities.

market risk The potential for an investor to experience losses owing to day-to-day fluctuations in the prices at which securities can be bought or sold. *See also* systematic risk.

market value The price at which investors buy or sell a share of common stock or a bond at a given time. Market value is determined by buyers' and sellers' interaction. *See also* current market value.

mark to the market To adjust the value of the securities in an account to the current market value of those securities; used to calculate the market value and equity in a margin account.

markup The difference between the lowest current offering price among dealers and the higher price a dealer charges a customer.

markup policy *See* NASD 5 percent markup policy.

married put The simultaneous purchase of a stock and a put on that stock specifically identified as a hedge.

matching orders Simultaneously entering identical (or nearly identical) buy and sell orders for a security to create the appearance of active trading in that security. This violates the antifraud provisions of the Securities Exchange Act of 1934.

material information Any fact that could affect an investor's decision to trade a security.

maturity date The date on which a bond's principal is repaid to the investor and interest payments cease. *See also* par; principal.

maximum loan value The percentage of market value a broker-dealer is permitted to lend a margin customer for the purchase of securities. Loan value is equal to the complement of the Regulation T requirement: if Reg T were 65 percent, the maximum loan value would be 35 percent. *Syn.* loan value.

maximum market value The market value to which a short sale position may advance before a margin maintenance call is issued. Maximum market value is set by the NASD/NYSE, and currently equals the credit balance divided by 130 percent. *Syn.* maximum short market value.

maximum short market value *See* maximum market value.

MBIA *See* Municipal Bond Investors Assurance Corp.

member (1) Of the New York Stock Exchange: one of the 1,366 individuals owning a seat on the Exchange. (2) Of the National Association of Securities Dealers: any broker or dealer admitted to membership in the Association.

member-at-the-takedown order In a municipal bond underwriting, a customer order submitted by one syndicate member, who will receive the entire takedown. Member-at-the-takedown orders receive the lowest priority when the securities of the issue are allocated. *Syn.* member order. *See also* designated order; group net order; presale order.

member firm A broker-dealer in which at least one of the principal officers is a member of the New York Stock Exchange, another exchange, a self-regulatory organization or a clearing corporation.

member order *See* member-at-the takedown order.

membership The members of the New York Stock Exchange, another exchange, a self-regulatory organization or a clearing corporation.

mini-max underwriting A form of best efforts underwriting in which the issuer sets a floor and a ceiling on the amount of securities to be sold. *See also* underwriting.

minimum death benefit The amount payable under a variable life insurance policy upon the policy owner's death, regardless of the separate account's investment performance. The insurance company guarantees the minimum amount.

minimum margin requirement *See* margin maintenance requirement.

minus tick A security transaction's execution price that is below the previous execution price, by a minimum amount. A short sale may not be executed on a minus tick. *Syn.* down tick. *See also* plus tick; plus tick rule; short sale; tick; zero-minus tick.

MIT *See* market-if-touched order.

MMI *See* Major Market Index.

modern portfolio theory (MPT) A method of choosing investments that focuses on the importance of the relationships among all of the investments in a portfolio rather than the individual merits of each investment. The method allows investors to quantify and control the amount of risk they accept and return they achieve.

Modified Accelerated Cost Recovery System (MACRS) An accounting method used to recover the cost of qualifying depreciable property by taking the larger deductions in the first years. The system eliminates the acceleration of deductions for real property. Deductions are based on percentages prescribed in the Internal Revenue Code. *See also* straight-line depreciation.

monetarist theory An economic theory holding that the money supply is the major determinant of price levels and that therefore a well-controlled money supply will have the most beneficial impact on the economy.

monetary policy The Federal Reserve Board's actions that determine the size and rate of the money supply's growth, which in turn affect interest rates. *See also* fiscal policy.

money market The securities market that deals in short-term debt. Money-market instruments are very liquid forms of debt that mature in less than one year. Treasury bills make up the bulk of money-market instruments.

money-market fund A mutual fund that invests in short-term debt instruments. The fund's objective is to earn interest while maintaining a stable net asset value of $1 per share. Generally sold with no load, the fund may also offer draft-writing privileges and low opening investments. *See also* mutual fund.

money supply The total stock of bills, coins, loans, credit and other liquid instruments in the economy. It is divided into four categories—L, M1, M2 and M3—according to the type of account in which the instrument is kept. *See also* M1; M2; M3.

Moody's Investors Service One of the best known investment rating agencies in the United States. A subsidiary of Dun & Bradstreet, Moody's rates bonds, commercial paper, preferred and common stocks, and municipal short-term issues. *See also* bond rating; Standard & Poor's Corporation.

moral obligation bond A municipal revenue bond for which a state legislature has the authority, but no legal obligation, to appropriate money in the event the issuer defaults.

mortgage bond A debt obligation secured by a property pledge. It represents a lien or mortgage against the issuing corporation's properties and real estate assets.

moving average chart A tool used by technical analysts to track the price movements of a commodity. It plots average daily settlement prices over a defined period of time (for example, over three days for a three-day moving average). *See also* bar chart; point-and-figure chart.

MSRB *See* Municipal Securities Rulemaking Board.

multiplier effect The expansion of the money supply that results from a Federal Reserve System member bank's being able to lend more money than it takes in. A small increase in bank deposits generates a far larger increase in available credit.

municipal bond A debt security issued by a state, a municipality or another subdivision (such as a school, a park, a sanitation or another local taxing district) to finance its capital expenditures. Such expenditures might include the construction of highways, public works or school buildings. *Syn.* municipal security.

municipal bond fund A mutual fund that invests in municipal bonds and operates either as a unit investment trust or as an open-end fund. The fund's objective is to maximize federally tax-exempt income. *See also* mutual fund; unit investment trust.

Municipal Bond Investors Assurance Corp. (MBIA) A public corporation offering insurance as to the timely payment of principal and interest on qualified municipal issues. Issues with MBIA insurance are generally rated AAA by Standard & Poor's.

municipal note A short-term municipal security issued in anticipation of funds from another source. *See also* municipal security.

Municipal Securities Rulemaking Board (MSRB) A self-regulatory organization that regulates the issuance and trading of municipal securities. The Board functions under the Securities and Exchange Commission's supervision; it has no enforcement powers. *See also* Securities Acts Amendments of 1975.

municipal security *See* municipal bond.

Munifacts A news wire service for the municipal bond industry; a product of *The Bond Buyer*.

mutual fund An investment company that continuously offers new equity shares in an actively managed portfolio of securities. All shareholders participate in the fund's gains or losses. The shares are redeemable on any business day at the net asset value. Each mutual fund's portfolio is invested to match the objective stated in the prospectus. *Syn.* open-end investment company; open-end management company. *See also* asset allocation fund; balanced fund; contractual plan; net asset value.

mutual fund custodian A national bank, a stock exchange member firm, a trust company or another qualified institution that physically safeguards the securities a mutual fund holds. It does not manage the fund's investments; its function is solely clerical.

N

N Consolidated Tape market identifier for the New York Stock Exchange.

naked The position of an option investor who writes a call or a put on a security he does not own. *Syn.* uncovered.

naked call writer An investor who writes a call option without owning the underlying stock or other related assets that would enable the investor to deliver the stock should the option be exercised. *Syn.* uncovered call writer. *See also* naked put writer.

naked put writer An investor who writes a put option without owning the underlying stock or other related assets that would enable the investor to purchase the stock should the option be exercised. *Syn.* uncovered put writer. *See also* naked call writer.

narrow-based index An index that is designed to reflect the movement of a market segment, such as a group of stocks in one industry or a specific type of investment. Examples include the Technology Index and the Gold/Silver Index. *See also* broad-based index; index.

NASD *See* National Association of Securities Dealers, Inc.

Nasdaq *See* National Association of Securities Dealers Automated Quotation System.

Nasdaq National Market (NNM) The most actively traded over-the-counter stocks quoted on Nasdaq. Trades in these stocks are reported as they occur.

Nasdaq 100 An index of the largest 100 nonfinancial stocks on Nasdaq, weighted according to capitalization.

NASD Bylaws The body of rules that describes how the NASD functions, defines its powers and determines the qualifications and registration requirements for brokers.

NASD District Business Conduct Committee (DBCC) A committee composed of up to 12 NASD members who each serves as administrator for one of the 13 local NASD districts. The DBCC has original jurisdiction for hearing and judging complaints.

NASD 5 percent markup policy A guideline for reasonable markups, markdowns and commissions for secondary over-the-counter transactions. According to the policy, all commissions on broker transactions and all markups or markdowns on principal transactions should equal 5 percent or should be fair and reasonable for a particular transaction. *Syn.* markup policy.

NASD Manual A publication that outlines NASD policies for regulating the over-the-counter market. Included are the Rules of Fair Practice, the Uniform Practice Code, the Code of Procedure and the Code of Arbitration Procedure.

NASD Regulation, Inc. Branch of the NASD organized in 1996 to supervise member broker-dealers, enforce laws and ethical standards and mete out disciplinary action.

NASD Rules of Fair Practice (Conduct Rules) Regulations designed to ensure that NASD member firms and their representatives follow fair and ethical trade practices when dealing with the public. The rules complement and broaden the Securities Act of 1933, the Securities Exchange Act of 1934 and the Investment Company Act of 1940.

National Association of Securities Dealers, Inc. (NASD) The self-regulatory organization for the over-the-counter market. The NASD was organized under the provisions of the 1938 Maloney Act. *See also* Maloney Act.

National Association of Securities Dealers Automated Quotation System (Nasdaq) The nationwide electronic quotation system for up-to-the-minute bid and asked quotations on approximately 5,500 over-the-counter stocks.

National List A list of securities for which Nasdaq will supply quotations for dissemination to the media; the list is compiled by the NASD Information Committee. Inclusion on the list is determined by size, float and price criteria. *See also* Additional List.

National Quotation Bureau The publisher of compiled quotes from market makers in over-the-counter stocks and bonds. The daily *Pink Sheets* report stock quotes and the daily Yellow Sheets report corporate bond quotes. *See also* Pink Sheets; *Yellow Sheets.*

National Securities Clearing Corporation (NSCC) An organization that acts as a medium through which member brokerage firms and exchanges reconcile accounts with each other.

National Securities Trading System (NSTS) An automated electronic execution system used by the Cincinnati Stock Exchange; it provides members with agency transactions of up to 1,099 shares at the best available quote prices.

NAV *See* net asset value.

NAV of fund The net total of a mutual fund's assets and liabilities; used to calculate the price of new fund shares.

NAV per bond A measure of a firm's ability to meet its long-term debt obligations by calculating the assets available to back the bonds issued.

NAV per share The value of a mutual fund share, calculated by dividing the fund's total net asset value by the number of shares outstanding.

negotiability A characteristic of a security that permits the owner to assign, give, transfer or sell it to another person without a third party's permission.

negotiable certificate of deposit (CD) An unsecured promissory note issued with a minimum face value of $100,000. It evidences a time deposit of funds with the issuing bank and is guaranteed by the bank.

negotiable order of withdrawal (NOW) account A bank account through which the customer can write drafts against money held on deposit; an interest-bearing checking account. *See also* M1.

negotiated underwriting A form of underwriting agreement in which a brokerage firm consults with the issuer to determine the most suitable price and timing of a forthcoming securities offering. *See also* competitive bid underwriting.

net asset value (NAV) A mutual fund share's value, calculated once a day, based on the closing market price for each security in the fund's portfolio. It is computed by deducting the fund's liabilities from the portfolio's total assets and dividing this amount by the number of shares outstanding. *See also* mutual fund.

net change The difference between a security's closing price on the trading day reported and the previous day's closing price. In over-the-counter transactions, the term refers to the difference between the closing bids.

net current asset value per share The calculation of book value per share that excludes all fixed assets. *See also* book value per share.

net debt per capita A measure of the ability of a municipality to meet its debt obligations; it compares

the debt issued by the municipality to its property values.

net debt to assessed valuation A measure of the financial condition of a municipality; it compares the municipality's debt obligations to the assessed value of its property. *See also* net debt to estimated valuation.

net debt to estimated valuation A measure of the financial condition of a municipality; it compares the municipality's debt obligations to the estimated value of its property. *See also* net debt to assessed valuation.

net direct debt The amount of debt obligations of a municipality, including general obligation bonds and notes and short-term notes. Self-supported debt from revenue bond issues is not included in the calculation.

net domestic product A measure of the annual economic output of a nation adjusted to account for depreciation. It is calculated by subtracting the amount of depreciation from the gross domestic product. *See also* gross domestic product.

net fixed assets per bond A measure of a bond's safety; it is a conservative measure because it excludes intangible assets, working capital and accumulated depreciation.

net income to net sales *See* net profit ratio.

net interest cost (NIC) A means of evaluating the competitive bids of prospective bond underwriting syndicates. It calculates the coupon interest to be paid by the issuer over the life of the bond. *See also* true interest cost.

net investment income The source of an investment company's dividend payments. It is calculated by subtracting the company's operating expenses from the total dividends and interest the company receives from the securities in its portfolio.

net investment return The rate of return from a variable life insurance separate account. The cumulative return for all years is applied to the benefit base when calculating the death benefit.

net operating profits interest A sharing arrangement in an oil and gas direct participation program whereby the general partner bears none of the program's costs but is entitled to a percentage of profits after all royalties and operating expenses have been paid. *See also* sharing arrangement.

net proceeds The amount of money received from a direct participation program offering less expenses incurred, such as selling commissions, syndicate fees and organizational costs.

net profit margin *See* net profit ratio.

net profit ratio A measure of a corporation's relative profitability. It is calculated by dividing aftertax income by net sales. *Syn.* net income to net sales; net profit margin; net profits to sales; profit after taxes; profit ratio.

net profits to sales *See* net profit ratio.

net revenue pledge The flow of funds arrangement in a municipal revenue bond issue pledging that operating and maintenance expenses will be paid before debt service. The pledge is contained in the trust indenture. *See also* gross revenue pledge.

net tangible assets per bond *See* book value per bond.

net tangible assets per share *See* book value per share.

net total debt The sum of the debt obligations of a municipality, calculated by adding the municipality's net direct debt to its overlapping debt. *See also* net direct debt; overlapping debt.

Network A A Consolidated Tape reporting system that provides subscribers with information on transactions in NYSE-listed securities. *See also* Consolidated Tape.

Network B A Consolidated Tape reporting system that provides subscribers with information on transactions in AMEX-listed and certain regional securities. *See also* Consolidated Tape.

net worth The amount by which assets exceed liabilities. *Syn.* owners' equity; shareholders' equity; stockholders' equity.

new account form The form that must be filled out for each new account opened with a brokerage firm. The form specifies, at a minimum, the account owner, trading authorization, payment method and types of securities appropriate for the customer.

new construction program A real estate direct participation program that aims to provide capital appreciation from building new property.

New Housing Authority bond (NHA) A municipal special revenue bond backed by the U.S. government and issued by a local public housing authority to develop and improve low-income housing. *Syn.* Housing Authority bond; Public Housing Authority bond.

new issue market The securities market for shares in privately owned businesses that are raising capital by selling common stock to the public for the first time. *Syn.* primary market. *See also* initial public offering; secondary market.

New Issues Act *See* Securities Act of 1933.

New York Stock Exchange (NYSE) The largest stock exchange in the United States. It is a corporation, operated by a board of directors, responsible for setting policy, supervising Exchange and member activities, listing securities, overseeing the transfer of members' seats on the Exchange and judging whether an applicant is qualified to be a specialist.

New York Stock Exchange Composite Index Index of common stocks listed on the NYSE, based on the price of each stock weighted by its total value of shares outstanding. *Syn.* NYSE Index.

NH *See* not held order.

NHA *See* New Housing Authority bond.

NIC *See* net interest cost.

nine bond rule An NYSE rule that requires orders for nine or fewer listed bonds to be sent to the floor of the NYSE before being traded in the over-the-counter market.

NNM *See* Nasdaq National Market.

no-load fund A mutual fund whose shares are sold without a commission or sales charge. The investment company distributes the shares directly. *See also* mutual fund; net asset value; sales load.

nominal owner The person in whose name securities are registered if that person is other than the beneficial owner. This is a brokerage firm's role when customer securities are registered in street name.

nominal quote A quotation on an inactively traded security that does not represent an actual offer to buy or sell, but is given for informational purposes only. *See also* bona fide quote; firm quote.

nominal yield The interest rate stated on the face of a bond that represents the percentage of interest the issuer pays on the bond's face value. *Syn.* coupon rate; stated yield. *See also* bond yield.

nonaccredited investor An investor not meeting the net worth requirements of Regulation D. Nonaccredited investors are counted for purposes of the 35-investor limitation for Regulation D private placements. *See also* accredited investor; private placement; Regulation D.

nonaffiliate A buyer of an unregistered public offering security who has no management or major ownership interest in the company being acquired. Nonaffiliates may sell this stock only after a specified holding period.

noncompetitive bid An order placed for Treasury bills in which the investor agrees to pay the average of the competitive bids and in return is guaranteed that the order will be filled.

noncumulative preferred stock An equity security that does not have to pay any dividends in arrears to the holder. *See also* convertible preferred stock; cumulative preferred stock; preferred stock.

nondiscrimination In a qualified retirement plan, a formula for calculating contributions and benefits that must be applied uniformly so as to ensure that all employees receive fair and equitable treatment. *See also* qualified retirement plan.

nondiversification A portfolio management strategy that seeks to concentrate investments in a particular industry or geographic area in hopes of achieving higher returns. *See also* diversification.

nondiversified investment company A management company that does not meet the diversification requirements of the Investment Company Act of 1940. These companies are not restricted in the choice of securities or by the concentration of interest they have in those securities. *See also* diversified investment company; management company; mutual fund.

nondiversified management company A management company that does not meet the diversification requirements of the Investment Company Act of 1940. Such a company is not restricted in the choice of securities or by the concentration of interest it has in those securities. *See also* diversified management company; management company; mutual fund.

noneligible security *See* nonmargin security.

nonequity option A security representing the right to buy or sell an investment instrument other than a common stock at a specified price within a specified time period. Examples of such investment instruments include foreign currencies, indexes and interest rates. *See also* equity option; foreign currency option; index option; interest rate option; option.

nonfixed unit investment trust An investment company that invests in a portfolio of securities and permits changes in the portfolio's makeup. *See also* fixed unit investment trust; unit investment trust.

nonmanaged offering A method of distributing direct participation program interests in which the program sponsor contracts with individual broker-dealers to offer the interests to the public. A wholesaler is often hired by the sponsor to arrange selling agreements with each firm.

nonmargin security A security that must be purchased in a cash account, that must be paid for in full, and that may not be used as collateral for a loan. Examples include put and call options, rights, insurance contracts and new issues. *See also* margin security.

nonqualified retirement plan A corporate retirement plan that does not meet the standards set by the Employee Retirement Income Security Act of 1974. Contributions to a nonqualified plan are not tax deductible. *See also* qualified retirement plan.

nonrecourse financing Debt incurred for the purchase of an asset which pledges the asset as security for the debt but that does not hold the borrower personally liable. *See also* recourse financing.

nonsystematic risk The potential for an unforeseen event to affect the value of a specific investment. Examples of such events include strikes, natural disasters, introductions of new product lines and attempted takeovers. *See also* systematic risk.

no-par stock An equity security issued without a stated value.

normal yield curve A chart showing long-term debt instruments having higher yields than short-term debt instruments. *Syn.* positive yield curve. *See also* flat yield curve; inverted yield curve; yield curve.

note A short-term debt security, usually maturing in five years or less. *See also* Treasury note.

not held order (NH) An order that gives the floor broker discretion as to the price and timing of the order's execution. Not held orders are often entered for large amounts of a security. *Syn.* market NH; market not held order.

notification *See* registration by filing.

NOW account *See* negotiable order of withdrawal account.

NSCC *See* National Securities Clearing Corporation.

NSTS *See* National Securities Trading System.

numbered account An account titled with something other than the customer's name. The title might be a number, symbol or special title. The customer must sign a form designating account ownership.

NYSE *See* New York Stock Exchange.

NYSE Composite Index *See* New York Stock Exchange Composite Index.

NYSE maintenance call *See* margin maintenance call.

NYSE maintenance requirement *See* margin maintenance requirement.

O

O Consolidated Tape market identifier for INSTINET.

OBO *See* order book official.

OCC *See* Office of the Comptroller of the Currency; Options Clearing Corporation.

OCC Disclosure Document *See* options disclosure document.

odd lot An amount of a security that is less than the normal unit of trading for that security. Generally, an odd lot is fewer than 100 shares of stock or five bonds. *See also* round lot.

odd lot differential The extra commission often charged when an odd lot order is executed on an exchange. Usually the charge is 12.5 cents (⅛ of a point) per share in addition to the broker's standard commission.

odd-lot theory A technical analysis theory based on the assumption that the small investor is always wrong. Therefore, if odd lot sales are up—that is, small investors are selling stock—it is probably a good time to buy.

offer (1) *See* ask. (2) Under the Uniform Securities Act, any attempt to solicit a purchase or sale in a security for value. *See also* bid; public offering price; quotation.

offering circular An abbreviated prospectus used by corporations issuing less than $5 million of stock. The SEC's Regulation A allows these offerings an exemption from the full registration requirements of the 1933 act. *See also* Regulation A.

office of supervisory jurisdiction (OSJ) The broker-dealer office responsible for supervising the activities of registered representatives and associated persons housed in that office and in other offices within the same region. The NASD requires a broker-dealer to assign these supervisory responsibilities to an office that carries out certain market making and customer service functions. *See also* branch office; satellite office.

Office of the Comptroller of the Currency (OCC) The bureau of the U.S. Treasury Department that is responsible for issuing and enforcing regulations governing the investing and lending practices of the nation's banks.

official notice of sale The invitation to bid on a municipal bond issue; the invitation is sent to prospective underwriters and specifies, among other things, the date, time and place of sale, description of the issue, maturities, call provisions and amount of good faith deposit required.

official statement (OS) A document concerning a municipal issue that must be provided to every buyer. The document is prepared by the underwriter from information provided by the issuer; typically included are the offering terms, descriptions of the bonds and the issuer, the underwriting spread, fees received by brokers, initial offering price and tax status.

OID *See* original issue discount bond.

oil and gas direct participation program A direct participation program formed to locate new oil and gas reserves, develop existing reserves or generate income from producing wells. A high return is the primary objective of such a program. *Syn.* oil and gas limited partnership.

oil depletion allowance An accounting procedure that reduces the taxable portion of revenues from the sale of oil to compensate for the decreased supply of oil in the ground. Depletion is the natural resource counterpart of depreciation.

omnibus account An account opened in the name of an investment adviser or a broker-dealer for the benefit of its customers. The firm carrying the account does not receive disclosure of the individual customers' names or holdings and does not maintain records for the individual customers. *Syn.* special omnibus account. *See also* introduced account.

one cancels other (OCO) *See* alternative order.

one-way lien Pledging a firm's securities as collateral for a bank loan to protect customer securities. *See also* cross lien.

open-end covenant A provision of a bond's trust indenture allowing the issuer to use the same collateral backing a bond as collateral for future bond issues. As a result, new creditors have the same claim on the collateral as existing creditors. *See also* closed-end covenant; junior lien debt.

open-end investment company *See* mutual fund.

open-end mortgage bond A secured bond issued with a trust indenture that permits the corporation to issue more bonds of the same class (and with the same collateral backing) at a later date. *See also* closed-end mortgage bond.

opening purchase Entering the options market by buying calls or puts. *See also* closing sale; opening sale.

opening sale Entering the options market by selling calls or puts. *See also* closing purchase; opening purchase.

open-market operations The buying and selling of securities (primarily government or agency debt) by the Federal Open Market Committee to effect control of the money supply. These transactions increase or decrease the level of bank reserves available for lending.

open order *See* good till canceled order.

operating expenses (1) The day-to-day costs incurred in running a business. (2) In an oil and gas program, any production or leasehold expense incurred in the operation of a producing lease, including district expense, direct out-of-pocket expenses for labor, materials and supplies and those shares of taxes and transportation charges not borne by overriding royalty interests.

operating income The profit realized from one year of operation of a business.

operating profit ratio *See* margin of profit ratio.

operating ratio The ratio of operating expenses to net sales; the complement to the margin of profit ratio.

operations and maintenance fund The account from which are paid current operating and maintenance expenses on a facility financed by a municipal revenue bond. *See also* flow of funds.

operator The person who supervises and manages the exploration, drilling, mining, production and leasehold operations of an oil and gas or mining direct participation program.

option A security that represents the right to buy or sell a specified amount of an underlying security—a stock, bond, futures contract, etc.—at a specified price within a specified time. The purchaser acquires a right, and the seller assumes an obligation.

option agreement The document a customer must sign within 15 days of being approved for options trading. In it the customer agrees to abide by the rules of the options exchanges and not to exceed position or exercise limits.

option contract adjustment An adjustment made automatically to the terms of an option on the ex-dividend date when a stock pays a stock dividend or if there is a stock split or a reverse split.

options account A customer account in which the customer has received approval to trade options.

Options Clearing Corporation (OCC) The organization that issues options, standardizes option contracts and guarantees their performance. The OCC made secondary trading possible by creating fungible option contracts.

options disclosure document A publication of the Options Clearing Corporation that outlines the risks and rewards of investing in options. The document must be given to each customer at the time of opening an options account, and must accompany any options sales literature sent to a customer. *Syn.* OCC Disclosure Document.

order book official (OBO) The title given to a specialist or market maker employed on the Pacific, Philadelphia and Chicago Board Options exchanges.

order department The department within a brokerage firm that transmits orders to the proper market for execution and returns confirmations to the appropriate representative. *Syn.* order room; wire room.

order memorandum The form completed by a registered rep that contains customer instructions regarding an order's placement. The memorandum contains such information as the customer's name and account number, a description of the security, the type of transaction (buy, sell, sell short, etc.) and any special instructions (such as time or price limits). *Syn.* order ticket.

order room *See* order department.

Order Routing System (ORS) The system the Chicago Board Options Exchange uses to collect, store, route and execute orders for public customers. ORS automatically routes option market and limit orders of up to 2,000 contracts to the CBOE member firm's floor booth, to the floor brokers in the trading crowd, to the order book official's electronic book or to the Retail Automatic Execution System. *See also* Chicago Board Options Exchange.

order ticket *See* order memorandum.

ordinary income Earnings other than capital gain.

organization and offering expense The cost of preparing a direct participation program for registration and subsequently offering and distributing it to the public; the cost includes sales commissions paid to broker-dealers.

original issue discount bond (OID) A corporate or municipal debt security issued at a discount from face value. The bond may or may not pay interest. The discount on a corporate OID bond is taxed as if accrued annually as ordinary income. The discount on a municipal OID bond is exempt from annual taxation; however, the discount is accrued for the purpose of calculating cost basis. *See also* zero-coupon bond.

ORS *See* Order Routing System.

OS *See* official statement.

OTC *See* over the counter.

OTC Bulletin Board An electronic quotation system for equity securities that are not listed on a national exchange or included in the Nasdaq system.

OTC margin security A security that is not traded on a national exchange but that has been designated by the Federal Reserve Board as eligible for trading on margin. The Fed publishes a list of such securities. *See also* margin security.

OTC market The security exchange system in which broker-dealers negotiate directly with one another rather than through an auction on an exchange floor. The trading takes place over computer and telephone networks that link brokers and dealers around the world. Both listed and OTC securities, as well as municipal and U.S. government securities, trade in the OTC market.

OTC option An option contract that is not listed on an exchange. All contract terms are negotiated between buyer and seller. *Syn.* nonstandard option. *See also* listed option.

out-of-the-money The term used to describe an option that has no intrinsic value, such as a call option when the stock is selling below the exercise price or a put option when the stock is selling above the exercise price. *See also* at-the-money; in-the-money; intrinsic value.

outstanding stock Equity securities issued by a corporation and in the hands of the public; issued stock that the issuer has not reacquired. *See also* treasury stock.

overbought A technical analysis term for a market in which more and stronger buying has occurred than the fundamentals justify. *See also* oversold.

overlapping debt A condition resulting when property in a municipality is subject to multiple taxing authorities or tax districts, each having tax collection powers and recourse to the residents of that municipality. *See also* coterminous.

overriding royalty interest A sharing arrangement whereby a person with a royalty interest in an oil and gas direct participation program takes no risks but receives a share of the revenues; the share is carved out of the working interest without liability for any costs of extraction. *See also* sharing arrangement.

oversold A technical analysis term for a market in which more and stronger selling has occurred than the fundamentals justify. *See also* overbought.

over the counter (OTC) The term used to describe a security traded through the telephone-linked and computer-connected OTC market rather than through an exchange. *See also* OTC market.

owners' equity *See* net worth.

P

P Consolidated Tape market identifier for the Pacific Stock Exchange.

Pacific Stock Exchange (PSE) The only SEC-registered stock exchange west of the Mississippi. It was registered in 1956, after merging four exchanges that served Los Angeles and San Francisco. *See also* regional exchange.

paid-in capital *See* capital surplus.

paid-in surplus *See* capital surplus.

par The dollar amount the issuer assigns to a security. For an equity security, par is usually a small dollar amount that bears no relationship to the security's market price. For a debt security, par is the amount repaid to the investor when the bond matures, usually $1,000. *Syn.* face value; principal; stated value. *See also* capital surplus; maturity date.

parity In an exchange market, a situation in which all brokers bidding have equal standing and the winning bid is awarded by a random drawing. *See also* precedence; priority.

parity price of common The dollar amount at which a common stock is equal in value to its corresponding convertible security. It is calculated by dividing the convertible security's market value by its conversion ratio.

parity price of convertible The dollar amount at which a convertible security is equal in value to its corresponding common stock. It is calculated by multiplying the market price of the common stock by its conversion ratio.

partial call The redemption by an issuer of a portion of an outstanding bond issue prior to the maturity date. *See also* catastrophe call; mandatory call.

participant (1) A person who advises stockholders in a proxy contest. (2) The holder of an interest in a direct participation program. *See also* limited partner.

participating preferred stock An equity security that offers the holder a share of corporate earnings remaining after all senior securities have been paid a fixed dividend. The payment is made in addition to the fixed dividend stated on the certificate, and may be cumulative or noncumulative. *See also* convertible preferred stock; cumulative preferred stock; noncumulative preferred stock; preferred stock.

participation The provision of the Employee Retirement Income Security Act of 1974 requiring that all employees in a qualified retirement plan be covered within a reasonable time of their dates of hire.

partnership A form of business organization in which two or more individuals manage the business and are equally and personally liable for its debts.

partnership account An account that empowers the individual members of a partnership to act on the behalf of the partnership as a whole.

partnership management fee The amount payable to the general partners of a limited partnership, or to other persons, for managing the day-to-day partnership operations. *Syn.* program management fee; property management fee.

par value The dollar amount assigned to a security by the issuer. For an equity security, par value is usually a small dollar amount that bears no relationship to the security's market price. For a debt security, par value is the amount repaid to the investor when the bond matures, usually $1,000. *Syn.* face value; principal; stated value. *See also* capital surplus; discount bond; premium bond.

passive income Earnings derived from a rental property, limited partnership or other enterprise in which the individual is not actively involved. Passive income therefore does not include earnings from wages or active business participation, nor does it include income from dividends, interest and capital gains. *See also* passive loss; unearned income.

passive investor *See* limited partner.

passive loss A loss incurred through a rental property, limited partnership or other enterprise in which the individual is not actively involved. Passive losses can be used to offset passive income only, not wage or portfolio income. *See also* passive income.

pass-through certificate A security representing an interest in a pool of conventional, VA, Farmers Home Administration or other agency mortgages. The pool receives the principal and interest payments, which it passes through to each certificate holder. Payments may or may not be guaranteed. *See also* Federal National Mortgage Association; Government National Mortgage Association.

pattern A repetitive series of price movements on a chart used by a technical analyst to predict future movements of the market.

payment date The day on which a declared dividend is paid to all stockholders owning shares on the record date.

payment period As defined by the Federal Reserve Board's Regulation T, the period of time corresponding to the regular way settlement period established by the NASD.

payout stage *See* distribution stage.

payroll deduction plan A retirement plan whereby an employee authorizes a deduction from his check on a regular basis. The plan may be qualified, such as a 401(k) plan, or nonqualified.

PE *See* price-earnings ratio.

peak The end of a period of increasing business activity throughout the economy, one of the four stages of the business cycle. *Syn.* prosperity. *See also* business cycle.

pegging (1) Stabilizing a country's currency through its purchase or sale by the country's central bank. (2) *See* fixing.

pension plan A contract between an individual and an employer, a labor union, a government entity or another institution that provides for the distribution of pension benefits at retirement.

Pension Reform Act *See* Employee Retirement Income Security Act of 1974.

PE ratio *See* price-earnings ratio.

percentage depletion A method of tax accounting for a direct participation program whereby a statutory percentage of gross income from the sale of a mineral resource is allowed as a tax-deductible expense. Percentage depletion is available to small producers only and not to purchasers of producing interests.

periodic payment plan A mutual fund sales contract in which the customer commits to buying shares in the fund on a periodic basis over a long time period in exchange for a lower minimum investment.

person As defined in securities law, an individual, a corporation, a partnership, an association, a fund, a joint stock company, an unincorporated organization, a trust, a government or a political subdivision of a government.

personal income (PI) An individual's total earnings derived from wages, passive business enterprises and investments. *See also* disposable income.

phantom income In a limited partnership, taxable income that is not backed by a positive cash flow. *See also* crossover point.

Philadelphia Automated Communication and Execution System (PACE) The computerized order routing system developed in 1975 by the Philadelphia Stock Exchange. The system routes and executes orders automatically; it provides electronic executions within approximately 15 seconds of order receipt and returns confirmations to the originating broker-dealer in only a few seconds more. PACE handles market and limit orders for actively traded stocks. *See also* Philadelphia Stock Exchange.

Philadelphia Stock Exchange (PHLX) Founded in 1790, the oldest stock exchange in the United States. Its three trading floors are devoted to equity securities, equity options and foreign currencies. *See also* Philadelphia Automated Communication and Execution System; regional exchange.

PHLX *See* Philadelphia Stock Exchange.

Pink Sheets A daily publication compiled by the National Quotation Bureau and containing interdealer wholesale quotations for over-the-counter stocks. *See also Yellow Sheets.*

pipeline theory *See* conduit theory.

placement ratio A ratio compiled by *The Bond Buyer* indicating the number of new municipal issues that have sold within the last week.

plan completion insurance An insurance contract purchased by a contractual plan investor naming the plan custodian as beneficiary. In the event of the investor's death, the insurance proceeds are used to complete the contractual plan payments.

plan custodian An institution retained by a contractual plan company to perform clerical duties. The custodian's responsibilities include safeguarding plan assets, sending out customer confirmations and issuing shares. *See also* custodian; mutual fund custodian.

plus tick A security transaction's execution price that is above the previous execution price, by a minimum amount. *Syn.* up tick. *See also* minus tick; plus tick rule; tick; zero-plus tick.

plus tick rule The SEC regulation governing the market price at which a short sale may be made. No short sale may be executed at a price below the price of the last sale. *Syn.* up tick rule. *See also* minus tick; short-exempt transaction; short sale; tick; zero-plus tick.

PN *See* project note.

point A measure of a bond's price; $10 or 1 percent of the par value of $1,000. *See also* basis point.

point-and-figure chart A tool used by technical analysts to track the effects of price reversals, or changes in the direction of prices, of a commodity over time. *See also* bar chart; moving average chart.

policy processing day The day on which charges authorized in a variable life insurance policy are deducted from the policy's cash value. These charges include administrative fees, taxes and cost of insurance.

POP *See* public offering price.

portfolio income Earnings from interest, dividends and all nonbusiness investments. *See also* earned income; passive income; unearned income.

portfolio insurance A method of hedging a portfolio of common stocks against market risk by selling stock index futures short. The technique is frequently used by institutional investors.

portfolio manager The entity responsible for investing a mutual fund's assets, implementing its investment strategy and managing day-to-day portfolio trading. *Syn.* fund manager.

position The amount of a security either owned (a long position) or owed (a short position) by an individual or a dealer. Dealers take long positions in specific securities to maintain inventories and thereby facilitate trading.

position limit The rule established by options exchanges that prohibits an investor from having a net long or short position of more than a specific number of contracts on the same side of the market.

position trader (1) A dealer who acquires or sells an inventory in a security. *See also* dealer; principal; make a market. (2) A commodities speculator who buys or sells positions in the futures markets as a means of speculating on long-term price movements. *See also* day trader; spreader.

positive yield curve *See* normal yield curve.

possession of securities *See* control of securities.

power of substitution *See* stock power.

Pr A message on the Consolidated Tape indicating that the trade being reported is in a preferred stock.

precedence In an exchange market, the ranking of bids and offers according to the number of shares involved. *See also* parity; priority.

preemptive right A stockholder's legal right to maintain her proportionate ownership by purchasing newly issued shares before the new stock is offered to the public. *See also* right.

preferred dividend coverage ratio An indication of the safety of a corporation's preferred dividend payments. It is computed by dividing preferred dividends by net income.

preferred stock An equity security that represents ownership in a corporation. It is issued with a stated dividend, which must be paid before dividends are paid to common stockholders. It generally carries no voting rights. *See also* callable preferred stock; convertible preferred stock; cumulative preferred stock.

preferred stock fund A mutual fund whose investment objective is to provide stable income with minimal capital risk. It invests in income-producing instruments such as preferred stock. *See also* bond fund.

preferred stock ratio One of several tools used by bond analysts to assess the safety of a corporation's bonds. It measures the percentage of the corporation's total capitalization that is composed of preferred stock by dividing the total face value of the preferred stock by the total capitalization.

preliminary prospectus An abbreviated prospectus that is distributed while the SEC is reviewing an issuer's registration statement. It contains all of the essential facts about the forthcoming offering except the underwriting spread, final public offering price and date on which the shares will be delivered. *Syn.* red herring.

premium (1) The amount of cash that an option buyer pays to an option seller. (2) The difference between the higher price paid for a security and the security's face amount at issue. *See also* discount.

premium bond A bond that sells at a higher price than its face value. *See also* discount bond; par value.

prerefunding *See* advance refunding.

presale order An order communicated to a syndicate manager prior to formation of the underwriting bid of a new municipal bond issue. If the syndicate wins the bid, the order takes the highest priority when orders are filled. *See also* designated order; group net order; member-at-the-takedown order.

price-earnings ratio (PE) A tool for comparing the prices of different common stocks by assessing how much the market is willing to pay for a share of each corporation's earnings. It is calculated by dividing the current market price of a stock by the earnings per share.

price risk The potential that the value of a currency or commodity will change between the signing of a delivery contract and the time delivery is made. The futures markets serve to manage price risk.

price spread *See* vertical spread.

primary distribution *See* primary offering.

primary earnings per share *See* earnings per share.

primary market *See* new issue market.

primary offering An offering in which the proceeds of the underwriting go to the issuing corporation, agency or municipality. The issuer seeks to increase its capitalization either by selling shares of stock, representing ownership, or by selling bonds, representing loans to the issuer. *Syn.* primary distribution.

prime rate The interest rate that commercial banks charge their prime or most creditworthy customers, generally large corporations.

principal (1) A person who trades for his own account in the primary or secondary market. (2) *See* dealer. (3) *See* par.

principal transaction A transaction in which a broker-dealer either buys securities from customers and takes them into its own inventory or sells securities to customers from its inventory. *See also* agency transaction; agent; broker; dealer; principal.

priority In an exchange market, the ranking of bids and offers according to the first person to bid or offer at a given price. Therefore, only one individual or firm can have priority. *See also* parity; precedence.

prior lien bond A secured bond that takes precedence over other bonds secured by the same assets. *See also* mortgage bond.

prior preferred stock An equity security that offers the holder stock that has prior claim over other preferred stock in receipt of dividends and in distribution of assets in the event of liquidation. *See also* preferred stock.

private placement An offering of new issue securities that complies with Regulation D of the Securities Act of 1933. According to Regulation D, a security generally is not required to be registered with the SEC if it is offered to no more than 35 nonaccredited investors or to an unlimited number of accredited investors. *See also* Regulation D.

productive well An oil or gas well that produces mineral resources that can be marketed commercially. *See also* dry hole.

profitability The ability to generate a level of income and gain in excess of expenses.

profitability ratio One of several measures of a corporation's relative profit or income in relation to its sales. *See also* margin of profit ratio; net profit ratio; return on equity.

profit after taxes *See* net profit ratio.

profit margin *See* margin of profit ratio.

profit ratio *See* net profit ratio.

profit-sharing plan An employee benefit plan established and maintained by an employer whereby the employees receive a share of the business's profits. The money may be paid directly to the employees or deferred until retirement. A combination of both approaches is also possible.

program trading A coordinated trading strategy involving the related purchases or sales of groups of stocks having a market value of $1 million or more. Program trading often involves arbitrage between the stock market and the futures market.

progressive tax A tax that takes a larger percentage of the income of high-income earners than that of low-income earners. An example is the graduated income tax. *See also* regressive tax.

project note (PN) A short-term municipal debt instrument issued in anticipation of a later issuance of New Housing Authority bonds. *See also* New Housing Authority bond.

property dividend A distribution made by a corporation to its stockholders of securities it owns in other corporations or of its products. *See also* dividend.

prospectus *See* final prospectus.

Prospectus Act *See* Securities Act of 1933.

proxy A limited power of attorney from a stockholder authorizing another person to vote on stockholder issues according to the first stockholder's instructions. To vote on corporate matters, a stockholder must either attend the annual meeting or vote by proxy.

proxy department The department within a brokerage firm that is responsible for sending proxy statements to customers whose securities are held in the firm's name, and for mailing financial reports received from issuers to their stockholders.

prudent man rule A legal maxim that restricts discretion in a fiduciary account to only those investments that a reasonable and prudent person might make.

PSA prepayment model A standard benchmark of prepayment speeds on mortgage loans, set forth by the Public Securities Association. Prices and interest rates of CMO securities are often based on these prepayment assumptions. *See also* Public Securities Association.

PSE *See* Pacific Stock Exchange.

Public Housing Authority bond (PHA) *See* New Housing Authority bond.

publicly traded fund *See* closed-end investment company.

public offering The sale of an issue of common stock, either by a corporation going public or by an offering of additional shares. *See also* initial public offering.

public offering price (POP) (1) The price of new shares that is established in the issuing corporation's prospectus. (2) The price to investors for mutual fund shares, equal to the net asset value plus the sales charge. *See also* ask; bid; mutual fund; net asset value.

public purpose bond A municipal bond that is exempt from federal income tax as long no more than 10 percent of the proceeds benefit private entities.

Public Securities Association (PSA) An organization of banks and broker-dealers that conduct business in mortgage-backed securities, money-market securities and securities issued by the U.S. government, government agencies and municipalities. *See also* PSA prepayment model.

purchasing power risk The potential that, due to inflation, a certain amount of money will not purchase as much in the future as it does today. *Syn.* inflation risk.

put (1) An option contract giving the owner the right to sell a certain amount of an underlying security at a specified price within a specified time. (2) The act of exercising a put option. *See also* call.

put bond A debt security requiring the issuer to purchase the security at the holder's discretion or within a prescribed time. *Syn.* tender bond.

put buyer An investor who pays a premium for an option contract and receives, for a specified time, the right to sell the underlying security at a specified price. *See also* call buyer; call writer; put writer.

put spread An option investor's position in which the investor buys a put on a particular security and writes a put on the same security but with a different expiration date, exercise price, or both.

put writer An investor who receives a premium and takes on, for a specified time, the obligation to buy the underlying security at a specified price at the put buyer's discretion. *See also* call buyer; call writer; put buyer.

pyramiding A speculative strategy whereby an investor uses unrealized profits from a position held to increase the size of the position continuously but by ever-smaller amounts.

Q

qualification *See* registration by qualification.

qualified legal opinion The statement of a bond attorney affirming the validity of a new municipal bond issue but expressing reservations about its quality. *See also* legal opinion of counsel; unqualified legal opinion.

qualified retirement plan A corporate retirement plan that meets the standards set by the Employee Retirement Income Security Act of 1974. Contributions to a qualified plan are tax deductible. *Syn.* approved plan. *See also* individual retirement account; Keogh plan; nonqualified retirement plan.

quick assets A measure of a corporation's liquidity that takes into account the size of the unsold inventory. It is calculated by subtracting inventory from current assets, and it is used in the acid-test ratio. *See also* acid-test ratio.

quick ratio *See* acid-test ratio.

quotation The price or bid a market maker or broker-dealer offers for a particular security. *Syn.* quote. *See also* ask; bid; bond quote; stock quote.

quote *See* quotation.

quote machine A computer that provides representatives and market makers with the information that appears on the Consolidated Tape. The information on the screen is condensed into symbols and numbers.

Quotron® One of several computerized financial information systems used by brokerage firms and market makers. *See also* quote machine.

R

RAN *See* revenue anticipation note.

random walk theory A market analysis theory that the past movement or direction of the price of a stock or market cannot be used to predict its future movement or direction.

range A security's low price and high price for a particular trading period, such as the close of a day's trading, the opening of a day's trading, or a day, month or year. *Syn.* opening range.

rate covenant A provision of a municipal revenue bond's trust indenture that helps ensure the safety of the issue by specifying the rates to be charged the user of the facility. *See also* insurance covenant; maintenance covenant.

rating An evaluation of a corporate or municipal bond's relative safety, according to the issuer's ability to repay principal and make interest payments. Bonds are rated by various organizations, such as Standard & Poor's and Moody's. Ratings range from AAA or Aaa (the highest) to C or D, which represents a company in default.

rating service A company, such as Moody's or Standard & Poor's, that rates various debt and preferred stock issues for safety of payment of principal, interest or dividends. The issuing company or municipality pays a fee for the rating. *See also* bond rating; rating.

ratio writing An option hedge position in which the investor writes more than one call option for every 100 shares of underlying stock that the investor owns. As a result, the investor has a partly covered position and a partly naked position.

raw land program A real estate direct participation program that aims to provide capital appreciation by investing in undeveloped land.

real estate investment trust (REIT) A corporation or trust that uses the pooled capital of many investors to invest in direct ownership of either income property or mortgage loans. These investments offer tax benefits in addition to interest and capital gains distributions.

real estate limited partnership A direct participation program formed to build new structures, generate income from existing property or profit from the capital appreciation of undeveloped land. Growth potential, income distributions and tax shelter are the most important benefits of such a program.

real estate mortgage investment conduit (REMIC) A corporation, trust or partnership that uses the pooled capital of many investors to invest in fixed portfolios of real estate mortgages. These investments offer tax benefits in addition to interest and capital gains distributions.

realized gain The amount a taxpayer earns when he sells an asset. *See also* unrealized gain.

reallowance *See* concession.

recapitalization Changing the capital structure of a corporation by issuing, converting or redeeming securities.

recapture The taxation as ordinary income of previously earned deductions or credits. Circumstances that may cause the IRS to require this tax to be paid include excess depreciation, premature sale of an asset or because a previous tax benefit is now disallowed.

recession A general economic decline lasting from 6 to 18 months.

reciprocal immunity *See* doctrine of mutual reciprocity.

reclamation The right of the seller of a security to recover any loss incurred in a securities transaction owing to bad delivery or other irregularity in the settlement process.

reclassification The exchange by a corporation of one class of its securities for another class of its securities. This shifts ownership control among the stockholders and therefore falls under the purview of the SEC's Rule 145. *See also* Rule 145.

record date The date a corporation's board of directors establishes that determines which of its stockholders are entitled to receive dividends or rights distributions.

recourse financing Debt incurred for the purchase of an asset and that holds the borrower personally liable for the debt. *See also* nonrecourse financing.

recovery *See* expansion.

redeemable security A security that the issuer redeems upon the holder's request. Examples include shares in an open-end investment company and Treasury notes.

redemption The return of an investor's principal in a security, such as a bond, preferred stock or mutual fund shares. By law, redemption of mutual fund shares must occur within seven days of receiving the investor's request for redemption.

redemption notice A published announcement that a corporation or municipality is calling a certain issue of its bonds.

red herring *See* preliminary prospectus.

refinancing Issuing equity, the proceeds of which are used to retire debt.

refunding Retiring an outstanding bond issue at maturity using money from the sale of a new offering. *See also* advance refunding.

regional exchange A stock exchange that serves the financial community in a particular region of the country. These exchanges tend to focus on securities issued within their regions, but also offer trading in NYSE- and AMEX-listed securities.

regional fund *See* sector fund.

registered The term describing a security that prints the owner's name on the certificate. The owner's name is stored in records kept by the issuer or a transfer agent.

registered as to principal only The term describing a bond that prints the owner's name on the certificate, but that has unregistered coupons payable to the bearer. *Syn.* partially registered. *See also* coupon bond; fully registered bond; registered.

registered options principal (ROP) The officer or partner of a brokerage firm who approves in writing accounts in which options transactions are permitted.

registered principal An associated person of a member firm who manages or supervises the firm's investment banking or securities business. This includes any individual who trains associated persons and who solicits business.

Unless the member firm is a sole proprietorship, it must employ at least two registered principals, one of whom must be registered as a general securities principal and one of whom must be registered as a financial and operations principal. If the firm does options business with the public, it must employ at least one registered options principal.

registered representative (RR) An associated person engaged in the investment banking or securities business. According to the NASD, this includes any individual who supervises, solicits or conducts business in securities or who trains people to supervise, solicit or conduct business in securities.

   Anyone employed by a brokerage firm who is not a principal and who is not engaged in clerical or brokerage administration is subject to registration and exam licensing as a registered representative. *Syn.* account executive; stockbroker. *See also* associated person of a member.

registrar The independent organization or part of a corporation responsible for accounting for all of the issuer's outstanding stock and certifying that its bonds constitute legal debt.

registration by coordination A process that allows a security to be sold in a state. It is available to an issuer that files for the security's registration under the Securities Act of 1933 and files duplicates of the registration documents with the state administrator. The state registration becomes effective at the same time the federal registration statement becomes effective.

registration by filing A process that allows a security to be sold in a state. Previously referred to as *registration by notification*, it is available to an issuer who files for the security's registration under the Securities Act of 1933, meets minimum net worth and certain other requirements, and notifies the state of this eligibility by filing certain documents with the state administrator. The state registration becomes effective at the same time the federal registration statement becomes effective.

registration by notification *See* registration by filing.

registration by qualification A process that allows a security to be sold in a state. It is available to an issuer who files for the security's registration with the state administrator, meets minimum net worth, disclosure and other requirements and files appropriate registration fees. The state registration becomes effective when the administrator so orders.

registration statement The legal document that discloses all pertinent information concerning an offering of a security and its issuer. It is submitted to the SEC in accordance with the requirements of the Securities Act of 1933, and it forms the basis of the final prospectus distributed to investors.

regressive tax A tax that takes a larger percentage of the income of low-income earners than that of high-income earners. Examples include gasoline tax and cigarette tax. *See also* progressive tax.

Reg T *See* Regulation T.

Reg T call *See* margin call.

regular complaint procedure The process for settling a charge or complaint under the NASD's Code of Procedure. *See also* Code of Procedure; summary complaint procedure.

regular way A settlement contract that calls for delivery and payment within a standard payment period from the date of the trade. The NASD's Uniform Practice Code sets the standard payment period. The type of security being traded determines the amount of time allowed for regular way settlement. *See also* cash transaction; settlement date.

regulated investment company An investment company to which Subchapter M of the Internal Revenue Code grants special status that allows the flow-through of tax consequences on a distribution to shareholders. If 90 percent of its income is passed through to the shareholders, the company is not subject to tax on this income.

Regulation A The provision of the Securities Act of 1933 that exempts from registration small public offerings valued at no more than $5 million worth of securities issued during a twelve-month period.

Regulation D The provision of the Securities Act of 1933 that exempts from registration offerings sold to a maximum of 35 nonaccredited investors during a twelve-month period. *See also* private placement.

Regulation G The Federal Reserve Board regulation that governs the extension of credit for securities transactions by commercial lenders and nonfinancial corporations. *See also* Regulation T; Regulation U.

Regulation Q The Federal Reserve Board regulation that established how much interest banks may pay on savings accounts. Regulation Q was phased out in 1986.

Regulation T The Federal Reserve Board regulation that governs customer cash accounts and the amount of credit that brokerage firms and dealers may extend to customers for the purchase of securities. Regulation T currently sets the loan value of marginable securities at 50 percent and the payment deadline at two days beyond regular way settlement. *Syn.* Reg T. *See also* Regulation G; Regulation U.

Regulation U The Federal Reserve Board regulation that governs loans by banks for the purchase of securities. Call loans are exempt from Regulation U. *See also* broker's loan; call loan; Regulation G; Regulation T; time loan.

Regulation X The Federal Reserve Board regulation that governs the use of borrowed money in securities transactions, mainly in connection with U.S. businesses borrowing from overseas lenders.

rehypothecation The pledging of a client's securities as collateral for a bank loan. Brokerage firms may rehypothecate up to 140 percent of the value of their customers' securities to finance margin loans to customers. *See also* hypothecation.

reinstatement privilege A benefit offered by some mutual funds, allowing an investor to withdraw money from a fund account and then redeposit the money without paying a second sales charge.

REIT *See* real estate investment trust.

rejection The right of the buyer of a security to refuse to accept delivery in completion of a trade because the security does not meet the requirements of good delivery.

REMIC *See* real estate mortgage investment conduit.

renewal and replacement fund The account that is used to fund major renewal projects and equipment replacements financed by a municipal revenue bond issue. *See also* flow of funds.

reoffering price The price or yield at which a municipal security is sold to the public by the underwriters.

reorganization department The department within a brokerage firm that handles transactions that represent a change in the securities outstanding, such as trades relating to tender offers, bond calls, preferred stock redemptions and mergers and acquisitions.

repo *See* repurchase agreement.

repurchase agreement A sale of securities with an attendant agreement to repurchase them at a higher price on an agreed-upon future date; the difference between the sale price and the repurchase price represents the interest earned by the investor. Repos are considered money-market instruments, and are used to raise short-term capital and as instruments of monetary policy. *Syn.* repo. *See also* reverse repurchase agreement.

reserve maintenance fund The account that holds funds that supplement the general maintenance fund of a municipal revenue bond issue. *See also* flow of funds.

reserve requirement The percentage of depositors' money that the Federal Reserve Board requires a commercial bank to keep on deposit in the form of cash or in its vault. *Syn.* reserves.

residual claim The right of a common stockholder to corporate assets in the event that the corporation ceases to exist. A common stockholder may claim assets only after the claims of all creditors and other security holders have been satisfied.

resistance level A technical analysis term describing the top of a stock's historical trading range. *See also* breakout; support level.

restricted account A margin account in which the equity is less than the Regulation T initial requirement. *See also* equity; initial margin requirement; margin account; retention requirement.

restricted security An unregistered, nonexempt security acquired either directly or indirectly from the issuer, or an affiliate of the issuer, in a transaction that does not involve a public offering. *See also* holding period; Rule 144.

retained earnings The amount of a corporation's net income that remains after all dividends have been paid to preferred and common stockholders. *Syn.* earned surplus; reinvested earnings.

retained earnings ratio A measure of a corporation's policy of accumulating profits, calculated by dividing the net income available for common stockholders by the dividends paid on common stock. The ratio is the complement of the dividend payout ratio. *See also* dividend payout ratio.

retention The percentage of a new issue that an underwriter holds to sell directly to its own customers. The securities that it underwrites but does not retain are turned back to the syndicate to be sold by the selling group.

retention requirement The provision of Regulation T that applies to the withdrawal of securities from a restricted account. The customer must deposit an amount equal to the unpaid portion of the securities being withdrawn, in order to reduce the debit balance. The retention requirement is the reciprocal of the initial margin requirement. *See also* restricted account.

retirement account A customer account established to provide retirement funds.

retiring bonds Ending an issuer's debt obligation by calling the outstanding bonds, by purchasing bonds in the open market, or by repaying bondholders the principal amount at maturity.

return on common equity A measure of a corporation's profitability, calculated by dividing aftertax income by common shareholders' equity.

return on equity A measure of a corporation's profitability, specifically its return on assets, calculated by dividing aftertax income by tangible assets.

return on investment (ROI) The profit or loss resulting from a security transaction, often expressed as an annual percentage rate.

return on sales *See* net profit ratio.

revaluation A change in the relative value of a country's currency owing to a decision by the country's government. *See also* devaluation.

revenue anticipation note (RAN) A short-term municipal debt security issued in anticipation of revenue to be received.

revenue bond A municipal debt issue whose interest and principal are payable only from the specific earnings of an income-producing public project. *See also* double-barreled bond; general obligation bond; municipal bond; special revenue bond.

reverse repo *See* reverse repurchase agreement.

reverse repurchase agreement A purchase of securities with an attendant agreement to resell them at a higher price on an agreed-upon future date; the difference between the purchase price and the resale price represents the interest earned by the investor. The purchaser initiates the deal. *Syn.* reverse repo. *See also* repurchase agreement.

reverse split A reduction in the number of a corporation's shares outstanding that increases the par value of its stock or its earnings per share. The market value of the total number of shares remains the same. *See also* stock split.

reversionary working interest A sharing arrangement whereby the general partner of a direct participation program bears none of the program's costs and does not share in revenues until the limited partners receive payment plus a predetermined rate of return. *Syn.* subordinated interest; subordinated reversionary working interest. *See also* sharing arrangement.

right A security representing a stockholder's entitlement to the first opportunity to purchase new shares issued by the corporation at a predetermined price (normally less than the current market price) in proportion to the number of shares already owned. Rights are issued for a short time only, after which they expire. *Syn.* subscription right; subscription right certificate. *See also* preemptive right; rights offering.

right of accumulation A benefit offered by a mutual fund that allows the investor to qualify for reduced sales loads on additional purchases according to the fund account's total dollar value.

right of withdrawal An Investment Company Act of 1940 provision that allows an investor in a mutual fund contractual plan to terminate the plan within 45 days from the mailing date of the written notice detailing the sales charges that will apply over the plan's life. The investor is then entitled to a refund of all sales charges. *See also* free-look letter.

rights agent An issuing corporation's agent who is responsible for maintaining current records of the names of rights certificate owners.

rights offering An issue of new shares of stock accompanied by the opportunity for each stockholder to maintain a proportionate ownership by purchasing additional shares in the corporation before the shares are offered to the public. *See also* right.

right to refund A benefit of a mutual fund front-end load plan that entitles an investor who cancels the plan within 18 months to receive the investment's current value and a refund of sales charges exceeding 15 percent.

risk arbitrage The purchase of stock in a company that is being acquired and the short sale of stock in the acquiring company, in order to profit from the anticipated increase in the acquired corporation's shares and decrease in the acquiring corporation's shares.

riskless and simultaneous transaction The buying or selling by a broker-dealer of a security for its own account so as to fill an order previously received from a customer. Although the firm is technically acting as a principal in the trade, the transaction is relatively riskless because the purchase and sale are consummated almost simultaneously. *Syn.* riskless transaction.

ROI *See* return on investment.

rollover The transfer of funds from one qualified retirement plan to another qualified retirement plan. If this is not done within a specified time period, the funds are taxed as ordinary income.

ROP *See* registered options principal.

round lot A security's normal unit of trading, which is generally 100 shares of stock or five bonds. *See also* odd lot.

royalty interest The right of a mineral rights owner to receive a share in the revenues generated by the resource if and when production begins. The royalty interest retained is free from production costs.

RR *See* registered representative.

RT A message on the Consolidated Tape indicating a right.

Rule 144 SEC rule requiring that persons who hold control or restricted securities may sell them only in limited quantities, and that all sales of restricted stock by control persons must be reported to the SEC by filing a Form 144, "Notice of Proposed Sale of Securities." *See also* control security; restricted security.

Rule 145 SEC rule requiring that, whenever the stockholders of a publicly owned corporation are solicited to vote on or consent to a plan for reorganizing the corporation, full disclosure of all material facts must be made in a proxy statement or prospectus that must be in the hands of the stockholders before the announced voting date. *See also* reclassification; transfer of assets.

Rule 147 SEC rule that provides exemption from the registration statement and prospectus requirements of the 1933 act for securities offered and sold exclusively intrastate.

Rule 15c2-1 SEC rule governing the safekeeping of securities in customer margin accounts. It prohibits broker-dealers from (1) using a customer's securities in excess of the customer's aggregate indebtedness as collateral to secure a loan without written permission from the customer, and (2) commingling a customer's securities without written permission from the customer. *See also* rehypothecation.

Rule 15c2-11 SEC rule governing the activities of market makers so as to ensure that investors receive enough information about a security's issuer to enable them to make a sound investment decision. The rule directs market makers to provide a prospectus unless financial reports of the issuer are available to the public.

Rule 15c3-1 SEC rule governing the net capital requirements of broker-dealers. The requirements vary for different types of broker-dealers and for different amounts of aggregate indebtedness. The rules define net capital and cover how to compute it, minimum dollar requirements, and maximum debt-to-equity ratios. *See also* aggregate indebtedness.

Rule 15c3-2 SEC rule requiring broker-dealers to inform customers of their free credit balances at least quarterly.

Rule 15c3-3 SEC Rule governing the location, segregation and handling of customer funds and securities. It requires broker-dealers to segregate all customer fully paid and excess margin securities in a special reserve bank account for the exclusive benefit of customers. *Syn.* customer protection rule.

Rule 17a-3 SEC rule governing the maintaining of records by a broker-dealer and the posting of reports and transactions to those records.

Rule 17a-4 SEC rule governing the retention and storage by a broker-dealer of records and reports.

Rule 405 NYSE rule requiring that each member organization exercise due diligence to learn the essential facts about every customer. *Syn.* know your customer rule.

Rule 415 SEC rule governing shelf offerings. The rule allows an issuer to sell limited portions of a new issue over a two-year period. *See also* shelf offering.

Rule 504 SEC rule providing that an offering of less than $1,000,000 during any twelve-month period may be exempt from full registration. The rule does not restrict the number of accredited or nonaccredited purchasers.

Rule 505 SEC rule providing that an offering of $1,000,000 to $5,000,000 during any twelve-month period may be exempt from full registration. The rule restricts the number of nonaccredited purchasers to 35 but does not restrict the number of accredited purchasers.

Rule 506 SEC rule providing that an offering of more than $5,000,000 during any twelve-month period may be exempt from full registration. The rule restricts the number of nonaccredited purchasers to 35 but does not restrict the number of accredited purchasers.

Rule G-1 MSRB rule that classifies as municipal securities dealers any separately identifiable departments of banks that engage in activities related to the municipal securities business. *See also* separately identifiable department or division.

Rule G-2 MSRB rule that sets professional qualification standards.

Rule G-3 MSRB rule governing the classification of municipal securities principals and representatives.

Rule G-4 MSRB rule that statutorily disqualifies members who have violated securities laws or regulations.

Rule G-5 MSRB rule governing disciplinary actions by regulatory agencies, including the SEC and other SROs.

Rule G-6 MSRB rule governing the fidelity bond requirements for member broker-dealers.

Rule G-7 MSRB rule governing the documentation that must be kept on each associated person.

Rule G-8 MSRB rule outlining the requirements for maintaining books and records.

Rule G-9 MSRB rule governing the preservation of books and records.

Rule G-10 MSRB rule requiring that an investor brochure be delivered in response to a customer complaint.

Rule G-11 MSRB rule governing the priority given to orders received for new issue municipal securities.

Rule G-12 MSRB rule governing the uniform practices for settling transactions between municipal securities firms.

Rule G-13 MSRB rule requiring broker-dealers to publish only bona fide quotations for municipal securities unless the quotations are identified as informational.

Rule G-14 MSRB rule prohibiting fictitious, deceptive or manipulative reports of municipal securities sales and purchases.

Rule G-15 MSRB rule governing the confirmation, clearance and settlement of customer municipal securities transactions.

Rule G-16 MSRB rule requiring inspections to be conducted every 24 months, to verify compliance.

Rule G-17 MSRB rule that sets ethical standards for conducting municipal securities business.

Rule G-18 MSRB rule requiring firms to make an effort to obtain the best price when executing municipal securities transactions for customers.

Rule G-19 MSRB rule governing discretionary accounts and the suitability of municipal securities recommendations and transactions.

Rule G-20 MSRB rule that sets a limit on the value of gifts and gratuities given by municipal securities firms.

Rule G-21 MSRB rule governing the advertising of municipal securities.

Rule G-22 MSRB rule requiring disclosures to customers of control relationships between municipal firms and issuers.

Rule G-23 MSRB rule that seeks to minimize conflicts of interest arising out of the activities of financial advisers that also act as municipal underwriters to the same issuer.

Rule G-24 MSRB rule prohibiting the misuse of confidential information about customers obtained by municipal securities firms acting in fiduciary capacities.

Rule G-25 MSRB rule prohibiting the improper use of assets by municipal securities firms and their representatives.

Rule G-26 MSRB rule governing municipal customer account transfers.

Rule G-27 MSRB rule requiring each municipal securities firm to designate a principal to supervise its municipal securities representatives.

Rule G-28 MSRB rule governing employee accounts held at other municipal securities firms.

Rule G-29 MSRB rule governing the availability of MSRB regulations.

Rule G-30 MSRB rule requiring prices and commissions charged by municipal securities firms to be fair and reasonable.

Rule G-31 MSRB rule prohibiting a municipal securities professional from soliciting business from an investment company portfolio in return for sales of that fund to its customers.

Rule G-32 MSRB rule requiring that customers receive a copy of the preliminary or final official statement when purchasing a new municipal issue.

Rule G-33 MSRB rule governing the calculation of accrued interest on municipal bonds using a 360-day year.

Rule G-34 MSRB rule requiring a managing underwriter to apply for a CUSIP number for a new municipal issue.

Rule G-35 MSRB rule governing the rules for arbitration to settle disputes between parties engaged in the municipal securities business.

Rule G-36 MSRB rule requiring the underwriter of a new municipal issue to file the final official statement with the MSRB.

Rule G-37 MSRB rule prohibiting municipal securities dealers from underwriting securities issued under the authority of a public official to whom an associated person of the dealer has contributed money.

Rule G-38 MSRB rule requiring municipal securities firms to disclose relationships with consultants hired to obtain business from municipal issuers.

Rules of Fair Practice (ROFP) NASD rules that outline ethical trade practices to be followed by member firms in their dealings with the public.

S

sale *See* sell.

sale-leaseback A method of raising cash by selling property to a buyer and then leasing it back from the buyer.

sales charge *See* commission.

sales literature Any written material a firm distributes to customers or the public in a controlled manner. Examples include circulars, research reports, form letters, market letters, performance reports and text used for seminars. *See also* advertisement; form letter; market letter.

sales load The amount added to a mutual fund share's net asset value to arrive at the offering price. *See also* mutual fund; net asset value; no-load fund.

Sallie Mae *See* Student Loan Marketing Association.

S&P *See* Standard & Poor's Corporation.

S&P 100 *See* Standard & Poor's 100 Stock Index.

S&P 500 *See* Standard & Poor's Composite Index of 500 Stocks.

satellite office A member location not identified as an office of supervisory jurisdiction or a branch office, or held out to the public as a place of business for the member. *See also* branch office; office of supervisory jurisdiction.

savings bond A government debt security that is not negotiable or transferable and that may not be used as collateral. *See also* Series EE bond; Series HH bond.

scale A list of each of the scheduled maturities in a new serial bond issue. The list outlines the number of bonds, maturity dates, coupon rates and yields. *See also* writing a scale.

scheduled premium policy A variable life insurance policy under which the insurer fixes both the amount and the timing of the premium payments.

Schedule 13D The form that must be filed by an individual (or individuals acting in concert) after acquiring beneficial ownership of 5 percent or more of any non-exempt equity security. It must be sent within ten business days to the issuing company, the exchange where the stock is trading and the SEC.

Schedule 13E-3 The form that must be filed by a public company when it engages in a strategy to take the company private; such a strategy includes a merger, tender offer, reverse stock split or transaction that would decrease the number of stockholders to fewer than 300. The results of such a transaction must be reported no later than ten days after the transaction.

Schedule 13E-4 The form that must be filed by a public company when it makes a tender offers for its own securities. Reporting must occur no later than ten days after termination of the tender. *Syn.* issuer tender offer statement.

Schedule 13G An abbreviated Schedule 13D used principally by a broker-dealer, bank or insurance company if it acquires a 5 percent position in the normal course of business and not for the purpose of changing or influencing control of the company. The schedule must be filed 45 days after the first calendar year end when the firm becomes subject to the requirement.

SEC *See* Securities and Exchange Commission.

secondary distribution (1) A distribution, with a prospectus, that involves securities owned by major stockholders (typically founders or principal owners of a corporation). The sale proceeds go to the sellers of the stock, not to the issuer. *Syn.* registered secondary distribution. (2) A procedure for trading very large blocks of shares of stock whereby the trade is executed off the floor of an exchange after the market closes.

secondary market The market in which securities are bought and sold subsequent to their being sold to the public for the first time. *See also* new issue market.

secondary offering A sale of securities in which one or more major stockholders in a company sell all or a large portion of their holdings; the underwriting proceeds are paid to the stockholders rather than to the corporation. Typically such an offering occurs when the founder of a business (and perhaps some of the original financial backers) determine that there is more to be gained by going public than by staying private. The offering does not increase the number of shares of stock outstanding. *See also* secondary distribution.

sector fund A mutual fund whose investment objective is to capitalize on the return potential provided by investing primarily in a particular industry or sector of the economy. *Syn.* industry fund; specialized fund.

secured bond A debt security backed by identifiable assets set aside as collateral. In the event that the issuer defaults on payment, the bondholders may lay claim to the collateral. *See also* debenture.

Securities Act of 1933 Federal legislation requiring the full and fair disclosure of all material information about the issuance of new securities. *Syn.* act of 1933; Full Disclosure Act; New Issues Act; Prospectus Act; Trust in Securities Act; Truth in Securities Act.

Securities Acts Amendments of 1975 Federal legislation that established the Municipal Securities Rulemaking Board. *See also* Municipal Securities Rulemaking Board.

Securities and Exchange Commission (SEC) Commission created by Congress to regulate the securities markets and protect investors. It is composed of five commissioners appointed by the President of the United States and approved by the Senate. The SEC enforces, among other acts, the Securities Act of 1933, the Securities Exchange Act of 1934, the Trust Indenture Act of 1939, the Investment Company Act of 1940 and the Investment Advisers Act of 1940.

Securities Exchange Act of 1934 Federal legislation that established the Securities and Exchange Commission. The act aims to protect investors by regulating the exchanges, the over-the-counter market, the extension of credit by the Federal Reserve Board, broker-dealers, insider transactions, trading activities, client accounts and net capital. *Syn.* act of 1934; Exchange Act.

Securities Industry Association (SIA) A nonprofit organization that represents the collective business interests of securities firms. The association's activities include government relations, industry research and educational and informational services for its members.

Securities Information Center (SIC) The organization designated by the SEC to act as a central data bank for records of lost and stolen securities.

Securities Investor Protection Corporation (SIPC) A nonprofit membership corporation created by an act of Congress to protect clients of brokerage firms that are forced into bankruptcy. Membership is composed of all brokers and dealers registered under the Securities Exchange Act of 1934, all members of national securities exchanges and most NASD members. SIPC provides brokerage firm customers up to $500,000 coverage for cash and securities held by the firms (although cash coverage is limited to $100,000).

securities record *See* stock record.

security Other than an insurance policy or a fixed annuity, any piece of securitized paper that can be traded for value. Under the act of 1934, this includes any note, stock, bond, investment contract, debenture, certificate of interest in a profit-sharing or partnership agreement, certificate of deposit, collateral trust certificate, preorganization certificate, option on a security, or other instrument of investment commonly known as a *security*.

security cage *See* cashiering department.

segregation Holding customer-owned securities separate from securities owned by other customers and securities owned by the brokerage firm. *See also* commingling.

selection risk The potential for loss on an investment owing to the particular security chosen performing poorly in spite of good overall market or industry performance.

self-regulatory organization (SRO) One of eight organizations accountable to the SEC for the enforcement of federal securities laws and the supervision of securities practices within an assigned field of jurisdiction. For example, the National Association of Securities Dealers regulates the over-the-counter market; the Municipal Securities Rulemaking Board supervises state and municipal securities; and certain exchanges, such as the New York Stock Exchange and the Chicago Board Options Exchange, act as self-regulatory bodies to promote ethical conduct and standard trading practices.

sell To convey ownership of a security or another asset for money or value. This includes giving or delivering a security with or as a bonus for a purchase of securities, a gift of assessable stock, and selling or offering a warrant or right to purchase or subscribe to another security. Not included in the definition is a bona fide pledge or loan or a stock dividend if nothing of value is given by the stockholders for the dividend. *Syn.* sale.

seller *See* writer.

seller's option A settlement contract that calls for delivery and payment according to a number of days specified by the seller. *See also* buyer's option.

selling a hedge Selling futures options as protection against a future decrease in commodities prices. *See also* hedge; long hedge; short hedge.

selling away An associated person engaging in private securities transactions without the employing broker-dealer's knowledge and consent. This violates the NASD Rules of Fair Practice.

selling concession *See* concession.

selling dividends (1) Inducing customers to buy mutual fund shares by implying that an upcoming distribution will benefit them. This practice is illegal. (2) Combining dividend and gains distributions when calculating current yield.

selling group Brokerage firms that help distribute securities in an offering but that are not members of the syndicate.

sell-out The procedure that the seller of a security follows when the buyer fails to complete the contract by accepting delivery of the security. The seller closes the contract by selling the security in the open market and charging the account of the buyer for transaction fees and any loss caused by changes in the market. *See also* buy-in.

sell stop order An order to sell a security that is entered at a price below the current market price and that is triggered when the market price touches or goes through the sell stop price.

senior lien debt A bond issue that shares the same collateral as is backing other issues but that has a prior claim to the collateral in the event of default.

senior registered options principal (SROP) The principal responsible for developing and enforcing a program for supervising customer options accounts. The SROP must review accounts for compliance with suitability rules and must approve all customer correspondence.

senior security A security that grants its holder a prior claim to the issuer's assets over the claims of another security's holders. For example, a bond is a senior security over common stock.

SEP *See* simplified employee pension plan.

separate account The account that holds funds paid by variable annuity contract holders. The funds are kept separate from the insurer's general account and are invested in a portfolio of securities that match the contract holders' objectives. *See also* accumulation unit; annuity; general account.

separately identifiable department or division A department of a bank that engages in the business of buying or selling municipal securities under the direct supervision of an officer of the bank. Such a department is classified by the Municipal Securities Rulemaking Board as a municipal securities dealer, and must comply with MSRB regulations. *See also* Rule G-1.

Separate Trading of Registered Interest and Principal of Securities (STRIPS) A zero-coupon bond issued and backed by the Treasury Department. *See also* zero-coupon bond.

SEP-IRA *See* simplified employee pension plan.

serial bond A debt security issued with a maturity schedule in which parts of the outstanding issue mature at intervals until the entire balance has been repaid. Most municipal bonds are serial bonds. *See also* maturity date; series bond.

series Options of the same class that have the same exercise price and the same expiration date. *See also* class; type.

Series 6 The investment company/variable contract products limited representative license, which entitles the holder to sell mutual funds and variable annuities and is used by many firms that sell primarily insurance-related products. The Series 6 can serve as the prerequisite for the Series 26 license.

Series 7 The general securities registered representative license, which entitles the holder to sell all types of securities products, with the exception of commodities futures (which requires a Series 3 license). The Series 7 is the most comprehensive of the NASD representative licenses and serves as a prerequisite for most of the NASD's principals examinations.

Series 8 The General Securities Sales Supervisor Limited Principal License, which entitles the holder to supervise the sale of all types of securities products except commodities.

Series 24 The General Securities Principal License, which entitles the holder to supervise the business of a broker-dealer. A Series 7 or a Series 62 qualification is a prerequisite for this license.

Series 26 The investment company/variable contract products limited principal license, which entitles the holder to supervise the sale of investment company and variable annuity products. A Series 6 or a Series 7 qualification is a prerequisite for this license.

Series 27 The Financial and Operations Limited Principal License, which entitles the holder to supervise the financial administration of a brokerage firm.

Series 52 The Municipal Securities Representative License, which entitles the holder to sell municipal and government securities and is used by many firms that sell primarily municipal debt products. The Series 52 license can serve as the prerequisite for the Series 53 license.

Series 53 The Municipal Securities Principal License, which entitles the holder to supervise the municipal and government securities business of a brokerage firm. A Series 7 or a Series 52 qualification is a prerequisite for this license.

Series 62 The Corporate Securities Limited Representative License, which entitles the holder to sell all types of corporate securities but not municipal securities, options, direct participation programs or certain other products. The Series 62 license can serve as the prerequisite for the Series 4 and the Series 24 licenses.

Series 63 The uniform securities agent state law exam, which entitles the successful candidate to sell securities and give investment advice in those states that require Series 63 registration. *See also* blue-sky laws; Uniform Securities Act.

Series 65 The uniform investment adviser law exam, which entitles the successful candidate to sell securities and give investment advice in those states that require Series 65 registration. *See also* blue-sky laws; Uniform Securities Act.

series bond A debt security issued in a series of public offerings spread over an extended time period. All the bonds in the series have the same priority claim against assets. *See also* serial bond.

Series EE bond A nonmarketable, interest-bearing U.S. government savings bond issued at a discount from par. Interest on Series EE bonds is exempt from state and local taxes. *See also* savings bond; Series HH bond.

Series HH bond A nonmarketable, interest-bearing U.S. government savings bond issued at par and purchased only by trading in Series EE bonds at maturity. Interest on Series HH bonds is exempt from state and local taxes. *See also* savings bond; Series EE bond.

settlement The completion of a trade through the delivery of a security or commodity and the payment of cash or other consideration.

settlement date The date on which ownership changes between buyer and seller. The NASD's Uniform Practice Code standardizes settlement provisions. *See also* cash transaction; regular way.

75-5-10 test The standard for judging whether an investment company qualifies as diversified under the Investment Company Act of 1940. Under this act, a diversified investment company must invest at least 75 percent of its total assets in cash, receivables or invested securities and no more than 5 percent of its total assets in any one company's voting securities. In addition, no single investment may represent ownership of more than 10 percent of any one company's outstanding voting securities. *See also* diversified management company.

shareholders' equity *See* net worth.

share identification An accounting method that identifies the specific shares selected for liquidation in the event that an investor wishes to liquidate shares. The difference between the buying and selling prices determines the investor's tax liability.

share of beneficial interest *See* unit of beneficial interest.

sharing arrangement A method of allocating the responsibility for expenses and the right to share in revenues among the sponsor and limited partners in a direct participation program. *See also* carried interest; disproportionate sharing; functional allocation; net operating profits interest; overriding royalty interest; reversionary working interest.

shelf offering An SEC provision allowing an issuer to register a new issue security without selling the entire issue at once. The issuer can sell limited portions of the issuer over a two-year period without reregistering the security or incurring penalties. *See also* Rule 415.

short The term used to describe the selling of a security, contract or commodity that the seller does not own. For example, an investor who borrows shares of stock from a broker-dealer and sells them on the open market is said to have a *short position* in the stock. *See also* long.

short against the box The term used to describe the selling of a security, contract or commodity that the seller owns but prefers not to deliver; frequently this is done to defer taxation.

short-exempt transaction An exception to the SEC plus tick rule that allows a short sale in an arbitrage account even if the price is declining. *See also* plus tick rule.

short hedge Selling options or futures as protection against a decrease in the value of a long securities or actuals position. *See also* hedge; long hedge; selling a hedge.

short-interest theory A technical analysis theory that examines the ratio of short sales to volume in a stock. Because the underlying stock must be purchased to close out the short positions, a high ratio is considered bullish.

short sale The sale of a security that the seller does not own, or any sale consummated by the delivery of a security borrowed by or for the account of the seller. *See also* plus tick rule.

short securities difference A shortfall between the number of shares reported in a broker-dealer's accounting records and the number of shares in a physical count of its securities. *See also* stock record break.

short straddle An option investor's position that results from selling a call and a put on the same stock with the same exercise price and expiration month. *See also* long straddle; spread; straddle.

short-term capital gain The profit realized on the sale of an asset that has been owned for twelve months or less. *See also* capital gain; capital loss; short-term capital loss.

short-term capital loss The loss incurred on the sale of a capital asset that has been owned for twelve months or less. *See also* capital gain; capital loss; short-term capital gain.

SIA *See* Securities Industry Association.

SIC *See* Securities Information Center.

simplified arbitration An expedient method of settling disputes involving claims not exceeding $10,000, whereby a panel of arbitrators reviews the evidence and renders a decision. All awards are made within 30 business days. *See also* arbitration.

simplified employee pension plan (SEP) A nonqualified retirement plan designed for employers with 25 or fewer employees. Contributions made to each employee's individual retirement account grow tax deferred until retirement. *See also* individual retirement account.

single account An account in which only one individual has control over the investments and may transact business.

sinking fund An account established by an issuing corporation or municipality into which money is deposited regularly so that the issuer has the funds to redeem its bonds, debentures or preferred stock.

SIPC *See* Securities Investor Protection Corporation.

SLD A message on the Consolidated Tape indicating that the sale being reported was not reported on time and is therefore out of sequence.

SLMA *See* Student Loan Marketing Association.

SMA *See* special memorandum account.

Small Order Execution System (SOES) The automatic order execution system the NASD uses to facilitate the trading of public market and executable limit orders of 1,000 or fewer shares. Any Nasdaq or Nasdaq National Market security with at least one active SOES market maker is eligible for trading through SOES. SOES electronically matches and executes orders, locks in a price and sends confirms directly to the broker-dealers on both sides of the trade. *See also* National Association of Securities Dealers, Inc.

SOES *See* Small Order Execution System.

solvency The ability of a corporation both to meet its long-term fixed expenses and to have adequate money for long-term expansion and growth.

special arbitrage account A margin account for arbitrage transactions. These transactions are exempt from Reg T and short sale requirements. *See also* arbitrage; market arbitrage; risk arbitrage.

special assessment bond A municipal revenue bond funded by assessments only on property owners who benefit from the services or improvements provided by the proceeds of the bond issue. *See also* revenue bond.

specialist A stock exchange member who stands ready to quote and trade certain securities either for his own account or for customer accounts. The specialist's role is to maintain a fair and orderly market in the stocks for which he is responsible. *See also* specialist's book.

specialist block sale A block trading procedure for smaller blocks in which the specialist sells the block in a private transaction.

specialist block trade A transaction in which a specialist purchases or sells a relatively small block of shares for a customer in a private transaction.

specialist's book A journal in which a specialist records the limit and stop orders that he holds for execution. The contents of the journal are confidential. *Syn.* limit order book. *See also* specialist.

specialized fund *See* sector fund.

special memorandum account (SMA) A notation on a customer's general or margin account indicating that funds are credited to the account on a memo basis; the account is used much like a line of credit with a bank. An SMA preserves the customer's right to use excess equity. *Syn.* special miscellaneous account.

special miscellaneous account *See* special memorandum account.

special offering A block trading procedure in which a large number of shares of stock is offered for sale after a prior announcement on the Consolidated Tape. *Syn.* special bid.

special omnibus account *See* omnibus account.

special reserve bank account A separate account maintained by a broker-dealer for the exclusive benefit of customers and for the required deposits of customer credit balances.

special revenue bond A municipal revenue bond issued to finance a specific project. Examples include industrial development bonds, lease rental bonds, special tax bonds and New Housing Authority bonds. *See also* revenue bond.

special situation fund A mutual fund whose objective is to capitalize on the profit potential of corporations in nonrecurring circumstances, such as those undergoing reorganizations or being considered as takeover candidates.

special tax bond A municipal revenue bond payable only from the proceeds of a tax on certain items, rather than an ad valorem tax. *See also* revenue bond.

speculation Trading a commodity or security with a higher than average risk in return for a higher than average profit potential. The trade is effected solely for the purpose of profiting from it and not as a means of hedging or protecting other positions.

speculator One who trades a commodity or security with a higher than average risk in return for a higher than average profit potential. *See also* speculation.

split offering A public offering of securities that combines aspects of both a primary and a secondary offering. A portion of the issue is a primary offering, the proceeds of which go to the issuing corporation; the remainder of the issue is a secondary offering, the proceeds of which go to the selling stockholders. *Syn.* combined distribution. *See also* primary offering; secondary offering.

sponsor A person who is instrumental in organizing, selling, or managing a limited partnership.

spousal account A separate individual retirement account established for a nonworking spouse. Contributions to the account made by the working spouse grow tax deferred until withdrawal. *See also* individual retirement account.

spread In a quotation, the difference between a security's bid and ask prices.

spread load A system of sales charges for a mutual fund contractual plan. It permits a decreasing scale of sales charges, with a maximum charge of 20 percent in any one year and of 9 percent over the life of the plan. Rights of withdrawal with no penalty exist for 45 days. *See also* contractual plan; front-end load.

spread order A customer order specifying two option contracts on the same underlying security or commodity and a price difference between them. A spread order takes priority over equal but separate bids and offers.

SRO *See* self-regulatory organization.

SROP *See* senior registered options principal.

SS A symbol on the Consolidated Tape indicating that the stock in question sold in 10-share units.

stabilizing Bidding at or below the public offering price of a new issue security. Underwriting managers

may enter stabilizing bids during the offering period to prevent the price from dropping sharply. *See also* fixing.

stagflation A period of high unemployment in the economy accompanied by a general rise in prices. *See also* deflation; inflation.

Standard & Poor's Composite Index of 500 Stocks (S&P 500) A value-weighted index that offers broad coverage of the securities market. It is composed of 400 industrial stocks, 40 financial stocks, 40 public utility stocks and 20 transportation stocks. The index is owned and compiled by Standard & Poor's Corporation. *See also* index; Standard & Poor's Corporation; Standard & Poor's 100 Stock Index.

Standard & Poor's Corporation (S&P) A company that rates stocks and corporate and municipal bonds according to risk profiles and that produces and tracks the S&P indexes. The company also publishes a variety of financial and investment reports. *See also* bond rating; Moody's Investors Service; rating; Standard & Poor's 100 Stock Index; Standard & Poor's Composite Index of 500 Stocks.

Standard & Poor's 100 Stock Index (S&P 100) A value-weighted index composed of 100 blue chip stocks. The index is owned and compiled by Standard & Poor's Corporation. *See also* index; Standard & Poor's Corporation; Standard & Poor's Composite Index of 500 Stocks.

standardized contract A futures contract in which all the contract terms are set by the exchange except for price.

standardized option *See* listed option.

standby underwriter An investment banker that agrees to purchase any part of an issue that has not been purchased by current stockholders through a rights offering. The firm exercises the remaining rights, maintains a trading market in the rights, and offers the stock acquired to the public. *See also* rights offering.

stated yield *See* nominal yield.

statement of claim A document filed by the party submitting a dispute for resolution under the NASD's Code of Arbitration Procedure; the document specifies the relevant facts about the dispute and the remedies sought by the claimant.

statement of intention *See* letter of intent.

statutory disqualification Prohibiting a person from associating with a self-regulatory organization because the person has been expelled, barred or suspended from association with a member of an SRO; has had his registration suspended, denied or revoked by the SEC; has been the cause of someone else's suspension, barment or revocation; has been convicted of certain crimes; or has falsified an application or a report that he must file with or on behalf of a membership organization.

statutory voting A voting procedure that permits stockholders to cast one vote per share owned for each position. The procedure tends to benefit majority stockholders. *See also* cumulative voting.

step-out well An oil or gas well or prospect adjacent to a field of proven reserves. *See also* developmental drilling program.

stock ahead The term used to describe the inability of a specialist to fill a limit order at a specific price because other orders at the same price were entered previously.

stockbroker *See* registered representative.

stock certificate Written evidence of ownership in a corporation.

stock dividend *See* dividend.

stockholders' equity *See* shareholders' equity.

stock loan agreement The document that an institutional customer must sign when the broker-dealer borrows stock from the customer's account; the document specifies the terms of the loan and the rights of both parties.

stock power A standard form that duplicates the back of a stock certificate and is used for transferring the stock to the new owner's name. A separate stock power is used if a security's registered owner does not have the certificate available for signature endorse-

ment. *Syn.* irrevocable stock power; power of substitution. *See also* assignment.

stock quote A list of representative prices bid and asked for a stock during a particular trading day. Stocks are quoted in points, where one point equals $1 and ⅛ of a point equals 12.5 cents. Stock quotes are listed in the financial press and most daily newspapers. *See also* bond quote.

stock record A broker-dealer's accounting system that shows separately for each security all long and short positions, as well as the location of each security, the holdings of all customers, and all securities due from or owed to other broker-dealers. *Syn.* securities record. *See also* customer ledger.

stock record break A discrepancy between the number of shares reported in a broker-dealer's accounting records and the number of shares in a physical count of its securities. The discrepancy can be due to a counting error or to missing securities.

stock record department The department within a brokerage firm responsible for maintaining the ledger that lists the owners of securities and the location of certificates.

stock split An increase in the number of a corporation's outstanding shares, which decreases its stock's par value. The market value of the total number of shares remains the same. The proportional reductions in orders held on the books for a split stock are calculated by dividing the stock's market price by the fraction that represents the split.

stop limit order A customer order that becomes a limit order when the market price of the security reaches or passes a specific price. *See also* limit order; stop order.

stop order (1) A directive from the SEC that suspends the sale of new issue securities to the public when fraud is suspected or filing materials are deficient. (2) A customer order that becomes a market order when the market price of the security reaches or passes a specific price. *See also* limit order; market order; stop limit order.

stopping stock The method used by a specialist to guarantee that a customer order will be executed at a specific price.

straddle An option investor's position that results from buying a call and a put or selling a call and a put on the same security with the same exercise price and expiration month. *See also* long straddle; short straddle; spread.

straight-line depreciation An accounting method used to recover the cost of a qualifying depreciable asset, whereby the owner writes off the cost of the asset in equal amounts each year over the asset's useful life. *See also* Modified Accelerated Cost Recovery System.

strangle An option investor's position that results from buying a call and a put when both options are out-of-the-money on either side of the current price of the underlying security. A strangle can be profitable only if the market is highly volatile and makes a major move in either direction.

strap Buying two calls and one put on the same security with the same exercise price and expiration month. *See also* strip.

strike price *See* exercise price.

striking price *See* exercise price.

strip Buying two puts and one call on the same security with the same exercise price and expiration month. *See also* strap.

stripped bond A debt obligation that has been stripped of its interest coupons by a brokerage firm, repackaged and sold at a deep discount. It pays no interest but may be redeemed at maturity for the full face value. *See also* zero-coupon bond.

stripper well An oil well that produces fewer than ten barrels per day.

STRIPS *See* Separate Trading of Registered Interest and Principal of Securities.

Student Loan Marketing Association (SLMA) A publicly owned corporation that purchases student loans from financial institutions and packages them for sale in the secondary market, thereby increasing the availability of money for educational loans. *Syn.* Sallie Mae.

Subchapter S corporation A small business corporation that meets certain requirements and is taxed as a partnership while retaining limited liability.

subject quote A securities quotation that does not represent an actual offer to buy or sell but is tentative, subject to reconfirmation by the broker-dealer. *See also* bona fide quote; firm quote; nominal quote; workout quote.

submission agreement A document filed by each party involved in a dispute submitted for resolution under the NASD's Code of Arbitration Procedure; the document must be filed by each party before proceedings may begin.

subordinated debenture A debt obligation, backed by the general credit of the issuing corporation, that has claims to interest and principal subordinated to ordinary debentures and all other liabilities. *See also* debenture.

subordinated debt financing A form of long-term capitalization used by broker-dealers, in which the claims of lenders are subordinated to the claims of other creditors. Subordinated financing is considered part of the broker-dealer's capital structure and is added to net worth when computing its net capital.

subordinated interest *See* reversionary working interest.

subordinated loan A loan to a broker-dealer in which the lender agrees to subordinate its claim to the claims of the firm's other creditors.

subordinated reversionary working interest *See* reversionary working interest.

subscription agreement A statement signed by an investor indicating an offer to buy an interest in a direct participation program. In the statement, the investor agrees to grant power of attorney to the general partner and to abide by the limited partnership agreement. The sale is finalized when the subscription agreement is signed by the general partner.

subscription amount The total dollar amount that a participant in a direct participation program has invested.

subscription right *See* right.

suitability A determination made by a registered representative as to whether a particular security matches a customer's objectives and financial capability. The rep must have enough information about the customer to make this judgment. *See also* Rule 405.

summary complaint procedure A process for settling a charge or complaint that is quicker and less formal than the NASD's regular complaint procedure. The maximum penalty imposed under the summary complaint procedure is $2,500 plus public censure. *See also* Code of Procedure; regular complaint procedure.

Super Designated Order Turnaround System The computerized trading and execution system used by the New York Stock Exchange. The system allows broker-dealers to choose the destinations of orders and the routes they will take; specialists or commission brokers executing the orders use the system to send reports back to the firms. Orders executed through the system are often confirmed back to the broker in less than 60 seconds. *Syn.* SuperDot. *See also* New York Stock Exchange.

SuperDot *See* Super Designated Order Turnaround System.

supervision A system implemented by a broker-dealer to ensure that its employees and associated persons comply with the applicable rules and regulations of the SEC, the exchanges and the SROs.

supply The total amount of a good or service available for purchase by consumers. *See also* demand.

supply-side theory An economic theory holding that bolstering an economy's ability to supply more goods is the most effective way to stimulate economic growth. Supply-side theorists advocate income tax reduction insofar as this increases private investment in corporations, facilities and equipment.

support level A technical analysis term describing the bottom of a stock's historical trading range. *See also* breakout; resistance level.

surplus fund An account that is used to pay a variety of a municipal revenue bond's expenses, including redeeming bonds, funding improvements and making tax payments. *See also* flow of funds.

syndicate A group of investment bankers formed to handle the distribution and sale of a security on behalf of the issuer. Each syndicate member is responsible for the sale and distribution of a portion of the issue. *Syn.* underwriting syndicate. *See also* Eastern account; Western account.

syndicate manager *See* underwriting manager.

synthetic option A combination of a stock position with an option position that simulates the risk and return potential of a single option purchase or sale.

synthetic stock An options position that simulates the risk and return potential of directly holding the underlying stock.

systemic risk The potential for a security to decrease in value owing to its inherent tendency to move together with all securities of the same type. Neither diversification nor any other investment strategy can eliminate this risk. *See also* market risk.

T

T Consolidated Tape market identifier for trades of exchange-listed securities executed over the counter.

takedown The discount from the public offering price at which a syndicate member buys new issue securities from the syndicate for sale to the public. *See also* concession.

TAN *See* tax anticipation note.

Tape *See* Consolidated Tape.

taxability The risk of the erosion of investment income through taxation.

taxable gain The portion of a sale or distribution of mutual fund shares subject to taxation.

tax and revenue anticipation note (TRAN) A short-term municipal debt security to be paid off from future tax receipts and revenues.

tax anticipation note (TAN) A short-term municipal or government debt security to be paid off from future tax receipts.

tax basis The amount that a limited partner has invested in a partnership.

tax credit An amount that can be subtracted from a tax liability, often in connection with real estate development, energy conservation and research and development programs. Every dollar of tax credit reduces the amount of tax due, dollar for dollar. *See also* deduction.

tax-deferred annuity *See* tax-sheltered annuity.

tax-equivalent yield The rate of return a taxable bond must earn before taxes in order to equal the tax-exempt earnings on a municipal bond. This number varies with the investor's tax bracket.

taxes per capita *See* taxes per person.

taxes per person A measure of the tax burden of a municipality's population, calculated by dividing the municipality's tax receipts by its population. *Syn.* taxes per capita.

tax-exempt bond fund A mutual fund whose investment objective is to provide maximum tax-free income. It invests primarily in municipal bonds and short-term debt. *Syn.* tax-free bond fund.

tax-free bond fund *See* tax-exempt bond fund.

tax liability The amount of tax payable on earnings, usually calculated by subtracting standard and itemized deductions and personal exemptions from adjusted gross income, then multiplying by the tax rate. *See also* adjusted gross income.

tax preference item An element of income that receives favorable tax treatment. The item must be added to taxable income when computing alternative minimum tax. Tax preference items include accelerated depreciation on property, research and development costs, intangible drilling costs, tax-exempt interest on municipal private purpose bonds, and certain incentive stock options. *See also* alternative minimum tax.

Tax Reform Act of 1986 (TRA 1986) Legislation enacted by Congress for the purpose of reducing the federal deficit. The legislation set income tax brackets and imposed various surcharges and special taxes.

tax-sheltered annuity (TSA) An insurance contract that entitles the holder to exclude all contributions from gross income in the year they are made. Tax payable on the earnings is deferred until the holder withdraws funds at retirement. TSAs are available to employees of public schools, church organizations and other tax-exempt organizations. *Syn.* tax-deferred annuity.

T bill *See* Treasury bill.

T bond *See* Treasury bond.

T call *See* margin call.

TDA *See* tax-sheltered annuity.

technical analysis A method of evaluating securities by analyzing statistics generated by market activity, such as past prices and volume. Technical analysts do not attempt to measure a security's intrinsic value. *See also* chartist; fundamental analysis.

technician *See* chartist.

Telephone Consumer Protection Act of 1991 (TCPA) Federal legislation restricting the use of telephone lines for solicitation purposes. A company soliciting sales via telephone, facsimile or E-mail must disclose its name and address to the called party and must not call any person who has requested not to be called.

tenants in common *See* joint tenants in common.

tender offer An offer to buy securities for cash or for cash plus securities.

term bond *See* term maturity.

term maturity A repayment schedule for a bond issue in which the entire issue comes due on a single date. *Syn.* term bond. *See also* maturity date.

testamentary trustee A person authorized to administer a fiduciary account, including a brokerage account, created by a decedent. The trustee's authority is granted by the last will of the decedent.

testimonial An endorsement of an investment or service by a celebrity or public opinion influencer. The use of testimonials in public communications is regulated by the NASD.

third market The exchange where listed securities are traded in the over-the-counter market. Institutional investors are the primary users of the third market.

third-party account (1) A customer account for which the owner has given power of attorney to a third party. (2) A customer account opened by an adult naming a minor as beneficial owner. (3) A customer account opened for another adult. This type of account is prohibited.

30-day visible supply *See* visible supply.

tick A minimum upward or downward movement in the price of a security. *See also* minus tick; plus tick; plus tick rule.

Ticker Tape *See* Consolidated Tape.

TIGR *See* Treasury Investors Growth Receipt.

time deposit A sum of money left with a bank (or borrowed from a bank and left on deposit) that the depositing customer has agreed not to withdraw for a specified time period or without a specified amount of notice. *See also* demand deposit.

time loan A collateral loan of a brokerage firm that matures on a date agreed upon by the lender and the borrower and that has a constant interest rate for the duration of the contract. *See also* broker's loan; call loan.

times fixed charges earned ratio *See* bond interest coverage ratio.

times interest earned ratio *See* bond interest coverage ratio.

time spread *See* horizontal spread.

time value The amount an investor pays for an option above its intrinsic value; it reflects the amount of time left until expiration. The amount is calculated by subtracting the intrinsic value from the premium paid. *See also* intrinsic value.

timing risk The potential for an investor to incur a loss as a result of buying or selling a particular security at an unfavorable time.

Title 1 One of the four parts of the Employee Retirement Income and Security Act of 1974. Title 1 protects employee benefit rights. *See also* Employee Retirement Income and Security Act of 1974.

Title 2 One of the four parts of the Employee Retirement Income and Security Act of 1974. Title 2 amends the pension and benefits sections of the Internal Revenue Code. *See also* Employee Retirement Income and Security Act of 1974.

Title 3 One of the four parts of the Employee Retirement Income and Security Act of 1974. Title 3 divides responsibilities among the agencies that administer pension laws. *See also* Employee Retirement Income and Security Act of 1974.

Title 4 One of the four parts of the Employee Retirement Income and Security Act of 1974. Title 4 deals with pension plan termination insurance, and established the Pension Benefit Guaranty Corporation. *See also* Employee Retirement Income and Security Act of 1974.

T note *See* Treasury note.

tombstone A printed advertisement that solicits indications of interest in a securities offering. The text is limited to basic information about the offering, such as the name of the issuer, type of security, names of the underwriters and where a prospectus is available.

top-heavy rule The provision of a Keogh plan that sets the maximum salary on which employer contributions may be based. The rule prevents great disparities in the dollar amounts contributed for employees at different salary levels. *See also* Keogh plan.

total capitalization The sum of a corporation's long-term debt, stock accounts and capital in excess of par.

TRA 1986 *See* Tax Reform Act of 1986.

trade comparison The memorandum sent by both broker-dealers engaged on either side of a trade; it confirms the details of the transaction. Comparison procedures are established by the NASD's Uniform Practice Code.

trade confirmation A printed document that contains details of a transaction, including the settlement date and amount of money due from or owed to a customer. It must be sent to the customer on or before the settlement date.

trade date The date on which a securities transaction is executed.

trading authorization *See* full trading authorization; limited trading authorization.

trading halt A pause in the trading of a particular security on one or more exchanges, usually in anticipation of a news announcement or to correct an order imbalance. During a trading halt, open orders may be canceled and options may be exercised. *See also* HALT.

TRAN *See* tax and revenue anticipation note.

tranche One of the classes of securities that form an issue of collateralized mortgage obligations. Each tranche is characterized by its interest rate, average maturity, risk level and sensitivity to mortgage prepayments. Neither the rate of return nor the maturity date of a CMO tranche is guaranteed. *See also* collateralized mortgage obligation.

transfer agent A person or corporation responsible for recording the names and holdings of registered security owners, seeing that certificates are signed by the appropriate corporate officers, affixing the corporate seal and delivering securities to the new owners.

transfer and hold in safekeeping A securities buy order settlement and delivery procedure whereby the securities bought are transferred to the customer's name, but are held by the broker-dealer. *See also* hold in street name; transfer and ship.

transfer and ship A securities buy order settlement and delivery procedure whereby the securities bought are transferred to the customer's name and sent to the

customer. *See also* hold in street name; transfer and hold in safekeeping.

transfer of assets Moving all the assets of one corporation to another corporation, thus dissolving the first corporation. This changes the structure of both corporations and therefore falls under the purview of Rule 145. *See also* Rule 145.

Transportation Average *See* Dow Jones Transportation Average.

Treasury bill A marketable U.S. government debt security with a maturity of less than one year. Treasury bills are issued through a competitive bidding process at a discount from par; they have no fixed interest rate. *Syn.* T bill.

Treasury bond A marketable, fixed-interest U.S. government debt security with a maturity of more than 10 years. *Syn.* T bond.

Treasury Bond Receipt (TBR) One of several types of zero-coupon bonds issued by brokerage firms and collateralized by Treasury securities. *See also* Treasury receipt.

Treasury Investors Growth Receipt (TIGR) One of several types of zero-coupon bonds issued by brokerage firms and collateralized by Treasury securities. *See also* Treasury receipt.

Treasury note A marketable, fixed-interest U.S. government debt security with a maturity of between 1 and 10 years. *Syn.* T note.

Treasury receipt The generic term for a zero-coupon bond issued by a brokerage firm and collateralized by the Treasury securities a custodian holds in escrow for the investor.

treasury stock Equity securities that the issuing corporation has issued and repurchased from the public at the current market price. *See also* issued stock; outstanding stock.

trendline A tool used by technical analysts to trace a security's movement by connecting the reaction lows in an upward trend or the rally highs in a downward trend.

triangle On a technical analyst's trading activity chart, a pattern that shows a narrowing of the price range in which a security is trading. The left side of the triangle typically shows the widest range, and the right side narrows to a point. *Syn.* pennant. *See also* ascending triangle; descending triangle.

trough The end of a period of declining business activity throughout the economy, one of the four stages of the business cycle. *See also* business cycle.

true interest cost (TIC) A means of evaluating the competitive bids of prospective bond underwriting syndicates. Each syndicate provides a calculation of the coupon interest to be paid by the issuer over the life of the bond, taking into account the time value of money. *See also* net interest cost.

trust agreement *See* trust indenture.

trustee A person legally appointed to act on a beneficiary's behalf.

trust indenture A legal contract between a corporation and a trustee that represents its bondholders that details the terms of a debt issue. The terms include the rate of interest, maturity date, means of payment and collateral. *Syn.* deed of trust; trust agreement.

Trust Indenture Act of 1939 The legislation requiring that all publicly offered, nonexempt debt securities be registered under the Securities Act of 1933 and be issued under a trust indenture that protects the bondholders.

Trust in Securities Act *See* Securities Act of 1933.

Truth in Securities Act *See* Securities Act of 1933.

TSA *See* tax-sheltered annuity.

12b-1 asset-based fees An Investment Company Act of 1940 provision that allows a mutual fund to collect a fee for the promotion or sale of or another activity connected with the distribution of its shares. The fee must be reasonable (typically ½ percent to 1 percent of net assets managed), up to a maximum of 8.5 percent of the offering price per share.

two-dollar broker An exchange member that executes orders for other member firms when their floor brokers are especially busy. Two-dollar brokers charge a commission for their services; the amount of the commission is negotiated.

type A term that classifies an option as a call or a put. *See also* class; series.

U

UGMA *See* Uniform Gifts to Minors Act.

UIT *See* unit investment trust.

uncovered *See* naked.

uncovered call writer *See* naked call writer.

uncovered put writer *See* naked put writer.

underlying securities The futures or securities that are bought or sold when an option, right or warrant is exercised.

underwriter An investment banker that works with an issuer to help bring a security to the market and sell it to the public.

underwriting The procedure by which investment bankers channel investment capital from investors to corporations and municipalities that are issuing securities.

underwriting compensation The amount paid to a broker-dealer firm for its involvement in offering and selling securities.

underwriting discount *See* underwriting spread.

underwriting manager The brokerage firm responsible for organizing a syndicate, preparing the issue, negotiating with the issuer and underwriters and allocating stock to the selling group. *Syn.* manager of the syndicate; managing underwriter; syndicate manager. *See also* agreement among underwriters; syndicate.

underwriting spread The difference in price between the public offering price and the price an underwriter pays to the issuing corporation. The difference represents the profit available to the syndicate or selling group. *Syn.* underwriting discount; underwriting split.

underwriting syndicate *See* syndicate.

undivided account *See* Eastern account.

unearned income Income derived from investments and other sources not related to employment services. Examples of unearned income include interest from a savings account, bond interest and dividends from stock. *See also* earned income; passive income; portfolio income.

uniform delivery ticket The document that must accompany securities when they are delivered to the buyer; it signifies good delivery. *See also* good delivery.

Uniform Gifts to Minors Act (UGMA) Legislation that permits a gift of money or securities to be given to a minor and held in a custodial account that an adult manages for the minor's benefit. Income and capital gains transferred to a minor's name are taxed at a lower rate. *See also* Uniform Transfers to Minors Act.

Uniform Investment Adviser Law Exam
See Series 65.

Uniform Practice Code (UPC) The NASD policy that establishes guidelines for a brokerage firm's dealings with other brokerage firms.

Uniform Securities Act (USA) Model legislation for securities industry regulation at the state level. Each state may adopt the legislation in its entirety or it may adapt it (within limits) to suit its needs. *See also* blue-sky laws; Series 63; Series 65.

Uniform Securities Agent State Law Exam (USASLE) *See* Series 63.

Uniform Transfers to Minors Act (UTMA) Legislation adopted in some states that permits a gift of money or securities to be given to a minor and held in a custodial account that an adult manages for the minor's benefit until the minor reaches a certain age (not necessarily the age of majority). *See also* Uniform Gifts to Minors Act.

unit A share in the ownership of a direct participation program that entitles the investor to an interest in the program's net income, net loss and distributions.

United States Department of Agriculture (USDA) The federal agency that promotes agriculture through setting quality standards and testing agricultural products for conformity.

unit investment trust (UIT) An investment company that sells redeemable shares in a professionally selected portfolio of securities. It is organized under a trust indenture, not a corporate charter. *See also* fixed unit investment trust; nonfixed unit investment trust; unit of beneficial interest.

unit of beneficial interest A redeemable share in a unit investment trust, representing ownership of an undivided interest in the underlying portfolio. *Syn.* share of beneficial interest. *See also* unit investment trust.

unit refund annuity An insurance contract in which the insurance company makes monthly payments to the annuitant over the annuitant's lifetime. If the annuitant dies before receiving an amount equal to the account's value, the money remaining in the account goes to the annuitant's named beneficiary.

unqualified legal opinion The statement of a bond counsel affirming the compliance of a new municipal bond issue with municipal statutes and tax regulations, and expressing no reservations about its validity. *See also* legal opinion of counsel; qualified legal opinion.

unrealized gain The amount by which a security appreciates in value before it is sold. Until it is sold, the investor does not actually possess the sale proceeds. *See also* realized gain.

unsecured bond *See* debenture.

unsecured receivable An amount that is owed to a broker-dealer by a customer or another broker-dealer and that is not fully collateralized by securities on deposit with the firm. An unsecured receivable is a nonallowable asset for net capital computation purposes.

UPC *See* Uniform Practice Code.

up tick *See* plus tick.

up tick rule *See* plus tick rule.

USA *See* Uniform Securities Act.

USASLE *See* Series 63.

U.S. government and agency bond fund A mutual fund whose investment objective is to provide current income while preserving safety of capital through investing in securities backed by the U.S. Treasury or issued by a government agency.

Utilities Average *See* Dow Jones Utilities Average.

UTMA *See* Uniform Transfers to Minors Act.

V

Value Line An investment advisory service that rates hundreds of stocks as to safety, timeliness and projected price performance. *See also* Value Line Composite Index.

Value Line Composite Index A market index composed of 1,700 exchange and over-the-counter stocks. *See also* index; Value Line.

variable annuity An insurance contract in which at the end of the accumulation stage, the insurance company guarantees a minimum total payment to the annuitant. The performance of a separate account, generally invested in equity securities, determines the amount of this total payment. *See also* accumulation stage; annuity; fixed annuity; separate account.

variable death benefit The amount paid to a decedent's beneficiary that depends on the investment performance of an insurance company's separate account. The amount is added to any guaranteed minimum death benefit.

variable life insurance policy An insurance contract that provides financial compensation to the insured's named beneficiary if the insured dies. The insurance company guarantees payment of a minimum amount plus an additional sum according to the performance of a separate account, usually invested in equities or other relatively high-yielding securities.

variable-rate demand note *See* variable-rate municipal security.

variable-rate municipal security A short-term municipal debt security issued when either general interest rates are expected to change or the length of time before permanent funding is received is uncertain. *Syn.* variable-rate demand note.

vertical spread The purchase and sale of two options on the same underlying security and with the same expiration date but with different exercise prices. *Syn.* money spread; price spread. *See also* spread.

vesting (1) An ERISA guideline stipulating that an employee must be entitled to her entire retirement benefits within a certain period of time even if she no longer works for the employer. (2) The amount of time that an employee must work before retirement or before benefit plan contributions made by the employer become the employee's property without penalty. The IRS and the Employee Retirement Income Security Act of 1974 set minimum requirements for vesting in a qualified plan.

visible supply (1) The disclosure, published in *The Bond Buyer*, of the total dollar amount of municipal securities known to be coming to market within the next 30 days. (2) All supplies of goods and commodities that are readily deliverable.

volatility The magnitude and frequency of changes in the price of a security or commodity within a given time period.

volume of trading theory A technical analysis theory holding that the ratio of the number of shares traded to total outstanding shares indicates whether a market is strong or weak.

voluntary accumulation plan A mutual fund account into which the investor commits to depositing amounts on a regular basis in addition to the initial sum invested.

voluntary contribution An additional contribution an employee makes to a Keogh Plan to supplement plan benefits. The contribution amount is limited to 10 percent of the employee's compensation. Although the contribution is not tax deductible, the resultant earnings are not subject to tax until retirement.

voting right A stockholder's right to vote for members of the board of directors and on matters of corporate policy—particularly the issuance of senior securities, stock splits and substantial changes in the corporation's business. A variation of this right is extended to variable annuity contract holders and mutual fund shareholders, who may vote on material policy issues.

voting trust A corporation that assumes common stock voting power of a second corporation for a limited time period, such as during a reorganization of the second corporation.

voting trust certificate A certificate issued in place of a stock certificate to stockholders of a corporation that is temporarily managed by a voting trust. The certificate represents all of the benefits of ownership except the power to vote. When the corporation resumes management of its own affairs, it replaces the voting trust certificate with a new stock certificate.

W

warrant A security that gives the holder the right to purchase securities from the warrant issuer at a stipulated subscription price. Warrants are usually long-term instruments, with expiration dates years in the future.

wash sale Selling a security at a loss for tax purposes and, within 30 days before or after, purchasing the same or a substantially identical security. The IRS disallows the claimed loss. *See also* bond swap.

Western account A securities underwriting in which the agreement among underwriters states that each syndicate member will be liable only for the sale of the portion of the issue allocated to it. *Syn.* divided account. *See also* Eastern account; syndicate.

when-, as- and if-issued security *See* when issued security.

when issued contract A trade agreement regarding a security that has been authorized but is not yet physically available for delivery. The seller agrees to make delivery as soon as the security is ready, and the contract includes provisions for marking the price to the market and for calculating accrued interest.

when issued security (WI) A securities issue that has been authorized and is sold to investors before the certificates are ready for delivery. Typically, such securities include new issue municipal bonds, stock splits and Treasury securities. *Syn.* when-, as- and if-issued security.

WI *See* when issued security.

W I A message on the Consolidated Tape indicating that the trade being reported is in when issued stock or is trading when issued.

wildcatting *See* exploratory drilling program.

Wilshire 5,000 Equity Index A value-weighted market indicator composed of 5,000 exchange-listed and over-the-counter common stocks. It is the broadest measure of the market. *See also* index.

wire room *See* order department.

withdrawal plan A benefit offered by a mutual fund whereby a customer receives the proceeds of periodic systematic liquidation of shares in the account. The amounts received may be based on a fixed dollar amount, a fixed number of shares, a fixed percentage or a fixed period of time.

workable indication The price at which a municipal securities dealer is willing to purchase securities from another municipal dealer. The price may be revised if market conditions change.

working capital A measure of a corporation's liquidity; that is, its ability to transfer assets into cash to meet current short-term obligations. It is calculated by subtracting total current liabilities from total current assets.

working capital ratio *See* current ratio.

working interest An operating interest in a mineral-bearing property entitling the holder to a share of income from production and carrying the obligation to bear a corresponding share of all production costs.

workout quote A qualified quotation whereby a broker-dealer estimates the price on a trade that will require special handling owing to its size or to market conditions. *See also* bona fide quote; firm quote; nominal quote; subject quote.

World Bank *See* International Bank for Reconstruction and Development.

writer The seller of an option contract. An option writer takes on the obligation to buy or sell the underlying security if and when the option buyer exercises the option. *Syn.* seller.

writing a scale The process by which a syndicate establishes the yield for each maturity in a new serial bond issue in order to arrive at its competitive bid. *See also* scale.

WS A message on the Consolidated Tape indicating that the trade being reported is for a warrant.

Y

Yellow Sheets A daily publication compiled by the National Quotation Bureau and containing interdealer wholesale quotations for over-the-counter corporate bonds. *See also Pink Sheets.*

yield The rate of return on an investment, usually expressed as an annual percentage rate. *See also* current yield; dividend yield; nominal yield.

yield-based option A security representing the right to receive, in cash, the difference between the current yield of an underlying U.S. government security and the strike price of the option. A yield-based option is used to speculate on or hedge against the risk associated with fluctuating interest rates; its strike price represents the anticipated yield of the underlying debt security.

yield curve A graphic representation of the actual or projected yields of fixed-income securities in relation to their maturities. *See also* flat yield curve; inverted yield curve.

yield to call (YTC) The rate of return on a bond that accounts for the difference between the bond's acquisition cost and its proceeds, including interest income, calculated to the earliest date that the bond may be called by the issuing corporation. *See also* bond yield.

yield to maturity (YTM) The rate of return on a bond that accounts for the difference between the bond's acquisition cost and its maturity proceeds, including interest income. *See also* bond yield.

YTC *See* yield to call.

YTM *See* yield to maturity.

Z

zero-coupon bond A corporate or municipal debt security traded at a deep discount from face value. The bond pays no interest; rather, it may be redeemed at maturity for its full face value. It may be issued at a discount, or it may be stripped of its coupons and repackaged.

zero-minus tick A security transaction's execution price that is equal to the price of the last sale but lower than the last different price. *See also* minus tick; plus tick; zero-plus tick.

zero-plus tick A security transaction's execution price that is equal to the price of the last sale but higher than the last different price. *See also* minus tick; plus tick; plus tick rule; zero-minus tick.

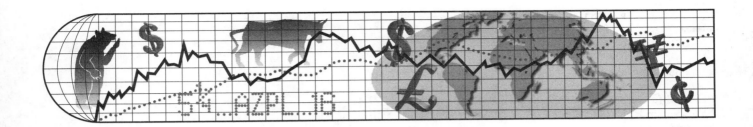

Index

Account
   employee of other broker, 195-96
   ownership, 188
   records, 194-95
   transfer, 120, 194, 491
   types of, 196-202
Account holder, death or
   incompetence of, 201-2
Accounting methods, 368
Accounts payable, 444
Accounts receivable, 444
Accredited investors, 257, 412
Accretion, 39, 480
Accrued interest, 121, 476, 323-26, 327
   360-day year calculations, 324-25
   365-day year calculations, 325-26
Accumulation plans, 370-71
Accumulation stage, 403
Accumulation units, 403
Acid-test ratio, 451
Active markets, 291
Additional bonds test, 80, 81
Additional issues, 248
Additional paid-in capital, 445
Additional takedown, 91
Adjustable-rate preferred, 11
Adjustment bonds, 45
Administrative messages,
   Consolidated Tape, 290-91
Administrator, 198, 492
ADRS, 21-22
Ad valorem taxes, 109
Advance/decline line, 435
Advertising, 517-26
   approval and filing requirements
      for, 519-20
   municipal securities, 97, 119

new issue, 246
recruitment, 524
returns, 522
SIPC membership, 492
Affiliated person, 258, 346
Aftermarket sales by prospectus, 246
After-tax rate of return, 78
Agency issues, 53-57, 475-76
   security funds, 353
   transactions, 103
Agent, 102, 275-76
Aggregate price, 103
Aggressive strategies, 472
Agreement among underwriters, 87
Agreement of limited partnership, 414
AIR, 405-6
All or none, 95, 253, 279, 285
Allied members, 514
Allocation priorities, 92-93
Alpha, 474
Alternative minimum tax (AMT), 476,
   481
Alternative order, 279
American depositary receipts (ADRs),
   21
American Stock Exchange (AMEX), 288
American style, 132-33
AMEX, 288
Amortization, 39, 479
AMT. *See* Alternative minimum tax
Annuitant, 399
Annuitized payments, 407
Annuity
   contract types, 399-402
   payout options, 404-5
   purchasing, 402-3
   receiving distributions from, 404-7

taxation of, 406-7
units, 405
Antidilution agreement, 7
Antifraud regulations, 259
Antireciprocal rule, 101-2
AON. *See* All or none
AP. *See* Associated person
Appeal, 511
Appreciation, 67
Apprenticeship, 114
Arbitrage, 274-75
Arbitration, 122, 512-14, 516
Arbitration awards, 513
As-issued trades, 316
Ask, 293
Assessments, 503
Asset allocation funds, 353
Assets, 2, 442-44
   residual claims to, 8
Assignment, of exercise, 177
Associated person (AP), 114, 461, 505-
   6, 509
Assumed interest rate (AIR), 405-6
At-the-market offers, 95
At-the-money, 134
At-the-open order, 279, 284-85
Auction market, 274
Audit, 81
Authorized stock, 3
Authorizing resolution, 83
Automatic exercise, 177
Average basis, 368
Award resolution, 83

BA, 61-62
Backdating letter, 362
Back-end load, 355, 359, 360

Equity Securities

Stock Classifications:	*Authorized:* number of shares corporation is permitted to issue *Issued:* has been sold to the public *Treasury:* repurchased by corporation; no voting rights, receives no dividends *Outstanding:* Number of shares held by the public Treasury = Issued – Outstanding; Outstanding = Issued – Treasury
Stock Valuations:	*Par:* assigned accounting value *Book:* liquidation or net worth value *Market:* value determined by supply and demand
Preemptive Rights:	Allow shareholders to maintain proportionate interest
Voting Rights:	Shareholders vote on directors, issuance of convertible bonds or preferred stock; <u>not</u> on dividend payment or amount
Stock Splits:	*Normal:* More shares, less value per share, same total value before and after *Reverse:* Less shares, more value per share, same total value before and after
Preferred Stock:	Par value = $100 Stated (fixed) dividend rate Priority over common in liquidation and dividend payment Typically no voting rights
Current Yield:	*Annual* dividends divided by current market price
Stock Points:	1 point = $1 1/8 =.125 1/4 =.25 3/8 =.375 1/2 =.5 5/8 =.625 3/4 =.75 7/8 =.875
Rights	30–45 day duration Strike price is below market Trade as separate security Available to existing shareholders only; One right per share outstanding
Warrants:	Long-term Strike price above market Trade as a separate security Offered as sweeteners
ADRs:	No preemptive rights Investors have voting rights Dividends in dollars
REITs:	Not a limited partnership Not an investment company Pass through income, not losses 75% of income must come from real estate Must distribute 95% or more of income to shareholders Trade on exchange or OTC

Debt Securities

Maturities:	*Term*: matures at one date in the future *Serial*: matures over a period of years, balloon has large lump payment at end *Series*: spread out issue, <u>not</u> a maturity
Investment Grade:	Baa or BBB and above, based on default risk, ability to pay interest and principal when due
Call Features:	Called by issuer when interest rates are falling; no interest after call Issuer cannot call during call protection period
Bond Yields:	Current Yield = annual income/current market price

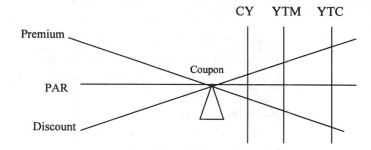

Refunding:	Refinancing at a lower rate Pre-refunded bonds are Triple A rated, considered defeased, funds escrowed in Treasuries
Corporate Bonds:	Called funded debt *Secured:* Mortgage, collateral trust (backed by securities), equipment trust certificates *Unsecured:* backed by full faith and credit, debentures and subordinated debentures
Trust Indenture:	Covenants between issuer and trustee for the benefit of the bondholders
Convertibles:	Par/conversion price = conversion ratio new price/conversion ratio = parity price of common conversion ratio x common stock price = parity price of bond
Governments:	Bills quoted at a discount, notes and bonds in 32nds notes/bonds are callable, bills are not Treasury STRIPS are backed in full by the U.S. government
Agencies:	Ginnie Maes are backed in full by U.S. government Interest taxable on all agency issues with nicknames
CMOs:	Corporate instrument with tranches; taxable monthly interest; PACs protect from prepayment risk; TACs have no protection from extension risk; subject to interest rate risk
Money Markets:	*Commercial paper:* most heavily traded; corporate issue; issued at a discount, 270 day maximum maturity *Negotiable CD:* minimum face of $100,000, trade with accrued interest *Bankers Acceptances:* Time draft, letter of credit for foreign trade; 270 day max maturity
Interest Rates:	Fed funds rate most volatile, established by market; Discount rate set by FRB
Interbank Market:	Establishes rates of exchange for foreign currency; decentralized; unregulated

Municipal Securities

GOs:	"Full faith and credit bonds" Backed primarily by taxes Generally safer than revenues Voter approval required Debt limits may restrict issuance Generally competitive bid underwriting Generally firm commitment underwriting Generally serial maturities with basis quotes Analysis based on taxes, debt statement, ratios
Revenues:	Self-supporting bonds Backed by user fees Generally less safe than GOs No voter approval, may be subject to additional bonds test Feasibility study to determine economic viability Generally negotiated underwriting Generally best efforts underwriting May be serial maturities with basis quotes or term maturities with dollar quotes Analysis based on feasibility study, debt service coverage ratio
PGDM:	Presale, Group, Designated, Member: Order allocation priority in syndicate letter
Bond Buyer:	Mostly primary market info includes 30 day visible supply placement ratios, official notices of sale
IDRs:	Backed by corporations, leaseback payments, interest may be taxable
Munifacts:	Wire service, provides general information relevant to muni market
Spread:	Compensation to syndicate Smallest portion is manager's fee Largest portion is takedown
60 days:	Settlement of syndicate account within 60 days of delivery of securities
2 bus. Days:	Time allowed for return of good faith deposit
Confirmations:	No later than settlement date for final confirmations
Unqualified:	Most desirable legal opinion; no reservations by bond counsel
3 years:	Required time for keeping advertising records 2 years in readily accessible location Advertising may be approved by muni or general securities principal
90 days:	Muni apprenticeship period; no commissions, no dealing with customers
Bond Swaps:	Change issuer, maturity or coupon and will not be wash sale
$100:	Maximum gift allowed to persons other than employees
TIC:	Includes time value of money; NIC method more commonly used for valuation of bid
Commissions:	Markups/commissions must be fair and reasonable; no 5% guideline for MSRB

Options

Single Options:

	Maximum Gain	Maximum Loss
Long Call	Unlimited	Premium
Short Call	Premium	Unlimited
Long Put	SP-Premium	Premium
Short Put	Premium	SP-Premium

Breakevens:	Calls: SP + Premium
	Puts: SP – Premium
Intrinsic Value:	Calls: Market Price – SP ("Call Up")
	Puts: SP – Market Price ("Put Down")

Hedging:

Best or Full Protection = Buy an option
Partial protection or improve rate of return: Sell an option
Long Stock Position: Risk is ↓, choose ↓ option to protect: buy puts or sell calls
Short Stock Position: Risk is ↑, choose ↑ option to protect: buy calls or sell puts

Long Stock, Long Put:
BE: Do T-chart. Stock Price + premium
Max Gain: Unlimited
Max Loss: (Stock price - strike price) + premium

Long Stock, Short Call:
BE: Do T-chart. Stock Price – premium
Max Gain: (Strike price - stock price) + premium
Max Loss: Stock price - premium

Short Stock, Short Put:
BE: Do T-chart. Stock Price + premium
Max Gain: (Stock price - strike price) + premium
Max Loss: Unlimited

Short Stock, Long Call:
BE: Do T-chart. Stock Price – premium
Max Gain: SP – premium
Max Loss: (Strike price - stock price) + premium

Spreads

Debits = widen = exercise
credits = narrow = expire

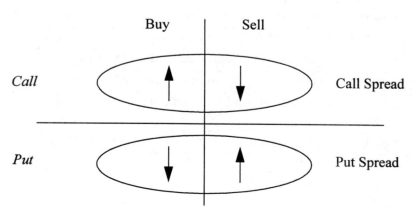

Do T-chart to determine net position

Options (continued)

Debit Spreads:	Max Gain = Initial Net Credit Max Loss = Diff. in Strike Prices minus the net credit
Credit Spreads:	Max Gain = Diff. in strike prices minus the net debit Max Loss = Initial net debit
Breakevens:	CAL: for call spreads add net premium to lower strike price PSH: for put spreads subtract net premium from higher strike price
Spreads with no premium:	Investor is bullish if long the lower strike price

---

Straddles: "Uncertain" investor
Same SP and Expiration

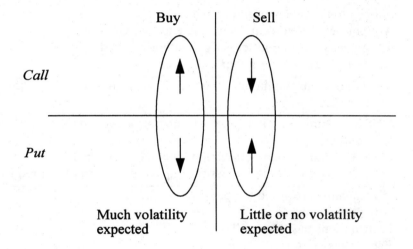

	Buy	Sell
Call	↑	↓
Put	↓	↑
	Much volatility expected	Little or no volatility expected

2 Breakevens: Call: SP + both premiums
Put: SP − both premiums

	Max Gain	Max Loss
Long Straddle	Unlimited	Both Premiums
Short Straddle	Both Premiums	Unlimited

Customer Accounts

New Account Forms:	Required for all accounts Birth date not required Customer signature not required for cash accounts; needed for margin accounts Signed by rep and approving principal
Account Approval:	By principal, either prior to or promptly after the first transaction
Unsolicited Transactions:	Must mark order ticket unsolicited Do not need to be suitable
Margin Agreement:	Credit Agreement – required, specifies loan terms Hypothecation Agreement – required, pledges customer securities as collateral Loan Consent Form – optional, allows B-D to loan customer margin securities Securities must be held in street name Not allowed for retirement accounts or UGMAs
Trading Authorization:	Limited – third party can trade only Full – third party can trade and withdraw cash and securities
Fiduciary Accounts:	Subject to prudent man rule or legal list All require written legal document, except UGMA/UTMA Margin accounts permitted only if authorized in document No short sales, naked options
Account Transfers:	Verify positions within three days; then freeze the account; four more days to transfer
Accounts for other B-D Employees:	NYSE – permission first, prior written notification, duplicate statements and confirms MSRB – prior written notification, duplicate confirms NASD – prior written notification, duplicate confirms upon request only
Joint Accounts:	All signatures required to open Any party can trade Distributions payable to all Each owns undivided interest
JTWROS:	equal ownership interest Passes to survivor(s) at death, no probate
JTIC:	unequal interests OK Passes by will to heirs, probate
Discretionary:	Authority from customer must be in writing Account must be approved before the first trade Principal must review discretionary accounts frequently for churning Time and price not discretionary
UGMA:	Cash accounts only Minor is beneficial owner; minor's Social Security number on account One minor, one custodian No short sales, no options, no margins

Margin Accounts

*Long and Short
T-Charts:*

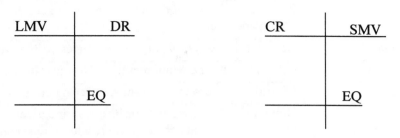

LMV	DR
	EQ

CR	SMV
	EQ

Reg T = 50% of LMV
Min. Mntnc. = 25% of LMV

Reg T = 50% of SMV
Min. Mntnc. = 30% of SMV

Account Status:

Excess Equity   *Creates SMA*

━━━━━━━━━━━━━━━━━━━━━━━━━━ **Reg T**

Restricted

Buy — Pay 50%
Sell — 50% retention
withdraw securities — deposit 50%

━━━━━━━━━━━━━━━━━━━━━━━━━━ **Min. Mtnc.**

Maintenance Call

Deposit Cash
Deposit Securities
Sell securities in account

Market Value at Maintenance:	**DR/.75**
Margin Agreement:	*Credit Agreement* — required, investor pays variable rate interest on money borrowed *Hypothecation Agreement* — required, investor pledges securities to BD, BD pledges to bank for loans to customers *Loan Consent Forms* — optional, if signed BD may loan customer securities for short sales
Reg T Exemptions:	Government securities, municipals subject to SRO requirements only
SMA in Long Account	*Increased by:* • Advance in market value of securities in account • Non required cash deposit ($1 for $1) • Sale of securities (50% of sales proceeds to SMA) *Decreased by:* Purchase of securities or withdrawal of cash, *not* market value decline
SMA Buying Power:	$1 of SMA buys $2 of stock (2 to 1)
Maintenance Call:	Must be met promptly; $1,000 exemption
New Account Deposit	Reg T or $2,000 whichever is greater (exception for long account: 100% of purchase price if less than $2,000)

Issuing Securities

Act of 1933:	Requires registration of all nonexempt issues Requires full and fair disclosure of new issues The "Paper Act"
Exempt Securities:	Commercial paper, bankers acceptances with maturities of less than 270 days
Exempt Issuers:	U.S. Government, Municipalities, Non-profits/Charities/Churches, Banks
Reg A:	$5 million or less in 12 months, Offering circular for disclosure
Rule 147:	Home office in state, 80% of business and assets in state Only state residents can buy, no resale to non-residents for 9 months
Reg D: *(Private Placements)*	No more than 35 non-accredited investors Unlimited accredited investors (Institutions, broker-dealers, individuals with income of more than $200,000 single, $300,000 married in last 2 years) Sign investment letter, hold for 1 year Private placement memorandum for disclosure
Rule 144:	1 year hold on restricted securities for insiders or non-insiders Volume limitations apply to all control stock sales Limits are greater of 1% of outstanding voting stock or average of preceding 4 weeks' weekly trading volume in 90 days Must file form 144 with SEC no later than sale date Insiders can't sell short; short-swing profits must be disgorged
Rule 144a:	No holding period on unregistered securities sold to institutional investors
Rule 145:	Proxy statement required to inform shareholders of mergers, acquisitions, reclassifications
Prospectus Delivery:	Final prospectus no later than confirmation of sale 90 days for IPOs 40 days for non-Nasdaq (Pink Sheet companies) 25 days for exchange listed and Nasdaq (includes NNM)
Cooling Off Period:	Minimum of 20 days No advertising, sales literature, orders, offers Tombstones, red herrings, indications of interest are OK
Underwriting:	Must be NASD members to underwrite corporate securities Firm commitment = principal capacity; underwriters have risk Best efforts = agent capacity; issuer has risk Syndicate members have liability; selling group members do not
Stabilizing:	One bid, at or below public offering price, only in underwriting period Must be stated in prospectus
Freeriding/ Withholding:	Firms, reps and financially supported persons cannot buy hot issues

Trading Securities

Act of 1934:	"People Act", regulates exchanges and OTC trading activity
Securities Markets:	*Exchanges*: listed securities, auction market *OTC*: unlisted securities, negotiated transactions *Third Market*: listed securities traded OTC, negotiated trades, trades reported in 90 seconds *Fourth Market*: Institutions trading direct through Instinet service
NYSE Trade Rule:	Priority, precedence and parity – determines which order is executed first
Specialist:	Maintains an orderly market, acts as agent and principal, priority to customer orders Holds book of stop and limit orders, sets opening quote
Nine Bond Rule:	Orders for fewer than 10 bonds must first be presented on the Exchange floor

Order Chart:

	BUY	SELL
	Buy stop Buy stop limits	Sell Limit
Current Mkt. price		
	Buy Limit	Sell stop Sell stop limit

Orders placed below the current market are adjusted for cash dividends (BLISS) unless marked DNR (do not reduce).
All orders are adjusted for stock splits and stock dividends.

Stop Orders:	*Buy stop* triggered at or above order price, executed at next price. If stop limit, same trigger, execution at or below order price; Buy stops protect short positions *Sell stop* triggered at or below order price, executed at next price. If stop limit, same trigger, execution at or above order price; Sell stops protect long positions
Time Sensitive Orders:	*FOK*: execute all immediately or cancel entire order *AON*: execute all, immediacy is not important; hold as GTC on book until filled *IOC*: execute whatever is available now, remainder is canceled
Short Sale Rules:	Must be executed on plus tick or zero-plus tick for exchanges, OTC has similar rule Short sale order tickets must be marked
Order Routing:	SuperDot for NYSE: up to 2,099 shares per order SOES: OTC automatic order execution, no more than 1000 shares per order
Pink Sheets:	Weekly publication of OTC equity with interdealer quotations; quotes are not firm Corporate bonds on yellow sheets
5% Policy:	Guide for OTC non-exempt (not munis or govs.) For markups, markdowns, commission Securities sold with prospectus are not subject

Brokerage Office Procedures

OPMC:	Order routing through B-D is: • Order dept. • Purchases and Sales • Margin dept. • Cashier
Order Tickets:	Must be approved by principal no later than the end of the trade date
Errors:	Report first to principal Reporting errors binding on customer at executed price Errors of execution are not binding on customer
Confirmations:	Customer: No later than settlement date B-D to B-D: No later than T + 1 Must disclose agent or principal Commissions must be disclosed; markups/downs are not disclosed
Customer Statements:	Minimum of quarterly, monthly statements for active accounts
Financial disclosure:	Customers entitled to most recent balance sheet upon written request
Settlement Dates:	Regular Way: Corps and Munis, T + 3 Governments, T + 1 Cash settlement: same day Reg T settlement: T + 5 DVP: no later than 35 calendar days Seller's option: no sooner than first day after regular way, no later than T + 60 calendar days When issued: no sooner than 3 business days after final confirmation
Frozen Accounts:	If no extension granted from SRO, 90 day freeze applies Amounts of less than $1,000 can be ignored
DERP:	Order of dates is Declaration, Ex, Record, Payable D, R and P determined by Board of Directors, NASD determines ex-date Buy before the ex-date to get the dividend
Ex-dates:	2 business days before record date (regular way) Business day after record date (cash settlement and mutual funds) Buy before the ex-date to get the dividend
Bonds traded flat:	No accrued interest Include income (adjustment) bonds, defaulted bonds, zeros
Accrued interest:	Corps and munis: 30 day months, regular way settlement is 3 business day Governments: Actual day months, regular way settlement is next business day Seller's interest includes prior payment date, up to (not including) settlement date
Invalid Signatures:	Dead persons, minors, persons declared legally incompetent

Investment Company Procedures

Inv. Co. Act of 40:	Defines and regulates investment companies 3 types: face amount certificate, unit investment trust, management company
Open-end company:	Mutual fund; continuous primary offering Redemption in seven calendar days Price by formula in prospectus Fractional shares
Closed-end company:	Trade in secondary market, issues debt and equity Fixed number of shares Sold with prospectus in IPO only
Diversified status:	75% invested in other companies Max of 5% in any one company Can own no more than 10% of a target company's voting stock Status applies to open- and closed-end companies
Registration requirements:	Minimum $100,000 capital, 100 investors Clearly defined investment objective Asset to debt ratio not less than 3 to 1 (300%)
Prohibited investing:	No purchases on margin, no short sales, no naked options sold
Shareholder votes:	Change investment objective, change sales load policy, change fund classification
Shareholder reports:	Annual audited report, semiannual unaudited report (2 per year)
Sector funds:	Minimum of 25% of assets in area of specialty; more aggressive
Money-market funds:	No load, fixed NAV, check-writing privileges, daily interest
Performance history:	1, 5, 10 years (or fund's life if less than 10 years)
Sales charge %:	POP — NAV/POP (NASD maximum of 8.5% of POP) settlement date
POP calculation:	NAV/100% - SC%
12b-1 charges:	Distribution fee approved annually and charged quarterly. Cannot be described as no-load fund if exceeds .25%
8½% Sales Charge:	Only if fund offers reinvestment at NAV, rights of accumulation, breakpoints
Letter of intent:	Must be in writing, maximum 13 months, can be backdated 90 days
Conduit theory:	IRC subchapter M. Fund is "regulated investment company" if it distributes a minimum of 90% of net investment income Fund taxed only on retained earnings
Ex-dividend date:	Determined by BOD, typically business day after record date.
Calculating yield:	Annual dividends/POP; capital gains distributions are not included
Dollar cost averaging:	Effective if average cost per share is lower than average price per share No guarantees

Retirement Plans

Nonqualified plans:	Non-deductible contributions, can be discriminatory Examples are payroll deduction, deferred compensation Risk of deferred compensation is employer failure
IRAs:	Maximum contribution is $2000, or 100% of earned income Spousal IRA allows $4,000 between 2 spouse filing joint returns, split between 2 accounts No life insurance or collectibles as contributions 10% penalty, plus applicable ordinary income tax, on withdrawals before age 59½ 6% excess contribution penalty 50% insufficient distribution penalty (insufficient if after 70½) One rollover allowed each 12 months to be completed within 60 days Unlimited trustee to trustee transfers
SEPs:	Qualified plan that allows employers to contribute money to employee IRAs Contribution max = 15% of employee salary up to $30,000 Contributions are immediately vested
Roth IRAs:	New IRA that allows after-tax contributions, possible tax-free distributions Maximum contribution of $2,000 per individual, $4,000 per couple Does not require distributions to begin at age 70½
Education IRAs:	New IRA that allows after-tax contributions for children under age 18 Maximum contribution is $500 per year Tax-free distributions if funds are used for higher education
Keoghs (HR-10):	Available to self-employed persons, owners of unincorporated businesses and professional practices Contribution max is lesser of 20% of gross for employer (25% for employee) or $30,000 All employees must participate if age 21 or older, employed more than 1 year, work more than 1000 hours per year Life insurance may be held within the plan Distributions in lump sums are eligible for 5-year income averaging through 1999
TSAs (403(b) plans):	Available to employees of non-profit organizations Typically funded by elective employee salary reductions, usually no cost basis
Pension Plans:	Require annual contribution *Defined benefit:* based on formula factoring age, salary years of service, calculated by actuary; favor older key employees *Defined contribution:* simpler to administer, contribution is typically a percent of salary 5-year income averaging available on distributions through 1999
Profit-Sharing Plans:	Annual contribution not required, great investment and contribution flexibility
Withholding Rule:	20% withholding applied to distributions from qualified plans made payable to participant
ERISA:	Protects participants in corporate (private) plans, not public plans Rules for funding, vesting, nondiscrimination, participation, communication

Variable Annuities

Fixed Annuity:	Guaranteed rate of return Insurance company has investment risk Subject to purchasing power risk Fixed income guaranteed for life Not a security
Variable Annuity:	Rate of return dependent on separate account performance Investor has investment risk Sold with prospectus Can keep pace with inflation Variable income guaranteed for life; principal is not guaranteed
Accumulation phase:	Investor pays money to insurer Units vary in number and in value
Annuity phase:	Investor receives payments from insurer Fixed number of units, vary in value
Purchase Methods:	*Periodic deferred*: paid in installments, payouts taken later *Single premium immediate*: lump sum payment, payouts begin immediately, no accumulation period *Single premium deferred*: lump sum, payment, payouts taken later
Payout Methods:	Lump sum or random withdrawals Annuitization (monthly income guaranteed for life) *Life Income*: no beneficiary, largest monthly payment *Life with Period Certain:* minimum guaranteed period *Joint Life with last Survivor*: annuity on two lives; smallest monthly payment
AIR:	Used to determine monthly income Income goes up from previous month if separate account performance is greater than AIR Income stays the same as previous month if separate account performance is equal to AIR Income falls from the previous month if separate account performance is less than the AIR
Taxation:	Monthly income: part return of cost basis, part taxable; proportion determined by exclusion ratio Lump sum/random withdrawals: LIFO applies; earnings withdrawn first, taxable as ordinary income; no tax on remainder because it is a return of cost basis
Regulated by:	Act of 1933; Act of 1934 Investment Company Act of 1940; Investment Advisers Act of 1940 State Insurance Departments; Federal insurance law
Maximum Sales Charge:	8 1/2%, except 9% on contractual plan

Direct Participation Programs

DPPs:	Not investment companies Distribute proportionate share of losses, gains and income
DPP Risk:	*Real Estate* • Raw land, most risky • Existing property, least risky • Tax credits from government assisted housing programs *Oil & Gas* • Exploratory, Most risky (high IDC write-offs) • Income programs, least risky (provide depletion allowances)
Sharing Arrangements:	Most common is functional allocation
Limited Partners:	No management Limited Liability Passive Investors only Can sue GP
General Partners:	Active management Fiduciary Responsibility Cannot borrow, compete or commingle
Syndicator:	Distributes LPs Compensation max is 10%
Documentation:	Certificate of Limited Partnership: Identifies GP and LPs Partnership Agreement: Rules of "the club", empowers GP to manage Subscription Agreement: "Application" for membership, effective when signed by GP, discloses income, net worth, understanding of risk
Partnership Democracy:	Special vote for switching GPs, dissolving partnership
Taxation:	Passive loss can only be used to shelter passive income LP's provide pass-through of all income, losses, gains to partners
Reason to Invest:	Economic viability is first concern
Methods of Analysis:	Cash flow analysis and internal rate of return computations
Liquidation Priority:	1) Secured creditors 2) Other creditors 3) Limited partners 4) General partner(s)

Economics and Analysis

Business Cycle:	• *Expansion:* low unemployment, increased business activity • *Peak* • *Contraction:* falling stock markets, rising inventories, decreasing GDP • *Trough:* accompanied by high unemployment (Recession = 6 months of declining GDP; Depression = 6 quarters of declining GDP)
CPI:	Measures inflation through comparison of constant dollars
Leading Indicators:	Money supply, building permits, number of unemployment claims, orders, stock prices
Coincident Indicators:	Personal income, GDP, agricultural unemployment, sales
Lagging Indicators:	Duration of unemployment, corporate profits, commercial loans outstanding
Economic Theories:	*Keynes*: aggregate demand, government intervention is encouraged *Friedman*: monetarist theory, quantity of money determines price levels *Laffer*: supply-side economics, government should reduce spending and taxes
Money Supply:	M1 = currency and demand deposits M2 = M1 + money markets, savings accounts, overnight repos M3 = M2 + large time deposits, longer repos
Fiscal Policy:	Taxation, spending by Congress and President
Monetary Policy:	FRB's tools: discount rate, reserve requirement (greatest impact) and FOMC (most used)
Technical Analysis:	Charting, market timing, price predictions based on trends
Technical Theories:	*Dow Theory*: confirms end of market trends, changes in stock prices reflected by indexes *Odd Lot Theory*: do the opposite of the small investor *Short Interest Theory*: large amount of short interest is bullish *MPT*: focuses on portfolio relationships, efficient markets *Random Walk*: direction of stock market or prices is unpredictable
Fundamental Analysis:	Study of a company's prospects based on overall economy, financial statements
Industry Analysis:	Defensive: food, tobacco, pharmaceuticals, energy Cyclical: heavy machinery Growth: technology (low dividend payouts)
Balance Sheet:	Assets – Liabilities = Net Worth; Assets = Liabilities + Net Worth Used to compute capitalization and liquidity ratios
Income Statement:	Summarizes revenues and expenses to determine efficiency and profitability
Ratios:	Capitalization: Debt/Equity, Bond ratio, Common Stock ratio Liquidity: Current ratio, Acid test ratio Valuation: PE ratio, Current Yield, Dividend Payout ratio Working Capital: Current assets – Current liabilities

Ethics, Recommendations and Taxation

Private Transactions:	Not allowed without B-D's knowledge and consent Prior written notice and disclosure of compensation required Passive investments not subject to this requirement
Gift Limit:	No more than $100 cash per year to employees of other member firms
Selling Dividends:	Prohibited practice due to tax liability
Breakpoint Sales:	Encouraging customer to purchase below the opportunity for a discount prohibited practice
Research Reports:	Must disclose if prepared by someone outside firm
Shared Accounts:	Allowable only if firm grants prior written approval sharing only in proportion to contribution
Prohibited Trading Practices:	*Painting the tape:* party sells with agreement from buyer that repurchase will occur the same day *Matching:* B-D stages a hot market by simultaneous purchases and sales *Front-running:* B-D order placed ahead of customer order for better price *Capping:* exerting selling pressure to keep stock prices from rising
Investment Objectives:	Preservation of capital; safety = Government securities or Ginnie Maes Growth = Common Stock or common stock mutual fund "balanced" or "moderate" growth = blue chip stocks "aggressive" growth = technology stocks or sector funds Income = Bonds (but not zero-coupons). Preferred stock and utilities also provide income. Tax free income = Municipal bonds or muni bond funds High yield income = Corporate bonds or corporate bond funds Liquidity = Money-market funds; (DPPs, CDs, real estate and annuities are illiquid)
Investment Risks:	*Purchasing power risk:* Inflation *Reinvestment risk:* Mortgage backed securities and callable bonds are susceptible *Market risk:* Also called systemic (or systematic) risk; diversification doesn't reduce *Credit risk:* Risk of issuer's default causing loss of principal *Liquidity risk:* Also called marketability risk; risk that investor cannot convert to cash quickly and at a fair price
CAPM:	Determines risk and reward from total portfolio; basis of modern portfolio theory
Beta:	Overall market has beta of 1. Beta higher than 1 is more volatile, aggressive
Foreign Stock:	Income taxed by country of investor's citizenship; 15% withholding on foreign distributions
Wash Sales:	Loss disallowed if substantially identical security purchased 30 days before or after sale for loss
Bond Cost Basis:	Amortize all premiums, accrete OID's only; secondary market discounts not accreted
Gifted/Inherited Stock:	For gift, cost basis is giver's original basis; Heir's cost basis is MV on date of death
Dividend Exclusion:	70% exclusion on corporate dividends; no dividend exclusion for individuals

U.S. Government and State Rules and Regulations

Act of 1933:	The Paper Act
	Nonexempt issuers must file registration statements with the SEC
	Requires use of prospectus when selling new issues
	Requires full and fair disclosure of new issues
	Regulates primary market activity (issuing and underwriting)
Act of 1934:	The People Act Regulates secondary market activity
	Created the SEC
	Requires registration of all reps and firms that trade securities for the public
	Oversees exchanges and OTC market
	Regulates extension of credit
	Prohibits fraudulent trading activities
	Regulates insider transactions, short sales, proxies and client accounts
	Prohibits use of inside information
	No security is exempt from antifraud provisions (even if exempt from 1933 registration)
Maloney Act:	Chartered the NASD as the SRO of the OTC
Trust Indenture Act of 1939:	Regulates senior corporate securities (bonds)
	Requires trust indenture/trustee for issues of more than $5 million in 12 months
	Trust indenture is covenants between issuer and trustee for protection of bondholders
Investment Advisers Act of 1940:	Requires registration of persons who receive flat fees or percentages for giving investment advice
Investment Company Act of 1940:	Regulates and defines investment companies
	Three types of investment companies: face amount certificate companies; unit investment trusts; management companies
	Requires clearly stated investment objectives
	Minimum of $100,000 assets, 100 shareholders
Insider Trading Act of 1988:	Tippers and tippees are guilty
	Penalties are up to the greater of $1,000,000 or 3 times profits made/losses avoided
	B-Ds must have written supervisory procedures
	Chinese Walls prohibit sensitive information passed between departments of B-Ds
Penny Stock Cold Calling Rule:	Persons that buy Non-Nasdaq stock of less than $5 must sign suitability statements before transactions
	Firms required to provide monthly statements of penny stock activity
	Customers receive disclosure of risk and commissions made by rep/firm
	Customers who opened account more than 12 months before, or made 3 different penny stock transactions with the firm
Uniform Securities Act:	Blue-Sky Laws — Coordination, Filing and Qualification for registering securities
	Requires registration of securities, B-Ds and reps at state level

Other SEC and SRO Regulations

NASD Manual:	*Conduct Rules* (formerly Rules of Fair Practice): fair and ethical dealing with the public
	Uniform Practice Code: standardizes practices between B-Ds, like DKs, settlements, ex- dates
	Code of Procedure (COP): handles complaints, disciplinary action; DBCC investigation
	Code of Arbitration: handles monetary disputes between BDs or within the industry
Principals:	Minimum of two per firm; manage, train and supervise
	Approve all accounts and client transactions
Felony Conviction:	May be disqualified for 10 years (also for cash/securities misdemeanor)
Continuing Commissions	Allowed to Reps or heirs with bona fide contract
Financial disclosure:	Customers entitled to most recent balance sheet upon written request
COP:	Respond to DBCC notice within 20 days
	DBCC can administer any penalty other than jail
	Appeal from DBCC to NBCC within 15 days
	Decision final after 45 days
	Summary Complaint: maximum fine $2,500 and/or censure; 10 days to respond
Code of Arbitration:	Between members, with public only with written consent
	Decisions are final and binding on all parties
	Awards after 30 days
	Simplified is $25,000 for public and industry
	Six year statute of limitations
NYSE Rules:	Prior permission for outside employment; no transfer of registration
NASD Communications:	Advertising = non-targeted communications Sales literature = targeted communications
	Both must be approved by principal before use, filed for three years, two years easily accessible
	Investment company material must be filed with NASD within 10 days of use
	1st year firms must file with NASD 10 days before first use
	Generic advertising is OK if product or service offered is available
	Name of member required except on recruitment ads
	Testimonials OK with disclosure of compensation
Recommendations:	Must be suitable; disclose current price; potential conflicts of interest
	"Past performance does not guarantee future results"
Investment Company Recommendations:	Advertising/sales literature must disclose 10 year period unless new fund
	Advertise based on highest charge, no breakpoint
	Yield = Annual dividend/POP
Telephone Consumer Protection Act:	Must call non-customers at home between 8 a.m. and 9 p.m.
	Firms must maintain "Do-Not-Call List" and written procedures
	Not applicable to non-profit organizations

How Many Business Days?

Same **Business** Day — The settlement date on cash transactions for securities

One **Business** Day — Regular way settlement on U.S. government securities

Two **Business** Days — The relationship of the normal ex-dividend date to the record date

Three **Business** Days — Regular way settlement for securities other than U.S. government securities (corporate and municipal)

Five **Business** Days — Regulation T settlement for cash account purchases

How Many Calendar Days?

Seven **Calendar** Days — The maximum time for mutual funds to redeem shares

Twenty **Calendar** Days — The minimum time between the filing date and the effective date of a security registration (cooling-off period)

Thirty **Calendar** Days — The IRS time restriction on purchases to avoid wash sale designation (thirty days before or thirty days after)

Forty-five **Calendar** Days — The maximum period within which one can receive a 100 percent refund of sales charges in an investment company contractual plan (free-look period)

Sixty **Calendar** Days — The maximum time within which the free-look letter can be sent by the custodian bank to the contractual planholder

The maximum time permitted to roll over qualified money from one qualified retirement plan to another qualified retirement plan

Ninety **Calendar** Days — The maximum length of time for a letter of intent to be backdated

How Many Months?

Six **Months** — The frequency with which investment companies must send reports to shareholders

Thirteen **Months** — The maximum duration of a letter of intent

Sixteen **Months** — The maximum time that an investment company prospectus may be used

Eighteen **Months** — The time after which refunds of sales charges in excess of 15 percent on front-end load contractual plans expire (act of 1940)